The Playbill® Broadway Yearbook

Seventh Annual Edition
2010-2011

Robert Viagas
Editor

Amy Asch
Assistant Editor

Kesler Thibert
Art Director

Brian Mapp   Joseph Marzullo
Photographers

David Gewirtzman
Production Coordinator

Samantha Souza
Photo Coordinator

The Playbill Broadway Yearbook: Seventh Annual Edition, June 1, 2010–May 31, 2011
Robert Viagas, Editor

©2011 Playbill® Incorporated
All rights reserved.

All PLAYBILL® covers in this book are from the magazine's archives.

ISBN 978-1-55783-783-7
ISSN 1932-1945

Published in 2011 by PLAYBILL® BOOKS
525 Seventh Avenue, Suite 1801
New York, NY 10018
Email: yearbook@playbill.com
Internet: www.playbill.com

Exclusively distributed by Applause Theatre & Cinema Books
An Imprint of Hal Leonard Corporation
7777 West Bluemound Road
Milwaukee, WI 53213

Trade Book Division Editorial Offices
33 Plymouth St., Montclair, NJ 07042

Printed in the United States of America

Book design by Kesler Thibert

www.applausebooks.com

Preface to the Seventh Edition

Broadway's 2010-2011 season was full of all kinds of riches for all kinds of theatre folk. From TV's "Glee" to the backstage dramas of *Spider-Man: Turn Off the Dark* to the hit status of *The Book of Mormon* and *War Horse*, Broadway put itself in the face of American pop culture.

And pop culture, in the form of visiting stars like Chris Rock, Al Pacino, Daniel Radcliffe, Kathy Griffin, Robin Williams, U2's Bono, Pee-wee Herman and Patrick Stewart, clearly put itself in Broadway's face as well. The Beatles were the subject of one show, and the Shirelles another. This was also the season when the National Football League made its Broadway debut as a producer of the biographical drama *Lombardi*, about coach Vince Lombardi.

A dozen new musicals made their debuts, on topics as varied as religion, banking fraud, Jewish theatre in the Holocaust, racism, marital infidelity, 19th century politics, 20th century pop music, the angst of Santa's elves and a grown-up Alice's adventures in Wonderland.

In the world of drama, addictions of many kinds were the preoccupation of our dramatists in plays like Jez Butterworth's *Jerusalem* and Stephen Adly Guirgis's confoundingly titled *The Motherf**cker With the Hat* (it had to be advertised as *The Mother With the Hat*, which sounds like something very different). As the musical *Wicked* moved into its eighth year pondering what it means to be wicked, David Lindsay-Abaire's social drama *Good People* asked us to consider the high price of trying to do what's good.

At a time when the general public associates Broadway with musical revivals, only two opened this season, *Anything Goes* and *How To Succeed in Business Without Really Trying*, both with bankable stars in the leads.

Play revivals were another story. The season offered a bumper crop that included Shaw and Shakespeare, David Mamet and Oscar Wilde, John Guare and Tom Stoppard.

Broadway shows sold $1.08 billion worth of tickets, the most ever. That wasn't just because of higher ticket prices (which grew toward a $155 non-premium top by Tony time). Broadway also sold more tickets, 12,534,595 of them, than ever in its history. Attendance has nearly doubled since the 1985-1986 season.

Forty-two shows opened on Broadway this season—the second-highest total in thirty years. Combined with the thirty-four shows held over from last season, plus one special case that previewed seven months without opening, that totaled seventy-seven shows—making for the most show chapters in a single

THE 2010-2011 YEARBOOK COMMITTEE
Top (L-R): David Gewirtzman, Robert Viagas, Brian Mapp
Bottom (L-R): Amy Asch, Samantha Souza, Joseph Marzullo
Not pictured: Kesler Thibert

Playbill Broadway Yearbook since it was founded six years ago.

This bounty affects the theatre world far beyond Broadway. New shows are being pumped into the touring pipeline and plans were being made to mount some of the bigger hits internationally.

The world immediately around Broadway continued to change this year as well. Construction scaffolding mushroomed around Times Square, particularly on the west side along Eighth Avenue, continuing to transform the Hell's Kitchen neighborhood of old brick low-rise apartment buildings into a spreading district of high-rise hotels and office towers. Most of the west end of the block bounded by 45th, 46th, Broadway and Eighth has been razed and awaits redevelopment.

The renaissance of live theatre in New York continued even as many other "old media" seemed to be withering in the face of a lingering national recession and the ever-burgeoning online world. Perhaps Broadway was busting out all over precisely because it learned early and well how to use the web to get the word out and create online communities around certain shows, personalities, viral videos and theatre companies. As the influence of print media continued to wane this

season, people turned more and more to the web to get information about shows and to find out what other people think about them.

As all this was going on, *The Playbill Broadway Yearbook* was, as usual, busily poking its nose backstage, to photograph the denizens of Broadway and to let them report on their activities. Check out these highlights:

Comedienne Kathy Griffin snarking about her two-week visit to Broadway in her solo show *Kathy Griffin Wants a Tony* (which wasn't nominated for one).

Colman Domingo eloquently defending his show, *The Scottsboro Boys*, against the charges of racism that helped truncate its run.

"Saturday Night Live" veteran Colin Quinn waxing philosophical about appearing in his own *Long Story Short* across the street from Al Pacino in Shakespeare's *The Merchant of Venice*.

Liz Pearce giving an understudy's view of life inside the stage door in *Billy Elliot*.

Leigh Ann Larkin sharing her account of an *A Little Night Music* cast party at Stephen Sondheim's house.

And so much more. As I write this we've already begun work on the eighth edition of the *Yearbook*. See you in 2012!

Robert Viagas
June 2011

Special Thanks

Special thanks to Amy Asch, David Gewirtzman, Samantha Souza, Brian Mapp, Joseph Marzullo, Kesler Thibert, Pam Karr, Jackie Jacobson, Benjamin Viagas, Krissie Fullerton, Matt Blank, Andrew Gans, Kenneth Jones, Adam Hetrick, Jean Kroeper Murphy, Brynn Cox, Maria Somma and Ellie Buck, whose help made this year's edition possible.

We also thank the Seventh Edition *Yearbook* Correspondents who shared their stories with such wit and insight: Erica Ash, Dorothy Atkinson, Hilary Austin, Robert Bennett, Kris Coleman, Nichole Capatasto, Jill Cordle (for the second time), Alvin Crawford, Joey Curatolo, Elizabeth DeRosa, Colman Domingo, Matt Doyle, John Treacy Egan (for the second time), Mary Faber, Meghann Fahy, Mike Farfalla, Matthew Farrell, Rebecca Faulkenberry, Bryan Fenkart, Micah Frank, Gabriela Garcia, Antonia Gianino, Gwendolyn M. Gilliam, Jane Grey, Kathy Griffin, Justin Guarini, Matthew Gumley, Roy Harris (for the fifth time), Zachary James (for the second time), Beverly Jenkins, Steve Landes, Leigh Ann Larkin (for the second time), Terry Lavell, Greta Lee, Shannon Lewis, Ellyn Marsh, Bryce McDonald (for the second time), Chuck Means, Kat Nejat, Keith Nobbs, Lindsay Northen, Kris Koop Ouellette (for the seventh time), Cambra Overend, Heather Parcells, Charlotte Parry, Liz Pearce, Bryce Pinkham, Drew Powell, Colin Quinn, John Robelen, Ryan Rossetto, Brian Sears, Tally Sessions, Hannah Sloat, Jessica Stone, Shaun Taylor-Corbett, Richard Topol, David Turner, Alex Lyu Volckhausen, Kristen Beth Williams, Phillippa Wilson and Denise Yaney.

And we thank the folks on each show who shared their photographs and other artwork that lent extra sparkle to the Scrapbook pages: Erica Ash, Linda Chin, Jill Cordle, Colleen Croft, Rebecca Faulkenberry, Roy Harris, Leigh Ann Larkin, Charlotte Parry, Shaun Taylor-Corbett, Tomas Vrzala, Aléna Watters, Phillippa Wilson, Peter James Zielinski and many others.

Also the Broadway press agents who helped set up interviews and photo sessions and helped track down the names of all the people in the crew photos: especially Chris Boneau, Adrian Bryan-Brown, Michael Hartman, Richard Kornberg, Jeffrey Richards, Marc Thibodeau, Philip Rinaldi, Sam Rudy, Tony Origlio, Rick Miramontez, Candi Adams, Whitney Tancred and their respective staffs.

Plus Joan Marcus, Paul Kolnik, Carol Rosegg, Ari Mintz, Anita Shevett, Steve Shevett, Michal Daniel and all the fine professional photographers whose work appears on these pages.

And, most of all, thanks to the great show people of Broadway who got into the spirit of the *Yearbook* and took time out of their busy days to pose for our cameras. There's no people like them.

Yearbook User's Manual

Which Shows Are Included? *The Playbill Broadway Yearbook 2010-2011* covers the Broadway season, which ran, as per tradition, from June 1, 2010 to May 31, 2011. Each of the seventy-seven shows that played at a Broadway theatre under a Broadway contract during that time are highlighted in this edition. That includes new shows that opened during that time, like *The Book of Mormon*; shows from last season that ran into this season, like *Memphis*; older shows from seasons past that closed during this season, like *In the Heights;* and older shows from seasons past that ran throughout this season and continue into the future (and into the next *Yearbook*), like *Mamma Mia!*

How Is It Decided Which Credits Page Will Be Featured? Each show's credits page (which PLAYBILL calls a "billboard page") changes over the year as cast members come and go. We use the opening-night billboard page for most new shows. For most shows that carry over from the previous season we use the billboard page from the first week in October.

Occasionally, sometimes at the request of the producer, we use a billboard page from another part of the season, especially when a major new star joins the cast.

What Are "Alumni" and "Transfer Students"? Over the course of a season some actors leave a production; others take their place. To follow our *Yearbook* concept, the ones who left a show before the date of the billboard page are listed as "Alumni"; the ones who joined the cast are called "Transfer Students." If you see a photo appearing in both "Alumni" and "Transfer Students" sections, it's not a mistake; it just means that they went in and out of the show during the season and were not present on the billboard date.

What Is a "Correspondent" and How Is One Chosen? We ask each show to appoint a Correspondent to record anecdotes of backstage life at their production. Sometimes the show's press agent picks the Correspondent; sometimes the company manager, the stage manager or the producer does the choosing. Each show gets to decide for itself. A few shows

decline to provide a correspondent, fail to respond to our request, or miss the deadline. Correspondents bring a richness of experience to the job and help tell the story of backstage life on Broadway from many different points of view.

Who Gets Their Picture in the Yearbook? Everyone who works on Broadway can get a picture in the *Yearbook*. That includes actors, producers, writers, designers, assistants, stagehands, ushers, box office personnel, stage doormen and anyone else employed at a Broadway show or a support organization. PLAYBILL maintains a database of headshots of all Broadway actors and most creators. We send our staff photographers to all opening nights and all major Broadway-related events. We also offer to schedule in-theatre photo shoots at every production. No one is required to appear in the *Yearbook*, but all are invited. A few shows declined to host a photo shoot this year or were unable to provide material by our deadline. We hope they'll join us in 2012.

TABLE OF CONTENTS

Timeline 2010-2011

Opening Nights, News Headlines and Other Significant Milestones of the Season

June 13, 2010 *Memphis* is named Best Musical and *Red* is named Best Play in the 64th annual Tony Awards.

July 15, 2010 The new season opens with *Harry Connick, Jr. in Concert on Broadway*, in which the crooner sings original pop songs and some of his favorite showtunes.

August 1, 2010 After a hiatus of several weeks, *A Little Night Music* reopens with Elaine Stritch and Bernadette Peters succeeding Angela Lansbury and Tony-winner Catherine Zeta-Jones in the roles of Madame Armfeldt her daughter Desirée.

August 18, 2010 One of the final performances of *South Pacific* is broadcast live on PBS.

August 21, 2010 The 2009 Tony Awards telecast executive-produced by Glenn Weiss and Ricky Kirshner and hosted by Neil Patrick Harris wins the Emmy for Outstanding Special Class Program.

August 29, 2010 The 2009 Tony Awards telecast wins the Emmy Award for Outstanding Writing for a Variety, Music or Comedy Special.

September 28, 2010 *Brief Encounter*, Emma Rice's expressionistic stage adaptation of Noël Coward's film about a bittersweet love affair between two married people, opens featuring members of the original U.K. Kneehigh Theatre cast.

September 30, 2010 Another West End-to-Broadway transfer, *The Pitmen Painters,* traces the lives of a group of miners who take an art class and wind up as world-famous artists.

October 3, 2010 Cherry Jones stars in a revival of George Bernard Shaw's scandalous 1894 play *Mrs. Warren's Profession*, about a proper English young lady who is shocked to discover that her family's business is running brothels. Directed by Doug Hughes.

October 5, 2010 Pakistani immigrant Faisal Shahzad, who tried to set off a car bomb near the Minskoff Theatre in Times Square May 1, 2010, is sentenced to life in prison.

October 7, 2010 Reopening of Donald Margulies' January 2010 drama *Time Stands Still*, with Christina Ricci joining original cast members Laura Linney, Brian d'Arcy James and Eric Bogosian.

October 12, 2010 In a revival of David Mamet's *A Life in the Theatre*, two actors—Robert (Patrick Stewart), nearing the end of his career, and John (T.R. Knight), at the dawn of his—share observations about acting, art and humanity as they ply their craft.

October 13, 2010 *Bloody Bloody Andrew Jackson* charts the brutal rise of the seventh president of the United States in an innovative musical that portrays him as a kind of rock star, and his followers as reminiscent of today's Tea Party movement.

(L-R): Songwriter Bono and director Julie Taymor at work on *Spider-Man: Turn Off the Dark*, which would become one of the most written-about shows of the season and would set a new record for previews. See November 28, 2010.

October 14, 2010 Mark Rylance, David Hyde Pierce and Joanna Lumley star in a revival of David Hirson's Moliere-esque comedy, *La Bête*.

October 21, 2010 The NFL makes its Broadway producing debut with *Lombardi*, Eric Simonson's new play about legendary football coach Vince Lombardi, starring Dan Lauria and Judith Light.

October 25, 2010 James Earl Jones is at the wheel under Vanessa Redgrave's steely eye in David Esbjornson's revival of Alfred Uhry's *Driving Miss Daisy*, also featuring Boyd Gaines.

October 26, 2010 *Rain—A Tribute to the Beatles on Broadway* offers a multi-media concert of the Fab Four's greatest hits, performed by a quartet of soundalikes.

October 31, 2010 *The Scottsboro Boys*, a new musical with a score by John Kander and the late Fred Ebb, uses the conventions of old-time minstrel shows to tell the real-life story of nine African-American men falsely accused of rape in the deep South. Directed and choreographed by Susan Stroman, with Joshua Henry and John Cullum.

November 1, 2010 Shannon Skye Tavarez, an 11-year-old who appeared on Broadway in *The Lion King* and whose battle with leukemia moved many on Broadway and in the pop world, passes away. During her final months, her fellow child performers from Broadway shows were seen selling bracelets and key chains that read, "Shine for Shannon," to help her family pay the medical bills. Broadway theatres dim their lights in her memory the following night.

November 3, 2010 Inspired by the "It Gets Better" campaign organized by columnist Dan Savage to prevent bullied gay teens from committing suicide, sixty-three members of the Broadway community share their stories of surviving bullying in a special "It Gets Better" video produced by Susan Blackwell, Hunter Bell and Matt Vogel, viewable at www.youtube.com/BroadwayItGetsBetter.

November 4, 2010 Patti LuPone, Brian Stokes Mitchell, Sherie Rene Scott, and Laura Benanti star in *Women on the Verge of a Nervous Breakdown*, a new David Yazbek-Jeffrey Lane musical inspired by the 1988 Pedro Almodóvar film.

November 6, 2010 A group of about thirty people picket the *The Scottsboro Boys*, saying that the musical, which uses the conventions of 19th century minstrel shows, is racist. Director Susan Stroman in *The New York Times* responds that the show's creators "were not celebrating the minstrel tradition but rather using it to reveal the evils of the system."

November 8, 2010 The original cast album of *Wicked* is certified double platinum by the Recording Industry Association of America, meaning it has sold more than two million copies.

November 9, 2010 Former "Saturday Night Live" comic Colin Quinn whisks audiences through a wry history of civilization in 75 minutes in his solo show *Colin Quinn Long Story Short.*

November 10, 2010 The Tony Awards announce the June 2011 ceremony will be held at the Beacon Theatre for the first time,

Timeline 2010-2011

moving from its longtime home at Radio City Music Hall, which has been booked that weekend by Cirque de Soleil.

November 11, 2010 Paul Reubens recreates his kids' TV show on Broadway with *The Pee-wee Herman Show*.

November 13, 2010 Al Pacino plays Shylock and Lily Rabe plays Portia in a revival of Shakespeare's *The Merchant of Venice*, following an acclaimed summer 2010 run in Central Park.

November 14, 2010 A musical adaptation of the movie comedy *Elf* stars Sebastian Arcelus as a boy who was raised to believe he was one Santa's elves, and now tries to find his true father in modern New York. The show fea-

Puppeteers working inside and beside creations by the South Africa's Handspring Puppet Company, seem to bring full-size horses to life in *War Horse*. Lincoln Center Theater's Tony-winning production is one of the sensations of the spring 2011 season. See April 14, 2011.

tures a score by Matthew Sklar and Chad Beguelin and book by Bob Martin and Thomas Meehan, and co-stars Amy Spanger, Mark Jacoby, Beth Leavel, Matthew Gumley and George Wendt.

November 18, 2010 Lincoln Center Theater hosts *A Free Man of Color*, John Guare's historical comedy that mixes fact and fiction in telling the adventures of a mixed-race rake in the high-society salons and bedrooms of early 19th-century New Orleans.

November 21, 2010 Brendan Fraser and Denis O'Hare play two inmates from a mental institution who, under the supervision of a social worker, are given a shot at living on their own in Simon Bent's U.K.-originated comedy,

Elling.

November 28, 2010 The first preview of *Spider-Man: Turn Off the Dark*. During the following seven months of previews—the most ever for a Broadway show—the $65 million production will weather headline-grabbing injuries to its cast, and will acquire a new director, librettist and leading lady, before the official opening is pushed into the 2011-2012 season. The show's difficulties become fodder for comedians and talk shows. Comedy Central's Stephen Colbert parodies the show's catchphrase saying, "With great power comes great medical bills."

December 9, 2010: *Donny and Marie: A Broadway Christmas* is a holiday music-and-dance revue featuring the brother/sister performers.

January 2, 2011 *Wicked* reports selling $2,228,235 worth of tickets for the week, the most of any Broadway show in history.

January 4, 2011 The Broadway League reports that Broadway sold a record 12.11 million tickets in 2010, worth a record $1.037 billion.

January 2011 Broadway cleans house. Fifteen shows close, making theatres available for a bumper crop of spring openings.

January 13, 2011 Brian Bedford dons drag to play the indomitable Lady Bracknell in a revival of Oscar Wilde's comedy of hidden identities, *The Importance of Being Earnest*, which he also directs.

March 3, 2011 A down-on-her-luck South Boston woman (Frances McDormand) finds herself in moral hot water when she hits up a successful old flame for a job in *Good People*, Manhattan Theatre Club's world-premiere presentation of David Lindsay-Abaire's drama.

March 6, 2011 Chris Noth and Kiefer Sutherland are among stars featured in a revival of the Pulitzer-winning drama, *That Championship Season*.

March 11, 2011 Standup comedian Kathy Griffin dishes the dirt on today's crop of celebrities in her solo show, *Kathy Griffin Wants a Tony*, marking the first time the Tony Awards have been mentioned by name in the title of a Broadway show.

March 17, 2011 A Broadway revival of Tom Stoppard's *Arcadia*, which jumps back and forth in time from the 19th century to the present. Featuring Billy Crudup, Raúl Esparza and Margaret Colin, the production is based on David Leveaux's 2009 London revival.

March 20, 2011 In the new musical *Priscilla Queen of the Desert*, three drag queens cross the dusty and often homophobic Australian Outback in a brightly painted bus named Priscilla so one of them can reunite with his son. The show was written by Stephan Elliott and Allan Scott, based upon the similarly titled film, using a score of pop hits.

March 22, 2011 Emmy Award-winning comic, writer and actor John Leguizamo brings his latest autobiographical solo show, *Ghetto Klown*, to Broadway.

March 24, 2011 Josh Gad and Andrew Rannells play mismatched missionaries in the irreverent original musical comedy *The Book of Mormon*, with a book and score by "South Park" creators Matt Stone and Trey Parker, and *Avenue Q* co-creator Robert Lopez.

March 27, 2011 *Harry Potter* star Daniel Radcliffe dons a bowtie and American accent to make his Broadway musical debut as J. Pierrepont Finch in Rob Ashford's revival of Frank Loesser's musical satire on corporate America, *How To Succeed in Business Without Really Trying*, opposite John Larroquette.

March 31, 2001 Rajiv Joseph's chilling and philosophical play *Bengal Tiger at the Baghdad Zoo* follows the intertwined stories of a tiger's ghost (Robin Williams), two American marines and an Iraqi gardener in wartime Baghdad as they try to make sense of a world gone to pieces.

April 7, 2011 Sutton Foster plays Reno Sweeney to Joel Grey's Moonface Martin in Kathleen Marshall's revival of Cole Porter's classic shipboard musical comedy *Anything Goes*.

April 10, 2011 *Catch Me If You Can*, the film

Timeline 2010-2011

comedy about a bold young con man, becomes a new musical from the *Hairspray* team of Marc Shaiman (Music, Lyrics), Scott Wittman (Lyrics) and Terrence McNally (Book). Jack O'Brien directs a cast headed by Norbert Leo Butz, Aaron Tveit, Tom Wopat, and Kerry Butler.

April 11, 2011 Chris Rock plays a duplicitous Alcoholics Anonymous sponsor in Stephen Adly Guirgis' comedy *The Motherf**ker with the Hat*, which also features Bobby Cannavale, Elizabeth Rodriguez, Annabella Sciorra and Yul Vázquez.

April 14, 2011 A young man crosses the battlefields of World War I to retrieve his pet horse who has been sold to the cavalry in Lincoln Center Theater's transfer of the National Theatre's *War Horse*, directed by Marianne Elliott and Tom Morris.

April 17, 2011 Lewis Carroll classic *Alice's Adventures in Wonderland* gets a new look as the grown Alice comes back for a second visit in Frank Wildhorn's and Jack Murphy's new musical *Wonderland*, starring Janet Dacal, Darren Ritchie, Karen Mason and Kate Shindle.

April 19, 2011 Kathleen Turner plays a nun who agrees to counsel a tough 19-year-old drug addict in Matthew Lombardo's drama *High*, also starring Stephen Kunken and Evan Jonigkeit.

April 20, 2011 Patina Miller and Victoria Clark star in a stage musical adaptation of the film *Sister Act*, about a singer on the run who transforms the lives of a convent full of nuns when she hides out among them. Jerry Zaks directed the show, which has a score by Alan Menken and Glenn Slater.

April 21, 2011 The hit London drama *Jerusalem* tells the story of a former daredevil motorcyclist (Mark Rylance) on a drug-and-booze-filled confrontation with the forces of civilization he is convinced are trying to bring him down.

April 24, 2011 Nina Arianda, Jim Belushi and Robert Sean Leonard star in a revival of the 1946 Garson Kanin comedy *Born Yesterday*, about a classic dumb-blonde character who smartens up enough to turn the tables on her corrupt businessman boyfriend.

April 25, 2011 A revival of John Guare's 1966 dark comedy *The House of Blue Leaves*, about people with big dreams headed for destinations that include Hollywood, Vietnam, heaven and the mental institution of the title. With Edie Falco, Ben Stiller and Jennifer Jason Leigh.

April 27, 2011 The new musical *Baby It's You!* tells the true-life story of a New Jersey housewife (Beth Leavel) who discovers the all-girl

Norbert Leo Butz jumps for joy after winning the Tony Award for Best Peformance by an Actor in a Leading Role in a Musical, for *Catch Me If You Can*. See June 12, 2011.

group the Shirelles and becomes a driving force in the early 1960s music business. With a book by Floyd Mutrux and Colin Escott (*Million Dollar Quartet*), and a score of hits from the period.

April 27, 2011 Actor Joel Grey crosses the footlights to co-direct with George C. Wolfe a revival of Larry Kramer's searing drama about the early days of the AIDS epidemic, *The Normal Heart*. Joe Mantello crosses the footlights in the other direction to star opposite John Benjamin Hickey and Ellen Barkin.

April 28, 2011 *The People in the Picture*, a new musical starring Donna Murphy as an American grandmother trying to keep alive her days in Polish Yiddish theatre through her granddaughter, has a book and lyrics by "Beaches" novelist Iris Rainer Dart and music by Mike Stoller (*Smokey Joe's Café*) and Artie Butler.

May 5, 2011 Following the Navy Seals' killing

of 9/11 mastermind Osama bin Laden, President Barack Obama visits NYFD Engine 54, Ladder 4, Battalion 9, the Manhattan firehouse that lost fifteen firefighters in the World Trade Center attack—the most of any New York firehouse. This is also the firehouse that protects the Broadway theatres and theatregoers.

May 31, 2011 Broadway ends its most lucrative season on record, selling $1,080,562,880 worth of tickets, according to the Broadway League. Total attendance hits a record 12,534,595.

June 12, 2011 The 65th Annual Tony Awards are given at the Beacon Theatre. *War Horse* is named Best Play and *The Book of Mormon* is named Best Musical.

—Robert Viagas

Head of the Class

Trends, Extraordinary Achievements and Peculiar Coincidences of the Season

Most Tony Awards to a Play: *War Horse* (5).
Most Tony Awards to a Musical: *The Book of Mormon* (9).
Shortest Run: *High* (8 performances).
Long Runs Say Farewell: *In the Heights* (1184 performances), *South Pacific* (996 performances), *West Side Story* (748 performances).
Some of the Stars You Could Have Seen This Season: Brian Bedford, Jim Belushi, Laura Benanti, Norbert Leo Butz, Harry Connick Jr., Barbara Cook, Edie Falco, Harvey Fierstein, Sutton Foster, Joel Grey, Kathy Griffin, Cherry Jones, James Earl Jones, John Leguizamo, Patti LuPone, Frances McDormand, Brian Stokes Mitchell, Chris Noth, Donny and Marie Osmond, Al Pacino, Estelle Parsons, Bernadette Peters, David Hyde Pierce, Colin Quinn, Lily Rabe, Daniel Radcliffe, Vanessa Redgrave, Paul Reubens (a.k.a. Pee-wee Herman), Chris Rock, Mark Rylance, Ben Stiller, Elaine Stritch, Kiefer Sutherland, Kathleen Turner, George Wendt, Robin Williams, et al.
Awards They Should Give: #1 Best New Showtune: Our nominees: "Go Back Home" from *The Scottsboro Boys*, "I Believe" from *The Book of Mormon*, "Don't Break the Rules" from *Catch Me If You Can*, "Raise Your Voice" from *Sister Act*, "One Knight" from *Wonderland*.
Drag: *La Cage aux Folles, Priscilla Queen of the Desert,* Brian Bedford in *The Importance of Being Earnest,* the "Welcome to Wonderland" number in *Wonderland*.
Comedians Doing Serious Roles: Chris Rock in *Motherf**ker With the Hat,* Robin Williams in *Bengal Tiger in the Baghdad Zoo,* Ben Stiller in *The House of Blue Leaves,* Bette Midler as producer of *Priscilla Queen of the Desert;* Whoopi Goldberg as producer of *Sister Act*.
Spanish Accents: *The Addams Family, Bloody Bloody Andrew Jackson, In the Heights, Women on the Verge.*
English Accents: *Arcadia, Billy Elliot, Brief Encounter, Jerusalem, A Life in the Theatre, Mary Poppins, Mrs. Warren's Profession, The Pitmen Painters, Rain, War Horse.*
Surprisingly Good American Accent: Daniel Radcliffe in *How to Succeed*.
Marital Infidelity As Plot or Major Subplot: *Baby It's You!, Brief Encounter, Catch Me If You Can, A Free Man of Color, Good People, The House of Blue Leaves, How To Succeed in Business Without Really Trying, The Motherf**ker With the Hat, The People in the Picture, Promises Promises, That Championship Season, Women on the Verge.*
Fish Out of Water: *Book of Mormon, Priscilla Queen, Scottsboro, Pitmen Painters, Sister Act, Catch Me If You Can.* Honorable Mention: Horse out of Water: *War Horse.*
Hey! Even Blue Collar People Like the Arts: *Pitmen Painters, Red, Billy Elliot.*
Shows Set in the South: *Bloody Bloody Andrew Jackson, Driving Miss Daisy, Free Man of Color, Memphis, Million Dollar Quartet, The Scottsboro Boys.*
Musicals Set in Africa: *The Lion King, The Book of Mormon, Fela!*
Alcoholics in and out of AA: *High, The*

Broadway's Longest Runs

By number of performances. Asterisk (*) indicates show still running as of May 31, 2011. Totals are for original runs except where otherwise noted.

* The Phantom of the Opera 9723
Cats 7485
Les Misérables 6680
A Chorus Line 6137
*Chicago (Revival) 6040
Oh! Calcutta! (Revival) 5959
* The Lion King 5672
Beauty and the Beast 5461
Rent 5123
Miss Saigon 4097
* Mamma Mia! 4000
42nd Street 3486
Grease 3388
Fiddler on the Roof 3242
Life With Father 3224
Tobacco Road 3182
* Wicked 3158
Hello, Dolly! 2844
My Fair Lady 2717
Hairspray 2642

Motherf**ker With the Hat, That Championship Season, War Horse, Jerusalem, Born Yesterday.
Awards They Should Give: #2 Best Special Effects: Our nominees: Flying over the Chrysler Building in *Spider-Man: Turn Off the Dark.* Live actors entering film scenes in *Brief Encounter.* The lifelike creation of horses through life-size puppets in *War Horse.* The titular bus making high-tech transformations in *Priscilla Queen of the Desert.* The magical entrance of the princess in *La Bête.* Santa's sleigh ride in *Elf.* Pervasive magical effects in *The Pee-wee Herman Show.*
Hating Blacks Is Bad: *Scottsboro Boys, Driving Miss Daisy, Race, Memphis, Baby It's You*
Hating Asians Is Bad: *South Pacific*
Hating Jews Is Bad: *The Merchant of Venice, The People in the Picture*
Hating Gays Is Bad: *Priscilla Queen of the Desert, Next Fall, The Normal Heart, La Cage*
Hating Elves Is Bad: *Elf*
Hating Talking Animals and Green People Is Bad: *Wicked*
Hating Indians, the Spanish, the French and the Eastern Establishment Is Good: *Bloody Bloody Andrew Jackson*
Men, Women, Boys, Sisters, Mothers and a Baby: *A Free Man of Color, Spider-Man, Pitmen Painters, Women on the Verge of a Nervous Breakdown, Scottsboro Boys, Jersey Boys, Sister Act, Mamma Mia!, The Motherf**ker With the Hat, Baby It's You!…and The Addams Family.*
Cute Little Girls in Danger of Being Kidnapped, Shot, Molested, Burned to Death, Raped, Trampled, Gassed by Nazis, Put on Trial by Their Toys or Anesthetized and Smothered (respectively): *Wonderland, War Horse, Jerusalem, Arcadia, Bengal Tiger at the Baghdad Zoo, The Lion King, People in the Picture,*

Mary Poppins. Honorable Mention: *Séance on a Wet Afternoon.* CLG death toll: 3.
The Song "Anything Goes": Heard in *Born Yesterday* and *Anything Goes.* Honorable mention: "Friendship" from *Anything Goes,* is heard in *House of Blue Leaves.*
Two Major Credits: Casey Nicholaw on *Book of Mormon* and *Elf.* Beth Leavel in *Elf* and *Baby Its You.* Joel Grey in *Anything Goes* and co-directing *The Normal Heart.* Mark Rylance in *Jerusalem* and *La Bête.* John McMartin in *Free Man of Color* and *Anything Goes.* George C. Wolfe staging *Free Man of Color* and *Normal Heart.*
Three Major Credits: Doug Hughes directing *Born Yesterday, Mrs. Warren's Profession* and *Elling.*
Provocative Songs and Show Titles: *The Motherf**ker with the Hat.* "Hasa Diga Eebowai" (Tr. "F**k You, God") in *The Book of Mormon.* "Lady in the Long Dress" (the seducing nuns song) in *Sister Act.* "Financial Advice" (a.k.a. "Jew Money") in *The Scottsboro Boys.*
Awards They Should Give: #3 Best New Rendition of an Old Song in a Revival or Jukebox Musical: "Grand Old Ivy" in *How To Succeed.* The title song in *Anything Goes.* "Dedicated to the One I Love" in *Baby It's You.* Honorable Mention: "I'll Take Manhattan" in *Spider-Man: Turn Off the Dark.*
Coups de Theatre: Bobby Cannavale can't bring himself to end a dysfunctional relationship in the final scene of *The Motherf**ker With the Hat*…watching the light go on over Josh Gad's head when he realizes he can convert more Africans to Mormonism by making up his own religion in *The Book of Mormon*…in the same musical, Andrew Rannells as Elder Price confronting a murderous warlord armed with only his faith in a lot of things that might seem absurd to outsiders, in the song "I Believe"…schlumpy Norbert Leo Butz catches fire as he and the chorus sing about obeying the law in "Don't Break the Rules" in *Catch Me If You Can*…Donna Murphy transforming from a fragile grandmother to a vibrant comic star in *The People in the Picture*…the tender deathbed wedding in *The Normal Heart* that prefigured the passage of a gay marriage bill in New York State…Brian Bedford as Lady Bracknell examining Jack Worthing's dubious suit for his/her niece in *The Importance of Being Earnest*…Frances McDormand stifling her conscience in *Good People*…Mark Rylance using the front of his pants and his gyrating hips to mix a morning concoction of drugs, booze and sour milk in *Jerusalem*…illicit lovers swinging on chandeliers in *Brief Encounter*…Laura Benanti's five-minute fast-talk marathon "Model Behavior" in *Women on the Verge*…Daniel Radcliffe dancing up a storm in "The Brotherhood of Man" from *How to Succeed*…the crazy cupcake costumes in *Priscilla Queen of the Desert*…the pony puppet Joey transforming into the fully-grown puppet Joey as it canters around the stage in *War Horse*…the climactic battle between Spider-Man and The Green Goblin in the air above the balcony in *Spider-man: Turn Off the Dark*…Alice tumbling down a magical elevator shaft instead of a rabbit hole in the New York-ified re-imagining of *Wonderland*.

Autographs

The Addams Family

First Preview: March 8, 2010. Opened: April 8, 2010.
Still running as of May 31, 2011.

PLAYBILL

The creepy, kooky gothic horror-comedy Addams Family faces a crisis when daughter Wednesday, now grown up, brings home the man she wants to marry. As Gomez and Morticia prepare to welcome his "normal" family for a get-acquainted dinner in their haunted house, they also face their own aging and the possibility of trouble in their own marriage.

CAST

THE ADDAMS FAMILY

Gomez Addams	ROGER REES
Morticia Addams	BEBE NEUWIRTH
Uncle Fester	BRAD OSCAR
Grandma	JACKIE HOFFMAN
Wednesday Addams	RACHEL POTTER
Pugsley Addams	ADAM RIEGLER
Lurch	ZACHARY JAMES

THE BEINEKE FAMILY

Mal Beineke	ADAM GRUPPER
Alice Beineke	HEIDI BLICKENSTAFF
Lucas Beineke	JESSE SWENSON

THE ADDAMS ANCESTORS

BECCA AYERS, TOM BERKLUND,
MO BRADY, ERICK BUCKLEY,
STEPHANIE GIBSON, FRED INKLEY,
LISA KARLIN, REED KELLY,
ALLISON THOMAS LEE, LOGAN ROWLAND,
CORTNEY WOLFSON

All puppetry is performed by members of
The Addams Family Company.

Continued on next page

LUNT-FONTANNE THEATRE

UNDER THE DIRECTION OF
JAMES M. NEDERLANDER AND JAMES L. NEDERLANDER

Stuart Oken   Roy Furman   Michael Leavitt   Five Cent Productions
Stephen Schuler   Decca Theatricals   Scott M. Delman   Stuart Ditsky   Terry Allen Kramer   Stephanie P. McClelland
James L. Nederlander   Eva Price   Jam Theatricals/Mary Lu Roffe   Pittsburgh CLO/Gutterman-Swinsky
Vivek Tiwary/Gary Kaplan   The Weinstein Company/Clarence, LLC   Adam Zotovich/Tribe Theatricals

by Special Arrangement with
Elephant Eye Theatrical

present

Roger Rees   Bebe Neuwirth

in

The Addams Family

A NEW MUSICAL
COMEDY

Book by	Music and Lyrics by
Marshall Brickman & **Rick Elice**	**Andrew Lippa**

Based on Characters Created by
Charles Addams

With

Heidi Blickenstaff Adam Grupper Zachary James Brad Oscar
Rachel Potter Adam Riegler Jesse Swenson and Jackie Hoffman

Merwin Foard Becca Ayers Tom Berklund Jim Borstelmann Mo Brady Erick Buckley
Colin Cunliffe Valerie Fagan Stephanie Gibson Fred Inkley Lisa Karlin Reed Kelly
Allison Thomas Lee Logan Rowland Samantha Sturm Cortney Wolfson

Lighting Design by	Sound Design by	Puppetry by
Natasha Katz	**Acme Sound Partners**	**Basil Twist**

Hair Design by	Make-up Design by	Special Effects by
Tom Watson	**Angelina Avallone**	**Gregory Meeh**

Orchestrations	Music Director	Dance Arrangements	Vocal Arrangements & Incidental Music
Larry Hochman	**Mary-Mitchell Campbell**	**August Eriksmoen**	**Andrew Lippa**

Casting	Press Representative	Marketing	Music Coordinator
Telsey + Company	**The Publicity Office**	**Type A Marketing**	**Michael Keller**

Production Supervisor	Production Management	General Management
Beverley Randolph	**Aurora Productions**	**101 Productions, Ltd.**

Creative Consultant
Jerry Zaks

Choreography by
Sergio Trujillo

Directed and Designed by
Phelim McDermott & **Julian Crouch**

NOW THAT'S BROADWAY!

3/22/11

(L-R): Adam Riegler, Jackie Hoffman,
Bebe Neuwirth, Roger Rees,
Brad Oscar, Rachel Potter

Photo by Jeremy Daniel

1

The Addams Family

MUSICAL NUMBERS

ACT ONE

Overture ....Orchestra
"When You're an Addams" ....The Addams Family, Ancestors
"Pulled" ....Wednesday, Pugsley
"Where Did We Go Wrong" ....Morticia, Gomez
"One Normal Night" ....Company
"Morticia" ....Gomez, Male Ancestors
"What If" ....Pugsley
"Full Disclosure" ....Company
"Waiting" ....Alice
"Full Disclosure – Part 2" ....Company

ACT TWO

Entr'acte ....Orchestra
"Just Around the Corner" ....Morticia, Ancestors
"The Moon and Me" ....Uncle Fester, Female Ancestors
"Happy/Sad" ....Gomez
"Crazier Than You" ....Wednesday, Lucas
"Let's Not Talk About Anything Else But Love" ....Mal, Gomez, Uncle Fester, Grandma
"In the Arms" ....Mal, Alice
"Live Before We Die" ....Gomez, Morticia
"Tango de Amor" ....Morticia, Gomez, Company
"Move Toward the Darkness" ....Company

(L-R): Heidi Blickenstaff, Zachary James, Adam Grupper

Photo by Jeremy Daniel

Photo by Jeremy Shaffer

CREW
(L-R): Paul Wimmer (Production Carpenter), David Gotwald (Production Sound), Jeremy Wahlers (Asst. Electrician), Holli Shevett (Deck Sound), Bryan Davis (Fly Automation), Mike Hyman (Head Electrician), Steve Long (Asst. Electrician), David Brickman (Spot Op), Scott Silvian (Asst. Sound), Brendan Lynch (Spot Op), Danny Viscardo (Props)

Cast Continued

STANDBY

Standby for Gomez Addams and Mal Beineke:
MERWIN FOARD

UNDERSTUDIES

For Gomez Addams: JIM BORSTELMANN
For Morticia Addams: BECCA AYERS,
    STEPHANIE GIBSON
For Uncle Fester: JIM BORSTELMANN,
    ERICK BUCKLEY
For Wednesday Addams: LISA KARLIN,
    CORTNEY WOLFSON
For Pugsley Addams: LOGAN ROWLAND
For Grandma: BECCA AYERS, VALERIE FAGAN
For Lurch: TOM BERKLUND, FRED INKLEY
For Mal Beineke: FRED INKLEY
For Alice Beineke: BECCA AYERS,
    VALERIE FAGAN
For Lucas Beineke: MO BRADY,
    COLIN CUNLIFFE

SWINGS

JIM BORSTELMANN, MICHAEL BUCHANAN,
COLIN CUNLIFFE, VALERIE FAGAN,
DONTEE KIEHN, SAMANTHA STURM

Dance Captain: COLIN CUNLIFFE
Puppet Performance Captain: COLIN CUNLIFFE
Assistant Dance Captain: SAMANTHA STURM

ORCHESTRA

Conductor: MARY-MITCHELL CAMPBELL
Associate Conductor: MARCO PAGUIA
Concertmaster: VICTORIA PATERSON
Violin: SEAN CARNEY
Viola: HIROKO TAGUCHI
Cello: ALLISON SEIDNER
Lead Trumpet: TONY KADLECK
Trumpet: BUD BURRIDGE
Trombones/Tuba: RANDY ANDOS
Reed 1: ERICA VON KLEIST
Reed 2: CHARLES PILLOW
Reed 3: MARK THRASHER
French Horn: ZOHAR SCHONDORF
Drums: DAMIEN BASSMAN
Bass: DAVE KUHN
Keyboard 1: CHRIS FENWICK
Keyboard 2: WILL VAN DYKE
Guitars: JIM HERSHMAN
Percussion: BILLY MILLER

Music Coordinator: MICHAEL KELLER
Music Copying: KAYE-HOUSTON MUSIC/
ANNE KAYE & DOUG HOUSTON

The Addams Family

THE MAN BEHIND THE FAMILY

Photo: Lane Stewart

"Are you unhappy, darling?" *"Oh yes, yes! Completely."*

The musical *The Addams Family* is inspired by the creations of the legendary American cartoonist Charles Addams, who lived from 1912 until 1988. In 1933, when he was just 21, his work was published in *The New Yorker*, and over the course of nearly six decades, he became one of the magazine's most cherished contributors.

Bizarre, macabre and weird are all words that have been used to describe Charles Addams' cartoons. Yet adjectives such as charming, enchanting and tender can just as accurately be employed to depict the same body of work, as well as the man himself.

His unique style and wonderfully crafted cartoons enabled his work to transcend such dichotomies for his millions of fans worldwide.

Charles Addams is most widely known for his characters that came to be called The Addams Family, a group that evolved into multiple television shows, motion pictures and now this Broadway musical. Gomez, Morticia, Uncle Fester, Wednesday, Pugsley, Grandma and Lurch existed in various forms and aspects of Addams' cartoons dating back to the 1930's but were not actually named by him until the early 1960's,

when the television series was created. Surprisingly, The Addams Family characters appear in only a small number of the artist's several thousand works. The majority of his cartoons are occupied by hundreds of other characters, but there is little doubt that those that come to life on this

stage are his most beloved creations. Over 15 books of his drawings have been published around the world, including the new collection, *The Addams Family: An Evilution*, the first complete history of The Addams Family, including more than 200 cartoons, many never previously published. The collection also

includes Addams' own incisive character descriptions (originally penned for the benefit of the television show producers) that

remind us where these oddly lovable characters came from and, in doing so, offer a lasting tribute to one of America's greatest humorists.

To learn more about Charles Addams, his life and his legacy, please visit our gallery in the second floor lounge.

All artwork © Charles Addams with permission of the Tee and Charles Addams Foundation

Roger Rees
Gomez Addams

Bebe Neuwirth
Morticia Addams

Heidi Blickenstaff
Alice Beineke

Adam Grupper
Mal Beineke

Jackie Hoffman
Grandma

Zachary James
Lurch

Brad Oscar
Uncle Fester

Rachel Potter
Wednesday Addams

Adam Riegler
Pugsley Addams

Jesse Swenson
Lucas Beineke

Merwin Foard
Standby Gomez Addams, Standby Mal Beineke

Becca Ayers
Ancestor

Tom Berklund
Ancestor

Jim Borstelmann
Swing

Mo Brady
Ancestor

Michael Buchanan
Swing

Erick Buckley
Ancestor

Colin Cunliffe
Swing, Puppet Performance Captain, Dance Captain

Valerie Fagan
Swing

Stephanie Gibson
Ancestor

Fred Inkley
Ancestor

The Addams Family

Lisa Karlin
Ancestor

Reed Kelly
Ancestor

Dontee Kiehn
*Associate
Choreographer/
Swing*

Allison Thomas Lee
Ancestor

Logan Rowland
Ancestor

Samantha Sturm
*Swing/Assistant
Dance Captain*

Cortney Wolfson
Ancestor

Marshall Brickman
Book

Rick Elice
Book

Andrew Lippa
Music and Lyrics

Phelim McDermott
Director/Designer

Julian Crouch
Director/Designer

Sergio Trujillo
Choreographer

Natasha Katz
Lighting Designer

Sten Severson, Tom Clark, Mark Menard and Nevin Steinberg,
Acme Sound Partners
Sound Designer

Basil Twist
Puppetry

Tom Watson
*Hair and Wig
Designer*

Angelina Avallone
Make-up Designer

Gregory Meeh
*Special Effects
Designer*

Mary-Mitchell
Campbell
Music Director

Larry Hochman
Orchestrations

August Eriksmoen
*Dance
Arrangements*

Bernard Telsey,
Telsey + Company
Casting

Michael Keller
Music Coordinator

Beverley Randolph
*Production
Supervisor*

Wendy Orshan,
101 Productions, Ltd.
General Manager

Stuart Oken
Producer

Roy Furman
Producer

Michael Leavitt
Producer

Stuart Ditsky/
Ditsky Productions,
LLC
Producer

Terry Allen Kramer
Producer

Stephanie P.
McClelland/
Green Curtain
Productions
Producer

James L.
Nederlander
Producer

The Addams Family

Eva Price/
Maximum
Entertainment
Producer

Arny Granat,
Jam Theatricals
Producer

Steve Traxler,
Jam Theatricals
Producer

Mary Lu Roffe
Producer

Van Kaplan,
Pittsburgh CLO
Producer

Jay and Cindy Gutterman
Producer

Morton Swinsky
Producer

Vivek J. Tiwary
Producer

Bob Weinstein,
The Weinstein
Company
Producer

Harvey Weinstein,
The Weinstein
Company
Producer

Adam Zotovich
Producer

Carl Moellenberg,
Tribe Theatricals
Producer

Wendy Federman,
Tribe Theatricals
Producer

Jamie deRoy,
Tribe Theatricals
Producer

Larry Hirschhorn,
Tribe Theatricals
Producer

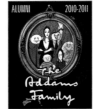

Carolee Carmello
Alice Beineke

Kevin Chamberlin
Uncle Fester

Rachel de Benedet
Ancestor

Matthew Gumley
Ancestor

Morgan James
Ancestor

Clark Johnsen
Ancestor

Nathan Lane
Gomez Addams

Terrence Mann
Mal Beineke

Barrett Martin
Ancestor

Jessica Lea Patty
Ancestor

Liz Ramos
*Ancestor,
Dance Captain*

Krysta Rodriguez
Wednesday Addams

Charlie Sutton
Ancestor

Wesley Taylor
Lucas Beineke

Aléna Watters
Ancestor

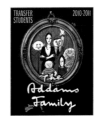

Mike Cannon
Swing

Curtis Holbrook
Ancestor

The Addams Family

Associate Scenic Designer ....Frank McCullough
Associate Costume Designers ....MaryAnn D. Smith,
                                          David Kaley
Associate Lighting Designer ....Yael Lubetzky
Automated Lighting Programmer ....Aland Henderson
Associate Sound Designer ....Jason Crystal
Associate Special Effects Designer ....Jeremy Chernick
Associate Puppetry Designer ....Ceili Clemens
Assistant Scenic Designers ....Lauren Alvarez,
                      Jeffrey Hinchee, Christine Peters,
                                          Rob Thirtle
Assistant Costume Designer ....Sarah Laux
Assistant Lighting Designer ....Joel Shier
Assistant Make-up Designer ....Jorge Vargas
Costume Assistant ....Jennifer A. Jacob
Assistant in Puppetry ....Meredith Miller
Production Carpenter ....Paul T. Wimmer
Assistant Carpenter/Automation ....Bill Partello
Flyman ....Bryan S. Davis
Production Electrician ....J. Michael Pitzer
Head Electrician ....Mike Hyman
Assistant Electrician ....Stephen R. Long
Lead Follow Spot ....Brent Oakley
Production Props ....Denise J. Grillo
Assistant Props ....Kevin Crawford
Production Sound ....David Gotwald
Assistant Sound ....Scott Silvian
Advance Sound ....Darin Stillman
Wardrobe Supervisor ....Linda Lee
Assistant Wardrobe Supervisor ....Andrea Gonzalez
Mr. Rees' Dresser ....Ken Brown
Ms. Neuwirth's Dresser ....Paula Davis
Dressers ....Jennifer Barnes, Ceili Clemens,
                      Joe Hickey, Betsy Waddell, John Webber
Hair & Make-up Supervisor ....Barry Ernst
Hair Dressers ....Kevin Phillips, Robin Baxter
Music Coordinator ....Michael Keller
Music Preparation ....Kaye-Houston Music, Inc./
                              Anne Kaye, Doug Houston
Music Preparation Assistants ....Russell Driscoll,
                                          Ernst Ebell, III,
                      Arthur Koening, Barry Lille
Electronic Music Programmer ....James Abbott
Additional Orchestrations ....August Eriksmoen,
                                          Danny Troob
Additional Drum & Percussion
    Arrangements ....Damien Bassman
Music Interns ....Ben Krauss, Tim Rosser,
                                          Adam Wiggins
Children's Guardian ....Katy Lathan
Stage Management
    Production Assistants ....Zac Chandler,
                      CJ LaRoche, Jenn McNeil,
                      Alison Roberts, Deanna Weiner
Company Management
    Assistants ....Johnny Milani, Kathleen Mueller
Lighting Design Production Assistant ....Alec Thorne
Sound Design Production Assistant ....Jessica Bauer
Assistant to Mr. Oken ....Missy Greenberg
Assistant to Mr. Furman ....Eileen Williams
Assistant to Mr. Leavitt ....Erlinda Vo
Assistant to Mr. Lippa ....Will Van Dyke
Assistant to Mr. Lane ....Andrea Wolfson
Legal Counsel ....Levine, Plotkin & Menin LLP/
                      Loren Plotkin, Esq., Susan Mindell,
                      Conrad Rippy, Cris Criswell

Accountant ....Rosenberg, Neuwirth,
                              & Kuchner, CPAs/
                              Christopher Cacace
Comptroller ....Jana Jevnikar
Advertising ....Serino Coyne/
                      Sandy Block, Angelo Desimini,
                              Matt Upshaw
Marketing ....Type A Marketing/
                      Anne Rippey, Michael Porto,
                      Elyce Henkin, Robin Steinthal
Interactive Marketing ....Situation Interactive/
                      Damian Bazadona, John Lanasa,
                      Jeremy Kraus, Jenn Elston
Educational Program ....Camp Broadway
101 Productions, Ltd. Staff ....Ingrid Kloss,
                      Meredith Morgan, Michael Rudd,
                      Mary-Six Rupert, Christine Stump
Children's Tutoring ....On Location Education/
                              Alan Simon, Muriel Kester
Banking ....City National Bank/Anne McSweeney
Insurance ....DeWitt Stern, Inc./Peter Shoemaker
Physical Therapy ....PhysioArts/Jennifer R. Green
Orthopedist ....David S. Weiss, MD
Immigration ......Traffic Control Group, Inc./David King
Merchandising ....Encore Merchandising, Inc./
                      Joey Boyles, Chris Paseka,
                              Maryana Geller
Production Photographer ....Joan Marcus
Payroll Services ....Castellana Services, Inc.

www.theaddamsfamilymusical.com

CREDITS

Scenery by Hudson Scenic Studios, Inc., Showman Fabricators, Chicago Scenic Studios, Inc. Automated scenery by Hudson Scenic Studios. Lighting equipment and special lighting effects from PRG Lighting. Sound equipment from Masque Sound. Costumes executed by Eric Winterling, Carelli Costumes, Jennifer Love. Costume painting by Jeffrey Fender. Props by the Paragon Innovation Group, Jerard Studios, Craig Grigg, Daedalus Design & Production, Zoe Morsette, ICBA, Inc. Men's shirts by Cego Custom Shirt. Millinery by Hugh Hanson for Carelli Costumes and Arnold S. Levine, Inc. Custom footwear by LaDuca Productions, Ltd.; Pluma Handmade Dance Footwear; Worldtone Dance; and Sam Vasili Custom Shoes. "Fester" custom work by Izquierdo Studio. "Grandma's" shawl by Vanessa Theriault. Additional men's tailoring by Paul Chang, Chicago. Special effects by Jauchem & Meeh, Inc. Flying by Foy Aerographic® Services. Make-up provided by M•A•C. Mr. Mann's wardrobe provided by Brooks Brothers. Cell phones courtesy of Nokia. Emergen-C super energy booster provided by Alacer Corp. Onstage merchandising by George Fenmore.

"Addams Family Theme" by Vic Mizzy, published by Unison Music Company (ASCAP). Administered by Next Decade Entertainment, Inc. All rights reserved, used by permission.

THE ADDAMS FAMILY rehearsed at
New 42nd Street Rehearsal Studios.

PUPPETRY BUILT BY
TANDEM OTTER PRODUCTIONS

Barbara Busackino, Project Manager
Ceili Clemens, Build Manager
BUILDERS: TV Alexander, Liz Cherry, Duncan Gillis, Kristin Gdula, Michael Kerns, Matthew Leabo, Vito Leanza, Nara Lesser, Laura Manns, Eric Novak, Adam Pagdon, Travis Pickett, Jon Mark Ponder, Jessica Scott, Ted Southern, Nikki Taylor, Will Pike

MUSIC CREDITS

"For What It's Worth" (Stephen Stills), ©1967 (renewed), Richie Furay Music (BMI), Springalo Toones (BMI), Ten East Music (BMI) and Cotillion Music Inc. (BMI), All rights administered by Warner-Tamerlane Publishing Corp. All rights reserved. Used by permission. **"Maniac"** (Dennis Matkosky and Michael Sembello), ©1983 WB Music Corp. (ASCAP), Sony/ATV Harmony (ASCAP) and Intersong-USA, Inc. (ASCAP). All rights administered by WB Music Corp. All rights reserved. Used by permission. **"Puff (The Magic Dragon)"** (Peter Yarrow, Leonard Lipton), ©1963 (renewed), 1991 Silver Dawn Music (ASCAP) and Honalee Melodies (ASCAP). All rights on behalf of Silver Dawn Music administered by WB Music Corp. Worldwide rights for Honalee Melodies administered by Cherry Lane Music Publishing Company, Inc. (ASCAP). All rights reserved. Used by permission. **"So Long, Farewell"** (music by Richard Rodgers, lyrics by Oscar Hammerstein II). This selection is used by special arrangement with The Rodgers and Hammerstein Organization. All rights reserved. Used by permission.

**Souvenir merchandise by
Encore Merchandising, Inc.**

**Original cast album now available on
Decca Records.**

For booking information, contact Meredith Blair:
www.thebookinggroup.com

NEDERLANDER

Chairman ....James M. Nederlander
President ....James L. Nederlander

Executive Vice President
Nick Scandalios

Vice President   Senior Vice President
Corporate Development   Labor Relations
Charlene S. Nederlander   **Herschel Waxman**

Vice President   Chief Financial Officer
Jim Boese   **Freida Sawyer Belviso**

STAFF FOR THE LUNT-FONTANNE

House Manager ....**Tracey Malinowski**
Treasurer ....Joe Olcese
Assistant Treasurer ....Gregg Collichio
House Carpenter ....Terry Taylor
House Electrician ....Dennis Boyle
House Propertyman ....Andrew Bentz
House Flyman ....Matt Walters
House Engineers ....Robert MacMahon,
                              Joseph Riccio III

The Addams Family
SCRAPBOOK

Correspondent: Zachary James, "Lurch"

Memorable Note, Fax or Fan Letter: Will you sing at my funeral?

Anniversary Party: One-year anniversary party at Blue Fin.

Most Exciting Celebrity Visitor and What She Said: Elaine Stritch: "You were a part of it."

Actor Who Performed the Most Roles in This Show: Allison Thomas Lee: "Native American Ancestor," "Monster Under the Bed," "Tassel," "Bird," "Star."

Actor Who Has Done the Most Shows in His Career: Merwin Foard

Special Backstage Rituals: Complaining. Eating.

Favorite Moment During Each Performance: When the curtain opens.

Favorite In-Theatre Gathering Place: Hair room.

Favorite Off-Site Hangout: Kodama, Glass House Tavern, Blue Fin.

Favorite Snack Foods: Trail mix, Cheez-Its.

Mascot: Adam Riegler.

Favorite Therapy: Jackie Hoffman: Tranquilizers.

Memorable Ad-Libs: "Fuck it. Go on to the next scene."

"I'm on a drug and it's called *Grandma*."

"Hey sailors. You can drop your anchor right here."

"This is why I couldn't be in *True Grit*."

"Ya ya ya ya ya ya ya ya ya ya ya ya ya."

Record Number of Cell Phone Rings, Cell Phone Photos or Texting Incidents During a Performance: Who can count? It's like a red carpet out there!

Memorable Press Encounter: Lovely Russian fella doing video interviews at the stage door.

Memorable Stage Door Fan Encounters: "Can I hug you?" "Make that noise you make." "How tall are you?"

Ancestor: "Do you want everyone's autograph or just the important people?"

Fan: "Just the important people."

What Did You Think of the Web Buzz on Your Show: It was tough to compete with our own reputation.

Fastest Costume Change: Ancestors changing every other minute.

Busiest Day at the Box Office: Wednesday.

Who Wore the Heaviest/Hottest Costume: Fester.

Who Wore the Least: Pugsley.

Catchphrase Only the Company Would Recognize: "Gawkahgah!"

Sweethearts Within the Company: Tassel & It.

Orchestra Member Who Played the Most Instruments: Damien Bassman, various percussion.

Orchestra Member Who Played the Most Consecutive Performances Without a Sub: Allison Seidner, cello.

Memorable Directorial Note: "Activate your lizard."

1. Kevin Chamberlin and Bebe Neuwirth at Sardi's Restaurant for the unveiling of his caricature, June 10, 2010.
2. Castmates Krysta Rodriguez and Wesley Taylor at Sardi's.
3. Chamberlin with the portrait.

Best In-House Parody Lyric: "When you're an Addams you have white makeup on your cell phone."

Company In-Jokes: Tell the story. Family. Journey.

Company Legend: Bebe Neuwirth.

Nickname: Melissa.

Ghostly Encounters Backstage: Nathan Lane.

Superstitions That Turned Out To Be True: Nathan Lane sells tickets.

Coolest Thing About Being in This Show: Making people laugh.

Fan Club President: Ronda.

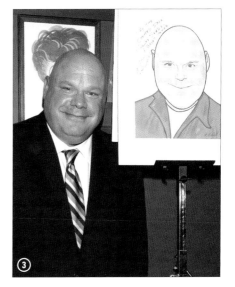

American Idiot

First Preview: March 24, 2010. Opened: April 20, 2010.
Closed April 24, 2011 after 26 Previews and 422 Performances.

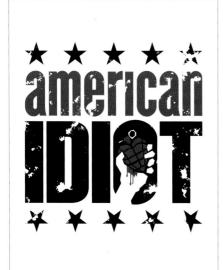

PLAYBILL®

Three young men, Johnny, Will and Tunny, try to find meaning in their lives despite living in what they see as the moral, intellectual and emotional wasteland of early 21st century America. Adapted from the rock album of the same name by the group Green Day.

CAST
(in order of appearance)

Johnny ....JOHN GALLAGHER, JR.
Will ....MICHAEL ESPER
Tunny ....STARK SANDS
Heather ....MARY FABER
Whatsername ....REBECCA NAOMI JONES
St. Jimmy ....TONY VINCENT
The Extraordinary Girl ....CHRISTINA SAJOUS
Ensemble ....DECLAN BENNETT,
ANDREW CALL,
GERARD CANONICO,
MIGUEL CERVANTES,
BRIAN CHARLES JOHNSON,
LESLIE McDONEL, CHASE PEACOCK,
WALLACE SMITH, THEO STOCKMAN,
BEN THOMPSON, ALYSHA UMPHRESS,
LIBBY WINTERS

Standby for Johnny, Will, Tunny: VAN HUGHES

Continued on next page

🍂 ST. JAMES THEATRE
A JUJAMCYN THEATRE

JORDAN ROTH
President

PAUL LIBIN
Producing Director

JACK VIERTEL
Creative Director

Tom Hulce & Ira Pittelman

Ruth and Stephen Hendel   Vivek J. Tiwary and Gary Kaplan   Aged In Wood and Burnt Umber
Scott M. Delman   Latitude Link   HOP Theatricals and Jeffrey Finn   Larry Welk
Bensinger Filerman and Moellenberg Taylor   Allan S. Gordon and Élan V. McAllister
Berkeley Repertory Theatre

In Association with
Awaken Entertainment   John Pinckard and John Domo

Present

american IDIOT

Music by
Green Day

Lyrics by
Billie Joe Armstrong

Book by
Billie Joe Armstrong and **Michael Mayer**

John Gallagher Jr.
Stark Sands   Michael Esper
Rebecca Naomi Jones   Christina Sajous   Mary Faber
and
Tony Vincent

with

Declan Bennett   Andrew Call   Gerard Canonico   Miguel Cervantes   Sydney Harcourt
Van Hughes   Brian Charles Johnson   Joshua Kobak   Lorin Latarro   Omar Lopez-Cepero
Leslie McDonel   Chase Peacock   Corbin Reid   Wallace Smith   Theo Stockman
Ben Thompson   Alysha Umphress   Aspen Vincent   Libby Winters

Scenic Design	Costume Design	Lighting Design	Sound Design	Video/Projection Design
Christine Jones	Andrea Lauer	Kevin Adams	Brian Ronan	Darrel Maloney

Casting	Production Stage Manager	Technical Supervisor	Music Coordinator
Jim Carnahan, C.S.A. Carrie Gardner, C.S.A.	James Harker	Hudson Theatrical Associates	Michael Keller

General Management	Press Representative	Marketing
Abbie M. Strassler	The Hartman Group	Type A Marketing

Music Director	Associate Choreographer	Associate Director
Carmel Dean	Lorin Latarro	Johanna McKeon

Associate Producers
SenovvA   Tix Productions   Tracy Straus and Barney Straus   Lorenzo Thione and Jay Kuo
Pat Magnarella   Christopher Maring

Musical Supervision, Arrangements, and Orchestrations
Tom Kitt

Choreographer
Steven Hoggett

Director
Michael Mayer

World Premiere produced by Berkeley Repertory Theatre, September 2009
Tony Taccone, Artistic Director   Susan Medak, Managing Director

10/1/10

(L-R): Stark Sands, John Gallagher Jr., Michael Esper and company

Photo by Paul Kolnik

American Idiot

SONG LIST

1. "American Idiot" .... Company
2. "Jesus of Suburbia"
   a. "Jesus of Suburbia" .... John Gallagher Jr. and Michael Esper
   b. "City of the Damned" .... Stark Sands, John Gallagher Jr., Michael Esper and Company
   c. "I Don't Care" .... John Gallagher Jr., Michael Esper, Stark Sands and Company
   d. "Dearly Beloved" .... Mary Faber and Men
   e. "Tales of Another Broken Home" .... John Gallagher Jr., Michael Esper, Stark Sands, Mary Faber and Company
3. "Holiday" .... John Gallagher Jr., Stark Sands, Theo Stockman and Company
4. "Boulevard of Broken Dreams" .... John Gallagher Jr., Rebecca Naomi Jones, Stark Sands and Men
5. "Favorite Son" .... Wallace Smith and Women
6. "Are We the Waiting" .... Stark Sands, Wallace Smith and Company
7. "St. Jimmy" .... John Gallagher Jr., Tony Vincent and Company
8. "Give Me Novacaine" .... Michael Esper, Stark Sands and Company
9. "Last of the American Girls"/"She's a Rebel" .... John Gallagher Jr., Rebecca Naomi Jones, Michael Esper, Tony Vincent, Chase Peacock and Company
10. "Last Night on Earth" .... Tony Vincent, Rebecca Naomi Jones, Mary Faber and Company
11. "Too Much Too Soon" .... Theo Stockman, Alysha Umphress, Michael Esper and Mary Faber
12. "Before the Lobotomy" .... Stark Sands, Chase Peacock, Wallace Smith and Ben Thompson
13. "Extraordinary Girl" .... Christina Sajous, Stark Sands and Company
14. "Before the Lobotomy" (reprise) .... Stark Sands, Chase Peacock, Wallace Smith, Ben Thompson and Company
15. "When It's Time" .... John Gallagher Jr.
16. "Know Your Enemy" .... Tony Vincent, Michael Esper, John Gallagher Jr. and Company
17. "21 Guns" .... Rebecca Naomi Jones, Christina Sajous, Mary Faber, Stark Sands, John Gallagher Jr., Michael Esper and Company
18. "Letterbomb" .... Rebecca Naomi Jones and Women
19. "Wake Me Up When September Ends" .... John Gallagher Jr., Michael Esper, Stark Sands and Company
20. "Homecoming"
    a. "The Death of St. Jimmy" .... Tony Vincent and John Gallagher Jr.
    b. "East 12th Street" .... John Gallagher Jr., Gerard Canonico, Theo Stockman and Company
    c. "Nobody Likes You" † .... Michael Esper and Company
    d. "Rock and Roll Girlfriend" * ...... Miguel Cervantes, Mary Faber, Michael Esper and Company
    e. "We're Coming Home Again" ...... John Gallagher Jr., Stark Sands, Michael Esper and Company
21. "Whatsername" .... John Gallagher Jr. and Company

† Lyrics by Mike Dirnt
* Lyrics by Tré Cool

Cast Continued

UNDERSTUDIES

For Johnny: CHASE PEACOCK
For Will: DECLAN BENNETT
For Tunny: BEN THOMPSON
For Heather: LESLIE McDONEL, LIBBY WINTERS
For Whatsername: LESLIE McDONEL, CORBIN REID, CHRISTINA SAJOUS
For St. Jimmy: ANDREW CALL, JOSHUA KOBAK
For The Extraordinary Girl: ASPEN VINCENT, LIBBY WINTERS

SWINGS

SYDNEY HARCOURT, JOSHUA KOBAK, LORIN LATARRO, OMAR LOPEZ-CEPERO, CORBIN REID, ASPEN VINCENT

DANCE CAPTAIN

LORIN LATARRO

BAND

Conductor/Keyboard/Accordion: CARMEL DEAN
Drums/Percussion: TREY FILES
Guitar 1: MICHAEL AARONS
Guitar 2: ALEC BERLIN
Bass: DAN GRENNES
Violin: CENOVIA CUMMINS
Viola: ALISSA SMITH
Cello: AMY RALSKE
Associate Conductor: JARED STEIN
Music Coordinator: MICHAEL KELLER
Keyboard Programmer: RANDY COHEN

TIME: The Recent Past
PLACE: Jingletown, USA

Developed by Berkeley Repertory Theatre, November-December 2008, and New York Stage and Film and the Powerhouse Theater at Vassar, July 2009.

John Gallagher, Jr.
Johnny

Tony Vincent
St. Jimmy

Stark Sands
Tunny

Michael Esper
Will

Rebecca Naomi Jones
Whatsername

Christina Sajous
The Extraordinary Girl

Mary Faber
Heather

American Idiot

Declan Bennett
Ensemble

Andrew Call
Ensemble

Gerard Canonico
Ensemble

Miguel Cervantes
Ensemble

Sydney Harcourt
Swing

Van Hughes
Standby for Johnny, Will, Tunny

Brian Charles Johnson
Ensemble

Joshua Kobak
Swing

Omar Lopez-Cepero
Swing

Leslie McDonel
Ensemble

Chase Peacock
Ensemble

Corbin Reid
Swing

Wallace Smith
Ensemble

Theo Stockman
Ensemble

Ben Thompson
Ensemble

Alysha Umphress
Ensemble

Aspen Vincent
Swing

Libby Winters
Ensemble

Carmel Dean
Music Director

Mike Dirnt, Billie Joe Armstrong, Tré Cool/ Green Day
Music & Lyrics (Green Day); Book & Lyrics (Billie Joe Armstrong)

Michael Mayer
Director, Book

Steven Hoggett
Choreographer

Tom Kitt
Music Supervisor/ Arrangements/ Orchestrations

Christine Jones
Scenic Design

Andrea Lauer
Costume Design

Kevin Adams
Lighting Design

Brian Ronan
Sound Design

Jim Carnahan
Casting

Lorin Latarro
Associate Choreographer

Liz Caplan Vocal Studios, LLC
Production Vocal Supervisor

Neil A. Mazzella, Hudson Theatrical Associates
Technical Supervisor

Michael Keller
Music Coordinator

Tom Hulce
Producer

Ira Pittelman
Producer

American Idiot

Ruth Hendel
Producer

Vivek J. Tiwary
Producer

Robyn Goodman,
Aged in Wood
Producer

Walt Grossman,
Aged in Wood
Producer

Judi Krupp,
Burnt Umber
Productions
Producer

Bill Gerber,
Burnt Umber
Productions
Producer

Ralph Bryan,
Latitude Link
Producer

Larry Kaye,
Hop Theatricals
Producer

Jeffrey Finn
Producer

Chris Bensinger
Producer

Michael Filerman
Producer

Carl Moellenberg
Producer

Deborah Taylor
Producer

Allan S. Gordon
Producer

Élan V. McAllister
Producer

Tony Taccone,
Artistic Director,
Berkeley Repertory
Theatre
Producer

Jennifer Maloney,
Awaken
Entertainment
Producer

John Pinckard
Producer

Lorenzo Thione
Associate Producer

Jay Kuo
Associate Producer

Joshua Henry
Ensemble

Sean Wing
Ensemble

Krystina Alabado
Ensemble

Billie Joe Armstrong
St. Jimmy

Jennifer Bowles
Swing

Jeanna de Waal
Heather

Melissa Etheridge
St. Jimmy

P.J. Griffith
Swing

Justin Guarini
Will

Joshua Henry
Ensemble

Davey Havok
St. Jimmy

Jason Kappus
Ensemble

David Larsen
Tunny

American Idiot

Sean Michael
Murray
Swing

Mikey Winslow
Swing

FRONT OF HOUSE STAFF
Front Row (L-R): Katie Siegmund, Margaret McElroy,
Julia Furay, Cynthia Lopiano

Second Row (L-R): Donna Vanderlinden, Blake Sherman,
Kendra McDuffie, Heather Jewels, Andrew Mackay,
Barbara Carrol, Caroline Choi, Jeff Hubbard

Back Row (L-R): Donnette Niles, Adam Young, Katie Schmidt,
Brian Veith, Jim Barry, Jeff Blim, Rafael Liriano

CREW
Front Row (L-R): Eric Castaldo, Dave Brown, Timothy McDonough, Mark Diaz

Second Row (L-R): Robert Griffin, Frasier Weir, Bob Miller, Albert Sayers, Susan Pelkofer, Tom Maloney,
Angelo Grasso, Timothy McDonough Jr., Ryan McDonough, Cody Spencer

Back Row: Greg Peeler

WARDROBE DEPARTMENT
(Bottom to Top, L-R): Christopher Thornton and
Angela Simpson, Jessica Dermody and
Polly Noble, Julienne Schubert-Blechman and
Meredith Benson, Ryan Oslak and
Doug MacArthur

MUSIC DIRECTOR
Jared Stein

HAIR SUPERVISOR
Kevin Maybee

PRODUCTION SOUND OPERATOR
David Dignazio

American Idiot

BOX OFFICE
(L-R): Vincent Sclafani, Jeff Nevin, Vincent Siniscalchi

STAFF FOR *AMERICAN IDIOT*

GENERAL MANAGER
Abbie M. Strassler

COMPANY MANAGER
Kimberly Helms

GENERAL PRESS REPRESENTATIVE
THE HARTMAN GROUP
Michael Hartman
Leslie Baden   Alyssa Hart

MARKETING
TYPE A MARKETING
Anne Rippey   Jenna Gilfoil   Robin Steinthal

TECHNICAL SUPERVISION
HUDSON THEATRICAL ASSOCIATES
Neil A. Mazzella   Sam Ellis

PRODUCTION VOCAL SUPERVISOR
Liz Caplan Vocal Studios, LLC

Production Stage Manager ....James Harker
Stage Manager ....Freda Farrell
Assistant Stage Manager ....Bethany Russell
Assistant Company Manager ....Rachel Scheer
Dance Captain ....Lorin Latarro
Assistant Dance Captain ....Ben Thompson
Assistant Director ....Austin Regan
Associate Set Designer ....Edward Coco
Assistant Set Designer ....Damon Pelletier
Associate Costume Designer ....Chloe Chapin
Assistant Costume Designer ....Janice Lopez
Associate Lighting Designer ....Aaron Sporer
Assistant Lighting Designer ....Benjamin C. Travis
Assistant to the Lighting Designer ....Barbara Samuels
Associate Sound Designer ....Ashley Hanson
Associate Video/Projection Designer ....Dan Scully
Assistant Editor ....Nico Sarudiansky
Moving Light Programmer ....Victor Seastone
Video and Projection Programmer ....Jeff Cady/
                                              SenovvA
Video and Projection Assistant ....Alex Marshall/
                                              SenovvA
Production Carpenter ....Donald J. Oberpriller
Flyman ....Dave Brown
Flying Automation/Deck Carpenter ....Mark Diaz
Production Electrician ....Greg Husinko

Head Electrician ....Eric Abbott
Followspots ....Sue Pelkofer, Tom Maloney, Bob Miller
Production Sound Operator ....David Dignazio
Assistant Sound ....Cody Spencer
Deck Sound ....Joe Lenihan
Production Video/Deck Audio ....Greg Peeler
Production Property Supervisor ....Joseph P. Harris Jr.
Head Properties ....Eric Castaldo
Wardrobe Supervisor ....Angela Simpson
Assistant Wardrobe Supervisor ....Jaki Harris
Dressers ....Meredith Benson, Yleana Nuñez,
                          Ryan Oslak, Danny Paul,
                   Julienne Schubert-Blechman, Jack Scott
Hair Designer ....Brandon Dailey
Wig Designer ....Leah Loukas
Makeup Designer ....Amy Jean Wright
Hair Supervisor ....Kevin Maybee
Craft Artisan ....Jennilee Houghton
Costume Interns ....Amy Sutton, Matt Allemon,
                                            Mikaela Holmes
Costume Shoppers ....Paloma Young, Kara Harmon
Assistant Synthesizer Programmer ....Bryan Cook
Music Preparation ....Colleen Darnall
Management Associate ....Scott Armstrong
Assistant to Mr. Hulce ....Christopher Maring
Assistant to Mr. Pittelman ....Dorothy Evins
Stage Management interns ....Clinton Harwood,
                                          Katie Klehr White
Production Office Interns .Jamie Caplan, Amanda Gagnon
Casting Associate ....Jillian Cimini
Advertising ....Serino Coyne, Inc./
                          Tom Callahan, Scott Johnson,
                                          Kristina Curatolo
Interactive Marketing ....Situation Interactive/
                                          Damian Bazadona,
                       Christopher Powers, John Lanasa,
                       Eric Bornemann, Jessica Dacchille
Press Associates ....Michelle Bergmann,
                       Nicole Capatasto, Tom D'Ambrosio,
                       Juliana Hannett, Bethany Larsen,
                 Matt Ross, Frances White, Wayne Wolfe
Banking ....JP Morgan Chase
Payroll ....Castellana Services, Inc./
                                          Lance Castellana
Accountant ....Fried & Kowgios Partners CPA's LLP/
                                          Robert Fried CPA
Comptroller ....Galbraith & Co., Inc/
                                          Sarah Galbraith
Insurance ....Tanenbaum Harber of Florida/
                                          Carol Bressi-Cilona

Legal Counsel ....Lazarus & Harris, LLP/
                                   Scott R. Lazarus, Esq.,
                                   Robert C. Harris, Esq.
Physical Therapy ....Performing Arts Physical Therapy/
                                          Sean Gallagher
Massage Therapist ....Russ Beasley
Group Sales ....Telecharge Group Sales
Merchandising ....Bravado
Media Licensing ....Eric Kulberg
Production Photography ....Doug Hamilton
Opening Night Coordination ....Suzanne Tobak
Travel Agency ....Tzell Travel/
                                   The "A" Team, Road Rebel

Flying by Foy

CREDITS AND ACKNOWLEDGEMENTS

Scenery and automation by Hudson Scenic Studio, Inc. Lighting equipment from Hudson Sound and Light LLC. Sound equipment from Masque Sound. Video technology and production by SenovvA, Inc. TV/displays provided by Sony Electronics, Inc. Media server technology by Green Hippotizers. Specialty props provided by The Spoon Group. Prosthetics constructed by Denscape Designs. Denim courtesy of Levis. Additional costumes by Donna Langman Costumes, John Kristiansen New York Inc., Saint Laurie Merchant Tailors NYC, World Tone Shoes. Special thanks to Bra*Tenders for hosiery and undergarments. Hair products provided by Bumble and Bumble, LLC, and Pravana. Makeup provided by M•A•C. Custom in-ear monitors provided by Ultimate Ears. Keyboards by Yamaha. Guitar strings provided by Ernie Ball. Guitars provided by Gibson and Epiphone Guitar Company. Cymbals by Agop Cymbals. Drumsticks by Pro-Mark Sticks. Opening audio sequence by Ira Pittelman and Wayne Hyde.

Rehearsed at the New 42nd Street Studios

SPECIAL THANKS

Adrienne Armstrong, Chris Bilheimer, Chris Dugan, Lorrin Golembieski, Doug Goodman, Brian Bumbery, Tom Pearl and the staff of Berkeley Rep. Theatre, Carole Pittelman, Bill Schneider, Maggie Whitaker, Wayne Hyde, Bryan Smith, Derek Brooks, MSG Entertainment and Madison Square Garden, Andrew Hans Buscher and Jordan Roth.

www.AmericanIdiotOnBroadway.com

JUJAMCYN THEATERS

JORDAN ROTH
President

PAUL LIBIN	**JACK VIERTEL**
Producing Director	Creative Director
DANIEL ADAMIAN	**JENNIFER HERSHEY**
General Manager	Director of Operations
MEREDITH VILLATORE	**JERRY ZAKS**
Chief Financial Officer	Resident Director

STAFF FOR THE ST. JAMES THEATRE

Manager ....Daniel Adamian
Associate Manager ....Jeff Hubbard
Treasurer ....Vincent Sclafani
Carpenter ....Timothy McDonough Jr.
Propertyman........................Timothy McDonough
Electrician ....Albert Sayers
Engineer......................................Anthony Pastore

Anything Goes

First Preview: March 10, 2011. Opened: April 7, 2011.
Still running as of May 31, 2011.

PLAYBILL®

When Billy Crocker learns that the girl of his dreams, Hope Harcourt, is sailing off to Europe to marry a rich twit, Billy stows away and adopts a series of disguises in hopes of winning her away from her fiancé and her disapproving mother. Along the way Billy gets help from gangster Moonface Martin and nightclub singer Reno Sweeney in a series of farcical plots that eventually win Hope's heart and hand.

CAST

(in order of appearance)

Elisha Whitney	JOHN McMARTIN
Fred, a bartender	JOSH FRANKLIN
Billy Crocker	COLIN DONNELL
Reno Sweeney	SUTTON FOSTER
Captain	WALTER CHARLES
Ship's Purser	ROBERT CREIGHTON
Crew	CLYDE ALVES, WARD BILLEISEN, DANIEL J. EDWARDS, JOSH FRANKLIN, KEVIN MUNHALL, ADAM PERRY, WILLIAM RYALL, ANTHONY WAYNE
A Reporter	ANTHONY WAYNE
A Photographer	CLYDE ALVES
Henry T. Dobson, a minister	WILLIAM RYALL
Luke	ANDREW CAO
John	RAYMOND J. LEE
Angels	
Purity	SHINA ANN MORRIS
Chastity	KIMBERLY FAURÉ
Charity	JENNIFER SAVELLI
Virtue	JOYCE CHITTICK

Continued on next page

STEPHEN SONDHEIM THEATRE

ROUNDABOUTTHEATRECOMPANY

Todd Haimes, Artistic Director
Harold Wolpert, Managing Director
Julia C. Levy, Executive Director

Presents

Sutton Foster
and
Joel Grey
in

Anything Goes

Music & Lyrics by
Cole Porter

Original Book by
P.G. Wodehouse & Guy Bolton
and Howard Lindsay & Russel Crouse

New Book by
Timothy Crouse & John Weidman

with

Colin Donnell   Adam Godley   Laura Osnes   Jessica Stone
Walter Charles   Robert Creighton   Andrew Cao   Raymond J. Lee

Clyde Alves   Ward Billeisen   Joyce Chittick   Nikki Renée Daniels   Margot De La Barre
Daniel J. Edwards   Kimberly Fauré   Josh Franklin   Justin Greer   Tari Kelly
Shina Ann Morris   Linda Mugleston   Kevin Munhall   Adam Perry
William Ryall   Jennifer Savelli   Anthony Wayne   Kristen Beth Williams

with

John McMartin
and
Jessica Walter

Set Design	*Costume Design*	*Lighting Design*	*Sound Design*
Derek McLane	Martin Pakledinaz	Peter Kaczorowski	Brian Ronan
Additional Orchestrations	*Original Orchestrations*	*Dance Arrangements*	*Music Director/Conductor* *Music Coordinator*
Bill Elliott	Michael Gibson	David Chase	James Lowe Seymour Red Press
Hair & Wig Design	*Makeup Design*	*Production Stage Manager*	*Casting*
Paul Huntley	Angelina Avallone	Peter Hanson	Jim Carnahan, C.S.A. & Stephen Kopel
Associate Director	*Associate Choreographer*	*Technical Supervisor*	*Executive Producer*
Marc Bruni	Vince Pesce	Steve Beers	Sydney Beers
Press Representative	*Director of Marketing & Sales Promotion*	*Director of Development*	*Founding Director* *Associate Artistic Director*
Boneau-Bryan/Brown	David B. Steffen	Lynne Gugenheim Gregory	Gene Feist Scott Ellis

Music Supervisor/Vocal Arranger
Rob Fisher

Directed and Choreographed by
Kathleen Marshall

Proud Sponsor BANK OF AMERICA

Anything Goes benefits from Roundabout's Musical Theatre Fund with gifts from Marty and Perry Granoff, HRH Foundation, Ted and Mary Jo Shen, Peter and Leni May, Tom and Diane Tuft, The Kaplen Foundation, and one anonymous donor. Roundabout gratefully acknowledges partial underwriting from Goldman Sachs Gives at the Recommendation of R. Martin Chavez. Major support for Anything Goes provided by The Blanche and Irving Laurie Foundation. Roundabout thanks the Henry Nias Foundation, courtesy of Dr. Stanley Edelman, for their support of Anything Goes.

Anything Goes was produced by Lincoln Center Theater in 1987.

4/7/11

(L-R): Shina Ann Morris, Joyce Chittick, Colin Donnell, Sutton Foster, Joel Grey, Kimberly Fauré, Jennifer Savelli

Photo by Joan Marcus

Anything Goes

SCENES & MUSICAL NUMBERS

ACT ONE

Overture

Scene 1: **A Smoky Manhattan Bar**

"I Get a Kick Out of You" ....Reno Sweeney

Scene 2: **The Afterdeck of an Ocean Liner**

"There's No Cure Like Travel" ....Captain, Purser and Sailors

"Bon Voyage" ....Sailors and Passengers

Scene 3: **On Deck, that evening**

"You're the Top" ....Reno Sweeney and Billy Crocker

"Easy to Love" ....Billy Crocker

Reprise: "Easy to Love" ....Hope Harcourt

Scene 4: **Whitney's Stateroom/Moon's Adjacent Cabin**

"The Crew Song" ....Elisha Whitney

Scene 5: **On Deck, mid-morning**

"There'll Always Be a Lady Fair" (Sailor's Chantey) ....Quartet

"Friendship" ....Moonface Martin and Reno Sweeney

Scene 6: **Evelyn's Stateroom**

Scene 7: **On Deck, at twilight**

"It's De-lovely" ....Billy Crocker and Hope Harcourt

Scene 8: **On Deck, early the following morning**

"Anything Goes" ....Reno Sweeney, Sailors and Passengers

ACT TWO

Entr'Acte

Scene 1: **The Ship's Nightclub**

"Public Enemy Number One" ....Captain, Purser and Passengers

"Blow, Gabriel, Blow" ....Reno Sweeney, Angels and Passengers

"Goodbye, Little Dream, Goodbye" ....Hope Harcourt

Scene 2: **The Ship's Brig**

"Be Like the Blue Bird" ....Moonface Martin

"All Through the Night" ....Billy Crocker, Hope Harcourt and Quartet

Scene 3: **On Deck, later that night**

"The Gypsy in Me" ....Lord Evelyn Oakleigh and Reno Sweeney

Scene 4: **The Ship's Brig**

Scene 5: **On Deck**

"Buddie, Beware" ....Erma and Sailors

Finale ....Full Company

ORCHESTRA

Conductor:
JAMES LOWE

Associate Conductor:
DAVID GURSKY

Music Coordinator:
SEYMOUR RED PRESS

Reeds:
JIM ERCOLE, RON JANNELLI,
RALPH OLSEN, DAVE YOUNG

Trumpets:
EARL GARDNER, KEN RAMPTON,
STU SATALOF

Trombone:
LARRY FARRELL, ROB FOURNIER,
WAYNE GOODMAN

Piano:
DAVID GURSKY

Bass:
JEFF CARNEY

Drums:
JOHN REDSECKER

Percussion:
BILL HAYES

Guitar:
ERIC DAVIS

Synthesizer Programmer:
BRUCE SAMUELS

Music Copying:
EMILY GRISHMAN MUSIC PREPARATION—
KATHARINE EDMONDS/EMILY GRISHMAN

Cast Continued

Hope Harcourt ....LAURA OSNES

Mrs. Evangeline Harcourt ....JESSICA WALTER

Lord Evelyn Oakleigh..............ADAM GODLEY

FBI Agents ...ADAM PERRY, KEVIN MUNHALL

Erma ....JESSICA STONE

Moonface Martin ....JOEL GREY

Old Lady in a Wheelchair ...LINDA MUGLESTON

Quartet ...WARD BILLEISEN, JOSH FRANKLIN,
DANIEL J. EDWARDS, WILLIAM RYALL

Ship's Passengers ....CLYDE ALVES,
WARD BILLEISEN, NIKKI RENÉE DANIELS,
DANIEL J. EDWARDS, JOSH FRANKLIN,
TARI KELLY, LINDA MUGLESTON,
KEVIN MUNHALL, ADAM PERRY,
WILLIAM RYALL, ANTHONY WAYNE,
KRISTEN BETH WILLIAMS

SWINGS

MARGOT DE LA BARRE, JUSTIN GREER

UNDERSTUDIES

For Reno Sweeney:
TARI KELLY

For Billy Crocker & Evelyn Oakleigh:
JOSH FRANKLIN

For Moonface Martin:
ROBERT CREIGHTON

For Hope Harcourt:
NIKKI RENÉE DANIELS

For Mrs. Evangeline Harcourt:
LINDA MUGLESTON

For Elisha Whitney & Captain:
WILLIAM RYALL

For the Purser:
CLYDE ALVES

For Erma:
JOYCE CHITTICK

For Luke & John:
DANIEL J. EDWARDS

Dance Captain:
JENNIFER SAVELLI

Assistant Dance Captain:
JUSTIN GREER

Production Stage Manager:
PETER HANSON

Stage Manager:
JON KRAUSE

Anything Goes

Sutton Foster
Reno Sweeney

Joel Grey
Moonface Martin

John McMartin
Elisha Whitney

Jessica Walter
*Mrs. Evangeline
Harcourt*

Colin Donnell
Billy Crocker

Adam Godley
Lord Evelyn Oakleigh

Laura Osnes
Hope Harcourt

Jessica Stone
Erma

Walter Charles
Captain

Robert Creighton
Purser

Andrew Cao
Luke

Raymond J. Lee
John

Clyde Alves
*Crew,
A Photographer,
Passenger*

Ward Billeisen
*Crew, Passenger,
Quartet*

Joyce Chittick
Virtue

Nikki Renée Daniels
Passenger

Margot de La Barre
Swing

Kimberly Fauré
Chastity

Josh Franklin
*Fred, Crew,
Passenger, Quartet*

Justin Greer
Swing

Daniel J. Edwards
Crew, Quartet

Tari Kelly
Passenger

Shina Ann Morris
Purity

Linda Mugleston
Passenger

Kevin Munhall
*FBI Agent,
Passenger*

Adam Perry
Crew, Passenger

William Ryall
*Crew,
Henry T. Dobson,
Passenger, Quartet*

Jennifer Savelli
*Charity,
Dance Captain*

Anthony Wayne
*Crew, Reporter,
Passenger*

Kristen Beth
Williams
Passenger

Cole Porter
Music & Lyrics

Guy Bolton

P.G. Wodehouse

Timothy Crouse
*Co-Author of the
New Book*

John Weidman
New Book

Anything Goes

Kathleen Marshall
*Director &
Choreographer*

Derek McLane
Scenic Design

Martin Pakledinaz
Costume Design

Peter Kaczorowski
Lighting Design

Brian Ronan
Sound Design

Rob Fisher
*Musical Supervisor,
Vocal Arranger*

Bill Elliott
*Additional
Orchestrations*

Seymour Red Press
Musical Coordinator

David Chase
Dance Arranger

James Lowe
*Musical Director/
Conductor*

Paul Huntley
Hair & Wig Design

Angelina Avallone
Make-Up Design

Marc Bruni
Associate Director

Vince Pesce
*Associate
Choreographer*

Jim Carnahan
Casting

Gene Feist
*Founding Director,
Roundabout Theatre
Company*

Todd Haimes
*Artistic Director,
Roundabout Theatre
Company*

CREW
Stairs (Top-Bottom):
Erika Warmbrunn (Followspot Operator),
John Patrick "JP" Nord (Deck Carpenter),
William Craven (Flyman), Paul Ashton
(Automation Operator), Nelson Vaughn
(Properties Running Crew),
Jessica Morton (Followspot Operator)

Left of Stairs (L-R):
Dan Mendeloff (Properties Running Crew),
Josh Weitzman (Production
Electrician/Moving Light Programmer)

Right of Stairs (Clockwise from Top):
Matt Gratz (Followspot Sub),
Donald "Buck" Roberts (Deck Carpenter),
Andrew Forste (House Properties),
Steve Beers (Production Carpenter),
Christopher Ford (Properties Running
Crew Sub), Shannon Slaton (Production
Sound Engineer/Sound Mixer),
Dorion Fuchs (Followspot Operator)

Photo by Brian Mapp

Anything Goes

WARDROBE
Stairs (Top-Bottom): Nadine Hettel (Wardrobe Supervisor),
Emily Merriweather (Dresser), Tara Delahunt (Dresser), Ruth Goya
(Dayworker), Polly Noble (Dayworker/Dresser Sub), Kevin Mark Harris
(Dresser), Jessie St. George (Dayworker)

Left of Stairs (L-R): Suzanne Delahunt (Dresser), Julien Havard (Dresser)

Right of Stairs (L-R): Pamela Pierzina (Dresser), James Cavanaugh
(Dayworker)

ORCHESTRA
Stairs (Top-Bottom): Bill Hayes (Percussion), James Lowe (Music Director/
Conductor), John Redsecker (Drums), James Ercole (Reeds)

Left of Stairs (L-R): Earl Gardner (Trumpet), Ronald Jannelli (Reeds),
Wayne Goodman (Trombone)

Right of Stairs (L-R): David Gursky (Associate Conductor/Keyboard),
Stu Satalof (Trumpet), Ken Rampton (Trumpet), David Young (Reeds)

STAGE MANAGEMENT/COMPANY MANAGEMENT
(Clockwise from Top): Peter Hanson (Production Stage Manager),
Jon Krause (Stage Manager), Doug Gaeta (Company Manager),
Rachel Bauder (Assistant Stage Manager), Jeffrey Rodriguez (Stage
Management Sub)

Not Pictured: David Solomon (Assistant Company Manager)

FRONT OF HOUSE STAFF
Standing on Stairs (Top-Bottom): Megan Kosmoski, Jehan O. Young,
Caroline Carbo, Michael Portman, Karen Murray

Seated on Stairs (L-R): Jessica Alverson, Billy Peña (Usher Sub)

Left of Stairs (L-R): Christopher Ruth, Johannah-Joy Magyawe (House
Manager)

Right of Stairs: Delores Danska (Usher Sub)

Anything Goes

HAIR DEPARTMENT
(L-R): Kelli Reid (Hair Assistant), Jessie Mojica (Hair Assistant), Heather Wright (Hair Assistant), Nathaniel Hathaway (Hair & Wig Supervisor)

Photos by Brian Mapp

BOX OFFICE STAFF
(Clockwise from Top): Ron Tobia (Box Office), Andrew Clements (Assistant Box Office Manager), Carlos Morris (Box Office)

Not pictured: Jaime Perlman (Head Treasurer)

ROUNDABOUT THEATRE COMPANY STAFF
ARTISTIC DIRECTOR ....TODD HAIMES
MANAGING DIRECTOR ....HAROLD WOLPERT
EXECUTIVE DIRECTOR ....JULIA C. LEVY
ASSOCIATE ARTISTIC DIRECTOR ...SCOTT ELLIS

ARTISTIC STAFF
DIRECTOR OF ARTISTIC DEVELOPMENT/
DIRECTOR OF CASTING ....Jim Carnahan
Artistic Consultant ....Robyn Goodman
Resident Director ....Doug Hughes
Associate Artists ....Mark Brokaw, Scott Elliott,
Sam Gold, Bill Irwin, Joe Mantello,
Kathleen Marshall, Theresa Rebeck
Literary Manager ....Jill Rafson
Casting Director ....Carrie Gardner
Casting Associate ....Kate Boka
Casting Associate ....Stephen Kopel
Casting Assistant ....Jillian Cimini
Artistic Assistant ....Amy Ashton
Literary Associate ....Josh Fiedler
The Blanche and Irving Laurie Foundation
Theatre Visions Fund Commissions ....Stephen Karam,
Nathan Louis Jackson
Educational Foundation of
America Commissions ....Bekah Brunstetter,
Lydia Diamond, Diana Fithian,
Julie Marie Myatt
New York State Council
on the Arts Commission ....Nathan Louis Jackson
Roundabout Commissions ....Steven Levenson,
Matthew Lopez, Kim Rosenstock
Casting Interns ....Devon Caraway, Kyle Eberlein,
Jonny Lang, Aaron Quinn
Script Readers ....Jay Cohen, Ben Izzo,
Alexis Roblan, Nicholas Stimler
Artistic Intern ....Becky Bicks

EDUCATION STAFF
EDUCATION DIRECTOR ....Greg McCaslin

Associate Education Director ....Jennifer DiBella
Education Program Associates ....Aliza Greenberg,
Sarah Malone
Education Assistant ....Holly Sansom
Education Dramaturg ....Ted Sod
Teaching Artists ....Cynthia Babak, Victor Barbella,
Grace Bell, LaTonya Borsay,
Mark Bruckner, Joe Clancy,
Vanessa Davis-Cohen, Joe Doran,
Jimena Duca, Elizabeth Dunn-Ruiz,
Carrie Ellman-Larsen, Deanna Frieman,
Natalie Gold, Sheri Graubert, Benton Greene,
Melissa Gregus, Adam Gwon, Devin Haqq,
Carrie Heitman, Karla Hendrick, Mary Hunt,
Jason Jacobs, Lisa Renee Jordan, Jamie Kalama,
Alvin Keith, Tami Mansfield, Erin McCready,
Kyle McGinley, Nick Moore, Andrew Ondrejcak,
Meghan O'Neill, Laura Poe, Nicole Press,
Jennifer Rathbone, Leah Reddy, Cassy Rush,
Nick Simone, Joe Skowronski, Heidi Stallings,
Daniel Sullivan, Carl Tallent, Vickie Tanner,
Jolie Tong, Larine Towler, Cristina Vaccaro,
Jennifer Varbalow, Leese Walker,
Eric Wallach, Michael Warner,
Christina Watanabe, Gail Winar,
Chad Yarborough
Teaching Artist Emeritus ....Reneé Flemings
Education Intern ....Erin Monahan

EXECUTIVE ADMINISTRATIVE STAFF
ASSOCIATE MANAGING
DIRECTOR ....Greg Backstrom
Assistant Managing Director ....Jill Boyd
Assistant to the Managing Director ....Zachary Baer
Assistant to the Executive Director ....Nicole Tingir

MANAGEMENT/ADMINISTRATIVE STAFF
GENERAL MANAGER ....Sydney Beers
General Manager,
American Airlines Theatre ....Rebecca Habel

General Manager, Steinberg Center ....Rachel E. Ayers
Human Resources Manager ....Stephen Deutsch
Operations Manager ....Valerie D. Simmons
Associate General Manager ....Maggie Cantrick
Office Manager ....Scott Kelly
Archivist ....Tiffany Nixon
Receptionists ....Dee Beider, Elisa Papa,
Allison Patrick, Monica Sidorchuk
Messenger ....Darnell Franklin
Management Intern ....Catherine Moreton
Archives Intern ....Carina Don

FINANCE STAFF
DIRECTOR OF FINANCE.................Susan Neiman
Payroll Director ....John LaBarbera
Accounts Payable Manager ....Frank Surdi
Payroll Benefits Administrator ....Yonit Kafka
Manager Financial Reporting ....Joshua Cohen
Business Office Assistant ....Jackie Verbitski
Business Interns ....Nicholas Barbato, Ayla Schermer

DEVELOPMENT STAFF
DIRECTOR OF
DEVELOPMENT ....Lynne Gugenheim Gregory
Assistant to the Director of Development ....Liz Malta
Director, Institutional Giving ....Liz S. Alsina
Director, Individual Giving ....Christopher Nave
Director, Special Events ....Steve Schaeffer
Associate Director, Individual Giving ....Tyler Ennis
Manager, Telefundraising ....Gavin Brown
Manager, Corporate Relations ....Sohyun Kim
Manager, Donor Information Systems ....Lise Speidel
Associate Manager, Patron Programs ....Marisa Perry
Patron Services Associate ....Joseph Foster
Institutional Giving Assistant ....Brett Barbour
Development Assistant ....Martin Giannini
Individual Giving Assistant ....Sophia Hinshelwood
Special Events Assistant ....Amy Rosenfield
Development Interns ....Bethany Nothstein,
Sara Valencia

Anything Goes

INFORMATION TECHNOLOGY STAFF
IT DIRECTOR ....Antonio Palumbo
IT Associates ....Jim Roma, Cary Kim
DIRECTOR DATABASE
   OPERATIONS........................Wendy Hutton
Database Administrator/Programmer ....Revanth Anne

MARKETING STAFF
DIRECTOR OF MARKETING
   AND SALES PROMOTION ....David B. Steffen
Associate Director of Marketing ....Tom O'Connor
Senior Marketing Manager ....Shannon Marcotte
Marketing Associate ....Eric Emch
Marketing Assistant ....Bradley Sanchez
Website Consultant ....Keith Powell Beyland
Director of Telesales Special Promotions ......Marco Frezza
Telesales Manager ....Patrick Pastor
Marketing Interns ....J. Samuel Horvath,
   Claire-Marine Sarner

TICKET SERVICES STAFF
DIRECTOR OF
   SALES OPERATIONS ....Charlie Garbowski, Jr.
Ticket Services Manager ....Ellen Holt
Subscription Manager ....Bill Klemm
Box Office Managers ....Edward P. Osborne,
   Jaime Perlman, Krystin MacRitchie,
   Nicole Nicholson
Group Sales Manager ....Jeff Monteith
Assistant Box Office Managers ....Robert Morgan,
   Andrew Clements,
   Catherine Fitzpatrick
Assistant Ticket Services Managers ....Robert Kane,
   Lindsay Ericson
Assistant Ticket Services Manager ....Jessica Pruett-Barnett
Customer Services Coordinator ....Thomas Walsh
Ticket Services ....Solangel Bido, Arianna Boykins,
   Lauren Carrelli, Joseph Clark,
   Nisha Dhruna, Adam Elsberry,
   Joe Gallina, James Graham,
   Tova Heller, Nicki Ishmael,
   Kate Longosky, Michelle Maccarone,
   Elisa Mala, Mead Margulies,
   Laura Marshall, Kenneth Martinez,
   Chuck Migliaccio, Carlos Morris,
   Bekah Nutt, Kaia Rafoss,
   Josh Rozett, Heather Siebert,
   Nalane Singh, Lillian Soto,
   Ron Tobia, Michael Valentine,
   Hannah Weitzman
Ticket Services Intern ....Lindsay Hoffman

SERVICES
Counsel ....Paul, Weiss,
   Rifkind, Wharton and Garrison LLP,
   Charles H. Googe Jr., Carol M. Kaplan
Counsel ....Rosenberg & Estis
Counsel ....Andrew Lance,
   Gibson, Dunn, & Crutcher, LLP
Counsel ....Harry H. Weintraub,
   Glick and Weintraub, P.C.
Counsel ....Stroock & Stroock & Lavan LLP
Counsel ....Daniel S. Dokos,
   Weil, Gotshal & Manges LLP
Counsel ....Claudia Wagner/
   Manatt, Phelps & Phillips, LLP

Immigration Counsel ....Mark D. Koestler and
   Theodore Ruthizer
House Physicians ....Dr. Theodore Tyberg,
   Dr. Lawrence Katz
House Dentist ....Neil Kanner, D.M.D.
Insurance ....DeWitt Stern Group, Inc.
Accountant ....Lutz & Carr CPAs, LLP
Advertising ....Spotco/
   Drew Hodges, Jim Edwards,
   Tom Greenwald, Kyle Hall,
   Cory Spinney
Interactive Marketing..................Situation Interactive/
   Damian Bazadona, John Lanasa,
   Eric Bornemann, Randi Fields
Events Photography ....Anita and Steve Shevett
Production Photographer ....Joan Marcus
Theatre Displays ....King Displays, Wayne Sapper
Lobby Refreshments ....Sweet Concessions
Merchandising ....Spotco Merch/
   James Decker

MANAGING DIRECTOR
   EMERITUS ....Ellen Richard

Roundabout Theatre Company
231 West 39th Street, New York, NY 10018
(212) 719-9393.

GENERAL PRESS REPRESENTATIVE
BONEAU/BRYAN-BROWN
Adrian Bryan-Brown
Matt Polk   Jessica Johnson   Amy Kass
Seena Hodges   Amanda De Souza

CREDITS FOR *ANYTHING GOES*
Company Manager ....Doug Gaeta
Assistant Company Manager ....David Solomon
Production Stage Manager ....Peter Hanson
Stage Manager ....Jon Krause
Dance Captain ....Jennifer Savelli
Assistant Dance Captain ....Justin Greer
Assistant Choreographer ....David Eggers
Assistant Set Designer ....Erica Hemminger
Associate Costume Designer ....Sara Jean Tosetti
Costume Design Assistant ....Carisa Kelly
Assistant to the
   Costume Designer ....Justin Hall
Costume Interns ....Hannah Kittel, Shannon Smith,
   Heather Mathiesen
Associate Lighting Designer ....Paul Toben
Assistant Lighting Designer ....Gina Scherr
Associate Wig and Hair Designer .....Giovanna Calabretta
Makeup Design Associate ....Jorge Vargas
Assistant Sound Designer ....John Emmett O'Brien
Production Sound Engineer ....Shannon Slaton
Music Department
   Interns ....Molly Gachignard, Ian Weinberger
Automation Operator ....Paul Ashton
Flyman ....William Craven
Production Electrician/
   Moving Light Programmer ....Josh Weitzman
Assistant Production Electricians ....John Wooding,
   Jocelyn Smith
Sound Mixer.................................Shannon Slaton
Followspot Operators ....Dorion Fuchs,
   Erika Warmbrunn, Jessica Morton

Deck Electricians ....Jocelyn Smith,
   Francis Elers
House Properties ....Andrew Forste
Properties Running Crew ....Dan Mendeloff,
   Nelson Vaughn
Associate Production Properties ....Carrie Mossman
Prop Artisans.....................Mike Billings, Tim Ferro,
   Cathy Small, Mary Wilson
Wardrobe Supervisor ....Nadine Hettel
Dressers ....Suzanne Delahunt, Tara Delahunt,
   Kevin Mark Harris, Julien Havard,
   Emily Merriweather, Pamela Pierzina,
   Stacy Sarmiento
Hair and Wig Supervisor ....Nathaniel Hathaway
Hair Assistants .... Monica Costea,
   Heather Wright
SDC Observer ....Adam Cates
Production Assistants ....Rachel Bauder,
   Hannah Dorfman
Physical Therapy ....Performing Arts Physical Therapy

CREDITS
Scenery fabrication by Hudson Scenic Studio, Inc. Scenic elements constructed by Global Scenic Services, Inc., Bridgeport, CT. Lighting equipment by PRG Lighting. Audio equipment by PRG Audio. Costumes by Arel Studio Inc.; Artur & Tailors Ltd.; Carelli Costumes Inc.; Helen Uffner Vintage Clothing, LLC; Krostyne Studio; Parson-Meares, Ltd; Paul Chang Custom Tailors; Tricorne, Inc. Millinery by Lynne Mackey Studio, Rodney Gordon, Inc. Men's hats by J.J. Hat Center. Shoes by JC Theatrical, LaDuca, Worldtone Dance. Shoe repair by Rostelle Shoe Repair. Mr. McMartin's glasses provided by Myoptics. Special thanks to Bra*Tenders for hosiery and undergarments. Specialty prop construction by Cigar Box Studios, Inc.; Costume Amour; Craig Grigg; Anne Guay; Aardvark Interiors. Flame treatment by Turning Star, Inc.

Flying by Foy

STEPHEN SONDHEIM THEATRE
SYDNEY BEERS   GREG BACKSTROM
General Manager   Associate Managing Director
VALERIE SIMMONS
Operations Manager

Make-up provided by M•A•C

STEPHEN SONDHEIM THEATRE STAFF
Operations Manager .... Valerie D. Simmons
House Manager .... Johannah-Joy G. Magyawe
Assistant House Manager ....Stephanie Ward
Head Treasurer ....Jaime Perlman
Associate Treasurer ....Andrew Clements
Assistant Treasurers ....Carlos Morris,
   Ronnie Tobia
House Carpenter ....Steve Beers
House Electrician ....Josh Weitzman
House Properties ....Andrew Forste
Engineer ....Deosarran
Security ....Gotham Security
Maintenance ....C+W Cleaning Services Inc.
Lobby Refreshments by ....Sweet Concessions

Anything Goes

SCRAPBOOK

Opening Night Curtain Call (front L-R): John McMartin, *Yearbook* Correspondent Jessica Stone, Colin Donnell, Sutton Foster, Joel Grey, Laura Osnes, Adam Godley, Jessica Walter, Robert Creighton, Andrew Cao.

Correspondent: Jessica Stone, "Erma"

Opening Night Party/Gifts: We had a lovely time on the aircraft carrier/museum Intrepid, which is huge. All agreed that the best opening night gift came from Kristen Beth Williams who made homemade cake pops: chocolate, red velvet cake and peanut butter. You've never tasted anything more delicious. After a week they became black market items. If anyone hid one in their room, it was like *Lord of the Flies*!

Most Exciting Celebrity Visitors: The way backstage area is laid out, most of us don't see which celebrities visit Sutton and Joel. They get off the elevator and go directly into their dressing rooms. However, the members of the company itself are celebrities. We're a very experienced, professional company and most of us have done eight, ten, twelve shows. Only a handful are making their Broadway debuts.

Which Actor Performed the Most Roles in This Show? Colin Donnell. His character, "Billy," is constantly pretending to be different people—a sailor, English guy, guy with beard, broker, gangster, et cetera.

Who Got the Gypsy Robe: Joyce Chittick.

Who Has Done the Most Shows in Their Career: Gotta be John McMartin.

Special Backstage Rituals: We're a very ritual-happy bunch, but it's very individualized. Laura Osnes and I at every intermission do a "plank." After we've been on stage tapping our butts off for ten minutes, we hold the plank for a minute and a half. The boys in the sailor dressing room are obsessed with the Wii game "King of Pong." They literally made a trophy and it travels from person to person. Linda Mugleston and Tari Kelly have a dance-off every night. Sutton Foster has a little chocolate hour with Joyce Chittick and Jennifer Savelli. They stretch out in Sutton's room and Sutton gives away her chocolates. Andrew Cao and Ray Lee do Krumping in the wings during "Bon Voyage."

Favorite Moments During Each Performance (On Stage or Off): I get to work with Clyde Alves and Anthony Wayne as the sailors in "Buddy Beware," which is a silly, flirty song. We make our entrance from a lifeboat and sometimes we are laughing so hard in there.

They are the best group of guys, amazing dancers, really present as actors and just a ball to work with on stage and off. Another highlight happens when the curtain comes down every night and the audience is screaming. Collectively as a group we scream "Hooray!" It's very sweet, really bonded company.

Favorite In-Theatre Gathering Place: The greenroom because there's food. You've never seen a more gluttonous group. We're dancing so much we just burn it off. There are bagels and cakes and cupcakes all the time.

Favorite Off-Site Hangouts: Un Deux Trois and Chop't for dinner.

Favorite Therapy: Cake pops.

Favorite Snack Food: Basically the answer to every question on this list should be "cake pops."

Most Memorable Ad-Libs: Joyce Chittick told me that her favorite ad-libs are mine, because during "Buddy Beware," when I'm walking on the boys' backs, I say things like "I see London, I see France, I've seen you all without your...never mind." I made them all up myself.

Favorite Mess-Up: In the stateroom scene, Walter Charles enters and is supposed to say "We have reason to believe there is no Murray Hill Flowers. We have reason to believe he is Public Enemy number one, 'Snake Eyes' Johnson."

Instead he said, "We have reason to believe he's Public Enemy number one, *Levi Johnston* [Bristol Palin's baby daddy]."

Memorable Stage Door Fan Encounter: We've had a lot of school groups: young kids in the middle of doing their own production of *Anything Goes*. They're usually so excited to be here. A couple of the groups actually danced for us out there.

Who Wore the Heaviest/Hottest Costume: Linda Mugleston as the old lady.

Who Wore the Least: Probably me in my little teddy. Costume designer Martin Pakledinaz says it's like I'm not really wearing anything. And here I'm 40 and have two children.

Catchphrase Only the Company Would Recognize: "Trixie."

Best In-House Parody Lyrics: The crew guys keep coming up with dirty lyrics. They had a whole lyric that began, "I like big boats and I cannot lie...." I think all the sailors should be doing that song!

Understudy Anecdotes: People started missing very early so it was only our second week of previews when Bobby Creighton had to go on for Joel. Justin and Margo, our swings, had to go on for a couple of different parts early without any rehearsals and all did amazingly well.

Sweethearts Within the Company: Andrew Cao and Ray Lee, play our two Chinese guys like they're Oscar and Felix. I've never seen such a bromance blossom.

Coolest Thing About Being in This Show: The company. I say this with much fatigue, but it really is a rare thing on Broadway to be in a show where everyone has been there before and knows what they're doing and trained to do, and it's in their blood.

Also: Besides the cake pops, I think the thing most profound for us was what happened after we had our gypsy run-through. It was clunky and quiet and sort of labored. At the end we all were feeling pretty dejected. Then, twenty-four hours later, came the first preview and the audience screamed and leapt to their feet. That twenty-four-hour turnaround was very, very memorable.

2010-2011 AWARDS

TONY AWARDS
Best Revival of a Musical
Best Performance by an Actress
in a Leading Role in a Musical
(Sutton Foster)
Best Choreography
(Kathleen Marshall)

OUTER CRITICS CIRCLE AWARDS
Outstanding Revival of a Musical
Outstanding Choreographer
(Kathleen Marshall)
Outstanding Actress in a Musical
(Sutton Foster)
Outstanding Featured Actor in a Musical
(Adam Godley)

DRAMA DESK AWARDS
Outstanding Revival of a Musical
Outstanding Actress in a Musical
(Sutton Foster)
Outstanding Choreography
(Kathleen Marshall)
Outstanding Set Design
(Derek McLane)
Outstanding Sound Design in a Musical
(Brian Ronan)

DRAMA LEAGUE AWARD
Distinguished Revival of a Musical

FRED AND ADELE ASTAIRE AWARD
Best Female Dancer on Broadway
(Sutton Foster)

Arcadia

First Preview: February 26, 2011. Opened: March 17, 2011.
Still running as of May 31, 2011.

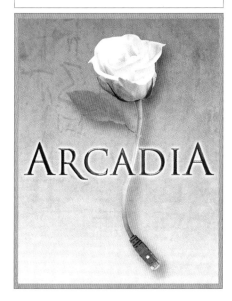

PLAYBILL

As characters in the present try to solve a literary mystery, the play jumps back in time to show us what really happened.

CAST
(in order of appearance)

Thomasina Coverly	BEL POWLEY
Septimus Hodge	TOM RILEY
Jellaby	EDWARD JAMES HYLAND
Ezra Chater	DAVID TURNER
Richard Noakes	BYRON JENNINGS
Lady Croom	MARGARET COLIN
Captain Brice	GLENN FLESHLER
Hannah Jarvis	LIA WILLIAMS
Chloë Coverly	GRACE GUMMER
Bernard Nightingale	BILLY CRUDUP
Valentine Coverly	RAÚL ESPARZA
Gus Coverly/Augustus Coverly	NOAH ROBBINS

Stage Manager: MATTHEW LACEY

UNDERSTUDIES

For Hannah Jarvis, Lady Croom: BIANCA AMATO
For Septimus Hodge, Augustus Coverly/
Gus Coverly: JACK CUTMORE-SCOTT
For Thomasina Coverly, Chloë Coverly:
ALYSSA MAY GOLD
For Bernard Nightingale, Valentine Coverly:
BAYLEN THOMAS
For Captain Brice, Ezra Chater, Richard Noakes,
Jellaby: RAY VIRTA

Bel Powley, Tom Riley and Lia Williams appeared
with the support of Actors' Equity Association
pursuant to an exchange program between
American Equity and UK Equity.

ⓖ ETHEL BARRYMORE THEATRE
243 West 47th Street
A Shubert Organization Theatre

Philip J. Smith, *Chairman*   **Robert E. Wankel,** *President*

Sonia Friedman Productions   Roger Berlind   Stephanie P. McClelland
Scott M. Delman   Nicholas Quinn Rosenkranz   Disney Theatrical Group
Robert G. Bartner   Olympus Theatricals   Douglas Smith
in association with Janine Safer Whitney

present

ARCADIA

By

Tom Stoppard

Margaret Colin   Billy Crudup   Raúl Esparza
Glenn Fleshler   Grace Gummer   Edward James Hyland
Byron Jennings   Bel Powley   Tom Riley
Noah Robbins   David Turner   Lia Williams

Set Hildegard Bechtler
Costumes Gregory Gale
Lighting Donald Holder
Sound David Van Tieghem
Hair David Brian Brown
Music Corin Buckeridge

Casting	*Press Representative*	*Advertising & Marketing*
Jim Carnahan, CSA	Boneau/Bryan-Brown	aka

US General Management	*UK General Management*
101 Productions, Ltd.	Sonia Friedman Productions

Production Stage Manager	*Technical Supervisor*	*Dialect Consultant*	*Choreographer*
Ira Mont	Peter Fulbright	Elizabeth Smith	Jodi Moccia

Directed by

David Leveaux

The producers wish to express their appreciation to Theatre Development Fund for its support of this production

3/17/11

(L-R): Billy Crudup, Lia Williams, Raúl Esparza, Grace Gummer

Photo by Carol Rosegg

Arcadia

Margaret Colin
Lady Croom

Billy Crudup
Bernard Nightingale

Raúl Esparza
Valentine Coverly

Glenn Fleshler
Captain Brice

Grace Gummer
Chloë Coverly

Edward James
Hyland
Jellaby

Byron Jennings
Richard Noakes

Bel Powley
Thomasina Coverly

Tom Riley
Septimus Hodge

Noah Robbins
*Gus/Augustus
Coverly*

David Turner
Ezra Chater

Lia Williams
Hannah Jarvis

Bianca Amato
*u/s Hannah Jarvis/
Lady Croom*

Jack Cutmore-Scott
*u/s Septimus Hodge/
Augustus Coverly/
Gus Coverly*

Alyssa May Gold
*u/s Thomasina
Coverly/
Chloë Coverly*

Baylen Thomas
*u/s Bernard
Nightingale/
Valentine Coverly*

Ray Virta
*u/s Jellaby/
Ezra Chater/
Richard Noakes/
Captain Brice*

Tom Stoppard
Playwright

David Leveaux
Director

Hildegard Bechtler
Set

Gregory Gale
Costumes

Donald Holder
Lighting

David Van Tieghem
Sound

David Brian Brown
Hair

Corin Buckeridge
Music

Elizabeth Smith
Dialect Consultant

Jodi Moccia
Choreographer

Jim Carnahan, CSA
Casting

Wendy Orshan,
101 Productions, Ltd.
General Manager

Sonia Friedman
Productions Ltd.
Producer

Roger Berlind
Producer

Stephanie P.
McClelland
Producer

Nicholas Quinn
Rosenkranz
Producer

2010-2011 AWARD

THEATRE WORLD AWARD
Outstanding Broadway
or Off-Broadway Debut
(Grace Gummer)

Arcadia

BOX OFFICE STAFF
(L-R): Diane Heatherington,
Chuck Loesche

Photos by Brian Mapp

CREW
(L-R): Darren Shaw (Sound Engineer), Robert Guy (Wardrobe Supervisor), Susan Cook (Dresser), Matthew Lacey (Stage Manager), Kevin O'Brien (Dresser), Rick Caroto (Hair Supervisor), Phillip Feller (Prop Man), Ira Mont (Production Stage Manager)

FRONT OF HOUSE STAFF
Front Row (L-R): Aileen Kilburn, Michael Reilly, Dan Landon (Manager), Monica Orellana (Porter), John Dancy

Back Row (L-R): Kate Reiter, John Barbaretti (Assistant Manager), Dexter Luke (Chief Usher), John Cashman

Arcadia

(L-R): David Turner, Tom Riley

Photo by Carol Rosegg

STAFF FOR *ARCADIA*

GENERAL MANAGEMENT
101 PRODUCTIONS, LTD.
Wendy Orshan   Jeffrey M. Wilson
David Auster
Elie Landau

COMPANY MANAGER
David van Zyll de Jong

GENERAL PRESS REPRESENTATIVE
BONEAU/BRYAN-BROWN
Adrian Bryan-Brown Aaron Meier
Emily Meagher

TECHNICAL SUPERVISION
TECH PRODUCTION SERVICES, INC.
Peter Fulbright, Mary Duffe
Colleen Houlehen, Kaitlyn Anderson

U.S. CASTING
JIM CARNAHAN CASTING
Jim Carnahan, CSA
Kate Boka, CSA, Carrie Gardner, CSA,
Stephen Kopel, Jillian Cimini

Makeup Designer ....Naomi Donne
Production Stage Manager ....**Ira Mont**
Stage Manager ....Matthew Lacey
Assistant Director ....Jason Lawson
UK Assistant Scenic Designer ....Luke Smith
US Assistant Scenic Designers ....Evan Adamson,
                                          Frank McCullough
Associate Costume Designer ....Colleen Kesterson
Assistants to Mr. Gale .... Julia Broer, Jennifer A. Jacob
Intern to Mr. Gale ....Kristy Leigh Hall
Associate Lighting Designer ....John Viesta
Assistant Lighting Designers...............Caroline Chao,
                                           Michael P. Jones
Assistant to Mr. Holder ....Cecelia Martin
Associate Sound Designer ....David Sanderson
Production Carpenter......................Rich Cocchiara
Production Electrician ....Michael LoBue
Production Sound ....Darin Stillman
Advance Props ....Dylan Foley, Robert Presley
Wardrobe Supervisor ....Robert Guy
Dressers ....Renee Borys, Kevin O'Brien

Wig and Hair Supervisor ....Rick Caroto
Production Assistant ....Jason Pelusio
Legal Counsel ....Lazarus & Harris, LLP/
               Scott R. Lazarus, Esq., Robert C. Harris, Esq.
Assistant to Mr. Berlind......................Jeffrey Hillock
Assistant to Ms. McClelland ....Lisa Traina
Olympus Theatricals Assistant. ....Megan Hawkins
Accountant ....Fried & Kowgios, CPA's LLP/
                                          Robert Fried, CPA
Comptroller ....Galbraith & Co. Inc./Kenny Noth
Advertising/Marketing ....aka/
                          Elizabeth Furze, Scott A. Moore,
                         Andrew Damer, Joshua Lee Poole,
                             Adam Jay, Janette Roush,
                               Jessica Albano-English
Digital & Interactive ....aka Connect/
                                     Terry Goldman, Erin Rech
101 Productions, Ltd. Staff ....Beth Blitzer,
                           Michael Rudd, Mary Six Rupert,
                                         Samara Ungar
101 Productions, Ltd. Interns ....Jennifer Hoguet,
                                        Malissa O'Donnell
Banking ....City National Bank/Anne McSweeney
Insurance ....DeWitt Stern/Peter Shoemaker
Theatre Displays ....King Displays, Inc.
Payroll Services ....Castellana Services, Inc.
Housing ....ABA Corporate Housing/Elizabeth Helke
Immigration ....Traffic Control Group, Inc./David King
Opening Night Coordination ....Serino Coyne LLC/
                              Suzanne Tobak, Gail Perlman
Production Photographer ....Carol Rosegg
Group Sales ....Telecharge.com Group Sales
                                          (212) 239-6262

FOR SONIA FRIEDMAN PRODUCTIONS
Producer ....Sonia Friedman
General Manager ....Diane Benjamin
Head of Production ....Pam Skinner
Associate Producer ....Sharon Duckworth
Literary Associate ....Jack Bradley
Assistant General Manager ....Martin Ball
Production Assistant ....Ross Nicholson
Production Assistant ....Fiona Stewart
General Management Assistant ....Ben Canning
Assistant to Sonia Friedman ....Sarah Hammond
Production Accountant ....Melissa Hay
Chief Executive Officer (New York) ....David Lazar
New York Assistant (SFP) ....Valerie Steinberg

SFP Board ....Helen Enright, Howard Panter,
                                          Rosemary Squire

Front cloth painting: Chalfont House, Buckinghamshire,
                     with a Shepherdess;
                 by Thomas Girtin (1775-1802)

CREDITS
London scenery by Souvenir Studios. U.S. scenery by PRG-
Scenic Technologies, a division of Production Resource
Group, LLC. Lighting by PRG Lighting. Sound equipment
by Masque Sound. UK props by Chris Marcus for Marcus
Hall Props. Costumes provided by Sands Films Costumes,
Ltd. Costumes constructed by Jennifer Love and Cosprop.
Custom embroidery and knitting by Hall-Craft Associates.
Costume crafts and painting by Jeff Fender Studio. Wigs
made by Ray Marston. Special thanks to Bra*Tenders for
hosiery and undergarments. Makeup provided by M•A•C.

To learn more about the production, please visit
arcadiabroadway.com

Arcadia rehearsed at Ballet Tech.

Arcadia wishes to thank Tekserve for their generous
donation of the laptop computers used onstage in this
production.

SPECIAL THANKS
Actors' Equity Association; Stephen Cabral and the TDF
Costume Collection; Andi Henig; Tom Stoppard, for the
Cornhill Review; Seasons Floral Design Studio

Staff for The Ethel Barrymore
House Manager ....Dan Landon

Arcadia
SCRAPBOOK

Correspondent: David Turner, "Ezra Chater," with answers supplied by various members of the cast.

Memorable Opening Night Note: BILLY: From President Obama. "Mr. Crudup, you are my light."

Opening Night Gifts: ALYSSA: Crumpets from Tom Stoppard.

MARGARET: Original edition of *The Castle of Otranto*.

BILLY: Congressional Medal of Honor.

Most Exciting Celebrity Visitor: GLENN: Tom Hanks—very firm handshake: "I'm Tom Hanks!!'

LIA: Anonymous: "I didn't understand a word but you were lovely."

BILLY: President Obama: "Mr. Crudup, you're the reason this great land is free."

Which Actor Performed the Most Roles in This Show: GLENN: The little guy. I forget his name.

BILLY: Noah.

Actor Who Has Done the Most Shows in Their Career: GLENN: Byron Jennings.

BEL: Everyone but me.

BILLY: Gotta be Carol Channing, right?

Special Backstage Rituals: JACK: Hiding Raúl Esparza's hair gel.

GRACE: Hanging out with David T. in the hospital.

TOM: Cleaning my teeth 'til my gums bleed.

Favorite Moment During Each Performance: Opening exchange between Septimus and Thomasina. And the waltz, hands down.

Favorite In-Theatre Gathering Places: Fifth floor and "Chez Raúl."

Favorite Off-Site Hangout: Glass House Tavern.

Favorite Snack Food: Sour Patch Kids, Yogurt-covered pretzels.

Mascot: Plautus.

Favorite Therapy: "Slings and Arrows."

Most Memorable Ad-Lib: None. You can't ad-lib Stoppard. We're not that smart.

Memorable Cell Phone Incident During a Performance: There was a lady in the front row who not only answered her cell phone but carried on a conversation, hung up, and made another call. She left at intermission.

Memorable Press Encounter: MARGARET: On opening night. An interviewer knew I played Lady Croom but thought I was a different actor entirely.

Memorable Stage Door Fan Encounter: Meryl Streep.

Fastest Costume Change: Leaving after the show.

Who Wore the Least: Noah, because he's the smallest.

Memorable Directorial Notes: "Sometimes it is necessary for the doctor to say 'You're not ill,' which is my English way of saying 'Things are going terribly well.'"

"Do the show like Brazilian soccer, not German soccer."

Company In-Jokes: "What happens when the cream goes in...?"

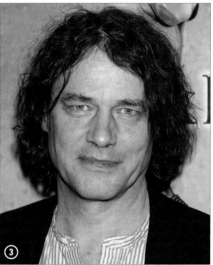

1. (L-R): Raúl Esparza, Lia Williams, Billy Crudup, Tom Riley and Grace Gummer take curtain calls on the Ethel Barrymore stage on opening night.
2. Playwright Tom Stoppard at the Gotham Hall cast party.
3. Director David Leveaux at Gotham Hall.
4. (L-R): Cast members Glenn Fleshler, Noah Robbins, David Turner and Edward James Hyland at the opening night party.

Company Legend: Billy Crudup.

Nicknames: Mute Boy (Noah Robbins)
Powskey (Bel Powley)
Gums (Grace Gummer)
John Riley (Tom Riley)
Croomy (Margaret Colin)
The B-Team (The Understudies)

Sweethearts Within the Company: GRACE: Grace & David

BEL: Bel & Byron

BILLY: Noah & Margaret

Embarrassing Moments: BILLY: Walking in on Noah & Margaret.

TOM: The front cloth rising as I rearranged my balls.

Ghostly Encounters Backstage: Hearing Harvey Fierstein (next door in *La Cage*) warm up in the alley where the Barrymore meets the Longacre. Spooky.

Coolest Thing About Being in This Show: Being in this show.

Also: Regarding a difficult passage in the play, a confused cast member asked Tom Stoppard, "I just want to know what you're thinking here?" Tom replied: "I wouldn't assume that I'm thinking."

Photos by Joseph Marzullo/WENN

Baby It's You!

First Preview: March 26, 2011. Opened: April 27, 2011.
Still running as of May 31, 2011.

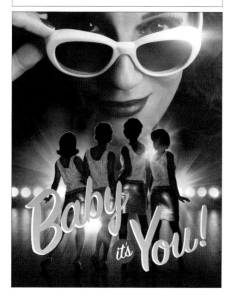

New Jersey housewife Florence Greenberg escapes a stifling marriage and becomes a major record producer when the group she represents, The Shirelles, rockets to the top of the pop charts in the early 1960s.

CAST

Florence Greenberg	BETH LEAVEL
Luther Dixon	ALLAN LOUIS
Jocko, Chuck Jackson, Ronald Isley, Gene Chandler	GENO HENDERSON
Micki, Romantic, Dionne Warwick	ERICA ASH
Mary Jane Greenberg, Lesley Gore	KELLI BARRETT
Beverly, Ruby	KYRA DA COSTA
Millie	ERICA DORFLER
Street Singer	JAHI A. KEARSE
Doris, Romantic	CRYSTAL STARR
Bernie Greenberg, Milt Gabler	BARRY PEARL
Shirley	CHRISTINA SAJOUS
Stanley Greenberg, Murray Schwartz, Kingsman	BRANDON URANOWITZ

Dance Captain: ERICA DORFLER

STANDBYS

For Florence Greenberg:
ALISON CIMMET
For Luther Dixon:
KEN ROBINSON, JAHI A. KEARSE
For Jocko/Chuck Jackson/
Ronald Isley/Gene Chandler:
JAHI A. KEARSE, KEN ROBINSON

Continued on next page

⑤ BROADHURST THEATRE

235 West 44th Street
A Shubert Organization Theatre

Philip J. Smith, *Chairman*   Robert E. Wankel, *President*

WARNER BROS. THEATRE VENTURES & AMERICAN POP ANTHOLOGY

in association with
UNIVERSAL MUSIC GROUP & PASADENA PLAYHOUSE

Present

Baby it's You!

Book by **FLOYD MUTRUX** & **COLIN ESCOTT**

Conceived by **FLOYD MUTRUX**

Starring
BETH LEAVEL
ALLAN LOUIS   GENO HENDERSON

Featuring
ERICA ASH   KELLI BARRETT   KYRA Da COSTA
ERICA DORFLER   JAHI A. KEARSE   BARRY PEARL
CHRISTINA SAJOUS   CRYSTAL STARR   BRANDON URANOWITZ

Scenic Design **ANNA LOUIZOS**	Costume Design **LIZZ WOLF**	Lighting Design **HOWELL BINKLEY**	Sound Design **CARL CASELLA**
Projection Design **JASON H. THOMPSON**	Hair & Wig Design **DAVID H. LAWRENCE**	Casting **TELSEY + COMPANY**	Production Stage Manager **JOSHUA HALPERIN**
Music Supervisor & Arrangements **RAHN COLEMAN**	Orchestrations **DON SEBESKY**	Music Director **SHELTON BECTON**	Music Coordinator **JOHN MILLER**
Marketing Direction **TYPE A MARKETING** **ANNE RIPPEY**	Advertising **SPOTCO**	Consulting Producer **RICHARD PERRY**	Producer for American Pop Anthology **JONATHAN SANGER**

Press Representative **THE HARTMAN GROUP**	Technical Director **BRIAN LYNCH**	General Management **ALAN WASSER · ALLAN WILLIAMS** **AARON LUSTBADER**

Choreographed by
BIRGITTE MUTRUX

Directed by
FLOYD MUTRUX
&
SHELDON EPPS

BABY IT'S YOU was originally produced at Pasadena Playhouse.
Sheldon Epps, Artistic Director; Stephen Eich, Executive Director

The producers wish to express their appreciation to Theatre Development Fund for its support of this production.

4/27/11

(L-R):
Crystal Starr,
Christina Sajous,
Beth Leavel,
Erica Ash,
Kyra Da Costa

Photo by Ari Mintz

Baby It's You!

SONG LIST

ACT ONE

"Mr. Lee," "Book of Love," "Rockin' Robin," "Dance With Me" ....The Company
"Mama Said" ....Florence
"Yakety Yak" ....Bernie
"Get a Job" ....Stanley
"I Met Him on a Sunday" ....Shirley, Beverly, Doris, Micki
"Dedicated to the One I Love" ....Florence, Stan, Shirley, Beverly, Doris, Micki
"Dedicated to the One I Love" (Reprise)* ....Florence, Stanley
"Sixteen Candles" ....Florence
"Tonight's the Night" ....Luther, Shirley, Beverly, Doris, Micki
"Dedicated to the One I Love" ....Shirley, Beverly, Doris, Micki
"Dedicated to the One I Love" (Reprise) ....Mary Jane
"Since I Don't Have You" ....Chuck Jackson
"Big John" ....Shirley, Beverly, Doris, Micki
"He's So Fine" ....Shirley, Beverly, Doris, Micki
"Soldier Boy" ....Florence, Luther, Shirley, Beverly, Doris, Micki

ACT TWO

"Shout" ....Ron Isley, Shirley, Beverly, Doris, Micki
"Mama Said" ....Shirley, Beverly, Doris, Micki, Luther, Florence
"Duke of Earl" ....Gene Chandler, Shirley, Micki, Beverly, Doris
"Foolish Little Girl" ....Shirley, Beverly, Doris, Micki
"It's My Party" ....Lesley Gore
"Our Day Will Come" ....Ruby & The Romantics
"The Dark End of the Street" ....Luther, Florence, Chuck Jackson, Shirley
"Rhythm of the Rain" ....Stanley, Mary Jane, Florence
"You're So Fine" ....Chuck Jackson, Shirley, Beverly, Doris, Micki
"Hey Paula" ....Chuck Jackson, Shirley, Beverly, Doris, Micki
"Louie, Louie" ....Kingsman, Chuck Jackson, Shirley, Beverly, Doris, Micki
"You Really Got a Hold on Me" ....Chuck Jackson, Beverly, Shirley, Micki, Doris, Mary Jane, Florence
"Baby It's You" ....Shirley, Beverly, Doris, Micki, Florence, Luther
"A Thing of the Past" ....Beverly, Micki, Shirley
"Don't Make Me Over" ....Dionne Warwick, Florence
"Walk on By" ....Dionne Warwick, Florence, Luther
"Baby It's You" (Reprise) ....Shirley, Beverly, Doris, Micki
"Tonight's the Night" (Reprise) ....Shirley, Beverly, Doris, Micki
"Dedicated to the One I Love" (Reprise) ....Shirley, Beverly, Doris, Micki, Florence
"I Say a Little Prayer" ....The Company
"Shout" (Reprise), "Twist and Shout" ....The Company

* Arrangement by Adam Irizarry

Cast Continued

For Bernie Greenberg/Milt Gabler:
ADAM HELLER
For Mary Jane Greenberg/Lesley Gore:
CHELSEA MORGAN STOCK
For Stanley Greenberg/Murray Schwartz/Kingsman:
ZACHARY PRINCE
For Shirley:
ERICA ASH, ERICA DORFLER,
BERLANDO DRAKE
For Beverly/Ruby:
ERICA DORFLER, BERLANDO DRAKE,
ANNETTE MOORE
For Doris/Romantics:
ERICA DORFLER, ANNETTE MOORE
For Micki/Bobbette/Romantics/
Dionne Warwick, Millie:
BERLANDO DRAKE, ANNETTE MOORE

Although this play is inspired by actual events, some material has been fictionalized for dramatic purposes.

SETTING
1958 - 1965
Passaic, New Jersey and New York City

ORCHESTRA
Conductor: SHELTON BECTON
Associate Conductor: JOEL SCOTT
Music Coordinator: JOHN MILLER
Reeds: TOM MURRAY
Trumpet/Flugel: RAVI BEST
Drums: RAYMOND POUNDS
Electric Bass: FRANCISCO CENTENO
Guitar: MICHAEL AARONS
Percussion: CHARLIE DESCARFINO
Synth 1: SHELTON BECTON
Synth 2/Associate Conductor: JOEL SCOTT
Synthesizer Programmer: KARL MANSFIELD
Music Preparation: EMILY GRISHMAN/
    KATHARINE EDMONDS
Music Copying: EMILY GRISHMAN

Photo by Colleen Croft

ORCHESTRA
Front Row (L-R): Francisco Centeno, Joel Scott, Shelton Becton, Rahn Coleman, Don Sebesky

Back Row (L-R): John Miller, Raymond Pounds, Charlie Descarfino, Ravi Best, Tom Murray, Emily Grishman, Michael Aarons

Baby It's You!

Beth Leavel
Florence Greenberg

Allan Louis
Luther Dixon

Geno Henderson
Jocko,
Chuck Jackson,
Ronald Isley,
Gene Chandler

Erica Ash
Micki, Romantic,
Dionne Warwick

Kelli Barrett
Mary Jane
Greenberg,
Lesley Gore

Kyra Da Costa
Beverly, Ruby

Erica Dorfler
Dance Captain,
Millie

Jahi A. Kearse
Street Singer

Barry Pearl
Bernie Greenberg,
Milt Gabler

Christina Sajous
Shirley

Crystal Starr
Doris, Romantic

Brandon Uranowitz
Stanley Greenberg,
Murray Schwartz,
Kingsman

Alison Cimmet
Standby for
Florence Greenberg

Berlando Drake
Standby Shirley,
Micki, Romantics,
Dionne Warwick,
Millie

Adam Heller
Standby
Bernie Greenberg,
Milt Gabler

Chelsea Morgan
Stock
Standby Mary Jane
Greenberg,
Lesley Gore

Annette Moore
Standby Beverly,
Ruby, Doris, Micki,
Dionne Warwick,
Millie, School Yard
Dancer

Zachary Prince
Standby
Stanley Greenberg,
Murray Schwartz

Ken Robinson
Standby
Luther Dixon, Jocko,
Chuck Jackson,
Ronald Isley,
Gene Chandler

Birgitte Mutrux and Floyd Mutrux
Choreography; Co-Author, Co-Director,
Conceiver

Colin Escott
Co-Author

Sheldon Epps
Co-Director

Shelton Becton
Music Director

John Miller
Music Coordinator

Anna Louizos
Scenic Design

Howell Binkley
Lighting Design

David Lawrence
Hair Design

Jason H. Thompson
Projections Design

Don Sebesky
Orchestrations

Brian Lynch
(Theatretech, Inc.)
Production/
Technical Supervisor

Bernard Telsey,
Telsey + Company
Casting

Alan Wasser
General Manager

Allan Williams
General Manager

Baby It's You!

COMPANY MANAGEMENT
(L-R): Matthew Sherr, Maia Sutton

STAGE MANAGEMENT
(L-R): Jason Brouillard, Joshua Halperin,
Matthew Aaron Stern

HAIR
(L-R): Linda Rice, Renee Kelly (in front),
David Lawrence, Patricia Marcus, Richard Fabris

WARDROBE

DOORMAN
Joe Trapasso

CREW
Front Row (L-R): Keith Buchanan, Brian Bullard,
Gregg Maday (Producer), Chris Kluth,
Janet Smith

Back Row (L-R): Jeff Turner, Patrick Harrington,
Rob Brenner, Leon Stieb, Chris Doornbos,
Charlie DeVerna, Ronnie Vitelli, Ty Lackey

Baby It's You!

BOX OFFICE
(L-R): Noreen Morgan, Manny Rivera

STAFF FOR *BABY IT'S YOU!*

FOR WARNER BROS.
Chairman & CEO ....Barry Meyer
President & COO ....Alan Horn

WARNER BROS. THEATRE VENTURES
Executive Vice President,
 Lead Producer ....Gregg Maday
Senior Vice President, Development and
 Head of Operations......................Raymond Wu
Chief Financial Officer ....Laura Valan
Senior Vice President, Finance ....Mark Coker
Director, Finance ....Maria Gonzalez
Senior Financial Analyst ....Arthur Yang
Staff ....Carol Wood, Jennifer Kim,
 Rachel Spenst, Susan Gary

AMERICAN POP ANTHOLOGY
Producer.......................................Jonathan Sanger
Executive Producer ....Gerald Katell
Historical Consultant ....Artie Ripp
Executive Angels...........................Abraham Aguchi,
 Annette Tapert Allen, Knut Bjorum,
 Richard & Lauren Schuler Donner,
 Joel & Jolie Keyser, Tom Pape,
 Yvonne & Brian Perera, Claudia Potamkin,
 Dorothy & Jill Schoelin,
 Mark Singer, Lynne Wasserman

THE PASADENA PLAYHOUSE
| **Sheldon Epps** | **Stephen Eich** |
| **Artistic Director** | **Executive Director** |

Director of Development ....Jennifer Berger
Director of Major Gifts ....Patti Eisenberg
Director of Marketing and
 Communications..........................Patty Onagan
Controller ....Stephanie Surabian
Operations Manager ....Victoria Watson
Patron Services Manager ....Carrie Gergely

GENERAL MANAGEMENT
ALAN WASSER ASSOCIATES
Alan Wasser   Allan Williams
Aaron Lustbader   Mark Shacket

GENERAL PRESS REPRESENTATIVE
THE HARTMAN GROUP
Michael Hartman   Wayne Wolfe   Nicole Capatasto

MARKETING DIRECTION

TYPE A MARKETING
Anne Rippey   Elyce Henkin
Sarah Ziering

COMPANY MANAGER
Matthew Sherr

PRODUCTION MANAGEMENT
Brian Lynch

CASTING
TELSEY + COMPANY
Bernie Telsey CSA, Will Cantler CSA, David Vaccari CSA,
Bethany Knox CSA, Craig Burns CSA,
Tiffany Little Canfield CSA, Rachel Hoffman CSA,
Justin Huff CSA, Patrick Goodwin CSA,
Abbie Brady-Dalton, David Morris, Cesar A. Rocha

PRODUCTION STAGE MANAGER
Joshua Halperin

Stage Manager ....Matthew Aaron Stern
Assistant Stage Manager ....Jason Brouillard
Assistant Company Manager ....Maia Sutton
Assistant to Mr. Epps ....Courtney Harper
Assistant to Mr. Mutrux ....Ashley Mutrux
Assistant Choreographer ....Tyrone A. Jackson
Dance Captain ....Erica Dorfler
Associate Scenic Designers ....Aimee B. Dombo,
 Jeremy W. Foil
Assistant Scenic Designer ....Melissa Shakun
Associate Costume Designer ....Sarah Sophia Lidz
Assistant Costume Designer ....Amanda Bujak
Costume Design Assistant ....Elizabeth Van Buren
Costume Design Interns ....Stella Mutrux, Laura Rios,
 Taylor Martin
Associate Lighting Designer ....Ryan O'Gara
Assistant to Howell Binkley ....Michael Rummage
Associate Sound Designer ....Wallace Flores
Assistant Sound Designers ....Josh Liebert,
 Robert Hanlon
Assistant Projections Designers ....Jeff Teeter,
 Resa Deverich
Automated Lighting Programmer ....David Arch
Associate Make-up Designer ....Oslyn Holder
Assistant Hair Designer ....Linda Rice
House Carpenter ....Brian McGarty
Production Carpenter/TheatreTech Assoc. .....Chris Kluth
Automation Carpenter ....Robert Hentze
House Electrician...........................Charlie DeVerna
Production Electrician ....Keith Buchanan
Spotlight Operator ....Patrick Harrington
Moving Light Programmer ....David Arch
Projection Programmer ....Matthew Mellinger
House Properties ....Ronnie Vitelli
Production Properties ....George Wagner
Production Sound Supervisor ....Jim Wilkerson
Production Sound Engineer ....Ty Lackey
Synthesizer Programmer ....Karl Mansfield
Wardrobe Supervisor ....James Hall
Dressers ....Jason Blair, Kay Gowenlock,
 Franklin Hollenbeck, Ginny Hounsel,
 Susan Kroeter, Yleana Nuñez, Katherine Sorg
Stitchers ....Angela Lehrer, Liam O'Brien
Hair Supervisor ....Renee Kelly
Hairstylists ....Patricia Marcus, Richard Fabris,

---

Linda Rice
Music Coordinator ....John Miller
Assistant to John Miller ....Jennifer Coolbaugh
Production Assistant ....Lisa Susanne Schwartz
Music Intern ....Rachel Lee
Music Clearances ....Jill Meyers Music
Projection Image Clearances ....Jay Floyd

Advertising ....Spotco/
 Drew Hodges, Jim Edwards,
 Tom Greenwald, Tom McCann,
 Josh Fraenkel
Theatre Displays..............BAM Signs Inc./Adam Miller
Website Design & Internet Marketing ....Spotco/
 Sara Fitzpatrick, Matt Wilstein,
 Michael Crowley, Marc Mettler,
 Christina Sees
Legal Counsel ....Loeb & Loeb, LLP/
 Seth Gelblum, Esq.
Audience Development ....Walk Tall Girl Productions/
 Marcia Pendelton, Diane Sanders;
 Walker International Communications Group Inc./
 Donna Walker-Kuhne, Cherine Anderson
Accounting ....Rosenberg, Neuwirth & Kuchner/
 Chris Cacace, Ruthie Skochil
General Management Associates ....Mark Barna,
 Dawn Kusinski
General Management Office.............Hilary Ackerman,
 Jake Hirzel, Nina Lutwick,
 Jennifer O'Connor

Production Photographer ....Ari Mintz
Rehearsal Pianist.................................Seth Farber
Insurance ....Reiff & Associates, LLC
Banking ....Signature Bank/
 Barbara von Borstel, Margaret Monigan,
 Mary Ann Fanelli, Janett Urena,
 Alicia Williams
Payroll ....Castellana Services, Inc.
Merchandising ....The Araca Group
Opening Night Coordination .....The Lawrence Company
Group Sales ....Broadway InBound/212-302-0995

CREDITS
Scenery and Automation by Hudson Scenic Studios.
Lighting equipment from PRG Lighting. Sound and video
by Sound Associates, Inc. Custom men's Tailoring by Arel
Studio and Western Costume Company. Millinery by Harry
Rotz. Custom knitwear by Maria Ficalora Knitwear Ltd.
Custom shoes by Worldtone Dance and LaDuca. Costumes
by Euro Co Costumes, Inc.; Donna Langman Costumes;
Jennifer Love Costumes Inc.; Katrina Patterns; Timberlake
Studios, Inc.; Tricorne, Inc. Special thanks to Bra*Tenders
for hosiery and undergarments. Custom fabric printing by
First2Print. Fur by Fur and Furgery. Custom fabric painting
by Jeff Fender. Custom fabric dyeing by Ellen Steingraber
and Eric Winterling, Inc. Eyewear by Fabulous Fanny's and
Myoptics. Men's shirts by Anto and L. Allmeier Inc.
Souvenir merchandise designed and created by The Araca
Group.

MUSIC CREDITS
"Mr. Lee" (Reather E. Dixon, Helen Gathers, Jannie
Pought, Laura E. Webb, Emma Ruth Pought), ©1957
(renewed) Unichappell Music Inc. (BMI) and Pre Music
Company (BMI). All rights administered by Unichappell

Baby It's You!

PHOTO CREDITS

SPECIAL THANKS

Janis Nelson; Genie Printing; Judy Strauss Schwarz; JSS Vision Consulting; Fabulous Fanny's; Jamie M. Brown; JJ Hat Center; New York Vintage; Playclothes Vintage Fashions; Right to the Moon Alice; Salette A. Corpuz; The Family Jewels Vintage Clothing; Pang Yun Tak; Pang Pik Wan; Mark S. Auerbach, Passaic City Historian; Chris Woelk, www.vietnamsoldier.com; Mark Nouhan; Cleopatra Records/Brian & Yvonne Perera; Joel & Jolie Keyser; Vader sticks; D'Addario Strings; Stan & Kay Greenberg; Mary Jane Greenberg-Goff; Wally Roker; Marvin Schlacter; Brenda Kaye; Paul Cantor; Lennie Bleecher; Kenny Vance

---

Makeup provided by M•A•C

Rehearsed at the New 42nd Street Studios and Ripley-Grier Studios

www.BabyItsYouonBroadway.com

Energy-efficient washer/dryer courtesy of LG Electronics.

Baby It's You!
SCRAPBOOK

Correspondent: Erica Ash, "Micki," "Romantic," "Dionne Warwick," "Bobbette"

Memorable Fan Letter: The heartfelt, personalized letter someone in the cast received from a fan… that over the next week every other cast member got from the same fan! Guess it wasn't so personal.

Anniversary Parties and/or Gifts: Christina Sajous's surprise birthday party/The jungle of gifts we all received on opening night… COACH for everyone!!

Most Exciting Celebrity Visitors: Melissa Etheridge came with her children and they LOVED the show!

Actor Who Performed the Most Roles in This Show: Me—four roles.

Actor Who Has Done the Most Shows: Beth Leavel (of COURSE!).

Special Backstage Ritual: Prayers and high-fives backstage left before the show.

Favorite Moments During Each Performance (On Stage or Off): Allan Louis's "Special" conducting during "Tonight's the Night." Beth Leavel skipping offstage after curtain call every night.

Favorite In-Theatre Gathering Place: The basement (hair & makeup and the wardrobe corral).

Favorite Off-Site Hangout: Sardi's.

Favorite Snack Foods: Homemade delights by Chelsea Morgan Stock, Erica Dorfler or Alison Cimmet.

Mascot: Chia Mutrux.

Favorite Therapy: Pastilles and Gummy Bears.

Memorable Ad-Lib: "Maybe a new man in your li…fe."—Kyra Da Costa

Memorable Press Encounter: Our very first press event during previews Beth turns to the Shirelles and says, "Girls, get ready to suck in your stomachs for five minutes straight!"

Memorable Stage Door Fan Encounter: Stanley Greenberg bringing his entire family to the show.

Latest Audience Arrival: Thirty minutes before the end of the show.

Fastest Costume Change: "Foolish Little Girl" 12-second quick change.

Busiest Day at the Box Office: Wednesday matinee.

Who Wore the Heaviest/Hottest Costume: Beth Leavel full-on winter coat with hat and gloves (we get hot just looking at her… poor thing!)

Who Wore the Least: Onstage: Kelli Barrett (we have to judge by amount of costumes because they're all pretty similar). Offstage: Erica Ash ("It's too hot for clothes!")

Catchphrase Only The Company Would Recognize: "I trust you."—Brandon Uranowitz

Sweethearts Within the Company: Adam Heller does not kiss and tell!

Orchestra Member Who Played the Most Consecutive Performances Without a Sub: Shelton Becton.

Orchestra Members Who Played the Most

1. The recording studio (L-R): Kelli Barrett, Erica Ash, Christina Sajous, Kyra Da Costa and Crystal Starr.
2. (L-R): Rahn Coleman, Barry Pearl, Allan Louis.
3. Brandon Uranowitz
4. Exterior of Broadhurst Theatre during the run of *Baby It's You!*

Instruments: Charlie plays a jungle-gym of percussion, Ravi plays two horns at once, Tom plays two flutes and a sax.

Memorable Directorial Note: P.U.H. (to be pronounced as a fart sound) but a very serious and effective note that stands for Precision, Urgency and Honesty. Love you Sheldon Epps!

Company In-Jokes: Der-mashield?
Company Legends: Richard Perry (a music mogul and legend) and Jane Fonda (need I say more??)

Understudy Anecdote: "We're in the cast too!"

Nicknames: "Betty Crocker" (Chelsea Morgan Stock). "Mr. Subliminal" (Zachary Prince),

Embarrassing Moments: Kyra takes a tumble on opening night, Allan Louis has a "Porky Pig" line flub onstage. Christina's shoe getting stuck in the stage floor.

Ghostly Encounters Backstage: Crystal and Kyra's water turning on by itself in their dressing room.

Coolest Thing About Being in This Show: Seeing how affected the audience is every single night.

Fan Club: BabyItsYouOnBroadway.com

Photos by Erica Ash

Bengal Tiger at the Baghdad Zoo

First Preview: March 11, 2011. Opened: March 31, 2011.
Still running as of May 31, 2011.

PLAYBILL

Rajiv Joseph's ferocious comedy follows the intertwined stories of a tiger's ghost (Robin Williams), two American marines and an Iraqi gardener-turned-translator in wartime Baghdad as they try to make sense of a world gone to pieces.

CAST
(in order of appearance)

Tiger	ROBIN WILLIAMS
Tom	GLENN DAVIS
Kev	BRAD FLEISCHER
Musa	ARIAN MOAYED
Iraqi Woman, Leper, Arabic vocals	NECAR ZADEGAN
Iraqi Man, Uday	HRACH TITIZIAN
Iraqi Teenager, Hadia	SHEILA VAND

TIME: 2003
PLACE: Baghdad

UNDERSTUDIES

For Iraqi Woman/Iraqi Teenager/Hadia/Leper:
HEND AYOUB
For Tom/Kev:
COREY BRILL
For Musa/Iraqi Man/Uday:
DAOUD HEIDAMI
For Tiger:
SHERMAN HOWARD

RICHARD RODGERS THEATRE
UNDER THE DIRECTION OF JAMES M. NEDERLANDER AND JAMES L. NEDERLANDER

ROBYN GOODMAN   KEVIN McCOLLUM   JEFFREY SELLER
SANDER JACOBS   RUTH HENDEL/BURNT UMBER   SCOTT & BRIAN ZEILINGER
CENTER THEATRE GROUP   STEPHEN KOCIS/WALT GROSSMAN

present

ROBIN WILLIAMS

in

BENGAL TIGER
AT THE BAGHDAD ZOO

by

RAJIV JOSEPH

with

GLENN DAVIS   BRAD FLEISCHER
HRACH TITIZIAN   SHEILA VAND   NECAR ZADEGAN
and **ARIAN MOAYED**

HEND AYOUB   COREY BRILL   DAOUD HEIDAMI   SHERMAN HOWARD

Scenic Design	Costume Design	Lighting Design	Sound Design
DEREK McLANE	**DAVID ZINN**	**DAVID LANDER**	**ACME SOUND PARTNERS** and **CRICKET S. MYERS**

Music By	Casting By	Press Representative
KATHRYN BOSTIC	**BONNIE GRISAN, CSA** and **MELCAP CASTING, CSA**	**SAM RUDY MEDIA RELATIONS**

Production Stage Manager	Original Fight Director	Technical Supervisor	General Management
BEVERLY JENKINS	**BOBBY C. KING**	**BRIAN LYNCH**	**RICHARDS/CLIMAN, INC.**

Directed By
MOISÉS KAUFMAN

The World Premiere of *Bengal Tiger at the Baghdad Zoo* was Originally Produced by Center Theatre Group, Los Angeles, Michael Ritchie, Artistic Director; Charles Dillingham, Managing Director

Developed at the Lark Play Development Center, New York City

3/31/11

(L-R): Robin Williams, Brad Fleischer, Glenn Davis

Photo by Carol Rosegg

Bengal Tiger at the Baghdad Zoo

Robin Williams
Tiger

Arian Moayed
Musa

Glenn Davis
Tom

Brad Fleischer
Kev, Fight Captain

Hrach Titizian
Iraqi Man, Uday

Sheila Vand
Hadia/Iraqi Teenager

Necar Zadegan
Leper, Iraqi Woman, Arabic vocals

Hend Ayoub
u/s Iraqi Woman/ Iraqi Teenager/ Hadia/Leper

Corey Brill
u/s Tom, Kev

Daoud Heidami
u/s Musa/Iraqi Man/ Uday

Sherman Howard
u/s Tiger

Rajiv Joseph
Playwright

Moisés Kaufman
Director

Derek McLane
Scenic Designer

David Zinn
Costume Designer

David Lander
Lighting Designer

Sten Severson, Tom Clark, Mark Menard and Nevin Steinberg, Acme Sound Partners
Sound Designer

Cricket S. Myers
Sound Designer

Kathryn Bostic
Composer

Bobby C. King
Original Fight Director

Brian Lynch/ Theatretech, Inc.
Production/ Technical Supervisor

David R. Richards and Tamar Haimes, Richards/Climan, Inc.
General Management

Robyn Goodman
Producer

Kevin McCollum
Producer

Jeffrey Seller
Producer

Sander Jacobs
Producer

Ruth Hendel
Producer

Judi Krupp, Burnt Umber Productions
Producer

Bill Gerber, Burnt Umber Productions
Producer

Scott Zeilinger
Producer

Brian Zeilinger
Producer

Michael Ritchie
Artistic Director, Center Theatre Group

Bengal Tiger at the Baghdad Zoo

Charles Dillingham
*Managing Director,
Center Theatre
Group*

Gordon Davidson
*Founding Artistic
Director,
Center Theatre
Group*

Walt Grossman
Producer

2010-2011 AWARDS

DRAMA DESK AWARDS
Outstanding Lighting Design
(David Lander)
Outstanding Sound Design
in a Play
(Acme Sound Partners
and Cricket S. Myers)

THEATRE WORLD AWARD
Outstanding Broadway
or Off-Broadway debut:
(Arian Moayed)

STAGE MANAGEMENT
(L-R): Erica Christensen, Johnny A. Milani, Beverly Jenkins, Alex Lyu Volckhausen

Photo by James Darrah

Photo by Brian Mapp

THE CREW
Front: Robin Williams

Middle Row (L-R): Beverly Jenkins (on side of cage), Steve Carver, Ronnie Knox, Rebecca E. Spencer, Jessica Reiner, Cletus Karamon, Alex Lyu Volckhausen, Justin Rathbun (kneeling)

Back Row (L-R): Steve DeVerna, Dave Camus, Kevin Camus, Lizz Cone, Tree Sarvay, Moira MacGregor-Conrad, McBrien Dunbar, Ron Groomes (leaning on cage)

Bengal Tiger at the Baghdad Zoo

Scrapbook

Correspondents: Beverly Jenkins, PSM, and Alex Lyu Volckhausen, SM

Memorable Opening Night Letter: The letter from Kirk Douglas from the original production's 2009 opening at the Kirk Douglas Theatre in Los Angeles.

Opening Night Gifts: Wine from Robin's grapes.

Most Exciting Celebrity Visitors: Whoopi Goldberg, Joy Behar, and Mario Cuomo all bid on and won photos with the cast for our Broadway Cares fundraising.

Who Has Done the Most Shows in Their Career: Stage management (between us 30 Broadway shows), and of course our crew…too many to count.

Special Backstage Rituals: At five, cast circles in the basement and cheers a line from the play. Full company flips each other the bird at Act II places.

Favorite Moment: The hand job.

Favorite In-Theatre Gathering Place: Stage Manager office, which is really the Greenroom.

Favorite Off-Site Hangouts: Bar Centrale, Glass House Tavern.

Favorite Snack Foods: All the gorgeous snacks sent by our lovely producers, Bill and Judi of Burnt Umber Productions. Or whatever is sitting on the file cabinet in the office.

Mascot: The fake hand that was cut in tech rehearsals—it looks like a costume piece Nipsey Russell wore in *The Wiz*.

Most Memorable Ad-Lib: "FUCK" (when the gun misfired).

Favorite Therapies: Tree and Moira's Magic Throat Elixir. Who needs Ricola?

Memorable Stage Door Fan Encounter: Sting. He stopped the cast outside because he wanted to talk to US.

Latest Audience Arrival: Our head carpenter's parents had tickets for the matinee and showed up for the evening show.

Heaviest/Hottest Costume: Necar Zadegan's burka with the leper makeup underdressed.

Catchphrase Only the Company Would Recognize: "Do they make that in men's sizes?"

Memorable Directorial Notes: To Arian Moayed: "Your Broadway Cares speech. It is not good." And during tech rehearsal: "Move two inches to the right…now split the difference."

Company In-Jokes: Ficky Fick! Chemo the Clown. The Cocksucker with the Fez.

Company Legend: Um…we're working with Robin Williams.

Understudy Anecdote: It's an actual quote: "You mean, I have to stay AFTER half hour???"

Sweethearts Within the Company: Glenn Davis and _____ (meaning anyone).

Coolest Thing About Being in This Show: Um…we're working with Robin Williams.

STAFF FOR
BENGAL TIGER AT THE BAGHDAD ZOO

GENERAL MANAGEMENT
RICHARDS/CLIMAN, INC.
David R. Richards   Tamar Haimes
Michael Sag   Kyle Bonder   Cesar Hawas

GENERAL PRESS REPRESENTATIVE
SAM RUDY MEDIA RELATIONS
Sam Rudy   Dale R. Heller

CASTING
MELCAP CASTING
Mele Nagler   David Caparelliotis
Lauren Port   Christina Wright

ORIGINAL CASTING
Bonnie Grisan, CSA

COMPANY MANAGER
Lizbeth Cone

Production Stage Manager ....Beverly Jenkins
Stage Manager ....Alex Lyu Volckhausen
Production Assistants ....Erica Christensen, Dwayne K. Mann, Johnny A. Milani
Assistant Director ....Timothy Koch
Technical Supervisor ....Brian Lynch/Theatretech Inc.
Arabic Coach ....Fajer Al-Kaisi
Translations/Cultural Consultants ....Raida Fahmi, Ammar Ramzi
Associate Scenic Designer ....Brett Banakis
Associate Costume Designer ....Jacob Climer
Associate Lighting Designer ....Heather Graf
Assistant Lighting Designer ....Ben Pilat
Associate Sound Designer ....Jason Crystal
Head Carpenter/Automation ....McBrien Dunbar
Head Electrician ....Cletus Karamon
Head Sound Operator ....Justin Rathbun
Moving Light Programmer ....Jay Pennfield
Properties Supervisor ....George Wagner
Head Properties ....Ron Groomes

Wardrobe Supervisor ....Moira MacGregor-Conrad
Dresser ....Tree Sarvay
Original Fight Direction ....Bobby C. King
Additional Fight Direction ....Ron Piretti
Fight Captain ....Brad Fleischer
Gunshot Blood Effects ....Hero Props/Seán McArdle
Hair and Makeup Supervisor ....Adam Bailey
Make-up Special Effects ....Adam Bailey
Assistant to Mr. Williams ....Rebecca Erwin Spencer
Advertising...........SpotCo/Drew Hodges, Jim Edwards, Tom Greenwald, Tom McCann, Beth Watson, Tim Falotico
Merchandising................Creative Goods Merchandise/ Pete Milano
Legal Counsel ....Levine Plotkin & Menin LLP/ Loren Plotkin
Accounting ....Fried and Kowgios CPA's LLC/ Robert Fried, CPA
Controller ....Elliott Aronstam
Payroll Service ....Castellana Services Inc./ Lance Castellana
Insurance ....DeWitt Stern Group/Anthony Pittari
Banking ....Signature Bank/Mary Ann Fanelli
Group Sales ....Group Sales Box Office
Production Photographer ....Carol Rosegg

Rehearsed at the New 42nd Street Studios

AGED IN WOOD, LLC
Robyn Goodman   Stephen Kocis
Josh Fiedler   Margaret Skoglund

THE PRODUCING OFFICE
Kevin McCollum   Jeffrey Seller
John Corker
Kaitlin Fine   Andrew Jones

CREDITS
Scenery fabricated and painted by Global Scenic Services Inc., Bridgeport CT. Show control and scenic motion control supplied by Global Scenic Services Inc. Show control and scenic motion control featuring Stage Command System® by PRG Scenic Technologies, a division of Production Resource Group, LLC, New Windsor, NY. Martin Albert Interiors, Inc. Lighting equipment and special lighting effects by PRG Lighting. Sound equipment from PRG Audio. Video equipment from PRG Video. Topiaries provided by John Creech Design and Production. *Bengal Tiger at the Baghdad Zoo* was originally developed with support from the NEA New Play Development Program, also a recipient of a 2008 Edgerton Foundation New American Plays Award. Original costumes constructed by the Center Theater Group costume shop.

SPECIAL THANKS
Manny Azenberg, Meg Simon, Seth Glewen, David Franklin, Bra*Tenders for hosiery and undergarments, Steven Hoggett

✦N✦
NEDERLANDER

Chairman ....**James M. Nederlander**
President ....**James L. Nederlander**

Executive Vice President
Nick Scandalios

Vice President Corporate Development	Senior Vice President Labor Relations
Charlene S. Nederlander	**Herschel Waxman**
Vice President	Chief Financial Officer
Jim Boese	**Freida Sawyer Belviso**

HOUSE STAFF FOR
THE RICHARD RODGERS THEATRE
House Manager ....Timothy Pettolina
Box Office Treasurer ....Fred Santore Jr.
Assistant Treasurer ....Corinne Dorso
Electrician ....Steve Carver
Carpenter ....Kevin Camus
Propertymaster ....Stephen F. DeVerna
Engineer ....Sean Quinn

Billy Elliot

First Preview: October 1, 2008. Opened: November 13, 2008.
Still running as of May 31, 2011.

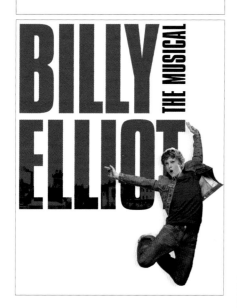

Young Billy has grown up in a union family living in a grim northern English coal-mining town torn by a year-long strike. Like a flower growing in a vacant lot, Billy conceives a desire to be a ballet dancer. He endures the teasing of his friends, the disapproval of his family and the derision of the town at large. But when it becomes apparent that Billy has a chance to get into the Royal Ballet Academy, the townsfolk pool their pennies so Billy can be the one among them who will get to fulfill his dream.

CAST

Billy	JACOB CLEMENTE, ALEX KO, PETER MAZUROWSKI, DAYTON TAVARES
Mrs. Wilkinson	KATE HENNIG
Dad	GREGORY JBARA
Grandma	CAROLE SHELLEY
Tony	WILL CHASE
George	JOEL HATCH
Michael	NEIL McCAFFREY, GABRIEL RUSH
Debbie	GEORGI JAMES
Small Boy	ALEX DREIER, SETH FROMOWITZ
Big Davey	BRAD NACHT
Lesley	AMBER STONE
Scab/Posh Dad	DREW McVETY
Mum	STEPHANIE KURTZUBA
Mr. Braithwaite	THOMMIE RETTER
Tracey Atkinson	RUBY RAKOS
Older Billy/Scottish Dancer	STEPHEN HANNA
Mr. Wilkinson	BRAD BRADLEY
Pit Supervisor	AUSTIN LESCH
Tall Boy/Posh Boy	BEN COOK
Clipboard Woman	LIZ PEARCE

Continued on next page

Continued on next page

⑧ **IMPERIAL THEATRE**
249 West 45th Street
A Shubert Organization Theatre

Philip J. Smith, *Chairman*   **Robert E. Wankel,** *President*

UNIVERSAL PICTURES STAGE PRODUCTIONS   WORKING TITLE FILMS   OLD VIC PRODUCTIONS
in association with WEINSTEIN LIVE ENTERTAINMENT present

BILLY ELLIOT THE MUSICAL

Based on the Universal Pictures/Studio Canal Film

**KATE HENNIG   GREGORY JBARA
CAROLE SHELLEY   WILL CHASE**

And Introducing
JACOB CLEMENTE   ALEX KO   PETER MAZUROWSKI   DAYTON TAVARES

With
STEPHEN HANNA • JOEL HATCH • GEORGI JAMES • STEPHANIE KURTZUBA • NEIL McCAFFREY • THOMMIE RETTER • GABRIEL RUSH
MICHAEL ARNOLD • GRADY McLEOD BOWMAN • BRAD BRADLEY • ALY BRIER • BEN COOK • JEREMY DAVIS • AVA DeMARY • ALEX DREIER
C.K. EDWARDS • EBONI EDWARDS • TIM FEDERLE • BRIANNA FRAGOMENI • SETH FROMOWITZ • CHELSEA GALEMBO
ERIC GUNHUS • CARA KJELLMAN • DAVID KOCH • DAVID LARSEN • AUSTIN LESCH • MERLE LOUISE • DREW McVETY • MARINA MICALIZZI
BRAD NACHT • TESSA NETTING • MADDY NOVAK • KARA OATES • LIZ PEARCE • RUBY RAKOS • ROBBIE ROBY • MICHAELJON SLINGER
JIMMY SMAGULA • AMBER STONE • KENDRA TATE • HOLLY TAYLOR • HEATHER TEPE • GRANT TURNER • NATALIE WISDOM

Press Representative	General Management	Advertising
THE HARTMAN GROUP	NINA LANNAN ASSOCIATES/DEVIN KEUDELL	SPOTCO

Production Stage Manager	Music Contractor	Production Supervisors
BONNIE L. BECKER	MICHAEL KELLER	ARTHUR SICCARDI PATRICK SULLIVAN

Adult Casting Director	Children's Casting Director	Associate Director (U.S.)	Resident Director
TARA RUBIN CASTING	NORA BRENNAN	JUSTIN MARTIN	MARK SCHNEIDER

Associate Set Designer	Associate Costume Designer	Associate Lighting Designer (Programmer)	Associate Sound Designer
PAUL ATKINSON	CLAIRE MURPHY	VIC SMERDON	JOHN OWENS

Associate Choreographer	Resident Choreographers	Assistant Choreographer	Hair, Wig and Make-Up Designer
KATHRYN DUNN	JEFF EDWARDS GREG GRAHAM	NIKKI BELSHER	CAMPBELL YOUNG

Musical Supervision and Orchestrations by
MARTIN KOCH

Music Director
DAVID CHASE

Costume Design by	Lighting Design by	Sound Design by
NICKY GILLIBRAND	RICK FISHER	PAUL ARDITTI

Executive Producers
DAVID FURNISH   ANGELA MORRISON

Produced by
TIM BEVAN   ERIC FELLNER   JON FINN   SALLY GREENE

Associate Director
JULIAN WEBBER

Set Design by
IAN MacNEIL

Choreography by
PETER DARLING

Directed by
STEPHEN DALDRY

Book and Lyrics by
LEE HALL

Music by
ELTON JOHN

PROUDLY SPONSORED BY FIDELITY INVESTMENTS

10/1/10

Dayton Tavares (center)
and Company

Photo by Carol Rosegg

Billy Elliot

MUSICAL NUMBERS

ACT 1

"The Stars Look Down" (The Eve of the Miners' Strike 1984) ....Full Company
"Shine" ....Mrs. Wilkinson, Ballet Girls, Billy
"We'd Go Dancing" ....Grandma, Men's Ensemble
"Solidarity" ....Full Company
"Expressing Yourself" ....Billy, Michael, Ensemble
"Dear Billy" (Mum's Letter) ....Billy, Mrs. Wilkinson, Mum
"Born to Boogie" ....Billy, Mrs. Wilkinson, Mr. Braithwaite
"Angry Dance" ....Billy, Men's Ensemble

ACT 2
Six Months Later

"Merry Christmas, Maggie Thatcher" ....Full Company
"Deep Into the Ground" ....Dad, Full Company
"He Could Go and He Could Shine" ....Dad, Tony, Ensemble
"Electricity" ....Billy
"Once We Were Kings" ....Full Company
"Dear Billy" (Billy's Reply) ....Billy, Mum
"Company Celebration" ....Full Company

Carole Shelley

(L-R): Alex Ko and Gregory Jbara

Photos by Carol Rosegg

ORCHESTRA

Conductor: DAVID CHASE
Associate Conductor: SHAWN GOUGH
Assistant Conductor: HOWARD JOINES,
    JOSEPH JOUBERT
Reeds: EDDIE SALKIN, RICK HECKMAN,
    MIKE MIGLIORE, JAY BRANDFORD
Trumpets: JAMES DELA GARZA, JOHN DENT,
    ALEX HOLTON
Trombones: DICK CLARK, JACK SCHATZ
French Horns: EVA CONTI, LARRY DiBELLO
Keyboards: JOSEPH JOUBERT,
    SHAWN GOUGH
Guitar: JJ McGEEHAN
Bass: RANDY LANDAU

Drums: GARY SELIGSON
Percussion: HOWARD JOINES
Music Coordinator: MICHAEL KELLER

In addition to playing trumpets, French horns and trombones, the brass section of the *Billy Elliot* Orchestra is also playing cornets, flugel horns, tenor horns and euphoniums. These unique brass instruments are the same instruments played in the Easington Colliery Band, which was founded in 1913. Brass players with band experience were encouraged by management to come from the west of Durham to work in the Colliery and play in the band, which continues to perform to this day.

Cast Continued

"Expressing Yourself"
    Dancers ....MICHAEL ARNOLD,
        GRADY McLEOD BOWMAN,
        BRAD BRADLEY, C.K. EDWARDS,
        DAVID LARSEN, AUSTIN LESCH,
        AMBER STONE, GRANT TURNER

ENSEMBLE

MICHAEL ARNOLD, GRADY McLEOD BOWMAN, BRAD BRADLEY, C.K. EDWARDS, ERIC GUNHUS, STEPHEN HANNA, STEPHANIE KURTZUBA, DAVID LARSEN, AUSTIN LESCH, MERLE LOUISE, DREW McVETY, BRAD NACHT, LIZ PEARCE, THOMMIE RETTER, JIMMY SMAGULA, AMBER STONE, GRANT TURNER

BALLET GIRLS

ALY BRIER, AVA DeMARY, EBONI EDWARDS, MARINA MICALIZZI, TESSA NETTING, MADDY NOVAK, KARA OATES, RUBY RAKOS, KENDRA TATE, HOLLY TAYLOR

SWINGS

JEREMY DAVIS, BRIANNA FRAGOMENI, CHELSEA GALEMBO, CARA KJELLMAN, DAVID KOCH, ROBBIE ROBY, MICHAELJON SLINGER, HEATHER TEPE, NATALIE WISDOM

UNDERSTUDIES

For Mrs. Wilkinson: CARA KJELLMAN,
    LIZ PEARCE
For Dad: JOEL HATCH, DREW McVETY
For Grandma: MERLE LOUISE
For Tony: DAVID LARSEN, AUSTIN LESCH
For George: ERIC GUNHUS, JIMMY SMAGULA
For Michael: JACOB CLEMENTE, BEN COOK,
    DAYTON TAVARES
For Debbie: ALY BRIER,
    BRIANNA FRAGOMENI
For Mum: LIZ PEARCE, NATALIE WISDOM
For Mr. Braithwaite: MICHAEL ARNOLD,
    ERIC GUNHUS
For Older Billy/Scottish Dancer:
    MICHAELJON SLINGER, GRANT TURNER

DANCE CAPTAINS

TIM FEDERLE, CARA KJELLMAN, ROBBIE ROBY, MICHAELJON SLINGER

Billy Elliot

Kate Hennig
Mrs. Wilkinson

Gregory Jbara
Dad

Carole Shelley
Grandma

Will Chase
Tony

Jacob Clemente
Billy

Alex Ko
Billy

Peter Mazurowski
Billy

Dayton Tavares
Billy

Stephen Hanna
Older Billy;
Scottish Dancer

Joel Hatch
George

Georgi James
Debbie

Stephanie Kurtzuba
Mum

Neil McCaffrey
Michael

Thommie Retter
Mr. Braithwaite

Gabriel Rush
Michael

Michael Arnold
Ensemble

Grady McLeod
Bowman
Ensemble/
Fight Captain

Brad Bradley
Mr. Wilkinson/
Ensemble

Aly Brier
Ballet Girl

Ben Cook
Tall Boy/Posh Boy

Jeremy Davis
Swing

Ava DeMary
Ballet Girl

Alex Dreier
Small Boy

C.K. Edwards
Ensemble

Eboni Edwards
Ballet Girl

Tim Federle
Dance Captain

Brianna Fragomeni
Swing

Seth Fromowitz
Small Boy

Chelsea Galembo
Swing

Eric Gunhus
Ensemble

Cara Kjellman
Swing/
Dance Captain

David Koch
Swing

David Larsen
Ensemble

Austin Lesch
Pit Supervisor/
Ensemble

Merle Louise
Ensemble

Billy Elliot

Drew McVety
Posh Dad/Scab

Marina Micalizzi
Ballet Girl

Brad Nacht
Big Davey/Ensemble

Tessa Netting
Ballet Girl

Maddy Novak
Ballet Girl

Kara Oates
Ballet Girl

Liz Pearce
*Clipboard Woman/
Ensemble*

Ruby Rakos
Tracey Atkinson

Robbie Roby
*Swing/
Dance Captain*

Michaeljon Slinger
*Swing/
Dance Captain*

Jimmy Smagula
Ensemble

Amber Stone
Lesley/Ensemble

Kendra Tate
Ballet Girl

Holly Taylor
Ballet Girl

Heather Tepe
Swing

Grant Turner
Ensemble

Natalie Wisdom
Swing

Elton John
Music

Lee Hall
Book & Lyrics

Stephen Daldry
Director

Peter Darling
Choreographer

Ian MacNeil
Set Design

Nicky Gillibrand
Costume Design

Rick Fisher
Lighting Designer

Paul Arditti
Sound Design

Martin Koch
*Musical Supervision
& Orchestrations*

David Chase
Music Director

Michael Keller
Music Coordinator

Greg Graham
*Resident
Choreographer*

Tara Rubin Casting
Casting

Nora Brennan
Children's Casting

Mark Schneider
Resident Director

David S. Leong
Fight Director

Nina Lannan
Associates
*General
Management*

Arthur Siccardi
Theatrical Services,
Inc.
*Production
Supervisor*

Billy Elliot

Sally Greene,
Old Vic Productions
PLC
Producer

David Furnish
Executive Producer

David Bologna
Michael

Michael Dameski
Billy

Kyle DesChamps
Swing

David Eggers
Swing

J. Austin Eyer
*Ensemble,
"Expressing
Yourself" Dancer,
Pit Supervisor*

Eugene Fleming
*Ensemble,
"Expressing
Yourself" Dancer*

Izzy Hanson-
Johnston
Debbie

Kylend Hetherington
Tall Boy/Posh Boy

David Hibbard
*Ensemble,
"Expressing
Yourself" Dancer,
Mr. Wilkinson*

Rick Hilsabeck
Big Davey, Ensemble

Aaron Kaburick
Ensemble

Donnie Kehr
*Ensemble,
Scab/Posh Dad*

Jeff Kready
Tony

Patti Perkins
Standby for Grandma

Liam Redhead
Billy

Jake Evan
Schwencke
Michael

Luke Trevisan
Small Boy

Jason Babinsky
*"Expressing
Yourself" Dancer*

Kevin Bernard
*Ensemble,
"Expressing
Yourself" Dancer,
Mr. Wilkinson*

Stephen Carrasco
Swing

Cameron Clifford
Michael

Lilla Crawford
Debbie

Laura Marie Duncan
Ensemble, Mum

David Eggers
*Ensemble,
"Expressing
Yourself" Dancer*

J. Austin Eyer
*Ensemble,
"Expressing
Yourself" Dancer,
Pit Supervisor*

Makenzi Rae
Fischbach
Ballet Girl

Joseph Harrington
Billy

Annabelle Kempf
Ballet Girl

Alison Levenberg
*Dance Captain,
Swing*

Zachary Maitlin
Small Boy

Jake Evan
Schwencke
Michael

Billy Elliot

Emily Skinner
Mrs. Wilkinson

Ryan Steele
Swing

Kayla Vanderbilt
Ballet Girl

Christopher Brian
Williams
Ensemble

Thad Turner Wilson
Ensemble

Caroline Workman
Swing

STAGE AND COMPANY MANAGEMENT
Front Row (L-R): Charlene Speyerer,
Scott Rowen (in frame), Gregg Arst,
Carol M. Oune

Back Row (L-R): Bonnie L. Becker,
Andrew Gottlieb

CREW
Front Row (L-R): Robert Breheny, Brad Robertson, Darryl Mull, Michael Wojchik, Alissa Zulvergold, Marcia McIntosh, Joby Horrigan, Tina Marie Clifton, Chris Noke, Jay Satterwite

Middle Row (L-R): Reginald Vessey, Pete Donovan, Amanda Grundy, Gerard Griffin, Jackie Pietro, Susan Corrado, Lisa Preston, Jay Gill, Margiann Flanagan, Paul Ludick, Jessica Scoblick, Paul Dean Jr., Renee Mariotti, Nanette Golia, David Bornstein

Back Row (L-R): Anthony Ferrer, John Funk, Todd Montgomery, Charles Heulitt III, Justin Sanok, David Mitchell, Margo Lawless, Kirsten Solberg, Ricardo Fernandez, Terri Purcell

Billy Elliot

Photo by Brian Mapp

FRONT OF HOUSE STAFF
Front Row (L-R): Fran Barberetti, Joan Seymour,
Michael Knowles, Lois Fernandez,
Marilyn Wassbotten, Martin Werner

Back Row (L-R): Ed Phillins, Larry Scharld,
Dennis Norwood, Julie Pazmino, Ron Albanese,
Doug Massell

STAFF FOR *BILLY ELLIOT THE MUSICAL*

GENERAL MANAGEMENT
NINA LANNAN ASSOCIATES
Devin Keudell

COMPANY MANAGER
Gregg Arst
Associate Company Manager ....Carol M. Oune

GENERAL PRESS REPRESENTATIVE
THE HARTMAN GROUP
Michael Hartman
Juliana Hannett   Frances White

CHILDREN'S CASTING
NORA BRENNAN CSA

ADULT CASTING
TARA RUBIN CASTING
Tara Rubin CSA, Eric Woodall CSA, Dale Brown
Merri Sugarman CSA, Laura Schutzel CSA,
Paige Blansfield, Kaitlin Shaw

Production Stage Manager ....Bonnie L. Becker
Stage Manager ....Scott Rowen
Assistant Stage Managers................Charlene Speyerer,
                                        Andrew C. Gottlieb

Supervising Dialect Coach (UK) ....William Conacher
Resident Dialect Coach ....Ben Furey

Resident Choreographers ......Jeff Edwards, Greg Graham
Dance Captains................Tim Federle, Cara Kjellman,
                        Robbie Roby, Michaeljon Slinger
Fight Captain ....Grady McLeod Bowman
Original Resident Director ....BT McNicholl
Choreographic Supervision ....Ellen Kane
Staging and Dance Assistant ....Lee Proud

Associate Set Designer ....Paul Atkinson
Assistant Set Designer ....Jaimie Todd
Associate Costume Designer (UK) ....Claire Murphy
Associate Costume Designer (US) ....Brian Russman

Assistant Costume Designer (US) ....Rebecca Lustig
Assistant to Ms. Gillibrand ....Rachel Attridge
Associate Lighting Designer (UK) ....Vic Smerdon
Associate Lighting Designer (US) ....Daniel Walker
Assistant Lighting Designer (US) ....Kristina Kloss
Associate Sound Designer (UK) ....John Owens
Associate Sound Designer (US) ....Tony Smolenski IV
Moving Light Programmer (US) ....David Arch
Costume Shopper (UK) ....Bryony Fayers
Props Shoppers (UK) ....Kathy Anders, Lisa Buckley

Fight Director ....David S. Leong

Production Carpenter ....Gerard Griffin
Production Flyman ....Brian Hutchinson
Production Automation Carpenter ......Charles Heulitt III
Assistant Carpenter ....Ben Horrigan
Production Electrician ....Jimmy Maloney, Jr.
Head Electrician ....Kevin Barry
Assistant Electrician ....Michael Taylor
Production Props Supervisor ....Joseph Harris, Jr.
Head Propmaster ....David Bornstein
Assistant Propmaster ....Reginald Vessey
Production Sound ....Bob Biasetti
Assistant Production Sound ....Stephanie Vetter,
                                        Michael Wojchik
Special Effects Consultant ....Greg Meeh

Wardrobe Supervisor ....Terri Purcell
Associate Wardrobe Supervisor ....Nanette Golia
Dressers ....Michael Berglund, Tina Marie Clifton,
                Lyssa Everett, Margiann Flanagan,
            Jay Gill, Joby Horrigan, Margo Lawless,
                Paul Ludick, Maureen McCloskey,
            Marcia McIntosh, Duduzile Ndlovu-Mitall,
            Lisa Preston, Leah Redmond, Jessica Scoblick
Hair & Makeup Supervisor ....Susan Corrado
Assistant Hair Supervisor ....Monica Costea
Hair Dresser ....Jackie Pietro
Head Children's Guardian....................Robert Wilson
Assistant Head Guardian ....Amanda Grundy
Guardians ....John V. Fahey, John Funk,
                    Andy Gale, Annie Grappone

Production Assistants ....Emily Andres,
                Andrew Gottlieb, Alison M. Roberts
Rehearsal Pianists ....Joseph Joubert, Aron Accurso
Music Copying/
    Library Services (US) ....Emily Grishman
                                    Music Preparation
Children's Tutoring ....On Location Education/
                                Alan Simon, Jodi Green
Tutors........................Jennifer Cutler, Abigale Dyer,
                Diane Hallman, Irene Karasik,
                Kim Karim, Lillian Purpi
Box Office Staff ....Bill Carrick, Paul Blaber,
            Carlin Blum, A. Greer Bond, Bryan Cobb,
                Kiki Lenoue, John Zameryka
Ballet Instructors..............Miranda Barker, Finis Jhung,
                                Francois Perron
Acrobatic Instructor ....Hector Salazar
Physical Therapy ....PhysioArts/Jenni Green
Company Physical Therapists...............Sarah Bingham,
                Ryanne Glasper, Suzanne Lynch
Orthopedic Consultant ....Dr. Phillip Bauman
Pediatric/ENT Consultant ....Dr. Barry Kohn
Health & Safety Consultants ....Eric D. Wallace,
                                Greg Petruska

Advertising ....SPOTCO/
        Drew Hodges, Jim Edwards, Tom McCann,
            Tom Greenwald, Josh Fraenkel,
                        Laura Ellis
Marketing ....Allied Live/
            Laura Matalon, Tanya Grubich,
            Victoria Cairl, Sara Rosenzweig
International Marketing Consultants ....AKA/
            Adam Kenwright, Liz Furze,
            Richard Howle, Adam Jay
Interactive Marketing Agency ....Situation Interactive/
                Damian Bazadona, Jenn Elston
Production Videographer ....Suspension Productions/
                                Joe Locarro
Production Photographers ....David Scheinmann,
                                Carol Rosegg
Accountant ....FK Partners/Robert Fried
Comptroller ....Sarah Galbraith and Co./
                                Sarah Galbraith

Billy Elliot

Immigration ....Kramer Levin Naftalis & Frankel LLP/
Mark D. Koestler, Esq., Allison Gray, Esq.
Legal Counsel ....Loeb & Loeb/
Seth Gelblum
Franklin, Weinrib, Rudell & Vassallo, PC/
Elliot H. Brown
General Management Associates................Steve Dow,
Libby Fox, David Roth,
Danielle Saks
General Management Intern ....Malissa O'Donnell
Production Supervisor Intern ....Lenora Hartley
Lighting Intern................................Trent Suidgeest
Sound Intern ....Rachel O'Connor
Press Associates ....Leslie Baden, Michelle Bergmann,
Tom D'Ambrosio, Alyssa Hart,
Matt Ross, Wayne Wolfe
Children's Casting Assistants ....Lindsay Levine,
Jamie Tuss
Payroll Services ....Castellana Services, Inc.
Travel Agent ....Tzell Travel/
The "A" Team, Andi Henig
Housing ....Premier Relocation Solutions/
Christine Sodikoff
Banking ....Bank of America/Glen Rylko
Insurance ....AON/
Albert G. Ruben Insurance Services, Inc./
Susan M. Weiss
Structural Engineering
Consultant ....McLaren Engineering Group/
Bill Gorlin
Demolition
Services ....JRM Construction Management, LLC/
Philip R. Arnold, Jr.
Theatre Displays ....BAM Signs
Merchandising ....Encore Merchandising/
Joey Boyles, Chris Paseka, Maryana Geller,
Jessie Bello, Claire Newhouse
Opening Night
Coordination ....The Lawrence Company Events, Inc./
Michael Lawrence

FOR UNIVERSAL PICTURES
STAGE PRODUCTIONS

President and COO, Universal Studios Inc. .....Ron Meyer
Chairman ....Adam Fogelson
Co-Chairman ....Donna Langley
President, Universal Pictures ....Jimmy Horowitz
President of Marketing.........................Eddie Egan
SVP, Production Finance ....Arturo Barquet
Legal Affairs ....Keith Blau

FOR WORKING TITLE FILMS

Marketing Director ....Susan Butterly
Vice President,
Legal and Business Affairs ....Gráinne McKenna
President of Production (U.S.) ....Liza Chasin
Head of Film ....Debra Hayward
Head of Production ....Michelle Wright
Head of Legal and Business Affairs ....Sheeraz Shah
Finance Director ....Tim Easthill
Assistant to Eric Fellner ....Katherine Pomfret
Assistant to Tim Bevan ....Chloe Dorigan
Assistant to Angela Morrison ....Kirsty Robinson
Associate Producer ....Marieke Spencer
Head of Finance, *Billy Elliot* ....Shefali Ghosh

FOR OLD VIC PRODUCTIONS

Chief Executive ....Sally Greene
Executive Producer ....Joseph Smith
Finance Director ....Vanessa Harrison
Assistant Producer............................Becky Barber
Assistant to Sally Greene ....Sophie Netchaef
Administrative Assistant ....Fiona Finlow
Legal Representative ....David Friedlander

CREDITS

Scenery constructed and automation equipment provided by Hudson Scenic Studios, Inc. Back wall by Souvenir Scenic Studios, Ltd. Miners' banner by Alaister Brotchie. Flying by Foy. Lighting equipment from PRG Lighting. Sound equipment by Masque Sound. Puppets designed and contracted by the Wright Stuff Theatre of Puppets. Costumes constructed by Mark Costello, London; Tricorne NYC; Jennifer Love Costumes; Baracath Customwear; Douglas Earl Costumes; David Quinn. Custom knitwear by Maria Ficalora and Karen Eifert. Custom footwear by T.O. Dey and Capezio. Millinery and costume crafts by Rodney Gordon, Inc. Undergarments provided by Bra*Tenders. "Express" dress puppet frames and Maggie Thatcher tank by Sophie Jones. Dancing dresses by Phil Reynolds Costumes, London. Ballet Girls clothing by Airy Fairy Costuming. Fabric painting and costume distressing by Nicola Killeen Textiles and Jeff Fender. Wigs made by Campbell Young Associates. Incidental and small props by the Spoon Group. Soft goods props by Mariah Hale. Musical instruments provided by Manny's Music, Pearl Drums, Mesa Boogie Guitar Amplifiers, Eden Electronics and Ernie Ball. Natural herb cough drops supplied by Ricola USA, Inc. Rehearsed at New 42nd Street Studios. Rehearsal scenery and props by the Technical Office Pty, Australia, and Adelaide Festival Centre Trust Workshops. Coal mining footage used by permission of British Pathé and BFI National Archive.

Billy Elliot on Broadway originally rehearsed at the Little Shubert Theatre, NYC; Ripley-Grier Studios, NYC; 3 Mills Studio, London.

Make-up Provided by
MAKE UP FOR EVER

To learn more about the production, please visit
www.BillyElliotBroadway.com

To become the next Billy Elliot, please visit
www.BeBilly.com

SPECIAL THANKS

The producers wish to thank the following partners for their generous support: HOTEL MELA, FIDELITY, CAPEZIO, STEPS ON BROADWAY.

Special thanks to Cass Jones (technical director Aus.); Stephen Rebbeck (technical director UK); Dennis Crowley; Maggie Brohn; Mark Vogeley, Michael Stewart and staff of the Little Shubert Theatre; Stanislav Iavroski and the staff of Ripley-Grier Studios; Steve Roath and the staff of Chelsea Studios; Chuck Vassallo and the staff of the Professional Performing Arts School, New York City; American Ballet Theatre; Youth America Grand Prix (YAGP); Ann Willis Ratray (Acting Consultant); Joan Lader; Ray Hesselink; Tim Federle; Callie Carter; Sara Brians; Stacy Caddell; Fred Lassen; Dorothy Medico and Dorothy's School of Dance – Long Island; Laurie Rae Waugh of Acocella Group; Lisa

Schuller of Halstead Property, LLC; Marie Claire Martineau of Maison International; the "Victoria Posse": Jackie Morgan, John Caswell, Tiffany Horton, Donald Ross, Peter Waterman, Gemma Thomas, Sarah Askew, Marian Lynch, Sian Farley; Treagus Stoneman Associates, Ltd.; Louise Withers and Associates; David Blandon; Diane Dawson; Donna Distefano Jewelry. With thanks to the National Coal Mining Museum for England, Wakefield, W. Yorkshire.
Working Title Films would like to thank Ron Meyer, Marc Shmuger, David Linde, Jimmy Horowitz, Donna Langley, Rick Finkelstein, Arturo Barquet, Allison Ganz, Stephanie Sperber, Stephanie Testa and Jonathan Treisman at Universal Pictures; Peter Bennett-Jones and Greg Brenman at Tiger Aspect Pictures; David Thompson at the BBC and Tessa Ross; Luke Lloyd Davies; Janine Shalom; all at Working Title Films for their continuing help and support; and especially to all the people who worked on the film *Billy Elliot*.
Old Vic Productions would like to thank Eric Fellner, Tim Bevan, Elton John, David Furnish, Lee Hall, Stephen Daldry, Peter Darling, Angela Morrison, Jon Finn and all at Working Title Films, Arthur Cohen, David Friedlander, Robert Reed, Marieke Spencer, Jimmy Horowitz, John Barlow, Adam Kenwright, Janine Shalom, and most of all, to David, Kiril and Trent.
Elton John would like to thank Lee Hall, Stephen Daldry, David Furnish, Matt Still, Eric Fellner, Tim Bevan, Jon Finn, Sally Greene, Angela Morrison, Frank Presland, Keith Bradley, Clive Banks, Todd Interland, Davey Johnstone, Bob Birch, Guy Babylon, John Mahon, Nigel Olsen. And a special thanks to Liam, James and George for bringing Billy to life on stage.

THE SHUBERT ORGANIZATION, INC.
Board of Directors

House Manager ....Joseph Pullara

Billy Elliot
Scrapbook

Correspondent: Hi! Liz Pearce here, from the cast of *Billy Elliot*. I am excited to be this year's *Yearbook* Correspondent. I play the part of "Clipboard Lady" in the show and understudy "Mrs. Wilkinson" and "Dead Mum." With the help of my cast mates, especially Kara Oates ("Ballet Girl"), Ben Cook ("Tall Boy") and Greg Jbara ("Dad") and my stage management team I have put together some of our memories from this past year.

Memorable Note, Fax or Fan Letter: We received the most incredible letter from an older gentleman who saw the show in the latter part of 2010. The letter was so touching our stage managers posted it on the call board for us all to read. In the handwritten note, the sender spoke of the scene in which Billy and his Mum sing "The Letter." As he watched the scene he said he began to weep uncontrollably. In that moment he realized he had never cried a single tear for his mother who had also died when he was a young boy, more than 70 years before. The catharsis that he found in the show that day was healing for him and he shared that experience so eloquently with us. For weeks we kept the letter up on the call board as a reminder of how we can touch people with our performances.

Anniversary Parties and/or Gifts: In November 2010 we celebrated the second anniversary of *Billy Elliot* at Tony's DiNapoli restaurant in Times Square. A commemorative painting was revealed of cast members Emily Skinner, Carole Shelley, Greg Jbara and Will Chase with a Billy leaping overhead. We had fabulous Italian food and drinks and partied late into the night!

Most Exciting Celebrity Visitors: My personal favorite was Kate Winslet who happened to be in the audience the first time I went on for the role of Mrs. Wilkinson. It was very exciting and she came backstage afterwards to congratulate me. It was a dream come true to meet an actress I have admired for such a long time.

Other favorite celebrity visitors include Sarah

Jessica Parker and her son; Harry Connick Jr.; Priscilla Presley; Betsey Johnson; and cast members from "So You Think You Can Dance."

Most Roles in This Show: In first place is our swing, Robbie Roby, who has performed 13 tracks in the show. That is all the men in the ensemble! In second place is myself, Liz Pearce, who has performed 6 tracks in the show including 4 roles. And in third place is ensemble member Eric Gunhus who has performed 5 roles in the show.

Most Performances in This Show: This record goes, without competition, to Merle Louise who has performed an incredible 930 out of 935 performances at the date of my filling out this questionnaire!

Special Backstage Rituals: When I go on for the part of Mrs Wilkinson I have the privilege to witness the ballet girls perform a series of rituals, chants and cheers that they do every night before making their entrance in "Shine." I have enlisted the help of ballet girl Kara Oates, who plays Keeley Gibson, to describe first hand the very important nightly ritual: "In the number 'Shine' all the Ballet Girls have birds that we dance with. Don't worry, they are fake! We have all named our birds. My bird's name is Lucky. One of my secret handshakes with Holly is: 'Ched and Lucky, Ched and Lucky, If we're good we'll get a ducky. Have a good show tweet tweet! Yeah!' Another one with Kendra is 'Lucky and Marley, Lucky and Marley. Oh yeah! Let's Go. Let's Go. L-E-T-S G-O!!!! Good Show! Come on, let's go!' We believe that if we do not do our sacred handshakes we will not have a very good show. As you can tell, our birds are very special to us."

Favorite Moments During Each Performance: I love the Walkdown in the moment the upstage trucks part and we walk downstage towards the audience. I also love watching small boy, Alex Dreier, mesmerized as he watches, and attempts to dance, "Electricity" every night in the wings.

1. Billys Liam Redhead, Alex Ko and Trent Kowalik with ensemble members C.K. Edwards and David Hibbard.
2. Swing Caroline Workman at the stage door.
3. (L-R): Stage Manager M.K. Flynt, Resident Director Mark Schneider and *Yearbook* correspondent Liz Pearce.

Margiann Flanagan (Dresser)—I love the quick change in "Shine" for the ballet girls as we change them into their pink tutus. It is like a flock of doves flies in and flock of flamingos flies out!

Kara Oates (Ballet Girl)—I love the Finale as I love to tap!

David Larsen (Ensemble)—"Saturday Night on Broadway" upstairs in the men's dressing room.

Natalie Wisdom (Swing)—Playing Bananagrams with the ballet girls.

Ben Cook (Tall Boy)—"Solidarity" and the moment backstage before "Kings" when I'm dancing with Small Boy!

Grant Turner (Ensemble)—The Finale, as it is a celebration of Dance.

Alex Dreier (Small Boy)—I like getting to watch "Electricity" from the wings every night before I enter in Soup Kitchen. (I think we have another Billy in the making!)

Thommie Retter (Mr. Braithwaite)—My favorite part of the show happens after the adjudicator asks Billy "What does it feel like

Billy Elliot
SCRAPBOOK

Some of the Ballet Girls on the stairs leading to the stage erected in Times Square for the September 2010 "Broadway on Broadway" event.

when you're dancing?" The moment Billy turns back with the determination and the love and happiness that consumes him when he's dancing. I find that moment so inspirational.

In-Theatre Gathering Place: The Ensemble Men's Dressing Room on a Saturday Night after the show.

Off-Site Hangouts: Glass House Tavern, Hour Glass Tavern, Room Service, Zigolini's, Schnipper's and Charlie Underhill (Stage Management) and David Hibbard's (Ensemble) lake house.

Favorite Snacks: As a company we tend to snack on Backstage pretzels, Twizzlers, Dove chocolates, popcorn, Saturday Bagels, Oreos, chips and queso and whatever incredible gourmet dish that Drew McVety (Posh Dad/Scab) has prepared for us to taste. It's fun to have a chef in the company!!

Mascots: Tessa Netting's (Ballet Girl) Rubber Chicken and "Shne-Ha" the hanging skull with a ponytail, courtesy of the Billy/Michael/Tall Boy/Small Boy dressing room. Don't ask!

Favorite Therapy: PhysioArts, our physical therapist team, are the company's favorite therapy and the only reason we can do the show eight times a week.

Memorable Press Encounters: Our Billys—Alex Ko, Dayton Tavares, Liam Redhead and Jacob Clemente—had the honor of meeting First Lady Michelle Obama at the White House Dance Series honoring Judith Jamison. Dayton performed "Electricity" in the East Room and all the boys got to take a tour of the White House. It was a very exciting day for them! Joseph Harrington (Billy) and Neil McCaffrey (Michael), along with the ballet girls got to film a performance of "Expressing Yourself" that aired during the Macy's Thanksgiving Day Parade on CBS. Pretty cool!! The ballet girls sang Christmas carols in the Time Warner Center at Columbus Circle in December. As a company we also performed at both "Broadway in Bryant Park" and "Broadway on Broadway" in Times Square.

Fastest Costume Change: According to Terri Purcell, our wardrobe supervisor, the fastest quick change is for the entire male ensemble during the riot into their Riot Police gear at a record 10 seconds! The second fastest change is my quick change into Clipboard Lady which comes in at 20 seconds!

Heaviest/Hottest Costume: The dancing dresses are the heaviest costumes in the show and are worn by David Larsen, Grady Bowman, Brad Bradley, Austin Lesch, Stephanie Kurtzuba, C.K. Edwards and our swings.

Catchphrases Only the Company Would Recognize: Stephanie Kurtzuba (Lesley): "Puppet, Puppet, Coconut, Puppet...."
Ben Cook (Tall Boy): "My dress really smells."
David Larsen (Ensemble): "Safety Fifth."
Aaron Kaburick (Ensemble): "Billy, get downstairs now!" (sung).

Sweethearts Within the Company: Stephanie Kurtzuba (Lesley) and her husband Josh Coakley (Props). Ben Cook (Tall Boy) is the object of all the Ballet Girls' desire, or so I hear!!

In-House Parody Lyrics: Every night Greg Jbara (Dad) sings these alternate lyrics to "The Stars Look Down" as he is putting his costume on: "Through the dark and through the fungus, through the night and through the fear which rhymes with Beer, Through the fights and years of Hardsh#@t! Through the storms and through the tears which rhymes with beers. And although your feet are stinky and although the soles of your shoes are worn and although your mother may shake and bake you and although you feel alone which rhymes with beer. We will always stand with Heather, eating duck pate on toast. We will stand with our over the shoulder boulder holders and eat some worms."

Company In-Jokes/Games: "The Gobbler" courtesy of David Larsen (Ensemble) and Greg Graham (Dance Captain). Too shocking to be described. Aaron Kaburick (Ensemble) created something called the "Riot Challenge" in which he would give a clue to his dresser in the two seconds he was off stage during the riot and they and the rest of wardrobe had to guess the word. For instance the clue might be "clown car," or the "mens ensemble dressing room" or "501 Jeans" and the winning word was "Tight Fit"! Ben Cook (Tall Boy) and the Billys and Michaels like to play a game in their dressing room called "Blind Man" which involves blindfolding one kid and hiding from each other. No easy task in a small dressing room!

Company Legend: Merle Louise (Ensemble) made her Broadway debut in the Imperial Theatre as Dainty June during the original run of *Gypsy* with Ethel Merman. Merle told me once that when she is on as Grandma she sometimes has flashbacks to singing "If Momma Was Married" on the very same stage. Amazing!

Tale from the Put-In: At Stephen Carrasco's (Swing) Put-In he accidentally fell off the stage while wearing a dancing dress into the front row of the house. It was very scary for a moment, but thank goodness he wasn't seriously hurt and we all had a good giggle afterwards!

Embarrassing Moments: There has been more than one occasion where the dressers have been caught onstage in the light during Dancing Dresses when the curtains have flown out prematurely. Very embarrassing for them!

Ghostly Encounters Backstage: Kara Oates (Ballet Girl) told me she had a ghostly encounter in the hallway of the fourth floor, while doing homework outside the dressing rooms—apparently the bathroom door opened and shut and no one was inside...spooooookky!

Fundraising Efforts: Not only did we raise money for Broadway Cares/Equity Fights AIDS, this past year we continue to send a portion of our money raised to The Place to Be organization in Easington, County Durham, where our story takes place. It supports arts education in the community there. We also sent money during our Easter Bonnet collecting this past year to the West Virginia Mining Disaster Relief Efforts. It was a incident that moved us here at *Billy Elliot* and we used our Easter Bonnet presentation to honor the miners who lost their lives.

Coolest Thing About Being in This Show: As an original company member I have worked with more than 13 Billys in the show. One of the most exciting things about being in *Billy Elliot* is having the privilege of not only knowing these amazing kids but being able to observe their growth as performers in the course of their time here. We, the adult members of the cast, watch our Billys like proud parents and witness their struggles and challenges and then have the profound joy of seeing them overcome them. It is truly a gift.

Bloody Bloody Andrew Jackson

First Preview: September 20, 2010. Opened: October 13, 2010.
Closed January 2, 2011 after 26 Previews and 94 Performances.

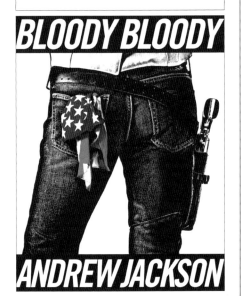

Profane and hallucinatory musical retelling of the life of the seventh U.S. president, Andrew Jackson, focusing on his populist rise to power battling Indians, the Spanish, the French and the Eastern establishment. Not coincidentally a commentary on the current Tea Party political movement, and recent American history in general.

THE COMPANY
(in speaking order)

Andrew Jackson	BENJAMIN WALKER
The Storyteller	KRISTINE NIELSEN
Elizabeth, Erica	KATE CULLEN ROBERTS
Andrew Sr., Calhoun	DARREN GOLDSTEIN
Cobbler, Messenger, John Quincy Adams, Tour Guide, Florida Man	JEFF HILLER
Toula, Female Ensemble	NADIA QUINN
Female Soloist, Announcer, Naomi	EMILY YOUNG
Monroe	BEN STEINFELD
Rachel, Florida Woman	MARIA ELENA RAMIREZ
Black Fox, Clay	BRYCE PINKHAM
Male Soloist, Citizen, Phil	JAMES BARRY
Red Eagle, University President	GREG HILDRETH
Keokuk, Van Buren	LUCAS NEAR-VERBRUGGHE
Lyncoya	CAMERON OCASIO

Continued on next page

♿ BERNARD B. JACOBS THEATRE
242 West 45th Street
A Shubert Organization Theatre

Philip J. Smith, *Chairman*   **Robert E. Wankel**, *President*

THE PUBLIC THEATER
OSKAR EUSTIS, ARTISTIC DIRECTOR   ANDREW D. HAMINGSON, EXECUTIVE DIRECTOR
JEFFREY RICHARDS   JERRY FRANKEL   NORTON HERRICK & HERRICK ENTERTAINMENT
STEWART LANE & BONNIE COMLEY   SUSAN QUINT GALLIN/MARY LU ROFFE/JENNIFER MANOCHERIAN
NANCY C. PADUANO/HAROLD THAU
JOEY PARNES, EXECUTIVE PRODUCER
AND
CENTER THEATRE GROUP

PRESENT

BLOODY BLOODY ANDREW JACKSON

WRITTEN BY   MUSIC & LYRICS BY
ALEX TIMBERS   **MICHAEL FRIEDMAN**

STARRING

BENJAMIN WALKER

WITH

JAMES BARRY   DARREN GOLDSTEIN   GREG HILDRETH   JEFF HILLER   LUCAS NEAR-VERBRUGGHE
CAMERON OCASIO   BRYCE PINKHAM   NADIA QUINN   MARIA ELENA RAMIREZ
KATE CULLEN ROBERTS   BEN STEINFELD   EMILY YOUNG
HEATH CALVERT   AIDEN EYRICK   ERIN FELGAR   ELI JAMES   JOE JUNG   MARIA-CHRISTINA OLIVERAS

AND

KRISTINE NIELSEN

SCENIC DESIGN	COSTUME DESIGN	LIGHTING DESIGN	SOUND DESIGN
DONYALE WERLE	**EMILY REBHOLZ**	**JUSTIN TOWNSEND**	**BART FASBENDER**

MUSIC DIRECTOR	MUSIC COORDINATOR	FIGHT DIRECTOR
JUSTIN LEVINE	**SEYMOUR RED PRESS**	**JACOB GRIGOLIA-ROSENBAUM**

BROADWAY CASTING	PRODUCTION STAGE MANAGER	DRAMATURGS
CARRIE GARDNER	**ARTHUR GAFFIN**	**ANNE DAVISON & MIKE SABLONE**

ASSOCIATE PRODUCERS
MANDY HACKETT   JEREMY SCOTT BLAUSTEIN   MICHAEL CREA
SD WAGNER   JOHN JOHNSON

PRESS REPRESENTATIVE
JEFFREY RICHARDS ASSOCIATES
IRENE GANDY/ALANA KARPOFF

CHOREOGRAPHY BY
DANNY MEFFORD

DIRECTED BY
ALEX TIMBERS

THE WORLD PREMIERE OF BLOODY BLOODY ANDREW JACKSON WAS PRESENTED BY CENTER THEATRE GROUP AND THE PUBLIC
THEATER AT THE KIRK DOUGLAS THEATRE IN LOS ANGELES, CA IN JANUARY 2008
AND SUBSEQUENTLY AT THE PUBLIC THEATER IN APRIL 2010.

BLOODY BLOODY ANDREW JACKSON WAS DEVELOPED IN ASSOCIATION WITH LES FRERES CORBUSIER.

THE PRODUCERS WISH TO EXPRESS THEIR APPRECIATION TO THEATRE DEVELOPMENT FUND
FOR ITS SUPPORT OF THIS PRODUCTION.

10/13/10

Benjamin Walker (center) with the company

Photo by Joan Marcus

Bloody Bloody Andrew Jackson

Cast Continued

MUSICIANS
Piano/Guitar/Conductor:
JUSTIN LEVINE
Bass/Associate Conductor:
CHARLIE ROSEN
Drums:
KEVIN GARCIA

SWINGS
HEATH CALVERT, ERIN FELGAR, ELI JAMES,
JOE JUNG, MARIA-CHRISTINA OLIVERAS

UNDERSTUDIES
For Andrew Jackson:
HEATH CALVERT, BRYCE PINKHAM
For Lyncoya:
AIDEN EYRICK
For The Storyteller:
NADIA QUINN, ERIN FELGAR

Dance Captain:
GREG HILDRETH

(L-R): Darren Goldstein, Bryce Pinkham, Ben Steinfeld, Jeff Hiller, Lucas Near-Verbrugghe

Photo by Joan Marcus

Benjamin Walker
Andrew Jackson

Kristine Nielsen
The Storyteller

James Barry
Male Soloist, Citizen, Phil

Darren Goldstein
Andrew Sr., Calhoun

Greg Hildreth
Red Eagle, University President

Jeff Hiller
Cobbler, Messenger, John Quincy Adams, Tour Guide, Florida Man

Lucas Near-Verbrugghe
Keokuk, Van Buren

Cameron Ocasio
Lyncoya

Bryce Pinkham
Black Fox, Clay

Nadia Quinn
Toula, Female Ensemble

Maria Elena Ramirez
Rachel, Florida Woman

Kate Cullen Roberts
Elizabeth, Erica

Ben Steinfeld
Monroe

Emily Young
Female Soloist, Announcer, Naomi

Heath Calvert
Swing

Aiden Eyrick
u/s Lyncoya

Erin Felgar
Swing

Eli James
Swing

Joe Jung
Swing

Maria-Christina Oliveras
Swing

Charlie Rosen
Bass/Associate Conductor

The Playbill Broadway Yearbook 2010-2011

51

Bloody Bloody Andrew Jackson

Kevin Garcia
Drums

Alex Timbers
Writer & Director

Michael Friedman
Music & Lyrics

Danny Mefford
Choreographer

Donyale Werle
Scenic Design

Justin Levine
*Music Director,
Bandleader*

Seymour Red Press
Music Coordinator

Oskar Eustis
*Artistic Director,
The Public Theater*

Andrew D.
Hamingson
*Executive Director,
The Public Theater*

Jeffrey Richards
Producer

Jerry Frankel
Producer

Norton Herrick &
Herrick
Entertainment
Producer

Stewart Lane/Bonnie Comley
Producers

Susan Quint Gallin
Producer

Mary Lu Roffe
Producer

Jennifer
Manocherian
Producer

Harold Thau
Producer

Joey Parnes
Executive Producer

Michael Ritchie
*Artistic Director,
Center Theatre
Group*

Charles Dillingham
*Managing Director,
Center Theatre
Group*

Gordon Davidson
*Founding Artistic
Director,
Center Theatre
Group*

CREW
(L-R): Gabe Wood, Bonnie Runk, Gretchen Metzloff, Herb Messing, Mike VanPraagh, Marc Schmittroth, Dylan Foley

Bloody Bloody Andrew Jackson

STAGE AND COMPANY MANAGEMENT
(L-R): Alaina Taylor, Maddie Felix,
Jamie Greathouse, Artie Gaffin

FRONT OF HOUSE STAFF
(L-R): Billy Mitchell, Patanne McEvoy,
Carrie Hart, Eva Laskow, Martha Rodriguez

MUSICIANS
(L-R): Kevin Garcia, Justin Levine, Charlie Rosen

BOX OFFICE
Karen Coscia

DRESSERS
(L-R): Clarion Overmoyer, Chip White

Photos by Brian Mapp

Bloody Bloody Andrew Jackson

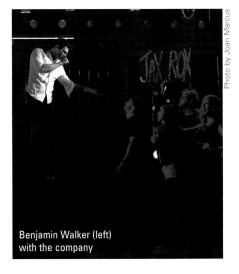

Benjamin Walker (left)
with the company

Photo by Joan Marcus

Bloody Bloody Andrew Jackson
SCRAPBOOK

1. The cast and creators roar approval on opening night.
2. A more subdued Benjamin Walker at the final curtain call on closing night twelve weeks later.
3. The creative team (L-R): Public Theater Artistic Director Oskar Eustis, author/director Alex Timbers, composer-lyricist Michael Friedman and Public Theater Executive Director Andrew D. Hamingson.

Correpondent: Bryce Pinkham, "Black Fox," "Clay"

Memorable Opening Night Note: Sign in the window of David Hyde Pierce's dressing room window across 45th Street at *La Bête* that read "Happy Bloody Opening."

Most Exciting Celebrity Visitor and What They Did/Said: Kirk Douglas who told us he actually voted for Jackson.

Who Got the Gypsy Robe and What They Put on It: Heath Calvert. Blood.

Who Wrote the Gypsy of the Year Sketch: Jeff Hiller and Nadia Quinn.

Which Actor Performed the Most Roles in This Show (and how many): Jeff Hiller (7 characters) and Emily Young (12 quick changes).

Ghostly Encounters Backstage: Constantly in search of Bert Lahr's ghost.

Who Has Done the Most Shows in Their Career (and how many): Kristine Nielsen. All of them.

Special Backstage Rituals: Shana-nana-coomba hesacoming-inahonda. Farting power-rangers. Singing rounds in dressing rooms. Running around naked. Dancing Indian nipple flick.

Favorite Moment During Each Performance: "The Wedge" at the top of the show when we're all together and Ben addresses the audience.

Favorite In-Theatre Gathering Place: The couches downstairs or anywhere that Artie has candy. The Gym in room 17.

Favorite Off-Site Hangout: Hurley's Bar.

Favorite Therapy: Hurley's Bar. The pull-up bar.

Mascot: The upside-down dead horse.

Favorite Snack Food: Chex Mix. Bagels. Candy.

Most Memorable Ad-Libs: "Miss Tickle." "Go Ahead Gus." "Let's take it from, 'My wife just died.'" "Did you say the phone was ringing?"

Record Number of Cell Phone Rings, Cell Phone Photos, Tweeting or Texting Incidents During a Performance: One. Ben only had to tell them once.

What Did You Think of the Internet Buzz on Your Show: What's the internet?

Memorable Press Encounter: Greg Hildreth on Fox5 Cleveland.

Memorable Stage Door Fan Encounter: James Barry signing a fan's forehead at the teenager's urgent request.

Fastest Costume Changes: The Cheerleaders. All of Walker's changes.

Busiest Day at the Box Office: Tomorrow.

Who Wore the Heaviest/Hottest Costume: Ben Walker's General coat with the shower-curtain lining.

Who Wore the Least: The Dancing Indians.

Catchphrases Only the Company Would Recognize: "Swagat!" "Topless of Show." "OhmyGawd" "No.Not.Right!" "RESULTS." "ART-AY!" "MyGreyNuts" "Zango" "Sacagawea!" "Muppence"

Which Orchestra Member Played the Most Instruments, and What Were They: Justin Levine and Charlie Rosen (guitar, bass and piano) followed closely by Greg Hildreth, a bassist on the Broadway level.

Best In-House Parody Lyrics: "Sometimes with Plumbs, Sometimes with Peaches Too." "A Matador That Says Welcome." "The Ironing is Killing Me." "There's nothing left in this hotel." "Poop-U-Loo-Zoom You, You." "Jackson wears gloves!"

Memorable Directorial Notes: "More micro-machiney." "Keanu Reeves-it like a declaration." "Do it like it's in a real play."

Company In-Jokes: Frank Messer. Couldn't Care Less. As a writer on the Broadway level. Cropdusting. Doing the show and not doing the show are exactly the same at this point.

Company Legends: Artie Gaffin.

Understudy Anecdote: Joe knows, everything.

Nicknames: Jeff Hiller: "Winky" Ben Steinfeld: "Styles" Chip: "Whitey"

Sweethearts Within the Company: Jeff Hiller and Greg Hildreth

Embarrassing Moments: When James Franco tripped Ben Walker in the audience

Superstitions That Turned Out To Be True: God.

Coolest Things About Being in This Show: All the Candy.

Also: The time in previews when everyone onstage broke during Washington Two. Find the Funny.

The Book of Mormon

First Preview: February 24, 2011. Opened: March 24, 2011.
Still running as of May 31, 2011.

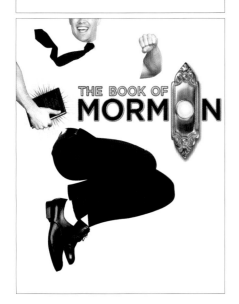

Elder Price, the smartest, most devout and most handsome young Mormon in missionary school, is stunned to find himself assigned, not to Orlando, Florida, as he had prayed, but to a small, miserable village in Africa. He's also shocked to find himself partnered with the dorkiest missionary student, Elder Cunningham. Things go from bad to worse—until Cunningham starts making up his own additions to the Mormon Bible.

CAST
(in order of appearance)

Mormon	JASON MICHAEL SNOW
Moroni	RORY O'MALLEY
Elder Price	ANDREW RANNELLS
Elder Cunningham	JOSH GAD
Price's Dad	LEWIS CLEALE
Cunningham's Dad	KEVIN DUDA
Mrs. Brown	REMA WEBB
Guards	JOHN ERIC PARKER, TOMMAR WILSON
Mafala Hatimbi	MICHAEL POTTS
Nabulungi	NIKKI M. JAMES
Elder McKinley	RORY O'MALLEY
General	BRIAN TYREE HENRY
Doctor	MICHAEL JAMES SCOTT
Mission President	LEWIS CLEALE
Ensemble	SCOTT BARNHARDT, JUSTIN BOHON, DARLESIA CEARCY, KEVIN DUDA, ASMERET GHEBREMICHAEL, BRIAN TYREE HENRY, CLARK JOHNSEN, JOHN ERIC PARKER, BENJAMIN SCHRADER, MICHAEL JAMES SCOTT, BRIAN SEARS, JASON MICHAEL SNOW,

Continued on next page

⬤ EUGENE O'NEILL THEATRE
A JUJAMCYN THEATRE

JORDAN ROTH
President

PAUL LIBIN
Executive Vice President

JACK VIERTEL
Senior Vice President

ANNE GAREFINO   SCOTT RUDIN

ROGER BERLIND   SCOTT M. DELMAN   JEAN DOUMANIAN
ROY FURMAN   IMPORTANT MUSICALS LLC   STEPHANIE P. McCLELLAND
KEVIN MORRIS   JON B. PLATT   SONIA FRIEDMAN PRODUCTIONS

EXECUTIVE PRODUCER STUART THOMPSON

PRESENT

THE BOOK OF MORMON

BOOK, MUSIC AND LYRICS BY

TREY PARKER, ROBERT LOPEZ AND MATT STONE

WITH

JOSH GAD   ANDREW RANNELLS

NIKKI M. JAMES   RORY O'MALLEY   MICHAEL POTTS

LEWIS CLEALE   SCOTT BARNHARDT   JUSTIN BOHON   GRAHAM BOWEN
TA'REA CAMPBELL   DARLESIA CEARCY   KEVIN DUDA   JARED GERTNER
ASMERET GHEBREMICHAEL   BRIAN TYREE HENRY   TYSON JENNETTE
CLARK JOHNSEN   JOHN ERIC PARKER   BENJAMIN SCHRADER
MICHAEL JAMES SCOTT   BRIAN SEARS   JASON MICHAEL SNOW   NICK SPANGLER
LAWRENCE STALLINGS   REMA WEBB   MAIA NKENGE WILSON   TOMMAR WILSON

SCENIC DESIGN	COSTUME DESIGN	LIGHTING DESIGN	SOUND DESIGN
SCOTT PASK	**ANN ROTH**	**BRIAN MacDEVITT**	**BRIAN RONAN**

HAIR DESIGN	CASTING	PRODUCTION STAGE MANAGER
JOSH MARQUETTE	**CARRIE GARDNER**	**KAREN MOORE**

ORCHESTRATIONS	DANCE MUSIC ARRANGEMENTS	MUSIC COORDINATOR
LARRY HOCHMAN & STEPHEN OREMUS	**GLEN KELLY**	**MICHAEL KELLER**

PRESS REPRESENTATIVE	PRODUCTION MANAGEMENT	GENERAL MANAGEMENT
BONEAU/BRYAN-BROWN	**AURORA PRODUCTIONS**	**STP/DAVID TURNER**

MUSIC DIRECTION AND VOCAL ARRANGEMENTS
STEPHEN OREMUS

CHOREOGRAPHED BY
CASEY NICHOLAW

DIRECTED BY
CASEY NICHOLAW AND TREY PARKER

3/24/11

Andrew Rannells (front center) and company

Photo by Joan Marcus

The Book of Mormon

Cast Continued

LAWRENCE STALLINGS, REMA WEBB,
MAIA NKENGE WILSON, TOMMAR WILSON

UNDERSTUDIES

For Elder Price:
KEVIN DUDA, NICK SPANGLER
For Elder Cunningham:
BENJAMIN SCHRADER
For Price's Dad/Mission President:
KEVIN DUDA, BENJAMIN SCHRADER
For Mafala Hatimbi:
TYSON JENNETTE, JOHN ERIC PARKER
For Nabulungi:
TA'REA CAMPBELL,
ASMERET GHEBREMICHAEL
For Elder McKinley:
SCOTT BARNHARDT, BRIAN SEARS
Standby for Elder Cunningham:
JARED GERTNER

SWINGS

GRAHAM BOWEN, TA'REA CAMPBELL,
TYSON JENNETTE, NICK SPANGLER

Dance Captain:
GRAHAM BOWEN
Assistant Dance Captain:
ASMERET GHEBREMICHAEL

ORCHESTRA

Conductor:
STEPHEN OREMUS
Associate Conductor:
ADAM BEN-DAVID

Keyboards:
STEPHEN OREMUS, ADAM BEN-DAVID
Guitars:
JAKE SCHWARTZ
Bass:
DAVE PHILLIPS
Drums/Percussion:
SEAN McDANIEL
Reeds:
BRYAN CROOK
Trumpet:
RAUL AGRAZ
Trombone:
RANDY ANDOS
Violin/Viola:
ENTCHO TODOROV

Music Coordinator:
MICHAEL KELLER
Keyboard Programmer:
RANDY COHEN
Copyist:
EMILY GRISHMAN MUSIC PREPARATION

Josh Gad
Elder Cunningham

Andrew Rannells
Elder Price

Nikki M. James
Nabulungi

Rory O'Malley
Elder McKinley

Michael Potts
Mafala Hatimbi

Lewis Cleale
*Price's Dad/
Mission President*

Scott Barnhardt
Ensemble

Justin Bohon
Ensemble

Graham Bowen
*Swing,
Dance Captain*

Ta'rea Campbell
Swing

Darlesia Cearcy
Ensemble

Kevin Duda
Ensemble

Jared Gertner
*Standby
Elder Cunningham*

Asmeret
Ghebremichael
*Ensemble, Assistant
Dance Captain*

Brian Tyree Henry
Ensemble

Tyson Jennette
Swing

Clark Johnsen
Ensemble

John Eric Parker
Ensemble

Benjamin Schrader
Ensemble

Michael James Scott
Ensemble

The Book of Mormon

Brian Sears
Ensemble

Jason Michael Snow
Ensemble

Nick Spangler
Swing

Lawrence Stallings
Ensemble

Rema Webb
Ensemble

Maia Nkenge Wilson
Ensemble

Tommar Wilson
Ensemble

Matt Stone and Trey Parker
*Book, Music and Lyrics;
Co-Director, Book, Music, Lyrics*

Robert Lopez
Book, Music, Lyrics

Casey Nicholaw
*Co-Director and
Choreographer*

Scott Pask
Scenic Design

Ann Roth
Costume Design

Brian MacDevitt
Lighting

Brian Ronan
Sound Design

Stephen Oremus
*Music Director/
Vocal Arranger/
Co-Orchestrator*

Larry Hochman
Orchestrations

Josh Marquette
Hair Design

Michael Keller
Music Coordinator

John MacInnis
*Associate
Choreographer*

David Turner
General Manager

Anne Garefino
Producer

Scott Rudin
Producer

Roger Berlind
Producer

Jean Doumanian
Producer

Sonia Friedman
Productions Ltd.
Producer

Roy Furman
Producer

Stephanie P.
McClelland
Producer

Jon B. Platt
Producer

Stuart Thompson
Executive Producer

Valisia LeKae
Swing

Douglas Lyons
Swing

The Book of Mormon

BOX OFFICE
(L-R): Rusty Owen, Stan Shaffer, Robert Riechiuti, Sonia Vazquez, Joe Nava, Gary Kenny

Photos by Brian Mapp

HAIR
(L-R): Matthew Wilson, Tod McKim, Joel Hawkins

COMPANY MANAGEMENT
(L-R): Adam Miller (Company Manager), Megan Curren (Assistant Company Manager)

REHEARSAL PIANIST
Brian Usifer

CREW
Front Row (L-R): Donald E. Robinson, Guy Patria, Damian Caza-Cleypool, Jake Mooney, Ken Keneally, Andrew Lanzarotta, Michael Martinez, Scott Dixon, Mary McGregor, Jason McKenna

Back Row (L-R): Bobby Terrill Jr., Kevin Maher, Christopher Beck, James Gardner, Todd J. D'Aiuto, Drayton Allison, Chris Sloan, Louis Igoe, Gregory Fedigan

The Book of Mormon

STAGE MANAGEMENT
(L-R): Rachel S. McCutchen, Karen Moore, Michael P. Zaleski, Sara Cox Bradley

FRONT OF HOUSE STAFF
Front Row (L-R): Kelly Green, Adam Hargua, Jeremy Benson

Second Row (L-R): Lorraine Wheeler, Charlotte Brauer, Verna Hobson

Third Row (L-R): Francisco Lopez, Kristin Griffith, Peter Hodgsen, John Nascenti

Fourth Row (L-R): Raymond Millan, Giovanni Monserrate, Bruce Lucoff

Fifth Row (L-R): Dorothy Lennon, Heather Jewels, Joann Mariani, Mili Vela

Back Row (L-R): Emily Hare, Saime Hodzic

WARDROBE
Front Row (L-R): Frank Scaccia, Grants Barrett, Eugene Nicks

Back Row (L-R): Michael Harrell, Veneda Truesdale, Virginia Ohnesorge, Dolly Williams, James Martin Williams Gunn, Jeff McGovney

---

STAFF FOR *THE BOOK OF MORMON*

GENERAL MANAGEMENT
STUART THOMPSON PRODUCTIONS
Stuart Thompson   David Turner   Marshall B. Purdy
Cassidy Briggs   Kevin Emrick   Geo Karapetyan
Brittany Levasseur   Andrew Lowy
Christopher Taggart

COMPANY MANAGER
Adam J. Miller

PRODUCTION MANAGEMENT
AURORA PRODUCTIONS INC.
Gene O'Donovan   W. Benjamin Heller II
Stephanie Sherline   Jarid Sumner
Liza Luxenberg   Jason Margolis
Ryan Stanisz   Melissa Mazdra

PRESS REPRESENTATIVE
BONEAU/BRYAN-BROWN
Chris Boneau   Jim Byk   Christine Olver

MAKEUP DESIGNER
Randy Houston Mercer

ASSOCIATE DIRECTOR
Jennifer Werner

ASSOCIATE CHOREOGRAPHER
John MacInnis

SCOTT RUDIN PRODUCTIONS
Eli Bush   Steven Cardwell   Max Grossman
Adam Klaff   Joshua Mehr
Allie Moore   Matt Nemeth
Jill Simon   Nora Skinner

Production Stage Manager	**Karen Moore**
Stage Manager	Rachel S. McCutchen
Assistant Stage Manager	Michael P. Zaleski
Assistant Company Manager	Megan Curren
Dance Captain	Graham Bowen
Assistant Dance Captain	Asmeret Ghebremichael
Associate Scenic Designer	Frank McCullough
Assistant Scenic Designers	Lauren Alvarez, Christine Peters
Associate Costume Designers	Matthew Pachtman, Michelle Matland
Costume Design Assistant	Irma Escobar
Associate Lighting Designer	Benjamin C. Travis
Assistant Lighting Designer	Carl Faber
Associate Sound Designer	Ashley Hanson
Production Carpenter	Mike Martinez
Production Electrician	Dan Coey
Head Electrician	Drayton Allison
Production Sound Engineer	Chris Sloan

The Book of Mormon

Moving Light Programmer ....David John Arch
Lead Front Electrics ....Damian Caza-Cleypool
Sound Engineer ....Jason McKenna
Deck Automation ....Andrew Lanzarotta
Fly Automation ....Scott Dixon
Production Props...........................Ken Keneally
Properties Coordinator ....Pete Sarafin
Wardrobe Supervisor ....Dolly Williams
Assistant Wardrobe Supervisor ....Fred Castner
Hair Supervisor ....Tod L. McKim
Dressers ....D'Ambrose Boyd, Michael Harrell,
　　　　　　　　Eugene Nicks, Melanie McClintock,
　　　　　　　　Jeff McGovney, Virginia Neininger,
　　　　　　　　　　　　　　Veneda Truesdale
Hair Dressers ....Joel Hawkins, Matthew Wilson
Associate Musical Director ....Adam Ben-David
Electronic Music Programmer ....Randy Cohen
Drum Programmer ....Sean McDaniel
Rehearsal Pianist ....Brian Usifer
Assistant to the Producers ....Kurt Nickels
Production Assistants ....Sara Cox Bradley,
　　　　　　　　　　　　　　　　Derek DiGregorio
Music Department Assistant ....Matthew Aument
Costume Shoppers ....Brenda Abbandandolo,
　　　　　　　　　　　　　　　　Kate Friedberg
Assistant to Ms. Roth ....Jonathan Schwartz
Research Assistant to Ms. Roth ....Debbe DuPerrieu
Assistants to Mr. MacDevitt ....Ariel Benjamin,
　　　　　　　　　　　　　　　Jonathan Dillard
Prop Shopper ....Buist Bickley
Casting Associate ....Jillian Cimini
General Management Interns ....Rikki Bahar,
　　　　　　　　　　　　　　　　Liz Shumate
Banking ....City National Bank/Michele Gibbons
Payroll ....Castellana Services, Inc.
Accountant ....Fried & Kowgios CPA's LLP/
　　　　　　　　　　　　　　Robert Fried, CPA
Controller ....　...................J.S. Kubala
Insurance ....DeWitt Stern Group
Legal Counsel ....Lazarus & Harris/
　　　　Scott Lazarus, Esq., Robert C. Harris, Esq.
Advertising ....Serino Coyne/Greg Corradetti,
　　　　　　　　　　Sandy Block, Scott Johnson,
　　　　　　　　　Lauren Pressman, Sarah Miller
Marketing, Web Interactive ....aka/Elizabeth Furze,
　　　　　　　　Scott A. Moore, Andrew Damer,
　　　　　　　　　Terry Goldman, Adam Jay,
　　　　　　　　Janette Roush, Meghan Bartley
Website Design ....South Park Digital Studios/aka
Production Photographer ....Joan Marcus
Company Physical Therapists ....PhysioArts
Company Orthopaedist ....David S. Weiss, M.D.
Theatre Displays ....BAM Signs, Inc.
Transportation ....IBA Limousines

CREDITS

Scenery fabrication by PRG-Scenic Technologies, a division of Production Resource Groups, LLC, New Windsor, NY. Lighting equipment provided by PRG Lighting, Secaucus, NJ. Sound equipment provided by Masque Sound. Costumes by Eric Winterling, Inc.; Giliberto Designs, Inc.; Katrina Patterns; Izquierdo Studios, Ltd.; Studio Rouge, Inc. Millinery by Rodney Gordon, Inc. Military clothing provided by Kaufman's Army & Navy. Custom military ammunition by Weapons Specialists, Ltd. Custom fabric printing by First 2 Print LLC. Custom fabric dyeing and

painting by Jeff Fender. Eyewear provided by Dr. Wayne Goldberg. Custom footwear by LaDuca Shoes, Inc.; Worldtone Dance. Props executed by Cigar Box Studios, Tom Carroll Scenery, Jerard Studios, Daedalus Design and Production, Joe Cairo, J&M Special Effects, Jeremy Lydic, Josh Yoccom. Wigs made by Hudson Wigs. Makeup provided by M•A•C Cosmetics.

SPECIAL THANKS

John Barlow, Lisa Gajda, Angela Howard, Bruce Howell, Beth Johnson-Nicely, Sarah Kooperkamp, Kristen Anderson-Lopez, Katie Lopez, Annie Lopez, Kathy Lopez, Frank Lopez, Billy Lopez, Brian Shepherd, Eric Stough, Boogie Tillmon, The Vineyard Theatre, Darlene Wilson

---

Souvenir merchandise designed and created by
The Araca Group.

Rehearsed at the New 42nd Street Studios

🎭 JUJAMCYN THEATERS

JORDAN ROTH
President

PAUL LIBIN　　　　　**JACK VIERTEL**
Executive Vice President　　Senior Vice President
MEREDITH VILLATORE　**JENNIFER HERSHEY**
Chief Financial Officer　　Vice President,
　　　　　　　　　　　Building Operations
MICAH HOLLINGWORTH　**HAL GOLDBERG**
Vice President,　　　　　Vice President,
Company Operations　　　Theatre Operations

Director of Business Affairs ....Albert T. Kim
Theatre Operations Managers ....Willa Burke,
　　　　　　　　　Susan Elrod, Hal Goldberg,
　　　　　　　　Jeff Hubbard, Albert T. Kim
Theatre Operations Associates ....Carrie Jo Brinker,
　　　　　　　　Emily Hare, Anah Jyoti Klate
Accounting ....Cathy Cerge, Erin Dooley,
　　　　　　　　　　　　　　Christian Sislian
Executive Producer, Red Awning ....Nicole Kastrinos
Director of Marketing, Givenik.com ....Joe Tropia
Building Operations Associate ....Erich Bussing

(L-R): Rema Webb, Andrew Rannells, Josh Gad

Photo by Joan Marcus

Assistant to Jordan Roth ....Ed Lefferson
Assistant to Paul Libin ....Clark Mims Tedesco
Assistant to Jack Viertel ....Marisol Rosa-Shapiro
Receptionist ....Kate Garst
Superintendent ....Ralph Santos
Security ....Rasim Hodzic, John Inzanti
Interns ....Ryan Bogner, Ben Cohen,
　　　　　　　　　　Michael Composto, Katie Young

STAFF FOR THE EUGENE O'NEILL THEATRE FOR THE BOOK OF MORMON

Theatre Manager ....Hal Goldberg
Associate Theatre Manager ....Emily Hare
Treasurer ...　.............................Stanley Shaffer
Head Carpenter ....Donald E. Robinson
Head Propertyman ....Christopher Beck
Head Electrician ....Todd J. D'Aiuto
Flyman ....Kevin Maher
Engineer ....Matthew DiBono
Assistant Treasurers ....Russell P. Owen,
　　　　　　　　Keith Stephenson, Sonia Vazquez
Carpenters ....Jake Mooney, Guy Patria
Propertymen ....Gregory Fedigan, Robert Terrill, Jr.
Electrician ....James Gardner
House Sound Engineer ....Mary McGregor
Head Usher ....Saime Hodzic
Ticket-Takers ....Dorothy Lennon, Scott Rippe
Ushers ....Charlotte Brauer, Verna Hobson,
　　　　　　　Bruce Lucoff, Giovanni Monserrate,
　　　　　　　　　Sandra Palmer, Mili Vela,
　　　　　　　Irene Vincent, Lorraine Wheeler
Doormen ....Emir Hodzic, Dmitri Ponomarev
Director(ess) ....Pamela F. Martin
Head Porter ....Byron Vargas
Porter ....Francisco Lopez
Head Cleaner ....Mara Mijat
Cleaners ....Mujesira Bicic, Maribel Cabrera

Lobby refreshments by Sweet Concessions.

Security provided by P & P Security.

Jujamcyn Theaters is a proud member of the
Broadway Green Alliance.

The Book of Mormon
SCRAPBOOK

1. Bows on opening night (front row, L-R): Rory O'Malley Josh Gad, co-director Casey Nicholaw, co-author Trey Parker, co-author Matt Stone, co-author Robert Lopez, Andrew Rannells, Nikki M. James and Michael Potts.
2. (L-R): James and Rannells at the cast party at Gotham Hall.
3. Cast members Kevin Duda, Rory O'Malley and Jason Michael Snow at Gotham Hall.

Correspondent: Brian Sears, "Ensemble"

Memorable Opening Note: "Fuck You ALL!!" from Marc Shaiman.

Most Exciting Celebrity Visitor and What They Did/Said: Jim Carrey, sent 12 orchids and candy with a very sweet card.

Who Got the Gypsy Robe: Michael James Scott .

Actor Who Performed the Most Roles in This Show: Lewis Cleale: Five roles.

Actor Who Has Done the Most Shows in Their Career: Tommar Wilson, seven Broadway shows.

Special Backstage Ritual: Josh Gad recites poetry as Maya Angelou.

Favorite In-Theatre Gathering Place: Room 402 for a sensible Cool Down every night.

Favorite Off-Site Hangout: Inc Lounge at the Time Hotel.

Mascot: Fucked frog.

Favorite Therapies: Maker's Mark and vodka with Fresca and 5-Hour Energy Drink.

Most Memorable Ad-Lib: Josh Gad calling Nabulungi "Nipple Cream."

Memorable Stage Door Fan Encounter: People asking us to sign actual Books of Mormon.

Who Wore the Heaviest/Hottest Costumes: Brian Tyree Henry—Satan Tommar Wilson—Darth Vader

Catchphrases Only the Company Would Recognize: "Black People!"

Orchestra Member Who Played the Most Instruments: We don't talk to those people.

Orchestra Member Who Played the Most Consecutive Performances Without a Sub: See above!

Sweethearts Within the Company: Asmeret and some guy.

Coolest Thing About Being in This Show: Being in this show. It's God's Favorite Musical.

2010-2011 AWARDS

TONY AWARDS
Best Musical
Best Performance by an Actress in a Featured Role in a Musical
(Nikki M. James)
Best Original Score (Music and/or Lyrics) Written for the Theatre
(Trey Parker, Robert Lopez and Matt Stone)
Best Book of a Musical
(Trey Parker, Robert Lopez and Matt Stone)
Best Direction of a Musical
(Casey Nicholaw and Trey Parker)
Best Scenic Design of a Musical
(Scott Pask)
Best Lighting Design of a Musical
(Brian MacDevitt)

Best Sound Design of a Musical
(Brian Ronan)
Best Orchestrations
(Larry Hochman and Stephen Oremus)

NEW YORK DRAMA CRITICS' CIRCLE AWARD
Best Musical

OUTER CRITICS CIRCLE AWARDS
Outstanding New Broadway Musical
Outstanding New Score (Broadway or OB)
(Trey Parker, Robert Lopez and Matt Stone)
Outstanding Director of a Musical
(Casey Nicholaw and Trey Parker)
Outstanding Actor in a Musical
(Josh Gad)

DRAMA LEAGUE AWARD
Distinguished Production of a Musical

DRAMA DESK AWARDS
Outstanding Musical
Outstanding Director of a Musical
(Casey Nicholaw and Trey Parker)
Outstanding Music
(Trey Parker, Robert Lopez and Matt Stone)
Outstanding Lyrics
(Trey Parker, Robert Lopez and Matt Stone)
Outstanding Orchestrations
(Larry Hochman and Stephen Oremus)

Born Yesterday

First Preview: March 31, 2011. Opened: April 24, 2011.
Still running as of May 31, 2011.

PLAYBILL

Billie Dawn, an ex-chorus girl derided as a dumb blonde by her crooked boyfriend, gets tutored by a handsome writer in the ways of Washington, DC —and the world—and turns out to be smarter than anyone expected.

CAST OF CHARACTERS

(in order of appearance)

Helen, a Maid ....JENNIFER REGAN
Paul Verrall ....ROBERT SEAN LEONARD
Eddie Brock ....MICHAEL McGRATH
Bellhop ....FRED ARSENAULT
Another Bellhop ....DANNY RUTIGLIANO
A Third Bellhop ....BILL CHRIST
Harry Brock ....JIM BELUSHI
Assistant Manager ....ANDREW WEEMS
Billie Dawn ....NINA ARIANDA
Ed Devery ....FRANK WOOD
Barber ....BILL CHRIST
Manicurist ....LIV ROOTH
Bootblack ....DANNY RUTIGLIANO
Senator Norval Hedges ....TERRY BEAVER
Mrs. Hedges...................PATRICIA HODGES

UNDERSTUDIES

For Billie Dawn: LIV ROOTH
Harry Brock: BILL CHRIST
Paul Verrall: FRED ARSENAULT
Ed Devery: ROBERT EMMET LUNNEY
Eddie Brock: DANNY RUTIGLIANO
Senator Norval Hedges: ANDREW WEEMS
Mrs. Hedges: JENNIFER REGAN
Assistant Manager, Bellhops, Barber, Bootblack:
ROBERT EMMET LUNNEY
Continued on next page

Continued on next page

CORT THEATRE

138 West 48th Street
A Shubert Organization Theatre

Philip J. Smith, *Chairman*   Robert E. Wankel, *President*

Philip Morgaman   Anne Caruso   Vincent Caruso   Frankie J. Grande
James P. MacGilvray   Brian Kapetanis   Robert S. Basso
in association with Peter J. Puleo

present

JIM BELUSHI   ROBERT SEAN LEONARD   NINA ARIANDA

in

Born Yesterday

a comedy by

GARSON KANIN

with

Frank Wood

Terry Beaver   Patricia Hodges   Michael McGrath
Fred Arsenault   Bill Christ   Jennifer Regan
Liv Rooth   Danny Rutigliano   Andrew Weems

Scenic Design	Costume Design	Lighting Design	Original Music/Sound Design
John Lee Beatty	Catherine Zuber	Peter Kaczorowski	David Van Tieghem

Hair/Wig Design	Casting	Fight Director	Production Stage Manager
Tom Watson	Jay Binder/ Jack Bowdan	J. David Brimmer	Tripp Phillips

Press Representative	Technical Supervisor	Company Manager	General Management
Richard Kornberg & Associates	Larry Morley	Brig Berney	Richards/Climan, Inc.

Directed by

Doug Hughes

The Producers wish to express their appreciation to Theatre Development Fund for its support of this production.

4/24/11

(L-R): Jim Belushi, Robert Sean Leonard and Nina Arianda

Photo by Carol Rosegg

Born Yesterday

The play is set in Washington, D.C.
The year is 1946.

ACT ONE
September

ACT TWO
About two months later

ACT THREE
Later that night

2010-2011 AWARD

OUTER CRITICS CIRCLE AWARD
Outstanding Actress in a Play
(Nina Arianda)

James Belushi
Harry Brock

Robert Sean Leonard
Paul Verrall

Nina Arianda
Billie Dawn

Frank Wood
Ed Devery

Terry Beaver
*Senator Norval
Hedges*

Patricia Hodges
Mrs. Hedges

Michael McGrath
Eddie Brock

Fred Arsenault
A Bellhop

Bill Christ
*A Third Bellhop,
Barber*

Jennifer Regan
Helen

Liv Rooth
Manicurist

Danny Rutigliano
*Another Bellhop,
Bootblack*

Andrew Weems
*Assistant Hotel
Manager*

Robert Emmet
Lunney
*u/s Ed Devery,
Assistant Manager,
Bellhops, Barber,
Bootblack*

Garson Kanin
Playwright

Doug Hughes
Director

John Lee Beatty
Scenic Designer

Catherine Zuber
Costume Designer

Peter Kaczorowski
Lighting Designer

David Van Tieghem
*Original Music/
Sound Designer*

Tom Watson
Hair/Wig Designer

Jay Binder C.S.A.
Casting

Jack Bowdan C.S.A.
Casting

J. David Brimmer
Fight Director

Richard Kornberg &
Associates
*Press
Representative*

David R. Richards and Tamar Haimes,
Richards/Climan, Inc.
General Management

Philip Morgaman
Producer

Anne Caruso
Producer

Vincent Caruso
Producer

Frankie J. Grande
Producer

Born Yesterday

BOX OFFICE STAFF
(L-R): Larry Staroff, Pete Damen

STAGE DOORMAN
Hills Smith

STAGE AND COMPANY MANAGEMENT
(L-R): Jason Hindelang, Tripp Phillips, Brig Berney

HAIR AND WARDROBE
(L-R): Carmel A. Vargyas, Lo Marriott, Claire Verlaet, Steve Chazaro

CREW
(L-R): David Levenberg, Scott DeVerna, Shannon January, Lonnie Gaddy

FRONT OF HOUSE STAFF

Born Yesterday

Jim Belushi
and Nina Arianda

Photo by Carol Rosegg

STAFF FOR *BORN YESTERDAY*

GENERAL MANAGEMENT
RICHARDS/CLIMAN INC.
David R. Richards   Tamar Haimes
Michael Sag   Kyle Bonder   Cesar Hawas

COMPANY MANAGER
Brig Berney

GENERAL PRESS REPRESENTATIVES
RICHARD KORNBERG & ASSOCIATES
Richard Kornberg   Don Summa   Billy Zavelson
Danielle McGarry

CASTING
BINDER CASTING
Jay Binder CSA,
Jack Bowdan CSA, Mark Brandon CSA,
Nikole Vallins CSA
Assistant: Patrick Bell

PRODUCTION STAGE MANAGER ...TRIPP PHILLIPS
Stage Manager ....Jason Hindelang
Assistant Director ....Alexander Greenfield
Fight Captain ....Fred Arsenault
Associate Scenic Designer ....Kacie Hultgren
Assistant Costume Designers ....Patrick Bevilacqua,
Nicole Moody, Ryan Park
Assistant Lighting Designer ....Jake DeGroot
Associate Sound Designer ....David Sanderson
Lighting Programmer ....Jay Penfield
Assistant Fight Director ....Turner Smith
Production Carpenter ....Edward Diaz
Production Electrician ....Shannon M.M. January
Production Sound ....Jens McVoy
Head Electrician ....Scott DeVerna
Head Props ....Lonnie Gaddy
Props Coordinators ....Scott Laule, Buist Bickley
Props Supervisor............................David Levenberg
Wardrobe Supervisor ....Patrick Bevilacqua
Hair Supervisor ....Carmel A. Vargyas
Make-Up Design ....Ashley Ryan

Dressers ....Erin Byrne, Steve Chazaro, Claire Verlaet
Production Assistants ....Robbie Peters, John Bantay
Assistant to Mr. Belushi ....Laura Marriott
Legal Counsel ....Frankfurt, Kurnit, Klein & Selz PC
S. Jean Ward
Advertising ....Serino-Coyne/
Greg Coradetti, Joe Alesi, Sandy Block,
Tom Callahan, Joaquin Esteva,
Sarah Marcus, Peter Gunther
Marketing Services ....Type A Marketing/
Anne Rippey, Michael Porto,
John McCoy
Digital Outreach, Online Media,
Video Production, Website Design ....Serino-Coyne/
Jim Glaub, Chip Meyrelles,
Laurie Connor, Kevin Keating,
Ryan Greer, Crystal Chase, Brad Coffman
Accountant ....Fried & Kowgios, CPAs, LLP/
Robert Fried, CPA
Controller ....Elliott Aronstam
Insurance ....DeWitt Stern Group/
Pete Shoemaker, Anthony Pittari
Banking ....City National Bank/
Michele Gibbons, Erik Piecuch
Payroll ....Castellana Services
Merchandise ....Broadway Merchandising LLC
Production Photographer ....Carol Rosegg
Additional Photography ....Joan Marcus
Event & Party Planner ....Jennifer Pate Gilbert

CREDITS
Scenery constructed by Showman Fabricators. Lighting equipment from LUCS Lighting. Sound Equipment from Masque Sound. Costumes built by Parsons Meares Costumes, Timberlake Studios, John Cowles, Brian Hemesath and DL Cerney. Shoes by JC Theatrical Custom Shoes. Millinery by Rodney Gordon and Arnold Levine. Some costumes provided by Angels of London.

MUSIC RIGHTS
"Anything Goes" music and lyrics by Cole Porter, copyright 1934 (renewed) by Warner Bros., Inc., used by permission of the Cole Porter Musical and Literary Property Trusts.

"Well Git It!" written by Cy Oliver. Embassy Music (BMI). Courtesy of Music Sales Corporation/G. Schirmer, Inc.

Born Yesterday rehearsed at the
Roundabout Rehearsal Studios.

Energy-efficient washer/dryer courtesy of
LG Electronics.

CORT THEATRE
House Manager ....Joseph Traina

Brief Encounter

First Preview: September 10, 2010. Opened: September 28, 2010.
Closed January 2, 2011 after 21 Previews and 111 Performances.

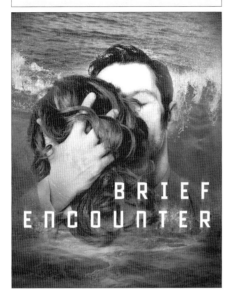

Stage adaptation of the 1945 Noël Coward film about a doomed romance between a man and woman who are married to others. They meet by chance in a railway station and fall fiercely in love, but the emotional damage and shame of their infidelity leads their "brief encounter" to a bittersweet end. Originated at the U.K.'s Kneehigh Theatre, this production expanded the roles of the supporting cast and added music.

CAST
(in order of appearance)

Laura	HANNAH YELLAND
Alec	TRISTAN STURROCK
Fred	JOSEPH ALESSI
Beryl	DOROTHY ATKINSON
Myrtle	ANNETTE McLAUGHLIN
Stanley	GABRIEL EBERT
Albert	JOSEPH ALESSI
Musicians	EDWARD JAY, ADAM PLEETH
Bill/Ensemble	DAMON DAUNNO

UNDERSTUDIES

For Fred/Albert, Stanley:
DAMON DAUNNO
For Alec:
GABRIEL EBERT

Production Stage Manager:
PETER HANSON

Stage Manager:
JON KRAUSE

The actors in *Brief Encounter* are appearing
with the permission of Actors' Equity Association.

STUDIO 54

ROUNDABOUT THEATRE COMPANY

Todd Haimes, Artistic Director
Harold Wolpert, Managing Director
Julia C. Levy, Executive Director
in association with
David Pugh & Dafydd Rogers and Cineworld
present
Kneehigh Theatre's Production of

Noël Coward's

BRIEF ENCOUNTER

with

Joseph Alessi Dorothy Atkinson Damon Daunno Gabriel Ebert Edward Jay
Annette McLaughlin Adam Pleeth Tristan Sturrock Hannah Yelland

Set & Costume Design Neil Murray	*Lighting Design* Malcolm Rippeth	*Sound Design* Simon Baker	*Projection Design* Jon Driscoll & Gemma Carrington
Original Music Stu Barker	*Production Stage Manager* Peter Hanson		*Technical Supervisor* Steve Beers
U.K. Casting Sam Jones	*U.S. Casting* Jim Carnahan, C.S.A. & Stephen Kopel	*Press Representative* Boneau/ Bryan-Brown	*General Manager* Sydney Beers
Director of Marketing & Sales Promotion David B. Steffen	*Director of Development* Lynne Gugenheim Gregory	*Founding Director* Gene Feist	*Associate Artistic Director* Scott Ellis

Adapted and Directed by
Emma Rice

Adapted from the play *Still Life* and the screenplay of *Brief Encounter*, both by Noël Coward.

This production was first produced in the United States on tour at American Conservatory Theater,
St. Ann's Warehouse and The Guthrie Theater.

Roundabout Theatre Company is a member of the League of Resident Theatres.
www.roundabouttheatre.org

9/28/10

Tristan Sturrock and
Hannah Yelland as
Alec and Laura in front
of a filmed image
of her husband.

Photo by Joan Marcus

Brief Encounter

SONG LIST

"Any Little Fish"
(words and music Noël Coward,
arr. Stu Barker)

"No Good at Love"
(words Noël Coward, music Stu Barker)

"Mad About the Boy"
(words and music Noël Coward)

"Wide Lagoon"
(words Noël Coward, music Stu Barker)

"Go Slow, Johnny"
(words and music Noël Coward,
arr. Stu Barker)

"Romantic Fool"
(words Noël Coward, music Stu Barker)

"So Good at Love"
(words Noël Coward, music Stu Barker)

"A Room With a View"
(words and music Noël Coward,
arr. Stu Barker)

"Always"
(words Noël Coward, music Stu Barker)

(L-R): Annette McLaughlin, Joseph Alessi

Photo by Joan Marcus

Joseph Alessi
Albert/Fred

Dorothy Atkinson
Beryl

Damon Daunno
Bill/Ensemble

Gabriel Ebert
Stanley

Edward Jay
Musician

Annette McLaughlin
Myrtle

Adam Pleeth
Musician

Tristan Sturrock
Alec

Hannah Yelland
Laura

Noël Coward
Playwright

Emma Rice
Adapted & Directed

Simon Baker
Sound Design

Jon Driscoll
Projection Design

Jim Carnahan
Casting

Gene Feist
*Founding Director,
Roundabout Theatre
Company*

Todd Haimes
*Artistic Director,
Roundabout Theatre
Company*

Carly Street
*u/s Laura, Beryl,
Myrtle*

2010-2011 AWARD

OUTER CRITICS CIRCLE AWARD
Outstanding Set Design
(Neil Murray)

Brief Encounter

Photos by Brian Mapp

HOUSE STAFF
Front Row (L-R): Jack Watanachaiyot, Alvin Vega, Stella Varrialle

Middle Row (L-R): Sara Rodriguez, Linda Gjonbalaj, LaConya Robinson, Luis Royo

Back Row (L-R): Felisha Whatts, Essence Mason, Delilah Rivera, Jason Battle

CREW
(L-R): Lawrence Jennino, John Wooding, Michael Widmer (seated), Steve Jones, Paul Coltoff, Wallace Flores, Dan Hoffman

STAGE MANAGEMENT
(L-R): Jon Krause, Peter Hanson

COMPANY MANAGEMENT
(L-R): Denise Cooper, David Solomon

Brief Encounter

WARDROBE/HAIR
(L-R): Stephanie Sleeper, Kelly Reed, Nadine Hettel

BOX OFFICE
(L-R): Benjamin Schneider, Scott Falkowski, Krystin MacRitchie, Joseph Clark

---

ROUNDABOUT THEATRE COMPANY STAFF
ARTISTIC DIRECTOR ....**TODD HAIMES**
MANAGING DIRECTOR ....**HAROLD WOLPERT**
EXECUTIVE DIRECTOR ....**JULIA C. LEVY**
ASSOCIATE ARTISTIC DIRECTOR ..**SCOTT ELLIS**

ARTISTIC STAFF

DIRECTOR OF ARTISTIC DEVELOPMENT/
   DIRECTOR OF CASTING ....Jim Carnahan
Artistic Consultant ....Robyn Goodman
Resident Director ....Doug Hughes
Associate Artists ....Mark Brokaw, Scott Elliott,
   Bill Irwin, Joe Mantello,
   Kathleen Marshall, Theresa Rebeck
Literary Manager ....Jill Rafson
Casting Director ....Carrie Gardner
Casting Associate ....Kate Boka
Casting Associate ....Stephen Kopel
Artistic Assistant ....Amy Ashton
Literary Associate ....Josh Fiedler
The Blanche and Irving Laurie Foundation
   Theatre Visions Fund Commissions ....Stephen Karam,
   Nathan Louis Jackson
Educational Foundation of
   America Commissions ....Bekah Brunstetter,
   Lydia Diamond, Diana Fithian,
   Julie Marie Myatt
New York State Council
   on the Arts Commission ....Nathan Louis Jackson
Roundabout Commissions ....Steven Levenson,
   Matthew Lopez, Kim Rosenstock
Casting Interns ....Kyle Bosley, Jillian Cimini,
   Erin Drake, Andrew Femenella,
   Lauren Lewis, Quinn Meyers
Script Readers ....Jay Cohen, Ben Izzo,
   Nicholas Stimler
Artistic Intern ....Alexis Roblan

EDUCATION STAFF

EDUCATION DIRECTOR ....Greg McCaslin
Associate Education Director ....Jennifer DiBella
Education Associate
   for Theatre-Based Programs ....Sarah Malone
Education Program Associate ....Aliza Greenberg
Education Dramaturg ....Ted Sod
Teaching Artists ....Cynthia Babak, Victor Barbella,
   Grace Bell, LaTonya Borsay,
   Mark Bruckner, Joe Clancy, Vanessa Davis,
   Joe Doran, Elizabeth Dunn-Ruiz,
   Carrie Ellman-Larsen, Kevin Free,
   Tony Freeman, Deanna Frieman,
   Natalie Gold, Sheri Graubert,
   Matthew A.J. Gregory, Melissa Gregus,
   Adam Gwon, Devin Haqq,
   Carrie Heitman, Karla Hendrick,
   Jim Jack, Jason Jacobs, Lisa Renee Jordan,
   Jamie Kalama, Alvin Keith,
   Tami Mansfield, Erin McCready, Kyle McGinley,
   Andrew Ondrejcak, Meghan O'Neill,
   Laura Poe, Nicole Press, Jennifer Rathbone,
   Leah Reddy, Amanda Rehbein,
   Bernita Robinson, Christopher Rummel,
   Cassy Rush, Nick Simone, Heidi Stallings,
   Daniel Sullivan, Carl Tallent, Vickie Tanner,
   Jolie Tong, Cristina Vaccaro, Jennifer Varbalow,
   Leese Walker, Eric Wallach, Michael Warner,
   Christina Watanabe, Gail Winar,
   Conwell Worthington, III
Teaching Artist Emeritus....................Reneé Flemings
Teaching Artist Apprentices ....Carrie Ellman-Larsen,
   Deanna Frieman, Meghan O'Neill
Education Intern ....Erin Monahan

ADMINISTRATIVE STAFF

GENERAL MANAGER.......................Sydney Beers

Associate Managing Director ....Greg Backstrom
General Manager,
   American Airlines Theatre ....Rebecca Habel
General Manager, Steinberg Center ....Rachel E. Ayers
Human Resources Manager ....Stephen Deutsch
Operations Manager ....Valerie D. Simmons
Associate General Manager ....Maggie Cantrick
Office Manager ....Scott Kelly
Management Associate ....Jill K. Boyd
Archivist ....Tiffany Nixon
Receptionists ....Dee Beider, Raquel Castillo,
   Elisa Papa, Allison Patrick,
   Monica Sidorchuk
Messenger ....Darnell Franklin
Management Intern ....Elizabeth Johnstone
Archives Intern ....Matthew Kagen

FINANCE STAFF

DIRECTOR OF FINANCE.................Susan Neiman
Payroll Director ....John LaBarbera
Accounts Payable Manager ....Frank Surdi
Payroll Benefits Administrator ....Yonit Kafka
Manager Financial Reporting ....Joshua Cohen
Business Office Assistant ....Jackie Verbitski
Business Intern ....Maurice Blackman

DEVELOPMENT STAFF

DIRECTOR OF
   DEVELOPMENT ....Lynne Gugenheim Gregory
Director, Institutional Giving ....Liz S. Alsina
Director, Special Events ....Steve Schaeffer
Associate Director, Individual Giving ....Tyler Ennis
Manager, Telefundraising ....Gavin Brown
Manager, Corporate Relations ....Roxana Petzold
Manager, Donor Information Systems ....Lise Speidel
Associate Manager, Patron Programs ....Marisa Perry
Patron Services Associate ....Joseph Foster

Brief Encounter

Assistant to the Executive Director ....Nicole Tingir
Assistant to the Director of Development ....Liz Malta
Institutional Giving Assistant ....Brett Barbour
Development Assistant ....Martin Giannini
Special Events Assistant ....Amy Rosenfield
Development Interns ....Emma Acciani,
Sophia Hinshelwood

INFORMATION TECHNOLOGY STAFF
IT DIRECTOR ....Antonio Palumbo
IT Associate ....Dylan Norden
IT Associate...................................Jim Roma
DIRECTOR DATABASE
OPERATIONS ....Wendy Hutton
Database Administrator/Programmer ....Revanth Anne

MARKETING STAFF
DIRECTOR OF MARKETING
AND SALES PROMOTION ....David B. Steffen
Associate Director of Marketing ....Tom O'Connor
Senior Marketing Manager ....Shannon Marcotte
Digital Marketing Manager ....Lauren Brender
Website Consultant ....Keith Powell Beyland
Director of Telesales Special Promotions ......Marco Frezza
Telesales Manager ....Patrick Pastor
Marketing Intern ....Bradley Sanchez

TICKET SERVICES STAFF
Director of Sales Operations ....Charlie Garbowski, Jr.
Ticket Services Manager ....Ellen Holt
Acting Subscription Manager....................Bill Klemm
Acting Assistant Ticket Services
Manager ....Jessica Pruett-Barnett
Box Office Managers ....Edward P. Osborne,
Jaime Perlman, Krystin MacRitchie,
Nicole Nicholson
Group Sales Manager ....Jeff Monteith
Assistant Box Office Managers ....Robert Morgan,
Andrew Clements, Scott Falkowski,
Catherine Fitzpatrick
Assistant Ticket Services Managers ....Robert Kane,
Lindsay Ericson
Customer Services Coordinator ....Thomas Walsh
Ticket Services ....Solangel Bido, Arianna Boykins,
Lauren Cartelli, Joseph Clark,
Nisha Dhruna, Adam Elsberry,
Joseph Gallina, James Graham,
Kara Harrington, Tova Heller,
Nicki Ishmael, Kate Longosky,
Michelle Maccarone, Elisa Mala,
Mead Margulies, Laura Marshall,
Chuck Migliaccio, Carlos Morris,
Bekah Nutt, Hillary Parker,
Kaia Rafoss, Josh Rozett,
Ben Schneider, Kenneth Senn,
Heather Siebert, Nalane Singh,
Lillian Soto, Ron Tobia,
Hannah Weitzman
Ticket Services Interns ....Jacqueline Battaglia,
Lindsay Hoffman

SERVICES
Counsel ....Paul, Weiss,
Rifkind, Wharton and Garrison LLP,
Charles H. Googe Jr., Carol M. Kaplan
Counsel ....Rosenberg & Estis

Counsel ....Andrew Lance,
Gibson, Dunn, & Crutcher, LLP
Counsel ....Harry H. Weintraub,
Glick and Weintraub, P.C.
Counsel ....Strook & Strook & Lavan LLP
Counsel ....Daniel S. Dokos,
Weil, Gotshal & Manges LLP
Immigration Counsel ....Mark D. Koestler and
Theodore Ruthizer
Counsel ....Claudia Wagner/
Manatt, Phelps & Phillips, LLP
House Physicians ....Dr. Theodore Tyberg,
Dr. Lawrence Katz
House Dentist ....Neil Kanner, D.M.D.
Insurance ....DeWitt Stern Group, Inc.
Accountant ....Lutz & Carr CPAs, LLP
Advertising ....Spotco/
Drew Hodges, Jim Edwards,
Tom Greenwald, Kyle Hall,
Cory Spinney
Interactive Marketing.................Situation Interactive/
Damian Bazadona, John Lanasa,
Eric Bornemann, Randi Fields
Events Photography ....Anita and Steve Shevett
Production Photographer ....Carol Rosegg
Theatre Displays ....King Displays, Wayne Sapper
Lobby Refreshments ....Sweet Concessions
Merchandising ....Spotco Merch/
James Decker

MANAGING DIRECTOR
EMERITUS ....Ellen Richard

Roundabout Theatre Company
231 West 39th Street, New York, NY 10018
(212) 719-9393.

GENERAL PRESS REPRESENTATIVES
BONEAU/BRYAN-BROWN
Adrian Bryan-Brown
Matt Polk   Jessica Johnson   Amy Kass

STAFF FOR *BRIEF ENCOUNTER*
Company Manager .... Denise Cooper
Company Manager Assistant .... David Solomon
Production Stage Manager ....Peter Hanson
Stage Manager ....Jon Krause
Associate Director ....Wes Grantom
UK Scenic/Costume Assistant ....Imogen Clöet
Associate Lighting Designer ....Daniel Walker
Associate Designer ....Michael Clark
Video Programmer ....Eric Norris
Production Carpenter ....Dan Hoffman
Flyman ....Steve Jones
Production Electrician ....John Wooding
Light Programmer ....Marc Polimeni
Followspot Operator ....Paul Coltoff
UK Sound Associate ....Andy Graham
Production Sound Engineer ....Wallace Flores
Deck Sound ................................T.J. McEvoy
House Properties ....Lawrence Jennino
Local 1 IATSE Apprentice ....Michael Widmer
Wardrobe Supervisor ....Nadine Hettel
Dresser ....Stephanie Sleeper
Hannah Yelland's Hair by ....John Barrett Salon
Dialect Coach ....Stephen Gabis

US Musical Director ....Andy Einhorn
UK Stage Managers ....Steph Curtis, Karen Habens
UK Musical Coordinator ....Pete Judge
UK Production Manager ....Dom Fraser
UK Deputy Production Manager ....Cath Bates
Production Assistant ....Hannah Dorfman

CREDITS
Bridge structure constructed by Weld-Fab Engineering. Set constructed and painted by Visual Scene. UJ cloth supplied by Claire Sanderson. Additional scenic elements by Global Scenic Services. Lighting equipment from PRG Lighting. Audio and video equipment from Sound Associates. Tristan Sturrock's suit by Giliberto Designs. Hannah Yelland's slip and blouse by Jennifer Love Costumes. Shoe repair by Rostelle.

EMMA RICE SPECIAL THANKS
With heartfelt thanks to Naomi Frederick, Tamzin Griffin, Andy Williams, Mandy Lawrence, Stu McLoughlan, Alex Vann, Pete Judge, Bev Rudd, Milo Twomey, Chris Price, Ian Ross, Dave Brown and all at Kneehigh. These valued friends and colleagues have helped to create this production. Their humanity, creativity and generosity run through the veins of this precious show. Thank you. ER

SPECIAL THANKS
Paul Huntley and Cynthia Demand for Wigs

STAFF FOR KNEEHIGH THEATRE
Joint Artistic Director & Chief Executive ...... Emma Rice
Joint Artistic Director .... Mike Shepherd
Producer .... Paul Crewes
General Manager .... Charlotte Bond
Communications Manager .... Anna Mansell
Finance Officer .... Sarah Comacchio
Development Officer .... Matt Armstrong
Project Administrator .... Elizabeth King
Office Administrator .... Chloe Rickard

M•A•C Cosmetics
Official Makeup of Roundabout Theatre Company

To learn more about Roundabout Theatre Company,
please visit roundabouttheatre.org
Find us on Facebook.
Follow us on Twitter @RTC_NYC

STUDIO 54 THEATRE STAFF
House Carpenter ....Dan Hoffman
House Electrician ....John Wooding
House Properties ....Lawrence Jennino
Box Office Manager....................Krystin MacRitchie
Assistant Box Office Manager ....Scott Falkowski
House Manager ....LaConya Robinson
Associate House Manager ....Jack Watanachaiyot
Head Usher...............................Jonathan Martineaz
Ushers......................Justin Brown, Linda Gjonbalaj,
Jennifer Kneeland, Hajjah Karriem,
Essence Mason, Nicole Ramirez,
Diana Trent, Stella Varrialle,
Nicholas Wheatley
Security ....Gotham Security
Maintenance ....Jason Battle, Ralph Mohan,
Eddie Perez, Reliable Cleaning
Lobby Refreshments ....Sweet Concessions

Brief Encounter
SCRAPBOOK

Correspondent: Dorothy Atkinson, "Beryl" and other roles

Memorable Opening Night Notes: It was fairly low-key because we'd done the show before. We got some nice "Hope it goes well" notes from our friends at St. Ann's Warehouse, where the show started its life in New York. Being on Broadway feels like the cherry on the cake. This show has had a long and varied life.

Opening Night Gifts: Annette McLaughlin's dressing room was a Florists. She gets the prize for most flowers. Roundabout gave us a framed photo of all the cast and crew. Annette gave us some real British teabags and British biscuits. David Pugh gave us Tiffany luggage tags.

Most Exciting Celebrity Visitors: Liza Minnelli was pretty special—she gave us all a hug. A visit from Sarah Jessica Parker was the origin of our catchphrase, "OMG SJP!" Other visitors included Stephen Sondheim and Hal Prince together. Mikhail Baryshnikov. Oliver Stone asked me where I got the false teeth, and I said, "No, they're mine!" Recently we have spotted Kirk Douglas, Glenn Close, Pierce Brosnan and my particular favourite Julia Louis-Dreyfus.

Actor Who Performed the Most Roles in This Show: Me. I play four: Beryl, a waitress, Hermione and Dolly. There used to be five, but one got cut. She was called Mildred and she was a Nosy Parker. I played her in the West End, but when we got here she was gone. Alas, Mildred is no more.

Actors Who Have Done the Most Shows in Their Careers: Joe, Tristan, myself and Annette are the "mature" members of the company. We've probably racked up quite a few miles on the show clock.

Who Has Been in the Most Performances of *Brief Encounter*: Bobby and Margaret, our two puppets. (They're *very* difficult to work with.)

Special Backstage Rituals: We warm up before every single show for about thirty minutes. When we're being good, we do yoga. The director used to run it but we take turns now. We also play games from the Kneehigh school of acting such as "Big Buddy." It's a clapping game in which we all clap in time in a circle. It helps keep us sharp. We also play the Fruit Game. Someone stands in the middle of a ring, everyone else takes the name of a fruit, the one in the middle has to say the name of the fruit three times before the corresponding person interrupts. It involves a lot of shouting. We like to modify this game by choosing expletives instead of fruits on occasion!

Favorite Moment During Each Performance (On Stage or Off): The boat scene, in which half the action takes place on the stage, and half on screen. The whole cast is on stage, all looking at Alec and Laura. It feels like a very communal moment. Off stage, our SM Jonny Krause finds elaborate, funny and at times macabre ways of delivering the prop bunch of

1. Curtain calls on opening night (L-R): Edward Jay, Adam Pleeth, Dorothy Atkinson, Hannah Yelland, Tristan Sturrock, Annette McLaughlin, Joseph Alessi, Gabriel Ebert and Damon Daunno.
2. Dressed up for the premiere (L-R): Dorothy Atkinson, Annette McLaughlin and Hannah Yelland.
3. Tristan Sturrock and Hannah Yelland in costume on opening night.

roses to Gabe.

Favorite In-Theatre Gathering Place: On stage. Studio 54 is the perfect place for our show. It has a big, quirky, cinematic quality, and it has brought that quality out in our production, which has mostly played smaller venues.

Favorite Off-Site Hangout: Adam's apartment, Cosmic Diner—we really need to get out more!

Favorite Snack Food: Pretzel sticks that wardrobe provides, which are brilliant. I've also got an infamous packet of chips in my dressing room, which has been aging nicely for more than a month.

Mascots: The rowing boat, the teapot and tea cosy.

Favorite Therapies: Yoga. And Ricola; we can't have one without shouting "Riiicola," like on the commercials. We also have a group sit-down with each one sitting on another's knee before the show. We also do quite a lot of jamming.

Memorable Ad-Libs: Each night when Tristan has to run across the train platform and explain why the train has been transferred to another track he mumbles a different excuse. There's so much noise that the audience can't hear it. But we can. He says things like, "Because there's a cheese-weighing contest on the platform" or "There's a pack of wolves on the line in Bumford."

Memorable Stage Door Fan Encounter: We had a chap who came four days running and

Brief Encounter
SCRAPBOOK

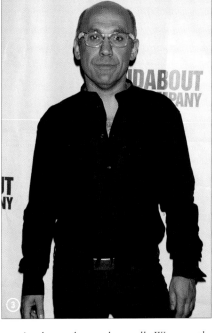

(Photo credit, vertical:)

1. Post-show performance at the premiere (L-R): Adam Pleeth, Gabriel Ebert, Edward Jay, Tristan Sturrock, Joseph Alessi, and Damon Daunno.
2. (L-R): Dorothy Atkinson, Annette McLaughlin and Hannah Yelland do a special opening night song.
3. Actor and spoon-player Joseph Alessi in party togs for the Studio 54 cast party.

got everyone's autograph.

Record Number of Cell Phone Rings, Cell Phone Photos or Texting Incidents During a Performance: We've had pretty few because of our pre-show announcement, which Joe does. He explains that the play is set in 1938, long before there were cell phones. "In keeping with this, please turn off all electronic devices." It always gets a laugh, and people go straight into their pockets.

Memorable Press Encounter: It's a novelty for us to have that "Broadway" sort of attention after the opening night. We're used to a more laid-back British sort of opening. Some of us were taken aback by it, but I really enjoyed it. It's nice for someone to ask questions about your show. I like to think we

acquitted ourselves rather well. We recently were interviewed as a group on Sirius radio's Broadway channel, and recorded our songs. That was a real highlight and a beautiful bonding moment.

What Did You Think of the Internet Buzz on Your Show? I tracked it, and it was great. Having so much media interest was kind of a novelty for us. A lot of Brits are much more staid and less vocal. We loved the enthusiasm that surrounded the show. The video stuff was very well done.

Latest Audience Arrival: Our pre-show when we sing "Oh, You Beautiful Doll" is geared to embrace that. If someone comes in late, the song signifies "Hurry up!"

Fastest Costume Change: We were arguing

about this. We all play lots of characters, so there are some real humdingers. Joe may have the fastest: He's out of Albert and into Fred in 10 seconds. I have to change my shoes about 20 times. A lot of this show is waiting in the dark to change our shoes.

Who Wore the Heaviest/Hottest Costume: We're all wearing period costumes, all wool and serge. Gabe has his Stanley outfit on, then a whole army uniform on top of that. That's pretty hot. Hannah's got quite a few layers on: a silk petticoat, a silk blouse, a wool suit and then a wool coat. And don't forget her wig and tights.

Who Wore the Least: Hannah when she's on the boat in her petticoat.

Catchphrases Only the Company Would Recognize: "OMG SJP!" "Make me an offer." "Plum, plum, plum." "I'm afraid I'll be terrified of the cushion." "Biffins." "Harry one blob."

Memorable Directorial Notes: There's one big one and we all stick by it: "Make each other look good." There's also, "Damon, please stop spitting in the teacups."

Company In-Jokes: Tristan is such a naughty tickler. When he asks for items from the tea bar he usually asks for obscene, rude things. To which Mrs. Bagger always replies, "Would you like milk with that?"

Company Legends: Noël Coward, whose music we use throughout the show. Also the piano on the set, which was given to us in the beginning in exchange for tickets to the show. We brought it with us. The boat has been all over Britain and all over the States. It's originally from Knee-High Barns in Gorran Haven, Cornwall, where this all started. It's really heavy and really cumbersome. We all either love it or hate it, but it's mainly love.

Nicknames: Hannah is "Gray Baby." Adam is called "Madame." Annette is "Nettie Pot."

Sweethearts Within the Company: It's such a romantic play I think we all are secretly in love with each other. We've seen two proper relationships develop over the time we've been doing it: Adam and Avye, and Annette and Chris.

Embarrassing Moments: I was quite embarrassed when I was in the middle of a full-on snog on the floor with Gabe who plays Stanley, the front of my costume came open and revealed my bright white, very big knickers to the whole world. Fortunately the light is quite low at that point.

Ghostly Encounters Backstage: We were hoping to find something from Studio 54's disco days but haven't yet. I will say that when Stanley and Beryl are on the bridge and look upward, we do sometimes see wispy ectoplasmic things that intrigue us. Annette also says she can sometimes see shadows of people backstage.

Coolest Thing About Being in This Show: Each other. The best group of people—trust, respect and humour on and off stage.

Catch Me If You Can

First Preview: March 11, 2011. Opened: April 10, 2011.
Still running as of May 31, 2011.

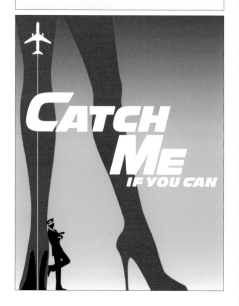

Based on a true story, this musical traces the life of Frank Abagnale, Jr., a young man who turns his father's twisted philosophy into a life of crime, becoming a master con man and forger and successfully posing as everything from an airline pilot to a doctor and a lawyer. He is pursued by dogged FBI agent Carl Hanratty, with whom he establishes a kind of respect and even affection, until Frank makes the fatal mistake of falling in love.

CAST

(in order of appearance)

Frank Abagnale, Jr. .... AARON TVEIT
Agent Branton .... JOE CASSIDY
Agent Dollar .... BRANDON WARDELL
Agent Carl Hanratty ....NORBERT LEO BUTZ
Agent Cod .... TIMOTHY McCUEN PIGGEE
Frank Abagnale, Sr. .... TOM WOPAT
Paula Abagnale .... RACHEL de BENEDET
Cheryl Ann .... RACHELLE RAK
Brenda Strong .... KERRY BUTLER
Roger Strong .... NICK WYMAN
Carol Strong .... LINDA HART
The Frank Abagnale, Jr. Players ...... JOE CASSIDY,
ALEX ELLIS, JENNIFER FRANKEL,
LISA GAJDA, BOB GAYNOR,
KEARRAN GIOVANNI,
GRASAN KINGSBERRY,
MICHAEL X. MARTIN, ALEKS PEVEC,
TIMOTHY McCUEN PIGGEE,
RACHELLE RAK, JOE AARON REID,
ANGIE SCHWORER, SABRINA SLOAN,
SARRAH STRIMEL, CHARLIE SUTTON,
BRANDON WARDELL, KATIE WEBBER,
CANDICE MARIE WOODS

Continued on next page

Continued on next page

NEIL SIMON THEATRE

UNDER THE DIRECTION OF JAMES M. NEDERLANDER AND JAMES L. NEDERLANDER

Margo Lion   Hal Luftig

Stacey Mindich   Yasuhiro Kawana   Scott & Brian Zeilinger   The Rialto Group   The Araca Group
Michael Watt   Barbara & Buddy Freitag   Jay & Cindy Gutterman/Pittsburgh CLO   Elizabeth Williams
Johnny Roscoe Productions/Van Dean   Fakston Productions/Solshay Productions   Patty Baker/Richard Winkler
Nederlander Presentations Inc. and Warren Trepp

IN ASSOCIATION WITH

Remmel T. Dickinson   Paula Herold/Kate Lear   Stephanie P McClelland   Jamie deRoy   Barry Feirstein   Rainerio J. Reyes
Rodney Rigby   Loraine Boyle   Amuse Inc.   Joseph & Matthew Deitch/Cathy Chernoff   Joan Stein/Jon Murray

The 5th Avenue Theatre

PRESENT

Norbert Leo Butz   **Aaron Tveit**

CATCH ME
IF YOU CAN
THE MUSICAL
Based on the DreamWorks Motion Picture

BOOK BY   MUSIC BY   LYRICS BY
Terrence McNally   **Marc Shaiman**   **Scott Wittman**
                                                              & Marc Shaiman

STARRING

Tom Wopat

Rachel de Benedet   Linda Hart   Nick Wyman   Jay Armstrong Johnson
        Joe Cassidy   Timothy McCuen Piggee   Brandon Wardell

Sara Andreas   Alex Ellis   Will Erat   Jennifer Frankel   Lisa Gajda
Bob Gaynor   Kearran Giovanni   Nick Kenkel   Grasan Kingsberry   Michael X. Martin
Aleks Pevec   Kristin Piro   Rachelle Rak   Joe Aaron Reid   Angie Schworer
Sabrina Sloan   Sarrah Strimel   Charlie Sutton   Katie Webber   Candice Marie Woods

AND

Kerry Butler

SCENIC DESIGN   COSTUME DESIGN   LIGHTING DESIGN   SOUND DESIGN
David Rockwell   **William Ivey Long**   **Kenneth Posner**   **Steve Canyon Kennedy**

CASTING   WIG & HAIR DESIGN   ASSOCIATE DIRECTOR   ASSOCIATE CHOREOGRAPHERS
Telsey + Company   **Paul Huntley**   **Matt Lenz**   **Joey Pizzi   Nick Kenkel**

PRODUCTION STAGE MANAGER   MUSIC COORDINATOR   TECHNICAL SUPERVISOR
Rolt Smith   **John Miller**   **Chris Smith/Smitty**

ASSOCIATE PRODUCERS   ADVERTISING   PRESS REPRESENTATIVE   GENERAL MANAGER
Brian Smith   T. Rick Hayashi   **SpotCo**   **The Hartman Group**   **The Charlotte Wilcox Company**

ARRANGEMENTS BY   ORCHESTRATIONS BY
Marc Shaiman   **Marc Shaiman & Larry Blank**

MUSIC DIRECTION BY
John McDaniel

CHOREOGRAPHED BY
Jerry Mitchell

DIRECTED BY
Jack O'Brien

The World Premiere of *Catch Me If You Can* was produced by The 5th Avenue Theatre,
David Armstrong, Executive Producer and Artistic Director; Bernadine Griffin, Managing Director; Bill Berry, Producing Director

4/10/11

Aaron Tveit and company

Catch Me If You Can

MUSICAL NUMBERS

ACT I

OVERTURE

"Live in Living Color" .... Frank, Jr. and Company
"The Pinstripes Are All That They See" .... Frank, Sr., Frank, Jr., Ladies
"Someone Else's Skin" .... Frank, Jr. and Company
"Jet Set" .... Frank, Jr. and Company
"Live in Living Color" (Reprise) .... Frank, Jr.
"Don't Break the Rules" .... Hanratty and Company
"The Pinstripes Are All That They See" (Reprise) .... The Ladies
"Butter Outta Cream" .... Frank, Sr., Frank, Jr.
"The Man Inside the Clues" .... Hanratty
"Christmas Is My Favorite Time of Year" .... Partygoers
"My Favorite Time of Year" .... Hanratty, Frank, Jr., Frank, Sr., Paula

ACT II

ENTR'ACTE

"Doctor's Orders" .... Nurses
"Live in Living Color" (Reprise) .... Frank, Jr.
"Don't Be a Stranger" .... Paula, Frank, Sr.
"Little Boy, Be a Man" .... Frank, Sr., Hanratty
"Seven Wonders" .... Frank, Jr., Brenda
"(Our) Family Tree" .... Carol, Roger, Brenda, Frank, Jr. and Strong Family Singers
"Fly, Fly Away" .... Brenda
"Good-Bye" .... Frank, Jr.
"Strange But True" .... Frank, Jr., Hanratty

(L-R): Brandon Wardell,
Timothy McCuen Piggee,
Norbert Leo Butz, Joe Cassidy

Cast Continued

Standby for Frank Abagnale, Jr.:
JAY ARMSTRONG JOHNSON

UNDERSTUDIES

For Frank Abagnale, Jr.:
BRANDON WARDELL
For Agent Carl Hanratty:
JOE CASSIDY, WILL ERAT
For Frank Abagnale, Sr.:
BOB GAYNOR, MICHAEL X. MARTIN
For Paula Abagnale:
RACHELLE RAK, ANGIE SCHWORER
For Brenda Strong:
ALEX ELLIS, KATIE WEBBER
For Carol Strong:
JENNIFER FRANKEL, LISA GAJDA
For Roger Strong:
WILL ERAT, MICHAEL X. MARTIN

SWINGS

SARA ANDREAS, WILL ERAT, NICK KENKEL,
KRISTIN PIRO

ORCHESTRA

Conductor:
JOHN McDANIEL
Associate Conductor:
LON HOYT
Woodwinds:
TODD GROVES, RICK HECKMAN,
ALDEN BANTA
Trumpets:
DAVE TRIGG, TREVOR NEUMANN
Trombone:
ALAN FERBER
Guitar:
LARRY SALTZMAN
Bass:
VINCENT FAY
Drums:
CLINT DE GANON
Percussion:
JOSEPH PASSARO
Keyboards:
LON HOYT, JASON SHERBUNDY
Keyboard/Guitar:
BRIAN KOONIN
Concert Master:
RICK DOLAN
Violin:
BELINDA WHITNEY
Cello:
CLAY RUEDE

Music Coordinator:
JOHN MILLER
Keyboard Programmer:
SYNTHLINK LLC, JIM HARP

Photo by Joan Marcus

Catch Me If You Can

Norbert Leo Butz
Agent Carl Hanratty

Aaron Tveit
Frank Abagnale, Jr.

Tom Wopat
Frank Abagnale, Sr.

Kerry Butler
Brenda Strong

Rachel de Benedet
Paula Abagnale

Linda Hart
Carol Strong

Nick Wyman
Roger Strong

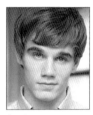
Jay Armstrong
Johnson
*Standby for Frank
Abagnale, Jr.*

Joe Cassidy
Agent Branton

Timothy McCuen
Piggee
Agent Cod

Brandon Wardell
Agent Dollar

Sara Andreas
Swing

Alex Ellis
Ensemble

Will Erat
Swing

Jennifer Frankel
Ensemble

Lisa Gajda
Ensemble

Bob Gaynor
Ensemble

Kearran Giovanni
Ensemble

Nick Kenkel
*Associate
Choreographer,
Swing*

Grasan Kingsberry
Ensemble

Michael X. Martin
Ensemble

Aleks Pevec
Ensemble

Kristin Piro
Swing

Rachelle Rak
*Cheryl Ann,
Ensemble*

Joe Aaron Reid
Ensemble

Angie Schworer
Ensemble

Sabrina Sloan
Ensemble

Sarrah Strimel
Ensemble

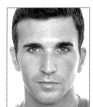
Charlie Sutton
Ensemble

Katie Webber
Ensemble

Candice Marie
Woods
Ensemble

Terrence McNally
Book

Marc Shaiman
*Music/Lyrics/
Arrangements/
Orchestrations*

Scott Wittman
Lyrics

Jack O'Brien
Director

Catch Me If You Can

Jerry Mitchell
Choreographer

David Rockwell
Scenic Design

William Ivey Long
Costume Design

Kenneth Posner
Lighting Design

Steve Canyon
Kennedy
Sound Design

Paul Huntley
Wig & Hair Design

John McDaniel
Music Director

Larry Blank
Co-Orchestrator

John Miller
Music Coordinator

Chris Smith/
Smitty
Technical Supervisor

Bernard Telsey,
Telsey + Company
Casting

The Charlotte Wilcox
Company
General Manager

Margo Lion
Producer

Hal Luftig
Producer

Yasuhiro Kawana
Producer

Scott Zeilinger
Producer

Brian Zeilinger
Producer

Lauren Stevens,
The Rialto Group
Producer

Wendy Federman,
The Rialto Group
Producer

Carl Moellenberg,
The Rialto Group
Producer

Barbara Freitag
Producer

Michael Rego, Hank Unger and
Matthew Rego,
The Araca Group
Producer

Buddy Freitag
Producer

Jay & Cindy Gutterman
Producers

Van Kaplan,
Pittsburgh CLO
Producer

Elizabeth Williams
Producer

Van Dean
Producer

Lorenzo Thione,
Sing Out, Louise!
Productions
Producer

Jay Kuo,
Sing Out, Louise!
Productions
Producer

Adam Blanshay,
Solshay Productions
Producer

Patty Baker
Producer

James M.
Nederlander,
Nederlander
Presentations, Inc.
Producer

James L.
Nederlander,
Nederlander
Presentations, Inc.
Producer

Catch Me If You Can

SCRAPBOOK

1. The cast takes bows on opening night.
2. Frank Abagnale Jr., on whom the show is based, addresses the crowd while Aaron Tveit (C), Norbert Leo Butz and the cast listen.
3. Butz and Tveit take a curtain call.
4. Rachel de Benedet and Tom Wopat.
5. (L-R): Lyricist Scott Wittman, composer Marc Shaiman, producer Hal Luftig, librettist Terrence McNally, choreographer Jerry Mitchell, producer Margo Lion and director Jack O'Brien.
6. Kerry Butler at Cipriani Restaurant for the cast party.
7. Butz and de Benedet.

Remmel T. Dickinson
Producer

Paula Herold
Producer

Kate Lear
Producer

Stephanie P. McClelland
Producer

Jamie deRoy
Producer

Rainerio J. Reyes
Producer

Loraine Alterman Boyle
Producer

Joseph Deitch
Producer

Matthew Deitch
Producer

T. Rick Hayashi
Associate Producer

David Armstrong,
Executive Producer
and Artistic Director,
5th Avenue Theatre
Originating Theatre

Bernadine Griffin,
Managing Director,
5th Avenue Theatre
Originating Theatre

Bill Berry,
Producing Director,
5th Avenue Theatre
Originating Theatre

Catch Me If You Can

(L-R): Jose Lopez (Porter),
Chris Langdon (TicketTaker)

SOUND ENGINEER/BOARD OP
Daniel Tramontozzi

BOX OFFICE
Marc Needleman, unidentified

HAIR, PROPS, WARDROBE
Front Row (L-R): Mark Trezza (Wardrobe), Douglas Petitjean (Wardrobe), Samantha Lawrence
(Wardrobe), Edward J. Wilson (Hair Dept), Steven Kirkham (Hair)

Back Row (L-R): John Rinaldi (Wardrobe), Julie Tobia (Wardrobe), Dede LaBarre (Wardrobe),
Scotty Cain (Wardrobe), Anna Hoffman (Hair Dept), Lolly Totero (Wardrobe), Pete Drummond (Props)

STAGE MANAGEMENT
Lisa Ann Chernoff, Carly J. Price,
Andrea O. Saraffian, Rolt Smith

Not Pictured: Holly Coombs

FRONT OF HOUSE STAFF
Front Row (L-R): Sierra Waxman, Marilyn Christie, Jean Manso, Grace Darbasie, Sally Dillon, Evie Gonzalez

Middle Row (L-R): Lauren Arellano, Joanne DeCicco, Robyn Corrigan, Evelyn Olivero, Kim Raccioppi, Rebecca Henning, Dorothy Marquette, Michelle Smith

Back Row (L-R): Tara Delasnueces, Ryan Conn (Bar), Steven Ouellette (House Manager), Angel Diaz (Chief Usher), Eddie Cuevas, Omar Aguilar (Porter),
Peter Hodgson and Jared St. Gelais (Merchandise), Amy Carcaterra

Chicago

MUSICAL NUMBERS

ACT I

"All That Jazz"	Velma and Company
"Funny Honey"	Roxie
"Cell Block Tango"	Velma and the Girls
"When You're Good to Mama"	Matron
"Tap Dance"	Roxie, Amos and Boys
"All I Care About"	Billy and Girls
"A Little Bit of Good"	Mary Sunshine
"We Both Reached for the Gun"	Billy, Roxie, Mary Sunshine and Company
"Roxie"	Roxie and Boys
"I Can't Do It Alone"	Velma
"My Own Best Friend"	Roxie and Velma

ACT II

Entr'acte	The Band
"I Know a Girl"	Velma
"Me and My Baby"	Roxie and Boys
"Mister Cellophane"	Amos
"When Velma Takes the Stand"	Velma and Boys
"Razzle Dazzle"	Billy and Company
"Class"	Velma and Matron
"Nowadays"	Roxie and Velma
"Hot Honey Rag"	Roxie and Velma
Finale	Company

ORCHESTRA

Orchestra Conducted by
LESLIE STIFELMAN
Associate Conductor:
SCOTT CADY
Assistant Conductor:
JOHN JOHNSON
Woodwinds:
SEYMOUR RED PRESS, JACK STUCKEY,
RICHARD CENTALONZA
Trumpets:
GLENN DREWES, DARRYL SHAW
Trombones:
DAVE BARGERON, BRUCE BONVISSUTO
Piano:
SCOTT CADY
Piano, Accordion:
JOHN JOHNSON
Banjo:
JAY BERLINER
Bass, Tuba:
DAN PECK
Violin:
MARSHALL COID
Drums, Percussion:
RONALD ZITO

Charlotte d'Amboise
as Roxie Hart

ROXIE ROCKS CHICAGO!

Photo by Jeremy Daniel

Cast Continued

THE SCENE
Chicago, Illinois. The late 1920s.

UNDERSTUDIES

For Roxie Hart:
MELISSA RAE MAHON, JILL NICKLAUS
For Velma Kelly:
DONNA MARIE ASBURY,
NICOLE BRIDGEWATER, SOLANGE SANDY
For Billy Flynn:
GREG REUTER, JASON PATRICK SANDS
For Amos Hart:
JAMES T. LANE, ADAM ZOTOVICH
For Matron "Mama" Morton:
DONNA MARIE ASBURY,
NICOLE BRIDGEWATER
For Mary Sunshine:
J. LOEFFELHOLZ
For Fred Casely:
DAVID KENT, JASON PATRICK SANDS,
BRIAN SPITULNIK
For "Me and My Baby":
DAVID KENT, GREG REUTER,
BRIAN SPITULNIK

For all other roles:
GABRIELA GARCIA, DAVID KENT,
SHARON MOORE, BRIAN SPITULNIK

Dance Captain:
DAVID KENT

Assistant Dance Captain:
MELISSA RAE MAHON

"Tap Dance" specialty performed by
GREG REUTER, JAMES T. LANE and
JASON PATRICK SANDS

"Me and My Baby" specialty performed by
MICHAEL CUSUMANO and JAMES T. LANE

"Nowadays" whistle performed by
JASON PATRICK SANDS

Original Choreography for "Hot Honey Rag" by
BOB FOSSE

Chicago

Charlotte d'Amboise
Roxie Hart

Amra-Faye Wright
Velma Kelly

Tom Hewitt
Billy Flynn

Raymond Bokhour
Amos Hart

Roz Ryan
Matron "Mama" Morton

R. Lowe
Mary Sunshine

Donna Marie Asbury
June

Nili Bassman
Hunyak

Nicole Bridgewater
Liz

Michael Cusumano
Martin Harrison

Gabriela Garcia
Swing

James Harkness
Fred Casely

David Kent
Swing/ Dance Captain

James T. Lane
Aaron

Dan LoBuono
Harry/The Jury

J. Loeffelholz
Standby Mary Sunshine

Melissa Rae Mahon
Go-To-Hell Kitty/ Assistant Dance Captain

Sharon Moore
Swing

Jill Nicklaus
Mona

Greg Reuter
Bailiff/Court Clerk

Jason Patrick Sands
Doctor/The Judge

Solange Sandy
Annie

Brian Spitulnik
Swing

Adam Zotovich
Sergeant Fogarty

John Kander & Fred Ebb
Music; Book/Lyrics

Bob Fosse
Book

Walter Bobbie
Director

Ann Reinking
Choreographer

John Lee Beatty
Set Design

William Ivey Long
Costume Designer

Ken Billington
Lighting Designer

Scott Lehrer
Sound Design

David Thompson
Script Adaptation

Rob Fisher
Supervising Music Director

Chicago

Leslie Stifelman
Musical Director

Seymour Red Press
Music Coordinator

Duncan Stewart
Casting Director

Arthur Siccardi,
Theatrical Services
Inc.
Technical Supervisor

Barry and Fran Weissler
Producers

Morton Swinsky/
Kardana Productions
Producer

John Gore,
CEO,
Broadway Across
America
Producer

Thomas B. McGrath,
Chairman,
Broadway Across
America
Producer

ALUMNI 2010-2011

Eddie Bennett
Swing

Dylis Croman
Swing

Colman Domingo
Billy Flynn

Shawn Emamjomeh
Harry, The Jury

Tom Riis Farrell
Amos Hart

Ruthie Henshall
Roxie Hart

Terra C. MacLeod
Velma Kelly

D. Micciche
Mary Sunshine

James Patric Moran
Fred Casely

John O'Hurley
Billy Flynn

Matthew Settle
Billy Flynn

D. Vogel
u/s Mary Sunshine

Terri White
*Matron "Mama"
Morton*

Carol Woods
*Matron "Mama"
Morton*

TRANSFER STUDENTS 2010-2011

Brent Barrett
Billy Flynn

Eddie Bennett
*Aaron, "Me and My
Baby" Specialty,
Sergeant Fogarty,
Swing, "Tap Dance"
Specialty*

Christie Brinkley
Roxie Hart

Robert Creighton
Amos Hart

Dylis Croman
Mona

Colman Domingo
Billy Flynn

Jennifer Dunne
*Hunyak, Mona,
Swing*

Shawn Emamjomeh
Harry, The Jury

LaVon Fisher-Wilson
*Matron "Mama"
Morton*

Bianca Marroquin
Roxie Hart

Chicago

Jeff McCarthy
Billy Flynn

D. Micciche
Mary Sunshine

Peter Nelson
Harry,
Martin Harrison

Brian O'Brien
Bailiff, Court Clerk,
"Tap Dance"
Specialty

Carol Woods
Matron "Mama"
Morton

Ryan Worsing
Aaron, "Me and My
Baby" Specialty,
"Tap Dance"
Specialty

Leigh Zimmerman
Velma Kelly

FRONT OF HOUSE STAFF
Front Row (L-R): Anthony Grandison (Bartender), Dorothea Bentley (Chief Usher), Danielle Banyai (Usher), Elizabeth Ulmer (Bartender)

Second Row (L-R): Manuel Levine (House Manager), Timothy Newsome (Usher), Chris Holmes (Bar Manager)

Third Row (L-R): Carol Bokun (Usher), Julie Pazmino (Usher), Tasha Allen (Usher), Tyrone Hendrix (Ticket Taker), Marilyn Wasbotten (Usher)

Fourth Row (L-R): David Loomis (Merchandise), Nicholas Fusco (Usher), Belen Bekker (Usher), Susan Snow (Usher)

Back Row (L-R): Lane Beauchamp (Merchandise), Dennis Cintron (Usher), Rita Sussman (Infrared Rep.), Bobbi Parker (Usher)

Photos by Jeremy Shaffer

WARDROBE AND HAIR
Front Row (L-R): Kathy Dacey (Dresser), Cleopatra Matheos (Dresser)

Back Row (L-R): Kevin Woodworth (Wardrobe Supervisor), Jenna Brauer (Hair Supervisor), Rick Meadows (Dresser)

Chicago

COMPANY MANAGER
Alexandra Gushin Agosta

STAGE MANAGEMENT
(L-R): Terry Witter (Stage Manager), David Hyslop (Production Stage Manager), Mindy Farbrother (Stage Manager)

STAFF FOR *CHICAGO*

GENERAL MANAGEMENT
B.J. Holt, General Manager
Nina Skriloff, International Manager

PRESS REPRESENTATIVE
THE PUBLICITY OFFICE
Jeremy Shaffer Marc Thibodeau Michael Borowski

COMPANY MANAGER
Alexandra Gushin Agosta

Production Stage Manager	**Gregg Kirsopp**
Stage Managers	Terrence J. Witter,
	Mindy Farbrother
Associate General Manager	Hilary Hamilton
General Management	
Associate	Stephen Spadaro
Assistant Director	Jonathan Bernstein
Associate Lighting Designer	John McKernon
Assistant Choreographer	Debra McWaters
Assistant Set Designers	Eric Renschler,
	Shelley Barclay
Wardrobe Supervisor	Kevin Woodworth
Hair Supervisor	Jenna Brauer
Costume Assistant	Donald Sanders
Personal Asst to Mr. Billington	Jon Kusner
Assistant to Mr. Lehrer	Thom Mohrman
Production Carpenter	Joseph Mooneyham
Production Electrician	James Fedigan
Head Electrician	Luciana Fusco
Front Lite Operator	Michael Guggino
Production Sound Engineer	John Montgomery
Production Props	Fred Phelan
Dressers	Jo-Ann Bethell,
	Kathy Dacey, Cleopatra Matheos,
	Rick Meadows, Eric Concklin
Banking	Chase Manhattan, Stephanie Dalton

Music Prep	Chelsea Music Services, Inc.
	Donald Oliver & Evan Morris
Payroll	Castellana Services, Inc.
Accountants	Rosenberg, Neuwirth & Kuchner
	Mark D'Ambrosi, Marina Flom
Insurance	Industrial Risk Specialists
Counsel	Seth Gelblum/Loeb & Loeb
Art Design	Spot Design
Advertising	SpotCo: Drew Hodges,
	Jim Edwards, Sara Fitzpatrick,
	Beth Watson, Tim Falotico
Press Assistant	Matthew Fasano
Education	Students Live/Amy Weinstein
Merchandising	Dewynters Advertising Inc.
Displays	King Display

NATIONAL ARTISTS MANAGEMENT CO.

Vice President of Marketing	Marci Kaufman
Chief Financial Officer	Bob Williams
Manager of Accounting/Admin.	Marian Albarracin
Assistant to Mrs. Weissler	Brett England
Assistants to Mr. Weissler	Eddie Pisapia,
	Roger Kuch
Director of Marketing	Ken Sperr
Receptionist	Michelle Coleman

SPECIAL THANKS
Additional legal services provided by Jay Goldberg, Esq. and Michael Berger, Esq. Dry cleaning by Ernest Winzer Cleaners. Hosiery and undergarments provided by Bra*Tenders. Tuxedos by Brioni.

CREDITS
Lighting equipment by PRG Lighting. Scenery built and painted by Hudson Scenic Studios. Specialty Rigging by United Staging & Rigging. Sound equipment by PRG Audio. Shoulder holster courtesy of DeSantis Holster and Leather Goods Co. Period cameras and flash units by George Fenmore, Inc. Colibri lighters used. Bible courtesy of Chiarelli's Religious Goods, Inc. Black pencils by Dixon-Ticonderoga. Gavel courtesy of The Gavel Co. Zippo lighters used. Garcia y Vega cigars used. Hosiery by Donna Karan. Shoes by T.O. Dey. Orthopaedic Consultant, David S. Weiss, M.D.

THE SHUBERT ORGANIZATION, INC.
Board of Directors

Philip J. Smith	**Robert E. Wankel**
Chairman	President
Wyche Fowler, Jr.	**John W. Kluge**
Lee J. Seidler	**Michael I. Sovern**

Stuart Subotnick

Elliot Greene	**David Andrews**
Chief Financial	Senior Vice President
Officer	Shubert Ticketing
Juan Calvo	**John Darby**
Vice President –	Vice President –
Finance	Facilities
Peter Entin	**Charles Flateman**
Vice President –	Vice President –
Theatre Operations	Marketing
Anthony LaMattina	**Brian Mahoney**
Vice President –	Vice President –
Audit & Production Finance	Ticket Sales

D.S. Moynihan
Vice President – Creative Projects

House Manager	Manuel Levine

Chicago
SCRAPBOOK

Correspondent: Gabriela Garcia, Swing

Memorable Fan Letter: A letter came to the theater addressed to Bob Fosse, I guess they just mailed it to every name on the Playbill without paying attention to who they were or if they were a choreographer that passed away in 1987.

Anniversary Gifts: Every year Annie Reinking sends each and every member of the company a rose on Christmas. Rob Fisher, our musical supervisor, sends ginger snaps every year. Our producers send us pies for Thanksgiving and we always wonder what our Christmas gift will be. Last year we got a *Chicago* gym bag, but my favorite Christmas gift has been the *Chicago* Snuggie. That was a winner.

Most Exciting Celebrity Visitor and What They Did/Said: I don't know what they said or if they said anything, but by far the most exciting celebrities to come backstage have been Beyoncé and Jay-Z when they came to see Michelle Williams as Roxie. I mean, c'mon!

Actors Who Performed the Most Roles in This Show: The swings definitely play the most roles, sometimes they have to play two roles when we need to have a cut show. For the lead roles, Donna Marie Asbury has been the only understudy to have played all three leading ladies, Velma, Roxie and Mama Morton. Donna has been with us the longest…almost 12 years! (She says she was 15 when she joined the cast).

Favorite Moment During Each Performance (On Stage or Off): Bobby Creighton, who played Amos, always did a little backstage dance during "Me and My Baby," which kept the girls sitting on stage left very entertained.

Mascot: We have a few schnauzers that frequent the theatre, Ruby, Berger, Stevie and Elie Mae, Chloe and a couple of new additions, Sammy an adorable French bulldog and Frankie the cutest little chihuahua.

Favorite Therapy: Emergen-C seems to be the winner around the theatre; there is always a box with assorted flavors in the stage management office.

Catchphrases Only the Company Would Recognize: "You got your trainables and your untrainables." "Things ain't what they used to be."

Memorable Directorial Note: "You want it, come and get it." Fourteen years later we still get that note.

Coolest Thing About Being in This Show: You get to make up your own improvs in certain moments AND the audience knows who you are because you wear only one costume.

Special Place in the Theatre: We are lucky to have Jeremy Shaffer as our publicist and amazing photographer. He has taken wonderful photos of the show and its company members, so now we have the *Chicago* gallery on the wall leading up to the dressing rooms where we display Jeremy's current photographs of the show. Gotta say it dresses up the wall nicely.

1. (L-R): Michael Cusumano, Brian Spitulnik, Christie Brinkley, Brian O'Brien and Adam Zotovich celebrate backstage March 25, 2011 as *Chicago* becomes the fifth longest-running show in Broadway history.
2. Producer Barry Weissler (center) and *Chicago* dancers welcome devotees of the show on Fan Day, January 30, 2011.
3. Alumnae Karen Ziemba and Amra-Faye Wright flank director Walter Bobbie on Fan Day.
4. Charlotte d'Amboise poses backstage Nov. 14, 2010 as the production celebrates its fourteenth anniversary on Broadway.

Favorite Snack Foods: There is a tin can that lives in the wardrobe room that is always filled with chocolatey goodness. Everyone looks forward to that. We also have a candy jar underneath the stage which Fred, our prop master, is in charge of.

Favorite In-Theatre Gathering Place: The basement. That's where you find the trashy magazines to keep you entertained with pop culture, the newspaper, the chocolates and other snacks. Often the TV will be on, tuned to "Dancing With the Stars."

Colin Quinn Long Story Short

First Preview: October 22, 2010. Opened: November 9, 2010.
Closed March 5, 2011 after 21 Previews and 135 Performances.

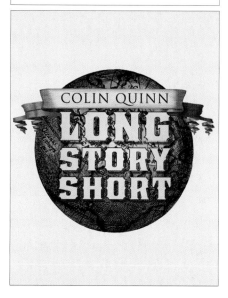

Standup comedian Colin Quinn recounts the
history of the world from his unique perspective.

Colin Quinn

Photo by Carol Rosegg

Colin Quinn
Author/Performer

Jerry Seinfeld
Director

David Gallo
*Scenic and
Projection Design*

Howell Binkley
Lighting Design

Hal Brooks
Creative Consultant

Jamie Cesa/
Cesa Entertainment
General Manager

Eva Price
Producer

Bruston Kade
Manuel
Producer

Will Dombrowski
Producer

THE HELEN HAYES THEATRE

MARTIN MARKINSON   DONALD TICK

EVA PRICE   RICHARD MARTINI

BRUSTON KADE MANUEL & WILL DOMBROWSKI   RICHARD WINKLER
GEORGE SHAPIRO   MATTHEW SALLOWAY   JACK THOMAS
BISNO/FRANKEL/FIREMAN   DAN FRISHWASSER
AVRAM FREEDBERG & MARY BETH DALE   ALLEN SPIVAK

present

WRITTEN AND PERFORMED BY
COLIN QUINN

| SCENIC AND PROJECTION DESIGN | LIGHTING DESIGN | SOUND DESIGN |
| DAVID GALLO | HOWELL BINKLEY | CHRISTOPHER "KIT" BOND |

| ORIGINAL COMPOSITIONS | PRODUCTION STAGE MANAGER | CREATIVE CONSULTANT |
| SCOTT ELMEGREEN | DANIEL J. KELLS | HAL BROOKS |

| PRESS REPRESENTATIVE | ADVERTISING | WEBSITE & SOCIAL MEDIA | MARKETING |
| RUBENSTEIN COMMUNICATIONS, INC. | HOFSTETTER+PARTNERS/ AGENCY 212 | BAY BRIDGE PRODUCTIONS | HHC MARKETING |

GENERAL MANAGER
CESA ENTERTAINMENT
KL MANAGEMENT • MAXIMUM ENTERTAINMENT

DIRECTED BY
JERRY SEINFELD

The producers wish to express their appreciation to Theatre Development Fund for its support of this production.

11/9/10

Colin Quinn Long Story Short
SCRAPBOOK

Correspondent: Colin Quinn

Opening Night Gifts: My managers gave me a mini trampoline, which I wanted. They're good for your circulation. I also got a $400 bottle of champagne, which is too bad since I haven't drunk in twenty-eight years.

Most Exciting Celebrity Visitors: Everybody came by at one time or another. There was Ben Stiller and Jimmy Fallon, who pretended to be drunk and started acting crazy in my dressing room. Whenever I see people from "Saturday Night Live" we just go into characters. One of my teachers from fifth grade showed up, and, of course, my boy Jerry [Seinfeld] showed.

Special Backstage Rituals: Usually I start the day by having an argument with Claire, my assistant. We just start yelling at each other. Then I go on the trampoline for two minutes.

Favorite Snack Food: Ricola, I use like eight Ricolas a night. They're so cool.

Favorite Therapy: I do Alexander technique once a week.

Most Memorable Ad-Lib: When people come in late, I ad-lib the whole show so far.

(L-R): Colin Quinn with director Jerry Seinfeld at a press reception.

Favorite Moment During Each Performance: It changes from week to week, but most of the time when I'm doing the Shakespeare dialog well, it's usually a good sign that you're hearing quality.

Record Number of Cell Phone Rings During a Performance: It's amazing how few there are.

Catchphrase Only the Company Would Recognize: "What new France?"

Favorite In-Theatre Gathering Place: The little greenroom. Guests gather there on Saturdays before the 2, 5 and 8 p.m. shows. The stagehands have a little section by the good food and stuff. I've seen them make submarine sandwiches that look like goddamn *Das Boot*.

Favorite Off-Site Hangouts: John's, Sardi's, the greenroom of *American Idiot*— pretty much anywhere on 44th Street.

Superstitions That Turned Out To Be True: I always do things in a certain order. For instance, I always take a sip of water and spit it out before I go on. And I always get to the theatre really early. I have to rely on the train, so maybe that's not actually a superstition.

Coolest Thing About Being in This Show: Every time I walk down my block, I get a small thrill when I look across the street at the Broadhurst Theatre and see that Al Pacino is doing *Merchant of Venice* there. Damn, that's big time. I think we can safely surmise that he doesn't get the same thrill when he looks across at my theatre.

STAFF FOR *COLIN QUINN LONG STORY SHORT*

GENERAL MANAGEMENT
CESA Entertainment
Jamie Cesa   Diane Alianiello

KL Management
Richard Martini   Elinor Prince
Sharon T. Pratt   Christy Ellingsworth

Maximum Entertainment
Avram Freedberg   Mary Beth Dale   Eva Price
Holly Sutton   Taylor James

GENERAL PRESS REPRESENTATIVE
RUBENSTEIN COMMUNICATIONS, INC.
Tom Keaney   Amy Jacobs

COMPANY MANAGER ....**Holly Sutton**
Production Stage Manager ....Daniel J. Kells
Associate Scenic Design ....Steven C. Kemp
Animator/
   Associate Projection Design ....Steve Channon
Assistant Projection Design ....Caite Hevner
Projection Assistant ....Scott Channon
Projection Design Intern ....Crystal Lee
Scenic Design Intern ....Ashley Cavadas

Design Studio Manager ....Sarah Zeitler
Associate Lighting Designer ....Ryan O'Gara
Lighting Board Programmer ....Sean Beach
Assistant Lighting Designer ....Amanda Zieve
Lighting Design Intern ....Michael Rummage
Spot Operator ....Brendan Keane
Master Electrician ....Joe Beck
Sound Technician ....Bob Etter
Legal Counsel ....Beigelman, Feiner & Feldman, PC/
                                      Ben Feldman, Esq.,
                                   Jordan Beckerman, Esq.
Accounting .. ..Rosenberg, Neuwirth & Kuchner
Advertising ....Hofstetter+Partners/
                                            Agency 212/
                            Bill Hofstetter, Jennifer Katz
Creative Directors ....Jules Evenson, Erin McParland
Press Assistants ....Elyse Weissman, Rachel Silverman
Marketing ....HHC Marketing/
                          Hugh Hysell, Michael Redman,
                          Todd Briscoe, Kiara Kincheloe,
                                     Christopher Rosenow
Website & Social Media ....Bay Bridge Productions/
                          Laura Wagner, Adam Magazine
Dramaturg ....Dani Vetere
Assistant to Colin Quinn ....Claire Gilbertsen
Assistant to Jerry Seinfeld ....Melissa Gastgaber
Banking ....JPMorgan Chase

Insurance ....DeWitt Stern
Payroll Services ....Castellana Services, Inc.
Bookkeeping.................................Elinor Prince
Souvenir Merchandise ....LTS/Max Merchandising
Stylist ....Brendan Cannon
Videography ....Frank Basile/
                               Fresh Produce Productions
Production Photographer ....Carol Rosegg
Opening Night Coordination ....Serino Coyne, LLC/
                          Suzanne Tobak, Gail Perlman

CREDITS

Rehearsed at Chelsea Studios, NYC. Lighting equipment provided by PRG Lighting, North Bergen, NJ. Sound equipment provided by Masque Sound. Projection equipment provided by Scharff Weisberg. Scenic shop: Showman Fabricators. Energy efficient washer/dryer courtesy of LG Electronics.

SPECIAL THANKS

Dave Quinn, Diane Sweeney, Lia Sweet, Carolyn Liebling, Rosemarie Ido, Nick Sparks, Erin Winebark, Brian Stern, Aaron Rhyne, Herrick Goldman, Perchik Kreiman-Miller, Ben Folstein, Chris Smith

THE HELEN HAYES THEATRE STAFF

Owned and Operated by Little Theatre Group LLC
Martin Markinson and Donald Tick
General Manager and Counsel..........Susan S. Myerberg
House Manager ....Alan R. Markinson
Engineer ....Hector Angulo
Treasurer....................................David Heveran
Assoc. Gen. Manager ....Sharon Fallon
Assistant Treasurer ....Chuck Stuis
Head Ushers ....Linda Maley, Berd Vaval,
                                          John Biancamano
Stage Door ....Robert Seymour, Jonathan Angulo,
                                             Luis Muniz
Accountant ....Chen-Win Hsu, CPA, PC
Intern ....Jacqueline Munoz

Continued from the previous page

Jack Thomas
Producer

Debbie Bisno
Producer

Jerry Frankel
Producer

Allen Spivak
Producer

Come Fly Away

John Selya
Sid

Hilary Gardner
Featured Vocalist

Rosena M. Hill
Featured Vocalist Alternate

Alexander Brady
Vico, Dance Captain

Todd Burnsed
Ensemble

Carolyn Doherty
Ensemble

Heather Hamilton
Ensemble

Meredith Miles
Ensemble

Eric Michael Otto
Ensemble

Justin Peck
Ensemble

Kristine Bendul
Alternate Slim

Colin Bradbury
Swing, Assistant Dance Captain

Jeremy Cox
Alternate Marty

Amanda Edge
Swing

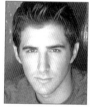
Cody Green
Alternate Sid

Laurie Kanyok
Alternate Babe

Marielys Molina
Alternate Kate

Mark Myars
Swing

Joel Prouty
Alternate Hank

Ron Todorowski
Alternate Chanos

Ashley Tuttle
Alternate Betsy

Twyla Tharp
Conception, Direction, Choreography

Frank Sinatra
Vocals

James Youmans
Scenic Design

Donald Holder
Lighting Design

Peter McBoyle
Sound Design

Don Sebesky
Additional Orchestrations and Arrangements

Dave Pierce
Additional Orchestrations and Arrangements

Patrick Vaccariello
Music Supervisor/ Music Coordinator

Russ Kassoff
Conductor/Pianist

Randall A. Buck
Production Executive

David Benken
Technical Supervisor

Kim Craven
Resident Director

The Charlotte Wilcox Company
General Manager

Susan V. Booth
Artistic Director, Alliance Theatre

Come Fly Away

James L. Nederlander
Producer

Terry Allen Kramer
Producer

Patrick Catullo
Producer

Jon B. Platt
Producer

Jerry Frankel
Producer

Roy Furman
Producer

Allan S. Gordon
Producer

Élan V. McAllister
Producer

Arny Granat,
Jam Theatricals
Producer

Steve Traxler,
Jam Theatricals
Producer

Stewart F. Lane and Bonnie Comley
Producer

Margo Lion
Producer

Daryl Roth
Producer

Hal Luftig
Producer

Yasuhiro Kawana
Producer

Van Kaplan,
Pittsburgh CLO
Producer

Jay and Cindy Gutterman,
GSFD
Producer

Mort Swinsky,
GSFD
Producer

Joseph Deitch,
GFSD
Producer

Matthew Deitch,
GFSD
Producer

Bob Weinstein,
The Weinstein
Company
Producer

Harvey Weinstein,
The Weinstein
Company
Producer

Barry and Fran Weissler
Producer

STAFF FOR *COME FLY AWAY*

GENERAL MANAGEMENT
CHARLOTTE WILCOX COMPANY
Charlotte W. Wilcox
Seth Marquette
Matthew W. Krawiec   Dina S. Friedler
Steve Supeck   Margaret Wilcox

COMPANY MANAGER
Heidi Neven

ASSISTANT COMPANY MANAGER
Michael Bolgar

GENERAL PRESS REPRESENTATIVE
THE HARTMAN GROUP
Michael Hartman
Tom D'Ambrosio   Michelle Bergmann

CASTING
STUART HOWARD ASSOCIATES, LTD.
Stuart Howard   Amy Schecter   Paul Hardt

Production Stage Manager ....Rick Steiger
Stage Manager ....Kevin Bertolacci
Assistant to Mr. Nederlander ....Ken Happel
Associate Set Designer ....Jerome Martin
Associate Costume Designer ....Amy Clark
Assistants to the Costume Designer ....Mike Floyd,
Caitlin Hunt
Associate Lighting Designers ....Jeanne Koenig,
Caroline Chao
Moving Light Programmer ....Joseph Allegro
Associate Sound Designer ....David Patridge
Assistant Sound Designer ....Daniel Fiandaca

Come Fly Away

Assistant Production Manager ....Rose Palombo
Assistant to the Production Manager ....Canara Price
Head Carpenter ....Rick Styles
Automation Carpenter ....Grigor Grigorov
Production Electrician ....James Maloney
Head Electrician ....Brad Robertson
Followspot Operator ....Justin McClintock
Head Sound ....Dillon Cody
Assistant Sound ....Jason Strangfeld
Production Props ....Jerry L. Marshall
Wardrobe Supervisor ....Edmund Harrison
Assistant Wardrobe Supervisor ....Jennifer Griggs
Dressers ....Tim Greer, Kay Gowenlock,
                    Maggie Horkey, Jeannie Naughton
Stitcher...Sue Hamilton
Production Assistants ....Morgan Hartley,
                              Jennifer O'Byrne
Rehearsal Programmer ....Joe DeVico
Rehearsal Pianist ....Jim Laev
Legal Counsel ....Levine, Plotkin & Menin LLP/
                    Loren Plotkin, Cris Criswell,
                    Susan Mindell, Conrad Rippy
Accountant ....Rosenberg, Neuwirth &
                    Kushner, CPA's/
                    Mark A. D'Ambrosi, Jana Jevnikar
Advertising ....SpotCo/Drew Hodges,
                    Jim Edwards, Tom McCann,
                    Josh Fraenkel, Tom Greenwald
Website Design ....SpotCo/
                    Sarah Fitzpatrick, Matt Wilstein,
                    Marc Mettler
Dance Press Representative Staff ....Dulce Shultz
Music Clearance ....Jill Meyers Music Consultants
Payroll Services ....Castellana Services, Inc.
Production Photographer ....Joan Marcus
Banking ....City National Bank/Michele Gibbons
Insurance Consultant ....Stockbridge Risk Management
Insurance ....Reiff & Associates, LLC./
                    Dennis Reiff, Regina Newsome
Physical Therapy ....PhysioArts/Jennifer Green
Massage Therapist ....Russell Beasley
Orthopedist ....Phillip Bauman, MD
Consulting Physician ....Dr. Karen Thorton
Group Sales ....Nederlander Group Sales
Merchandise ....Creative Goods/
                    Pete Milano, Mike D'Arcy
Information Management
    Services ....Marion Finkler Taylor
Travel Services ....Tzell Travel/Andi Henig
Theatre Displays ....King Displays, Inc.

CREDITS

Scenery by Hudson Scenic, I. Weiss NY and Showman Fabrication. Automation by Hudson Scenic. Lighting equipment from Production Resource Group. Sound equipment from Production Resource Group. Costumes by Eric Winterling, Saint Laurie Merchant Tailors NYC. Undergarments by Bra*Tenders. Custom footwear by LaDuca, T.O. Dey, JC Theatrical, Zoraide. Custom headwear by Lynne Mackey Studio, Worth and Worth. Custom jewelry by Abby Kong. Special thanks to Alliance Costume Shop, Mark Happel, John Kristiansen. Music consultation by Frank Sinatra Enterprises. Piano by Steinway & Sons.

MUSIC CREDITS

Air Mail Special written by Benny Goodman, Jimmy Mundy and Charles Christian. Used by permission of Rytvoc, Inc. (ASCAP), Regent Music Corp. and Ragbag Music Publ. Corp. ©1941. **Body and Soul**, Frank Eyton, John Green, Edward Heyman and Robert B. Sour. Range Road Music Inc. o/b/o itself and Quartet Music, WB Music Corp., and Druropetal Music. **Come Fly With Me** (Sammy Cahn and Jimmy Van Heusen), ©1958 (renewed), Cahn Music Co. (ASCAP) and Maraville Music Corp. (ASCAP). All rights on behalf of Cahn Music Co. administered by WB Music Corp. **Fly Me to the Moon (In Other Words)** words and Music by Bart Howard, TRO ©1954 (renewed), Hampshire House Publishing Corp., New York, NY. International copyright secured. Made in U.S.A. All rights reserved including public performance for profit. **I'm Gonna Live Till I Die** words and music by Al Hoffman, Walter Kent and Manny Kurtz. Copyright ©1950 (renewed) by Al Hoffman Songs, Inc., Barton Music Corp., Walter Kent Music and Mann Curtis Music Company. **I've Got a Crush On You** (George Gershwin and Ira Gershwin), ©1930 (renewed), WB Music Corp. (ASCAP). **I've Got the World on a String** music by Harold Arlen, lyrics by Ted Koehler. Published by S.A. Music (ASCAP). Published and administered in Canada by EMI Mills Music, Inc. (ASCAP). **I've Got You Under My Skin** words and music by Cole Porter, ©1936 by Chappell & Company, Inc. Copyright renewed. Assigned to Robert H. Montgomery, Jr., trustee of the Cole Porter Musical & Literary Property Trusts, Chappell & Co., publisher. International copyright secured. **It's All Right With Me** words and music by Cole Porter, ©1953 by Cole Porter. Copyright renewed. Assigned to Robert H. Montgomery, Jr., trustee of the Cole Porter Musical & Literary Property Trusts, Chappell & Co., publisher. International copyright secured. **Jumpin' at the Woodside** (Count Basie and Jon Hendricks), ©1959 (renewed) WB Music Corp. (ASCAP). **Just Friends** written by John Klenner and Sam M. Lewis. Published and administered by EMI Robbins Catalog Inc. (ASCAP). **Lean Baby** by Roy Alfred and Billy May. Used by permission of Morley Music Co. (ASCAP). **Learnin' the Blues** (Dolores "Vicki" Silvers), Barton Music Corp. **Let's Face the Music and Dance** music and lyrics by Irving Berlin. Used by special arrangement with The Rodgers and Hammerstein Organization on behalf of the Estate of Irving Berlin. **Let's Fall in Love** by Ted Koehler and Harold Arlen ©1933 by Bourne Co. (ASCAP). Copyright renewed. International copyright secured. **Makin' Whoopee** by Walter Donaldson and Gus Kahn. Donaldson Publishing Co., LLC, and Gilbert Keyes Music Company. All rights on behalf of Gilbert Keyes Music Company administered by WB Music Corp. **Moonlight Becomes You** written by Johnny Burke and James Van Heusen, ©1942 Sony/ATV Harmony (ASCAP). **My Funny Valentine** music and lyrics by Richard Rodgers and Lorenz Hart, ©1937 (renewed), Chappell & Co., Inc. (ASCAP) and Williamson Music, Inc. (ASCAP). Used by special arrangement with The Rodgers and Hammerstein Organization on behalf of the Family Trust u/w of Richard Rodgers. **My Way** written by Paul Anka, Claude Francois, Jacques Revaux and Gilles Thibault. Chrysalis Standards, Inc. (BMI), Architectural Music Co. (BMI), and Jingoro Co. (BMI). **New York, New York (Theme)** written by John Kander and Fred Ebb. Published and administered EMI Unart Catalog Inc. (BMI). **Nice 'n' Easy** written by Lew Spence, Alan Bergman and Marilyn Bergman. Spirit Two Music, Inc. on behalf of Lew Spence Music and Threesome Music Company (ASCAP). **One for**

My Baby (And One More for the Road) by Johnny Mercer and Harold Arlen. Used by permission of Harwin Music Co. (ASCAP). **Pick Yourself Up** (Dorothy Fields and Jerome Kern). Used by permission of Shapiro, Bernstein & Co., Inc. o/b/o Aldi Music. Universal Music Publishing. **Saturday Night Is the Loneliest Night in the Week** (Sammy Cahn and Jule Styne), ©1944 (renewed). Cahn Music Co. (ASCAP) and Producers Music Publ. Co., Inc. (ASCAP). All rights on behalf of Cahn Music Co. administered By WB Music Corp. All rights on behalf of Producers Music Publ. Co., Inc. administered By Chappell & Co., Inc. **The September of My Years** (Sammy Cahn and Jimmy Van Heusen), ©1965 (renewed), Cahn Music Co. (ASCAP) and Van Heusen Music Corp. (ASCAP). All rights on behalf of Cahn Music Co. administered by WB Music Corp. **Summer Wind** (Johnny Mercer, Henry Mayer and Hans Bradtke), ©1965 (renewed), the Johnny Mercer Foundation (ASCAP) and Edition Primus Rolf Budde KG (GEMA). All rights administered by WB Music Corp. **Take Five** written by Paul Desmond, published in the United States by Desmond Music Company. Published in Canada by Derry Music Company. **Teach Me Tonight** (Sammy Cahn and Gene De Paul), ©1954 (renewed), Cahn Music Co. (ASCAP) and The Hub Music Co., Inc. (ASCAP). All rights on behalf of Cahn Music Co. administered by WB Music Corp. **That's Life** (Dean Kay, Kelly L. Gordon), Universal-Polygram Int. Publ., Inc. ©1964, renewed 1992. **Wave** music and lyrics by Antonio Carlos Jobim, published by Corcovado Music Corp. (BMI). **Witchcraft** by Carolyn Leigh and Cy Coleman. Used by permission of Morley Music Co. (ASCAP). **Yes Sir, That's My Baby** by Walter Donaldson and Gus Kahn, ©1925 Donaldson Publishing Co., LLC, and Gilbert Keyes Music Company (ASCAP). All rights on behalf of Gilbert Keyes Music Company administered by WB Music Corp. **You Make Me Feel So Young** (Josef Joe Myrow and Mack Gordon), ©1946 (renewed), WB Music Corp. (ASCAP). All rights reserved. Used by permission.

To learn more about the production, please visit ComeFlyAway.com

NEDERLANDER

Chairman ....James M. Nederlander
President ....James L. Nederlander

Executive Vice President
Nick Scandalios

Vice President   Senior Vice President
Corporate Development   Labor Relations
Charlene S. Nederlander   **Herschel Waxman**

Vice President   Chief Financial Officer
Jim Boese   **Freida Sawyer Belviso**

STAFF FOR THE MARQUIS THEATRE

Manager ....David Calhoun
Associate Manager ....Austin Nathaniel
Treasurer ....Rick Waxman
Assistant Treasurer ....John Rooney
Carpenter ....Joseph P. Valentino
Electrician ....James Mayo
Property Man ....Scott Mecionis

Donny & Marie: A Broadway Christmas

First Performance: December 9, 2010.
Closed January 2, 2011 after 20 Performances.

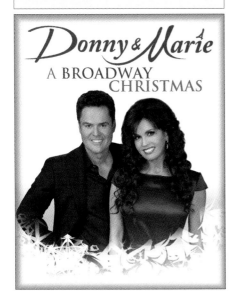

A holiday music and dance revue featuring the brother/sister singing team.

CAST AND MUSICIANS

DANCERS

MATTHEW FISH, KARL HENDRICKSON, JERMAINE JOHNSON, KELENE JOHNSON, MAKINZEE LOVE, RICHARD MCAMISH, JESSIE THACKER, JAYMZ TUAILEVA, ASHLEY WILLIAMS, IVY MICHELLE WILLIAMS

Dance Captain: JAYMZ TUAILEVA

MUSICIANS

Musical Director	JERRY WILLIAMS
Drums	JOEY FINGER
Guitar	STEVEN LEE
Percussion	GABRIEL FALCON
Sax	ROCCO BARBATO, ROBERT MADER
Trombone	MIKE TURNBULL
Trumpet	GIL KAUPP
Bass	ROCHON WESTMORELAND

MARQUIS THEATRE

UNDER THE DIRECTION OF JAMES M. NEDERLANDER AND JAMES L. NEDERLANDER

GREGORY YOUNG
THE PRODUCTION OFFICE

JON B. PLATT
ON THE LINE COMPANY

MAGIC ARTS & ENTERTAINMENT
NEWSPACE ENTERTAINMENT

IN ASSOCIATION WITH

GREG SPERRY AND ERIC GARDNER

PRESENT

DONNY OSMOND   MARIE OSMOND

Donny & Marie
A BROADWAY CHRISTMAS

PRODUCTION DESIGN	SET AND VIDEO DESIGN	COSTUME DESIGN	LIGHTING DESIGN
PERRY "BUTCH" ALLEN & PETER MORSE	PERRY "BUTCH" ALLEN	KIRSTIN GALLO	PETER MORSE

GENERAL MANAGEMENT	PRODUCTION MANAGEMENT	PRODUCTION COORDINATOR
ALCHEMY PRODUCTION GROUP LLC CARL PASBJERG FRANK SCARDINO	EBERG STAGE SOLUTIONS	DAVID NOVICH

GENERAL PRESS REPRESENTATIVES	DIRECTOR OF MARKETING
THE HARTMAN GROUP	BRUCE GRANATH

MUSICAL DIRECTOR
JERRY WILLIAMS

DIRECTED AND CHOREOGRAPHED BY
BARRY LATHER

12/15/10

(Center, L-R): Marie Osmond and Donny Osmond

Photo by Kim Goodwin

Donny & Marie: A Broadway Christmas

Marie Osmond and Donny Osmond

Carl Pasbjerg,
Alchemy Production
Group LLC
*General
Management*

Gregory Young
Producer

Jon B. Platt
Producer

STAFF FOR
DONNY & MARIE - A BROADWAY CHRISTMAS

GENERAL MANAGEMENT
ALCHEMY PRODUCTION GROUP LLC
Carl Pasbjerg   Frank P. Scardino

PRODUCTION MANAGEMENT
Eberg Stage Solutions
Steven Ehrenberg

GENERAL PRESS REPRESENTATIVE
THE HARTMAN GROUP
Michael Hartman   Wayne Wolfe   Matt Ross

DIRECTOR OF MARKETING
Bruce Granath

Company Manager ....Erik Birkeland

Executive Assistant to Marie Osmond ....Darla Sperry
Assistants to Marie Osmond ....Rachael Lauren,
Kim Goodwin
Managerial Associate ....Tegan Meyer
Assistant to General Managers ....Amanda Coleman
Head Writer ....Marcia Wilkie
Video Director ....Simon Greaves
Assistant Choreographer ....Bryan Anthony
Assistant to Eric Gardner ....Lynn Robnett
Production Monitor Engineer ....Joe Webster
Lighting Programmer ....Joseph Eddy
Backline Technician ....Michael "Micro" Shaw
Video Shader ....Jesus "Chuy" Guerrero
Head Wardrobe ....Maria Gomez
Dressers ....Moira Conrad,
Julien Havard,
Daryl Stone
Press Associates ....Michelle Bergmann,
Nicole Capatasto, Tom D'Ambrosio,
Juliana Hannett, Alyssa Hart,
Bethany Larsen, Leslie Papa,
Frances White
Merchandising ....Michelle Sloan, Pete Milano
Travel Agent ....Roy Ericson/Starflight Travel
Trucking Company ....Scott Frutrell/
Riverwood Management Inc.
Production Audio Engineer ....David Bullard
Production Carpenter ....Joseph P. Valentino
Sound Engineer ....Lucas "Rico" Corrubia Jr.
Production Props ....Scott Mecionis
Advertising.............................Serino Coyne, LLC/
Roger Micone, Jim Russek,
Becca Goland-Van Ryn, Nick Nolte

Post Production ....Creative Group, Inc./
Joe Franze
Sponsorships ....EMCI/
Jay Coleman
Accountants ....Fried & Kowgios Partners, LLP/
Robert Fried, CPA
Controller ....Sarah Galbraith
Legal Counsel ....Brooks & Distler
Insurance ....DeWitt Stern Group, Inc./
Anthony Pittari, Peter Shoemaker
Banking ....Signature Bank/Barbara von Borstel
Payroll ....Castellana Services, Inc.
Production Photographers ......Kim Goodwin, Erik Kabik
Group Sales ....Nederlander Group Sales
Theatre Displays ....King Displays, Inc.

STAFF FOR ON THE LINE COMPANY
President ....Jon B. Platt
General Manager ....Terrie Lootens Hyde

STAFF FOR MAGIC ARTS & ENTERTAINMENT/
NEWSPACE ENTERTAINMENT
Co-CEO .... Lee D. Marshall
Co-CEO .... Joe Marsh
Chief Operating Officer .... Steve Boulay
President .... John W. Ballard
Marketing Director .... Bruce Granath
Sales Director ....Michael Braxton
Operations Manager ....Mary Ann Porcaro
Controller ....Patty Vartenuk
General Manager ....Dave Stinson
Director of Ticketing .... Tracie Yagi
Production Manager ....Cate Kizerian
Accounting ....Sandy Winchester

CREDITS
Scenery constructed by All Access Staging and Productions
and Hudson Scenic Studio Inc. Sound equipment from
Sound Associates, Inc. Star drop provided by I. Weiss.
Lighting provided by Epic Production Technologies. Video
screen provided by Creative Technology. Video control
room equipment provided by Tours By Sloan. Automation
by SGPS.

SPECIAL THANKS FROM MARIE OSMOND
To Greg Young: Just like me, you grew up in this business.
I've had the honor of being included in the Young legacy of
shows, both father and son, for over 17 years. As always,
your wonderful personal qualities of vision, persistence and
loyal dedication to our friendship have made this amazing
opportunity happen. I'm so grateful for you and our
friendship.

SPECIAL THANKS FROM GREGORY YOUNG
Greg would like to thank both Donny & Marie and their
families, friends and fans for without whose support we
would not be here. He would also like to thank Donny &
Marie's production crew, Eric Gardner, Lee Marshall and
team, for all their hard work and dedication in bringing this
production to the stage. He is grateful that during his 20-
year career he has had mentors in both his father, Robert
Young, and his friend and producing partner, Jon Platt, who
introduced him to Marie whom Greg considers a dear friend
and true inspiration. Greg admires both the intention and
tireless dedication to entertain by both Donny & Marie as
they always rise to shine and give the audience a warm
embrace. A cornerstone to Greg's foundation is his 20-year
partnership with Atanas Ilitch, who has supported Greg's
endeavors and stood by his side. And a special note of
gratitude to friends Greg & Darla Sperry, who over the past
year have always, so kindly, put up with the persistence
needed to bring this Broadway production to life.

NEDERLANDER

Chairman	**James M. Nederlander**
President	**James L. Nederlander**

Executive Vice President
Nick Scandalios

Vice President	Senior Vice President
Corporate Development	Labor Relations
Charlene S. Nederlander	**Herschel Waxman**

Vice President	Chief Financial Officer
Jim Boese	**Freida Sawyer Belviso**

STAFF FOR THE MARQUIS THEATRE
Manager ....David Calhoun
Associate Manager ....Austin Nathaniel
Treasurer ....Rick Waxman
Assistant Treasurer ....John Rooney
Carpenter...............................Joseph P. Valentino
Electrician ....James Mayo
Property Man ....Scott Mecionis

Driving Miss Daisy

First Preview: October 7, 2010. Opened: October 25, 2010.
Closed April 9, 2011 after 20 Previews and 180 Performances.

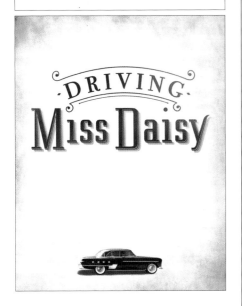

An elderly black man and an elderly white woman gradually grow to know, understand, respect, and perhaps even love one another over the years that he serves as her chauffeur in Atlanta, Georgia during the years of the Civil Rights movement. The first Broadway revival of the Pulitzer Prize-winning drama whose movie adaptation won the Academy Award as Best Picture.

CAST
(in alphabetical order)

Boolie Werthan ....BOYD GAINES
Hoke Coleburn ....JAMES EARL JONES
Daisy Werthan ....VANESSA REDGRAVE

UNDERSTUDIES AND STANDBYS

Standby for Daisy Werthan:
MAUREEN ANDERMAN
Standby for Boolie Werthan:
ALLEN FITZPATRICK
Standby for Hoke Coleburn:
COUNT STOVALL

SETTING

Atlanta, Georgia, in the 1950s and 1960s
at the height of the Civil Rights Movement

Vanessa Redgrave is appearing with the permission of
Actors' Equity Association.

---

⑤ GOLDEN THEATRE
A Shubert Organization Theatre
Philip J. Smith, *Chairman*   **Robert E. Wankel,** *President*

JED BERNSTEIN   ADAM ZOTOVICH
ELIZABETH IRELAND McCANN   ROGER BERLIND   BETH KLOIBER
ALBERT NOCCIOLINO   JON B. PLATT   STYLESFOUR PRODUCTIONS
RUTH HENDEL/SHAWN EMAMJOMEH   LARRY HIRSCHHORN/SPRING SIRKIN
CARL MOELLENBERG/WENDY FEDERMAN   DARYL ROTH/JANE BERGÈRE
IN ASSOCIATION WITH MICHAEL FILERMAN

present

JAMES EARL JONES   VANESSA REDGRAVE
BOYD GAINES

in

by
ALFRED UHRY

Scenic Design	Costume Design	Lighting Design	Projection Design
JOHN LEE BEATTY	JANE GREENWOOD	PETER KACZOROWSKI	WENDALL K. HARRINGTON

Music	Sound Design	Casting
MARK BENNETT	CHRISTOPHER CRONIN	DAVE CLEMMONS, C.S.A.

Production Stage Manager	Technical Supervisor	Marketing Services	Advertising
KAREN ARMSTRONG	LARRY MORLEY	ABOVE THE TITLE ENTERTAINMENT	SPOTCO

Press Representative	Company Manager	General Management
O&M CO.	BRUCE KLINGER	RICHARDS/CLIMAN, INC.

Directed by
DAVID ESBJORNSON

DRIVING MISS DAISY WAS FIRST PRODUCED BY PLAYWRIGHTS HORIZONS, AND SUBSEQUENTLY BY JANE HARMON/NINA KENEALLY, IVY PROPERTIES, LTD./RICHARD FRANKEL, GENE WOLSK/ALAN M. SHORE AND SUSAN S. MYERBERG IN ASSOCIATION WITH PLAYWRIGHTS HORIZONS, OFF-BROADWAY IN 1987.

10/25/10

(L-R): Vanessa Redgrave
and James Earl Jones

Photo by Annabel Clark

Driving Miss Daisy

James Earl Jones
Hoke Coleburn

Vanessa Redgrave
Daisy Werthan

Boyd Gaines
Boolie Werthan

Maureen Anderman
Standby for Daisy Werthan

Allen Fitzpatrick
Standby for Boolie Werthan

Count Stovall
Standby for Hoke Coleburn

Alfred Uhry
Playwright

David Esbjornson
Director

John Lee Beatty
Scenic Design

Jane Greenwood
Costume Design

Peter Kaczorowski
Lighting Design

Wendall K. Harrington
Projection Design

Mark Bennett
Music

Christopher Cronin
Sound Design

Dave Clemmons Casting
Casting

David R. Richards and Tamar Haimes, Richards/Climan, Inc.
General Manager

Jed Bernstein
Producer

Adam Zotovich
Producer

Elizabeth Ireland McCann
Producer

Roger Berlind
Producer

Beth Kloiber
Producer

Albert Nocciolino
Producer

Jon B. Platt
Producer

John Styles, StylesFour Productions
Producer

Jason Styles, StylesFour Productions
Producer

Ruth Hendel
Producer

Shawn Emamjomeh
Producer

Larry Hirschhorn
Producer

Spring Sirkin
Producer

Carl Moellenberg
Producer

Wendy Federman
Producer

Daryl Roth
Producer

Jane Bergère
Producer

Michael Filerman
Producer

Driving Miss Daisy

CREW
Front: Amelia Haywood (Dresser)

Middle Row (L-R): Nathaniel Hathaway (Hair),
Matthew Farrell (Stage Manager),
Karen Armstrong (Production Stage Manager),
Maureen Anderman (Honorary Crew Member/
"Daisy" Standby)

Back Row (L-R): Laura Beattie (Dresser),
Bruce Klinger (Company Manager)

Not pictured: John Robelen
(Wardrobe Supervisor)

CREW
Front Row (L-R): Terrance McGarty (Carpenter),
Sylvia Yoshioka (Electrician), Steve McDonald
(Props)

Back Row (L-R): Brien Brannigan (Sound),
John Kilgore (Sub)

STAGE DOORMAN
John Green
Not pictured: Joe Kasper (Day Stage Doorman)

BOX OFFICE
(L-R): Chip Jorgensen (Treasurer), Melissa Jorgensen, Gary Powers
Not pictured: Craig Panella

Photos by Brian Mapp

Driving Miss Daisy

FRONT OF HOUSE STAFF
Front Row (L-R): Paula Parente, Thomas Pollock, Patrick Marran, Helen Bentley

Back Row (L-R): Edytha Harlin, Yuri Fernandez, Veronica Morrissey, Patricia Byrne, Mae Smith-Hendrix, Shelia Miller

HOUSE MANAGER
Carolyne Jones

STAFF FOR *DRIVING MISS DAISY*

GENERAL MANAGEMENT
RICHARDS/CLIMAN, INC.
DAVID R. RICHARDS   TAMAR HAIMES
Michael Sag   Kyle Bonder
Cesar Hawas   Julianna Slaten

COMPANY MANAGER
Bruce Klinger

GENERAL PRESS REPRESENTATIVE
O&M CO.
Rick Miramontez
Molly Barnett   Elizabeth Wagner

PRODUCTION STAGE
   MANAGER ....KAREN ARMSTRONG
Stage Manager ....Matthew Farrell
Dialect Coaches ....Deborah Hecht, Kate Wilson
Assistant Technical Supervisor ....Amanda Raymond
Associate Scenic Designer ....Kacie Hultgren
Assistant Scenic Designer ....Yoshinori Tanokura
Associate Costume Designer ....Moria Clinton
Associate Composer ....Matthew Henning
Assistant Lighting Designer ....Keri Thibodeau
Assistant Projection Designer ....Tim Brown
Assistant Sound Designer ....Alex Neumann
Assistant to Mr. Esbjornson ....Nick Minas
Production Assistants ....Deanna Weiner, Jojo Karlin
Casting Assistant ....Alan Lane
Production Carpenter ....Jordan Gable
Production Electrician ....Brian GF McGarity
Lighting Programmer ....Josh Weitzman
Projection Programmer ....Paul Vershbow
Production Props ....Neil Rosenberg
Prop Shoppers ....Shelley Barclay, Buist Bickley
Wardrobe Supervisor ....John Robelen
Mr. Jones' Dresser ....Amelia Heywood
Ms. Redgrave's Dresser ....Laura Beattie
Costume Shopper ....Lisa Loen
Hair Supervisor ....Nathaniel Hathaway
Assistant to Mr. Bernstein ....Matthew Troillett
Assistant to Mr. Jones ....Flynn Earl Jones

Assistant to Ms. Redgrave ....Eamonn Burke
For EI McCann LLC:
   Executive Producer ....Joey Parnes
   Associate Producers .........S.D. Wagner, John Johnson
   Assistant to EI McCann ....Kristen Luciani
Advertising ....SpotCo/
   Drew Hodges, Jim Edwards,
   Tom Greenwald, Y. Darius Suyama,
   Kristen Rathbun
Website/Interactive Marketing ....SpotCo/
   Sara Fitzpatrick, Matt Wilstein
Marketing Service ....Above The Title Entertainment/
   Jed Bernstein, Britt Marden
Marketing Consultants ....Donna Walker Kuhne,
   Cherine Anderson
Press Associates ....Dusty Bennett, Jaron Caldwell,
   Philip Carrubba, Sam Corbett,
   Jon Dimond, Richard Hillman,
   Yufen Kung, Andy Snyder
Banking ....City National Bank/
   Michele Gibbons
Insurance ....DeWitt Stern Group Inc./
   Joseph Bower, Anthony Pittari
Accountants ....Fried & Kowgios, CPA's LLP,
   Robert Fried, CPA
Comptroller ....Elliott Aronstam
Legal Counsel ....Levine Plotkin & Menin LLP/
   Loren H. Plotkin, Esq.
Payroll ....CSI/Lance Castellana
Production Photographer ....Carol Rosegg
Photographer ....Annabel Clark
Opening Night Coordination ....Suzanne Tobak,
   Gail Perlman, Serino Coyne, LLC

CREDITS
Scenery constructed by Showman Fabricators, Inc., Long Island City, NY. Computer motion control and automation of scenery and rigging by Showman Fabricators, Inc. using Raynok motion control. Projection and lighting equipment from PRG Lighting. Sound equipment from Sound Associates. Costumes by Eric Winterling, Inc. Rehearsed at the Roundabout Rehearsal Studios. Recordings engineered at John Kilgore Studios. "White Christmas" music and lyrics by Irving Berlin. This selection is used by special arrangement with The Rodgers and Hammerstein Organization, on behalf of the Estate of Irving Berlin, www.irvingberlin.com. All rights reserved.

SPECIAL THANKS
Roundabout Theatre Company, Ani V'ata NYU Vocal Ensemble, Cantor Deborah Numark, Barbara Bennett

---

www.DaisyOnBroadway.com

 **THE SHUBERT ORGANIZATION, INC.**
Board of Directors

Philip J. Smith Chairman	**Robert E. Wankel** President
Wyche Fowler, Jr.	**John W. Kluge**
Lee J. Seidler	**Michael I. Sovern**

Stuart Subotnick

Elliot Greene Chief Financial Officer	**David Andrews** Senior Vice President – Shubert Ticketing
Juan Calvo Vice President – Finance	**John Darby** Vice President – Facilities
Peter Entin Vice President – Theatre Operations	**Charles Flateman** Vice President – Marketing
Anthony LaMattina Vice President – Audit & Production Finance	**Brian Mahoney** Vice President – Ticket Sales

D.S. Moynihan
Vice President – Creative Projects

House Manager ....Carolyne Jones

Driving Miss Daisy
Scrapbook

Correspondents: Matthew Farrell (Stage Manager) and John Robelen (Wardrobe Supervisor).

Memorable Opening Night Letter, Fax or Note: A personalized "form letter" describing how honored Boyd Gaines was to work with each and every member of the company—the letter was in a self addressed envelope from Mr. Gaines.

Opening Night Gifts: A bound special edition copy of the play from the producers; champagne from Ms. Redgrave; champagne with a straw from our wardrobe supervisor John Robelen; personalized travel mugs with a map of the "Ride to Mobile" from Amelia (dresser), Piggly Wiggly key chains with Daisy Keys from Laura (dresser), car mezuzahs from Boyd Gaines, pumpkin pies from Matthew (stage manager), flowers from the world….

Most Exciting Celebrity Visitor: An extraordinary number of exciting artists have come to our production. Of all of the wonderful people who have graced the Golden Theatre for a visit, we would say Julie Harris was exceptionally exciting. Boyd saw Ms. Harris standing in the front row at the curtain call, cheering our play. He immediately got the audience's attention and announced to the house that we had an honored guest among us. As soon as he said, "Miss Julie Harris" the crowd jumped to their feet again. The ovation for Ms. Harris was unforgettable. Afterwards, Ms. Harris came backstage and gave each and every crew and company member a kiss on the hand, a kiss on the cheek and a great big hug (as well as a beautiful memory that we all treasure).

Actor Who Performed the Most Roles in This Show: Onstage each actor portrays one role. Offstage crew members and stage managers perform all of the unseen characters mentioned in the play: Idella, Uncle Walter, Miriam, Beulah, Minnie, Oscar, Florine and the ever-popular Miss McClatchey. We don't know exactly who has portrayed the most characters in one evening but we guarantee the casting is completely non-traditional and hysterically funny (to us anyway).

Who Has Done the Most Shows in Their Career: This question broke our calculators… did you see the cast list?

Special Backstage Rituals: A nightly shoulder scrunch for Vanessa, a dirty joke from Boyd, a big smile and huge laugh from James.

Favorite Moment During Each Performance: We can't tell you how much fun we have throughout the show each night… too difficult to chose one moment.

Favorite In-Theatre Gathering Place: Daisy's Green Room.

Favorite Off-Site Hangout: The bar in the InterContinental.

Favorite Snack Food: Anything baked by our production assistant, Jojo. Corn Bread. Smoked Salmon.

Fastest Costume Change: Boyd's trip to Mobile!

Favorite Therapies: Ricolas, Ginger Tea, Chamomile Tea, Scotch, Massage, Scotch, Red Wine, Limoncello, and more Red Wine….

Memorable Ad-Lib: After a major problem with the sound system the phones wouldn't ring on cue. In one call Vanessa said, "I think I heard the phone ring." For the next call, Boyd said "Mama, pick up the phone" and Vanessa, as Miss Daisy, did.

Memorable Cell Phone Incident: Actually, the audience has been very respectful and has for the most part followed the stage manager's direction at the top of the show to shut those devices off. However, there was one time when a cell phone went off right after the announcement. It was incredibly loud as though it was right next to her. When our stage manager looked around for the source she discovered it was her own phone that she had forgotten to turn off!

Memorable Press Encounter: The New Yorker photo shoot with Brigitte Lacombe.

Memorable Stage Door Fan Encounter: Cloris Leachman came backstage to visit with the company one night. After sharing a glass of wine with Ms. Leachman, Ms. Redgrave left for the evening via a neighboring theatre's stage door exit. Ms. Leachman exited our stage door. The *Driving Miss Daisy* fans cheered her and Ms. Leachman signed all of the fans' PLAYBILLS (we assume as Miss Daisy—but we don't know for sure).

Busiest Day at the Box Office: November 23, Variety reported that *Driving Miss Daisy* broke the Golden Theatre house record for Box Office gross: $727,178 for the prior week.

Who Wore the Heaviest/Hottest Costume: Boyd's three-piece suit with coat and hat.

Who Wore the Least: Boyd (a costume trifecta!) in Bermuda shorts, polo shirt, and black knee socks.

Catchphrases Only the Company Would Recognize: "Hidey, Miss McClatchey"

Company In-Jokes: House Propman Steve McDonald is the "real" offstage cook, Idella. He makes the coffee and the deviled eggs. And Idella's stuffed eggs are good!

1. Bows on opening night (L-R): James Earl Jones, Vanessa Redgrave and Boyd Gaines.
2. Playwright Alfred Uhry takes a curtain call.
3. Redgrave waves thanks to the first night audience for her flowers.

Photos by Joseph Marzullo/WENN

Elf

First Preview: November 2, 2010. Opened: November 14, 2010.
Closed January 2, 2011 after 15 Previews and 57 Performances.

PLAYBILL

Up at the North Pole, Buddy, one of Santa's perkiest toymakers, gets the shocking news that he's not really an elf at all, but was raised from babyhood by elves. The news launches him on an odyssey to New York City to find his real family and eventually to reawaken the holiday spirit in the jaded New Yorkers.

CAST

(in order of appearance)

Santa	GEORGE WENDT
Mrs. Claus	NANCY JOHNSTON
Buddy	SEBASTIAN ARCELUS
Charlie	NOAH WEISBERG
Shawanda	ASMERET GHEBREMICHAEL
Walter Hobbs	MARK JACOBY
Sam	NOAH WEISBERG
Matthews	MATT LOEHR
Chadwick	BLAKE HAMMOND
Emily	BETH LEAVEL
Michael	MATTHEW GUMLEY
Deb	VALERIE WRIGHT
Macy's Manager	MICHAEL MANDELL
Jovie	AMY SPANGER
Fake Santa	TIMOTHY J. ALEX
Policemen	LEE WILKINS, NOAH WEISBERG
Mr. Greenway	MICHAEL McCORMICK
Charlotte Dennon	EMILY HSU

Ensemble ....TIMOTHY J. ALEX, LISA GAJDA,
ASMERET GHEBREMICHAEL,
BLAKE HAMMOND, JENNY HILL,

Continued on next page

Continued on next page

---

9 AL HIRSCHFELD THEATRE
A JUJAMCYN THEATRE

JORDAN ROTH
President

PAUL LIBIN
Executive Vice President

JACK VIERTEL
Senior Vice President

Warner Bros. Theatre Ventures, Inc.
in association with
Unique Features
Present

elf

Book by
Thomas Meehan and **Bob Martin**

Music by
Matthew Sklar

Lyrics by
Chad Beguelin

Based upon the New Line Cinema film written by David Berenbaum

Starring
Sebastian Arcelus
Amy Spanger
Mark Jacoby

Michael Mandell   Michael McCormick   Valerie Wright
Matthew Gumley   Matthew Schechter

With

Timothy J. Alex   Callie Carter   Cara Cooper   Lisa Gajda
Asmeret Ghebremichael   Blake Hammond   Jenny Hill   Stacey Todd Holt
Emily Hsu   Nancy Johnston   Marc Kessler   Matt Loehr
Michael James Scott   Noah Weisberg   Lee Wilkins   Kirsten Wyatt

Also Starring
Beth Leavel
And
George Wendt
as
Santa

Scenic Design
David Rockwell	Costume Design
Gregg Barnes	Lighting Design
Natasha Katz	Sound Design
Peter Hylenski
Casting
Telsey & Co.	Projection Design
Zachary Borovay	Hair Design
Josh Marquette	Dance Arrangements
David Chase
Production Stage Manager
Karen Moore	Associate Director
Casey Hushion	Music Coordinator
John Miller	Technical Supervisor
Chris Smith/Smitty
Executive Producer
Mark Kaufman	Marketing Direction
aka	Press Representative
The Hartman Group	General Manager
Charlotte Wilcox Company

Orchestrations
Doug Besterman

Music Direction & Vocal Arrangements
Phil Reno

Directed and Choreographed by
Casey Nicholaw

11/14/10

Sebastian Arcelus
(center) and ensemble

Elf

MUSICAL NUMBERS

ACT ONE

Overture .... The Orchestra
Prologue: The North Pole - Santa's home
Scene 1: The North Pole - Christmastown
  "Christmastown" .... Santa, Buddy & Company
Scene 2: The North Pole - Santa's workshop
Scene 3: The North Pole - Christmastown
Scene 4: The North Pole/New York City
  "World's Greatest Dad" .... Buddy
Scene 5: Empire State Building. The offices of Greenway Press
  "In the Way" .... Deb, Walter, Emily, Michael & Company
Scene 6: Macy's department store
  "Sparklejollytwinklejingley" .... Buddy, Store Manager & Company
Scene 7: The Hobbs' apartment
  "I'll Believe in You" .... Michael & Emily
Scene 8: The Hobbs' apartment, the next day
  "In the Way" (Reprise) .... Emily & Walter
Scene 9: The offices of Greenway Press
  "Just Like Him" .... Buddy, Deb & Company
Scene 10: Rockefeller Center
  "A Christmas Song" .... Buddy, Jovie & Company
Scene 11: Walter's office
Scene 12: The streets of New York
  "I'll Believe in You" (Reprise) .... Buddy & Company

ACT TWO

Entr'acte .... The Orchestra
Prologue: The streets of New York .... Buddy & Santa
Scene 1: Chung Fu Palace
  "Nobody Cares About Santa" .... Fake Santas, Store Manager & Buddy
Scene 2: Exterior, The Tavern on the Green
  "Never Fall in Love" .... Jovie
Scene 3: The Hobbs' apartment
  "There Is a Santa Claus" .... Michael & Emily
Scene 4: The offices of Greenway Press
  "The Story of Buddy the Elf" .... Buddy, Michael, Walter, Greenway,
                                     Emily, Deb & Company
Scene 5: Central Park, the woods near the Boathouse
  "Nobody Cares About Santa" (Reprise) .... Santa
Scene 6: Central Park
  "A Christmas Song" (Reprise) .... Jovie, Buddy, Emily, Michael, Walter & Company
Epilogue: The North Pole - Santa's house
  Finale .... Company

Cast Continued

EMILY HSU, NANCY JOHNSTON,
MATT LOEHR, MICHAEL JAMES SCOTT,
NOAH WEISBERG, LEE WILKINS,
KIRSTEN WYATT

UNDERSTUDIES
For Santa: BLAKE HAMMOND
For Buddy: MATT LOEHR, NOAH WEISBERG
For Walter: TIMOTHY J. ALEX,
  STACEY TODD HOLT
For Emily: CARA COOPER,
  NANCY JOHNSTON
For Deb: JENNY HILL, KIRSTEN WYATT
For Macy's Manager: BLAKE HAMMOND,
  MICHAEL JAMES SCOTT
For Jovie: CARA COOPER, KIRSTEN WYATT
For Mr. Greenway: TIMOTHY J. ALEX

Standby for Michael: MATTHEW SCHECHTER

SWINGS
CALLIE CARTER, CARA COOPER,
STACEY TODD HOLT, MARC KESSLER

Dance Captain: CALLIE CARTER
Assistant Dance Captain: MARC KESSLER

ORCHESTRA
Conductor: PHIL RENO
Associate Conductor: MAT EISENSTEIN
Concert Master: RICK DOLAN
Violin: BELINDA WHITNEY
Cello: SARAH HEWITT-ROTH
Bass: MICHAEL KUENNEN
Woodwinds: TOM MURRAY,
  RICK HECKMAN, MARK THRASHER
Trumpets: CRAIG JOHNSON,
  SCOTT HARRELL
Trombones: ALAN FERBER, JEFF NELSON
Percussion: CHARLES DESCARFINO
Drums: PERRY CAVARI
Keyboards: MAT EISENSTEIN,
  MARK C. MITCHELL, PHIL RENO
Music Coordinator: JOHN MILLER

(L-R):
Sebastian Arcelus
and Amy Spanger

Photo by Joan Marcus

Elf

Sebastian Arcelus
Buddy

Amy Spanger
Jovie

Beth Leavel
Emily

George Wendt
Santa

Mark Jacoby
Walter

Michael Mandell
Store Manager

Michael McCormick
Mr. Greenway

Valerie Wright
Deb

Matthew Gumley
Michael

Matthew Schechter
Michael Standby

Timothy J. Alex
Ensemble

Callie Carter
Swing/
Dance Captain

Cara Cooper
Swing

Lisa Gajda
Ensemble

Asmeret
Ghebremichael
Ensemble

Blake Hammond
Ensemble

Jenny Hill
Ensemble

Stacey Todd Holt
Swing

Emily Hsu
Ensemble

Nancy Johnston
Ensemble

Marc Kessler
Swing

Matt Loehr
Ensemble

Michael James Scott
Ensemble

Noah Weisberg
Ensemble

Lee Wilkins
Ensemble

Kirsten Wyatt
Ensemble

Thomas Meehan
Book

Bob Martin
Book

Matthew Sklar
Music

Chad Beguelin
Lyrics

Casey Nicholaw
Director/
Choreographer

David Rockwell
Scenic Design

Gregg Barnes
Costume Design

Natasha Katz
Lighting Design

Peter Hylenski
Sound Design

Elf

Zachary Borovay
Projection Design

Josh Marquette
Hair Design

Bernard Telsey,
Telsey + Company
Casting

Doug Besterman
Orchestrations

Phil Reno
*Music Director/
Vocal Arranger*

David Chase
Dance Arranger

John Miller
Music Coordinator

Chris Smith/
Theatersmith, Inc.
Technical Supervisor

Charlotte Wilcox,
The Charlotte Wilcox
Company
General Manager

Casey Hushion
Associate Director

Gregg Maday,
Warner Bros.
Theatre Ventures
Producer

Raymond Wu,
Warner Bros.
Theatre Ventures
Producer

Robert Shaye,
Unique Features
Producer

Michael Lynne,
Unique Features
Producer

Mark Kaufman
Executive Producer

FRONT OF HOUSE STAFF
Front Row (L-R): Anah Klate, Lorraine Feeks, Jose Nunez

Second Row (L-R): Brian Gold, Jennifer DiDonato, Julie Burnham,
Janice Rodriguez, Elizabeth Harvey

Third Row (L-R): Roberto Ellington, Tamica Yates, Mary Marzan,
Theresa Lopez, Henry Menendez

Back Row (L-R): Albert Kim, Matthew Cohn, Donald Royal,
Bill Meyers, Alex Gutierrez, Bart Ryan, Terry Monahan

CREW
Front Row (L-R): Liam O'Brien, Jeffrey Johnson, Franklin Hollenbeck, Kristin Farley, Michael Norris, Karen Moore, Karen Evanouskas, Brian Bogin,
Rachel McCutchen

Middle Row (L-R): Jesse Stevens, Eileen MacDonald, Patrick Shea, John Blixt, Elisa Acevedo

Back Row: Joel Hawkins, Chris Robinson, Gabe Harris, Joe Mooneyham, Fran Rapp, Gene Manford, Tom Burke, Joshua Burns, Anthony Hoffman, Sal Sclafani,
Will Sweeney, Pete Drummond, Mark Thrasher (Musician), Brian Schweppe, Richard Orton

Elf

STAFF FOR *ELF*

FOR WARNER BROS.

Chairman & CEO ....Barry Meyer
President & COO ....Alan Horn

WARNER BROS. THEATRE VENTURES

Executive Vice President ....Gregg Maday
Senior Vice President,
    Development and Head of Operations ...Raymond Wu
Chief Financial Officer ....Laura Valan
Senior Vice President, Finance ....Mark Coker
Director, Finance ....Maria Gonzalez
Senior Financial Analyst ....Arthur Yang
Staff ....Carol Wood, Jennifer Kim,
                            Rachel Spenst, Susan Gary

FOR UNIQUE FEATURES

Michael Lynne, Principal
Bob Shaye, Principal
Mark Kaufman
Dylan Sellers   Julie Crowne   Christina Delgado
Jonna Smith   Leah Holzer

GENERAL MANAGEMENT
CHARLOTTE WILCOX COMPANY
Charlotte W. Wilcox
Seth Marquette
Matthew W. Krawiec   Dina S. Friedler
Regina Mancha   Steve Supeck   Margaret Wilcox
Stephen Donovan   Francesca De La Vega

COMPANY MANAGER
Heidi Neven

ASSOCIATE COMPANY MANAGER
Michael Bolgar

GENERAL PRESS REPRESENTATIVE
THE HARTMAN GROUP
Michael Hartman
Juliana Hannett   Frances White

CASTING
TELSEY + COMPANY
Bernie Telsey CSA, Will Cantler CSA, David Vaccari CSA,
Bethany Knox CSA, Craig Burns CSA,
Tiffany Little Canfield CSA, Rachel Hoffman CSA,
Justin Huff CSA, Patrick Goodwin CSA,
Abbie Brady-Dalton, David Morris, Cesar A. Rocha

Production Stage Manager ....Karen Moore
Stage Manager ....Rachel S. McCutchen
Assistant Stage Manager ....Brian Bogin
Associate Choreographer ....Brian J. Marcum
Assistant Choreographer ....Callie Carter
Associate Set Designer ....Richard Jaris
Assistant Set Designers ....Ann Bartok,
                            Charles Corcoran, Christine Peters
Assistant to the Set Designer ....Anne Colice
Associate Costume Designer ....Matthew Pachtman
Assistant Costume Designers ....Sarah Sophia Lidz,
                                        Sky Switser
Associate Lighting Designer ....Peter Hoerburger
Assistant Lighting Designer ....Kathleen Dobbins

Moving Light Programmer ....Hillary Knox
Associate Sound Designer ....Keith Caggiano
Assistant Projection Designer ....Driscoll Otto
Makeup Consultant ....Joe Dulude II
Skating Coach ....Marni Halasa

Production Electrician ....James Fedigan
Production Property Supervisor ....Emiliano Pares
Advance Sound ....Jason Strangfeld
Head Carpenter ....Patrick Shea
Automation Carpenter ....Mike Norris
Head Electrician ....Brian Dawson
Assistant Electrician ....Chris Robinson
Head Sound ....Jesse Stevens
Head Props ....Brian Schweppe
Assistant Props ....Peter Drummond
Wardrobe Supervisor ....James Hall
Assistant Wardrobe Supervisor ....Franklin Hollenbech
Dressers ....Joshua Burns, Suzanne Delahunt,
                    Kristin Farley, Dan Foss,
                    Kay Gowenlock, Jennifer Griggs,
                    Anthony Hoffman, Kate Sorg
Hair Supervisor ....Richard Orton
Hair Dressers ....Elisa Acevedo,
                        Monica Costea, Joel Hawkins
Production Assistants ....Karen Evanouskas,
                    Sara Cox Bradley, Leanne Deaver,
                    Irma Escobar, Ben Philipp,
                    Blair Baker
Intern ....Sara Ryer
Legal Counsel ....Loeb & Loeb LLP/
                                Seth Gelblum
Accountant ....Rosenberg, Neuwirth & Kushner, CPAs/
                    Mark D'Ambrosio, Jana Jevnikar
Advertising ....Serino Coyne, LLC/
                    Greg Corradetti, Tom Callahan,
                    Joe Alesi, Andrea Prince,
                    Sarah Marcus
Website & Online Marketing ....Art Meets Commerce/
                    Jim Glaub, Chip Meyrelles,
                    Laurie Connor, Kevin Keating,
                    Jacqui Kaiser, Crystal Chase
Payroll Services ....Castellana Services, Inc.
Production Photographer ....Joan Marcus
Press Representative Staff ....Leslie Baden,
                    Michelle Bergmann,
                    Nicole Capatasto, Tom D'Ambrosio,
                    Alyssa Hart, Bethany Larsen,
                    Matt Ross, Wayne Wolfe
Banking ....JPMorgan Chase Bank/
                                Salvatore Romano
Insurance ....Reiff & Associates, LLC/
                        Dennis Reiff, Regina Newsome
Physical Therapy ....PhysioArts/
                                Jennifer Green
Orthopedist ....Dr. Weiss, MD
Children's Tutoring ....On Location Education
Children's Tutor ....Muriel Kester
Children's Guardian ....Felicia Velasco
Group Sales ....Telecharge Group Sales
Merchandise ....Araca Merchandise
Information Management
    Services ....Marion Finkler Taylor
Travel Services ....Tzell Travel/Andi Henig
Theatre Displays ....King Displays, Inc.

CREDITS

Scenery by Hudson Scenic and Showman Fabrication.
Automation by Hudson Scenic. Projection equipment by
Scharff Weisberg, Inc. Souvenir merchandise designed and
created by The Araca Group. Costumes by Arel Studios,
Barbara Matera, Ltd., Baltogs Dancewear, Carelli Costumes,
Giliberto Designs, Inc., Katrina Patterns, Inc., Shafton, Inc.,
Tricorne, Inc. Millinery by Carelli Costumes. Custom
knitwear by Thea Eschliman. Custom footwear by LaDuca
Shoes, Rodney Gordon, Inc., Worldtone Dance. Ice skates
by Klingbeil Shoe Labs, Inc. Custom fabric printing by
First2Print. Custom fabric dyeing and painting by Eric
Winterling, Inc., Jeff Fender. Fur by Fur & Furgery, Inc.
Eyewear by Dr. Wayne Goldberg. Undergarments and
hosiery provided by Bra*Tenders, On Stage Dancewear.
Lighting equipment from Production Resource Group.
Sound equipment from Production Resource Group. Car
service by IBA Limousine.

To learn more about the production, please visit
ELFMUSICAL.com

Rehearsed at New 42nd Street Studios

🔊 JUJAMCYN THEATERS

JORDAN ROTH
President

PAUL LIBIN   **JACK VIERTEL**
Executive Vice President   Senior Vice President
MEREDITH VILLATORE   **JENNIFER HERSHEY**
Chief Financial Officer   Vice President,
                                Building Operations

MICAH HOLLINGWORTH   **HAL GOLDBERG**
Vice President,   Vice President,
Company Operations   Theatre Operations

Staff for the Al Hirschfeld Theatre

Manager ....Albert T. Kim
Associate Manager ....Anah Jyoti Klate
Treasurer ....Carmine La Mendola
Carpenter ....Joseph J. Maher, Jr.
Propertyman ....Sal Sclafani
Electrician ....Michele Gutierrez
Engineer ....Brian DiNapoli

George Wendt
as Santa Claus

Photo by Joan Marcus

Elf
Scrapbook

Photos courtesy Matthew Gumley

1. The leads ring the closing bell at the New York Stock Exchange.
2. *Yearbook* correspondent Matthew Gumley hoists something sweet with Katherine McNamara of *A Little Night Music*.
3. (L-R): Leading man Sebastian Arcelus with Gumley.
4. Celebrity guest Joan Rivers with Gumley.

Correspondent: Matthew Gumley, "Michael"

Memorable Opening Night Letter: One I received could actually be considered an opening night gift, but in letter form. A member of our cast, Michael McCormick, wrote a memo to everyone in the cast as his character, Mr. Greenway. The letter was an official notice of termination from the Greenway Press Offices. The pink slip included a very wonderful note with beautiful words and was very touching but at the end, it said, "That being said, the above still stands. You're fired." I decided to make hand-crafted elf boots with a wooden rose sticking out the top for everyone in the company. The rose had a ribbon on it that said "*Elf* Opening Night 11/14/10."

Memorable Opening Night Gift: A very special opening night gift was from our director, Casey Nicholaw. It was the brand new Nerf gun, the Stampede. My alternate, Matthew Schechter, and I went around the theatre playing with it all night.

Most Exciting Celebrity Vistor: Probably Joan Rivers, who absolutely loved the show! My mother is a huge fan so it was funny when I introduced her to Joan.

Who Got the Gypsy Robe: Lisa Gajda.

"Carols for a Cure" Song: Sebastian Arcelus and Amy Spanger performed "The First Noel."

Most Roles in This Show: Matt Loehr, coming in at a whopping six!

Most Shows in Their Career: Lisa Gajda.

Special Backstage Ritual: At every show's intermission my wrangler, Felicia Velasco and I perform "Team Tango." This is when I change out of my white undershirt and into my Superman undershirt, while wearing my mic! I take off and put on my shirts while Felicia holds my mic pack and feeds it through the collars of my shirts while I put them on. It is literally a tango, how we have to finagle the pack!

Favorite Moment During the Show: It has got to be before my song with Beth Leavel when we test each other's reflexes and see how hard our feet can kick our coffee table set piece before it goes on stage…it is fun and kind of naughty… good thing Santa likes me!

Favorite In-Theatre Meeting Place: The cast's favorite has got to be the upper lobby. We always meet there for notes and other social gatherings.

Off-Site Hangout: My personal favorite has got to be the Westway Diner between 43rd and 44th Street on Ninth Avenue. I go there all the time! They are open seven days a week, 24 hours a day. Perfect for a working actor's schedule.

Favorite Snack Food: My top-ranking snack food is chocolate. All the way, baby!

Favorite Therapy: The best has got to be Dr. Kessler's Vapors. Dr. K is the theatre's local fix-'em-up guru. He can make the show go on!

Most Memorable Ad-Lib: This has got to be when our Buddy the Elf, Sebastian Arcelus, was performing a scene with our Jovie, Amy Spanger. They were doing what could be considered the quietest scene in the show, when a light broke and sounded, literally, as loud as a jackhammer. They tried to do the scene over the deafening noise but it really didn't work, so Sebastian says, "Why is there so much construction in New York City?" They eventually solved the problem and continued with the scene.

Memorable Press Encounter: At the New York Stock Exchange when Sebastian, Amy, Beth, and I got to ring the closing bell on the day of the 87th Annual Christmas Tree Lighting.

Fastest Costume Change: The fastest I can think of belongs to some of our ensemble members who quickly switch from their New York street clothes to their office attire in about 15 to 20 seconds. Yikes!!

Who Wore the Heaviest/Hottest Costume: George Wendt in the second act when he is in his full Santa Claus suit and coat.

Who Wore the Least: I probably wear the lightest costume in the show in the second act. I wear jeans, a light dress shirt and an undershirt. It's so nice.

Catchphrase Only the Company Would Recognize: "Let's take it from snowflake girls!" This was a cue given by Casey Nicholaw, our director.

Orchestra Member Who Plays the Most Instruments: Charlie Descarfino. He plays the glockenspiel, the xylophone, the tympani, the chimes, the conga, the bell tree, the triangle (go triangle! It's the one instrument I have mastered…), the flexatone, and the vibraphone.

Orchestra Member Who Played the Most Consecutive Performances Without a Sub: Mark Mitchell, our pianist. Way to go, Mark!

Memorable Directorial Note: Casey Nicholaw told us, "Pick up the pace. The pace is sooooo sloooow…."

Company In-Joke: "Is Michael Mandell here?" Michael is a very funny cast member who has a voice that can carry quite far. You always know when he is in the building.

Company Legend: We are our own company legends.

Nicknames: My favorite is for Matthew Schechter. We call him "Schex mix" or "Schex party mix."

Embarrassing Moment: It came in the song "Nobody Cares about Santa Claus" in the kick line. Matt Loehr accidentally tore off his wig when the fake Santas tear off their hats and their beards and throw them on the ground. All he had left was his wig cap! He recovered his wig and put it back on, but it was funny to see a bald Santa!

Coolest Thing About Being in This Show: When you hear a lone child laugh at something that they think is funny. It's really a rewarding feeling.

Also: One other memorable moment I can think of was when a few cast members from the show went and sang Christmas carols with children from the Ronald McDonald House. It was so amazing to be able to put such a big smile on so many faces. Not to mention I got my butt whooped in ping pong by one of the children there.

Elling
SCRAPBOOK

Rocco Landesman,
Dodger Theatricals
Producer

Des McAnuff,
Dodger Theatricals
Producer

Bob Boyett
Producer

Opening night curtain call (L-R):
Richard Easton, Denis O'Hare,
Brendan Fraser, Jennifer Coolidge
and Jeremy Shamos.

Photo by Joseph Marzullo/WENN

STAFF FOR *ELLING*

GENERAL MANAGEMENT
STUART THOMPSON PRODUCTIONS
Stuart Thompson   Marshall B. Purdy   David Turner

Cassidy Briggs   Megan Curren   Kevin Emrick
Geo Karapetyan   Brittany Levasseur
Christopher Taggart

COMPANY MANAGER
Adam J. Miller

PRODUCTION MANAGEMENT
AURORA PRODUCTIONS INC.
Gene O'Donovan   W. Benjamin Heller II
Stephanie Sherline   Jarid Sumner   Liza Luxenberg
Ryan Stanisz   Jason Margolis   Melissa Mazdra

PRESS REPRESENTATIVE
BONEAU/BRYAN-BROWN
Adrian Bryan-Brown   Susanne Tighe   Kelly Guiod

Production Stage Manager ....Barclay Stiff
Stage Manager ....Kelly Beaulieu
Assistant Director ....Alexander Greenfield
Associate Scenic Designer ....Christine Peters
Associate Costume Designers ....Nicole Moody,
Ryan Park
Associate Lighting Designer ....Justin Partier
Associate Sound Designer ....David Sanderson
Production Carpenter ....Mike Martinez
Production Electrician ....Dan Coey
Production Sound Engineer ....Phil Lojo/
Paul Delcioppo
Electrician ....Stephen Allain
Properties Coordinator ....Pete Sarafin
Wardrobe Supervisor ....Kathleen Gallagher
Hair Supervisor ....Lisa Weiss
Dressers ....Paul Riner, Katt Masterson
Makeup Consultants.................Dick Page, Ashley Ryan
Production Assistant ....Michael Padden
General Management Interns ....Andrew Lowy,
Diana Merek

AMBASSADOR THEATRE GROUP
Life President ....Sir Eddie Kulukundis OBE
Executive Chairman ....Greg Dyke
Joint Chief Executive &
Creative Director ....Howard Panter

Joint Chief Executive ....Rosemary Squire OBE
Operations & Building
Development Director ....David Blyth
Financial & Commercial Director ....Helen Enwright
Executive Director ....Michael Lynas
Business Affairs Director ....Peter Kavanagh
Director ....Richard Lenane
Director ....Chris Graham
Director ....Simon Davidson
Director ....Peter Beckwith OBE
Director ....Bill Benjamin
Chief Executive Officer (New York) ....David Lazar
Producer (London) ....Tali Pelman
Production Associate ....Mike Forte
Creative Assistant (London) ....Sarah Gimblett
Production Assistant ....Alex Bisker

Banking ....City National Bank/Michele Gibbons
Payroll ....Castellana Services, Inc.
Accountant ....Fried & Kowgios CPA's LLP/
Robert Fried, CPA
Controller ....Joe Kubala
Insurance ....DeWitt Stern Group
Legal
Counsel .....Franklin, Weinrib, Rudell & Vassallo, PC/
Elliot Brown Esq., Dan Wasser Esq.
Advertising...SpotCo/
Drew Hodges, Jim Edwards,
Tom Greenwald, Kyle Hall, Cory Spinney
Marketing/Partnerships ....SpotCo/
Nick Pramik, Kristen Rathbun
Website/Interactive Marketing ....SpotCo/
Sara Fitzpatrick, Matt Wilstein
Key Art Design ....Art Machine
Production Photographer ....Joan Marcus
Theatre Displays ....King Displays, Inc.
Transportation ....IBA Limousines,
Attitude Limousines Inc.

CREDITS
Scenery constructed by Hudson Scenic Studios, Inc.,
Yonkers, NY. Furniture by John O'Donovan. Prop house by
Craig Grigg. Lighting equipment provided by PRG
Lighting, North Bergen, NJ. Sound equipment provided by
Masque Sound, East Rutherford, NJ. Costumes by EuroCo
Costumes, Brian Hemesath, Arnold Levine and Alice Bee.
Hosiery and undergarments by Bra*Tenders. Makeup
provided by M•A•C. Coffee makers and K-cups generously
provided by Keurig. Water sponsorship by VOSS Artesian
Water from Norway. Pizza by John's Pizzeria. Rehearsed at

Lincoln Center Institute and BalletTech Studios. Special
thanks to Jerrod, Alecia and Knox Pace. Special thanks to
Trond Bækken and Trine Nikolaisen of the New York
Norwegian Consulate General.

Souvenir merchandise designed and created by
The Araca Group.

www.EllingOnBroadway.com

Follow *Elling*
On Twitter: http://Twitter.com@EllingBroadway
On Facebook:
http://www.facebook.com/EllingOnBroadway

 THE SHUBERT ORGANIZATION, INC.
Board of Directors

Philip J. Smith	**Robert E. Wankel**
Chairman	President
Wyche Fowler, Jr.	**Lee J. Seidler**
Michael I. Sovern	**Stuart Subotnick**

Elliot Greene	**David Andrews**
Chief Financial Officer	Senior Vice President Shubert Ticketing
Juan Calvo	**John Darby**
Vice President – Finance	Vice President – Facilities
Peter Entin	**Charles Flateman**
Vice President – Theatre Operations	Vice President – Marketing
Anthony LaMattina	**Brian Mahoney**
Vice President – Audit & Production Finance	Vice President – Ticket Sales

D.S. Moynihan
Vice President – Creative Projects

Staff for The Ethel Barrymore
House Manager ....Dan Landon

Fela!

First Preview: October 19, 2009. Opened: November 23, 2009.
Closed January 2, 2011 after 34 Previews and 463 Performances.

This show chronicles the short, intense, musical and political life of real-life activist Fela Anikulapo-Kuti and his fight for freedom from oppression in his native Nigeria during the 1960s and 1970s. The score consists mainly of Kuti's own "Afrobeat" hits.

CAST

Fela Anikulapo-Kuti ....KEVIN MAMBO,
SAHR NGAUJAH

Funmilayo Anikulapo-Kuti,
   his mother ....PATTI LaBELLE

Sandra Isadore ....SAYCON SENGBLOH

Ismael, Geraldo Piño, Orisha,
   Ensemble ....ISMAEL KOUYATÉ

J.K. Braimah (Tap Dancer), Egungun,
   Ensemble ....GELAN LAMBERT

Jembe Drummer ....TALU GREEN

Ensemble .COREY BAKER, HETTIE BARNHILL,
LAUREN DE VEAUX,
NICOLE CHANTAL DE WEEVER*,
ELASEA DOUGLAS,
RUJEKO DUMBUTSHENA,
CATHERINE FOSTER, TALU GREEN,
SHANEEKA HARRELL,
ABENA KOOMSON, GELAN LAMBERT,
SHAKIRA MARSHALL, AFI MCCLENDON,
ADESOLA OSAKALUMI, JEFFREY PAGE,
DANIEL SOTO, IRIS WILSON,
AIMEE GRAHAM WODOBODE

Continued on next page

🎭 EUGENE O'NEILL THEATRE
A JUJAMCYN THEATRE

JORDAN ROTH
President

PAUL LIBIN
Producing Director

JACK VIERTEL
Creative Director

SHAWN "JAY-Z" CARTER AND WILL & JADA PINKETT SMITH
RUTH & STEPHEN HENDEL, ROY GABAY, SONY PICTURES ENTERTAINMENT, EDWARD TYLER NAHEM, SLAVA SMOLOKOWSKI
CHIP MEYRELLES/KEN GREINER, DOUGLAS G. SMITH, STEVE SEMLITZ/CATHY GLASER
DARYL ROTH/TRUE LOVE PRODUCTIONS, SUSAN DIETZ/M. SWINSKY/J. DEITCH, KNITTING FACTORY ENTERTAINMENT

PRESENT

FELA!

BOOK
JIM LEWIS & BILL T. JONES

MUSIC AND LYRICS
FELA ANIKULAPO-KUTI

ADDITIONAL LYRICS BY
JIM LEWIS

ADDITIONAL MUSIC BY
AARON JOHNSON & JORDAN McLEAN

BASED ON THE LIFE OF
FELA ANIKULAPO-KUTI

CONCEIVED BY
BILL T. JONES, JIM LEWIS & STEPHEN HENDEL

SAHR NGAUJAH   **KEVIN MAMBO**

SAYCON SENGBLOH

COREY BAKER, HETTIE VYRINE BARNHILL, LAUREN DE VEAUX, NICOLE CHANTAL DEWEEVER, ELASEA DOUGLAS, RUJEKO DUMBUTSHENA,
CATHERINE FOSTER, RASAAN-ELIJAH "TALU" GREEN, SHANEEKA HARRELL, CHANON JUDSON, ABENA KOOMSON, ISMAEL KOUYATÉ, GELAN LAMBERT,
FARAI MALIANGA, SHAKIRA MARSHALL, AFI McCLENDON, ADESOLA OSAKALUMI, JEFFREY PAGE, ONEIKA PHILLIPS, JUSTIN PRESCOTT,
RYAN H. RANKINE, DANIEL SOTO, JILL M. VALLERY, IRIS WILSON, J.L. WILLIAMS, AIMEE GRAHAM WODOBODE

AND

PATTI LaBELLE

SCENIC & COSTUME DESIGNER	LIGHTING DESIGNER	SOUND DESIGNER	PROJECTION DESIGNER
MARINA DRAGHICI	ROBERT WIERZEL	ROBERT KAPLOWITZ	PETER NIGRINI

WIG, HAIR & MAKEUP DESIGNER	PRODUCTION SUPERVISOR	CASTING
COOKIE JORDAN	LINDA MARVEL	MUNGIOLI THEATRICALS ARNOLD J. MUNGIOLI, CSA

PRESS REPRESENTATIVE	ADVERTISING & NEW MEDIA SERVICES	MARKETING
RICHARD KORNBERG & ASSOCIATES	ART MEETS COMMERCE	HHC MARKETING WALK TALL GIRL PRODUCTIONS

TECHNICAL SUPERVISION	ASSOCIATE TECHNICAL SUPERVISION	GENERAL MANAGER
HUDSON THEATRICAL ASSOCIATES	JAY JANICKI JOHN TIGGELOVEN	ROY GABAY

MUSIC DIRECTION & SUPERVISION/ORCHESTRATIONS/ARRANGEMENTS	MUSIC COORDINATOR	ASSOCIATE PRODUCER
AARON JOHNSON	MICHAEL KELLER	AHMIR "QUESTLOVE" THOMPSON

ASSOCIATE MUSICAL DIRECTOR & ARRANGER	MUSIC CONSULTANT	ASSOCIATE DIRECTOR	ASSOCIATE CHOREOGRAPHER
JORDAN McLEAN	ANTIBALAS	NIEGEL SMITH	MAIJA GARCIA

DIRECTED AND CHOREOGRAPHED BY
BILL T. JONES

10/1/10

Sahr Ngaujah as Fela Kuti with the Ensemble

Photo by Monique Carboni

Fela!

MUSICAL NUMBERS

ACT 1

Welcome Na De Shrine
"Everything Scatter" ....Fela and Company

B.I.D. (Breaking It Down)
"Iba Orisa": Traditional Yoruba chant...................Ismael, Fela and Company
Hymn by Reverend J.J. Ransome-Kuti ....Fela, Company and Band
"Medzi Medzi" by E.T. Mensah ....Company and Band
"Mr. Syms" by John Coltrane ....Company and Band
"Manteca" by Chano Pozo ....Company and Band
"I Got the Feeling" by James Brown...................Ismael and Company

Underground Spiritual Game (The Clock)
"Originality/Yellow Fever" ....Fela and Company

Trouble
"Trouble Sleep" ....Fela, Funmilayo and Company
"Teacher Don't Teach Me Nonsense" ....Fela, Funmilayo and Company

Black President
"Lover"* ....Fela and Sandra
"Upside Down"..Fela, Sandra and Company
"Expensive Shit" ....Fela and Company
"Pipeline"*/"I.T.T. (International Thief Thief)" ....Fela and Company
"Kere Kay" ....Fela and Company

ACT 2

Water
"Water No Get Enemy" ....Fela, Sandra and Company
"Egbe Mio" ....Fela, Queens and Funmilayo

The Game
"Zombie" ....Fela and Company
"Trouble Sleep" (reprise) ....Fela, Funmilayo and Queens

Wedding
"Na Poi" ....Fela and Queens

The Storming of Kalakuta
"Sorrow Tears and Blood" ....Fela and Company

Dance of the Orisas
"Iba Orisa/Shakara" ....Company and Band
"Rain"** ....Funmilayo and Company

B.Y.O.C. (Bring Your Own Coffin)
"Coffin for Head of State" ....Fela and Company
"Kere Kay" (reprise) ....Fela and Company

*"Lover" and "Pipeline," English lyrics by Jim Lewis
***"Rain" music by Aaron Johnson and Jordan McLean, lyrics by Bill T. Jones and Jim Lewis

Cast Continued

SWINGS
CHANON JUDSON, FARAI M. MALIANGA, ONEIKA PHILLIPS*, JUSTIN PRESCOTT, RYAN H. RANKINE, JILL M. VALLERY, J.L. WILLIAMS

DANCE CAPTAINS
JILL M. VALLERY, DANIEL SOTO

UNDERSTUDIES
For Fela Anikulapo-Kuti:
ADESOLA OSAKALUMI
For Funmilayo:
ABENA KOOMSON, ONEIKA PHILLIPS
For Sandra:
ELASEA DOUGLAS, ONEIKA PHILLIPS

*Nicole Chantal De Weever and Oneika Phillips are appearing with the permission of Actors' Equity Association.

SETTING
Fela's final concert at the Shrine in Lagos, Nigeria
The Summer of 1978, six months after the death of Funmilayo, Fela's mother

BAND
Conductor/Trombone/Keyboard:
AARON JOHNSON
Assistant Conductor/Drums/Percussion:
GREG GONZALEZ
Trumpet:
JORDAN McLEAN
Bass/Keyboards/Percussion:
JEREMY WILMS
Guitar/Percussion:
OREN BLOEDOW
Guitar/Percussion:
RICARDO QUINONES
Percussion:
YOSHIHIRO TAKEMASA
Baritone Saxophone/Percussion:
ALEX HARDING
Tenor Saxophone/Percussion/
Featured Saxophone Soloist:
STUART BOGIE
Percussion:
DYLAN FUSILLO
Music Coordinator:
MICHAEL KELLER

Kevin Mambo as Fela Kuti

Photo by Monique Carboni

Fela!

Sahr Ngaujah
Fela Anikulapo-Kuti

Kevin Mambo
Fela Anikulapo-Kuti

Patti LaBelle
Funmilayo Anikulapo-Kuti

Saycon Sengbloh
Sandra Isadore

Corey Baker
Ensemble

Hettie Vyrine Barnhill
Ensemble

Lauren De Veaux
Ensemble

Nicole Chantal De Weever
Ensemble

Elasea Douglas
Ensemble

Rujeko Dumbutshena
Ensemble

Catherine Foster
Ensemble

Rasaan-Elijah "Talu" Green
Ensemble

Shaneeka Harrell
Ensemble

Chanon Judson
Swing

Abena Koomson
Vocal Captain, Ensemble

Ismael Kouyaté
Ensemble

Gelan Lambert
Ensemble

Farai Malianga
Swing

Shakira Marshall
Ensemble

Afi McClendon
Ensemble

Adesola Osakalumi
Ensemble

Jeffrey Page
Ensemble

Oneika Phillips
Swing

Justin Prescott
Swing

Ryan H. Rankine
Swing

Daniel Soto
Ensemble/Assistant Dance Captain

Jill M. Vallery
Swing/ Dance Captain

Iris Wilson
Ensemble

J.L. Williams
Swing

Aimee Graham Wodobode
Ensemble

Fela Anikulapo-Kuti
Music/Lyrics

Bill T. Jones
Conceiver/Director/ Choreographer/ Book Writer

Jim Lewis
Conceiver/ Book Writer/ Additional Lyrics

Marina Draghici
Set & Costume Design

Robert Wierzel
Lighting Designer

Fela!

Robert Kaplowitz
Sound Design

Peter Nigrini
Projection Design

Neil A. Mazzella/
Hudson Theatrical
Associates
*Technical
Supervision*

Aaron Johnson
Musical Director

Jordan McLean
*Associate Musical
Director*

Michael Keller
Music Contractor

Maija Garcia
*Associate
Choreographer*

Arnold Mungioli,
Mungioli Theatricals,
Inc.
Casting

Richard Kornberg &
Associates
*Press
Representative*

Shawn "Jay-Z"
Carter
Producer

Will Smith
Producer

Jada Pinkett Smith
Producer

Ruth Hendel
Producer

Roy Gabay
*Producer/
General Manager*

Edward Tyler Nahem
Producer

Chip Meyrelles
Producer

Ken Greiner
Producer

Daryl Roth
Producer

Jeanne Donovan
Fisher/
True Love
Productions
Producer

Laurie Gilmore/
True Love
Productions
Producer

Susan Dietz
Producer

Mort Swinsky
Producer

Lillias White
*Funmilayo
Anikulapo-Kuti*

BOX OFFICE
(L-R): Harry Keith Stephenson, Stan Shaffer

MANAGEMENT
(L-R): Jon Goldman (PSM), Linda Marvel (SM), Hilary Austin (ASM)

Fela!

DOORMAN
Emir Hodzic

HAIR
(L-R): Heather Wright, Anna Hoffmann

FRONT OF HOUSE STAFF
Front Row (L-R): Lorraine Wheeler, Verna Hobson, Saime Hodzic, Bruce Lucoff

Second Row (L-R): Pamela Martin, Sandra Palmer, Mili Vela, Heather Gilles

Third Row (L-R): Giovanni Monserrate, Scott Rippe, Dorothy Lennon, Byron Vargas

Back Row (L-R): Hal Goldberg, Russ Ramsey, Elise Gainer, Ray Segal

CREW
Front Row (L-R): Damian Caza-Cleypool, Kevin Maher, Susie Ghebresillassie, Sue Stepnik, Heather Wright, Anna Hoffmann, Linda Marvel, Sue Cerceo, Reid Hall, Hilary Austin

Back Row (L-R): Jordan Gable, James Gardener, Mary Chesterman, Guy Patria, Shannon Slayton, Mary McGregor, Emile LaFargue, Christopher Beck, Ken Keneally, Jon Goldman

A Free Man of Color

First Preview: October 23, 2010. Opened: November 18, 2010.
Closed January 9, 2011 after 29 Previews and 61 Performances.

PLAYBILL

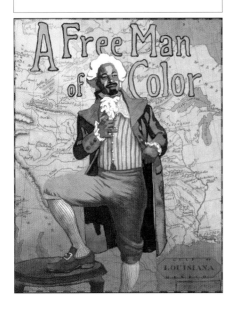

This historical comedy mixes fact and fiction in telling the adventures of a mixed-race rake in the high-society salons and bedrooms of early 19th century New Orleans.

CAST

Jacques Cornet	JEFFREY WRIGHT
Cupidon Murmur, his slave	MOS
Zeus-Marie Pincepousse, his half-brother	REG ROGERS
Margery Jolicoeur, a country wife	NICOLE BEHARIE

Citizens of New Orleans:

Dr. Toubib	JOSEPH MARCELL
Intendante Juan Ventura Morales	TRINEY SANDOVAL
Doña Smeralda, his wife	JUSTINA MACHADO
Orphee and Leda, their slaves	ESAU PRITCHETT TEYONAH PARRIS
Doña Athene, Jacques' wife	SARA GETTELFINGER
Remy Dorilante	ARNIE BURTON
Mme. Dorilante, his wife	TEYONAH PARRIS
Jonathan Sparks	BRIAN REDDY
Mrs. Sparks, his wife	ROSAL COLÓN
Lord Harcourt	ROBERT STANTON
Lady Harcourt, his wife	WENDY RICH STETSON
Alcibiade	DAVID EMERSON TONEY
Pythagore	NICK MENNELL
Mercure	PETER BARTLETT
Mme. Mandragola	VEANNE COX

Continued on next page

LINCOLN CENTER THEATER AT THE VIVIAN BEAUMONT

A Free Man of Color

A New Play by
John Guare

With deep bows to Ariadne, Aphra Behn, Napoleon Bonaparte, Barbara Bush,
Lady Byron, Lord Byron, Calderón de la Barca, Susannah Centlivre,
William Congreve, George Etherege, Euripides, Thomas Jefferson, Ben Jonson,
Lamartine, John Milton, Molière, Ossian, Lorenzo da Ponte, Thomas Shadwell,
William Shakespeare, Virgil, John Wilmot, Second Earl of Rochester
And
William Wycherley

with (in alphabetical order)

Yao Ababio   Peter Bartlett   Nicole Beharie   Arnie Burton   Rosal Colón
Veanne Cox   Paul Dano   Sara Gettelfinger   Derric Harris   Justina Machado
Joseph Marcell   John McMartin   Nick Mennell   Mos   Teyonah Parris
Postell Pringle   Esau Pritchett   Brian Reddy   Reg Rogers
Triney Sandoval   Robert Stanton   Wendy Rich Stetson   Jerome Stigler
Senfuab Stoney   David Emerson Toney   Jeffrey Wright

Sets	Costumes	Lighting
David Rockwell	**Ann Hould-Ward**	**Jules Fisher & Peggy Eisenhauer**

Original Music	Sound	Choreography
Jeanine Tesori	**Scott Stauffer**	**Hope Clarke**

Stage Manager	Casting	General Press Agent
Gwendolyn M. Gilliam	**Daniel Swee**	**Philip Rinaldi**

General Manager	Production Manager	Director of Development	Director of Marketing
Adam Siegel	**Jeff Hamlin**	**Hattie K. Jutagir**	**Linda Mason Ross**

Directed by
George C. Wolfe

Originally commissioned by The Public Theater
George C. Wolfe, Producer; Mara Manus, Executive Director

A FREE MAN OF COLOR is sponsored by The National Actors Theatre Foundation.

This play is a recipient of an "Edgerton Foundation New American Plays" award.

Special thanks to The Harold and Mimi Steinberg Charitable Trust
for supporting new American plays at LCT.

American Airlines is the Official Airline of Lincoln Center Theater.

LCT wishes to express its appreciation to Theatre Development Fund for its support of this production.

11/18/10

(L-R): Robert Stanton, Arnie Burton, Brian Reddy, Reg Rogers, Mos and Jeffrey Wright

A Free Man of Color

UNDERSTUDIES

For Jacques Cornet:
HOWARD W. OVERSHOWN
For Cupidon Murmur:
POSTELL PRINGLE
For Margery Jolicoeur:
TEYONAH PARRIS
For Dr. Toubib:
DAVID EMERSON TONEY
For Toussaint Louverture:
ESAU PRITCHETT
For Juan Ventura Morales, Remy Dorilante,
Jonathan Sparks, Napoleon Bonaparte,
Major Walter Reed:
KYLE FABEL
For Doña Smeralda, Josephine:
ROSAL COLÓN
For Orphee, Alcibiade:
DERRIC HARRIS
For Leda, Melpomene, Mme. Dorilante:
ASHLEY BRYANT
For Doña Athene, Mrs. Sparks, Euterpe, Calliope,
Terpsichore, The Infanta, Lady Harcourt:
STEPHANIE DiMAGGIO
For Lord Harcourt, Pythagore, Meriwether Lewis,
James Monroe, General LeClerc,
King Carlos Cuarto, Georges Feydeau,
LeClerc's Captain:
DAVID GRAHAM JONES
For Mercure, Count Achille Creux,
Thomas Jefferson:
DAVID MANIS
For Mme. Mandragola, Doña Polissena,
Robert Livingston:
WENDY RICH STETSON

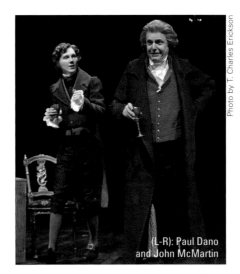

(L-R): Paul Dano and John McMartin

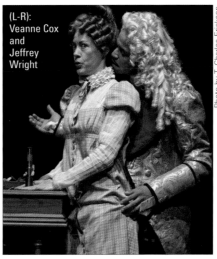

(L-R): Veanne Cox and Jeffrey Wright

FRONT OF HOUSE STAFF

Front Row (L-R): Lydia Tchornobai, Donna Zurich, Jessica Clough, Ann Danilovics, Barbara Hart, Jeff Goldstein, Margareta Shakeridge, Mim Pollock (Chief Usher)
Middle Row (L-R): Eleanore Rooks, Mildred Terrero, Nick Andors, Beatrice Gilliard, Billie Stewart, Clinton Kennedy, Judith Fanelli, Ruby Jaggernauth

Back Row (L-R): Francesco Visconti, Farida Asencio, Margie Blair, Security Officer Douglas Charles

Cast Continued

Her girls:
Melpomene ....TEYONAH PARRIS
Euterpe ....WENDY RICH STETSON
Calliope ....SARA GETTELFINGER
Terpsichore ....ROSAL COLÓN

Citizens of Sante Domingue:
Count Achille Creux ....PETER BARTLETT
Doña Polissena, his wife, a scientist .VEANNE COX
Toussaint Louverture, Haitian revolutionary ....MOS

The Americans:
Thomas Jefferson ....JOHN McMARTIN
Meriwether Lewis, his secretary ....PAUL DANO
Robert Livingston,
   Minister to France..................VEANNE COX
James Monroe, future president ...ARNIE BURTON
Major Walter Reed ....BRIAN REDDY

The French:
Napoleon Bonaparte ....TRINEY SANDOVAL
Josephine, his wife............JUSTINA MACHADO
Tallyrand, his foreign minister ....REG ROGERS
General LeClerc,
   his brother-in-law ....NICK MENNELL
LeClerc's Captain ....ROBERT STANTON
Georges Feydeau, playwright .ROBERT STANTON

The Spanish:
King Carlos Cuarto ....NICK MENNELL
The Infanta ....ROSAL COLÓN

Slaves of New Orleans ....YAO ABABIO
                      DERRIC HARRIS
                      POSTELL PRINGLE
                      JEROME STIGLER
                      SENFUAB STONEY

Assistant Stage Manager .....KEVIN BERTOLACCI

TIME
1801-1806

PLACE
New Orleans, and other locations
in Europe and America

In the New World at this time, there was a
vocabulary of more than 100 terms for people of
mixed-race, extending back seven generations in an
individual's heritage.
For example:
"pure" white and "pure" black = mulatto
mulatto and black = sambo
mulatto and white = quadroon
a mamelouc was "113 of 120 parts white," etc.

A Free Man of Color

Yao Ababio
Slave

Peter Bartlett
*Count Achille Creux,
Mercure*

Nicole Beharie
Margery Jolicoeur

Arnie Burton
*Remy Dorilante,
James Monroe*

Rosal Colón
*Mrs. Sparks,
Terpsichore,
The Infanta*

Veanne Cox
*Doña Polissena,
Mme. Mandragola,
Robert Livingston*

Paul Dano
Meriwether Lewis

Sara Gettelfinger
*Doña Athenee,
Calliope*

Derric Harris
Slave

Justina Machado
*Doña Smeralda,
Josephine*

Joseph Marcell
Dr. Toubib

John McMartin
Thomas Jefferson

Nick Mennell
*Jacques Pythagore,
General LeClerc,
King Carlos Cuarto*

Mos
*Cupidon Murmur,
Toussaint Louverture*

Teyonah Parris
*Leda,
Mme. Dorilante,
Melpomene*

Postell Pringle
Slave

Esau Pritchett
Orphee

Brian Reddy
*Jonathan Sparks,
Major Walter Reed*

Reg Rogers
*Zeus-Marie
Pincepousse,
Talleyrand*

Triney Sandoval
*Juan Ventura
Morales,
Napoleon Bonaparte*

Robert Stanton
*Lord Harcourt,
LeClerc's Captain,
Georges Feydeau*

Wendy Rich Stetson
*Lady Harcourt,
Euterpe*

Jerome Stigler
Slave

Senfuab Stoney
Slave

David Emerson Toney
Achille Alcibiade

Jeffrey Wright
Jacques Cornet

Ashley Bryant
Understudy

Stephanie DiMaggio
Understudy

Kyle Fabel
Understudy

David Graham Jones
Understudy

David Manis
Understudy

Howard W.
Overshown
Understudy

John Guare
Playwright

George C. Wolfe
Director

David Rockwell
Sets

A Free Man of Color

Ann Hould-Ward
Costumes

Jules Fisher & Peggy Eisenhauer
Lighting

Jeanine Tesori
Original Music

Hope Clarke
Choreographer

Paul Huntley
Hair and Wigs

Thomas Schall
Fight Director

André Bishop and Bernard Gersten,
Lincoln Center Theater
Producer

Photos by Brian Mapp

HAIR
(L-R): April Schuller, Carrie Lynn Rohm (Supervisor), Tim Miller, John McNulty, Chelsea Roth

Not pictured: Erin Hicks

WARDROBE
Dressers (L-R): Shannon Koger, Adam Adelman, Rosie Wells, Sarah Rochford, Donna Holland, Melinda Suarez-White, unidentified

Not pictured: Lynn Bowling (Wardrobe Supervisor), Richard Gross (Dresser), Patti Luther (Dresser), James Nadeaux (Dresser)

CREW
Front Row (L-R): Gerard Fortunato (Carpenter), Andrew Belits (Carpenter), Matt Henderson (Carpenter), Ray Skillin (Deck Carpenter), Juan Bustamante (Deck Automation), Joe Pizzuto (Follow Spot Operator), Rudy Wood (Props), John Ross (Props), Adam Smolinski (Deck Sound), Luis Lojo (Elec. Sub.), Bill Burke (Deck Electrician), Matt Altman (Follow Spot)

Back Row (L-R): Jeff Ward (Follow Spot Operator), Greg Cushna (Flyman), John Howie (Carpenter), Bill Nagle (Production Carpenter), Kyle Barrineau (Carpenter), Pat Merryman (Production Electrician), John Weingart (Production Flyman), Charles Rausenberger (Props), Karl Rausenberger (Production Propman), Fred Bredenbeck (Carpenter), Marc Salzberg (Production Soundman), Larry White (Deck Electrician), Bruce Rubin (Electrician/Board Operator), Frank Linn (Electrician/Automation Tech)

Not pictured: Mark Dignam (Props)

A Free Man of Color

ADMINISTRATIVE STAFF

GENERAL MANAGER .... ADAM SIEGEL
  Associate General Manager .... Jessica Niebanck
  General Management Assistant .... Meghan Lantzy
  Facilities Manager .... Alex Mustelier
  Associate Facilities Manager .... Michael Assalone
GENERAL PRESS AGENT .... PHILIP RINALDI
  Press Associates .... Barbara Carroll, Amanda Dekker
PRODUCTION MANAGER .... JEFF HAMLIN
  Associate Production Manager .... Paul Smithyman
DIRECTOR OF
   DEVELOPMENT .... HATTIE K. JUTAGIR
  Associate Director of Development ..... Rachel Norton
  Manager of Special Events and
   LCT Young Angels .... Karin Schall
  Grants Writer .... Neal Brilliant
  Manager, Patron Program .... Sheilaja Rao
  Assistant to the
   Director of Development ...... Raelyn R. Lagerstrom
  Development Associate/Special Events
   & LCT Young Angels .. Jennifer H. Rosenbluth-Stoll
  Development Assistant/
   Individual Giving .... Sydney Rais-Sherman
DIRECTOR OF FINANCE .... DAVID S. BROWN
  Controller .... Susan Knox
  Systems Manager .... Stacy Valentine
  Finance Assistant .... Kristen Parker
DIRECTOR OF MARKETING .LINDA MASON ROSS
  Marketing Associate .... Ashley M. Dunn
  Marketing Assistant .... John Casavant
DIRECTOR OF EDUCATION .... KATI KOERNER
  Associate Director of Education .... Alexandra Lopez
  Assistant to the Executive Producer ..... Barbara Hourigan
  Office Manager .... Brian Hashimoto
  Office Assistant .... Stephen McFarland
  Messenger .... Esau Burgess
  Reception .... Brenden Rogers, Michelle Metcalf

ARTISTIC STAFF

ASSOCIATE DIRECTORS ...... GRACIELA DANIELE,
                   NICHOLAS HYTNER,
                   JACK O'BRIEN,
                   SUSAN STROMAN,
                   DANIEL SULLIVAN
RESIDENT DIRECTOR .... BARTLETT SHER
DRAMATURG and DIRECTOR,
   LCT DIRECTORS LAB .... ANNE CATTANEO
CASTING DIRECTOR .... DANIEL SWEE, CSA
MUSICAL THEATER
   ASSOCIATE PRODUCER .... IRA WEITZMAN
ARTISTIC DIRECTOR/LCT3 .... PAIGE EVANS
  Artistic Administrator .... Julia Judge
  Casting Associate .... Camille Hickman
  Lab Assistant .... Kate Marvin

HOUSE STAFF

HOUSE MANAGER .... RHEBA FLEGELMAN
  Production Carpenter .... William Nagle
  Production Electrician .... Patrick Merryman
  Production Propertyman .... Karl Rausenberger
  Production Flyman .... John Weingart
  House Technician .... Linda Heard

Chief Usher .... M.L. Pollock
Box Office Treasurer .... Fred Bonis
Assistant Treasurer .... Robert A. Belkin

SPECIAL SERVICES

Advertising .... Serino-Coyne/
       Jim Russek, Roger Micone,
       Becca Goland-Van Ryn
Principal Poster Artist .... James McMullan
Poster Artwork for *A Free Man of Color* ... James McMullan
Counsel .... Peter L. Felcher, Esq.;
       Charles H. Googe, Esq.;
     and Carol Kaplan, Esq. of
  Paul, Weiss, Rifkind, Wharton & Garrison
Immigration Counsel .... Theodore Ruthizer, Esq.;
       Mark D. Koestler, Esq.
  of Kramer, Levin, Naftalis & Frankel LLP
Labor Counsel .... Michael F. McGahan, Esq.
  of Epstein, Becker & Green, P.C.
Auditor .... Frederick Martens, C.P.A.
      Lutz & Carr, L.L.P.
Insurance .... Jennifer Brown of
      DeWitt Stern Group
Photographer .... T. Charles Erickson
Video Services .... Fresh Produce Productions/
      Frank Basile
Travel .... Tygon Tours
Consulting Architect .... Hugh Hardy,
   H3 Hardy Collaboration Architecture
Construction Manager .... Yorke Construction
Payroll Service .... Castellana Services, Inc.
Merchandising .... Marquee Merchandise, LLC/
      Matt Murphy
Lobby Refreshments .... Sweet Concessions

STAFF FOR *A FREE MAN OF COLOR*

COMPANY
  MANAGER .. JESSICA PERLMETER COCHRANE
Associate Company Manager .... Daniel Hoyos
Assistant Director .... Saheem Ali
Assistant to Mr. Guare .... Stella Powell Jones
Associate Set Designer .... Richard Jaris
Assistant Set Designers .... T.J. Greenway,
      Gaetane Bertol, Ann Bartok,
      Christine Peters, Todd Potter
Set Modelmakers .... Eric Beauzay, Morgan Moore,
    Mike Dereskewicz, Jim Waterhouse
Assistant Costume Designer .... Christopher Vergara

Assistant to Ms. Hould-Ward .... Robin McGee
Assistant Lighting Designer .... Tricia Nichols,
      Dan Ozminkowski
Assistant to the Composer .... Peter Lerman
Assistant Sound Designers .... Benjamin Furiga,
      Bridget O'Connor
Automated Light Programmer .... Timothy F. Rogers
Props .... Scott Laule
Props Assistant .... Julie Sandy
Fight Captain .... Howard W. Overshown
Wardrobe Supervisor .... Lynn Bowling
Dressers .... Adam Adelman, Richard Gross,
     Donna Holland, Peggy Danz Kazdan,
   Shannon Koger, Patti Luther, James Nadeaux,
     Chuck ReCar, Sarah Rochford,
    Melinda Suarez-White, Rosie Wells
Hair Supervisor .... Carrie Lynn Rohm
Hair Assistants .... Erin Hicks, John McNulty,
     Tim Miller, Chelsea Roth,
     April Schuller
Make-up .... Cynthia Demand
Production Assistants .... Cliff Moller, Laura Wilson
Costume Interns .... Caitlyn Raines, Anastasia Armes
SDC Directing Fellow .... Tome Cousin

Projections .... batwin + robin productions

Dialect Coach .... Deborah Hecht

Fight Director .... Thomas Schall

Hair and Wig Design .... Paul Huntley

CREDITS

Scenery and scenic effects built, painted, electrified and automated by Show Motion, Inc., Norwalk, Connecticut. Costumes by EuroCo, Tricorne, Eric Winterling, James Nadeaux, and Barbara Matera. Millinery by Lynn Mackey. Costume crafts by Martin Izquierdo Studios and Arnold S. Levine, Inc. Sound equipment by Masque Sound. Lighting equipment from PRG Lighting. Natural herb cough drops courtesy of Ricola USA, Inc.

Visit www.lct.org

For groups of 20 or more:
Caryl Goldsmith Group Sales
(212) 889-4300

STAGE MANAGEMENT
(L-R): Cliff Moller (Production Assistant), Gwendolyn M. Gilliam (Stage Manager), Laura Wilson (Production Assistant), Kevin Bertolacci (Assistant Stage Manager)

A Free Man of Color

SCRAPBOOK

Correspondent: Gwendolyn M. Gilliam, Stage Manager

Memorable Opening Night Gifts: From John Guare: foie gras. From David Rockwell: A scarf that replicated one of the set pieces

Most Exciting Celebrity Visitors: Cornel West came backstage with Tavis Smiley.

Actor Who Performed the Most Roles in This Show: Veanne (four): Mme. Mandragola, Polissena, Livingston, Nun.

Who Has Done the Most Shows in Their Career: John McMartin, 25 shows.

Special Backstage Ritual: Mos playing his preshow music.

Favorite In-Theatre Gathering Place: The Hair Room.

Favorite Off-Site Hangouts: P.J. Clarke's and Ed's Chowder House.

Favorite Snack Food: Beignets.

Favorite Therapy: Honey, Honey, Honey.

Memorable Ad-Lib: John McMartin's.

What Did You Think of the Web Buzz on Your Show: Unfair. Many of the things that were said were by folks who came in previews while the show was undergoing massive changes.

Fastest Costume Change: Reg Rogers, from Pincepousse into Tallyrand.

Heaviest/Hottest Costume: Triney Sandoval: full Napoleon get-up plus cape with four-foot train.

Who Wore the Least: Triney Sandoval: Napoleon bathtub strategically placed cannon costume.

Company Legends: Jeffrey Wright, Mos, John McMartin.

Nicknames: "Crazy Latins."

Sweethearts Within the Company: What happens at *Free Man* stays at *Free Man*.

Scariest Moment: When Triney Sandoval fell off the stage during a performance.

Coolest Thing About Being in This Show: Working with George C. Wolfe and John Guare.

1. Jeffrey Wright and Mos at the opening night party at Avery Fisher Hall.
2. Playwright John Guare.
3. Director George C. Wolfe with Rosie Perez.
4. Joseph Marcell and Wendy Rich Stetson.
5. Nicole Beharie.
6. John McMartin.

Ghetto Klown
SCRAPBOOK

Correspondent: Micah Frank, Assistant Director

Memorable Opening Night Letter: The cast of *How to Succeed* sent over a letter and it had Daniel Radcliffe's signature on it. I was always roughly the same age as Harry Potter growing up so I was really excited about that. But somebody recently took it from backstage. I'm on a hunt to track it down. I've put up missing posters.

Opening Night Gifts: Fisher Stevens gave these beautiful original movie posters. I got the original subway art of Fellini's *Amarcord*. It's beautiful. And ginormous—it's bigger than me. And John gave these beautiful personalized Murano glass clowns.

Most Exciting Celebrity Visitors: Sting recently saw the show which was pretty awesome. He loved it and was really touched by it. He said some beautiful things to John backstage afterwards. I also got really excited when Howard Schultz (CEO of Starbucks) came. You can't get any bigger than that!

Which Actor Performed the Most Roles in This Show: Tough one. I'm gonna have to go with John Leguizamo. During one performance I counted how many roles he plays—I think it was 37 different characters.

Who Has Done the Most Shows in Their Career: I think Danny Paul (John's dresser) has probably done the most.

Special Backstage Rituals: John gets to the theatre four or five hours early. He usually does some writing, plays solitaire, takes a nap, and relaxes. About two hours before, he begins his warm-up and runs through all the musical sections of the show on the stage. He then roams the hallways talking and doing vocal warm-ups before going on.

Favorite Moment During Each Performance: I love the end of Act I. The moment of silence is chilling. You can see the energy between John and the audience.

Favorite In-Theatre Gathering Place: John's dressing room is pretty poppin'.

Favorite Off-Site Hangouts: John's favorite is Orso. He goes there with his family after every matinee. Fisher holds court at Bar Centrale—he loves it there.

Favorite Snack Food: There always seem to be lots of almonds backstage. I don't know why. There seems to be a bag in every dressing room.

Favorite Therapies: John gets a ridiculous amount of therapy. He gets physical therapy twice a week, neck therapy and vocal therapy once a week, and then performing the show every night is basically therapy in itself.

Memorable Ad-Libs: His best ad-libs are always when he interacts with the audience. The biggest issue is people yelling during the show. People yell all sorts of crazy things at John during the performances. He's feisty with them—he yells back.

Memorable Fan Encounter: A fan jumped onstage during the curtain call and tackled John into the wing. The guy claimed he was John's cousin...which he was not.

1. Display window outside the Lyceum Theatre showing PLAYBILLS from Leguizamo's Broadway shows through the years.
2. Leguizamo takes his curtain call on opening night.
3. (L-R): Lucas Leguizamo, Justine Maurer Leguizamo (whose courtship by Leguizamo is the centerpiece of the show) and Allegra Sky Leguizamo.

Who Wore the Least: Although he is fully clothed the whole show, John is always emotionally naked (rim shot).

Catchphrase Only the Company Would Recognize: "Incendiary."

Memorable Directorial Notes: There's a lot of "mature humor" in the show and so some of the notes are hilarious. An outsider might find them offensive. They say things like: "Level marks, checking emails, and menstrual cycle need to go faster."

Understudy Anecdote: Fish always says that he wants to be John's understudy. I'm pretty sure he isn't kidding.

Embarrassing Moment: We did the show at the La Jolla Playhouse in a 100-seat black box. It was really an intimate experience...maybe too intimate. One night while onstage, John was wearing his pants low (really low) and his boxers ripped.

Coolest Thing About Being in This Show: I met John and Fisher about a year ago—I was their intern while they did the show at the La Jolla Playhouse. I am so appreciative and thankful to both of them for taking a chance on a 19-year-old and giving me this unbelievable opportunity and amazing experience. I would have never believed you in a million years if you had told me that I would be working on Broadway while I was a sophomore in college. It's just surreal. I go to class during the day and the show at night. I can't believe how lucky I am.

Also: Once during tech rehearsal on tour, Fish had to step out to make a phone call. When he came back, we resumed teching but Fisher started freaking out. He was yelling that it was too dark and that he couldn't see anything. The SM and Lighting Designer frantically started raising all the levels. The SM finally looked over at Fish and realized Fisher was still wearing his sunglasses.

High
SCRAPBOOK

1. The marquee of the Booth Theatre.
2. (L-R): Director Rob Ruggiero, Stephen Kunken, Kathleen Turner, Evan Jonigkeit and playwright Matthew Lombardo at SD26 restaurant for the opening night party.

Photos by Joseph Marzullo/WENN

STAFF FOR *HIGH*

GENERAL MANAGER
Leonard Soloway

COMPANY MANAGER
Jennifer Hindman Kemp

GENERAL PRESS REPRESENTATIVE
BONEAU/BRYAN-BROWN
Chris Boneau   Jessica Johnson   Amanda de Souza

CASTING
Pat McCorkle, CSA

PRODUCTION SUPERVISOR
Arthur Siccardi/Patrick Sullivan

Production Stage Manager ....Bess Marie Glorioso
Stage Manager ....Ana M. Garcia
Assistant Director ....Nick Eilerman
Associate Set Design ....Steven C. Kemp
Assistant Set Design ....Thomas George
Set Design Studio Manager ....Sarah Zeitler
Set Design Intern ....Brian Dudkiewicz
Associate Costume Designer ....China Lee
Assistant Lighting Designer ....Keri Thibodeau
Lighting Design Intern ....Jeffrey Small
Associate Sound Designer ....Christopher Cronin
Production Properties Supervisor ....Mike Pilipski
Automation Carpenter........................Chad Hershey
Production Electrician ....Neil McShane
Wardrobe Supervisor ....Jesse Galvin
Dresser....................................Dawn Marcoccia
Legal Counsel ....Cowan, DeBaets, Abrahams &
Sheppard LLP/
Frederick P. Bimbler, Esq.;
David Ashley

Accountant ....Rosenberg, Neuwirth &
Kuchner CPAs/
Mark A. D'Ambrosi, Patricia Pedersen
Advertising & Marketing ....aka/
Elizabeth Furze, Scott A. Moore,
Clint Bond, Jr., Andrew Damer,
Richard Arnold, Adam Jay, Janette Roush,
Erik Alden, Meghan Bartley
Digital & Interactive ....aka Connect/
Terry Goldman, Erin Rech
Production Photographer ....Joan Marcus
Production B-roll ....David Kane
Press Office ....Adrian Bryan-Brown, Chris Boneau,
Jim Byk, Jackie Green, Joe Perrotta,
Matt Polk, Susanne Tighe, Aaron Meier,
Heath Schwartz, Jessica Johnson,
Kelly Guiod, Amy Kass, Emily Meagher,
Christine Olver, Michael Strassheim,
Amanda de Souza, Seena Hodges,
Brandi Cornwell, Linnae Hodzic,
Kevin Jones, Amanda Sales
Banking ....JPMorgan Chase/Alan J. Petrilli
Insurance ....NFP Property & Casualty Services/
Sue Wattenberg
Theatre Displays ....King Displays
Payroll ....CSI/Lance Castellana
Rehearsal Studio ....Ripley-Grier Studios

CREDITS
Scenery by Hudson Scenic Studio, Inc. Lighting equipment from PRG Lighting. Sound equipment from Sound Associates. Video footage by Carr Rundle. Kathleen Turner's shoes by Oliver Moore Bootmakers. Knitwear by Maria Ficalora. Transportation provided by Ready to Roll Transportation.

SPECIAL THANKS
Champe Leary; Carl Zyskowski; Central Optica, Hartford,

CT; Robert Hamelin; Rev. Richard D. Baker at St. Malachy's, Mike Isaacson, Melanie T. Morgan

---

Energy-efficient washer/dryer courtesy of
LG Electronics.

THE SHUBERT ORGANIZATION, INC.
Board of Directors

Philip J. Smith Chairman	**Robert E. Wankel** President
Wyche Fowler, Jr.	**Lee J. Seidler**
Michael I. Sovern	**Stuart Subotnick**

Elliot Greene Chief Financial Officer	**David Andrews** Senior Vice President – Shubert Ticketing
Juan Calvo Vice President – Finance	**John Darby** Vice President – Facilities
Peter Entin Vice President – Theatre Operations	**Charles Flateman** Vice President – Marketing
Anthony LaMattina Vice President – Audit & Production Finance	**Brian Mahoney** Vice President – Ticket Sales

D.S. Moynihan
Vice President – Creative Projects

House Manager ....Laurel Ann Wilson

The House of Blue Leaves

First Preview: April 4, 2011. Opened: April 25, 2011.
Still running as of May 31, 2011.

PLAYBILL®

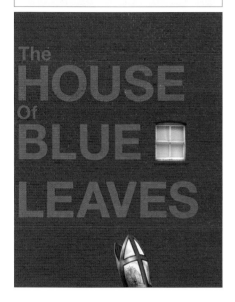

A black comedy about a middle-aged man who makes one last grab for happiness by leaving his mentally ill wife and running away with his girlfriend to pursue his dream of becoming a songwriter—just as the pope arrives in town.

CAST

(in order of appearance)

Artie Shaughnessy	BEN STILLER
Ronnie Shaughnessy	CHRISTOPHER ABBOTT
Bunny Flingus	JENNIFER JASON LEIGH
Bananas Shaughnessy	EDIE FALCO
Corrinna Stroller	ALISON PILL
Head Nun	MARY BETH HURT
Second Nun	SUSAN BENNETT
Little Nun	HALLEY FEIFFER
Policeman	JIMMY DAVIS
White Man	TALLY SESSIONS
Billy Einhorn	THOMAS SADOSKI

UNDERSTUDIES

For Artie Shaughnessy: JIM BRACCHITTA
For Bananas Shaughnessy: KATIE KREISLER
For Bunny Flingus: SUSAN BENNETT
For Billy Einhorn: TALLY SESSIONS
For Corrinna Stroller: AMELIA McCLAIN
For Head Nun: KATIE KREISLER
For Ronnie Shaughnessy: JIMMY DAVIS
For Little Nun: AMELIA McCLAIN
For Second Nun: KATIE KREISLER

SETTING

A cold apartment in Sunnyside, Queens,
New York City
Time: October 4, 1965

WALTER KERR THEATRE

A JUJAMCYN THEATRE

JORDAN ROTH
President

PAUL LIBIN
Executive Vice President

JACK VIERTEL
Senior Vice President

Scott Rudin   Stuart Thompson   Jean Doumanian
Mary Lu Roffe/Susan Gallin/Rodger Hess
The Araca Group   Scott M. Delman   Roy Furman
Ruth Hendel   Jon B. Platt   Sonia Friedman Productions/Scott Landis

present

BEN   EDIE   JENNIFER
STILLER FALCO JASON LEIGH

in

THE HOUSE OF
BLUE LEAVES

by
JOHN GUARE

with

THOMAS SADOSKI
MARY BETH HURT   CHRISTOPHER ABBOTT   HALLEY FEIFFER
SUSAN BENNETT   JIMMY DAVIS   TALLY SESSIONS
ALISON PILL

Scenic Design	Costume Design	Lighting Design	Sound Design
SCOTT PASK	JANE GREENWOOD	BRIAN MACDEVITT	FITZ PATTON & JOSH SCHMIDT

Hair/Wig Design	Casting	Fight Direction	Production Stage Manager
TOM WATSON	MELCAP CASTING	THOMAS SCHALL	BARCLAY STIFF

Production Management	Press Representative	General Management
AURORA PRODUCTIONS	BONEAU/ BRYAN-BROWN	STP/ MARSHALL B. PURDY

Directed by
DAVID CROMER

The Producers wish to express their appreciation to Theatre Development Fund for its support of this production.

4/25/11

(L-R): Ben Stiller, Edie Falco and Jennifer Jason Leigh

Photo by Joan Marcus

The House of Blue Leaves

Ben Stiller
Artie Shaughnessy

Edie Falco
Bananas Shaughnessy

Jennifer Jason Leigh
Bunny Flingus

Thomas Sadoski
Billy Einhorn

Alison Pill
Corrinna Stroller

Mary Beth Hurt
Head Nun

Christopher Abbott
Ronnie Shaugnessy

Halley Feiffer
Little Nun

Susan Bennett
Second Nun

Jimmy Davis
Policeman

Tally Sessions
White Man

Jim Bracchitta
u/s Artie Shaughnessy

Katie Kreisler
u/s Bananas Shaughnessy, u/s Head Nun, u/s Second Nun

Amelia McClain
u/s Corrinna Stroller, u/s Little Nun

John Guare
Playwright

David Cromer
Director

Scott Pask
Scenic Design

Jane Greenwood
Costume Design

Brian MacDevitt
Lighting Design

Josh Schmidt
Sound Design

Tom Watson
Hair/Wig Design

Thomas Schall
Fight Director

Scott Rudin
Producer

Stuart Thompson
Producer

Jean Doumanian
Producer

Mary Lu Roffe
Producer

Susan Gallin
Producer

Rodger Hess
Producer

Michael Rego, Hank Unger and Matthew Rego, The Araca Group
Producer

Roy Furman
Producer

Ruth Hendel
Producer

Jon B. Platt
Producer

Sonia Friedman Productions
Producer

Scott Landis
Producer

The House of Blue Leaves

CREW
Front Row (L-R): Jennifer Hohn, William King, David Stollings, Jill Heller, Kate Dalton, Vincent Valvo

Back Row (L-R): George Fullum, Brian Munroe, Amelia Haywood, Kelly Beaulieu, Barclay Stiff, Joshua First, P.J. Iacovello, Timothy Bennet

ENGINEER
Michael Tooze

BOX OFFICE
(L-R): Harry Jaffie, Gail Yerkovich, Michael Loiacono

COMPANY AND STAGE MANAGEMENT
(L-R): Barclay Stiff, Kelly Beaulieu, Chris Morey

FRONT OF HOUSE STAFF
Front Row (L-R): Jason Aguirre, Manuel Sandridge

2nd Row (L-R): Aaron Kendall, Jeffrey Blim, Mallory Sims

3rd Row (L-R): Katie Siegmund, Alison Traynor, Joy Sandell, Theresa Aceves

4th Row (L-R): T.J. D'Angelo, Tatiana Gomberg

Back Row (L-R): Jared Pike, Victoria Lauzun, Robert Zwaschka

The House of Blue Leaves

Photo by Joan Marcus

Alison Pill

STAFF FOR *THE HOUSE OF BLUE LEAVES*

GENERAL MANAGEMENT
STUART THOMPSON PRODUCTIONS
Stuart Thompson   Marshall B. Purdy   David Turner
Cassidy Briggs   Kevin Emrick   Geo Karapetyan
Brittany Levasseur   Andrew Lowy
Christopher Taggart

COMPANY MANAGER
Chris Morey

SCOTT RUDIN PRODUCTIONS
Eli Bush   Steven Cardwell   Max Grossman
Adam Klaff   Joshua Mehr
Allie Moore   Matt Nemeth
Jill Simon   Nora Skinner

PRESS REPRESENTATIVE
BONEAU/BRYAN-BROWN
Chris Boneau   Heath Schwartz   Michael Strassheim

PRODUCTION MANAGEMENT
AURORA PRODUCTIONS INC.
Gene O'Donovan   Ben Heller
Stephanie Sherline   Jarid Sumner
Liza Luxenberg   Jason Margolis
Ryan Stanisz   Melissa Mazdra

Production Stage Manager ....Barclay Stiff
Stage Manager ....Kelly Beaulieu
Assistant Director ....Michael Padden
Associate Scenic Designers ....Christine Peters,
                                            Lauren Alvarez
Associate Costume Designer ....Moria Clinton
Associate Lighting Designer ....Jennifer Schriever
Associate Sound Designers ....Joshua Reid,
                                        Joanna Lynne Staub
Hair Stylist for Mr. Stiller ....Lori Guidroz

Makeup Consultants ....Naomi Donne, Alice Lane
Production Carpenter ....Brian Munroe
Production Electrician ....Dan Coey
Head Electrician ....Will King
Moving Light Programmer ....Timothy Rogers
Production Properties Coordinator ....Propstar/
                                            Kathy Fabian
Advance Properties ....Andrew Meeker
Head Sound Engineer ....David Stollings
Wardrobe Supervisor ....John A Robelen III
Dressers ....Amelia Haywood, Jill Heller,
                            Daniel Eaton, Jennifer Hohn
Hair Supervisor ....Joshua First
Hairdresser ....April Schuller
Dialect Coach ....Howard Samuelsohn
Piano Coaches ....Gerard D'Angelo, Garry Dial
Music Coach ....Richard Carsey
Production Assistant ....Davin De Santis
Costume Assistant ....Kristina Makowski
Casting Assistant ....Lauren Port
General Management Interns ....Rikki Bahar,
                            Liz Shumate, Brett Janecek
Banking ....City National Bank/Michele Gibbons
Payroll ....Castellana Services, Inc.
Accountant ....Fried & Kowgios CPA's LLP/
                                        Robert Fried, CPA
Controller ....Joe Kubala
Insurance ....DeWitt Stern Group
Legal Counsel ....Lazarus & Harris, LLP
            Scott Lazarus, Esq., Robert C. Harris, Esq.
Advertising ....Serino Coyne Inc./
                            Greg Corradetti, Sandy Block,
                            Tom Callahan, Scott Johnson,
                            Robert Jones, Danielle Boyle,
                            Zack Kinney, Andrei Oleinik,
                                            Jeff Alphin
Marketing ....aka/
                Elizabeth Furze, Scott A. Moore,
            Adam Jay, Janette Roush, Andrew Damer,
            Sara Rosenzweig, Meghan Bartley
Digital and Interactive Marketing ....aka Connect/
                            Terry Goldman, Erin Rech
Production Photographer ....Joan Marcus
Theatre Displays ....King Displays, Inc.
Transportation ....Attitude Limousines Inc.

SPECIAL THANKS
Coffee makers and K-Cups generously provided by Keurig;
Mama Donna Henes, urban shaman.

CREDITS
Scenery and scenic effects built, painted and electrified by
Showmotion Inc., Milford, CT. Automation and show
control by Showmotion, Inc., using the AC² computerized
motion control system. Costumes by Eric Winterling, Inc.
Lighting equipment from PRG Lighting. Sound equipment
by Masque Sound. Special electronics equipment by
Perfection Electricks. Fur coat by Ritz Furs.

Music and Lyrics by John Guare.

The House of Blue Leaves first opened in New York on
February 10, 1971, and was produced by Warren Lyons and
Betty Ann Besch. Mel Shapiro was the director. John Guare
dedicates this production to them.

Rehearsed at New 42nd Street Studios.

Souvenir merchandise designed and created by
The Araca Group

www.HouseOfBlueLeaves.com

JUJAMCYN THEATERS

JORDAN ROTH
President

PAUL LIBIN   **JACK VIERTEL**
Executive Vice President   Senior Vice President
MEREDITH VILLATORE   **JENNIFER HERSHEY**
Chief Financial Officer   Vice President,
                                  Building Operations
MICAH HOLLINGWORTH   **HAL GOLDBERG**
Vice President,   Vice President,
Company Operations   Theatre Operations

Director of Business Affairs ....Albert T. Kim
Theatre Operations Managers ....Willa Burke,
                            Susan Elrod, Hal Goldberg,
                            Jeff Hubbard, Albert T. Kim
Theatre Operations Associates ....Carrie Jo Brinker,
                            Emily Hare, Anah Jyoti Klate
Accounting ....Cathy Cerge, Erin Dooley,
                                        Christian Sislian
Executive Producer, Red Awning ....Nicole Kastrinos
Director of Marketing, Givenik.com ....Joe Tropia
Building Operations Associate ....Erich Bussing
Assistant to Jordan Roth ....Ed Lefferson
Assistant to Paul Libin ....Clark Mims Tedesco
Assistant to Jack Viertel ....Marisol Rosa-Shapiro
Receptionist ....Kate Garst
Superintendent ....Ralph Santos
Security ....Rasim Hodzic, John Inzanti
Interns ....Ryan Bogner, Ben Cohen,
                            Michael Composto, Katie Young

Staff for the Walter Kerr Theatre for
The House of Blue Leaves
Theatre Manager ....Susan Elrod
Treasurer ....Harry Jaffie
Head Carpenter ....George E. Fullum
Head Electrician ....Vincent J. Valvo
Head Props ....Timothy Bennet
Assistant Treasurers ....Michael Loiacono,
                            Joseph Smith, Gail Yerkovich
Ushers/Ticket Takers/Doormen ....Florence Arcaro,
                            Juliette Cipriatti, TJ D'Angelo,
                            Michele Fleury, Brandon Houghton,
                            Victoria Lauzun, Joy Sandell,
                            Alison Traynor, Kevin Wallace,
                            Robert Zwaschka
Head Porter ....Marcio Martinez
Head Cleaner ....Sevdija Pasukanovic
Porter ....Rudy Martinez
Cleaner ....Lourdes Perez

Lobby refreshments by Sweet Concessions.

Security provided by P and P Security.

Jujamcyn Theaters is a proud member of the
Broadway Green Alliance.

House of Blue Leaves

Scrapbook

Correspondent: Tally Sessions, "White Man"

Opening Night Gifts: We had several memorable opening night gifts! Among them: a newly bound edition of the script, commemorating our opening night, including a title page listing the 2011 Broadway revival's cast and creative team (a gift from our lovely producers); a beautiful sterling silver key chain engraved with "*HOBL* 2011" and decorated with a blue leaf ornament (a gift from our peerless Bananas, Edie Falco); and a t-shirt (from me, Tally Sessions) featuring a small house with three blue leaves on the front, and one of the play's lines (courtesy of our phenomenal playwright, John Guare), "Be An Audience."

Most Exciting Celebrity Visitors: We've had a ton! Robert De Niro, Nicole Kidman, Patti LuPone, Matthew Broderick, Laura Linney, Nathan Lane, Mark Rylance, Chris Rock, Liza Minnelli, Terrence McNally, Phoebe Cates, Colin Quinn, and on and on….

Actor Who Performed the Most Roles in This Show: We all play one part, but our off-stage understudies cover multiple roles. Katie Kreisler covered Bananas Shaughnessy, Head Nun and Second Nun. Jim Bracchitta covered Artie Shaughnessy, Military Policeman and White Man. Amelia McClain covered Corrinna Stroller and Little Nun.

Who Has Done the Most Shows in Their Career: I imagine that would be our lovely Mary Beth Hurt!

Special Backstage Rituals: Our fight call before half-hour is an exercise in hilarity. And some new, bizarre, often unintelligible interpretations of John Guare's text. And Jimmy Davis does a funny dance.

Favorite Moments During Each Performance: The explosion at the end of Act II, Scene 1. Also the prologue during the El Dorado (written expressly for the 2011 revival).

Favorite In-Theatre Gathering Place: Onstage for a little vocal and physical warm-up.

Favorite Off-Site Hangout: Saturday nights at Bettibar, the upstairs bar at the Hourglass Tavern on 46th Street between Eighth and Ninth Avenues.

Favorite Snack Food: The gigantic jar of candy provided by our wonderful house manager at the Walter Kerr, Susan Elrod. Alison Pill liked to hoard the candy. Did she ever eat all of it? Who knows?

Memorable Ad-Lib: During Ronnie's

2010-2011 AWARDS

Drama Desk Award
Outstanding Featured Actress in a Play
(Edie Falco)

Theatre World Award
Outstanding Broadway
or Off-Broadway Debut
(Halley Feiffer)

1. (L-R): Ben Stiller, Edie Falco and Alison Pill take a curtain call on opening night.
2. Playwright John Guare at the premiere party at Sardi's.
3. Guests on opening night, the comedy team of Stiller & Meara (L-R): Anne Meara and Jerry Stiller, parents of Ben.

monologue at the top of Act II, the top of the box containing the bomb Ronnie plans to use to blow up the Pope fell into the audience. Christopher Abbott (the actor playing Ronnie) improvised the line to an audience member, "Could you hand me that? I need it for my bomb."

Memorable Directorial Note: David Cromer, our genius director (literally, he was awarded a MacArthur "Genius" Grant) constantly gave this one piece of direction that really hit home, "You have to explain your point to the person you're talking to." Sounds basic, but it really forced every actor to communicate specifically and achieve his/her goals in the scene.

Nicknames: Christopher Abbott earned the nickname "Thrustopher" after our rake training (training for working on a raked stage). He thrusts his pelvis forward to compensate for the rake.

Embarrassing Moments: There are two that I can think of and they were more shocking than embarrassing. Firstly, after the explosion during

Act II, Ben Stiller falls to the lip of the stage. His head was hanging offstage during one performance, and a female audience member reached up and tapped him on the top of the head. Perhaps she just wanted to say she'd touched the head of Gaylord Focker. The second is also strange: At the curtain call of one performance, a woman stood up and alternately screamed "Bravo!" at Edie Falco and "You son of a bitch!" at Ben Stiller. I don't think she enjoyed Artie's treatment of Bananas, particularly during the play's climax.

Coolest Thing About Being in This Show: The coolest thing about being in this show? BEING IN THIS SHOW! We are on Broadway (several of us making our debuts), doing this brilliant American play by John Guare, a theatrical treasure, with a genius director and design team, tireless producers, wonderful stage and company management, and a cast that is, simply put, fearless. I am and will always be humbled to have been included.

How to Succeed in Business Without Really Trying

First Preview: February 26, 2011. Opened: March 27, 2011.
Still running as of May 31, 2011.

PLAYBILL

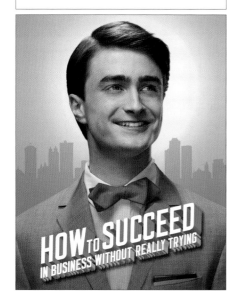

J. Pierrepont Finch is a lowly window washer at the World Wide Wicket Company, but he's got a dream. He bought himself the book "How To Succeed in Business Without Really Trying," and decides to follow its precepts and see how far they take him. Starting in the mailroom, he uses a combination of flattery, insincere friendship-building and bare-faced chutzpah to leap upward through the ranks in just a few days, dazzling stenographer Rosemary, who sets her cap for him, and horrifying the older climbers in the company hierarchy as he breezes past them on the way to the president's chair. Just before J. Pierrepont takes over the company completely, he makes one fatally flawed move that threatens to send him plunging back to the mailroom. But not to worry: his magical book has the right answer for everything.

CAST
(in order of appearance)

The Voice of the Narrator	ANDERSON COOPER
J. Pierrepont Finch	DANIEL RADCLIFFE
Mr. Gatch	NICK MAYO
Mr. Jenkins	CHARLIE WILLIAMS
Mr. Johnson/TV Announcer	KEVIN COVERT
Mr. Matthews	RYAN WATKINSON
Mr. Peterson	MARTY LAWSON
Mr. Tackaberry	JOEY SORGE
Mr. Toynbee	DAVID HULL
Mr. Andrews	BARRETT MARTIN
J.B. Biggley	JOHN LARROQUETTE
Rosemary Pilkington	ROSE HEMINGWAY
Mr. Bratt	MICHAEL PARK
Smitty	MARY FABER

Continued on next page

The Playbill Broadway Yearbook 2010-2011

---

❾ AL HIRSCHFELD THEATRE
A JUJAMCYN THEATRE

JORDAN ROTH
President

PAUL LIBIN
Executive Vice President

JACK VIERTEL
Senior Vice President

BROADWAY ACROSS AMERICA   CRAIG ZADAN   NEIL MERON
JOSEPH SMITH   MICHAEL McCABE
CANDY SPELLING   TAKONKIET VIRAVAN / SCENARIO THAILAND   HILARY A. WILLIAMS
JEN NAMOFF / FAKSTON PRODUCTIONS   TWO LEFT FEET PRODUCTIONS / POWER ARTS
HOP THEATRICALS, LLC / PAUL CHAU / DANIEL FRISHWASSER / MICHAEL JACKOWITZ
MICHAEL SPEYER - BERNIE ABRAMS / JACKI BARLIA FLORIN - ADAM BLANSHAY / ARLENE SCANLAN / TBS SERVICE

DANIEL RADCLIFFE   JOHN LARROQUETTE

Music & Lyrics by	Book by
FRANK LOESSER	**ABE BURROWS, JACK WEINSTOCK & WILLIE GILBERT**

Based on the book by SHEPHERD MEAD

TAMMY BLANCHARD   CHRISTOPHER J. HANKE

ROB BARTLETT   MARY FABER   ELLEN HARVEY   MICHAEL PARK

CAMERON ADAMS	CLEVE ASBURY	TANYA BIRL	KEVIN COVERT	PAIGE FAURE
DAVID HULL	JUSTIN KEYES	MARTY LAWSON	ERICA MANSFIELD	BARRETT MARTIN
NICK MAYO	SARAH O'GLEBY	STEPHANIE ROTHENBERG	MEGAN SIKORA	MICHAELJON SLINGER
JOEY SORGE	MATT WALL	RYAN WATKINSON	CHARLIE WILLIAMS	SAMANTHA ZACK

and introducing
ROSE HEMINGWAY

featuring
ANDERSON COOPER
as the Voice of the Narrator

Scenic Design by	Costume Design by	Lighting Design by	Sound Design by
DEREK McLANE	**CATHERINE ZUBER**	**HOWELL BINKLEY**	**JON WESTON**

Hair & Design by	Orchestrations by	Music Coordinator
TOM WATSON	**DOUG BESTERMAN**	**HOWARD JOINES**

Production Stage Manager	Associate Director	Associate Choreographer	Assistant Choreographers
MICHAEL J. PASSARO	**STEPHEN SPOSITO**	**CHRISTOPHER BAILEY**	**SARAH O'GLEBY CHARLIE WILLIAMS**

Casting by	Production Manager	Press Representative	Marketing
TARA RUBIN CASTING	**JUNIPER STREET PRODUCTIONS**	**THE HARTMAN GROUP**	**TYPE A MARKETING ANNE RIPPEY**

General Management	Associate Producers	Executive Producer
ALAN WASSER - ALLAN WILLIAMS MARK SHACKET	**STAGE VENTURES 2010 LIMITED PARTNERSHIP**	**BETH WILLIAMS**

Music Direction & Arrangements by
DAVID CHASE

Directed & Choreographed by
ROB ASHFORD

3/27/11

(L-R): Rose Hemingway, Daniel Radcliffe, Mary Faber and company.

Photo by Ari Mintz

How to Succeed in Business Without Really Trying

MUSICAL NUMBERS

ACT I

"Overture" ....Orchestra
"How to Succeed" ....Finch and Company
"Happy to Keep His Dinner Warm" ....Rosemary
"Coffee Break" ....Bud, Smitty and Company
"Company Way" ....Finch and Twimble
"Company Way" (Reprise) ....Bud and Company
"Rosemary's Philosophy" ....Rosemary
"A Secretary Is Not a Toy" ....Bratt, Smitty, Bud and Company
"Been a Long Day" ....Smitty, Finch, Rosemary and Company
"Been a Long Day" (Reprise) ....Biggley, Bud and Hedy
"Grand Old Ivy" ....Finch and Biggley
"Paris Original" ....Rosemary, Smitty, Miss Krumholtz, Miss Jones and the Secretaries
"Rosemary" ....Finch and Rosemary
"Act I Finale" ....Finch, Rosemary and Bud

ACT II

"Cinderella Darling" ....Smitty and the Secretaries
"Happy to Keep His Dinner Warm" (Reprise) ....Rosemary
"Love From a Heart of Gold" ....Biggley and Hedy
"I Believe in You" ....Finch and the Men
"Pirate Dance" ....Company
"I Believe in You" (Reprise) ....Rosemary
"Brotherhood of Man" ....Finch, Miss Jones, Wally Womper and Men
"Finale" ....Company

(L-R): Michael Park, Daniel Radcliffe, John Larroquette and company

Photo by Ari Mintz

ORCHESTRA

Conductor:
DAVID CHASE
Associate Conductor:
MATT PERRI
Music Coordinator:
HOWARD JOINES
Reeds:
STEVE KENYON, LAWRENCE FELDMAN,
MARK THRASHER
Trumpets:
NICHOLAS MARCHIONE,
SCOTT WENDHOLT
Trombones:
JOHN ALLRED, GEORGE FLYNN
Horn:
DAVID PEEL

Drums:
PAUL PIZZUTI
Bass:
NEAL CAINE
Guitars:
SCOTT KUNEY
Percussion:
ERIK CHARLSTON
Harp:
GRACE PARADISE
Piano/Synth/Associate Conductor:
MATT PERRI
Keyboard Programmer:
RANDY COHEN
Music Preparation:
ANIXTER RICE MUSIC SERVICE

Cast Continued

Miss Jones ....ELLEN HARVEY
Miss Krumholtz ....MEGAN SIKORA
Bud Frump ....CHRISTOPHER J. HANKE
Mr. Twimble/Wally Womper ....ROB BARTLETT
Hedy La Rue ....TAMMY BLANCHARD
Mr. Davis ....JUSTIN KEYES
Meredith ....STEPHANIE ROTHENBERG
Kathy/Scrub Woman ....CAMERON ADAMS
Miss Grabowski/Scrub Woman .....PAIGE FAURE
Nancy ....TANYA BIRL
Lily ....SAMANTHA ZACK
Mr. Ovington ....CLEVE ASBURY

Dance Captain: SARAH O'GLEBY
Assistant Dance Captain: MATT WALL

SWINGS
ERICA MANSFIELD, SARAH O'GLEBY,
MICHAELJON SLINGER, MATT WALL

UNDERSTUDIES
For J. Pierrepont Finch:
DAVID HULL, JUSTIN KEYES
For J.B. Biggley:
ROB BARTLETT, MICHAEL PARK
For Rosemary Pilkington:
CAMERON ADAMS,
STEPHANIE ROTHENBERG
For Bud Frump:
JUSTIN KEYES, CHARLIE WILLIAMS
For Hedy La Rue, Smitty:
PAIGE FAURE, MEGAN SIKORA
For Miss Jones:
ERICA MANSFIELD, MEGAN SIKORA
For Twimble/Womper:
CLEVE ASBURY, KEVIN COVERT
For Bert Bratt:
NICK MAYO, JOEY SORGE

Daniel Radcliffe is appearing with the permission of
Actors' Equity Association.

How to Succeed in Business Without Really Trying

Daniel Radcliffe
J. Pierrepont Finch

John Larroquette
J.B. Biggley

Rose Hemingway
Rosemary Pilkington

Tammy Blanchard
Hedy LaRue

Christopher J. Hanke
Bud Frump

Rob Bartlett
*Mr. Twimble/
Wally Womper*

Mary Faber
Smitty

Ellen Harvey
Miss Jones

Michael Park
Bert Bratt

Anderson Cooper
*The Voice of the
Narrator*

Cameron Adams
Kathy/Scrub Woman

Cleve Asbury
Mr. Ovington

Tanya Birl
Nancy

Kevin Covert
*Mr. Johnson/
TV Announcer*

Paige Faure
*Miss Grabowski/
Scrub Woman*

David Hull
Mr. Toynbee

Justin Keyes
Mr. Davis

Marty Lawson
Mr. Peterson

Erica Mansfield
Swing

Barrett Martin
Mr. Andrews

Nick Mayo
Mr. Gatch

Sarah O'Gleby
*Swing/
Dance Captain*

Stephanie
Rothenberg
Meredith

Megan Sikora
Miss Krumholtz

Michaeljon Slinger
Swing

Joey Sorge
Mr. Tackaberry

Matt Wall
*Swing/
Asst. Dance Captain*

Ryan Watkinson
Mr. Matthews

Charlie Williams
Mr. Jenkins

Samantha Zack
Lily

Frank Loesser
Music and Lyrics

Abe Burrows
Book

Shepherd Mead
Original Author

Rob Ashford
*Director/
Choreographer*

Derek McLane
Scenic Design

How to Succeed in Business Without Really Trying

Catherine Zuber
Costume Designer

Howell Binkley
Lighting Design

Tom Watson
Hair and Wig Design

Stephen Sposito
Associate Director

Doug Besterman
Orchestrations

David Chase
*Music Director and
Arranger*

Howard Joines
Music Contractor

Joseph DeLuise, Alexandra Paull,
Hillary Blanken, Ana Rose Greene,
Kevin Broomell, Guy Kwan,
Juniper Street Productions
Production Manager

Tara Rubin Casting
Casting

Alan Wasser
General Manager

Allan Williams
General Manager

John Gore,
CEO,
Broadway Across
America
Producer

Thomas B. McGrath
Chairman,
Broadway Across
America
Producer

Craig Zadan
Producer

Neil Meron
Producer

Candy Spelling
Producer

Hilary A. Williams
Producer

Joel Dodge,
Two Left Feet
Productions
Producer

Jonathan Feder,
Two Left Feet
Productions
Producer

Larry Kaye,
Hop Theatricals, LLC
Producer

Paul Chau
Producer

Michael Speyer
Producer

Bernie Abrams
Producer

Jacki Barlia Florin
Producer

(L-R): Daniel Radcliffe
and John Larroquette

Photo by Ari Mintz

Arlene Scanlan
Producer

Beth Williams
Executive Producer

Adam Blanshay
Producer

How to Succeed in Business Without Really Trying

CARPENTRY
(L-R): Gus Poitras, Erik Hansen, Joseph Maher, Jr., Gabe Harris, Chris Conrad

Photos by Brian Mapp

STAGE MANAGEMENT
(L-R): Jim Athens, Michael J. Passaro, Pat Sosnow, Shannon Hammons

DOORMAN
Neil Perez

BOX OFFICE
(L-R): Gloria Diabo, Jeff Nevin

HAIR
(L-R): Katie Beatty, Carla Muniz, Gabrielle Vincent

WARDROBE
Front Row (L-R): Nesreen Mahmoud, Barry Hoff

Middle Row (L-R): Sandy Binion, Debbie Cheretun, Jeff Johnson, Anthony Hoffman

Back Row (L-R): Brendan Cooper, Icey Parks, Trevor McGinness, Kristin Farley, Shana Albery

CREW
Standing (L-R): Rocco Williams, Paul Ker, Gretchen Metzloff, Jason Strangfeld, Charles Grieco, Tom Burke, Brian Dawson, Emile LaFargue

Top: Michele Gutierrez

How to Succeed in Business Without Really Trying

FRONT OF HOUSE STAFF
Front Row (L-R): Julie Burnham, Lorraine Feeks, Donald Royal, Theresa Lopez

Second Row (L-R): Jennifer DiDonato, Heather Gilles, Elizabeth Harvey, Steven Mooney, Mary Marzan

Third Row (L-R): Pat Tarpey, Janice Rodriguez, Jose Nunez, Roberto Ellington, William Meyers

Fourth Row (L-R): Bart Ryan, Carrie Jo Brinker, Lawrence Levens, Tristan Blacer

Back Row (L-R): Hollis Miller, Henry E. Menendez, Alexander Gutierrez, Albert Kim

ORCHESTRA
Seated (L-R): Neal Caine, Erik Charlston, Matt Perri, David Chase

Standing (L-R): David Peel, Mark Thrasher, Lawrence Feldman, Nick Marchione, George Flynn, John Allred, Grace Paradise, Scott Wendholt, Paul Pizzuti, Steve Kenyon, Scott Kuney

PROPERTIES
Kneeling: Jim Kane

Standing (L-R): Christopher Pantuso, Richard Anderson, Sal Sclafani, Will Sweeney

---

STAFF FOR
HOW TO SUCCEED IN BUSINESS WITHOUT REALLY TRYING

GENERAL MANAGEMENT
ALAN WASSER ASSOCIATES
Alan Wasser   Allan Williams
Mark Shacket   Aaron Lustbader

GENERAL PRESS REPRESENTATIVE
THE HARTMAN GROUP
Michael Hartman
Wayne Wolfe   Matt Ross   Nicole Capatasto

COMPANY MANAGER
Penelope Daulton

MARKETING
TYPE A MARKETING
Anne Rippey   Michael Porto
Elyce Henkin   Sarah Ziering

CASTING
TARA RUBIN CASTING
Tara Rubin CSA, Merri Sugarman CSA
Eric Woodall CSA, Laura Schutzel CSA, Dale Brown CSA
Lindsay Levine, Kaitlin Shaw

PRODUCTION MANAGEMENT
JUNIPER STREET PRODUCTIONS
Hillary Blanken   Guy Kwan
Joseph DeLuise   Kevin Broomell   Ana Rose Greene

Production Stage Manager	Michael J. Passaro
Stage Manager	Pat Sosnow
Assistant Stage Manager	Jim Athens
Assistant Company Manager	Cathy Kwon
Dance Captain	Sarah O'Gleby
Assistant Dance Captain	Matt Wall
SDC Traube Fellow	Sara-Ashley Bischoff
Associate Scenic Designer	Shoko Kambara

How to Succeed in Business Without Really Trying

Assistant Scenic Designer ....Brett Banakis
Scenic Design Assistant ....Paul Depoo
Assistant Costume Designers ....Nicole Moody,
 David Newell, Liam O'Brian, Ryan Park
Costume Design Intern......................Peter Dolhas
Associate Lighting Designer ....Ryan O'Gara
Assistant Lighting Designers ....Sean Beach,
 Amanda Zieve
Associate Sound Designer/
 Sound Engineer ....Jason Strangfeld
Assistant Sound Designer ....Michael Eisenberg
Moving Lights Programmer ....Eric Norris
Make-up Design ....Ashley Ryan
Aerial Design ....Sonja Rzepski
Stunt Coordinator ....Mike Russo
Production Carpenter..........................Erik Hansen
Automation Carpenter ....Scott "Gus" Poitras
Production Electricians ....James J. Fedigan,
 Randall Zaibek
Head Electrician ....Brian Dawson
Production Properties Supervisor ......Christopher Pantuso
Assistant Properties Supervisor ....Jim Kane
Production Sound Engineers ....Paul Delcioppo,
 Phil Lojo
Deck Audio ....Charles Grieco
Wardrobe Supervisor ....Debbie Cheretun
Assistant Wardrobe Supervisor ....Brendan Cooper
Mr. Radcliffe's Dresser ....Sandy Binion
Mr. Larroquette's Dresser ....Barry Hoff
Dressers ....Shana Albery, Joshua Burns,
 Kristin Farley, Anthony Hoffman,
 Jeffrey Johnson, Nesreen Mahmoud,
 Icey Parks
Hair Supervisor ....Katie Beatty
Hair Dressers ....Carla Muniz, Brendan O'Neal
Music Coordinator ....Howard Joines
Music Copying ....Anixter Rice Music Service/
 Russ Anixter
Advertising ....Serino Coyne/Nancy Coyne,
 Sandy Block, Greg Corradetti,
 Robert Jones, Danielle Boyle
International Marketing ....Joe Public
Theatre Displays ....King Displays
Website Design &
 Internet Marketing ....Art Meets Commerce/
 Jim Glaub, Chip Meyrelles,
 Laurie Connor, Kevin Keating,
 Whitney Manalio Creighton, Mark Seeley
Legal Counsel ....Levine Plotkin & Menin LLP/
 Loren Plotkin, Esq.
Accounting ....Rosenberg, Neuwirth & Kuchner/
 Chris Cacace, Ruthie Skochil
For Daniel Radcliffe in London
 Vocal Coach ....Mark Meylan
 Dance Tutor ....Spencer Soloman
 Voice Work ....Barbara Houseman
 Dialect Coach ....Penny Dyer
General Management Associates ....Lane Marsh,
 Steve Greer
General Management Office..............Hilary Ackerman,
 Mark Barna, Jake Hirzel,
 Dawn Kusinski, Nina Lutwick,
 Jennifer O'Connor
Production Photographer.......................Ari Mintz
Production Assistants ....Shannon Bonds,
 Steve Chazaro, Melissa Hansen,

 Morgan Holbrook, Jeff Siebert
Physical Therapist ....Encore Physical Therapy PC/
 Marc Hunter-Hall
Orthopaedist ....David S. Weiss, MD
Insurance ....Ventura Insurance Brokerage/
 Christine Sadofsky
Banking ....Signature Bank/
 Barbara von Borstel, Margaret Monigan,
 Mary Ann Fanelli, Janett Urena
Payroll ....Castellana Services, Inc.
Opening Night
 Coordination ....Serino Coyne, LLC/
 Suzanne Tobak, Gail Perlman
Group Sales ....Broadway Inbound/212-302-0995
Transportation ....IBA Limousine

CREDITS AND ACKNOWLEDGEMENTS

Scenery constructed and show control and scenic motion control featuring Stage Command® Systems by PRG Scenic Technologies, a division of Production Resources Group, LLC, New Windsor, NY. Scenery constructed by Global Scenic Services, Bridgeport, CT. Lighting equipment provided by PRG Lighting. Audio equipment provided by PRG Audio. Props built by the Spoon Group, the Ken Larson Co. TV camera provided by the Museum of Broadcast Technology, Paul Beck, Pres. Costumes by Parsons-Meares, Ltd.; EuroCo Costumes, Inc., John Cowles; Center Stage Costume Shop. Millinery by Rodney Gordon, Inc.; Arnold Levine Millinery. Men's tailoring by Brooks Brothers, Brian Hemesath, Edward Dawson. Men's shirts by Cego Custom Shirts, Jared Bleese. Custom footwear by JC Theatrical and Custom, T.O. Dey, World Tone Dance. Fabric painting and dyeing by Jeffrey Fender. Custom knitwear by Maria Ficalora. Custom jewelry by Larry Vrba. Vintage eyewear by Fabulous Franny's. Special thanks to Bra*Tenders for hosiery and undergarments.

Makeup provided by M·A·C Cosmetics

Piano by Steinway & Sons

Rehearsed at the New 42nd Street Studios

Souvenir Merchandise designed and created by Creative Goods Merchandise

www.HowToSucceedBroadway.com

Energy efficient washer/dryer courtesy of LG Electronics.

JUJAMCYN THEATERS

JORDAN ROTH
President

PAUL LIBIN
Executive Vice President

JACK VIERTEL
Senior Vice President

MEREDITH VILLATORE
Chief Financial Officer

JENNIFER HERSHEY
Vice President,
Building Operations

MICAH HOLLINGWORTH
Vice President,
Company Operations

HAL GOLDBERG
Vice President,
Theatre Operations

Director of Business Affairs ....Albert T. Kim
Theatre Operations Managers ....Willa Burke,
 Susan Elrod, Hal Goldberg,
 Jeff Hubbard, Albert T. Kim
Theatre Operations Associates ....Carrie Jo Brinker,
 Emily Hare, Anah Jyoti Klate
Accounting ....Cathy Cerge, Erin Dooley,
 Christian Sislian
Executive Producer, Red Awning ....Nicole Kastrinos
Director of Marketing, Givenik.com ....Joe Tropia
Building Operations Associate ....Erich Bussing
Assistant to Jordan Roth ....Ed Lefferson
Assistant to Paul Libin ....Clark Mims Tedesco
Assistant to Jack Viertel ....Marisol Rosa-Shapiro
Receptionist ....Kate Garst
Superintendent ....Ralph Santos
Security ....Rasim Hodzic, John Inzanti
Interns ....Ryan Bogner, Ben Cohen,
 Michael Composto, Katie Young

Staff for the Al Hirschfeld Theatre for
How to Succeed in Business Without Really Trying

Theatre Manager ....Albert T. Kim
Associate Theatre Manager ....Carrie Jo Brinker
Treasurer....................................Carmine LaMendola
Head Carpenter ....Joseph J. Maher, Jr.
Head Propertyman ....Sal Sclafani
Head Electrician ....Michele Gutierrez
Flyman...Gabe Harris
Engineer ....Brian DiNapoli
Assistant Treasurers ....Vicci Stanton, Gloria Diabo,
 Joseph Smith, Janette Wernegreen
Carpenters ....Joe Mooneyham, Gene Manford
Propertyman ....Will Sweeney
Electricians ....John Blixt, Tom Burke,
 Emile LaFargue, Rocco Williams
Head Usher ....Janice Rodriguez
Ticket-Takers ....Tristan Blacer, Lorraine Feeks
Doormen.......................Zaim Hodzic, Neil Perez
Directress......................................Julie Burnham
Head Porter ....Jose Nunez
Head Cleaner ....Bethania Alvarez
Ushers ....Peter Davino, Jennifer DiDonato,
 Alexander Gutierrez, Elizabeth Harvey,
 Theresa Lopez, Mary Marzan,
 Henry E. Menendez, William Meyers,
 Donald Royal, Bart Ryan
Porters ....Tereso Avila, Roberto Ellington
Cleaners............Michelina Annarumma, Mirjan Aquino

Lobby refreshments by Sweet Concessions.

Security provided by P and P Security.

Jujamcyn Theaters is a proud member of the Broadway Green Alliance.

How to Succeed in Business Without Really Trying
SCRAPBOOK

Correspondent: Mary Faber, "Smitty"

Memorable Fan Letter: Daniel Radcliffe's fans get pretty crafty when attempting to contact him. A girl from Denmark sent letters to Rose, Tammy, and myself in which she basically said: "I guess you thought this fan letter would be for you! You'd be wrong. Can you get Daniel to sign this? Also, here's a dollar for your trouble and a picture of me on a dolphin." I'm paraphrasing, but that was the gist.

Most Exciting Celebrity Visitors: We've gotten plenty of celebrity visitors, but my favorite has to be Liza Minnelli. She's been to the show twice, and she's incredibly enthusiastic. She hoots and hollers "Yeah!" and "All right!" after every big number. Great lady, and so supportive.

Actor Who Performed The Most Roles in This Show: Nick Mayo performs a total of six characters in the show. Twelve if you account for the fact that one of his characters has a multiple personality disorder.

Who Has Done the Most Shows: Cleve Asbury has done a total of nine Broadway shows and tons of non-Broadway shows. He has the best stories. Ask him about the 1980 revival of *West Side Story* and "Black Sunday."

Special Backstage Ritual: Every night before the show, we circle up, put our hands in the circle and shout: "Say, Wickets!" The World Wide Wicket Company is where the show is set.

Favorite Moment During Each Performance: The last 30 seconds of "Brotherhood of Man."

Favorite In-Theatre Gathering Place: The ladies' ensemble dressing room has a large sitting room known as Chez Va.

Favorite Off-Site Hangouts: We've been known to frequent quite a few places in the neighborhood. Glass House Tavern is one of our favorites. We also caused a festive, margarita-fueled stir at a Mexican restaurant that shall remain nameless, but it was big fun.

Mascot: "Big Beaver"

Memorable Ad-Lib: John Larroquette loves to throw in ad-libs to break up the company onstage. One of my favorite recurring ad-libs is "Now, about my..." and then he says something like: "bocce ball court," "terrarium," "rumpus room," "Ferris wheel," or "bomb shelter."

Memorable Stage Door Fan Encounters: Every night, the stage door is mobbed by fans eager to get Dan and John's autographs. It takes three police officers just to keep people from going nuts. People will run into oncoming traffic just to get a picture!

Fastest Costume Change: Ellen Harvey, who plays Miss Jones, has the fastest quick change in the show. Between "Brotherhood of Man" and the final scene, she has a total of 35 seconds.

Heaviest/Hottest Costumes: The men in the number "Grand Old Ivy" have to wear old-fashioned football gear like leather helmets, wool pants, and big leather shoulder pads. Then they do a high energy dance in all of that.

Who Wore the Least: The women in "The Pirate Dance" wear cute Polynesian-style bikini tops and sarongs.

Sweethearts Within the Company: Barrett Martin and Megan Sikora are married.

Orchestra Member Who Played the Most Instruments: Mark Thrasher plays seven instruments: flute, alto flute, clarinet, bass clarinet, contrabass clarinet, bassoon, and baritone sax.

1. (L-R): Rose Hemingway, Daniel Radcliffe, director Rob Ashford, John Larroquette and cast take bows on opening night.
2. Tammy Blanchard takes her curtain call.
3. (L-R): Rose Hemingway meets Michele Lee, who played Rosemary on Broadway at in the film.
4. (L-R): Cast members Ellen Harvey and *Yearbook* correspondent Mary Faber at the premiere party at the Plaza Hotel.
5. News anchor Katie Couric visits Radcliffe backstage.

Understudy Anecdote: During our last week of previews, our Rosemary, Rose Hemingway, got sick. Her understudy, Stephanie Rothenberg, had had no rehearsal save for about 45 minutes right before curtain. She was cool as a cucumber and she nailed it.

Coolest Thing About Being in This Show: The audience is so enthusiastic every night! It's really great to have that energy in the air, it helps fuel the performance.

The Importance of Being Earnest

First Preview: December 17, 2010. Opened: January 13, 2011.
Still running as of May 31, 2011.

PLAYBILL

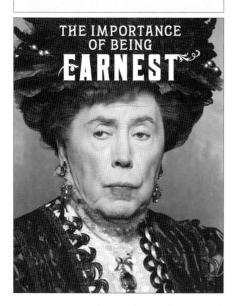

THE IMPORTANCE OF BEING EARNEST

Proper country gentleman John Worthing pretends to have a wild-spirited brother Earnest so he can have fun in town. But when he tries to straighten out his life and marry the lovely Gwendolen, the matter of his true identity causes concern for her imperious aunt, Lady Bracknell. Long-buried secrets resurface in this classic comedy of manners by Oscar Wilde.

CAST

(in order of appearance)

Lane ....PAUL O'BRIEN
Algernon Moncrieff ....SANTINO FONTANA
John Worthing ....DAVID FURR
Lady Bracknell ....BRIAN BEDFORD
Gwendolen Fairfax ....SARA TOPHAM
Cecily Cardew ....CHARLOTTE PARRY
Miss Prism ....DANA IVEY
Rev. Canon Chasuble .....PAXTON WHITEHEAD
Merriman ....TIM MACDONALD
Servant ....AMANDA LEIGH COBB

UNDERSTUDIES

For John Worthing, Algernon Moncrieff:
SEAN ARBUCKLE
For Gwendolen Fairfax, Cecily Cardew:
AMANDA LEIGH COBB
For Merriman, Lane, Servant:
COLIN McPHILLAMY
For Rev. Canon Chasuble:
PAUL O'BRIEN
For Lady Bracknell, Miss Prism:
SANDRA SHIPLEY
Production Stage Manager: ROBYN HENRY
Stage Manager: BRYCE McDONALD

AMERICAN AIRLINES THEATRE

ROUNDABOUT THEATRE COMPANY

Todd Haimes, Artistic Director
Harold Wolpert, Managing Director
Julia C. Levy, Executive Director

Presents

Brian Bedford

in

THE IMPORTANCE OF BEING EARNEST

By

Oscar Wilde

with

Paxton Whitehead

Santino Fontana   David Furr   Tim MacDonald   Paul O'Brien
Charlotte Parry   Sara Topham   Amanda Leigh Cobb

and

Dana Ivey

Set & Costume Design	Lighting Design	Sound Design	Original Music
Desmond Heeley	Duane Schuler	Drew Levy	Berthold Carrière

Hair & Wig Design	Dialect Consultant	Production Stage Manager	Production Management
Paul Huntley	Elizabeth Smith	Robyn Henry	Aurora Productions

Casting by	General Manager	Press Representative
Jim Carnahan, C.S.A.	Rebecca Habel	Boneau/Bryan-Brown
Carrie Gardner, C.S.A.		
Kate Boka, C.S.A.		

Director of Marketing & Sales Promotion	Director of Development	Founding Director	Associate Artistic Director
David B. Steffen	Lynne Gugenheim Gregory	Gene Feist	Scott Ellis

Directed by

Brian Bedford

The Stratford Shakespeare Festival presented an acclaimed production of *The Importance of Being Earnest*, directed by and starring Brian Bedford, in 2009.
Roundabout Theatre Company is a member of the League of Resident Theatres.
www.roundabouttheatre.org

1/13/11

(L-R): Sara Topham, David Furr, Brian Bedford

Photo by Joan Marcus

The Importance of Being Earnest

Brian Bedford
Director,
Lady Bracknell

Dana Ivey
Miss Prism

Paxton Whitehead
Rev. Canon Chasuble

Santino Fontana
Algernon Moncrieff

David Furr
John Worthing

Tim MacDonald
Merriman

Paul O'Brien
Lane

Charlotte Parry
Cecily Cardew

Sara Topham
Gwendolen Fairfax

Sean Arbuckle
u/s John Worthing,
Algernon Moncrieff

Amanda Leigh Cobb
Servant

Colin McPhillamy
u/s Merriman, Lane,
Servant

Sandra Shipley
u/s Lady Bracknell,
Miss Prism

Oscar Wilde
Playwright

Desmond Heeley
Set & Costume
Design

Duane Schuler
Lighting Design

Paul Huntley
Hair and Wig
Designer

Angelina Avallone
Make-up Designer

Jim Carnahan
Casting

Des McAnuff
Artistic Director,
The Stratford
Shakespeare
Festival

Todd Haimes
Artistic Director,
Roundabout Theatre
Company

Jessie Austrian
Gwendolen Fairfax

Richard Gallagher
u/s John Worthing,
Algernon Moncrieff,
Servant

2010-2011 AWARDS

TONY AWARD
Best Costume Design of a Play
(Desmond Heeley)

DRAMA DESK AWARD
Outstanding Featured Actor in a Play
(Brian Bedford)

OUTER CRITICS CIRCLE AWARD
Outstanding Featured Actor in a Play
(Brian Bedford)

CLARENCE DERWENT AWARD
Most promising male performer on
the New York metropolitan scene
(Santino Fontana)

SECURITY
(L-R): Adolf Torres, Malik Howell

Jeffrey Hayenga
u/s Rev. Canon
Chasuble, Merriman,
Lane

Jayne Houdyshell
Miss Prism

Brian Murray
Rev. Canon Chasuble

BOX OFFICE
(L-R): Robert Morgan, Solangel Bido, Mead
Margulies

The Importance of Being Earnest

FRONT OF HOUSE STAFF
(L-R): Chris Busch, Crystal Suarez, Jazmine Perez, Celia Perez, Lance Andrade, Zipporah Aguasvivas

CREW AND MANAGEMENT
Front Row (L-R): Sara Cox Bradley (PA), Bryce McDonald (ASM), Sarah Conyers (IA Apprentice), Carly DiFulvio (Company Manager), Susan Fallon (Wardrobe Supervisor), Lauren Gallitelli (Dresser), Kat Martin (Dresser)

Middle Row (L-R): Robyn Henry (PSM), Dann Wojnar (Sound Operator), Manuela LaPorte (Hair and Wig Supervisor), Robert W. Dowling II (Production Properties), Glenn Merwede (Production Carpenter), Mike Allen (Flyman), Dale Carman (Wardrobe Dayworker)

Back Row (L-R): Yolanda Ramsay (Hair and Wig Assistant), Brian Maiuri (Production Electrician)

ROUNDABOUT THEATRE COMPANY STAFF
ARTISTIC DIRECTOR ....TODD HAIMES
MANAGING DIRECTOR ......HAROLD WOLPERT
EXECUTIVE DIRECTOR ....JULIA C. LEVY
ASSOCIATE ARTISTIC DIRECTOR ...SCOTT ELLIS

ARTISTIC STAFF
DIRECTOR OF ARTISTIC DEVELOPMENT/
    DIRECTOR OF CASTING ....Jim Carnahan
Artistic Consultant ....Robyn Goodman
Resident Director ....Doug Hughes
Associate Artists ....Mark Brokaw, Scott Elliott,
        Sam Gold, Bill Irwin, Joe Mantello,
        Kathleen Marshall, Theresa Rebeck
Literary Manager ....Jill Rafson
Casting Director ....Carrie Gardner
Casting Associate ....Kate Boka
Casting Associate ....Stephen Kopel
Artistic Assistant ....Amy Ashton
Literary Associate ....Josh Fiedler
The Blanche and Irving Laurie Foundation
    Theatre Visions Fund Commissions ....Stephen Karam,
                Nathan Louis Jackson
Educational Foundation of
    America Commissions ....Bekah Brunstetter,
        Lydia Diamond, Diana Fithian,
                Julie Marie Myatt
New York State Council
    on the Arts Commission ....Nathan Louis Jackson
Roundabout Commissions ....Steven Levenson,
        Matthew Lopez, Kim Rosenstock
Casting Interns ....Kyle Bosley, Jillian Cimini, Erin Drake,
        Andrew Femenella, Lauren Lewis, Quinn Meyers

Script Readers ....Jay Cohen, Ben Izzo,
                Nicholas Stimler
Artistic Intern ....Alexis Roblan

---

EDUCATION STAFF
EDUCATION DIRECTOR ....Greg McCaslin
Associate Education Director ....Jennifer DiBella
Education Program Associates ....Aliza Greenberg,
                Sarah Malone
Education Assistant ....Holly Sansom
Education Dramaturg ....Ted Sod
Teaching Artists ....Cynthia Babak, Victor Barbella,
        Grace Bell, LaTonya Borsay,
        Mark Bruckner, Joe Clancy,
        Vanessa Davis-Cohen, Joe Doran,
        Jimena Duca, Elizabeth Dunn-Ruiz,
        Carrie Ellman-Larsen, Deanna Frieman,
        Natalie Gold, Sheri Graubert, Benton Greene,
        Melissa Gregus, Adam Gwon, Devin Haqq,
        Carrie Heitman, Karla Hendrick, Mary Hunt,
        Jason Jacobs, Lisa Renee Jordan,
        Jamie Kalama, Alvin Keith, Tami Mansfield,
        Erin McCready, Kyle McGinley, Nick Moore,
        Andrew Ondrejcak, Meghan O'Neil,
        Laura Poe, Nicole Press, Jennifer Rathbone,
        Leah Reddy, Nick Simone, Joe Skowronski,
        Heidi Stallings, Daniel Sullivan,
        Carl Tallent, Vickie Tanner, Jolie Tong,
        Larine Towler, Cristina Vaccaro,
        Jennifer Varbalow, Leese Walker,
        Eric Wallach, Michael Warner,
        Christina Watanabe, Gail Winar,
                Chad Yarborough

Teaching Artist Emeritus ....Reneé Flemings
Teaching Artist Apprentices ....Carrie Ellman-Larsen,
        Deanna Frieman, Meghan O'Neill
Education Intern ....Erin Monahan

EXECUTIVE ADMINISTRATIVE STAFF
ASSOCIATE MANAGING
    DIRECTOR...........................Greg Backstrom
Assistant Managing Director.........................Jill Boyd
Assistant to the Managing Director ....Zachary Baer
Assistant to the Executive Director ....Nicole Tingir

MANAGEMENT/ADMINISTRATIVE STAFF
GENERAL MANAGER ....Sydney Beers
General Manager,
    American Airlines Theatre ....Rebecca Habel
General Manager, Steinberg Center ....Rachel E. Ayers
Human Resources Manager ....Stephen Deutsch
Operations Manager ....Valerie D. Simmons
Associate General Manager ....Maggie Cantrick
Office Manager ....Scott Kelly
Archivist ....Tiffany Nixon
Receptionists ....Dee Beider, Raquel Castillo,
        Elisa Papa, Allison Patrick,
                Monica Sidorchuk
Messenger ....Darnell Franklin
Management Intern ....Elizabeth Johnstone

FINANCE STAFF
DIRECTOR OF FINANCE.................Susan Neiman
Payroll Director ....John LaBarbera
Accounts Payable Manager ....Frank Surdi
Payroll Benefits Administrator ....Yonit Kafka

The Importance of Being Earnest

Manager Financial Reporting ....Joshua Cohen
Business Office Assistant ....Jackie Verbitski
Business Intern ....Nicholas Barbato

DEVELOPMENT STAFF
DIRECTOR OF
    DEVELOPMENT ....Lynne Gugenheim Gregory
Assistant to the Director of Development ....Liz Malta
Director, Institutional Giving ....Liz S. Alsina
Director, Individual Giving ....Christopher Nave
Director, Special Events ....Steve Schaeffer
Associate Director, Individual Giving ....Tyler Ennis
Manager, Telefundraising ....Gavin Brown
Manager, Donor Information Systems ....Lise Speidel
Associate Manager, Patron Programs ....Marisa Perry
Patron Services Associate ....Joseph Foster
Institutional Giving Assistant ....Brett Barbour
Development Assistant ....Martin Giannini
Individual Giving Assistant ....Sophia Hinshelwood
Special Events Assistant ....Amy Rosenfield
Development Intern ....Sara Valencia

INFORMATION TECHNOLOGY STAFF
IT DIRECTOR ....Antonio Palumbo
IT Associates ....Jim Roma, Cary Kim
DIRECTOR DATABASE
    OPERATIONS...........................Wendy Hutton
Database Administrator/Programmer ....Revanth Anne

MARKETING STAFF
DIRECTOR OF MARKETING
    AND SALES PROMOTION ....David B. Steffen
Associate Director of Marketing ....Tom O'Connor
Senior Marketing Manager ....Shannon Marcotte
Marketing Associate ....Eric Emch
Website Consultant ....Keith Powell Beyland
Director of Telesales Special Promotions ......Marco Frezza
Telesales Manager ....Patrick Pastor
Marketing Interns ....Bradley Sanchez,
    Gabriel Jaquier

TICKET SERVICES STAFF
Director of Sales Operations ....Charlie Garbowski, Jr.
Ticket Services Manager ....Ellen Holt
Acting Subscription Manager ....Bill Klemm
Box Office Managers ....Edward P. Osborne,
    Jaime Perlman, Krystin MacRitchie,
    Nicole Nicholson
Group Sales Manager ....Jeff Monteith
Assistant Box Office Managers ....Robert Morgan,
    Andrew Clements, Scott Falkowski,
    Catherine Fitzpatrick
Assistant Ticket Services Managers ....Robert Kane,
    Lindsay Ericson
Acting Assistant Ticket Services
    Manager ....Jessica Pruett-Barnett
Customer Services Coordinator ....Thomas Walsh
Ticket Services ....Solangel Bido, Arianna Boykins,
    Lauren Cartelli, Joseph Clark,
    Nisha Dhruna, Adam Elsberry,
    James Graham, Kara Harrington,
    Tova Heller, Nicki Ishmael,
    Kate Longosky, Michelle Maccarone,
    Elisa Mala, Mead Margulies,
    Laura Marshall, Chuck Migliaccio,
    Carlos Morris, Bekah Nutt,

Kaia Rafoss, Josh Rozett,
    Ben Schneider, Kenneth Senn,
    Heather Siebert, Nalane Singh,
    Lillian Soto, Ron Tobia,
    Hannah Weitzman
Ticket Services Intern ....Lindsay Hoffman

SERVICES
Counsel ....Paul, Weiss,
    Rifkind, Wharton and Garrison LLP,
    Charles H. Googe Jr., Carol M. Kaplan
Counsel ....Rosenberg & Estis
Counsel ....Andrew Lance,
    Gibson, Dunn, & Crutcher, LLP
Counsel ....Harry H. Weintraub,
    Glick and Weintraub, P.C.
Counsel ....Stroock & Stroock & Lavan LLP
Counsel ....Daniel S. Dokos,
    Weil, Gotshal & Manges LLP
Counsel ....Claudia Wagner/
    Manatt, Phelps & Phillips, LLP
Immigration Counsel ....Mark D. Koestler and
    Theodore Ruthizer
House Physicians ....Dr. Theodore Tyberg,
    Dr. Lawrence Katz
House Dentist ....Neil Kanner, D.M.D.
Insurance ....DeWitt Stern Group, Inc.
Accountant ....Lutz & Carr CPAs, LLP
Advertising ....Spotco/
    Drew Hodges, Jim Edwards,
    Tom Greenwald, Kyle Hall,
    Cory Spinney
Interactive Marketing ....Situation Interactive/
    Damian Bazadona, John Lanasa,
    Eric Bornemann, Randi Fields
Events Photography ....Anita and Steve Shevett
Production Photographer ....Joan Marcus
Theatre Displays ....King Displays, Wayne Sapper
Lobby Refreshments ....Sweet Concessions
Merchandising ....Spotco Merch/
    James Decker

MANAGING DIRECTOR EMERITUS ....Ellen Richard

Roundabout Theatre Company
231 West 39th Street, New York, NY 10018
(212) 719-9393.

GENERAL PRESS REPRESENTATIVES
BONEAU/BRYAN-BROWN
Adrian Bryan-Brown
Matt Polk   Jessica Johnson   Amy Kass

STAFF FOR
THE IMPORTANCE OF BEING EARNEST
Company Manager ....Carly DiFulvio
Production Stage Manager ....Robyn Henry
Stage Manager ....Bryce McDonald
Production Management by ......Aurora Productions Inc./
    Gene O'Donovan, Ben Heller,
    Stephanie Sherline, Jarid Sumner,
    Liza Luxenberg, Ryan Stanisz,
    Jason Margolis, Melissa Mazdra
Assistant Director ....Robert Beard
Make-Up Designer ....Angelina Avallone
Associate Set Designer ....Michael Carnahan

Assistant Scenic Designers ....Rachel Nemec,
    Shana Burns
Associate Costume Designer ....Devon Painter
Associate Lighting Designer ....Justin Partier
Associate Sound Designer ....Will Pickens
Assistant Make-Up Artist ....Jorge Vargas
Assistant to Mr. Heeley ....Ren LaDassor
Production Properties Supervisor ....Peter Sarafin
Production Consultant ....Campbell Baird
Period Movement Consultant ....Frank Ventura
Production Carpenter ....Glenn Merwede
Production Electrician ....Brian Maiuri
Running Properties ....Robert W. Dowling II
Sound Operator ....Dann Wojnar
Flyman ....Mike Allen
Wardrobe Supervisor ....Susan J. Fallon
Dressers ....Lauren Gallitelli, Kat Martin
Wardrobe Dayworker ....Dale Carman
Hair and Wig Supervisor ....Manuela Laporte
Hair and Wig Assistant ....Yolanda Ramsay
Production Assistant ....Sara Cox Bradley
IA Apprentice ....Sarah K. Conyers
Scenery Fabrication by ....Scenic Technologies,
    a division of Production Resource Group, LLC
Lighting Equipment provided by ....PRG Lighting,
    a division of Production Resource Group, LLC
Sound Equipment provided by ....Sound Associates
Costumes constructed by ....Tricorne, Inc. and EuroCo
Milliner ....Rodney Gordon
Special Thanks ....Santo Loquasto, Judy Richardson
    and the Stratford Production Staff

M•A•C Cosmetics
Official Makeup of Roundabout Theatre Company

To learn more about Roundabout Theatre Company,
please visit roundabouttheatre.org
Find us on Facebook.
Follow us on Twitter @RTC_NYC

AMERICAN AIRLINES THEATRE STAFF
Company Manager ....Carly DiFulvio
House Carpenter ....Glenn Merwede
House Electrician ....Brian Maiuri
House Properties ....Robert W. Dowling II
House Sound ....Dann Wojnar
IA Apprentice ....Sarah K. Conyers
Wardrobe Supervisor ....Susan J. Fallon
Box Office Manager ....Ted Osborne
Assistant Box Office Manager ....Robert Morgan
House Manager ....Stephen Ryan
Associate House Manager ....Zipporah Aguasvivas
Head Usher ....Ilia Diaz
House Staff ....Anne Ezell, Denise Furbert,
    Edlyn Gonzalez, Lee Henry,
    Paul Krasner, Rebecca Knell,
    Taylor Martin, Joaquin Melendez,
    Ariana Murphy, Argenis Peguero,
    Celia Perez, Fatimah Robinson,
    Crystal Suarez, Adam Wier
Security ....Julious Russell
Additional Security provided by ....Gotham Security
Maintenance ....Jerry Hobbs, Daniel Pellew,
    Willie Philips, Magali Western
Lobby Refreshments....................Sweet Concessions

The Importance of Being Earnest
Scrapbook

Correspondent: Charlotte Parry, "Cecily Cardew"

Anniversary Party: We celebrated our 100th show with a huge cake made by Wardobe Supervisor Sue Fallon (see pictures, right).

Most Exciting Celebrity Visitor and What They Did/Said: Stephen Fry, Haley Mills and James Earl Jones. I have no idea what they said as I was too busy drooling.

Who Has Done the Most Shows: Brian, Dana and Paxton have played pretty much every role in the play at some point, so I assume that prize goes to them.

Special Backstage Ritual: Our SM Bryce throws me a ball of "goodstuff" at "places" on the Act II set before curtain up. Then we both assume downhill skiing positions and fart out the "badstuff" (see picture, lower right!).

Favorite Moments During Each Performance: The backstage crew are so cold in the hallway offstage right that they huddle in gloves and scarves by an imaginary "campfire." Fallon knits. I haven't yet seen any signs of 'Smores but no doubt someone will get around to it.

Favorite In-Theatre Gathering Place: By the chocolate tin on top of the microwave. Unless there's cake.

Favorite Off-Site Hangout: The local strip clubs. And if they're full, Rosie O'Grady's on 46th for Thirsty Thursday.

Favorite Snack Food: Fallon's cake, whenever there's a birthday, or any other excuse.

Mascot: Gerald the blue fish on the first floor of the dressing rooms and Baldrick, Cecily's imaginary rabbit from the Act II rose bed.

Favorite Therapies: A stiff whiskey and a good moan. Oh, and Fallon's homemade ginger and lemon tea.

Memorable Ad-Libs: References to Gwendolen as "Miss Fairfox" and "Mist Fairfax." Both Sara Topham and I dragging chairs across the stage that have become attached to our costumes. A mystery piece of toilet paper on the stage which had arrived courtesy of the bottom of someone's shoe.

Memorable Press Encounter: Brian did an NPR interview detailing his transformation into Lady Bracknell. And, if this counts, we were filmed for release in cinemas across the world during three performances in late March.

Memorable Stage Door Fan Encounter: Not quite stage door, but we had a seeing eye dog that gave us a standing ovation on the front row, and leapt up onto his hind legs at curtain call. Unfortunately his owner didn't.

Busiest Days at the Box Office: Sundays.

Who Wore the Heaviest/Hottest Costume: Brian Bedford as Lady Bracknell. He calls it the equivalent of a Moroccan Rug.

Catchphrases Only the Company Would Recognize: "Topham has her chat on" (Sara is talking too much), "Are you Thirsty Thursdaying one off?" (Will you be attending drinks on Thursday?), "I can't be trouted" (I

1. Cake celebrating the 100th performance.
2. The cast poses for photos on opening night.
3. Brian Bedford in his dressing room getting into costume as Lady Bracknell.
4. The cast poses backstage with the 100th performance cake.
5. Stage Manager Bryce McDonald and *Yearbook* correspondent Charlotte Parry assume skiing positions backstage before Act II.

don't have the energy), "I don't give a trout" (I couldn't care less).

Sweethearts Within the Company: Sandra Shipley and Paul O'Brien have been together for 25 years. I suppose that counts?!

Nicknames: Troy (Bryce), Topspam (Sara), Furzle (David), His Nibs (Brian).

Coolest Thing About Being in This Show: Having a killer brunch every Sunday downstairs in the traproom, courtesy of Fallon.

In the Heights

First Preview: February 14, 2008. Opened: March 9, 2008.
Closed January 9, 2011 after 29 Previews and 1184 Performances.

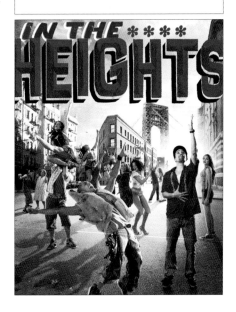

PLAYBILL®

In the upper Manhattan neighborhood of Washington Heights, Spanish-speaking immigrants from throughout the Caribbean seek love, a way to better themselves, and the best plan for what to do with $96,000 that one of them has won in the lottery.

CAST

(in order of appearance)

Graffiti Pete	SETH STEWART
Usnavi	LIN-MANUEL MIRANDA
Piragua Guy	TONY CHIROLDES
Abuela Claudia	OLGA MEREDIZ
Carla	COURTNEY REED
Daniela	ANDRÉA BURNS
Kevin	RICK NEGRÓN
Camila	PRISCILLA LOPEZ
Sonny	SHAUN TAYLOR-CORBETT
Benny	CHRISTOPHER JACKSON
Vanessa	MARCY HARRIELL
Nina	ARIELLE JACOBS
Bolero Singer	DOREEN MONTALVO
Ensemble	TONY CHIROLDES,

SHARONA D'ORNELLAS,
ROSIE LANI FIEDELMAN, RUBÉN FLORES,
MARCUS PAUL JAMES, JENNIFER LOCKE,
DOREEN MONTALVO, NOAH RIVERA,
GABRIELLE RUIZ, MARCOS SANTANA,
RICKEY TRIPP, WILLIS WHITE

Continued on next page

RICHARD RODGERS THEATRE
UNDER THE DIRECTION OF JAMES M. NEDERLANDER AND JAMES L. NEDERLANDER

KEVIN McCOLLUM   JEFFREY SELLER   JILL FURMAN
SANDER JACOBS   GOODMAN/GROSSMAN   PETER FINE   EVERETT/SKIPPER

PRESENT

IN THE
HEIGHTS

MUSIC AND LYRICS BY
LIN-MANUEL MIRANDA

BOOK BY
QUIARA ALEGRÍA HUDES

CONCEIVED BY
LIN-MANUEL MIRANDA

WITH

LIN-MANUEL MIRANDA

ANDRÉA BURNS   MARCY HARRIELL   CHRISTOPHER JACKSON   ARIELLE JACOBS   PRISCILLA LOPEZ
OLGA MEREDIZ   RICK NEGRÓN   COURTNEY REED   SETH STEWART   SHAUN TAYLOR-CORBETT

AND

TONY CHIROLDES   SHARONA D'ORNELLAS   ROSIE LANI FIEDELMAN   RUBÉN FLORES
MARCUS PAUL JAMES   JENNIFER LOCKE   DOREEN MONTALVO   NOAH RIVERA
GABRIELLE RUIZ   MARCOS SANTANA   RICKEY TRIPP   WILLIS WHITE
MICHAEL BALDERRAMA   BLANCA CAMACHO   ALLISON THOMAS LEE
ALEJANDRA REYES   DANIEL J. WATTS

SET DESIGN	*COSTUME DESIGN*	*LIGHTING DESIGN*	*SOUND DESIGN*
ANNA LOUIZOS	PAUL TAZEWELL	HOWELL BINKLEY	ACME SOUND PARTNERS

ARRANGEMENTS & ORCHESTRATIONS	*MUSIC COORDINATOR*	*MUSIC DIRECTOR*
ALEX LACAMOIRE & BILL SHERMAN	MICHAEL KELLER	ZACHARY DIETZ

CASTING	*PRESS REPRESENTATIVE*	*MARKETING*	*COMPANY MANAGER*
TELSEY + COMPANY	THE HARTMAN GROUP	SCOTT A. MOORE	BRIG BERNEY

GENERAL MANAGEMENT	*TECHNICAL SUPERVISOR*	*PRODUCTION STAGE MANAGER*	*ASSOCIATE PRODUCERS*
JOHN S. CORKER	BRIAN LYNCH	BEVERLY JENKINS	RUTH HENDEL
LIZBETH CONE			HAROLD NEWMAN

MUSIC SUPERVISION
ALEX LACAMOIRE

CHOREOGRAPHED BY
ANDY BLANKENBUEHLER

DIRECTED BY
THOMAS KAIL

DEVELOPMENT OF *IN THE HEIGHTS* WAS SUPPORTED BY THE EUGENE O'NEILL THEATER CENTER
DURING A RESIDENCY AT THE MUSIC THEATER CONFERENCE OF 2005.

INITIALLY DEVELOPED BY BACK HOUSE PRODUCTIONS.

INTHEHEIGHTSTHEMUSICAL.COM
BROADWAY CAST ALBUM AVAILABLE ON GHOSTLIGHT RECORDS.

1/9/11

(L-R): Priscilla Lopez and Lin-Manuel Miranda

Photo by Joan Marcus

In the Heights

MUSICAL NUMBERS

Cast Continued

ACT I	
"In the Heights"	Usnavi, Company
"Breathe"	Nina, Company
"Benny's Dispatch"	Benny, Nina
"It Won't Be Long Now"	Vanessa, Usnavi, Sonny
"Inutil"	Kevin
"No Me Diga"	Daniela, Carla, Vanessa, Nina
"96,000"	Usnavi, Benny, Sonny, Vanessa, Daniela, Carla, Company
"Paciencia y Fe" ("Patience and Faith")	Abuela Claudia, Company
"When You're Home"	Nina, Benny, Company
"Piragua"	Piragua Guy
"Siempre" ("Always")	Camila
"The Club/Fireworks"	Company

ACT II	
"Sunrise"	Nina, Benny, Company
"Hundreds of Stories"	Abuela Claudia, Usnavi
"Enough"	Camila
"Carnaval del Barrio"	Daniela, Company
"Atencion"	Kevin
"Alabanza"	Usnavi, Nina, Company
"Everything I Know"	Nina
"No Me Diga (Reprise)"	Daniela, Carla, Vanessa
"Piragua (Reprise)"	Piragua Guy
"Champagne"	Vanessa, Usnavi
"When the Sun Goes Down"	Nina, Benny
"Finale"	Usnavi, Company

BAND

Conductor:
ZACHARY DIETZ
Associate Conductor:
JOSEPH CHURCH
Lead Trumpet:
RAUL AGRAZ
Trumpet:
SCOTT WENDHOLT
Trombones:
JOE FIEDLER, RYAN KEBERLE
Reeds:
DAVE RICHARDS, KRISTY NORTER
Drums:
ANDRES FORERO
Percussion:
DOUG HINRICHS, WILSON TORRES
Bass:
IRIO O'FARRILL
Guitar:
MANNY MOREIRA
Keyboard 1:
ZACHARY DIETZ
Keyboard 2:
JOSEPH CHURCH

(L-R): Courtney Reed and Andréa Burns

Photo by Joan Marcus

SWINGS

MICHAEL BALDERRAMA,
BLANCA CAMACHO,
ALLISON THOMAS LEE,
ALEJANDRA REYES,
DANIEL J. WATTS

UNDERSTUDIES

For Usnavi:
MICHAEL BALDERRAMA, NOAH RIVERA,
SETH STEWART, SHAUN TAYLOR-CORBETT
For Abuela Claudia:
BLANCA CAMACHO, DOREEN MONTALVO
For Nina, Vanessa:
COURTNEY REED, GABRIELLE RUIZ
For Benny:
MARCUS PAUL JAMES, WILLIS WHITE
For Camila, Daniela:
BLANCA CAMACHO, DOREEN MONTALVO
For Kevin:
TONY CHIROLDES, RUBÉN FLORES
For Carla:
ALLISON THOMAS LEE, ALEJANDRA REYES,
GABRIELLE RUIZ
For Sonny:
NOAH RIVERA, SETH STEWART
For Graffiti Pete:
MICHAEL BALDERRAMA, RICKEY TRIPP,
DANIEL J. WATTS
For Piragua Guy:
RUBÉN FLORES, NOAH RIVERA

DANCE CAPTAIN

MICHAEL BALDERRAMA

ASSISTANT DANCE CAPTAIN

ALEJANDRA REYES

In the Heights

Lin-Manuel Miranda
Usnavi;
Music and Lyrics;
Original Concept

Andréa Burns
Daniela

Marcy Harriell
Vanessa

Christopher Jackson
Benny

Arielle Jacobs
Nina

Priscilla Lopez
Camila

Olga Merediz
Abuela Claudia

Rick Negrón
Kevin

Courtney Reed
Carla

Seth Stewart
Graffiti Pete

Shaun Taylor-Corbett
Sonny

Tony Chiroldes
Piragua Guy

Sharona D'Ornellas
Ensemble

Rosie Lani Fiedelman
Ensemble

Rubén Flores
Ensemble

Marcus Paul James
Ensemble

Jennifer Locke
Ensemble

Doreen Montalvo
Bolero Singer/
Ensemble

Noah Rivera
Ensemble

Gabrielle Ruiz
Ensemble

Marcos Santana
Ensemble

Rickey Tripp
Ensemble

Willis White
Ensemble

Michael Balderrama
Resident Supervisor/
Fight Captain/Swing

Blanca Camacho
Swing

Allison Thomas Lee
Swing

Alejandra Reyes
Swing; Assistant
Dance Captain

Daniel J. Watts
Swing

Quiara Alegría Hudes
Book

Thomas Kail
Director

Andy
Blankenbuehler
Choreographer

Alex Lacamoire
Music Supervisor,
Arranger,
Orchestrator

Anna Louizos
Set Designer

Paul Tazewell
Costume Designer

Howell Binkley
Lighting Designer

In the Heights

Sten Severson, Tom Clark, Mark Menard and Nevin Steinberg,
Acme Sound Partners
Sound Designer

Bill Sherman
*Arranger/
Orchestrator*

Bernard Telsey,
Telsey + Company
Casting

John Corker
General Manager

Brian Lynch/
Theatretech, Inc.
Technical Supervisor

Charles LaPointe
Wig Designer

Ron Piretti
Fight Director

Casey Hushion
Assistant Director

Kevin McCollum
Producer

Jeffrey Seller
Producer

Jill Furman
Producer

Sander Jacobs
Producer

Robyn Goodman,
Goodman/Grossman
Producer

Walt Grossman,
Goodman/Grossman
Producer

Sonny Everett,
Everett/Skipper
Producer

Ruth Hendel
Associate Producer

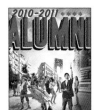

Sandy Alvarez
Swing

Kyle Beltran
Usnavi

Corbin Bleu
Usnavi

Danny Bolero
Kevin

Dwayne Clark
Ensemble

Janet Dacal
Nina

David Del Rio
Sonny

Kristina Fernandez
Swing

Michael Fielder
*Swing, Assistant
Dance Captain*

Afra Hines
Swing

Nina Lafarga
Ensemble

Bianca Marroquin
Daniela

Clifton Oliver
Benny

Antuan Raimone
Ensemble, Swing

Eliseo Román
*Piragua Guy,
Ensemble*

Jon Rua
Graffiti Pete, Sonny

In the Heights

Luis Salgado
Ensemble

Jordin Sparks
Nina

Nancy Ticotin
Swing

Alicia Taylor
Tomasko
Ensemble, Swing

William B. Wingfield
Graffiti Pete

STAGE DOOR
Angelo Gonzalez

Photos by Brian Mapp

WARDROBE
Seated: Alon Ben-David

Standing (L-R): Leslie Moulton, Kirsten Solberg,
Susan Checklick

HAIR
Jamie Stewart

CREW
Seated (L-R): Dan Tramontozzi, Justin Rathbun,
Chris Kurtz, David Speer, Brian Frankel

Standing (L-R): Steve DeVerna, Kevin Camus, Jae Day

STAGE AND COMPANY MANAGEMENT
Front: Heather Hogan

Back Row (L-R): Kenneth J. McGee,
Brig Berney, Beverly Jenkins

ORCHESTRA
Front Row (L-R): Joe Fiedler, Doug Hinrichs, Andres Forero, Zachary Dietz

Back Row (L-R): Richard Bouka, Dave Miller, Irio O'Farrill, Kristy Norter, Wilson Torres, Matt Gallagher,
Carl Fischer

In the Heights

STAFF FOR *IN THE HEIGHTS*

GENERAL MANAGEMENT
John S. Corker
Lizbeth Cone

GENERAL PRESS REPRESENTATIVES
THE HARTMAN GROUP
Michael Hartman
Wayne Wolfe   Matt Ross

DIRECTOR OF MARKETING
Scott A. Moore

CASTING
TELSEY + COMPANY
Bernie Telsey CSA, Will Cantler CSA, David Vaccari CSA,
Bethany Knox CSA, Craig Burns CSA,
Tiffany Little Canfield CSA, Rachel Hoffman CSA,
Carrie Rosson CSA, Justin Huff CSA, Bess Fifer CSA,
Patrick Goodwin CSA, Abbie Brady-Dalton

COMPANY MANAGER ....Brig Berney
TECHNICAL SUPERVISION ....Brian Lynch/
Theatretech, Inc.
PRODUCTION STAGE MANAGER .....Beverly Jenkins
WIG DESIGNER ....Charles LaPointe
Assistant Director...........................Casey Hushion
Associate Choreographer ....Joey Dowling
Fight Director ....Ron Piretti
Resident Supervisor ....Michael Balderrama
Assistant Dance Captain ....Alejandra Reyes
Stage Manager ....Kenneth J. McGee
Assistant Stage Manager ....Heather Hogan
Latin Assistant Choreographer ....Luis Salgado
Fight Captain ....Michael Balderrama
Associate Scenic Designers ....Donyale Werle,
Todd Potter
Assistant Scenic Designers....................Hilary Noxon,
Heather Dunbar
Associate Costume Designer ....Michael Zecker
Assistant Costume Designer ....Caitlin Hunt
Associate Lighting Designer ....Mark Simpson
Assistant Lighting Designer ....Greg Bloxham,
Ryan O'Gara
Associate Sound Designer ....Sten Severson
Moving Light Programmer ....David Arch
Advance Carpenter ....McBrien Dunbar
Advance Flyman ....Cheyenne Benson
Production Electrician ....Keith Buchanan
Head Electrician ....Christopher Kurtz
Production Sound..........................Dan Robillard
Production Propmaster ....George Wagner
Head Propmaster ....David Speer
Follow Spot Operator ....Jason Wilkosz
Sound Engineer ....Justin Rathbun
Wardrobe Supervisor ....Susan Checklick
Hair Supervisor ....Jamie Stewart
Dressers ....Alon Ben-David, Jake Fry,
Jennifer Hohn, Kirsten Solberg
Rehearsal Pianists ....Joseph Church, Matt Gallagher,
Carmine Giglio, Daniel Moctezuma, Kat Sherrell, Jeff Tanski
Musical Coordinator ....Michael Keller
"The Club" Dance Arrangement ....Oscar Hernandez
Copyist ....Emily Grishman Music Preparation/
Emily Grishman, Katharine Edmonds

Keyboard Programming ....Randy Cohen
Rehearsal Drummer ....Doug Hinrichs
Music Assistant ....Colleen Darnell
Management Assistant ....Andy Jones
Production Assistants ....Jess Slocum, Mark Barna
Assistant to Messrs. McCollum & Seller ....Kait Fine
Assistant to Mr. Corker ....Kim Marie Vasquez
Legal Counsel ....Levine Plotkin Menin, LLP/
Loren Plotkin, Susan Mindell,
Conrad Rippy, Cris Criswell
Marketing Associate ....Joshua Lee Poole
Advertising ....SpotCo/Drew Hodges, Jim Edwards,
Darius Suyama, Kristen Rathbun, Tom Greenwald
Accountant ....FK Partners/Robert Fried
Controller ....Sarah Galbraith and Co.
Insurance ...........................D.R. Reiff & Associates
Banking ....Signature Bank/
Margaret Monigan, Mary Ann Fanelli
Payroll ....Castellana Services
Merchandise ....Marquee Merchandise LLC/
Matt Murphy
Travel Arrangements ....Tzell Travel
Flyer Distribution ....Laura Cosentino/Roselily
Website/Internet Marketing ....SpotCo/
Sara Fitzpatrick, Matt Wilstein
Production Photographer ....Joan Marcus
Physical Therapy ....Mark Hunter Hall
Merchandising ....George Fenmore/
More Merchandising International

THE PRODUCING OFFICE
Kevin McCollum   Jeffrey Seller
John S. Corker   Debra Nir
Kait Fine

SPECIAL THANKS
Luis Miranda; John Buzzetti; Mark Sendroff;
Nick Lugo; LaVie Productions/R. Erin Craig,
Off-Broadway General Manager

CREDITS
Scenery constructed by Centerline Studio, Inc. Lighting equipment from PRG Lighting. Sound equipment from PRG Audio. New York Daily News, L.P., used with permission. Chain motors from Show Motion. Trucking by Clark Transfer, Inc. Percussion equipment and drum programming by Dan McMillan. Latin percussion supplied by Pearl Drum Company. Andres Patrick Forero plays Yamaha Drum heads, Sabian cymbals, Vic Firth sticks and Reunion Blues, exclusively. Wireless handsets by Verizon. Costumes built by Donna Langman Costumes; Tricorne, Inc.; Paul Chang Custom Taylor. Millinery by Lynne Mackey Studio. Hosiery and undergarments from Bra*Tenders. Goya products furnished by Goya Foods, Inc. Lottery items courtesy of NY State Lottery. Cell phones courtesy of Motorola. Cups, straws and stirrers courtesy of Solo, Inc. Mars Inc. products used. Adams gum and Cadbury chocolates used. Werthers Original courtesy of Storck USA. MASTERFOODS USA products used. Unilever N.A. products used. Kraft Foods products used. Massimo-Zanetti beverages used. Country Club cola products and Iberia Food products courtesy of Luis Botero, North Shore Bottling Company, Brooklyn, NY. Beauty salon supplies provided by Ray Beauty Supply. Piragua Cart, artificial food props, other props provided by John Creech

Design and Production. Local trucking provided by Prop Transport. Flicker candles provided by Clara Sherman, Kinnelon, NJ. Car service counter, bodega counter provided by Blackthorne Studio. Various bodega prop dressing courtesy of Rock Ice Café and Catering, Dunellen, NY. Food display hanging racks courtesy of Green Acres Health Food Store, Piscataway, NJ. Additional set and hand props courtesy of George Fenmore, Inc. Steel security gates by Steelcraft Folding Gate Corp. Raul Agraz exclusively uses Cannonball trumpets.

Makeup provided by M•A•C

Bolero singer is Doreen Montalvo. Radio voices by Joshua Henry, Eliseo Roman and Daphne Rubin-Vega

Smoke, haze and strobe lights are used
in this production.

Performance rights to *In the Heights*
are licensed by R&H Theatricals:
www.rnhtheatricals.com

In the Heights rehearsed at
The New 42nd Street Studios.

NEDERLANDER

Chairman ....James M. Nederlander
President ....James L. Nederlander

Executive Vice President
Nick Scandalios

Vice President   Senior Vice President
Corporate Development   Labor Relations
Charlene S. Nederlander   **Herschel Waxman**

Vice President   Chief Financial Officer
Jim Boese   **Freida Sawyer Belviso**

HOUSE STAFF FOR
THE RICHARD RODGERS THEATRE
House Manager ....Timothy Pettolina
Box Office Treasurer ....Fred Santore Jr.
Assistant Treasurer ....Corinne Dorso
Electrician ....Steve Carver
Carpenter ....Kevin Camus
Propertymaster ....Stephen F. DeVerna
Engineer ....Sean Quinn

Christopher Jackson

Photo by Joan Marcus

In the Heights
SCRAPBOOK

Correspondent: Shaun Taylor-Corbett, "Sonny"

Most Vivid Memory of the Final Performance: Lin-Manuel Miranda calling out, "No Pare," and the entire house at the Richard Rodgers screaming back, "Sigue Sigue." And the entire house screaming back "Freaky, Freaky," after Lin asks, "Did you see me get...." The look of pure joy on his face was unforgettable.

During Blackout, as the cast opens up their phones on stage, the entire audience of over 1,400 people, opening up their phones and waving them around as the cast sings, "Oh, no...Oh, no." It was a sea of lights waving back and forth, connecting the audience and the cast in a moment that will last in our memories forever. It was the stuff that dreams are made of.

Memorable Quotes from Farewell Stage Speeches: "And everything that I've ever wanted to know about saying goodbye, I realized we wrote over these last eight years. Because this is a show about how we say goodbye. This is a show about how you walk away from something with your head up, and your heart full, and your eyes clear and the little piece of something in every single step you take."— Thomas Kail (director)

"I know how upset some of y'all are getting, but *In the Heights* ain't closing, it's just spreadin'...somewhere chillin' in some outer theatre lobby, some little high-schooler's gonna be playin' Usnavi. That's why I want all of y'all to grab this. That little white kid's gonna know what a Puerto Rican flag is!"—Lin-Manuel Miranda

"When David heard music, he danced!"—Chris Jackson

Memorable Note, Fax or Fan Letter in the Final Weeks: Lin read a letter to us in the last two weeks of the show from a fan who had a friend that bought tickets to see the tour for all four shows of the weekend. This man was Latino and desired more than anything to see and experience *In the Heights*. He came to both shows on Saturday and was overfilled with joy to see and hear his culture up on that Broadway stage. The next day, Sunday, his friends came to meet him at the theatre and couldn't find him. They later found out that he had a heart attack and passed away that Saturday night. They were deeply saddened, but happy to know that he got to fulfill his dream of seeing *In the Heights* for the first time earlier that day.

Farewell Parties: Jordin Sparks' karaoke farewell party and Corbin Bleu's farewell party.

Most Exciting Celebrity Visitors: Bill and Hillary Clinton. The whole audience gave them a standing ovation as they entered the theatre. After the show, they met the cast on stage and shook each and every one of our hands. Also, Marc Anthony, who said that Eliseo Román had an incredible voice, and running into Leonardo DiCaprio in the stage manager's office where he dropped $100 into the BCEFA bucket.

Special Backstage Rituals: Before every show,

1. The cast forms its final prayer circle beneath the stage on closing night.
2. Composer Lin-Manuel Miranda juggles his Tony Award and a snack backstage at the final performance.
3. Memorabilia from closing night.

the entire cast would gather in the basement/cross-under area and "circle up," holding hands and checking in with one another. We would breathe together and share inspiring thoughts and ideas, or hardships that we needed help with. Our leader, Chris Jackson (Andréa Burns when Chris was away) or anyone who wanted to lead that day, would unify us and lead us in a prayer that would prepare us as a community to express the truth of family, home, and the pride of this amazing story. It was our duty and job to fulfill the responsibility each night of living and breathing as a community of real people, not only for the sake of a whole culture, but for the sake of all cultures around the world. One prayer we often said, passed to us by Debbie Allen, and recited on our closing night was, "unify us, don't divide us; may this ring, of our love, remain complete, around the world, amen!" We would say this in call-and-response fashion.

A funny ritual that's dear to us all: Marcus Paul James's vocal warm-up would be to sing, "On the Wings of Love," and from our dressing rooms we'd all yell, "Higher!" He would raise the pitch a half-step, and repeat "On the Wings of Love," and so on until his voice would crack or he would reach his dressing room.

Favorite Moments During the Final Weeks: After Sonny's "96,000" rap, holding the pose for a good thirty seconds while the crowd went crazy, and the end of "96,000." Marcy dropping the Shiraz, and pulling up her skirt by accident as she picked it up during closing night.

Favorite In-Theatre Gathering Place: Jamie Stewart, who was the head of our hair department, and our dear friend, decorated her whole area in the basement next to where we had our prayer circle. She put up pictures of birthday parties, weddings, and newspaper clippings involving cast members. We used to hang out by her chair and she kept us all laughing and full of spirit.

Favorite Off-Site Hangout: We rotated our parties from Bourbon Street, Brazil Brazil and we had many a farewell party and birthday party at the Time Hotel.

Favorite Snack Foods: Red Velvet Cake,

In the Heights
SCRAPBOOK

Lin-Manuel Miranda speaks to the audience during the final curtain calls.

cookies made by fans, Jordin Sparks' cupcakes! Jamie Stewart's sweet potato pie.

Nancy Ticotin's guacamole and her chocolate chip cookies.

Blanca Camacho's blueberry cobbler, Texas Caviar, and hummus.

Marcus Paul James' famous 4th of July Barbecue Parties.

Javier Muñoz's parents' coquito (coconut eggnog).

Tony Chiroldes's partner Peter's coquito and Tres Leches Cake.

Magnolia cupcakes and banana pudding.

And boy did we love pernil—roast pork, from any source. Justin Rathbun made a mean one!

Once the Puerto Rican restaurant El Deportivo closed, thank goodness the Colombian restaurant, Farmer's Rotisserie, opened. Rice, beans, plantains, soup were popular items from both places.

Mascot: Voltron...Alex Lacamoire, arranger and first musical conductor, kept a huge Voltron next to his chair in the pit. Each body part was an individual character, forming the full-bodied Voltron, and represented each person that formed the artistic powerhouse of *In the Heights*: Lin-Manuel Miranda (composer/lyricist), Alex Lacamoire (co-orchestrator/musical director), Bill Sherman (co-orchestrator), Tommy Kail (director), Quiara Alegría Hudes (book writer).

Favorite Therapies: We always had buckets of Ricola backstage and small tin cans of Altoids. There were mugs of hot water all around the theatre at any given time, and Icy-Hot. PT with Mark Hall was always a must every week.

Memorable Ad-Lib: The classic: "You are all subject to my mice" as opposed to "You are all my guinea pigs"—Priscilla Lopez

Sweethearts Within the Company: Blanca Camacho, Janet Dacal, Tony Chiroldes, Jen Hohn, Jake Fry, Afra Hines, Jimmy Russell

(Doorman), Brig Berney (company manager), Beverly Jenkins, Ken McGee, Heather Hogan.

Record Number of Cell Phone Rings, Cell Phone Photos or Texting Incidents During a Performance: Too many to count and they really frustrated Lin.

Memorable Press Encounters: The press parade when Britney came to the show, and Stephen Holt's interview with the cast of *Heights* at the Drama Desk Awards. Please look it up on YouTube!

Web Buzz: It was amazing. Lin's YouTube videos promoting the show captured the world's attention. He had a *Heights* song for Rihanna's "Umbrella" and "Run This" tour.

Catchphrases Only the Company Would Recognize: "Packin' up and pickin' up." "I've got today....off!!!" "Let's go from...waste... taste..face." "Ah no."

Orchestra Member Who Played the Most Consecutive Performances Without a Sub: Wilson Torres.

Best In-House Parody Lyrics: "Look at my fiber work." "I'm washing my tights." "He stood there staring at me toothless...he stood there staring at me juiceless." During "Champagne," Vanessa and Usnavi sing, "Are you done for the day, no way, 'cause we've got a date, OKAY." We had it like this: "Are you done for the day, no way, 'cause we've got a date, I'M GAY."

Company In-Jokes: Pre-fight call song to the theme of the old "Batman" TV series. During the club scene, everyone singing "booty, booty, and a little more booty." During "Paciencia y Fe," when Abuela sings, "Nueva York was far, but Nueva York had work," people would reply "WERK" with a snap.

Memorable Stage Door Fan Encounter: One matinee I went on for Usnavi and totally rapped gibberish during "96,000," saying, "You're now...tuckatoka took took...Washington

Hiznits," instead of, "You're now the youngest tycoon in Washington Hiznits." That night, as I was entering the stage door for the second show, a fan yelled really loudly in front of the whole audience entering the theater, "Hey Shaun, I heard you really screwed up '96,000' today!" That did *not* feel good right before going on for Usnavi that night.

Memorable Directorial Note: Alex Lacamoire used to tell us to cut off sung notes "like a soft serve ice-cream cone": Basically, the way you swirl the tip right before it stops coming out of the machine. The many ways and times choreographer Andy Blankenbuehler spoke of the ultimate pride we needed to muster and feel in "Carnaval" on the stop during the line "We rep our people and the beat go." Another memorable choreographic note happened at the end of the opening scene when the whole ensemble sang and repeated "In the Heights," while lifting their arms, feeling the music playing inside of them. Andy called this the "*Shawshank* Moment."

Nicknames: Priscilla Lopez: PLo. Mandy: The Beast" Gonzalez. Antuan "Magic" Raimone. Luis "Passion" Salgado. Josh "Chocolate Thunder" Henry. Shaun Taylor-Corbett: Shauntay La Corbett. Daniel J. Watts: "DeWatts." Michael Balderrama: "Baldy."

Ghostly Encounter Backstage: Luis Salgado claims to have seen the ghost of a small child just off stage during a show.

Embarrassing Moments: Robin De Jesús, the original Sonny, handing Lin-Manuel Miranda, the original Usnavi, and then Javier Muñoz on a separate occasion, a Coke can instead of a coffee cup which he has to then give to Vanessa, originated by Karen Olivo during "It Won't Be Long Now." The line is supposed to be, "Coffee, whole milk, very sweet, little bit of cinnamon?" Instead he had to say, "Coke, very sweet, just like you like it?" When she said, "Just like my abuela used to do," we all fell out laughing. Karen was so mad the first time that she could have pushed Robin into the pit, and his face was the color of a Coke can. The second time, he danced out of range of her swing, and from then on Javi hid the Coke can as far away from Robin as possible for every show.

Coolest Thing About Being in This Show: If you could pinpoint the supreme essence of what the word "home" means to every human being on this planet, that would be *In the Heights*. It is our home, and our family. It taught us how to love, and showed us what it was really like to be loved. We have had weddings and births throughout the course of the show, and more parties than can be counted. We celebrate life through performing the show on stage, but also through living by the messages of the show offstage with each other. We represent a proud Latino culture, and unheard voices that can finally shout out with joy: "We are here!" Ultimately what it gave us was something noble, and honorable to live by and say, "If I never do anything else, I did this."

Jersey Boys

First Preview: October 4, 2005. Opened: November 6, 2005.
Still running as of May 31, 2011.

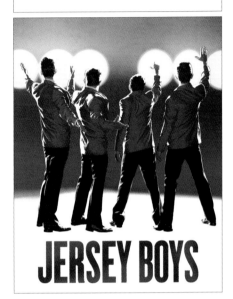

PLAYBILL

JERSEY BOYS

A musical based on the lives and careers of the close-harmony pop group The Four Seasons. We meet founder Tommy DeVito, a bad boy who is constantly in trouble with the law, supportive Nick Massi, songwriter Bob Gaudio, and finally lead singer Frankie Valli, whose soulful falsetto helps loft the foursome to international success. That success, along with DeVito's troubles with the mob and changes in the public's musical taste, helps splinter the original group. But the indefatigable Valli and the prolific Gaudio help make sure that the music lives on.

CAST

(in alphabetical order)

Nick DeVito, Stosh, Billy Dixon, Norman Waxman,
    Charlie Calello (and others) .....MILES AUBREY
Officer Petrillo, Hank Majewski, Crewe's PA,
    Joe Long (and others) ....ERIK BATES
Mary Delgado,
    Angel (and others) ....BRIDGET BERGER
Nick Massi ....MATT BOGART
French Rap Star, Detective One, Hal Miller,
    Barry Belson, Police Officer,
    Davis (and others) ....KRIS COLEMAN
Joey, Recording Studio Engineer
    (and others) ....RUSSELL FISCHER
Bob Crewe (and others) ....PETER GREGUS
Bob Gaudio ....RYAN JESSE
Gyp DeCarlo (and others) ....MARK LOTITO
Tommy DeVito ....DOMINIC NOLFI
Church Lady, Miss Frankie Nolan, Bob's Party Girl,
    Angel, Lorraine (and others) ......JESSICA RUSH

Continued on next page

162

---

❾ AUGUST WILSON THEATRE

A JUJAMCYN THEATRE

JORDAN ROTH
President

PAUL LIBIN
Producing Director

JACK VIERTEL
Creative Director

Dodger Theatricals   Joseph J. Grano   Tamara and Kevin Kinsella   Pelican Group
in association with Latitude Link   Rick Steiner/Osher/Staton/Bell/Mayerson Group

present

JERSEY BOYS

The Story of Frankie Valli & The Four Seasons

Book by	Music by	Lyrics by
Marshall Brickman & Rick Elice	**Bob Gaudio**	**Bob Crewe**

with

Matt Bogart   Ryan Jesse   Dominic Nolfi   Jarrod Spector

Miles Aubrey   Erik Bates   Bridget Berger   Scott J. Campbell   Kris Coleman
Ken Dow   Russell Fischer   John Hickman   Katie O'Toole   Joe Payne
Jessica Rush   Dominic Scaglione Jr.   Sara Schmidt   Taylor Sternberg
with Peter Gregus and Mark Lotito

Scenic Design	Costume Design	Lighting Design	Sound Design
Klara Zieglerova	Jess Goldstein	Howell Binkley	Steve Canyon Kennedy

Projection Design	Wig and Hair Design	Fight Director	Production Supervisor
Michael Clark	Charles LaPointe	Steve Rankin	Richard Hester

Orchestrations	Music Coordinator	Conductor	Production Stage Manager
Steve Orich	John Miller	Andrew Wilder	Michelle Bosch

Technical Supervisor	East Coast Casting	West Coast Casting	Company Manager
Peter Fulbright	Tara Rubin Casting	Sharon Bialy C.S.A. Sherry Thomas C.S.A.	Sandra Carlson

Associate Producers	Executive Producer	Promotions	Press Representative
Lauren Mitchell Rhoda Mayerson Stage Entertainment	Sally Campbell Morse	HHC Marketing	Boneau/Bryan-Brown

Music Direction, Vocal Arrangements & Incidental Music
Ron Melrose

Choreography
Sergio Trujillo

Directed by
Des McAnuff

World Premiere Produced by La Jolla Playhouse, La Jolla, CA
Christopher Ashley, Artistic Director & Michael S. Rosenberg, Managing Director

The producers wish to thank Theatre Development Fund for its support of this production.

10/1/10

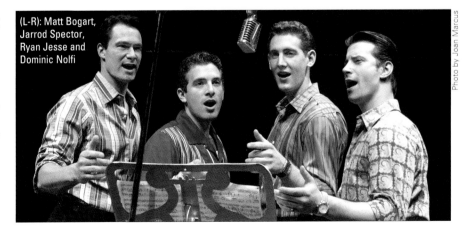

(L-R): Matt Bogart, Jarrod Spector, Ryan Jesse and Dominic Nolfi

Photo by Joan Marcus

Jersey Boys

MUSICAL NUMBERS

ACT ONE

"Ces Soirées-La (Oh What a Night)" – Paris, 2000 ....French Rap Star, Backup Group
"Silhouettes" ....Tommy DeVito, Nick Massi, Nick DeVito,
Frankie Castelluccio
"You're the Apple of My Eye" ....Tommy DeVito, Nick Massi, Nick DeVito
"I Can't Give You Anything But Love" ....Frankie Castelluccio
"Earth Angel" ....Tommy DeVito, Full Company
"Sunday Kind of Love" ....Frankie Valli, Tommy DeVito, Nick Massi, Nick's Date
"My Mother's Eyes" ....Frankie Valli
"I Go Ape" ....The Four Lovers
"(Who Wears) Short Shorts" ....The Royal Teens
"I'm in the Mood for Love/Moody's Mood for Love" ....Frankie Valli
"Cry for Me" ....Bob Gaudio, Frankie Valli, Tommy DeVito, Nick Massi
"An Angel Cried" ....Hal Miller and The Rays
"I Still Care" ....Miss Frankie Nolan and The Romans
"Trance" ....Billy Dixon and The Topix
"Sherry" ....The Four Seasons
"Big Girls Don't Cry" ....The Four Seasons
"Walk Like a Man" ....The Four Seasons
"December, 1963 (Oh What a Night)" ....Bob Gaudio, Full Company
"My Boyfriend's Back" ....The Angels
"My Eyes Adored You" ....Frankie Valli, Mary Delgado, The Four Seasons
"Dawn (Go Away)" ....The Four Seasons
"Walk Like a Man" (reprise) ....Full Company

ACT TWO

"Big Man in Town" ....The Four Seasons
"Beggin'" ....The Four Seasons
"Stay" ....Bob Gaudio, Frankie Valli, Nick Massi
"Let's Hang On (To What We've Got)" ....Bob Gaudio, Frankie Valli
"Opus 17 (Don't You Worry 'Bout Me)" ....Bob Gaudio, Frankie Valli and
The New Seasons
"Bye Bye Baby" ....Frankie Valli and The Four Seasons
"C'mon Marianne" ....Frankie Valli and The Four Seasons
"Can't Take My Eyes Off You" ....Frankie Valli
"Working My Way Back to You" ....Frankie Valli and The Four Seasons
"Fallen Angel" ....Frankie Valli
"Rag Doll" ....The Four Seasons
"Who Loves You" ....The Four Seasons, Full Company

(L-R): Jarrod Spector, Ryan Jesse, Dominic Nolfi and Matt Bogart

Cast Continued

Frankie Valli (Wed. &
Sat. matinees) ......DOMINIC SCAGLIONE JR.
Frankie's Mother, Nick's Date, Angel,
Francine (and others) ....SARA SCHMIDT
Frankie Valli ....JARROD SPECTOR
Thugs.......................KEN DOW, JOE PAYNE

SWINGS

SCOTT J. CAMPBELL, JOHN HICKMAN,
KATIE O'TOOLE, TAYLOR STERNBERG

Dance Captain:
PETER GREGUS
Assistant Dance Captain:
KATIE O'TOOLE

UNDERSTUDIES

For Tommy DeVito:
ERIK BATES, SCOTT J. CAMPBELL
For Nick Massi:
MILES AUBREY, JOHN HICKMAN
For Frankie Valli:
RUSSELL FISCHER,
DOMINIC SCAGLIONE JR.,
TAYLOR STERNBERG
For Bob Gaudio:
SCOTT J. CAMPBELL, JOHN HICKMAN
For Gyp DeCarlo:
MILES AUBREY, JOHN HICKMAN
For Bob Crewe:
ERIK BATES, SCOTT J. CAMPBELL,
JOHN HICKMAN

ORCHESTRA

Conductor:
ANDREW WILDER
Associate Conductor:
DEBORAH N. HURWITZ
Keyboards:
DEBORAH N. HURWITZ,
STEPHEN "HOOPS" SNYDER
Guitars:
JOE PAYNE
Bass:
KEN DOW
Drums:
KEVIN DOW
Reeds:
MATT HONG, BEN KONO
Trumpet:
DAVID SPIER
Music Coordinator:
JOHN MILLER

Jersey Boys

Matt Bogart
Nick Massi

Ryan Jesse
Bob Gaudio

Dominic Nolfi
Tommy DeVito

Jarrod Spector
Frankie Valli

Peter Gregus
Bob Crewe and others

Mark Lotito
Gyp DeCarlo and others

Miles Aubrey
Norm Waxman and others

Erik Bates
Hank Majewski and others

Bridget Berger
Mary Delgado and others

Scott J. Campbell
Swing

Kris Coleman
Hal Miller and others

Ken Dow
Thug, Bass

Russell Fischer
Joey, Recording Studio Engineer and others

John Hickman
Swing

Katie O'Toole
Swing

Joe Payne
Thug, Guitars

Jessica Rush
Lorraine and others

Dominic Scaglione Jr.
Frankie Valli on Wed. & Sat. Mats.

Sara Schmidt
Francine and others

Taylor Sternberg
Swing

Marshall Brickman
Book

Rick Elice
Book

Bob Gaudio
Composer

Bob Crewe
Lyricist

Des McAnuff
Director

Sergio Trujillo
Choreographer

Ron Melrose
Music Direction, Vocal Arrangements and Incidental Music

Klara Zieglerova
Scenic Design

Jess Goldstein
Costume Design

Howell Binkley
Lighting Design

Steve Canyon Kennedy
Sound Design

Charles LaPointe
Wig/Hair Design

Steve Rankin
Fight Director

Richard Hester
Production Supervisor

Steve Orich
Orchestrations

Jersey Boys

John Miller
Music Coordinator

Andrew Wilder
Conductor

Peter Fulbright/
Tech Production
Services
Technical Supervisor

Tara Rubin Casting
Casting

Sharon Bialy and
Sherry Thomas
West Coast Casting

Stephen Gabis
Dialect Coach

Michael David,
Dodger Theatricals
Producer

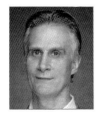

Edward Strong,
Dodger Theatricals
Producer

Rocco Landesman,
Dodger Theatricals
Producer

Joseph J. Grano
Producer

Kevin and Tamara Kinsella
Producers

Ivor Royston,
The Pelican Group
Producer

Rick Steiner
Producer

John and Bonnie
Osher
Producer

Dan Staton
Producer

Marc Bell
Producer

Frederic H.
Mayerson
Producer

Lauren Mitchell
Associate Producer

Rhoda Mayerson
Associate Producer

Joop van den Ende,
Stage Entertainment
Producer

Christopher Ashley,
Artistic Director,
La Jolla Playhouse
Original Producer

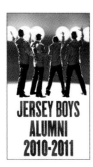

Michelle Aravena
Swing

Sebastian Arcelus
Bob Gaudio

Jared Bradshaw
Swing

Heather Ferguson
*Church Lady,
Miss Frankie Nolan,
Bob's Party Girl,
Angel, Lorraine (and
others)*

Jake Speck
Swing

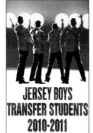

Sebastian Arcelus
Bob Gaudio

Brad Bass
Swing

Cara Cooper
*Assistant Dance
Captain; Mary
Delgado, Angel (and
others)*

Cory Grant
*Frankie Valli
at certain
performances*

Merissa Haddad
*Mary Delgado, Angel
(and others)*

Nathan Scherich
Swing

Jersey Boys

STAGE DOOR
Christine Snyder

HOUSE MANAGEMENT
(L-R): Willa Burke (House Manager),
Anah Jyoti Klate (Assistant House Manager)

STAGE MANAGEMENT
(L-R): Brendan M. Fay (Stage Manager), Michelle Bosch
(Production Stage Manager), Michelle Reupert (Assistant
Stage Manager)

HAIR
(L-R): Jason Hayes (Hair Department), Hazel Higgins
(Asst. Hair Supervisor), Fred Waggoner (Hair Supervisor)

ORCHESTRA
(L-R): Steve Gibb (802 Sub), Debra Barsha (Assoc. Conductor), Joe Payne (Guitar), Andy Wilder
(Conductor)

CARPENTRY
(L-R): Peter Wright (Flyman), Michael Kelly (Production Carpenter),
Ron Fucarino (Fly Automation), Greg Burton (Deck Automation)

PROPS
(L-R): Ken Harris (Production Props), Dylan Foley Props), Emiliano Pares
(Production Props), Scott Mulrain (House Property-person)

WARDROBE
Front Row (L-R): Lee Austin (Wardrobe
Supervisor), Nancy Ronan (Asst. Wardrobe
Supervisor)

Back Row (L-R): Nick Staub (Dresser),
Ricky J. Yates (Dresser),
Michelle Sesco (Dresser), Kelly Kinsella
(Dresser), Davis Duffield (Dresser)

Jersey Boys

FRONT OF HOUSE STAFF

Front Row (L-R): Jorge Castillo (Bartender), Raymond Polanco (Usher), Rose Balsamo (Head Usher), Carmella Galante (Ticket-Taker), Mellie Kaul (Bartender), Janet Polanco (Bartender)

Back Row (L-R): Tom Schwans (Bartender), Barbara Hill (Usher), Robert Fowler (Director), Andrew Mackay (Usher), Eli Phillips (Usher), Katie Schmidt (Usher), Amy Marquez (Director), Travis Navarra (Usher), Russell Saylor (Usher), Ariel Martinez (Usher)

SOUND AND ELECTRICS

Front (L-R): Jan Nebozenko (Assistant House Sound), Gary Marlin (Assistant Electrician), Al Sayers (Follow Spot), Bob Fehribach (House Electrician), David Shepherd (House Sound), Sean Fedigan (Lead Follow Spot)

Stairs (L-R): Bob Miller (Follow Spot), Brian Aman (Production Electrician), Julie Sloan (Production Sound)

STAFF FOR *JERSEY BOYS*

GENERAL PRESS REPRESENTATION
BONEAU/BRYAN-BROWN
Adrian Bryan-Brown   Susanne Tighe
Heath Schwartz

COMPANY MANAGER
Sandra Carlson

PRODUCTION STAGE
  MANAGER ....MICHELLE BOSCH
Stage Manager ....Michelle Reupert
Assistant Stage Manager ....Brendan M. Fay
Senior Associate General Manager ......Jennifer F. Vaughan
Associate General Manager.................Flora Johnstone
Assistant General Manager ....Dean A. Carpenter
Production Manager ....Jeff Parvin
Associate Company Manager ....Tim Sulka
Technical Supervision ....Tech Production Services/
        Peter Fulbright, Mary Duffe,
        Colleen Houlehen, Lauren A. Duffy

Music Technical Design ....Deborah N. Hurwitz
Musician Swing ....Steve Gibb
Associate Director ....West Hyler
Assistant Directors ....Holly-Anne Ruggiero,
        Daisy Walker
Second Assistant Director ....Alex Timbers
Associate Choreographers ....Danny Austin,
        Kelly Devine
Associate Music Supervisor ....Michael Rafter
Dialect Coach ....Stephen Gabis
Fight Captain ....Peter Gregus
Associate Scenic Designers ....Nancy Thun, Todd Ivins
Assistant Scenic Designers ....Sonoka Gozelski,
        Matthew Myhrum
Associate Costume Designer ....Alejo Vietti
Assistant Costume Designers ....China Lee,
        Elizabeth Flauto
Associate Lighting Designer ....Patricia Nichols
Assistant Lighting Designer ....Sarah E. C. Maines
Associate Sound Designer ....Andrew Keister
Associate Projection Designer ....Jason Thompson
Assistant Projection Designer ....Chris Kateff

Story Board Artist ....Don Hudson
Casting Directors ....Tara Rubin, CSA;
        Merri Sugarman, CSA
Casting Associates ....Eric Woodall, CSA;
        Laura Schutzel, CSA
Casting Assistants ....Paige Blansfield;
        Dale Brown, CSA; Kaitlin Shaw
Automated Lighting Programmer ....Hillary Knox
Projection Programming ....Paul Vershbow
Set Model Builder ....Anne Goelz
Costume Intern ....Jessica Reed
Production Carpenter ....Michael W. Kelly
Deck Automation ....Greg Burton
Fly Automation ....Ron Fucarino
Flyman ....Peter Wright
Production Electrician ....James Fedigan
Head Electrician ....Brian Aman
Assistant Electrician ....Gary L. Marlin
Follow Spot Operator ....Sean Fedigan
Production Sound Engineer ....Andrew Keister
Head Sound Engineer....................Julie M. Randolph
Production Props ....Emiliano Pares

Jersey Boys

Assistant Props..............................Kenneth Harris Jr.
Production Wardrobe Supervisor.............Lee J. Austin
Assistant Wardrobe Supervisor................Nancy Ronan
Wardrobe Department......Davis Duffield, Kelly Kinsella,
　　　　　　　　　　　Shaun Ozminski, Michelle Sesco,
　　　　　　　　　　　Nicholas Staub, Ricky Yates
Hair Supervisor.....................Frederick C. Waggoner
Hair Department............Hazel Higgins, Richard Fabris
Assistant to John Miller......................Charles Butler
Synthesizer Programming............Deborah N. Hurwitz,
　　　　　　　　　　　Steve Orich
Music Copying................Anixter Rice Music Service
Music Production Assistant.............Alexandra Melrose
Dramaturg......................................Allison Horsley
Associate to Messrs. Michael David
　　and Ed Strong..............................Pamela Lloyd
Advertising..................................Serino Coyne, Inc./
　　　　　　　　　　　Scott Johnson, Sandy Block, Lauren D'Elia
Marketing..............................Dodger Marketing/
　　　　　　　　　　　Jessica Ludwig, Jessica Morris
Promotions...............................HHC Marketing/
　　　　　　　　　　　Hugh Hysell, Michael Redman
Banking..............Signature Bank/Barbara von Borstel
Payroll..............................Castellana Services Inc./
　　　　　　　　　　　Lance Castellana, Norman Sewell, James Castellana
Accountants..................Schall and Ashenfarb, C.P.A.
Finance Director............................Paula Maldonado
Insurance......AON/Albert G. Rubin Insurance Services/
　　　　　　　　　　　George Walden, Claudia Kaufman
Counsel......................................Nan Bases, Esq.
Special Events................................John L. Haber
Travel Arrangements.........The "A" Team at Tzell Travel/
　　　　　　　　　　　Andi Henig
MIS Services...................Rivera Technics: Sam Rivera
Web Design.....................Curious Minds Media, Inc.
Production Photographer......................Joan Marcus
Theatre Displays..............................King Displays

DODGERS
DODGER THEATRICALS
Richard Biederman, Sandra Carlson, Dean A. Carpenter, Benjamin Cohen, Michael David, Anne Ezell, Lauren Freed, John L. Haber, Richard Hester, Flora Johnstone, Jennifer Hindman Kemp, Abigail Kornet, Tony Lance, Pamela Lloyd, James Elliot Love, Jessica Ludwig, Paula Maldonado, Lauren Mitchell, Jessica Morris, Sally Campbell Morse, Ed Nelson, Jeff Parvin, Samuel Rivera, R. Doug Rodgers, Maureen Rooney, Andrew Serna, Bridget Stegall, Edward Strong, Tim Sulka, Ashley Tracey, Ann E. Van Nostrand, Jennifer F. Vaughan, Lauren White, Laurinda Wilson, Josh Zeigler

Dodger Group Sales.....................1-877-5DODGER
Exclusive Tour Direction...................Steven Schnepp/
　　　　　　　　　　　Broadway Booking Office NYC

CREDITS
Scenery, show control and automation by ShowMotion, Inc., Norwalk, CT. Lighting equipment from PRG Lighting. Sound equipment by Masque Sound. Projection equipment by Sound Associates. Selected men's clothing custom made by Saint Laurie Merchant Tailors, New York City. Costumes executed by Carelli Costumes, Studio Rouge, Carmen Gee, John Kristiansen New York, Inc. Selected menswear by Carlos Campos. Props provided by The Spoon Group, Downtime Productions, Tessa Dunning.

Select guitars provided by Gibson Guitars. Laundry services provided by Ernest Winzer Theatrical Cleaners. Additional set and hand props courtesy of George Fenmore, Inc. Rosebud matches by Diamond Brands, Inc., Zippo lighters used. Rehearsed at the New 42nd Street Studios. Emergen-C by Alacer Corporation. PLAYBILL® cover photo by Chris Callis.

Grammy Award-winning cast album now available on Rhino Records.

www.jerseyboysinfo.com

Scenic drops adapted from *George Tice: Urban Landscapes*/W.W. Norton. Other photographs featured are from *George Tice: Selected Photographs 1953–1999*/David R. Godine. (Photographs courtesy of the Peter Fetterman Gallery/Santa Monica.)

SONG CREDITS
"Ces Soirees-La ("Oh What a Night")" (Bob Gaudio, Judy Parker, Yannick Zolo, Edmond David Bacri). Jobete Music Company Inc., Seasons Music Company (ASCAP). **"Silhouettes"** (Bob Crewe, Frank Slay, Jr.), Regent Music Corporation (BMI). **"You're the Apple of My Eye"** (Otis Blackwell), EMI Unart Catalog Inc. (BMI). **"I Can't Give You Anything But Love"** (Dorothy Fields, Jimmy McHugh), EMI April Music Inc., Aldi Music Company, Cotton Club Publishing (ASCAP). **"Earth Angel"** (Jesse Belvin, Curtis Williams, Gaynel Hodge), Embassy Music Corporation (BMI). **"Sunday Kind of Love"** (Barbara Belle, Anita Leanord Nye, Stan Rhodes, Louis Prima), LGL Music Inc./Larry Spier, Inc. (ASCAP). **"My Mother's Eyes"** (Abel Baer, L. Wolfe Gilbert), Abel Baer Music Company, EMI Feist Catalog Inc. (ASCAP). **"I Go Ape"** (Bob Crewe, Frank Slay, Jr.), MPL Music Publishing Inc. (ASCAP). **"(Who Wears) Short Shorts"** (Bob Gaudio, Bill Crandall, Tom Austin, Bill Dalton), EMI Longitude Music, Admiration Music Inc., Third Story Music Inc., and New Seasons Music (BMI). **"I'm in the Mood for Love"** (Dorothy Fields, Jimmy McHugh), Famous Music Corporation (ASCAP). **"Moody's Mood for Love"** (James Moody, Dorothy Fields, Jimmy McHugh), Famous Music Corporation (ASCAP). **"Cry for Me"** (Bob Gaudio), EMI Longitude Music, Seasons Four Music (BMI). **"An Angel Cried"** (Bob Gaudio), EMI Longitude Music (BMI). **"I Still Care"** (Bob Gaudio), Hearts Delight Music, Seasons Four Music (BMI). **"Trance"** (Bob Gaudio), Hearts Delight Music, Seasons Four Music (BMI). **"Sherry"** (Bob Gaudio), MPL Music Publishing Inc. (ASCAP). **"Big Girls Don't Cry"** (Bob Gaudio, Bob Crewe), MPL Music Publishing Inc. (ASCAP). **"Walk Like a Man"** (Bob Crewe, Bob Gaudio), Gavadima Music, MPL Communications Inc. (ASCAP). **"December, 1963 (Oh What a Night)"** (Bob Gaudio, Judy Parker, Jobete Music Company Inc, Seasons Music Company (ASCAP). **"My Boyfriend's Back"** (Robert Feldman, Gerald Goldstein, Richard Gottehrer), EMI Blackwood Music Inc. (BMI). **"My Eyes Adored You"** (Bob Crewe, Kenny Nolan), Jobete Music Company Inc, Kenny Nolan Publishing (ASCAP), Stone Diamond Music Corporation, Tannyboy Music (BMI). **"Dawn, Go Away"** (Bob Gaudio, Sandy Linzer), EMI Full Keel Music, Gavadima Music, Stebojen Music Company (ASCAP). **"Big Man in Town"** (Bob Gaudio), EMI Longitude Music (BMI), Gavadima Music (ASCAP). **"Beggin'"** (Bob Gaudio, Peggy Farina), EMI Longitude Music, Seasons Four

Music (BMI). **"Stay"** (Maurice Williams), Cherio Corporation (BMI). **"Let's Hang On (To What We've Got)"** (Bob Crewe, Denny Randell, Sandy Linzer), EMI Longitude Music, Screen Gems-EMI Music Inc., Seasons Four Music (BMI). **"Opus 17 (Don't You Worry 'Bout Me)"** (Denny Randell, Sandy Linzer) Screen Gems-EMI Music Inc, Seasons Four Music (BMI). **"Everybody Knows My Name"** (Bob Gaudio, Bob Crewe), EMI Longitude Music, Seasons Four Music (BMI). **"Bye Bye Baby"** (Bob Crewe, Bob Gaudio), EMI Longitude Music, Seasons Four Music (BMI). **"C'mon Marianne"** (L. Russell Brown, Ray Bloodworth), EMI Longitude Music and Seasons Four Music (BMI). **"Can't Take My Eyes Off You"** (Bob Gaudio, Bob Crewe), EMI Longitude Music, Seasons Four Music (BMI). **"Working My Way Back to You"** (Denny Randell, Sandy Linzer), Screen Gems–EMI Music Inc, Seasons Four Music (BMI). **"Fallen Angel"** (Guy Fletcher, Doug Flett), Chrysalis Music (ASCAP). **"Rag Doll"** (Bob Crewe, Bob Gaudio), EMI Longitude Music (BMI), Gavadima Music (ASCAP). **"Who Loves You?"** (Bob Gaudio, Judy Parker), Jobete Music Company Inc, Seasons Music Company (ASCAP).

SPECIAL THANKS
Peter Bennett, Elliot Groffman, Karen Pals, Janine Smalls, Chad Woerner of La Jolla Playhouse, Alma Malabanan-McGrath and Edward Stallsworth of the New 42nd Street Studios, David Solomon of the Roundabout Theatre Company, Dan Whitten. The authors, director, cast and company of *Jersey Boys* would like to express their love and thanks to Jordan Ressler.

IN MEMORY
It is difficult to imagine producing anything without the presence of beloved Dodger producing associate James Elliot Love. Friend to everyone he met, James stood at the heart of all that is good about the theatrical community. He will be missed, but his spirit abides.

The producers would like to use this space to remember Mark Fearon, and in the spirit of this production, to contemplate the abiding joy of youth.

In memory of Jairo "Jay" Santos

🜂 JUJAMCYN THEATERS
JORDAN ROTH
President

PAUL LIBIN	**JACK VIERTEL**
Producing Director	Creative Director
DANIEL ADAMIAN	**JENNIFER HERSHEY**
General Manager	Director of Operations
MICAH HOLLINGWORTH	**JERRY ZAKS**
Chief Financial Officer	Resident Director

STAFF FOR THE AUGUST WILSON THEATRE
Manager...Willa Burke
Treasurer...Nick Russo
Associate Manager...........................Justin L. Karr
Carpenter..Dan Dour
Propertyman....................................Scott Mulrain
Electrician.....................................Robert Fehribach
Engineer.......................................Ralph Santos

Jersey Boys
SCRAPBOOK

Photos by Joseph Marzullo/WENN

Correspondent: Kris Coleman, "French Rap Star, Detective One, Hal Miller, Barry Belson, Police Officer, Davis (and others)."

Anniversary Gift: We received a copy of the street sign "Jersey Boys Walk," formerly known as 52nd Street. From a fan.

Most Exciting Celebrity Visitors: David Beckham, Victoria Beckham and Tom Cruise. They all came together. The paparazzi was insane! The audience kept looking back at their reaction to the show. Tom Cruise sent us cupcakes from Magnolia Bakery the next day.

Actor Who Performed the Most Roles in This Show: Dominic Nolfi covered nine roles. Currently plays Tommy DeVito.

Who Has Done the Most Shows in Their Career: Tie among Sara Schmidt, Peter Gregus, and Mark Lotito.

Special Backstage Ritual: Running. Everyone has a million costume changes.

Favorite Moment During Each Performance: Sitting in the cafe.

Favorite In-Theatre Gathering Place: Stage Management's office.

Favorite Off-Site Hangout: Tonic Bar.

Favorite Snack Food: Anything Gummi.

Mascot: Our Christmas Rat.

Favorite Therapy: Grether's Vocal Pastilles.

Memorable Ad-Lib: "I'm just too good to be true, Can't take my eyes off of me."

Memorable Stage Door Fan Encounter: Kris Coleman was asked if he was in the show. Being the only black man in the show, he replied, "I'll give you one guess as to who I played."

What Did You Think of the Web Buzz on Your Show? Love it!

Fastest Costume Change: Katie O'Toole. In a split show played Mary Delgado, and Francine Valli, had to change her dress, wig, and character in twenty seconds.

Busiest Day at the Box Office: Every day! Woohoo!!!

1. Backstage on September 15, 2010 the cast and crew of *Jersey Boys* celebrated the show's 2000th performance, which took place on September 11.
2. Members of the creative team get their caricatures hung at Sardi's restaurant, November 8, 2010. Standing (L-R): Michelle Bosch, Ryan Jesse, Marshall Brickman, Rick Elice, Bob Gaudio, Frankie Valli, Dominic Scaglione Jr., Andrew Wilder. Kneeling: Peter Gregus, Katie O'Toole, Russell Fischer.
3. Frankie Valli with his Sardi's caricature.

Who Wore the Heaviest/Hottest Costume: All three girls. Their Angels costumes are the smallest dresses but are weighed down with beads. They feel like ten pounds each.

Who Wore the Least: Sara Schmidt, in "Oh What a Night."

Catchphrase Only the Company Would Recognize: "2 show on a 1 show."

Best In-House Parody Lyric: "Squawk like a man!"

Ghostly Encounters Backstage: We like to think August Wilson comes in from time to time and starts playing with the lights.

Memorable Directorial Note: "We recognize you as the Broadway company and don't want to change things to the tour... But on the tour we found this works."

Tales From the Put-in: Bring Snacks!

Embarrassing Moment: Heather Ferguson, slipping on beads that broke from a bracelet during the opening.

Company In-Jokes: Head Voice.

Coolest Thing About Being in This Show: The reaction we get from our audience.

Fan Club Head and Website: Susie Skarl http://www.jerseyboysblog.com.

Jerusalem

First Preview: April 2, 2011. Opened: April 21, 2011.
Still running as of May 31, 2011.

PLAYBILL

JERUSALEM

Local wild man Johnny "Rooster" Byron drinks, smokes and whores his way through life with joyous abandon surrounded by a tribe of his closest friends and hangers-on until at last the forces of civil order threaten to bulldoze his mobile home and drag him off to justice. Is this the way for a grown man to behave, especially one with an impressionable young son? Byron has to figure out a way to stay true to the legends he has concocted about himself while living up to his responsibilities as a grownup...or not.

CAST

Phaedra	AIMEÉ-FFION EDWARDS
Ms. Fawcett	SARAH MOYLE
Mr. Parsons	HARVEY ROBINSON
Johnny "Rooster" Byron	MARK RYLANCE
Ginger	MACKENZIE CROOK
The Professor	ALAN DAVID
Lee	JOHN GALLAGHER, JR.
Davey	DANNY KIRRANE
Pea	MOLLY RANSON
Tanya	CHARLOTTE MILLS
Wesley	MAX BAKER
Marky	AIDEN EYRICK

(Tues., Fri., Sat. mat. and eve.)
MARK PAGE
(Wed. mat. and eve., Thurs., Sun.)

Dawn	GERALDINE HUGHES
Troy Whitworth	BARRY SLOANE
Frank Whitworth	JAY SULLIVAN
Danny Whitworth	RICHARD SHORT

⊛ THE MUSIC BOX
239 W. 45th Street
A Shubert Organization Theatre
Philip J. Smith, *Chairman*   **Robert E. Wankel,** *President*

Sonia Friedman Productions   Stuart Thompson   Scott Rudin   Roger Berlind
Royal Court Theatre Productions   Beverly Bartner/Alice Tulchin   Dede Harris/Rupert Gavin
Broadway Across America   Jon B. Platt   1001 Nights/Stephanie P. McClelland
Carole L. Haber/Richard Willis   Jacki Barlia Florin/Adam Blanshay

present the **ROYAL COURT THEATRE** production of

Mark Rylance
in

JERUSALEM
by
Jez Butterworth

with

Mackenzie Crook   John Gallagher, Jr.

Max Baker   Alan David   Aimeé-Ffion Edwards   Aiden Eyrick   Geraldine Hughes
Danny Kirrane   Charlotte Mills   Sarah Moyle   Mark Page   Molly Ranson
Harvey Robinson   Barry Sloane
Frances Mercanti-Anthony   James Riordan   Richard Short   Jay Sullivan   Libby Woodbridge

Scenic & Costume Design	Lighting Design	Sound Design	Original Music
Ultz	**Mimi Jordan Sherin**	**Ian Dickinson for Autograph**	**Stephen Warbeck**

UK Casting	Casting	Production Stage Manager
Amy Ball	**Jim Carnahan, C.S.A.**	**Jill Cordle**

Press Representative	Production Management	General Management	UK General Management
Boneau/Bryan-Brown	**Aurora Productions**	**STP / David Turner**	**Sonia Friedman Productions**

Directed by
Ian Rickson

The Producers wish to express their appreciation to Theatre Development Fund for its support for this production.

4/21/11

UNDERSTUDIES

For Davey/Troy: RICHARD SHORT
For Dawn/Ms. Fawcett:
FRANCES MERCANTI-ANTHONY
For Ginger: HARVEY ROBINSON
For Lee/Mr. Parsons: JAY SULLIVAN
For Pea/Tanya/Phaedra: LIBBY WOODBRIDGE
For Wesley/The Professor: JAMES RIORDAN

SETTING

Flintock, Wiltshire, England 2011

Mark Rylance

Photo by Simon Annand

Jerusalem

Mark Rylance
Johnny "Rooster" Byron

Mackenzie Crook
Ginger

John Gallagher, Jr.
Lee

Max Baker
Wesley

Alan David
The Professor

Aimeé-Ffion Edwards
Phaedra

Aiden Eyrick
Marky

Geraldine Hughes
Dawn

Danny Kirrane
Davey

Charlotte Mills
Tanya

Sarah Moyle
Ms. Fawcett

Mark Page
Marky

Molly Ranson
Pea

Harvey Robinson
Mr. Parsons

Barry Sloane
Troy Whitworth

Frances Mercanti-Anthony
u/s Dawn, Ms. Fawcett

James Riordan
u/s Wesley, The Professor

Richard Short
Danny Whitworth

Jay Sullivan
Frank Whitworth

Libby Woodbridge
u/s Pea, Tanya, Phaedra

Jez Butterworth
Playwright

Ian Rickson
Director

Ultz
Set and Costume Design

Mimi Jordan Sherin
Lighting Design

Ian Dickinson
for Autograph
Sound Design

Stephen Warbeck
Composer

Charmian Hoare
Voice and Dialect Coach

Jim Carnahan C.S.A.
Casting

David Turner
General Manager

Sonia Friedman
Productions Ltd.
Producer

Stuart Thompson
Producer

Scott Rudin
Producer

Roger Berlind
Producer

Dede Harris
Producer

John Gore,
Broadway Across America
Producer

Jerusalem

Thomas B. McGrath,
Broadway Across
America
Producer

Jon B. Platt
Producer

Stephanie P.
McClelland
Producer

Richard Willis
Producer

Jacki Barlia Florin
Producer

Adam Blanshay
Producer

STAFF FOR *JERUSALEM*

GENERAL MANAGEMENT
STUART THOMPSON PRODUCTIONS
Stuart Thompson   David Turner   Marshall B. Purdy
Cassidy Briggs   Kevin Emrick   Geo Karapetyan
Brittany Levasseur   Andrew Lowy
Christopher Taggart

COMPANY MANAGER
Christopher D'Angelo

PRODUCTION MANAGEMENT
AURORA PRODUCTIONS INC.
Gene O'Donovan   Ben Heller
Jeremiah Thies   Stephanie Sherline
Jarid Sumner   Liza Luxenberg   Jason Margolis
Ryan Stanisz   Melissa Mazdra

PRESS REPRESENTATIVE
BONEAU/BRYAN-BROWN
Chris Boneau   Jim Byk   Christine Olver

CASTING
Jim Carnahan

Production Stage Manager ....Jill Cordle
Stage Manager ....Kenneth McGee
U.K. Stage Manager ....Cath Bates
U.K. Stage Manager ....Maddy Grant
U.S. Associate Scenic Designer ....Josh Zangen
U.S. Associate Scenic Designer ....Ryan Trupp
U.S. Associate Costume Designer ....Katie Irish
U.K. Associate Lighting Designer ....Steve Andrews
U.S. Associate Lighting Designer ..............D.M. Wood
U.S. Assistant Lighting Designer ....Gordon Olson
U.S. Associate Sound Designer ....Joanna Lynne Staub
U.K. Production Management ....Paul Handley
U.K. Costume Supervisor ....Iona Kenrick
U.K. Costume Supervisor ....Rana Fowler
Production Carpenter ....Jim Fossi
Production Electrician ....Brendan Quigley
Light Board Programmer ....Eric Norris
Production Props ....Scott Monroe
Production Sound ....Beth Berkeley
House Carpenter ....Dennis Maher
House Props ....Kim Garnett
House Electrician ....William K. Rowland
Wardrobe Supervisor ....Kay Grunder
Dressers ....Kimberly Prentice, Chip White
U.K. Production Assistant ....Hannah Gore
U.S. Production Assistant ....Jason Pelusio

Dialect Coach ....Charmian Hoare
U.S. Vocal Coach ....Andrew Wade
Casting Associate ....Jillian Cimini
General Management Interns ....Rikki Bahar,
Liz Shumate
Banking ....City National Bank/
Michele Gibbons
Accountant ....Fried & Kowgios CPA's LLP/
Robert Fried CPA
Controller ....J. S. Kubala
Insurance ....DeWitt Stern, Inc./
Peter Shoemaker, Lory Yan,
Ellen Fong, Sandra Salinas
Music Rights...............................Yolanda Ferraloro
Legal Counsel ....Davis Wright Tremaine LLP/
M. Graham Coleman, Robert Driscoll,
Andrew Owens
U.S. Immigration ....Traffic Control Group/David King
U.K. Immigration ....Visa Consultants/Lisa Carr
Advertising ....aka/
Scott A. Moore, Liz Furze, Clint Bond Jr.,
Melissa Marano, Richard Arnold,
Adam Jay, Janette Roush
Digital & Interactive Marketing..............aka Connect/
Terry Goldman, Erin Rech
Production Photographer ....Joan Marcus
Travel Agent ....Tzell Travel/
Andi Henig, Jeanne Lafond
Long Term Housing Agent ....ABA – Ideal/
Elizabeth Helke
Short Term Housing Agent ....Road Concierge, Inc./
Lisa Morris
Child Wrangler ....Brooke Engen
Tutoring Services ....On Location Education/
Muriel Kester, Jodi Green, Anna Smith
Theatre Displays ....King Displays
Transportation ....IBA Limousines
Payroll Services ....Castellana Services

SONIA FRIEDMAN PRODUCTIONS
Producer ....Sonia Friedman
General Manager ....Diane Benjamin
Head of Production ....Pam Skinner
Literary Associate ....Jack Bradley
Production Associate ....Peter Huntley
Production Coordinator ....Fiona Stewart
Production Assistant ....Thea Foster
General Management Assistant ....Ben Canning
Assistant to Sonia Friedman ....Sarah Hammond
Production Accountant ....Melissa Hay
Chief Executive Officer (New York) ....David Lazar
New York Assistant (SFP) ....Valerie Steinberg

Sonia Friedman Productions Board ....Helen Enright,
Howard Panter, Rosemary Squire

CREDITS
Scenery by PRG Scenic Technologies. Lighting equipment from PRG Lighting. Sound equipment from Sound Associates. Rehearsed at Jerwood Studios. McClaren Engineering. Foliage provided by American Foliage. Special thanks to Bra*Tenders for hosiery and undergarments. Micky Lay, Scottie Lay, Mr. John Hobbs and students of Pewsey Vale Secondary School; Jerry Kunkler, the landlord of Moonrakers

Souvenir merchandise designed and created by
The Araca Group

Energy-efficient washer/dryer courtesy of
LG Electronics.

 THE SHUBERT ORGANIZATION, INC.
Board of Directors

House Manager ....Jonathan Shulman

Jerusalem

BOX OFFICE
(L-R): Bob Kelly, John Stange

Photos by Brian Mapp

DOORMAN
Tim Barrett

FRONT OF HOUSE STAFF
Front Row (L-R): John Seid, Laura Scanlon, Nick Fusco, Jonathan Shulman (House Manager)

Middle Row (L-R): Joe Amato, Tim Shelton, Lottie Dennis, Tom Murdoch, Mike Composto

Back Row (L-R): Kenny Kelly, Dennis Scanlon

CREW
(L-R): Ken McGee (Stage Manager), Beth Berkeley (Production Sound), Kim Garnett (House Props), Billy Rowland (House Electrician), Dennis Maher (House Carpenter), Mark Diaz (Flyman), Jill Cordle (Production Stage Manager), Chris D'Angelo (Company Manager), Scott Monroe (Production Props)

Jerusalem
SCRAPBOOK

Photo courtesy Jill Cordle

Correspondent: Jill Cordle, Production Stage Manager

Opening Night Gifts: Drums from our producers.

Special Backstage Ritual: Pre-show volleyball games in the orchestra with full company. Slapbacks count as 2 points.

Favorite Moment During Each Performance: "The Rave": The whole company onstage at the top of the show.

Favorite In-Theatre Gathering Place: Boys' dressing room.

Favorite Off-Site Hangout: Hurley's on 48th Street.

Favorite Snack Food: Anything with sugar or salt in it.

Favorite Therapy: Post-show whiskey or tequila.

Memorable Ad-Lib: Once during the show when a lighting malfunction happened, Mark Rylance remarked, "It's a cloudy day."

Catchphrases Only the Company Would Recognize: "Put a name on it." "Classic zigzag." "I do not want to see it."

Memorable Directorial Note: "That was good….but do it one in ten shows."

Company Legend: Sir Alan David.

Coolest Thing About Being in This Show: It's the best play that's ever been written. Fact.

Photo by Joseph Marzullo/WENN

Photo by Krissie Fullerton

2010-2011 AWARDS

TONY AWARD
Best Performance by an Actor in a Leading Role in a Play
(Mark Rylance)

NEW YORK DRAMA CRITICS' CIRCLE AWARDS
Best Foreign Play
Special Citation
(Mark Rylance)

OUTER CRITICS CIRCLE AWARD
Outstanding Actor in a Play
(Mark Rylance)

DRAMA LEAGUE AWARD
Distinguished Performance Award
(Mark Rylance)

Photo courtesy Jill Cordle

1. (L-R): Mark Rylance, playwright Jez Butterworth, producer Jon B. Platt and actor Alan David on opening night.
2. Molly Ranson, Mark Page and Mark Rylance taking bows at the premiere.
3. Exterior of the Music Box theatre during the show's run.
4. (L-R): Alan David, Charlotte Mills, Barry Sloane, Harvey Robinson and Mackenzie Crook at the cast party.

Kathy Griffin Wants a Tony

First performance: March 11, 2011.
Closed March 19, 2011 after 10 Performances.

PLAYBILL

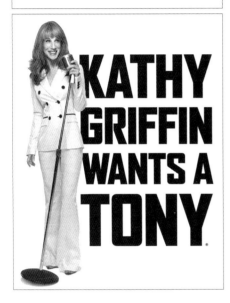

Standup comedian Kathy Griffin dishes today's celebrities in her limited-run solo show.

CAST
(in order of appearance)
Kathy Griffin ....KATHY GRIFFIN

UNDERSTUDY
For Kathy Griffin:
MAGGIE GRIFFIN

Photo by Krissie Fullerton

Kathy Griffin

⊛ **BELASCO THEATRE**
111 West 44th Street
A Shubert Organization Theatre

Philip J. Smith, *Chairman*   Robert E. Wankel, *President*

Robert Ahrens   Eva Price
Manny Kladitis
present

KATHY GRIFFIN WANTS A TONY.

Lighting Design	Sound Design
Matt Berman	**Matt Kraus**

Press Representative	General Manager
Sunshine Sachs & Associates	**Niko Companies**
Whitney Tancred	

ABROADWAYCONCERTEVENT.

TONY® is a registered trademark of the American Theatre Wing, Inc. Used with permission. All rights reserved.

3/11/11

Kathy Griffin
Kathy Griffin

Robert Ahrens
Presenter

Eva Price/
Maximum
Entertainment
Presenter

Manny Kladitis
Presenter

Kathy Griffin Wants a Tony

SCRAPBOOK

Correspondent: Kathy Griffin

Memorable Opening Night Letter, Fax or Note: Jay Leno sent me gorgeous flowers; however they were not delivered in one of his antique cars.

Opening Night Gifts: I received a two-and-a-half foot life size chocolate leg from someone named John, or just one of my "johns." Girl's gotta make a living.

Most Exciting Celebrity Visitor: Gloria Vanderbilt. Besides being a legend, icon and delightful dinner guest, she's also my future mother-in-law.

Special Backstage Ritual: Listening to Justin Bieber's "U Smile" on repeat on my iPod before every show, much to the chagrin of anyone who came back to visit me, except for–ironically–Justin Bieber, who came to my show every night.

Favorite Moment During Each Performance: Getting a standing ovation every night. Correction: every show, even the matinee, bitches.

Favorite In-Theatre Gathering Place: The glorified port-a-potty I used while everyone in my dressing room listened to me take what I lovingly call my pre-show pee.

Favorite Off-Site Hangout: The Donut Pub on 14th and Seventh. Here's a dollar, buy a clue and a donut.

Favorite Snack Food: See above.

Mascot: The ghost of David Belasco. By the way, I fucked him.

Favorite Therapy: Cortisone shot in my hip, like I was Barry Bonds telling dick jokes.

Memorable Ad-Lib: You don't understand, my entire show is ad-libbed. My next one will be, too.

Record Number of Cell Phone Rings During a Performance: Only one, and I Patti LuPone'd his ass out of there.

Memorable Press Encounter: I got stumped when several interviewers asked me which iconic role I'd like to play on Broadway. I panicked and said Porgy. What???

Memorable Stage Door Fan Encounter: Once someone was waiting for me dressed exactly as Sarah Palin. I'm just glad it wasn't really her.

What Did You Think of the Internet Buzz on Your Show: It was almost as good as the internet buzz about my topless photos in Miami. Go ahead, I'll wait while you Google them.

Latest Audience Arrival: Me. Some nights I wouldn't go on stage until 8:04pm. And don't think the union guys weren't up my ass for that.

Fastest Costume Change: I wore tights and a t-shirt. Sometimes I had to change my camel toe halfway through a good Lindsay Lohan story.

Busiest Day at the Box Office: Ten shows in eight days, $1 million gross. Cha-ching, bitch.

Who Wore the Heaviest/Hottest Costume: It's a tie between me and my camel toe.

Who Wore the Least: I required one nude stagehand and the union approved it.

Catchphrase Only the Company Would Recognize: My loyal staff, waiting backstage for me each night, yelling "the show's started, let's go to the Olive Garden for two hours, she'll never know."

Memorable Directorial Note: Since I was the director, producer, writer and only actor, my biggest note was "where is everybody?"

Company In-Jokes: Are you not paying attention to my previous answers?

Company Legend: I got a text message from Cher on opening night. Does that count?

Understudy Anecdote: My 90-year-old alcoholic mother Maggie was my understudy for every performance. It was only stressful because she was in her retirement village three thousand miles away, halfway through a box of wine. But she does know my act by heart, she could have Skyped it.

Nicknames: Britney, Christina, Ke$ha.

Sweethearts Within the Company: You mean who was I banging? It was a one-woman show so I guess that would be my right hand.

Embarrassing Moments: Well, the show started at 8 and ended at 10, so you have two hours to choose from.

Ghostly Encounter Backstage: I saw Kelsey Grammer out of drag.

Superstitions That Turned Out To Be True: Never look Angela Lansbury in the eyes. She WILL cut you.

Coolest Thing About Being in This Show: Changing the material every show and changing my panties every third show.

Also: Since the title of the show was *Kathy Griffin Wants a Tony*, my good friend Joan Rivers walked onstage one night with a bag of Tony Curtis' ashes, threw them on the stage and said "there's your Tony." You ain't gonna see that in *The Lion King*.

La Bête

First Preview: September 23, 2010. Opened: October 14, 2010.
Closed January 9, 2011 after 24 Previews and 101 Performances.

The French court playwright tries to put up with the new royal favorite: a rival who not only has repulsive personal habits but is ignorant, conceited, illiterate, crude, rude, clueless, talentless ... and maddeningly popular.

CAST

(in order of appearance)

Elomire ....DAVID HYDE PIERCE
Bejart ....STEPHEN OUIMETTE
Valere ....MARK RYLANCE
Dorine ....GRETA LEE
The Princess ....JOANNA LUMLEY
Madeleine Bejart ....SALLY WINGERT
Rene Du Parc ....ROBERT LONSDALE
Marquise-Therese Du Parc ....LISA JOYCE
De Brie ....MICHAEL MILLIGAN
Catherine De Brie ....LIZA SADOVY

UNDERSTUDIES

For Elomire:
MICHAEL MILLIGAN
For Bejart, De Brie, Rene Du Parc:
STEVE ROUTMAN
For Valere:
ROBERT LONSDALE, STEVE ROUTMAN
For Dorine:
LISA JOYCE
For The Princess:
DEANNE LORETTE, LIZA SADOVY
For Madeleine Bejart, Catherine De Brie,
Marquise-Therese Du Parc:
DEANNE LORETTE

SETTING

France, 1654

THE MUSIC BOX
239 W. 45th Street
A Shubert Organization Theatre

Philip J. Smith, *Chairman*   Robert E. Wankel, *President*

Scott Landis & Sonia Friedman Productions, Roger Berlind
Bob Bartner/Norman Tulchin, Bob Boyett/Tim Levy, Roy Furman, Max Cooper,
Dan Frishwasser, Bud Martin, Philip Morgaman/Frankie J. Grande,
Stephanie P. McClelland/Hagemann-Rosenthal
In association with 1001 Nights, Richard Winkler
present

Mark   David   Joanna
Rylance   Hyde Pierce   Lumley

in

by

David Hirson

with

Stephen Ouimette

Greta Lee   Lisa Joyce   Robert Lonsdale
Michael Milligan   Liza Sadovy   Sally Wingert
Deanne Lorette   Steve Routman

Hair/Makeup Design	US Casting	UK Casting
Campbell Young	Jim Carnahan, CSA	Lisa Makin
Production Stage Manager	**Technical Supervisor**	**Associate Director**
Ira Mont	Aurora Productions	Beatrice Terry
Press Representative	**Advertising**	**Marketing**
The Hartman Group	SpotCo	Type A / Anne Rippey

UK General Management	US General Management
Sonia Friedman Productions	Richards/Climan, Inc.

Lighting Design	Composer	Sound Design
Hugh Vanstone	Claire van Kampen	Simon Baker

Set and Costume Design
Mark Thompson

Director
Matthew Warchus

The Producers wish to express their appreciation to Theatre Development Fund for its support of this production.

10/14/10

(L-R): Mark Rylance, Joanna Lumley, David Hyde Pierce

Photo by Joan Marcus

La Bête

Mark Rylance
Valere

David Hyde Pierce
Elomire

Joanna Lumley
The Princess

Stephen Ouimette
Bejart

Greta Lee
Dorine

Lisa Joyce
*Marquise-Therese
Du Parc*

Robert Lonsdale
Rene Du Parc

Michael Milligan
De Brie

Liza Sadovy
Catherine De Brie

Sally Wingert
Madeleine Bejart

Deanne Lorette
*u/s The Princess,
Madeleine Bejart,
Catherine De Brie,
Marquise-Therese
Du Parc*

Steve Routman
*u/s Valere, Bejart,
De Brie, Rene Du
Parc*

David Hirson
Playwright

Matthew Warchus
Director

Mark Thompson
*Set and Costume
Design*

Hugh Vanstone
Lighting Design

Simon Baker
Sound Design

Jim Carnahan, CSA
Casting

David R. Richards and Tamar Haimes,
Richards/Climan, Inc.
U.S. General Manager

Scott Landis
Producer

Sonia Friedman
Productions
*Producer and
UK General Manager*

Roger Berlind
Producer

Bob Boyett
Producer

Roy Furman
Producer

Max Cooper
Producer

Frankie J. Grande
Producer

Stephanie P.
McClelland,
Green Curtain
Productions
Producer

**2010-2011
AWARDS**

NEW YORK
DRAMA CRITICS
CIRCLE AWARD
Special Citation
(Mark Rylance)

DRAMA
LEAGUE AWARD
Distinguished
Performance
(Mark Rylance)

(L-R): David Hyde Pierce
and Mark Rylance

Photo by Manoel Harlan

La Bête

Joanna Lumley and company

Photo by Joan Marcus

La Bête
SCRAPBOOK

Photos by Joseph Marzullo/WENN

1. The cast takes bows at the premiere.
2. David Hyde Pierce looking Fosse-esque for a press interview at Sardi's.
3. Cast members Lisa Joyce and *Yearbook* correspondent Greta Lee at Gotham Hall for the opening night party.
4. (L-R): Cast members Michael Milligan, Robert Lonsdale and Mark Rylance enjoy some celebratory stogies at Gotham Hall.

Correspondent: Greta Lee, "Dorine"

Memorable Note, Fax or Fan Letter: From Liza Sadovy, post-appendectomy.

Opening Night Parties and Gifts: Opening Night Gala at Gotham Hall. *La Bête* wine, framed copy of Valere's opening monologue, bath robes, volleyball gear—shoes, shirts.

Most Exciting Celebrity Visitors: Vanessa Redgrave, Joely Richardson, Alan Cumming, Dylan Baker, Angela Lansbury, Glenn Close, Patrick Stewart, Daniel Radcliffe, Jude Law, Sienna Miller, Tobey Maguire, Natalie Portman, F. Murray Abraham, Jennifer Saunders, The Archbishop of Canterbury, Philip Seymour Hoffman, and Leonardo DiCaprio who asked, "Will you marry me?" I

mean, I think that happened. It *might* have happened. Let's just say it happened.

Who Has Done the Most Shows: Kay Grunder: 25 Broadway shows.

Special Backstage Ritual: Thirty minutes of volleyball before every show.

Favorite Moment During Each Performance: Getting blasted in the face with glitter while trying to shut my mouth.

Favorite In-Theatre Gathering Place: The boys' dressing room where there are cookies, tea, coffee, and a shirtless boy from York who plays the guitar, sings angsty songs, and does push-ups.

Favorite Off-Site Hangouts: Bond 45, Hurley's, O'Flaherty's, Bar Centrale, Jimmy's

Corner, Angus, Sardi's, Kodama, Zen Palate, 5 Napkin Burger (when we force Mark to come sit under the meat hooks and surround him with burgers), and DHP's pad.

Favorite Snack Foods: Digestives from the UK, baked goods from Milly's mom, anything leftover from Sunday brunch.

Mascots: Beauregard the hump, Babba the doll.

Favorite Therapy: Deanne's Chinese Herbal Cough Syrup.

Memorable Ad-Libs: Mark's "The Pair of Balls of Two Boys from Cadiz" instead of "The Parable of Two Boys from Cadiz." DHP's "Blue thighs" to complete the verse, after "Blue Skies." And my personal favorite: during Babba the clown: Mark's "Ahhhhh... he's dying... I am dying... a death."

Memorable Stage Door Fan Encounter: Getting a stuffed meerkat doll wearing a red velvet robe from a fan.

Who Wore the Heaviest/Hottest Costume: Joanna had the heaviest and Mark had the hottest.

Who Wore the Least: Apparently I do, when I'm not in costume. But Mark wears shorts in the winter too.

Catchphrases Only the Company Would Recognize: Surprise serve—black slap back—bait the bear—ace-backwards salmon—smush—daylight lobbery—set 'um up, set 'um up, don't mess your hairdo—franchesca, stagechesca, netchesca, chestchesca, crotch-chesca—kill the trip.

Nicknames: Oo-my-eye, Bobby, Rejoice, Wayne, DHP, Sauce-Pot, Milly the Muff, Sal, Alan Gratis-Rock, Hank Tollman, The Luminator, The Master-Baiter.

Embarrassing Moments: "Someone" farting behind the curtain.

Sweethearts Within the Company: Joanna, Mark, and DHP, who threw a triple wedding opening night party in London at Bocca di Lupo.

Memorable Directorial Note: "You're a weird, important, dangerous mouse." Which was further explained with, "You're not important, what's going on is important."

Company In-Joke: Bobby's hair.

Company Legends: After training for weeks, playing a very competitive game of volleyball against the UK cast of *Jerusalem*. Even though Mark played on their side, *La Bête* won, but only to feel just like the Americans did when USA beat England in the World Cup. Not really able to celebrate.

Superstitions That Turned Out To Be True: The ceiling might fall on your head.

Coolest Things About Being in This Show: Being the "victim" of DHP, Mark, and Joanna's truly endless generosity. And for the Brits, being on Broadway, and for the Yanks, the West End. But most importantly, hearts bursting with transatlantic love, which actually just means hours of making fun of each other's accents.

La Cage aux Folles

First Preview: April 6, 2010. Opened: April 18, 2010.
Closed May 1, 2011 after 15 Previews and 433 Performances.

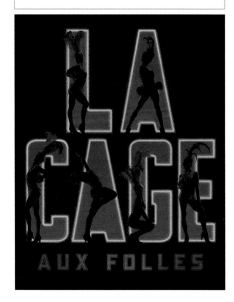

A middle-aged gay couple runs the La Cage aux Folles nightclub. Georges acts as emcee while Albin transforms each night into the club's star attraction, the glamorous Zaza. Offstage, Albin serves as surrogate mother to Georges' son Jean-Michel who is dating the beautiful Anne. But then Anne's deeply conservative parents demand to meet his folks. Farcical complications ensue before Jean-Michel realizes that you should always honor your mother—even if she's a man.

CAST
(in order of appearance)

Georges	CHRISTOPHER SIEBER
"Les Cagelles"	
Angelique	MATT ANCTIL
Bitelle	LOGAN KESLAR
Chantal	SEAN PATRICK DOYLE
Hanna	KARL WARDEN
Mercedes	TERRY LAVELL
Phaedra	YUREL ECHEZARRETA
Francis	CHRIS HOCH
Babette	CHERYL STERN
Jacob	WILSON JERMAINE HEREDIA
Albin	HARVEY FIERSTEIN
Jean-Michel	A.J. SHIVELY
Anne	ELENA SHADDOW
Colette	HEATHER LINDELL
Etienne	MICHAEL LOWNEY
Tabarro	BRUCE WINANT
Jacqueline	CHRISTINE ANDREAS
M. Renaud	MIKE McSHANE
Mme. Renaud	ALLYCE BEASLEY

Continued on next page

 LONGACRE THEATRE
220 West 48th Street
A Shubert Organization Theatre

Philip J. Smith, *Chairman* **Robert E. Wankel,** *President*

SONIA FRIEDMAN PRODUCTIONS, DAVID BABANI, BARRY AND FRAN WEISSLER and
EDWIN W. SCHLOSS, BOB BARTNER/NORMAN TULCHIN, BROADWAY ACROSS AMERICA, MATTHEW MITCHELL,
RAISE THE ROOF 4 RICHARD WINKLER/BENSINGER TAYLOR/LAUDENSLAGER BERGÈRE,
ARLENE SCANLAN/JOHN O'BOYLE, INDEPENDENT PRESENTERS NETWORK, OLYMPUS THEATRICALS,
ALLEN SPIVAK, JERRY FRANKEL/BAT-BARRY PRODUCTIONS, NEDERLANDER PRESENTATIONS, INC/HARVEY WEINSTEIN
Present the MENIER CHOCOLATE FACTORY Production

with

HARVEY FIERSTEIN   CHRISTOPHER SIEBER

in

LA CAGE AUX FOLLES

MUSIC & LYRICS BY
JERRY HERMAN

BOOK BY
HARVEY FIERSTEIN

BASED ON THE PLAY "LA CAGE AUX FOLLES" BY **JEAN POIRET**

Starring

MIKE McSHANE   ALLYCE BEASLEY
CHRIS HOCH   ELENA SHADDOW   A.J. SHIVELY

with
CHRISTINE ANDREAS
and
WILSON JERMAINE HEREDIA

DALE HENSLEY	HEATHER LINDELL	MICHAEL LOWNEY	CAITLIN MUNDTH	CHERYL STERN	BRUCE WINANT

And featuring the notorious and dangerous Cagelles

MATT ANCTIL	CHRISTOPHE CABALLERO	SEAN A. CARMON	SEAN PATRICK DOYLE	YUREL ECHEZARRETA	LOGAN KESLAR	TODD LATTIMORE	TERRY LAVELL	KARL WARDEN

Scenic Design	Costume Design	Lighting Design	Sound Design	Wig & Makeup Design
TIM SHORTALL	MATTHEW WRIGHT	NICK RICHINGS	JONATHAN DEANS	RICHARD MAWBEY

Associate Choreographer	Technical Supervisors	Production Stage Manager	Associate Producers
NICHOLAS CUNNINGHAM	ARTHUR SICCARDI & PATRICK SULLIVAN	KRISTEN HARRIS	CARLOS ARANA ROBERT DRIEMEYER

Music Director
TODD ELLISON

Music Coordinator
JOHN MILLER

Casting	Press Representative	Advertising	UK General Management
DUNCAN STEWART	BONEAU/BRYAN-BROWN	SPOTCO	DIANE BENJAMIN, PAM SKINNER & TOM SIRACUSA

General Manager
B.J. HOLT

Executive Producer
ALECIA PARKER

Music Supervision, Orchestrations & Dance Arrangements
JASON CARR

Choreography by
LYNNE PAGE

Directed by
TERRY JOHNSON

This production premiered at the Menier Chocolate Factory November 23, 2007
and transferred to the Playhouse Theatre October 30, 2008.
Original Chocolate Factory Set Design by David Farley.

3/14/11

Christopher Sieber and Harvey Fierstein (center) with
'Les Cagelles' (L-R): Yurel Echezarreta, Logan Keslar,
Karl Warden, Terry Lavell, Matt Anctil, Sean Patrick Doyle

Photo by Joan Marcus

La Cage aux Folles

MUSICAL NUMBERS

ACT ONE

Scene 1 La Cage Aux Folles Nightclub
"We Are What We Are" .... Cagelles, Georges

Scene 2 Georges and Albin's Apartment
"A Little More Mascara" .... Albin, Georges

Scene 2a La Cage Aux Folles Nightclub

Scene 3 Georges and Albin's Apartment
"With Anne on My Arm" .... Georges, Jean-Michel
"With You on My Arm" .... Albin, Georges

Scene 4 The Promenade
"Song on the Sand" .... Georges

Scene 5 Backstage at La Cage Aux Folles

Scene 5a La Cage Aux Folles Nightclub
"La Cage aux Folles" .... Company

Scene 6 Backstage at La Cage Aux Folles

Scene 6a La Cage Aux Folles Nightclub
"I Am What I Am" .... Albin

ACT TWO

Scene 1 Promenade
"Song on the Sand" (Reprise) .... Albin, Georges
"Masculinity" .... Albin, Georges, M. Renaud, Mme. Renaud, Tabarro

Scene 2 Georges and Albin's Apartment
"Look Over There" .... Georges
"Cocktail Counterpoint" .... Anne, M. Dindon, Mme. Dindon, Georges, Jacob, Jean-Michel

Scene 3 Chez Jacqueline Restaurant
"The Best of Times" .... Company

Scene 4 Georges and Albin's Apartment
"Look Over There" (Reprise) .... Georges, Jean-Michel

Scene 5 La Cage Aux Folles Nightclub
Finale .... Company

(L-R): A.J. Shively and Wilson Jermaine Heredia

Photo by Joan Marcus

Cast Continued

M. Dindon .... MIKE McSHANE
Mme. Dindon .... ALLYCE BEASLEY
Waiter .... DALE HENSLEY

SWINGS
CHRISTOPHE CABALLERO,
SEAN A. CARMON, TODD LATTIMORE,
CAITLIN MUNDTH

ASSISTANT DANCE CAPTAIN
CAITLIN MUNDTH

UNDERSTUDIES
For Georges, Albin:
DALE HENSLEY, CHRIS HOCH
For M. Dindon/M. Renaud:
DALE HENSLEY, BRUCE WINANT
For Mme. Dindon/Mme. Renaud:
HEATHER LINDELL, CHERYL STERN
For Francis:
CHRISTOPHE CABALLERO, DALE HENSLEY
For Anne:
HEATHER LINDELL, CAITLIN MUNDTH
For Jean-Michel:
LOGAN KESLAR, MICHAEL LOWNEY
For Jacqueline:
HEATHER LINDELL, CHERYL STERN
For Jacob:
CHRISTOPHE CABALLERO,
SEAN PATRICK DOYLE

ORCHESTRA
Conductor:
TODD ELLISON
Associate Conductor:
ANTONY GERALIS
Keyboards:
TODD ELLISON, ANTONY GERALIS
Woodwinds:
TOM CHRISTENSEN, ROGER ROSENBERG
Trumpet:
BOB MILLIKAN
Tenor Trombone:
KEITH O'QUINN
Acoustic Bass:
MARC SCHMIED
Drums/Percussion:
ERIC POLAND

Synthesizer Programmer:
RANDY COHEN

Music Coordinator:
JOHN MILLER

La Cage aux Folles

Harvey Fierstein
Albin and Author

Christopher Sieber
Georges

Mike McShane
*M. Dindon/
M. Renaud*

Allyce Beasley
*Mme. Dindon/
Mme. Renaud*

Chris Hoch
Francis

Elena Shaddow
Anne

A.J. Shively
Jean-Michel

Christine Andreas
Jacqueline

Wilson Jermaine
Heredia
Jacob

Heather Lindell
Colette

Michael Lowney
Etienne

Bruce Winant
Tabarro

Matt Anctil
Angelique

Sean Patrick Doyle
Chantal

Yurel Echezarreta
Phaedra

Logan Keslar
Bitelle

Terry Lavell
Mercedes

Karl Warden
Hanna

Christophe Caballero
Swing

Sean A. Carmon
Swing

Dale Hensley
Waiter, Swing

Todd Lattimore
Swing

Caitlin Mundth
Swing

Cheryl Stern
Babette

Jerry Herman
Music and Lyrics

Terry Johnson
Director

Lynne Page
Choreographer

Todd Ellison
Music Director

Tim Shortall
Scenic Design

Matthew Wright
Costume Design

Nick Richings
Lighting Design

Jonathan Deans
Sound Design

Richard Mawbey
*Wig & Makeup
Design*

Jason Carr
*Musical Supervision,
Orchestrations &
Dance
Arrangements*

John Miller
Music Coordinator

La Cage aux Folles

Duncan Stewart
Casting Director

Arthur Siccardi
Theatrical Services,
Inc.
Technical Supervisor

Sonia Friedman
Productions Ltd.
Producer

David Babani
Producer

Fran and Barry Weissler
Producer

Alecia Parker
Executive Producer

Edwin W. Schloss
Producer

John Gore,
Broadway Across
America
Producer

Thomas B. McGrath,
Broadway Across
America
Producer

Harriet Newman
Leve,
Raise The Roof 4
Producer

Jennifer
Manocherian,
Raise The Roof 4
Producer

Elaine Krauss,
Raise The Roof 4
Producer

Chris Bensinger
Producer

Deborah Taylor
Producer

Jane Bergère
Producer

Arlene Scanlan
Producer

John O'Boyle
Producer

Allen Spivak
Producer

Jerry Frankel
Producer

Barry Weisbord
Producer

James L.
Nederlander,
Nederlander
Presentations Inc.
Producer

Bob Weinstein,
The Weinstein
Company
Producer

Harvey Weinstein,
The Weinstein
Company
Producer

Nick Adams
Angelique

Fred Applegate
*M. Renaud,
M. Dindon*

Veanne Cox
*Mme. Dindon,
Mme. Renaud*

Nicholas
Cunningham
*Dance Captain,
Hanna*

Robin De Jesús
Jacob

Kelsey Grammer
Georges

Douglas Hodge
Albin

Bill Nolte
Tabarro

David Nathan Perlow
Etienne

Jeffrey Tambor
Georges

La Cage aux Folles

Ashley Kate Adams
Colette

Veanne Cox
Mme. Dindon,
Mme. Renaud

Harvey Fierstein as Zaza.

Photo by Joan Marcus

STAFF FOR *LA CAGE AUX FOLLES*

COMPANY MANAGER
Hilary Hamilton

GENERAL PRESS REPRESENTATIVE
BONEAU/BRYAN-BROWN
Adrian Bryan-Brown   Jim Byk   Michael Strassheim

Production Stage Manager	Kristen Harris
Stage Manager	Glynn David Turner
Assistant Stage Manager	Neveen Mahmoud
Associate General Manager	Hilary Hamilton
General Management Associate	Stephen Spadaro
Associate Scenic Designer	Bryan Johnson
Associate Lighting Designer	Vivien Leone
Assistant Lighting Designer	Ben Hagen
Associate Costume Designer	David Kaley
Moving Lights Programmer	Michael Hill
UK Production Consultant	Kirsten Turner
Head Carpenter	Karl Schuberth
Production Electricians	James J. Fedigan, Randall Zaibek
Head Electrician	Eric Norris
Head Properties	Robert Presley
Sound Engineer	Carin M. Ford
Advance Sound	Simon Matthews
Production Costume Coordinator	Brigid Guy
Wardrobe Supervisor	Jessica Neumann
Dressers	Jason Bishop, Cherie Cunningham, Tracey Diebold, Kimberly Mark, William Hubner, Deborah Black, Anastasya Jula, Marybeth Irons
Hair & Makeup Supervisor	John Curtin
Hair & Makeup Assistants	Brittnye Batchelor, Mark Manalansan
Production Assistants	Aaron Elgart, Beth Stegman
Assistant to John Miller	David A. Vandervliet
Casting Associate	Benton Whitley
Vice President of Marketing	Deirdre Hoetmer
Director of Marketing	Ken Sperr
Manager of Promotions & Marketing Partnerships	Matt Sicoli
Advertising	SpotCo/ Drew Hodges, Jim Edwards, Tom Greenwald, Vinny Sainato, Jim Aquino, Stacey Maya
Website Design/ Online Marketing Strategy	SpotCo/ Sara Fitzpatrick, Matt Wilstein, Marc Mettler, Christine Sees
Production Photography	Joan Marcus

Legal Counsel	Loeb & Loeb, Seth Gelblum
Merchandising	SpotCo Merch/Dewynters
Insurance	Stockbridge Risk Management DeWitt Stern
Accounting	Rosenberg, Neuwirth & Kuchner/ Mark D'Ambrosi, Marina Flom
Business Affairs Consultant	Daniel Posener
Banking	City National Bank/ Michele Gibbons
Resident Director	Tony Spinosa
Fight Director	Tom Schall
Skating Instruction	Lezly Skate School
Skate Trainer	James H. Singley
Physical Therapy	Performing Arts Physical Therapy
Travel Services	Tzell Travel/Andi Henig
Payroll Service	Castellana Services, Inc.

Promotional Support	Maybelline New York

SONIA FRIEDMAN PRODUCTIONS

Associate Producer	Sharon Duckworth
Literary Associate	Jack Bradley
Assistant to Sonia Friedman	Sarah Hammond
Assistant General Manager	Martin Ball
General Management Assistant	Ben Canning
Production Accountant	Melissa Hay
Chief Executive Officer-NY	David Lazar
New York Assistant	Valerie Steinberg

MENIER CHOCOLATE FACTORY

Marketing & Production Coordinator	Lucy McNally
Marketing & Production Assistant	Sarah Mannion
Restaurant General Manager	Nik Whybrew
Head Chef	Anthony Falla
Restaurant Manager	Douglas Hyde
Box Office Supervisor	Jane Elizabeth

NATIONAL ARTISTS MANAGEMENT COMPANY

Chief Financial Officer	Bob Williams
International Manager	Nina Skriloff
Executive Assistant to the Weisslers	Brett England
Accounting Associate	Marian Albarracin
Receptionist	Michelle Coleman
Assistant to B.J. Holt	Katharine Hayes
Creative Associate	Eli Gonda
Assistant to Barry Weissler	Irene Cabrera
Executive Assistant to Barry Weissler	Eddie Pisapia
Messenger	Victor Ruiz
Assistant to Alecia Parker	Marilyn Stout
Accounting Associate	Marion Taylor

CREDITS
Scenery executed by Hudson Scenic Studio, RK Resource. Plumage by Mark Wheeler. Lighting equipment from PRG Lighting. Sound equipment from PRG Audio. Costumes executed by Jane Gonin, Dennis & Shirley Fitzgerald, Theatrical Shoemakers, Theatre Royal Plymouth, Amanda Barrow, Keith Watson, Richard Handscombe, Glenn Hills, Judy Ward, Caroline Hughes, Elsa Threadgold, Sten Vollmuller, Shultz & Wiremu, Saint Laurie Merchant Tailors New York City. Millinery by Jenny Adey. Shoes by T.O. Dey, Capezio. Rollerskates by Lezly. Acrylic drinkware by U.S. Acrylic, LLC. Additional hand props by George Fenmore, Inc. Special thanks to Bra*Tenders for hosiery and undergarments. Make-up provided by M•A•C Cosmetics.

SPECIAL THANKS
Gary Murphy, Stas Iavorski at Ripley-Grier Studios, Elizabeth Helke, Will Dailey, John Darby.

Energy-efficient washer/dryer courtesy of LG Electronics.

 **THE SHUBERT ORGANIZATION, INC.**
Board of Directors

House Manager	Bob Reilly

La Cage aux Folles
SCRAPBOOK

Correspondent: Terry Lavell, "Mercedes"

Memorable Note, Fax or Fan Letter: Whoopi Goldberg came backstage and met the Cagelles and told me she thought we were fabulous. The next day she sent us a note and chocolate chip cookies.

Milestone Parties and Celebrations: We had our anniversary party Hurley's bar where we had celebrated winning the Tony Award.

Most Exciting Celebrity Visitors: Barbra Streisand came. She loved the show and I got a chance to meet her. She was probably our biggest celebrity, but we also have had James Earl Jones, Angela Lansbury, Whoopi Goldberg and Barbara Walters. Walters said she loved the show and thought we were great. Whoopi said we had great bodies and Sarah Jessica Parker said I had fabulous legs.

Actor Who Performed the Most Roles in This Show: Dale Hensley performs four different ensemble tracks. Harvey Fierstein has probably done the most over his whole career.

Special Backstage Rituals: We usually do a circle-up before the show. We pray or we do this thing that our English dance captain taught us: "Un, deux, trois, Oh, miss honey!" And then you add different phrases to it.

Favorite Moment During Each Performance (On Stage or Off): The beach ball section, because it's so improv and so random, we never know whether the audience is going to throw it back or not. It's the only section where, when you do it, you just don't know what's going to happen. It's totally different every night.

Favorite In-Theatre Gathering Place: The greenroom, which is in the basement under the stage.

Favorite Off-Site Hangouts: Hurley's for the most part. And Glass House Tavern.

Favorite Snack Foods: Harvey has snacks in his dressing room for everybody, everything from Reese's Pieces to jellybeans to cashew nuts to Jolly Rancher lollipops to chocolate to Starbursts.

Mascot: Barbie. Each of us has our own. For a long time, the Cagelles would dress their Barbie dolls and we had Barbie competitions. Harvey has two Barbies in his dressing room. At Halloween everybody in the company came in Barbie Doll costumes.

Favorite Therapies: Singer's Saving Grace, Throat Coat Tea, Hall's, Ricolas, honey and good old water.

Memorable Ad-Libs: The Cagelles love to insert comments into the show, and people love them: "I'm hungry." "Honey, that whip!" "Hell no!" "You wish!" They started as ad-libs, but they're written into the show now.

Memorable Press Encounter: We did a Garnier Fructis promotion in the middle of Times Square, which consisted of us throwing empty Garnier bottles in the air. It was so random!

Memorable Stage Door Fan Encounter: One girl made each of the Cagelles a photo album that chronicled each of us from beginning of

1. (L-R): Matt Anctil, Yurel Echezarreta, Terry Lavell, Douglas Hodge, Logan Kesler, Sean Patrick Doyle and Nicholas Cunningham celebrate Hodge's final performance February 13, 2011 at Hurley's.
2. Kelsey Grammer at curtain calls for his final performance on the same date.
3. (Foreground L-R): Chris Sieber and Harvey Fierstein celebrate the show's anniversary, April 18, 2011.

the show to the end. It has photos of the company and press events, and it's absolutely beautiful. There are six of us on stage and three swings, and everybody's book is different. She's a real fan.

What Did You Think of the Web Buzz on Your Show: Web buzz has always been great. We were just a hit, a great show, a better revival than the last revival, a smaller production but done so much better. Hats off to the company!

Fastest Costume Change: At the end of the can-can Hanna (Karl Warden) actually changes on stage. He takes off his can-can skirt, corset and wig and puts on black high heels, a cat suit, gloves and wig. All in twenty seconds.

Who Wore the Heaviest Costume? The Cagelles, in our finale headdresses.

Who Wore the Least? Matt Anctil strips down to just his panties.

Catchphrases Only the Company Would Recognize: "Not today, girl!"

Sweethearts Within the Company: No showmances!

Memorable Directorial Note: When Doug and Kelsey were in the show, we were rehearsing the scene at the end of the can-can when Doug

Hodge is holding a martini glass. Director asked me, "Terry, would you mind if we use your ass as a prop?" I'm supposed to have a large bum. I turned around and he rested the cocktail on my butt.

Tale From the Put-In: Christopher Sieber learned our show in one week. At put-in he did it like he'd been rehearsing for three weeks. He never called for a line. I don't think I ever saw anybody work like that.

Nicknames: We call Harvey "Mama." Sieber called the Cagelles "Kittens." The Cagelles call each other "Trannie."

Embarrassing Moments: I fell off the cabaret table opening night. Didn't hurt that bad but the excitement got me through. Harvey, when he opened his coat at the end of can-can number, had twirling tassels on his boobs. One night only one was working. That was pretty funny, but embarrassing. Wigs are always coming off. When Jeffrey Tambor forgot his lines, he was like a deer in the headlights: he just stared.

Coolest Thing About Being in This Show: It's the first time I was ever in a show where people really really loved the show.

A Life in the Theatre

First Preview: September 21, 2010. Opened: October 12, 2010.
Closed November 28, 2010 after 24 Previews and 56 Performances.

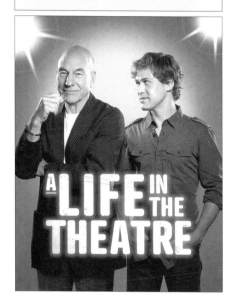

PLAYBILL®

In a series of backstage scenes over the course of years, two actors—Robert nearing the end of his career and John at the dawn of his—share observations about acting, art and humanity as they ply their craft.

THE COMPANY

Robert ....PATRICK STEWART
John ....T.R. KNIGHT

Production Stage Manager:
MATTHEW SILVER

Stage Manager:
JILLIAN M. OLIVER

UNDERSTUDIES

For Robert:
CONAN McCARTY

For John:
SEAN McNALL

---

⑤ GERALD SCHOENFELD THEATRE
236 West 45th Street
A Shubert Organization Theatre

Philip J. Smith, *Chairman*   **Robert E. Wankel,** *President*

JEFFREY RICHARDS   JERRY FRANKEL   JAM THEATRICALS
DEBBIE BISNO   EVA PRICE

LARRY MAGID   KATHLEEN K. JOHNSON   HERBERT GOLDSMITH PRODUCTIONS, INC.
ROGER KASS   BARRY & CAROLE KAYE   KELPIE ARTS   TERRY ALLEN KRAMER
BLACK-PEREIRA   FREEDBERG-DALE/DOMBROWSKI-MANUEL   KATHLEEN SEIDEL

present

PATRICK   T.R.
STEWART   KNIGHT

in

A LIFE IN THE THEATRE

by
DAVID MAMET

Scenic Design	Costume Design	Lighting Design
SANTO LOQUASTO	LAURA BAUER	KENNETH POSNER

Wig Design	Casting	Fight Choreographer
CHARLES LaPOINTE	TELSEY + COMPANY	J. DAVID BRIMMER

Production Stage Manager	Technical Supervision	Press Representative
MATTHEW SILVER	HUDSON THEATRICAL ASSOCIATES	JEFFREY RICHARDS ASSOCIATES IRENE GANDY/ALANA KARPOFF

Associate Producers	Company Manager	General Management
JEREMY SCOTT BLAUSTEIN SHANE MARSHALL BROWN MATTHEW SALLOWAY	MARY MILLER	RICHARDS/CLIMAN, INC.

Directed by
NEIL PEPE

The World Premiere of A LIFE IN THE THEATRE was presented by Goodman Theatre Stage 2–February, 1977.
The Producers wish to express their appreciation to the Theatre Development Fund for its support of this production.

10/12/10

(L-R): Patrick Stewart and T.R. Knight

Photo by Carol Rosegg

A Life in the Theatre

Patrick Stewart
Robert

T.R. Knight
John

Conan McCarty
u/s Robert

Sean McNall
u/s John

David Mamet
Playwright

Neil Pepe
Director

Kenneth Posner
Lighting Designer

Santo Loquasto
Scenic Design

Laura Bauer
Costume Design

Obadiah Eaves
*Original Music and
Sound Designer*

Neil A. Mazzella/
Hudson Theatrical
Associates
*Technical
Supervision*

David R. Richards and Tamar Haimes,
Richards/Climan, Inc.
General Manager

Charles LaPointe
Hair and Wig Design

Bernard Telsey,
Telsey + Company
Casting

J. David Brimmer
Fight Choreographer

Jeffrey Richards
Producer

Jerry Frankel
Producer

Arny Granat,
Jam Theatricals
Producer

Steve Traxler,
Jam Theatricals
Producer

Debbie Bisno
Producer

Eva Price/
Maximum
Entertainment
Producer

Valerie Gordon-
Johnson,
Kelpie Arts
Producer

Doug Johnson,
Kelpie Arts
Producer

Terry Allen Kramer
Producer

(L-R): T.R. Knight and
Patrick Stewart

Photo by Carol Rosegg

Bruston Kade
Manuel
Producer

Will Dombrowski
Producer

Jeremy Scott
Blaustein
Associate Producer

Shane Marshall
Brown
Associate Producer

A Life in the Theatre

CREW

Front Row (L-R): Leslie Kilian (House Electrician), Tim McWilliams (House Carp), Jason Hayes (Hair Supervisor)

Middle Row (L-R): Jillian Oliver (Stage Manager), Sandy Binion (Wardrobe Supervisor), Catherine Lynch (Stage Management P.A.), Laura McGarty (Props), Glen Scott Monroe (Carp)

Back Row (L-R): Glenn Ingram (Flyman), Justin Freeman (Light Board Op), Heidi Brown (House Props), Julien Havard (T.R.'s Dresser), Matthew Silver (Stage Manager), Moira MacGregor-Conrad (Patrick's Dresser), Chad Hershey (Automation)

Photo by Brian Mapp

STAFF FOR *A LIFE IN THE THEATRE*

GENERAL MANAGEMENT
RICHARDS/CLIMAN, INC.

DAVID R. RICHARDS	TAMAR HAIMES
Michael Sag	Kyle Bonder
Cesar Hawas	Julianna Slaten

COMPANY MANAGER
MARY MILLER

GENERAL PRESS REPRESENTATIVE
JEFFREY RICHARDS ASSOCIATES
IRENE GANDY/ALANA KARPOFF
Elon Rutberg   Diana Rissetto

CASTING
TELSEY + COMPANY, C.S.A.
Bernie Telsey CSA, Will Cantler CSA,
David Vaccari CSA,
Bethany Knox CSA, Craig Burns CSA,
Tiffany Little Canfield CSA,
Rachel Hoffman CSA,
Carrie Rosson CSA, Justin Huff CSA,
Patrick Goodwin CSA,
Abbie Brady-Dalton, David Morris,
Cesar A. Rocha

PRODUCTION MANAGEMENT
HUDSON THEATRICAL ASSOCIATES
Neil Mazzella   Sam Ellis   Irene Wang

PRODUCTION STAGE
   MANAGER ....MATTHEW SILVER
Stage Manager ....Jillian M. Oliver
Original Music...........................Obadiah Eaves
Assistant Director ....Cat Williams
Associate Scenic Designer ....Jenny Sawyers
Associate Costume Designer ....Bobby Tilley
Associate Lighting Designer ....John Viesta
Movement/Dance Consultant ....Kelly Maurer

Fight Choreographer Assistants ....Dan O'Driscoll,
    John Robichau, Michael Yahn
Dialect Coach ....Deborah Hecht
Production Assistant ....Catherine Lynch
Production Carpenters ....Chad Hershey, Scott Monroe
Production Electrician ....Justin Freeman
Production Props ....Kathy Fabian/Propstar
Head Props ....Laura McGarty
Wardrobe Supervisor ....Sandy Binion
Hair Supervisor ....Jason P. Hayes
Dressers ....Moira Conrad, Julien Havard
Assistant Scenic Designer ....Antje Ellerman
Associate Props Coordinator ....Carrie Mossman
Props Assistants ....Tim Ferro, Sarah Bird
Costume Intern ....Suzie Kondi
Assistants to Mr. Mamet ....Pam Susemiehl,
    Justin Fair
Assistant Producer ....Michael Crea
Assistant to Mr. Richards ....Will Trice
Assistant to Mr. Traxler ....Brandi Preston
Advertising ....Serino Coyne, Inc./
    Greg Corradetti, Tom Callahan,
    Robert Jones, Danielle Boyle
Interactive Marketing Agency ....Situation Interactive/
    Damian Bazadona, John Lanasa,
    Miriam Naggar, Victoria Gettler
Creative Director,
   Broadway's Best Shows ....'.....Andy Drachenberg
Merchandising ....Max Merchandising
Banking...............................City National Bank/
    Michele Gibbons
Accountants ....Fried & Kowgios,
    CPA's LLP, Robert Fried, CPA
Comptroller ....Elliott Aronstam
Legal Counsel ....Lazarus & Harris LLP./
    Scott R. Lazarus, Esq.,
    Robert C. Harris, Esq.
Insurance ....DeWitt Stern Group Inc./
    Joseph Bower, Anthony Pittari
Payroll ....CSI/Lance Castellana
Production Photographer ....Carol Rosegg
Company Mascots ....Skye, Franco and Stella

CREDITS
Scenery constructed by Hudson Scenic Studios, Inc. Lighting equipment from Hudson Lighting & Sound, LLC. Sound equipment from Sound Associates, Inc. Costume Shop: John Kristiansen NY, Inc. Costumes supplied by Western Costumes. Production rehearsed at Atlantic Theater Company.

The Lion King

First Preview: October 15, 1997. Opened: November 13, 1997.
Still running as of May 31, 2011.

When the evil lion Scar kills his brother Mufasa, and seizes the kingship of the African Pridelands, young prince Simba flees into the wilderness. There he is transformed by some new friends and finally returns to reclaim his crown. Performed by actors in puppetlike costumes designed by director Julie Taymor.

CAST

(in order of appearance)

RAFIKI .... Tshidi Manye
MUFASA .... Alton Fitzgerald White
SARABI .... Jean Michelle Grier
ZAZU .... Cameron Pow
SCAR .... Gareth Saxe
YOUNG SIMBA .... Alphonso Romero Jones II
                    (Wed., Fri., Sat. Eve., Sun. Mat.)
                                         Joshua J. Jackson
                    (Tues., Thurs., Sat. Mat., Sun. Eve.)
YOUNG NALA .... Eden Sanaa Duncan-Smith
                    (Wed., Thurs., Sat. Eve., Sun. Eve.)
                                            Khail Toi Bryant
                    (Tues., Fri., Sat. Mat., Sun. Mat.)
SHENZI .... Bonita J. Hamilton
BANZAI .... James Brown-Orleans
ED .... Enrique Segura
TIMON .... Fred Berman
PUMBAA .... Ben Jeffrey
SIMBA .... Dashaun Young
NALA .... Chaunteé Schuler
ENSEMBLE SINGERS .... Alvin Crawford,
                    Lindiwe Dlamini, Bongi Duma,
            Jean Michelle Grier, Joel Karie, Ron Kunene,
Continued on next page

Continued on next page

MINSKOFF THEATRE

UNDER THE DIRECTION OF
JAMES M. NEDERLANDER, JAMES L. NEDERLANDER,
SARA MINSKOFF ALLAN AND THE MINSKOFF FAMILY

Disney
PRESENTS

THE LION KING

Music & Lyrics by
ELTON JOHN & TIM RICE

Additional Music & Lyrics by
LEBO M. MARK MANCINA, JAY RIFKIN, JULIE TAYMOR, HANS ZIMMER

Book by
ROGER ALLERS & IRENE MECCHI

Starring
GARETH SAXE   ALTON FITZGERALD WHITE   TSHIDI MANYE
CAMERON POW   BEN JEFFREY   FRED BERMAN
DASHAUN YOUNG   CHAUNTEÉ SCHULER
JAMES BROWN-ORLEANS   BONITA J. HAMILTON   ENRIQUE SEGURA
KHAIL TOI BRYANT   EDEN SANAA DUNCAN-SMITH   JOSHUA J. JACKSON   ALPHONSO ROMERO JONES II

SANT'GRIA BELLO   IZELL O. BLUNT   CAMILLE M. BROWN   MICHELLE BRUGAL   ALVIN CRAWFORD   GABRIEL CROOM
GARLAND DAYS   CHARITY de LOERA   LINDIWE DLAMINI   BONGI DUMA   ANGELICA EDWARDS   JIM FERRIS
CHRISTOPHER FREEMAN   JEAN MICHELLE GRIER   KENNY INGRAM   NICOLE ADELL JOHNSON   DENNIS JOHNSTON
JOEL KARIE   CHARLAINE KATSUYOSHI   RON KUNENE   BRIAN M. LOVE   SHERYL McCALLUM   RAY MERCER
WILLIA-NOEL MONTAGUE   S'BU NGEMA   NTELISENG NKHELA   SELLOANE A. NKHELA   JAMES A. PIERCE III
JACQUELINE RENE'   KELLEN STANCIL   L. STEVEN TAYLOR   NATALIE TURNER   THOM CHRISTOPHER WARREN
REMA WEBB   KENNY REDELL WILLIAMS   CAMILLE WORKMAN

Adapted from the screenplay by
IRENE MECCHI & JONATHAN ROBERTS & LINDA WOOLVERTON

Produced by
PETER SCHNEIDER & THOMAS SCHUMACHER

Scenic Design RICHARD HUDSON	*Costume Design* JULIE TAYMOR	*Lighting Design* DONALD HOLDER	*Mask & Puppet Design* JULIE TAYMOR & MICHAEL CURRY
Sound Design STEVE CANYON KENNEDY	*Hair & Makeup Design* MICHAEL WARD	*Associate Director* JOHN STEFANIUK	*Associate Choreographer* MAREY GRIFFITH
Associate Producer ANNE QUART	*Technical Director* DAVID BENKEN	*Production Stage Manager* RON VODICKA	*Production Supervisor* DOC ZORTHIAN

Music Supervisor CLEMENT ISHMAEL	*Music Director* KARL JURMAN	*Associate Music Producer* ROBERT ELHAI	*Music Coordinator* MICHAEL KELLER	*Orchestrators* ROBERT ELHAI DAVID METZGER BRUCE FOWLER

Music Produced for the *Stage & Additional Score by* MARK MANCINA	*Additional Vocal Score,* *Vocal Arrangements* *& Choral Director* LEBO M	*Casting* BINDER CASTING/ MARK BRANDON, C.S.A.	*Fight Director* RICK SORDELET

Choreography by
GARTH FAGAN

Directed by
JULIE TAYMOR

©Disney

Disney
ON BROADWAY

10/1/10

(L-R): Fred Berman as Timon and Ben Jeffrey as Pumbaa

Photo by Joan Marcus

The Lion King

Moya Angela
*Ensemble Singer,
Lioness/Hyena
Shadow Puppet*

Shaylin Becton
*Young Nala
at certain
performances*

Judah Bellamy
*Young Simba
at certain
performances*

Kristina Bethel-Blunt
*Ant Hill Lady,
Ensemble Dancer*

Trista Dollison
*Ensemble Singer,
Lioness/Hyena
Shadow Puppet*

**Keisha Lauren Clarke
Gray**
Swing

Andrea Jones
*Ensemble Singer,
Lioness/Hyena
Shadow Puppet*

Cornelius Jones Jr.
*Ensemble Singer,
Giraffe Shadow
Puppet, Pumbaa
Pole Puppet, Scar
Shadow Puppet*

**Aubrey Omari
Joseph**
*Young Simba
at certain
performances*

Lisa Lewis
*Cheetah,
Ensemble Dancer,
Nala Pole Puppet*

Jaysin McCollum
*Ensemble Dancer,
Gazelle, Giraffe
Shadow Puppet,
Scar Shadow Puppet*

Clifton Oliver
Simba

**Brandon Christopher
O'Neal**
*Ensemble Dancer,
Gazelle, Giraffe
Shadow Puppet,
Scar Shadow Puppet*

Tom Alan Robbins
Pumbaa

Vusi Sondiyazi
*Circle of Life Vocals,
Ensemble Singer,
Giraffe Shadow
Puppet, Pumbaa
Pole Puppet, Scar
Shadow Puppet*

Torya
*Cheetah,
Ensemble Dancer,
Nala Pole Puppet*

Phillip W. Turner
*Ensemble Dancer,
Simba Shadow
Puppets*

**Lisa Nicole
Wilkerson**
*Ensemble Singer,
Lioness/Hyena
Shadow Puppet*

FRONT OF HOUSE STAFF
(L-R): Afton Boggiano, Gordon Eng-Wong

Photos by Brian Mapp

FRONT OF HOUSE STAFF
Front Row (L-R): Jennie Andrea, David Eschinger,
Elaine Healy, Marion Mooney

Second Row (L-R): Maria (Flo) Compton,
Magdalena Clavano, Joanne Shannon, Judy Pirouz

Third Row (L-R): Louis Musano, Cheryl Budd,
Fanny (Jing) Zhang, Mathew Maine

Back Row (L-R): Victor Irving, Christopher Quartana

The Lion King

CREW

Front Row (L-R): Kathryn Rohe, Myriah Perkins, Fred Hemminger, Amy McCraney, Thomas Schlenk, Carmen Abrazado, Mary Patricia "Pixie" Esmonde, Rita Acuna, Ruthlyn Salomons, Scott Scheidt, Ron Kunene (Actor)

Back Row: Santos Acuna, Ron Vodicka, Sheila Little Terrell, Tom Reynolds, Mark Houston, Mike Lynch, Karl Jurman, Dave Holliman, Ilya Vett, Stephen Speer, Jay Lynch, Douglas Graf, Walter Weiner, Dawn Reynolds, Herman Rivera, James Holvath, Scott Harrington, Alain Van Achte, George Zegarsky, Narda Alcorn, Frank Illo, Don McKennan, William Brennan, Vusi Sondiyazi (Actor), Kenny Ingram (Actor)

Staff for *THE LION KING* Worldwide

Associate Producer ....Anne Quart
Production Supervisor ....Doc Zorthian
Production Manager ....Myriah Perkins
Associate Director ....John Stefaniuk
Associate Choreographer ....Marey Griffith
Music Supervisor ....Clement Ishmael
Dance Supervisor ....Celise Hicks
Associate Music Supervisor ....Jay Alger
Associate Scenic Designer ....Peter Eastman
Associate Costume Designer ....Mary Nemecek Peterson
Associate Mask & Puppet Designer ....Louis Troisi
Associate Sound Designer ....John Shivers
Associate Hair & Makeup Designer ....Carole Hancock
Associate Lighting Designer ....Jeanne Koenig
Assistant Lighting Designer ....Marty Vreeland
Assistant Sound Designer ....Shane Cook
Automated Lighting Programmer ....Aland Henderson
Production Coordinator ....Tara Engler
Management Assistant ....Elizabeth Fine

DISNEY ON BROADWAY PUBLICITY

Senior Publicist ....Dennis Crowley
Publicist ....Adriana Douzos

Staff for *THE LION KING* New York

Company Manager ....THOMAS SCHLENK
Associate Company Manager ....Christopher A. Recker
Production Stage Manager ....Ron Vodicka
Resident Director ....Darren Katz
Resident Dance Supervisor ....Ruthlyn Salomons
Musical Director/Conductor ....Karl Jurman

Stage Managers ....Carmen I. Abrazado,
Antonia Gianino, Narda Alcorn,
Tom Reynolds
Dance Captains ......Garland Days, Willia-Noel Montague
Fight Captain ....Ray Mercer
Assistant Choreographers ....Norwood J. Pennewell,
Natalie Rogers
South African Dialect Coach ....Ron Kunene
Casting Associates ....Jack Bowdan, C.S.A.;
Mark Brandon, C.S.A.;
Nikole Vallins, C.S.A.
Casting Assistant ....Patrick Bell
Corporate Counsel ....Michael Rosenfeld
Physical Therapy ....Neuro Tour Physical Therapy/
Maria Shrime
Consulting Orthopedist ....Neil Roth, M.D.
Child Wrangler ....Rick Plaugher
Executive Travel ....Robert Arnao, Patt McRory
Production Travel ....Jill Citron
Web Design Consultant ....Joshua Noah
Advertising ....Serino/Coyne Inc.
Interactive Marketing ....Situation Marketing/
Damian Bazadona, Lisa Cecchini,
Miriam Gardin

Production Carpenter ....Drew Siccardi
Head Carpenter ....Michael Trotto
House Carpenter ....Patrick Sullivan
Assistant Carpenters ....Kirk Bender, Michael Phillips
Automation Carpenters ....Aldo "Butch" Servilio,
George Zegarsky
Carpenters ....Giuseppe Iannello, Daniel Macormack,
Duane Mirro
Flying Supervision ....Dave Hearn

Production Flymen ....Kraig Bender, Dylan Trotto
House Flyman ....Richard McQuail
Production Electrician ....James Maloney
House Electrician ....Michael Lynch
Board Operator ....Edward Greenberg
House Assistant Electrician ....Stephen Speer
Automated Lighting Technician ....Sean Strohmeyer
Key Spot Operator ....Doug Graf
Assistant Electricians ....William Brennan,
David Holliman, David Lynch,
Joseph P. Lynch
Production Propman ....Victor Amerling
House Propman ....Frank Illo
Props ....Matthew Lavaia, Michael Lavaia,
Robert McCauley
Head Sound ....Alain Van Achte
Sound Assistants ....Donald McKennan, Scott Scheidt
Production Wardrobe Supervisor ....Kjeld Andersen
Assistant Wardrobe Supervisor ....Cynthia Boardman
Puppet Supervisor ....Anne Salt
Puppet Dayworkers ....Islah Abdul-Rahiim,
Ilya Vett
Mask/Puppet Studio ....Jeff Curry
Dressers ....Meredith Chase-Boyd,
Andy Cook, Tom Daniel, Donna Doiron,
Pixie Esmonde, April Fernandez-Taylor,
Michelle Gore-Butterfield,
Douglas Hamilton, Mark Houston,
Sara Jablon, Chad C. Jason,
Mark Lauer, Dawn Reynolds,
Kathryn Rohe, Sheila Terrell,
Dave Tisue, Walter Weiner
Stitcher ....Janeth Iverson
Production Hair Supervisor ....Jon Jordan

The Lion King

Assistant Hair Supervisor ....Adenike Wright
Production Makeup Supervisor ....Elizabeth Cohen
Assistant Makeup
    Supervisor ....Marian Torre
Makeup Artist ....Rebecca Kuzma

Music Development ....Nick Glennie-Smith
Music Preparation ....Donald Oliver and Evan Morris/
    Chelsea Music Service, Inc.
Synthesizer Programmer...........................Ted Baker
Orchestral Synthesizer
    Programmer ....Christopher Ward
Electronic Drum Programmer ....Tommy Igoe
Addt'l Percussion Arrangements ....Valerie Dee Naranjo
Music Assistant ....Elizabeth J. Falcone
Personal Assistant to Elton John ....Bob Halley
Assistant to Tim Rice ....Eileen Heinink
Assistant to Mark Mancina ....Chuck Choi

Associate Scenic Designer ....Jonathan Fensom
Assistant Scenic Designer ....Michael Fagin
Lighting Design Assistant ....Karen Spahn
Automated Lighting Tracker ....Lara Bohon
Projection Designer ....Geoff Puckett
Projection Art ....Caterina Bertolotto
Assistant Sound Designer ....Kai Harada
Assistant Costume Designer ....Tracy Dorman
Stunt Consultant ....Peter Moore
Children's Tutoring ....On Location Education
Production Photography ....Joan Marcus,
    Marc Bryan-Brown
Associate Producer 1996–1998 ....Donald Frantz
Project Manager 1996–1998 ....Nina Essman
Associate Producer 1998–2002 ....Ken Denison
Associate Producer 2000-2003 ....Pam Young
Associate Producer 2002-2007 ....Todd Lacy
Associate Producer 2003-2008 ....Aubrey Lynch
Original Music Director ....Joseph Church

The Lion King is a proud member of the Broadway Green Alliance.

Disney's *The Lion King* is a registered trademark owned by The Walt Disney Company and used under special license by Disney Theatrical Productions.

HOUSE STAFF FOR THE MINSKOFF THEATRE

House Manager ....Victor Irving
Treasurer ....Nicholas Loiacono
Assistant Treasurer ....Cheryl Loiacono

CREDITS

Scenery built and mechanized by Hudson Scenic Studio, Inc. Additional scenery by Chicago Scenic Studios, Inc.; Edge & Co., Inc.; Michael Hagen, Inc.; Piper Productions, Inc.; Scenic Technologies, Inc.; I. Weiss & Sons, Inc. Lighting by Westsun, vari*lite® automated lighting provided by Vari-Lite, Inc. Props by John Creech Design & Production. Sound equipment by Pro-Mix, Inc. Additional sound equipment by Walt Disney Imagineering. Rehearsal Scenery by Brooklyn Scenic & Theatrical. Costumes executed by Barbara Matera Ltd., Parsons-Meares Ltd., Donna Langman, Eric Winterling, Danielle Gisiger, Suzie Elder. Millinery by Rodney Gordon, Janet Linville, Arnold Levine. Ricola provided by Ricola, Inc. Shibori dyeing by Joan Morris. Custom dyeing and painting by Joni Johns, Mary Macy, Parsons-Meares Ltd., Gene Mignola. Additional Painting by J. Michelle Hill. Knitwear by Maria Ficalora. Footwear by Sharlot Battin, Robert W. Jones, Capezio, Vasilli Shoes. Costume Development by Constance Hoffman. Special Projects by Angela M. Kahler. Custom fabrics developed by Gary Graham and Helen Quinn. Puppet Construction by Michael Curry Design, Inc. and Vee Corporation. Shadow puppetry by Steven Kaplan. Pumbaa Puppet Construction by Andrew Benepe. Flying by Foy. Trucking by Clark Transfer. Wigs created by Wig Workshop of London. Marimbas by De Morrow Instruments, Ltd. Latin Percussion by LP Music Group. Drumset by DrumWorkshop. Cymbals by Zildjian. Bass equipment by Eden Electronics. Paper products supplied by Green Forest.

SONG EXCERPTS (used by permission): "Supercalifragilisticexpialidocious" written by Richard M. Sherman and Robert B. Sherman; "Five Foot Two, Eyes of Blue" written by Sam Lewis, Joe Young, and Ray Henderson; "The Lion Sleeps Tonight" written by Hugo Peretti, George David Weiss, Luigi Creatore and Solomon Linda.

NEDERLANDER

Chairman ....James M. Nederlander
President ....James L. Nederlander

Executive Vice President
Nick Scandalios

Vice President   Senior Vice President
Corporate Development   Labor Relations
Charlene S. Nederlander   **Herschel Waxman**

Vice President   Chief Financial Officer
Jim Boese   **Freida Sawyer Belviso**

DISNEY THEATRICAL PRODUCTIONS

President ....Thomas Schumacher
EVP & Managing Director ....David Schrader

Senior Producer ....Michele Steckler
Senior Vice President, International ....Ron Kollen
Vice President, Operations ....Dana Amendola
Vice President, Worldwide Publicity
    & Communications ....Joe Quenqua
Vice President, Domestic Touring...............Jack Eldon
Vice President, Creative Development
    & Licensing ....Steve Fickinger
Vice President, Human Resources ....June Heindel
Director, Domestic Touring ....Michael Buchanan
Director, Labor Relations ....Edward Lieber
Manager, Labor Relations ....Stephanie Cheek
Manager, Human Resources ....Jewel Neal
Manager, Publicity &
    Communications ....Lindsay Braverman
Manager, Information Systems ....Scott Benedict
Senior Computer Support Analyst ....Kevin A. McGuire
IT/Business Analyst ....William Boudiette

Production

Executive Music Producer ....Chris Montan
Director, International ....Michael Cassel

Director, International Production ....Felipe Gamba
Manager, Physical Production ....Karl Chmielewski
Creative Development Manager ....Jane Abramson
Dramaturg & Literary Manager ....Ken Cerniglia

Marketing

Vice President, Broadway ....Andrew Flatt
Vice President, International.................Fiona Thomas
Director, Internet Strategy &
    Online Marketing ....Kyle Young
Director, Broadway ....Michele Groner
Director, Domestic Tour Marketing ......Deborah Warren
Director, Customer Relationship
    Management & Strategy ....Kelly Colbert
Assistant Manager, Advertising ....Lauren Daghini

Sales

Director, National Sales ....Bryan Dockett
National Sales Manager ....Victoria Cairl
Manager, Sales & Ticketing ....Nick Falzon
Manager, Sales & Ticketing ....David Felsen
Manager, Group Sales ....Hunter Robertson

Business and Legal Affairs

Senior Vice President ....Jonathan Olson
Director ....Daniel M. Posener
Senior Counsel ....Seth Stuhl
Paralegal ....Jessica White

Finance

VP Finance & Business Development ....Mario Iannetta
Director ....Joe McClafferty
Manager, Finance ....John Fajardo
Production Accountants ....Joy Sims Brown,
    Nick Judge
Assistant Production Accountant ....Isander Rojas
Senior Sales Analyst ....Liz Jurist Schwarzwalder
Senior Business Analyst ....Sven Rittershaus
Director, Accounting ....Leena Mathew
Sr. Financial Analyst ....Adrineh Ghoukassian

Administrative Staff

Sarah Bills, Amy Caldamone, Michael Dei Cas, Preston Copley, Alanna Degner, Brittany Dobbs, Cristi Finn, Jonathan Flood, Gregory Hanoian, Abbie Harrison, Cyntia Leo, Colleen McCormack, Lisa Mitchell, Brendan Padgett, Ryan Pears, David Scott, Anji Taylor, Christina Tuchman, Kyle Wilson, Jason Zammit

DISNEY THEATRICAL MERCHANDISE

Vice President ....Steven Downing
Operations Manager ....Shawn Baker
Merchandise Manager ....Neil Markman
Associate Buyer ....Violet Burlaza
Assistant Manager, Inventory ....Suzanne Jakel
On-Site Retail Manager ....Jeff Knizer
On-Site Assistant Retail Manager ....Jana Cristiano

Disney Theatrical Productions
c/o New Amsterdam Theatre
214 W. 42nd St.
New York, NY 10036

guestmail@disneytheatrical.com

The Lion King
SCRAPBOOK

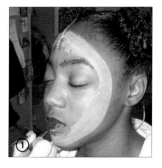
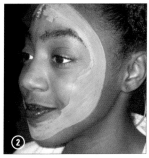

Makeup photos by Joseph Marzullo/WENN

Photo by Joan Marcus

Correspondent: Alvin Crawford, Ensemble, understudy for "Mufasa"

Most Vivid Memory: Tuesday November 2, 2010. The first performance after our beloved Young Nala, Shannon Skye Tavarez, lost her battle with acute myeloid leukemia. At the five-minute call, the entire company gathered on stage to hug and gain strength. We recited the Serenity Prayer and shared stories about Shannon. I was on as Mufasa that evening. Mufasa sings "They Live in You," explaining to his young son Simba whenever he ever feels alone, he must remember to look up at the stars because they represent his ancestors. I looked up and saw Shannon's smiling face. I will never forget her big, beautiful voice and her bright, shining spirit.

Milestone Parties, Celebrations and/or Company Gifts: My *Lion King* robe!

Most Exciting Celebrity Visitor and What They Did/Said: Tracy Morgan from "30 Rock." His quote: "Man, you guys work hard!" Yes we do!

Special Backstage Ritual: My fist-bump with Elaine the usher at the places call. She's our good luck charm!

Special Intermission Activity: Birthday cake. With a cast and crew of more than one hundred people, odds are it's always somebody's birthday!

Favorite Moment in the Show: "Circle of Life." I'm literally the second wildebeest walking down the left orchestra aisle. I have the pleasure of seeing how our opening number moves the audience to tears of joy. What an honor!

Favorite Off-Site Hangout: Bourbon Street on West 46th Street. It's a big place and they have my favorite beverage, the Dark and Stormy (dark rum and ginger beer, the best!)

Favorite Snack Food: Apples. Hey, an apple a day keeps the doctor away.

Memorable Stage Door Fan Encounter: After a matinee, I came out of the stage door to find my Eighth Grade music teacher who taught me how to play tuba! I hadn't seen Ms. Hauser in years! It was so nice to catch up.

Coolest Thing About Being in This Show: Singing this amazing music!

1-7. Jade Milan getting into makeup for Young Nala, as designed by Elizabeth Cohen, Production Makeup Supervisor.

8. Shannon Skye Tavarez in costume as Young Nala.

9. Helping raise money in the PIX 11 Morning News Bone Marrow Drive for Shannon Tavarez (Rear L-R): Jean Michelle Grier, Joel Karie, Alvin Crawford, Dennis Johnston. (Front L-R): Rema Webb, Charity de Loera, Willia-Noel Montague.

A Little Night Music

First Preview: November 24, 2009. Opened: December 13, 2009.
Closed January 9, 2011 after 20 Previews and 425 Performances.

Bernadette Peters
Desirée Armfeldt

Elaine Stritc[h]
Madame A[rmfeldt]

Ramona Mallory
Anne Egerman

Ron Bohmer
Frid

Kevin David Thomas
Mr. Erlanson

Keaton Whitta[ker]
Fredrika Armf[eldt]

Trevor Nunn
Director

Lynne Page
Choreographer

Gareth Owen
Sound Design

Paul Huntley
Wig & Hair Desi[gn]

Musical adaptation of the 1955 Ingmar Bergman film Smiles of a Summer Night, *about lawyer Fredrik Egerman who is torn between his still-virgin child bride and his former lover, the actress Desirée Armfeldt. Over the course of a weekend in the country, the various mismatched romances are reordered and the right people wind up with the right partners.*

CAST

(in order of appearance)

Henrik Egerman ...HUNTER RYAN HERDLICKA
Mr. Lindquist ....BEN DAVIS
Mrs. Nordstrom ....JAYNE PATERSON
Mrs. Anderssen ....JESSICA GROVÉ
Mr. Erlanson ....KEVIN DAVID THOMAS
Mrs. Segstrom ....GINA LAMPARELLA
Fredrika Armfeldt ......KATHERINE McNAMARA
(Tues., Wed. mat., Fri., Sat. mat.)
KEATON WHITTAKER
(Wed. eve., Thurs., Sat. eve., Sun.)
Madame Armfeldt ....ELAINE STRITCH
Frid ....RON BOHMER
Anne Egerman.................RAMONA MALLORY
Fredrik Egerman........STEPHEN R. BUNTROCK
Petra ....LEIGH ANN LARKIN
Desirée Armfeldt ....BERNADETTE PETERS
Count Carl-Magnus Malcolm ....BRADLEY DEAN
Countess Charlotte Malcolm ....ERIN DAVIE

SWINGS

KAREN MURPHY, ERIN STEWART,
KEVIN VORTMANN

Continued on next page

 WALTER KERR THEATRE
A JUJAMCYN THEATRE

JORDAN ROTH
President

PAUL LIBIN
Producing Director

JACK VIERTEL
Creative Director

Tom Viertel   Steven Baruch   Marc Routh   Richard Frankel   The Menier Chocolate Factory
Roger Berlind   David Babani   Sonia Friedman Productions   Andrew Fell
Daryl Roth/Jane Bergère   The Weinstein Company/Raise the Roof 3
Beverly Bartner/Dancap Productions, Inc.   Nica Burns/Max Weitzenhoffer
Eric Falkenstein/Anna Czekaj   Jerry Frankel/Ronald Frankel   James D. Stern/Douglas L. Meyer
present

BERNADETTE PETERS   ELAINE STRITCH
STEPHEN R. BUNTROCK
in

A LITTLE NIGHT MUSIC

Music and Lyrics by
Stephen Sondheim

Book by
Hugh Wheeler

Suggested by a Film by Ingmar Bergman
Originally Produced and Directed on Broadway by Harold Prince

starring
Erin Davie   Leigh Ann Larkin
Hunter Ryan Herdlicka   Ramona Mallory
and
Bradley Dean

Ron Bohmer   Ben Davis   Jessica Grové   Gina Lamparella   Katherine McNamara
Jayne Paterson   Kevin David Thomas   Keaton Whittaker
Karen Murphy   Erin Stewart   Kevin Vortmann

Set and Costume Design by
David Farley

Lighting Design by
Hartley T A Kemp

Sound Design by
Dan Moses Schreier
Gareth Owen

Wigs and Hair Design by
Paul Huntley

Make-up Design by
Angelina Avallone

Casting by
Tara Rubin Casting

Production Stage Manager
Julia P. Jones

Associate Director
Seth Sklar-Heyn

Associate Choreographer
Scott Taylor

Music Direction by
Rob Bowman

Orchestrations by
Jason Carr

Music Coordination by
John Miller

General Management by
Frankel Green
Theatrical Management

Technical Supervision by
Aurora Productions

Press Representative
Boneau/Bryan-Brown

Associate Producers
Broadway Across America
Dan Frishwasser
Jam Theatricals
Richard Winkler

Music Supervision by
Caroline Humphris

Choreography by
Lynne Page

Directed by
Trevor Nunn

This production premiered at the Menier Chocolate Factory November 22, 2008;
transferred to the Garrick Theatre on March 28, 2009

10/1/10

(L-R): Stephen R. Buntrock,
Bernadette Peters
and Bradley Dean

A Little N

A Little Night Music

A Little N

MUSICAL NUMB

Overture ....

"Night Waltz" ....
"Now" ....
"Later" ....
"Soon" ....
"The Glamorous Life" ......

"Remember?" ....

"You Must Meet My Wife" ....
"Liaisons" ....
"In Praise of Women" ....
"Every Day a Little Death" .
"A Weekend in the Country"

"The Sun Won't Set" ....

"Night Waltz II" ....

"It Would Have Been Wonder
"Perpetual Anticipation" .....
"Send in the Clowns" ....
"The Miller's Son" ....
Finale ....

(L-R): Elaine Stritch and Bernadette Peters

Laura Green, Frankel Green Theatrical Management
General Management

Tom Viertel
Producer

Steve Baruch
Producer

Marc Routh
Producer

Richard Frankel
Producer

Roger Berlind
Producer

David Babani
Producer

Sonia Friedman Productions Ltd.
Producer

Daryl Roth
Producer

Jane Bergère
Producer

Bob Weinstein, The Weinstein Company
Producer

Harvey Weinstein, The Weinstein Company
Producer

Harriet Newman Leve, Raise The Roof 3
Producer

Jennifer Manocherian, Raise The Roof 3
Producer

Elaine Krauss, Raise The Roof 3
Producer

Aubrey Dan, Dancap Productions, Inc.
Producer

Nica Burns
Producer

Max Weitzenhoffer
Producer

Eric Falkenstein
Producer

Jerry Frankel
Producer

Douglas L. Meyer
Producer

A Little Night Music
ALUMNI 2010-2011

Matt Dengler
Swing

Sara Jean Ford
Mrs. Anderssen

Alexander Hanson
Fredrik Egerman

Angela Lansbury
Madame Armfeldt

Aaron Lazar
Count Carl-Magnus Malcolm

Marissa McGowan
Mrs. Anderssen

Betsy Morgan
Mrs. Segstrom

Catherine Zeta-Jones
Desirée Armfeldt

A Little Night Music
TRANSFER STUDENTS 2010-2011

Heather Ayers
Swing

Justin Patterson
Swing

A Little Night Music

BOX OFFICE
(L-R): Gail Yerkovich, Michael Loiacono

FRONT OF HOUSE STAFF
Front Row (L-R): Juliette Cipriatti, T.J. D'Angelo

Back Row (L-R): Adam Ferguson, Dayris Fana, Brandon Houghton, Joy Sandell

CREW
Sitting (L-R): Brian McGarity, Enrique Vega, Samantha Lawrence, Mary MacLeod, Douglas Petitjean, Lolly Totero, Julia Jones

Standing (L-R): Tony Menditto, Ira Mont, Allen Sanders, George Fullum, Vinnie Valvo, Rachel Maier, John Dory, Josh Burns, Matt Maloney, Tanya Guercy-Blue, Karl Lawrence, Jim Kane, Maeve Butler, Tim Bennet, Mike Bennet

A Little Night Music

(L-R):
Leigh Ann Larkin
and Ramona Mallory

Photo by Joan Marcus

A Little Night Music
SCRAPBOOK

1. (L-R): Elaine Stritch and Bernadette Peters take a curtain call on "re-opening night" August 1, 2010.
2. Members of the cast including "Yearbook" correspondent Leigh Ann Larkin (second from left) and Angela Lansbury (third from right) during a party at the home of composer Stephen Sondheim.
3. Hunter Herdlicka and Ramona Mallory take a bow on "re-opening night."
4. (L-R): Herdlicka with Larkin and Erin Davie at the recording session for the cast album.

Correspondent: Leigh Ann Larkin, "Petra"
Memorable Note, Fax or Fan Letter: I loved the opening night faxes from all of the Broadway shows! Especially the ones that came from *Ragtime* and the message that Laura Benanti wrote to me from *In the Next Room, or the Vibrator Play*.
Anniversary Parties and/or Gifts: For our re-opening night, Bernadette gave the cast leather bound, personalized *A Little Night Music* scripts. They are gorgeous and unbelievably special. We have had some incredible parties thrown by our leading ladies! A lovely, intimate dinner thrown by Angela, a "let your hair down and dance" bash thrown by Catherine, and a classic New York gathering on the breathtaking terrace of Bernadette Peters!
Most Exciting Celebrity Visitor and What They Did/Said: I would say that would have

been Rachael Ray. She was hanging out in Catherine's dressing room before the show and EVERYONE came to visit her! She was so gracious! When Patti LuPone came to see the show I was terrified and excited at the same time. She LOVED the show and was so com-plimentary! I absolutely loved seeing her again after we were in *Gypsy*, and miss her so much!!!
Actor Who Performed the Most Roles in This Show: Erin Stewart. She has gone on for every female except me, Bernadette and Elaine!
Actor Who Has Done the Most Shows: It's probably safe to say Elaine, but I bet Bernadette is a close second.
Special Backstage Rituals: Steaming, warming up, praying and stepping onto the stage with the same foot every night!
Favorite Moment During Each Performance:

Hands down, singing "The Miller's Son."
In-Theatre Gathering Place: Vinnie Valvo's room!! He has a huge flat screen tv which is great for watching games during football season.
Favorite Off-Site Hangout: Hurley's.
Favorite Snack Foods: Organic vanilla animal cookies, kale chips, fruit of any kind.
Favorite Therapies: Entertainer's Secret, Lemon echinacea Throat Coat Tea, Olbas, Ricola, pastilles and steaming.
Fastest Costume Change: Probably, Kevin David Thomas and the two ladies into the Theater scene.
Record Number of Cell Phone Rings, Cell Phone Photos or Texting Incidents During a Performance: Don't have an exact number, buta handful of cell phones have definitely gone off during some of the quietest moments of the play. Turn off your phones, peeps!!

A Little Night Music
SCRAPBOOK

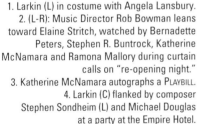

1. Larkin (L) in costume with Angela Lansbury.
2. (L-R): Music Director Rob Bowman leans toward Elaine Stritch, watched by Bernadette Peters, Stephen R. Buntrock, Katherine McNamara and Ramona Mallory during curtain calls on "re-opening night."
3. Katherine McNamara autographs a PLAYBILL.
4. Larkin (C) flanked by composer Stephen Sondheim (L) and Michael Douglas at a party at the Empire Hotel.

Memorable Press Encounter: For me it was definitely opening night. But a close second was our "re-opening" night for Bernadette and Elaine. Another one would have to be when we "met the press" back in rehearsals. So exciting!

Memorable Stage Door Fan Encounter: That would have to be when I met these men at the stage door who had Elaine Stritch t-shirts on that they had made. They were awesome! I know this is going to sound cheesy, but I love when my parents are visiting from out of town and wait behind the barricades for me to come out. They pass fans' Playbills forward and point out people that I missed. It's so cute. I have dreamed of being on Broadway for so long and I think it feels full circle for all of my family.

Memorable Ad-Lib: Pretty much any ad-lib that comes out of Elaine's mouth!

Company In-Joke: "Betsy Johnson."

Latest Audience Arrival: Usually during the first scene for Hunter and me.

Who Wore the Heaviest/Hottest Costume: Erin Davie. It's wool.

Who Wore the Least: Probably me during "The Miller's Son."

Sweethearts Within the Company: Kevin David Thomas and Ramona Mallory.

Orchestra Member Who Played the Most Instruments: David Young. Clarinet, alto sax, flute, bass clarinet.

Orchestra Member Who Played the Most Consecutive Performances Without a Sub: David Young

Memorable Directorial Note: All notes that Trevor gives are memorable. I keep my pad with my notes from past sessions in my dressing room to always remind myself of what was set from the beginning. Trevor is a genius and I feel so lucky

to have had the opportunity to work with him. Here's to many more.

Company Legends: Elaine Stritch and Bernadette Peters.

Tale from the Put-in: Watching Sondheim work with Elaine on "Liaisons" is a moment that I will never forget. Incredible and historic.

Nickname: Stephen Buntrock = "Bunty."

Embarrassing Moments: Any time I forget my words.

Ghostly Encounters Backstage: None backstage but Keaton says she has seen some activity in the house :)

Coolest Thing About Being in This Show: Being in a Sondheim show on Broadway!!

Who Heads Your Fan Club and What Is the Website: Callie Tresser runs my website leighannlarkin.com and has pretty much pioneered all fan-based web activity. She rocks!

Lombardi

First Preview: September 23, 2010. Opened: October 21, 2010.
Closed May 22, 2011 after 31 Previews and 244 Performances.

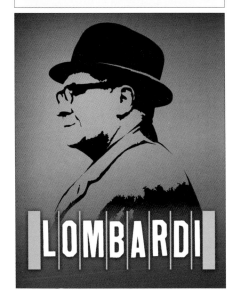

A biographical portrait of legendary Green Bay Packers football coach Vince Lombardi as seen through the eyes of his wife and a magazine writer sent to profile him. The production was notable for marking the Broadway producing debut of the National Football League.

CAST

(in order of appearance)

Vincent Lombardi ....DAN LAURIA
Michael McCormick ....KEITH NOBBS
Marie Lombardi ....JUDITH LIGHT
Dave Robinson .ROBERT CHRISTOPHER RILEY
Paul Hornung............................BILL DAWES
Jim Taylor ....CHRIS SULLIVAN

THE TIME:
Mostly November, 1965,
but also 1958, 1959 and 1964

THE PLACE:
Various locations in Green Bay, WI,
and Englewood, NJ

UNDERSTUDIES
For Vincent Lombardi:
JEFF STILL
For Marie Lombardi:
HENNY RUSSELL
For Michael McCormick, Paul Hornung, Jim Taylor:
BRAD SCHMIDT
For Dave Robinson:
JAVON JOHNSON

CIRCLE IN THE SQUARE

UNDER THE DIRECTION OF
THEODORE MANN and PAUL LIBIN
SUSAN FRANKEL, General Manager

Fran Kirmser   Tony Ponturo

Friends of Lombardi

IN ASSOCIATION WITH
The National Football League

PRESENT

Dan Lauria   Judith Light

IN

LOMBARDI

BY

Eric Simonson

BASED ON THE BOOK *When Pride Still Mattered: A Life of Vince Lombardi*
WRITTEN BY David Maraniss

ALSO STARRING
Keith Nobbs

Bill Dawes   Robert Christopher Riley   Chris Sullivan
Javon Johnson   Henny Russell   Brad Schmidt   Jeff Still

SCENIC DESIGN	COSTUME DESIGN	LIGHTING DESIGN	SOUND DESIGN
David Korins	Paul Tazewell	Howell Binkley	Acme Sound Partners

PROJECTION DESIGN	HAIR DESIGN	DIALECT COACH
Zachary Borovay	Charles LaPointe	Stephen Gabis

CASTING	TECHNICAL SUPERVISOR	PRODUCTION STAGE MANAGER
Laura Stanczyk, CSA	Peter Fulbright	Tripp Phillips

PRESS REPRESENTATIVE	MARKETING	GENERAL MANAGEMENT	EXECUTIVE PRODUCER
Boneau/Bryan-Brown	HHC Marketing	101 Productions, Ltd.	Red Awning

ASSOCIATE PRODUCERS
Joseph Favorito   Andrew Frank & John Mara, Jr.   Rebecca Gold   Al Kahn
Myla Lerner   Lauren Stevens   S.D. Wagner & John Johnson

DIRECTED BY
Thomas Kail

First performed at the Mahaiwe Performing Arts Center in Great Barrington, Massachusetts
The producers wish to express their appreciation to Theatre Development Fund for its support of this production.
Vince Lombardi c/o Luminary Group LLC. www.VinceLombardi.com

10/21/10

(L-R): Robert Christopher Riley, Bill Dawes, Chris Sullivan, Dan Lauria, Keith Nobbs, Judith Light

Photo by Joan Marcus

Lombardi

Dan Lauria
Vincent Lombardi

Judith Light
Marie Lombardi

Keith Nobbs
Michael McCormick

Bill Dawes
Paul Hornung

Robert Christopher Riley
Dave Robinson

Chris Sullivan
Jim Taylor

Javon Johnson
u/s Dave Robinson

Henny Russell
u/s Marie Lombardi

Brad Schmidt
u/s Michael McCormick, Paul Hornung, Jim Taylor

Jeff Still
u/s Vince Lombardi

Thomas Kail
Director

Eric Simonson
Playwright

David Maraniss
Author, Source Material

David Korins
Scenic Design

Paul Tazewell
Costume Design

Howell Binkley
Lighting Designer

Sten Severson, Tom Clark, Mark Menard and Nevin Steinberg, Acme Sound Partners
Sound Design

Zachary Borovay
Projection Design

Charles G. LaPointe
Hair Design

Stephen Gabis
Dialect Coach

Peter Fulbright
Technical Supervision

David Ruttura
Associate Director

Wendy Orshan, 101 Productions, Ltd.
General Manager

Fran Kirmser
Producer

Tony Ponturo
Producer

Roger Goodell
Commissioner, National Football League

Andrew Frank
Associate Producer

John Mara, Jr.
Associate Producer

Myla Lerner
Associate Producer

Lauren Stevens
Associate Producer

"FRIENDS OF LOMBARDI" PRODUCERS
Joe Abruzzese, Doug Albrecht, Stephen Bell, Mark Bobak, Tom Brosnan, Joe Castellano, Jamie Cesa, Jonathan Reinis, Tom Christophul, Tim Cohane & Joe Moglia, Ed Erhardt, Dennis Fitzsimmons, Fox Cities Performing Arts Center, Tim Kashani, Larry Kramer, Bob Lachky, Scott McCuaig, Scott McGraw, Robert Pollock & Anh-Tuyet Nguyen, Ruthe Ponturo, John Russell, Tom Santel, Robert Saxner & Keni Fine, Gary Stevenson, Pat Stokes

Lombardi

Photos by Brian Mapp

FRONT OF HOUSE STAFF
Front Row (L-R): Patricia Kennedy,
Georgia Keghlian, Sophie Koufakis,
Laurel Brevoort, Panagiota Thomatos,
Heidi Giovine

Back Row (L-R): Kelly Varley, Xavier Young,
Nirvana Diaz, Gertrude Galschjodt,
Mandy Gagedeen

CREW
(L-R): Robert Dagna, Owen Parmele, Stewart Wagner, David Cohen, Thomas Lawrey, Anthony Menditto,
James Bay

BOX OFFICE
(L-R): Timothy Moran, Patricia Kenary,
Kathleen Drury

COMPANY AND STAGE MANAGEMENT
(L-R): Barbara Crompton (Company Manager),
Tripp Phillips (Production Stage Manager),
Diane DiVita (Stage Manager)

HAIR AND WARDROBE
(L-R): Eileen Miller (Wardrobe Supervisor), Katie Beatty (Hair Supervisor), Charlie Catanese (Judith
Light's Dresser), Kelly Saxon (Dan Lauria's Dresser), Maura Clifford (3 Players Dresser)

Lombardi

STAFF FOR *LOMBARDI*

GENERAL MANAGEMENT
101 PRODUCTIONS, LTD.
Wendy Orshan   Jeffrey M. Wilson
David Auster
Elie Landau

EXECUTIVE PRODUCER
RED AWNING
Nicole Kastrinos

COMPANY MANAGER
Barbara Crompton

GENERAL PRESS REPRESENTATIVE
BONEAU/BRYAN-BROWN
Chris Boneau   Jackie Green   Kelly Guiod

TECHNICAL SUPERVISION
TECH PRODUCTION SERVICES
Peter Fulbright   Mary Duffe
Colleen Houlehen

Make-Up Design	**Marilyn Jordan**

Associate Director	**David Ruttura**

Production Stage Manager	**Tripp Phillips**
Stage Manager	Diane DiVita
Associate Scenic Designer	Rod Lemmond
Assistants to Mr. Korins	Sarah Miles, Amanda Stephens
Associate Costume Designer	Valerie Marcus Ramshur
Assistant Costume Designer	Daryl Stone
Associate Lighting Designers	Mark Simpson, Ryan O'Gara
Moving Light Programmer	Sean Beach
Associate Sound Designer	Jason Crystal
Associate Projection Designer	Daniel Brodie
Projection Editing Assistant	Hannelore Williams
Assistant to Mr. LaPointe	Leah Loukas
Casting Assistant	Anika Chapin
Music Consultants	Jesse Lagrazie, Debbie Markowitz
Production Carpenter	Anthony Menditto
Automation Carpenter	David Cohen
Production Electrician	Thomas Lawrey
Production Sound Engineer	Jim Bay
Production Props Supervisor	Robert Presley
Deck Props	Rob Dagna
Production Wardrobe Supervisor	Eileen Miller
Production Hair & Make-Up Supervisor	Katie Beatty
Dressers	Charles Catanese, Maura Clifford, Kelly Saxon
Legal Counsel	Loeb & Loeb LLP/ Seth Gelblum, Esq.
Accountant	Fried & Kowgios, LLP
Controller	Galbraith & Co. Inc./ Kenny Noth
Advertising & New Media Marketing	Art Meets Commerce/ Jim Glaub, Chip Meyrelles, Laurie Connor, Kevin Keating, Whitney Manalio Creighton, Mark Seeley
Brand Consultant	Bob Lachky

Marketing	HHC Marketing/ Hugh Hysell, Matt Sicoli, Nicole Pando Ponturo Management Group LLC
Manager of Operations	Mina Hu
101 Productions, Ltd. Staff	Beth Blitzer, Michael Rudd, Mary Six Rupert, Samara Ungar
101 Productions, Ltd. Interns	Malissa O'Donnell, Brittany O'Neill
Production Assistants	Andrew Zachary Cohen, Robbie Peters
Lombardi Interns	Kate Bodenheimer, Emily Peterson, Dana Wilson
Banking	City National Bank/ Anne McSweeney
Insurance	Tanenbaum Harber Insurance Group of FL, Inc./Carol Bressi
Payroll Services	Castellana Services, Inc.
Merchandising	Max Merchandising LLC
Production Photographer	Joan Marcus
Music Clearances	BZ Rights & Permissions, Inc.

Lobby display made possible by the generosity of the National Football League and the Pro Football Hall of Fame, Canton, OH.

CREDITS
Scenery fabrication by PRG-Scenic Technologies, a division of Production Resource Group, LLC, New Windsor, NY. Lighting by PRG Lighting. Sound equipment by Sound Associates. Media projection system provided by Scharff Weisberg, Inc. Fur coat by Fur and Furgery. Tailoring by Artur and Tailors. Tailoring for Mr. Lauria by Brian Hemesath. Ms. Light's costumes by Donna Langman Costumes. Distressing by Hochi Asiatico. Period NFL uniforms by Sports Studio LLC. Makeup provided by M•A•C.

MUSIC CREDITS
"The Battle of New Orleans" composed by Jimmy Driftwood. Courtesy of Warden Music Co., Inc. "I'll Be Home for Christmas" composed by Kim Gannon, Walter Kent, Buck Ram. Courtesy of Gannon & Kent Music and Piedmont Music Co. "The Seventh Son" composed by Willie Dixon. Courtesy of Hoochie Coochie Music (BMI) administered by Bug Music. "Shake" written and performed by Sam Cooke. Published by ABKCO Music, Inc. Courtesy of ABKCO Music & Records, Inc. www.samcooke.com.

"Stand By Me" composed by Ben E. King, Jerry Leiber and Mike Stoller. Courtesy of Sony/ATV Music Publishing.

TV Broadcaster Voices	Wayne Larrivee, Jeff Still

SPECIAL THANKS
National Football League; NFL Films; Luminary Group, LLC — www.VinceLombardi.com; Actors' Equity Association; The Gallery of Sports Art.

Lombardi rehearsed at New York City Center.

www.lombardibroadway.com

☐ CIRCLE IN THE SQUARE THEATRE
Thespian Theatre, Inc.
Under the direction of
Theodore Mann and Paul Libin
Susan Frankel, General Manager

House Manager	Cheryl Dennis
Head Carpenter	Anthony Menditto
Head Electrician	Stewart Wagner
Prop Master	Owen E. Parmele
FOH Sound Engineer	Jim Bay
Box Office Treasurer	Tim Moran
Administrative Assistant	Courtney Kochuba
Assistant to Paul Libin	Clark Mims Tedesco
Assistant to Theodore Mann	Eric P. Vitale

☐ CIRCLE IN THE SQUARE THEATRE SCHOOL
President	Paul Libin
Artistic Director	Theodore Mann
Theatre School Director	E. Colin O'Leary
Arts Education/Development	Jonathan Mann
Administrative Assistant	David Pleva
Administrative Assistant	Virginia Tuller

GOVERNMENT, FOUNDATION & PATRON SUPPORT
NYS Council on the Arts, NYC Dept. of Cultural Affairs, Stephen and Mary Birch Foundation, The Friars Foundation, Jewels of Charity, Thomas L. Kelly, Blanche and Irving Laurie Foundation, Frederick Loewe Foundation, Edith Meiser Foundation, Newman's Own Foundation, Patrick J. Patek Fund, Jerome Robbins Foundation, Ross Family Fund, Geraldine Stutz Trust, C. Daniel Chill, John DiMenna, A.R. Gurney, Vera Stern

(L-R): Keith Nobbs and Dan Lauria

Photo by Joan Marcus

Lombardi

SCRAPBOOK

Correspondent: Keith Nobbs, "Michael McCormick"

Memorable Opening Night Letter, Fax or Note: The notes from the cast, playwright and director always get me. It is comforting to know that whatever experience has happened up to that point, it has been shared.

Opening Night Gifts: A giant *Lombardi* cookie cake from my parents, a crystal football from Tiffany's, pretty nifty Converse sneakers in the Packer colors, a *Lombardi* jersey, a flask, and lots of flowers and bottles of champagne and wine, framed pictures and enough candy and chocolate to go into a sugar coma. Opening night is an exercise in what it's like to have unconditional love.

Most Exciting Celebrity Visitors: We've had Mark Sanchez, Vince Vaughn, Dennis Miller, Faith Hill, Tim McGraw, Frank Gifford and Kathie Lee and Hoda, Regis and Kelly, Charles Durning and Jack Klugman.... And then tons of players and NFL celebrities.

Who Has Done the Most Shows in Their Career: I would say Dan—he loves supporting new playwrights so he has been on the ground floor of developing a lot of new work. Judith too is an actress who went to Carnegie Mellon and cut her teeth on theatre. I think people are just beginning to realize how much of a deeply gifted actress she is onstage. With Dan and Judith, I hope they get all great things coming to them. No one deserves it more.

Special Backstage Rituals: Taking a nap on the Equity cot, getting my hair blow-dried by Katie, waiting till the last possible minute to put on my costume, doing a little '60s dance to the opening music while telling bad jokes to Charlie and Maura (our dressers). The usual backstage shenanigans.

Favorite Moment During Each Performance: At the end of the play, Dan and I get a short minute before the bows. It is a nice moment to exhale after living onstage for ninety minutes.

Favorite In-Theatre Gathering Place: Judith's dressing room. She has chairs and nuts. And drinks. Hers is a woman's dressing room. It smells nice and has an ambience. The rest of our rooms look like something from *Lord of the Flie*s. Five boys, one girl. Expected, I guess.

Favorite Off-Site Hangout: Bar Centrale is great. Or we go to the Irish pub Emmett O'Lunney's across the street.

Favorite Snack Food: Coke Zero.

Mascot: Bill Dawes.

Favorite Therapy: I love me some massage. And steaming too when the voice feels rough.

Most Memorable Ad-Lib: Dan was supposed to say the line, "This camp is for rookies and walk-ons only!" He said, "This camp is for wookies and rock-ons only!" Memorable.

Record Number of Cell Phone Rings During a Performance: I think there were about four rings in one scene once. Four too many.

Memorable Press Encounter: I play a sports reporter in the play and I got to sit in the press box at the new Giants stadium. That was great.

Company In-Jokes: A bunch. We laugh a lot.

1. Curtain call on opening night (L-R): Bill Dawes, Keith Nobbs (*Yearbook* correspondent), Dan Lauria, Judith Light, Robert Christopher Riley and Chris Sullivan.
2. Playwright Eric Simonson at the premiere.

Memorable Stage Door Fan Encounters: The people who come from Wisconsin are avid fans. One man had Vince Lombardi tattooed on his forearm. Another man sat in the front row in his Jersey with a Packer helmet perched on his knee. Often you hear, "This is the first play I've ever seen." It is moving to see theatre affecting a whole new group of people.

Internet Buzz: Some people didn't know what to make of it—the NFL and theatre? How does that work? But what has been humbling is to see people from the sports world and theatre world sitting next to each other both laughing and truly moved by the show.

Latest Audience Arrival: The late arrivals are fine—it's when people get up to go to the bathroom that can be distracting.

Fastest Costume Change: I wear the same suit. Dan has something like 18 changes. I put on an overcoat. And hat.

Who Wore the Heaviest/Hottest Costume: Gotta be the players: full-on pads under Broadway lights. Yikes.

Who Wore the Least: Bill Dawes gets to come out in a tank top and show off his guns.

Catchphrases Only the Company Would Recognize: "Allen! Allen!"

Memorable Directorial Note: Tommy's got tons of them. One night when my voice cracked: "Amazing that you hit it right on that line, Peter Brady." Or to Judith when someone brought a baby to the show: "Why did you make that baby cry?" Or at one point I think he said: "Talk like a human."

Company Legends: Dan's stories about old movies and the golden age of Hollywood.

Understudy Anecdote: Brad Schmidt—he covers Bill Dawes, Chris Sullivan and me. Three

very different parts. During understudy rehearsals, he goes back and forth. It's amazing—kinda like *Sybil.*

Nickname: One that can't be printed here made up by someone in the cast. You know who you are.

Sweethearts Within the Company: It's pretty much a love fest all the way around.

Embarrassing Moments: Had hair sticking up out of the back of my head for the whole last half of the show. I'm talking about Vince dying of cancer and I look like Alfalfa from "The Little Rascals."

Ghostly Encounters Backstage: Circle in the Square is incredible because it has an amazing performance history. George C. Scott in *Death of a Salesman.* A lot of old Tennessee Willliams. The history is in the air.

Coolest Thing About Being in This Show: Getting to work with such a talented, generous ensemble and creative team. Being a lead on Broadway has been a dream of mine since I was 7 so it is amazing to be doing it night after night.

Mamma Mia!

First Preview: October 5, 2001. Opened: October 18, 2001.
Still running as of May 31, 2011.

As her wedding approaches, Sophie decides to figure out which among three of her free-spirited mother's ex-lovers is her actual father. So she invites all three men to the wedding without telling mom. Set to the hits of the music group ABBA.

CAST

(in order of speaking)

Sophie Sheridan .... LIANA HUNT
Ali .... TRACI VICTORIA
Lisa .... HALLE MORSE
Tanya .... JUDY McLANE
Rosie .... GINA FERRALL
Donna Sheridan .... LISA BRESCIA
Sky .... COREY GREENAN
Pepper .... MARK DANCEWICZ
Eddie .... ANDREW CHAPPELLE
Harry Bright .... CLARKE THORELL
Bill Austin .... PATRICK BOLL
Sam Carmichael .... JOHN DOSSETT
Father Alexandrios ....BRYAN SCOTT JOHNSON

THE ENSEMBLE

BRENT BLACK, TIMOTHY BOOTH,
ALLYSON CARR, FELICITY CLAIRE,
STACIA FERNANDEZ, NATALIE GALLO,
HEIDI GODT, ALBERT GUERZON,
BRYAN SCOTT JOHNSON,
MONICA KAPOOR, MONETTE McKAY,
IAN PAGET, GERARD SALVADOR,
SHARONE SAYEGH, LAURIE WELLS,
BLAKE WHYTE

Continued on next page

WINTER GARDEN

1634 Broadway

 A Shubert Organization Theatre

Philip J. Smith, *Chairman*   Robert E. Wankel, *President*

JUDY CRAYMER, RICHARD EAST AND BJÖRN ULVAEUS
FOR LITTLESTAR IN ASSOCIATION WITH UNIVERSAL

PRESENT

MAMMA MIA!

MUSIC AND LYRICS BY
BENNY ANDERSSON
BJÖRN ULVAEUS

AND SOME SONGS WITH STIG ANDERSON

BOOK BY CATHERINE JOHNSON

PRODUCTION DESIGNED BY
MARK THOMPSON

LIGHTING DESIGNED BY
HOWARD HARRISON

SOUND DESIGNED BY
**ANDREW BRUCE &
BOBBY AITKEN**

MUSICAL SUPERVISOR, ADDITIONAL MATERIAL
& ARRANGEMENTS
MARTIN KOCH

CHOREOGRAPHY
ANTHONY VAN LAAST

DIRECTED BY
PHYLLIDA LLOYD

10/22/10

(L-R):
Judy McLane,
Lisa Brescia and
Gina Ferrall

Photo by Joan Marcus

Mamma Mia!

MUSICAL NUMBERS

(in alphabetical order)

CHIQUITITA
DANCING QUEEN
DOES YOUR MOTHER KNOW
GIMME! GIMME! GIMME!
HONEY, HONEY
I DO, I DO, I DO, I DO, I DO
I HAVE A DREAM
KNOWING ME, KNOWING YOU
LAY ALL YOUR LOVE ON ME
MAMMA MIA
MONEY, MONEY, MONEY
ONE OF US
OUR LAST SUMMER
SLIPPING THROUGH MY FINGERS
S.O.S.
SUPER TROUPER
TAKE A CHANCE ON ME
THANK YOU FOR THE MUSIC
THE NAME OF THE GAME
THE WINNER TAKES IT ALL
UNDER ATTACK
VOULEZ-VOUS

(L-R): Corey Greenan and Liana Hunt

Photo by Joan Marcus

Cast Continued

UNDERSTUDIES

For Sophie Sheridan:
FELICITY CLAIRE, NATALIE GALLO
For Ali:
NATALIE GALLO, MONETTE MCKAY
For Lisa:
FELICITY CLAIRE, MONICA KAPOOR,
SHARONE SAYEGH
For Tanya:
STACIA FERNANDEZ, HEIDI GODT,
LAURIE WELLS
For Rosie:
STACIA FERNANDEZ, HEIDI GODT
For Donna Sheridan:
HEIDI GODT, LAURIE WELLS
For Sky:
TONY GONZALEZ, BLAKE WHYTE
For Pepper:
IAN PAGET, GERARD SALVADOR
For Eddie:
TONY GONZALEZ, ALBERT GUERZON
For Harry Bright:
TIMOTHY BOOTH,
BRYAN SCOTT JOHNSON
For Bill Austin:
BRENT BLACK, TIMOTHY BOOTH,
BRYAN SCOTT JOHNSON
For Sam Carmichael:
BRENT BLACK, TIMOTHY BOOTH
For Father Alexandrios:
BRENT BLACK, TIMOTHY BOOTH,
TONY GONZALEZ

SWINGS

RACHEL FRANKENTHAL, ERIC GIANCOLA,
JON-ERIK GOLDBERG, TONY GONZALEZ,
ERICA MANSFIELD, COLLETTE SIMMONS

DANCE CAPTAINS

JANET ROTHERMEL, TONY GONZALEZ

On a Greek Island, a wedding is about to take place...

PROLOGUE
Three months before the wedding

ACT ONE
The day before the wedding

ACT TWO
The day of the wedding

THE BAND
Music Director/Conductor/Keyboard 1:
WENDY BOBBITT CAVETT

Associate Music Director/Keyboard 3:
ROB PREUSS

Keyboard 2:
STEVE MARZULLO

Keyboard 4:
MYLES CHASE

Guitar 1:
DOUG QUINN

Guitar 2:
JEFF CAMPBELL

Bass:
PAUL ADAMY

Drums:
RAY MARCHICA

Percussion:
DAVID NYBERG

Music Coordinator:
MICHAEL KELLER

Synthesizer Programmer:
NICHOLAS GILPIN

Lisa Brescia
Donna Sheridan

Liana Hunt
Sophie Sheridan

Gina Ferrall
Rosie

Judy McLane
Tanya

John Dossett
Sam Carmichael

Patrick Boll
Bill Austin

Clarke Thorell
Harry Bright

Mamma Mia!

Corey Greenan
Sky

Traci Victoria
Ali

Halle Morse
Lisa

Mark Dancewicz
Pepper

Andrew Chappelle
Eddie

Brent Black
Ensemble

Timothy Booth
Ensemble

Allyson Carr
Ensemble

Felicity Claire
Ensemble

Stacia Fernandez
Ensemble

Rachel Frankenthal
Swing

Natalie Gallo
Ensemble

Heidi Godt
Ensemble

Jon-Erik Goldberg
Swing

Tony Gonzalez
*Dance Captain,
Swing*

Albert Guerzon
Ensemble

Bryan Scott Johnson
*Father Alexandrios,
Ensemble*

Monica Kapoor
Ensemble

Erica Mansfield
Swing

Monette McKay
Ensemble

Ian Paget
Ensemble

Janet Rothermel
Dance Captain

Gerard Salvador
Ensemble

Sharone Sayegh
Ensemble

Collette Simmons
Swing

Laurie Wells
Ensemble

Blake Whyte
Ensemble

Björn Ulvaeus
Music & Lyrics

Benny Andersson
Music & Lyrics

Catherine Johnson
Book

Phyllida Lloyd
Director

Anthony Van Laast,
MBE
Choreographer

Mark Thompson
Production Designer

Howard Harrison
Lighting Designer

Andrew Bruce
Sound Designer

Mamma Mia!

Bobby Aitken
Sound Designer

Martin Koch
*Musical Supervisor;
Additional Material;
Arrangements
Musical Supervisor*

David Holcenberg
*Associate Music
Supervisor*

Nichola Treherne
*Associate
Choreographer*

Martha Banta
Resident Director

Tara Rubin Casting
Casting

David Grindrod
Casting Consultant

Arthur Siccardi
Theatrical Services,
Inc.
Production Manager

Judy Craymer
Producer

Richard East
Producer

Nina Lannan
Associates
*General
Management*

Andrew Treagus
*International
Executive Producer*

ALUMNI
2010-2011

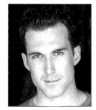

Matthew Farver
Eddie

Todd Galantich
Ensemble

Beth Leavel
Donna Sheridan

Raymond J. Lee
Eddie

Alyse Alan Louis
Sophie Sheridan

David Andrew
MacDonald
Harry Bright

Annie Edgerton
Ensemble

Corinne Melançon
Ensemble

Michael Mindlin
Pepper

Eric William Morris
Sky

Ryan Sander
*Dance Captain,
Swing*

Leah Zepel
Ensemble

TRANSFER
STUDENTS
2010-2011

Meredith Akins
Ensemble

Michelle Dawson
Ensemble

Annie Edgerton
Ensemble, Swing

Adrienne Jean Fisher
Swing

Corinne Melançon
Ensemble

Michael Mindlin
Pepper

Jennifer Perry
Rosie

Catherine Ricafort
Ali, Ensemble

Ryan Sander
*Dance Captain,
Swing*

Mamma Mia!

Allison Strong
Ensemble

Leah Zepel
Ensemble, Swing

1. (L-R): John Dossett, Clarke Thorell and
Patrick Boll as the three possible dads.
2. Mark Dancewicz as Pepper
and Judy McLane as Tanya.
3. (L-R): Halle Morse as Lisa,
Liana Hunt as Sophie
and Traci Victoria as Ali.

Photos by Joan Marcus

In loving memory of Daniel McDonald, a cast member of
the *Mamma Mia!* Broadway Company 2004-2005.

LITTLESTAR SERVICES LIMITED

Directors . . . . Judy Craymer
Richard East
Benny Andersson
Björn Ulvaeus
International Executive Producer . . . . Andrew Treagus
Business & Finance Director . . . . Ashley Grisdale
Administrator . . . . Peter Austin
PA to Judy Craymer . . . . Katie Wolfryd

Marketing & Communications Manager . . . . Claire Teare
Marketing & Communications Coordinator . Liz McGinity
Head of Accounts . . . . Jo Reedman
Accountant . . . . Sheila Egbujie
Administrative Assistant . . . . Matthew Willis
Receptionist . . . . Kimberley Wallwork
Legal Services . . . . Barry Shaw
Howard Jones at Sheridans
Production Insurance Services . . . . W & P Longreach
Business Manager for
Benny Andersson and
Björn Ulvaeus
& Scandinavian Press . . . . Görel Hanser

Consultant International
Associate Producer . . . . Julian Stoneman

NINA LANNAN ASSOCIATES

GENERAL MANAGERS . . . . DEVIN M. KEUDELL,
AMY JACOBS
Company Manager . . . . J. ANTHONY MAGNER
Assistant Company Manager . . . . Ryan Conway

ANDREW TREAGUS ASSOCIATES LIMITED

General Manager . . . . Philip Effemey

Mamma Mia!

International Manager ....Mark Whittemore
PA to Andrew Treagus ....Jacki Harding
International Travel Manager ....Lindsay Jones
Production Coordinator ....Felicity White

PRODUCTION TEAM
ASSOCIATE
    CHOREOGRAPHER ....NICHOLA TREHERNE
DANCE SUPERVISOR ....JANET ROTHERMEL
RESIDENT DIRECTOR ....MARTHA BANTA
ASSOCIATE
    MUSIC SUPERVISOR ......DAVID HOLCENBERG
ASSOCIATE
    SCENIC DESIGNER (US) ....NANCY THUN
ASSOCIATE
    SCENIC DESIGNER (UK) ....JONATHAN ALLEN
ASSOCIATE
    COSTUME DESIGNERS ....LUCY GAIGER
        SCOTT TRAUGOTT
ASSOCIATE HAIR DESIGNER ...JOSH MARQUETTE
ASSOCIATE
    LIGHTING DESIGNERS ....DAVID HOLMES
        ED MCCARTHY
        ANDREW VOLLER
ASSOCIATE
    SOUND DESIGNERS ....BRIAN BUCHANAN
        DAVID PATRIDGE
MUSICAL TRANSCRIPTION ......ANDERS NEGLIN
CASTING CONSULTANT ....DAVID GRINDROD

CASTING
TARA RUBIN CASTING
Tara Rubin CSA, Eric Woodall CSA,
Laura Schutzel CSA, Merri Sugarman CSA,
Dale Brown, Paige Blansfield, Kaitlin Shaw

PRESS REPRESENTATIVE
BONEAU/BRYAN-BROWN
Adrian Bryan-Brown   Joe Perrotta
Kelly Guiod

MARKETING U.S.
ALLIED LIVE
TANYA GRUBICH   LAURA MATALON
Uma McCrosson   James Viggiano

MUSIC PUBLISHED BY
EMI GROVE PARK MUSIC, INC. AND
EMI WATERFORD MUSIC, INC.

STAFF FOR MAMMA MIA!
PRODUCTION
    STAGE MANAGER ....ANDREW FENTON
Stage Managers ....Sherry Cohen, Dean R. Greer
Assistant Dance Captain ....Tony Gonzalez
PRODUCTION MANAGER ......ARTHUR SICCARDI

Head Carpenter ....Chris Nass
Assistant Carpenters ....Stephen Burns,
        Clark Middleton
Production Electrician ....Rick Baxter
Head Electrician ....Don Lawrence
Assistant Electrician ....Andy Sather
Vari*Lite Programmer ....Andrew Voller

Production Sound ....David Patridge
Head Sound ....Craig Cassidy
Assistant Sound ....Pitsch Karrer
Production Properties ....Simon E.R. Evans
Head Properties ....Gregory Martin
Wardrobe Supervisor ....Irene L. Bunis
Assistant Wardrobe ....Ron Glow
Dressers ....Carey Bertini, Jim Collum,
    Lauren Kievit, Robert Krauss,
    Trevor McGinness, Chasity Neutze,
    Christine Richmond, I Wang
Hair Supervisor ....Sandy Schlender
Assistant Hair Supervisor ....Vickey Walker
Assistant Lighting Designer ....Jeffrey Lowney
Assistant Costume Designer ....Robert J. Martin
House Crew ....Richard Carney, Reginald Carter,
    Holly Hanson, Mai-Linh Lofgren,
    Meredith Kievit, Aarne Lofgren,
    Francis Lofgren, John Maloney,
    Michael Maloney, Glenn Russo,
    Dennis Wiener
Rehearsal Pianist ....Sue Anschutz
Box Office ....Mary Cleary, Lee Cobb,
    Steve Cobb, James Drury, Sue Giebler,
    Bob McCaffrey, Ron Schroeder
Casting Directors ....Tara Rubin CSA,
    Eric Woodall CSA
Casting Associates ....Laura Schutzel CSA,
    Merri Sugarman CSA
Casting Assistants ....Dan Brown CSA,
    Paige Blansfield, Kaitlin Shaw
Canadian Casting ....Stephanie Gorin Casting, C.D.C.
Associate to Casting Consultant ....Stephen Crockett
London Casting Assistant ....Will Burton
Legal Counsel (U.S.) ....Lazarus & Harris LLP
    Scott Lazarus, Esq.
    Robert Harris, Esq.
Immigration Counsel ....Mark D. Koestler/
    Kramer Levin Naftalis & Frankel LLP
Accounting ....Rosenberg, Neuwirth and Kuchner/
    Chris Cacace, In Woo
Advertising ....Serino Coyne, Inc./
    Nancy Coyne, Greg Corradetti,
    Andrea Prince, Ruth Rosenberg
Interactive Marketing ....Situation Interactive/
    Damian Bazadona, John Lanasa,
    Jenn Elston, Randi Fields
Press Office Staff ....Chris Boneau, Jim Byk,
    Brandi Cornwell, Jackie Green,
    Linnae Hodzic, Jessica Johnson,
    Amy Kass, Kevin Jones, Emily Meagher,
    Aaron Meier, Christine Olver,
    Matthew Polk, Heath Schwartz,
    Michael Strassheim, Susanne Tighe
Production Photographer ....Joan Marcus
Merchandising ....Max Merchandise, LLC/
    Randi Grossman, Victor Romero
Theater Displays ....King Display
Insurance ....Dewitt, Stern/
    Walton & Parkinson Ltd.
Orthopedic Consultant ....Dr. Phillip Baumann
Banking ....City National Bank
Travel Agent ....Tzell Travel
Original Logo Design ....© Littlestar Services Limited

CREDITS AND ACKNOWLEDGMENTS
Scenery constructed and painted by Hudson Scenic Studio, Inc. and Hamilton Scenic Specialty. Computer motion control and automation by Feller Precision, Inc. SHOWTRAK computer motion control for scenery and rigging. Sound equipment supplied by Masque Sound. Lighting equipment supplied by Fourth Phase and Vari*Lite, Inc. Soft goods by I. Weiss and Sons. Costumes by Barbara Matera, Ltd., Tricorne New York City and Carelli Costumes, Inc. Additional costume work by Allan Alberts Productions. Millinery by Lynn Mackey. Wet suits by Aquatic Fabricators of South Florida. Custom men's shirts by Cego. Custom knitting by C.C. Wei. Custom fabric printing and dyeing by Dye-namix and Gene Mignola. Shoes by Native Leather, Rilleau Leather and T. O. Dey. Gloves by Cornelia James - London. Hair color by Redken. Properties by Paragon Theme and Prop Fabrication. Cough drops provided by Ricola U.S.A. Physical therapy provided by Sean Gallagher. Drums provided by Pearl. Cymbals provided by Zildjian. Drumsticks provided by Vic Firth. Drum heads provided by Remo.

Mamma Mia! was originally produced in London by
LITTLESTAR SERVICES LIMITED on April 6, 1999.

Experience *Mamma Mia!* around the world:
London/Prince of Wales Theatre/mamma-mia.com
Broadway/Winter Garden Theatre/telecharge.com
North American Tour/ticketmaster.com
International Tour/mamma-mia.com
For more information on all our
global productions visit: www.mamma-mia.com

Mary Poppins

First Preview: October 14, 2006. Opened: November 16, 2006.
Still running as of May 31, 2011.

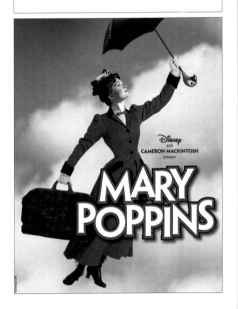

PLAYBILL

Into the lives of the dysfunctional Banks family of 17 Cherry Tree Lane, London, floats the magical nanny Mary Poppins, who uses her supercalifragilisticexpialidocious powers to escort them on a series of marvelous adventures, accompanied by a friendly chimney sweep named Bert. Along the way she teaches the Bankses the meaning and value of family togetherness. Based on both original P.L. Travers stories and the Disney film musical, with several new songs.

CAST OF CHARACTERS

(in order of appearance)

Bert	GAVIN LEE
George Banks	KARL KENZLER
Winifred Banks	MEGAN OSTERHAUS
Jane Banks	ROZI BAKER, CATHERINE MISSAL or RACHEL RESHEFF
Michael Banks	CHRISTOPHER FLAIM, ETHAN HABERFIELD or DAVID GABRIEL LERNER
Katie Nanna	KRISTIN CARBONE
Policeman	COREY SKAGGS
Miss Lark	KATE CHAPMAN
Admiral Boom	JONATHAN FREEMAN
Mrs. Brill	VALERIE BOYLE
Robertson Ay	MARK PRICE
Mary Poppins	LAURA MICHELLE KELLY
Park Keeper	JAMES HINDMAN
Neleus	NICK KEPLEY
Queen Victoria	ANN ARVIA

Continued on next page

NEW AMSTERDAM THEATRE

Disney
and
CAMERON MACKINTOSH
present

MARY POPPINS

A MUSICAL BASED ON THE STORIES OF P.L. TRAVERS AND THE WALT DISNEY FILM

With

LAURA MICHELLE KELLY   GAVIN LEE
KARL KENZLER   MEGAN OSTERHAUS
ANN ARVIA   MARK PRICE   JESSICA SHERIDAN   JONATHAN FREEMAN
and
VALERIE BOYLE

ROZI BAKER CHRISTOPHER FLAIM ETHAN HABERFIELD DAVID GABRIEL LERNER CATHERINE MISSAL RACHEL RESHEFF
KATE CHAPMAN JAMES HINDMAN NICK KEPLEY JANELLE ANNE ROBINSON CHAD SEIB COREY SKAGGS TOM SOUHRADA

AARON J. ALBANO TIA ALTINAY DAVID BAUM BRANDON BIEBER PAM BRADLEY CATHERINE BRUNELL KATHY CALAHAN
KRISTIN CARBONE BRIAN COLLIER BARRETT DAVIS ELIZABETH DeROSA SUZANNE HYLENSKI JUSTIN KEYES MARK LEDBETTER BRIAN LETENDRE
KATHLEEN NANNI AMBER OWENS T. OLIVER REID ROMMY SANDHU LAURA SCHUTTER JAMES TABEEK

Original Music and Lyrics by
RICHARD M. SHERMAN and ROBERT B. SHERMAN

Book by
JULIAN FELLOWES

New Songs and Additional Music and Lyrics by
GEORGE STILES and ANTHONY DREWE

Co-created by
CAMERON MACKINTOSH

Produced for Disney Theatrical Productions by
THOMAS SCHUMACHER

Music Supervisor	Music Director
DAVID CADDICK	BRAD HAAK

Orchestrations by
WILLIAM DAVID BROHN

Broadway Sound Design	Dance and Vocal Arrangements
STEVE CANYON KENNEDY	GEORGE STILES

Associate Choreographer	Associate Director	Associate Producer	Makeup Design
GEOFFREY GARRATT	ANTHONY LYN	ANNE QUART	NAOMI DONNE

Technical Director	Production Stage Manager	Casting
DAVID BENKEN	MARK DOBROW	TARA RUBIN CASTING

Co-choreographer	Lighting Design
STEPHEN MEAR	HOWARD HARRISON

Scenic and Costume Design
BOB CROWLEY

Co-direction and Choreography
MATTHEW BOURNE

Directed by
RICHARD EYRE

©Disney/CML

Disney ON BROADWAY

10/1/10

(L-R): Laura Michelle Kelly and Gavin Lee

Photo by Joan Marcus

Mary Poppins

MUSICAL NUMBERS

Mary Poppins takes place in and around the Banks' household
somewhere in London at the turn of the last century.

ACT I

"Chim Chim Cher-ee" † ....Bert
"Cherry Tree Lane" (Part 1)* ....George and Winifred Banks,
Jane and Michael, Mrs. Brill, and Robertson Ay
"The Perfect Nanny" ....Jane and Michael
"Cherry Tree Lane" (Part 2) ....George and Winifred Banks, Jane, and Michael,
Mrs. Brill, and Robertson Ay
"Practically Perfect"* ....Mary Poppins, Jane, and Michael
"Jolly Holiday" † ....Bert, Mary Poppins, Jane, Michael, Neleus, and the Statues
"Cherry Tree Lane" (Reprise),
   "Being Mrs. Banks,"*
   "Jolly Holiday" (Reprise) ....George, Winifred, Jane, and Michael
"A Spoonful of Sugar" ....Mary Poppins, Jane, Michael, Robertson Ay, and Winifred
"Precision and Order"* ....Bank Chairman and the Bank Clerks
"A Man Has Dreams" † ....George Banks
"Feed the Birds" ....Bird Woman and Mary Poppins
"Supercalifragilisticexpialidocious" † ....Mary Poppins, Mrs. Corry, Bert, Jane,
Michael, Fannie, Annie, and Customers
"Playing the Game"* ....Mary Poppins, Valentine and other Toys
"Chim Chim Cher-ee" (Reprise) ....Bert and Mary Poppins

ACT II

"Cherry Tree Lane" (Reprise) ....Mrs. Brill, Michael, Jane, Winifred,
Robertson Ay, and George
"Brimstone and Treacle" (Part 1)* ....Miss Andrew
"Let's Go Fly a Kite" ....Bert, Park Keeper, Jane, and Michael
"Cherry Tree Lane" (Reprise),
   "Being Mrs. Banks" (Reprise) ....George and Winifred
"Brimstone and Treacle" (Part 2) ....Mary Poppins and Miss Andrew
"Practically Perfect" (Reprise) ....Jane, Michael, and Mary Poppins
"Chim Chim Cher-ee" (Reprise) ....Bert
"Step in Time" † ....Bert, Mary Poppins, Jane, Michael, and the Sweeps
"A Man Has Dreams,"
   "A Spoonful of Sugar" (Reprise) ....George and Bert
"Anything Can Happen"* ....Jane, Michael, Mary Poppins, and the Company
"A Spoonful of Sugar" (Reprise) ....Mary Poppins
"A Shooting Star" † ....Orchestra

* New Songs   † Adapted Songs

SONG CREDITS

"The Perfect Nanny," "A Spoonful of Sugar," "Feed the Birds," "Let's Go Fly a Kite"
written by Richard M. Sherman and Robert B. Sherman.

"Chim Chim Cher-ee," "Jolly Holiday," "A Man Has Dreams," "Supercalifragilisticexpialidocious," "Step in
Time" written by Richard M. Sherman and Robert B. Sherman,
with new material by George Stiles and Anthony Drewe.

"Cherry Tree Lane," "Practically Perfect," "Being Mrs. Banks," "Precision and Order," "Playing the Game,"
"Brimstone and Treacle," "Anything Can Happen" written by George Stiles and Anthony Drewe.

Cast Continued

Bank Chairman ....JONATHAN FREEMAN
Miss Smythe ....ANN ARVIA
Von Hussler ....TOM SOUHRADA
Northbrook ....CHAD SEIB
Bird Woman ....JESSICA SHERIDAN
Mrs. Corry ....JANELLE ANNE ROBINSON
Fannie ....AMBER OWENS
Annie ....CATHERINE BRUNELL
Valentine ....AARON J. ALBANO
Miss Andrew ....ANN ARVIA

ENSEMBLE

AARON J. ALBANO, TIA ALTINAY,
DAVID BAUM, BRANDON BIEBER,
CATHERINE BRUNELL, KRISTIN CARBONE,
KATE CHAPMAN, ELIZABETH DeROSA,
JAMES HINDMAN, NICK KEPLEY,
JUSTIN KEYES, MARK LEDBETTER,
BRIAN LETENDRE, KATHLEEN NANNI,
AMBER OWENS, T. OLIVER REID,
JANELLE ANNE ROBINSON, CHAD SEIB,
LAURA SCHUTTER, COREY SKAGGS,
TOM SOUHRADA

SWINGS

PAM BRADLEY, KATHY CALAHAN,
BRIAN COLLIER, BARRETT DAVIS,
SUZANNE HYLENSKI, ROMMY SANDHU,
JAMES TABEEK

*Statues, bank clerks, customers, toys, chimney sweeps,
lamp lighters and inhabitants of Cherry Tree Lane played
by members of the company.*

Laura Michelle Kelly is appearing with the permission
of Actors' Equity Association pursuant to an exchange
program between American Equity and UK Equity.

UNDERSTUDIES

Mary Poppins: CATHERINE BRUNELL,
   ELIZABETH DeROSA
Bert: BRIAN COLLIER, MARK LEDBETTER,
   SAM STRASFELD
George Banks: JAMES HINDMAN,
   COREY SKAGGS, TOM SOUHRADA
Winifred Banks: KRISTIN CARBONE,
   LAURA SCHUTTER
Mrs. Brill: ANN ARVIA, PAM BRADLEY
Robertson Ay: AARON J. ALBANO,
   BRIAN COLLIER, BARRETT DAVIS
Bird Woman; Miss Andrew/Queen Victoria/
   Miss Smythe: KATE CHAPMAN,
   JANELLE ANNE ROBINSON,
   JESSICA SHERIDAN

Continued on next page

Mary Poppins

Cast Continued

Admiral Boom/Bank Chairman:
  JAMES HINDMAN, COREY SKAGGS,
  TOM SOUHRADA
Mrs. Corry: PAM BRADLEY,
  CATHERINE BRUNELL,
  KATHY CALAHAN
Katie Nanna: PAM BRADLEY,
  KATHY CALAHAN, SUZANNE HYLENSKI
Miss Lark: PAM BRADLEY, KATHY CALAHAN,
  LAURA SCHUTTER
Neleus: BRIAN COLLIER, BARRETT DAVIS,
  JAMES TABEEK
Von Hussler: T. OLIVER REID,
  ROMMY SANDHU, COREY SKAGGS
Northbrook: CHAD SEIB, COREY SKAGGS
Policeman: ROMMY SANDHU,
  TOM SOUHRADA
Park Keeper: ROMMY SANDHU,
  CHAD SEIB, COREY SKAGGS
Valentine: BRIAN COLLIER, BARRETT DAVIS,
  NICK KEPLEY

DANCE CAPTAIN

Brian Collier

ASSISTANT DANCE CAPTAIN

Barrett Davis

ORCHESTRA

Conductor: BRAD HAAK
Associate Conductor/2nd Keyboard:
  DALE RIELING
Assistant Conductor/Piano: MILTON GRANGER
Bass: PETER DONOVAN
Drums: DAVE RATAJCZAK
Percussion: DANIEL HASKINS
Guitar/Banjo/E-Bow: NATE BROWN
Horns: RUSSELL RIZNER, SHELAGH ABATE
Trumpets: JASON COVEY, JOHN SHEPPARD
Trombone/Euphonium: MARC DONATELLE
Bass Trombone/Tuba: JEFF CASWELL
Clarinet: PAUL GARMENT
Oboe/English Horn: ALEXANDRA KNOLL
Flutes: BRIAN MILLER
Cello: STEPHANIE CUMMINS
Music Contractor: DAVID LAI

Laura Michelle Kelly
Mary Poppins

Gavin Lee
Bert

Karl Kenzler
George Banks

Megan Osterhaus
Winifred Banks

Valerie Boyle
Mrs. Brill

Ann Arvia
*Miss Andrew,
Queen Victoria,
Miss Smythe*

Mark Price
Robertson Ay

Jessica Sheridan
Bird Woman

Jonathan Freeman
*Admiral Boom,
Bank Chairman*

Rozi Baker
*Jane Banks
at certain
performances*

Christopher Flaim
*Michael Banks
at certain
performances*

Ethan Haberfield
*Michael Banks
at certain
performances*

David Gabriel Lerner
*Michael Banks
at certain
performances*

Catherine Missal
*Jane Banks
at certain
performances*

Rachel Resheff
*Jane Banks
at certain
performances*

Kate Chapman
Miss Lark, Ensemble

James Hindman
*Park Keeper,
Ensemble*

Nick Kepley
Neleus, Ensemble

Janelle Anne
Robinson
Mrs. Corry, Ensemble

Chad Seib
*Northbrook,
Ensemble*

Mary Poppins

Corey Skaggs
*Policeman,
Ensemble*

Tom Souhrada
*Von Hussler,
Ensemble*

Aaron J. Albano
Valentine, Ensemble

Tia Altinay
Ensemble

David Baum
Ensemble

Brandon Bieber
Ensemble

Pam Bradley
Swing

Catherine Brunell
Annie, Ensemble

Kathy Calahan
Swing

Kristin Carbone
*Katie Nanna,
Ensemble*

Brian Collier
*Swing,
Dance Captain*

Barrett Davis
Swing

Elizabeth DeRosa
Ensemble

Suzanne Hylenski
Swing

Justin Keyes
Ensemble

Mark Ledbetter
Ensemble

Brian Letendre
Ensemble

Kathleen Nanni
Ensemble

Amber Owens
Fannie, Ensemble

T. Oliver Reid
Ensemble

Rommy Sandhu
Swing

Laura Schutter
Ensemble

James Tabeek
Swing

P.L. Travers
*Author of the
Mary Poppins stories*

Cameron Mackintosh
*Producer and
Co-Creator*

Thomas Schumacher
*Producer
and President
Disney Theatrical
Productions*

Richard M. Sherman and Robert B. Sherman
Original Music & Lyrics

Julian Fellowes
Book

George Stiles
*New Songs,
Additional Music,
Dance & Vocal
Arrangements*

Anthony Drewe
*New Songs &
Additional Lyrics*

Richard Eyre
Director

Matthew Bourne
*Co-Director &
Choreographer*

Bob Crowley
*Scenic and Costume
Design*

Stephen Mear
Co-Choreographer

Mary Poppins

Howard Harrison
Lighting Designer

Steve Canyon
Kennedy
*Broadway Sound
Designer*

William David Brohn
Orchestrations

David Caddick
Music Supervisor

Brad Haak
Music Director

Naomi Donne
Makeup Designer

Angela Cobbin
Wig Creator

Geoffrey Garratt
*Associate
Choreographer*

Anthony Lyn
Associate Director

David Benken
Technical Director

Tara Rubin Casting
Casting

ALUMNI
2010-2011

Christian Borle
Bert

Nick Corley
*Ensemble,
Park Keeper*

Nicolas Dromard
Bert

Ruth Gottschall
*Miss Andrew,
Miss Smythe,
Queen Victoria*

Jeremiah Kissane
Michael Banks

Melissa Lone
Ensemble

Michelle Lookadoo
Ensemble

Sean McCourt
*Ensemble,
Von Hussler*

Jeff Metzler
Ensemble

Sam Strasfeld
*Ensemble,
Northbrook*

TRANSFER
STUDENTS
2010-2011

Julie Barnes
Swing

Ashley Brown
Mary Poppins

Case Dillard
Ensemble

Ed Dixon
*Admiral Boom,
Bank Chairman*

Ruth Gottschall
*Miss Andrew,
Miss Smythe,
Queen Victoria*

Lewis Grosso
Michael Banks

Brigid Harrington
Jane Banks

Garett Hawe
Ensemble, Neleus

Kelly Jacobs
Ensemble

Regan Kays
Ensemble

Andrew
Keenan-Bolger
Robertson Ay

Laird Mackintosh
George Banks

Mary Poppins

Tyler Maynard
Ensemble

Kara Oates
Jane Banks

Catherine Walker
Annie, Ensemble

Kevin Samual Yee
Ensemble, Valentine

Brian Ogilvie
Ensemble, Valentine

Shua Potter
Robertson Ay

Anthony
Scarpone-Lambert
Michael Banks

Sadie Seelert
Jane Banks

Sam Strasfeld
*Ensemble,
Northbrook*

Photos by Brian Mapp

FRONT OF HOUSE STAFF
Front Row (L-R): Michael Gilbert, Carina Don, Kevin Shinnick, Jason Blanche, Kenneth Miller
Back Row (L-R): Jeryl Costello, Audrey Terrell, Carla Dawson, Bryan Plummer, Debbie Vogel

BOX OFFICE
(L-R): Charles Luff, Michael Hughes, Anthony Oliva, Andrew Grennan

MERCHANDISE
(L-R): Nikki Dillon, Thad Wilkes, Tatiana Diaz, Anna Lewgood

Mary Poppins

Photo by Brian Mapp

STAFF AND CREW
Front Row (L-R): Marshall Servilio, Alexis R. Prussack, Mark Dobrow, Liza Vest, Terry Alexander, David Sugarman, Steve Epstein

Middle Row (L-R): Amy Porter, Barbara Hladsky, Chris Lavin, Karen Zabinski, Kurt Fischer, Steve Stackle, John Loiacono, Brett Daley, Jimmy Maloney III, Tony Goncalves

Back Row (L-R): Bill Romanello, Carlos Martinez, Andy Catron (in the chimney) Joe Bivone, Marie Renee Foucher, Kevin Strohmeyer

---

THE ORIGINAL FILM SCREENPLAY
FOR WALT DISNEY'S *MARY POPPINS*
BY BILL WALSH * DON DA GRADI

DESIGN CONSULTANT
TONY WALTON

STAFF FOR *MARY POPPINS*

COMPANY MANAGER ....DAVE EHLE
Assistant Company Manager ....Laura Eichholz
Production Manager ....Eduardo Castro
Production Stage Manager ....Mark Dobrow
Stage Manager ....Jason Trubitt
Assistant Stage
    Managers ....Terence Orleans Alexander,
        Valerie Lau-Kee Lai, Alexis R. Prussack
Dance Supervisor ....Brian Collier
Assistant Dance Captain ....Barrett Davis
Assistant to the Associate Producer ....Kerry McGrath

DISNEY ON BROADWAY PUBLICITY
Senior Publicist...............................Dennis Crowley

Publicist ....Adriana Douzos

Associate Scenic Designer ....Bryan Johnson
Scenic Design Associate .... Rosalind Coombes
US Scenic Assistants ....Dan Kuchar,
                Rachel Short Janocko,
                Frank McCullough
UK Scenic Assistants ....Al Turner,
            Charles Quiggin, Adam Wiltshire
Associate Costume Designer ....Christine Rowland
Associate Costume Designer .... Mitchell Bloom
Assistant Costume Designer ....Patrick Wiley
Assistant Costume Designer .... Rick Kelly
Associate Lighting Designer ....Daniel Walker
Assistant Lighting Designer .... Kristina Kloss
Lighting Programmer .... Rob Halliday
Associate Sound Designer ....John Shivers
Wig Creator ....Angela Cobbin
Illusions Designer ....Jim Steinmeyer
Technical Director ....David Benken
Scenic Production Supervisor .... Patrick Eviston
Assistant Technical Supervisor ....Rosemarie Palombo
Production Carpenter ....Drew Siccardi

Production Flyman ....Michael Corbett
Foy Flying Operator ....Raymond King
Automation ....Steve Stackle, David Helck
Carpenters ....Eddie Ackerman, Frank Alter,
                Brett Daley, Tony Goncalves,
                Gary Matarazzo
Production Electrician ....James Maloney
Key Spot Operator ....Joseph P. Garvey
Lighting Console Operator ....Carlos Martinez
Pyro Operator .... Kevin Strohmeyer
Automated Lighting Technician .... Andy Catron
Assistant Electricians ....Gregory Dunkin,
            Al Manganaro, Chris Passalacqua
Production Propman ....Victor Amerling
Assistant Propman ....Tim Abel
Props ....Joe Bivone, John Saye,
                John Taccone, Gary Wilner
Production Sound Engineer .... Andrew Keister
Sound Engineer .... Kurt Fischer
Sound Engineer.......................... Marie Renee Foucher
Sound Assistant ....Bill Romanello, Karen Zabinski
Production Wardrobe Supervisor ....Helen Toth
Assistant Wardrobe Supervisor ....Abbey Rayburn

224

The Playbill Broadway Yearbook 2010-2011

Mary Poppins

Dressers ....Richard Byron, Vivienne Crawford, Marjorie Denton, Russell Easley, Steven Epstein, Maya Hardin, Carly Hirschberg, Barbara Hladsky, Laura Horner, Peggie Kurz, Janet Netzke, Tom Reiter, Frank Scaccia, Gary Seibert
Production Hair Supervisor ....Tod L. McKim
Hair Dept Assistants ....Chris Calabrese, Ashley Leitzel-Reichenbach, Matthew B. Wilson
Production Makeup Supervisor ....Amy Porter
Child Guardian ....Christina Huschle
UK Prop Coordinators ....Kathy Anders, Lisa Buckley
UK Wig Shop Assistant ....Beatrix Archer

Music Copyist ....Emily Grishman Music Preparation – Emily Grishman/ Katharine Edmonds
Keyboard Programming ....Stuart Andrews

MUSIC COORDINATOR ....DAVID LAI

DIALECT & VOCAL COACH ....DEBORAH HECHT

Resident Dialect Coach ....Shane-Ann Younts
Associate General Manager ....Alan Wasser
Production Co-Counsel ....F. Richard Pappas
Casting Directors ....Tara Rubin, Eric Woodall
Children's Tutoring ....On Location Education, Muriel Kester
Physical Therapy ....Physioarts
Advertising ....Serino Coyne, Inc
Interactive Marketing ....Situation Marketing/ Damian Bazadona, Lisa Cecchini, Miriam Gardin
Web Design Consultant ....Joshua Noah
Production Photography ....Joan Marcus
Production Travel ....Jill L. Citron
Payroll Managers ....Anthony DeLuca, Cathy Guerra
Corporate Counsel ....Michael Rosenfeld

CREDITS

Scenery by Hudson Scenic, Inc.; Adirondack Studios, Inc.; Proof Productions, Inc.; Scenic Technologies, a division of Production Resource Group, LLC, New Windsor NY. Drops by Scenic Arts. Automation by Hudson Scenic, Inc. Lighting equipment by Hudson Sound & Light, LLC. Lighting truss by Showman Fabricators, Inc. Sound Equipment by Masque Sound. Projection equipment by Sound Associates Inc. Magic props by William Kennedy of Magic Effects. Props by The Spoon Group, LLC; Moonboots Productions Inc.; Russell Beck Studio Ltd. Costumes by Barbara Matera Ltd.; Parsons-Meares, Ltd.; Eric Winterling; Werner Russold; Studio Rouge; Seamless Costumes. Millinery by Rodney Gordon, Arnold Levine, Lynne Mackey Studio. Shoes by T.O. Dey. Shirts by Cego. Puppets by Puppet Heap. Flying by Foy. Ricola cough drops courtesy of Ricola USA, Inc. Emergen-C super energy booster provided by Alacer Corp. Makeup provided by M•A•C.

MARY POPPINS rehearsed at the New 42nd Street Studios.

THANKS

Thanks to Marcus Hall Props, Claire Sanderson, James Ince and Sons, Great British Lighting, Bed Bazaar, The Wakefield Brush Company, Heron and Driver, Ivo and Kay Coveney, Mike and Rosi Compton, Bebe Barrett, Charles Quiggin, Nicola Kileen Textiles, Carl Roberts Shaw, David Scotcher Interiors, Original Club Fenders Ltd., Lauren Pattison, Robert Tatad.

Mary Poppins is a proud member of the Broadway Green Alliance.

FOR CAMERON MACKINTOSH LIMITED

Directors ....Nicholas Allott, Richard Johnston
Deputy Managing Director ....Robert Noble
Executive Producer & Casting Director .....Trevor Jackson
Technical Director ....Nicolas Harris
Financial Controller ....Richard Knibb
Associate Producer ....Darinka Nenadovic
Sales & Marketing Manager ....David Dolman
Head of Musical Development ....Stephen Metcalfe
Production Associate ....Shidan Majidi

DISNEY THEATRICAL PRODUCTIONS

President ....Thomas Schumacher
EVP & Managing Director ....David Schrader

Senior Producer ....Michele Steckler
Senior Vice President, International ....Ron Kollen
Vice President, Operations ....Dana Amendola
Vice President, Worldwide Publicity & Communications ....Joe Quenqua
Vice President, Domestic Touring................Jack Eldon
Vice President, Creative Development & Licensing ....Steve Fickinger
Vice President, Human Resources ....June Heindel
Director, Domestic Touring ....Michael Buchanan
Director, Labor Relations ....Edward Lieber
Manager, Labor Relations ....Stephanie Cheek
Manager, Human Resources ....Jewel Neal
Manager, Publicity & Communications ....Lindsay Braverman
Manager, Information Systems ....Scott Benedict
Senior Computer Support Analyst ....Kevin A. McGuire
IT/Business Analyst ....William Boudiette

Production

Executive Music Producer ....Chris Montan
Director, International ....Michael Cassel
Director, International Production ....Felipe Gamba
Manager, Physical Production ....Karl Chmielewski
Creative Development Manager ....Jane Abramson
Dramaturg & Literary Manager ....Ken Cerniglia

Marketing

Vice President, Broadway ....Andrew Flatt
Vice President, International ....Fiona Thomas
Director, Internet Strategy & Online Marketing ....Kyle Young
Director, Broadway ....Michele Groner
Director, Domestic Tour Marketing ....Deborah Warren

Director, Customer Relationship Management & Strategy ....Kelly Colbert
Assistant Manager, Marketing ....Lauren Daghini

Sales

Director, National Sales ....Bryan Dockett
National Sales Manager ....Victoria Cairl
Manager, Sales & Ticketing ....Nick Falzon
Manager, Sales & Ticketing ....David Felsen
Manager, Group Sales ....Hunter Robertson

Business and Legal Affairs

Senior Vice President ....Jonathan Olson
Director ....Daniel M. Posener
Senior Counsel ....Seth Stuhl
Paralegal ....Jessica White

Finance

VP Finance & Business Development ....Mario Iannetta
Director ....Joe McClafferty
Manager, Finance ....John Fajardo
Production Accountants ....Joy Sims Brown, Nick Judge
Assistant Production Accountant ....Isander Rojas
Director, Accounting ....Leena Mathew
Sr. Financial Analyst ....Adrineh Ghoukassian
Senior Sales Analyst ....Liz Jurist Schwarzwalder
Senior Business Analyst ....Sven Rittershaus

Administrative Staff

Sarah Bills, Amy Caldamone, Michael Dei Cas, Preston Copley, Alanna Degner, Brittany Dobbs, Cristi Finn, Jonathan Flood, Gregory Hanoian, Abbie Harrison, Cyntia Leo, Colleen McCormack, Lisa Mitchell, Brendan Padgett, Ryan Pears, David Scott, Anji Taylor, Christina Tuchman, Kyle Wilson, Jason Zammit

DISNEY THEATRICAL MERCHANDISE

Vice President ....Steven Downing
Operations Manager ....Shawn Baker
Merchandise Manager ....Neil Markman
Associate Buyer ....Violet Burlaza
Assistant Manager, Inventory ....Suzanne Jakel
On-Site Retail Manager ....Scott Koonce

Disney Theatrical Productions
c/o New Amsterdam Theatre
214 W. 42nd St.
New York, NY 10036

guestmail@disneytheatrical.com

STAFF FOR THE NEW AMSTERDAM THEATRE

Theatre Manager ....John M. Loiacono
Guest Services Manager ....Kenneth Miller
Box Office Treasurer ....Andrew Grennan
Assistant Treasurer ....Anthony Oliva
Chief Engineer ....Frank Gibbons
Engineer ....Dan Milan
Security Manager ....Carl Lembo
Head Usher ....Jeryl Costello
Lobby Refreshments ....Sweet Concessions
Special thanks ....Sgt. Arthur J. Smarsch, Det. Adam D'Amico

Mary Poppins
SCRAPBOOK

Photo by Amanda Schwab/StarPix celebrity images

Correspondent: Elizabeth DeRosa, "Ensemble" and understudy for "Mary Poppins"

Most Vivid Memory of a Recent Performance: A few nights ago we got a standing ovation after "Step in Time" from the first five rows or so of the center orchestra, which were filled with a high school musical theatre group. It was an incredibly gratifying and energizing moment. After the bows, they all wanted signatures from our conductor, Brad Haak, which he says does not happen very often!

Most Exciting Celebrity Visitors: A while back we had Brangelina and their gang at the show! Unfortunately, they had to leave before the end of the bows to avoid the crowds, but it was certainly a thrill! We also had Teresa Giudice from Bravo's "The Real Housewives of New Jersey" which was hilarious as she could not stop posing for the cameras. Perhaps the most exciting backstage celebrity encounter was Cate Blanchett. She is simply gorgeous, statuesque, completely lovely and so composed. I was in awe of her stunning aura. I suppose you could say I was the one who was star-struck.

Special Intermission Activity: Every Sunday matinee, Valerie Boyle hosts "Tea Club" in her dressing room. Along with hot tea, she serves little treats, cookies or cakes.

Photo by Krissie Fullerton

Photo by Joseph Marzullo/WENN

Favorite Moment in the Show: When I have the honor of playing the role of Mary, my favorite moment is "Feed the Birds." The song is so special and such an important lesson for Mary to teach the children (and in turn, the adults). I believe it was Walt Disney's favorite song. The message is a beautiful one: all human beings and creatures of the Earth need and deserve love.

Favorite Off-Site Hangout: The *Mary Poppins* crew will often get together at Jack's. It's around the corner from the New Am and the space is intimate, the food is great and the bartenders clear drinks they can't reach using the parrot head neck of a Mary Poppins umbrella. Is that inappropriate??

Favorite Snack Food: I eat at least one piece of fruit every show. I love apples, pears, oranges, bananas, melon, anything really!

Memorable Stage Management Note: "QUIET IN THE BUNKER." We have a lot of fun—maybe too much at times. :-)

Coolest Thing About Being in This Show: The cast and crew are an amazing group of people. We are very fortunate to enjoy each other's company and truly call ourselves friends. It's also pretty cool to be in a long-running show that will most likely be around for years to come!

Photo by Joseph Marzullo/WENN

1. In the rehearsal studio (L-R): Catherine Brunell, Kathleen Nanni, Amber Owens, Teresa Giudice of Bravo-TV, Barrett Davis, Tom Souhrada, Tia Altinay, Chris Lavin (wardrobe) and Elizabeth DeRosa.
2. Laura Michelle Kelly welcomes Lee back to the cast August 24, 2010 with a flute of champagne.
3. Gavin Lee (R) welcomes Ashley Brown (original Broadway Mary Poppins) back to the cast March 8, 2011.
4. Curtain call March 8, 2011.

Memphis

First Preview: September 23, 2009. Opened: October 19, 2009.
Still running as of May 31, 2011.

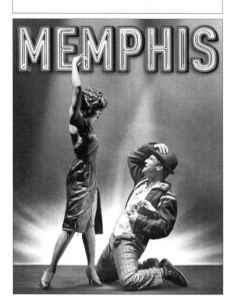

At the dawn of the rock 'n' roll era a white deejay in Memphis, Tennessee falls in love with "black" music, and then falls in love with a beautiful black singer. The two become pioneers in promoting the new musical sound, and become pioneers in interracial romance in a deeply racist society. When things go better for the music than for the romance, the two have to make some soul-shaking choices.

CAST
(in order of appearance)

White DJ/Mr. Collins/White Father/
   Gordon Grant/Ensemble ...... JOHN JELLISON
Black DJ/Be Black Trio/
   Ensemble .... RHETT GEORGE
Delray .... J. BERNARD CALLOWAY
Gator .... DERRICK BASKIN
Bobby .... JAMES MONROE IGLEHART
Ensemble/Wailin' Joe/
   Reverend Hobson .... JOHN ERIC PARKER
Ensemble/
   Someday Backup Singer .... TRACEE BEAZER
Ensemble/Someday Backup Singer/
   Double Dutch Girl .... DIONNE FIGGINS
Ensemble .... BAHIYAH SAYYED GAINES
Ensemble/Ethel .... TANYA BIRL
Ensemble .... TODRICK HALL
Ensemble/Be Black Trio .... SAM J CAHN
Ensemble/
   Be Black Trio .... PRESTON W. DUGGER III

Continued on next page

SAM S. SHUBERT THEATRE
225 West 44th Street
A Shubert Organization Theatre

Philip J. Smith, *Chairman*   **Robert E. Wankel,** *President*

Junkyard Dog Productions   Barbara and Buddy Freitag   Marleen and Kenny Alhadeff
Latitude Link   Jim and Susan Blair   Demos Bizar Entertainment   Land Line Productions
Apples and Oranges Productions   Dave Copley   Dancap Productions, Inc   Alex and Katya Lukianov   Tony Ponturo   2 Guys Productions   Richard Winkler

IN ASSOCIATION WITH

Lauren Doll   Eric and Marsi Gardiner   Linda and Bill Potter   Broadway Across America   Jocko Productions   Patty Baker   Dan Frishwasser
Bob Bartner/Scott and Kaylin Union   Loraine Boyle/Chase Mishkin   Remmel T. Dickinson/Memphis Orpheum Group   ShadowCatcher Entertainment/Vijay and Sita Vashee

PRESENT

MEMPHIS

BOOK AND LYRICS BY
JOE DIPIETRO

MUSIC AND LYRICS BY
DAVID BRYAN

BASED ON A CONCEPT BY
GEORGE W. GEORGE

STARRING

CHAD KIMBALL   MONTEGO GLOVER

WITH

DERRICK BASKIN   J. BERNARD CALLOWAY   JAMES MONROE IGLEHART   ALLEN FITZPATRICK   CASS MORGAN

JENNIFER ALLEN   BRAD BASS   TRACEE BEAZER   TANYA BIRL   SAM J CAHN   KEVIN COVERT   PRESTON W. DUGGER III
HILLARY ELK   BRYAN FENKART   DIONNE FIGGINS   BAHIYAH SAYYED GAINES   RHETT GEORGE   TODRICK HALL   TYRONE A. JACKSON
JOHN JELLISON   BRYAN LANGLITZ   CANDICE MONET McCALL   PAUL McGILL   ANDY MILLS   JILL MORRISON   SYDNEY MORTON
JOHN ERIC PARKER   JERMAINE R. REMBERT   BETSY STRUXNESS   DAN'YELLE WILLIAMSON

| SCENIC DESIGN | COSTUME DESIGN | LIGHTING DESIGN | SOUND DESIGN |
| DAVID GALLO | PAUL TAZEWELL | HOWELL BINKLEY | KEN TRAVIS |

| PROJECTION DESIGN | HAIR & WIG DESIGN | FIGHT DIRECTOR | CASTING | ASSOCIATE CHOREOGRAPHER |
| DAVID GALLO & SHAWN SAGADY | CHARLES G. LaPOINTE | STEVE RANKIN | TELSEY + COMPANY | KELLY DEVINE |

| ORCHESTRATIONS | MUSICAL DIRECTOR | DANCE ARRANGEMENTS | MUSIC CONTRACTOR | PRODUCTION STAGE MANAGER |
| DARYL WATERS & DAVID BRYAN | KENNY J. SEYMOUR | AUGUST ERIKSMOEN | MICHAEL KELLER | ARTURO E. PORAZZI |

| GENERAL MANAGER | PRODUCTION MANAGEMENT | PRESS AGENT | MARKETING DIRECTION |
| ALCHEMY PRODUCTION GROUP CARL PASBJERG & FRANK SCARDINO | JUNIPER STREET PRODUCTIONS, INC. | THE HARTMAN GROUP | aka |

ASSOCIATE PRODUCERS

EMILY AND AARON ALHADEFF   ALISON AND ANDI ALHADEFF   KEN CLAY   JOSEPH CRAIG   RON AND MARJORIE DANZ   CYRENA ESPOSITO   BRUCE AND JOANNE GLANT   MATT MURPHY

MUSIC PRODUCER/MUSIC SUPERVISOR
CHRISTOPHER JAHNKE

CHOREOGRAPHER
SERGIO TRUJILLO

DIRECTOR
CHRISTOPHER ASHLEY

THIS PRODUCTION OF MEMPHIS ORIGINALLY CO-PRODUCED BY LA JOLLA PLAYHOUSE, CHRISTOPHER ASHLEY, ARTISTIC DIRECTOR, MICHAEL S. ROSENBERG, MANAGING DIRECTOR
AND 5TH AVENUE THEATRE, SEATTLE, WA, DAVID ARMSTRONG, PRODUCING ARTISTIC DIRECTOR, MARILYNN SHELDON, MANAGING DIRECTOR
ORIGINALLY PRODUCED AS A JOINT WORLD PREMIERE AT NORTH SHORE MUSIC THEATRE, JON KIMBELL, EXECUTIVE PRODUCER
AND THEATREWORKS, ROBERT KELLEY, ARTISTIC DIRECTOR AND PHIL SANTORA, MANAGING DIRECTOR

10/1/10

Chad Kimball (center)
with the cast

Photo by Joan Marcus

Memphis

MUSICAL NUMBERS

ACT I

"Underground" ....Delray, Felicia and Company
"The Music of My Soul" ....Huey, Felicia and Company
"Scratch My Itch" ....Wailin' Joe and Company
"Ain't Nothin' But a Kiss" ....Felicia and Huey
"Hello, My Name Is Huey" ....Huey
"Everybody Wants to Be Black on a Saturday Night" ....Company
"Make Me Stronger" ....Huey, Mama, Felicia and Company
"Colored Woman" ....Felicia
"Someday" ....Felicia and Company
"She's My Sister" ....Delray and Huey
"Radio" ....Huey and Company
"Say a Prayer" ....Gator and Company

ACT II

"Crazy Little Huey" ....Huey and Company
"Big Love" ....Bobby
"Love Will Stand When All Else Falls" ....Felicia and Company
"Stand Up" ....Delray, Felicia, Huey, Gator, Bobby and Company
"Change Don't Come Easy" ....Mama, Delray, Gator and Bobby
"Tear Down the House" ....Huey and Company
"Love Will Stand/Ain't Nothin' But a Kiss" (Reprise) ....Felicia and Huey
"Memphis Lives in Me" ....Huey and Company
"Steal Your Rock 'n' Roll" ....Huey, Felicia and Company

BOX OFFICE
(L-R): Craig Bowley, Jennifer Holze

STAGE DOOR
Rose Alaio

Photos by Brian Mapp

FRONT OF HOUSE STAFF
Front Row (L-R): Joanne Blessington, Jason Weixelman, Maura Gaynor, Tomas Ortiz, Delia Pozo, Martin Cooper, Alexis Stewart

Middle Row (L-R): Linda Ruik, Giovanni LaDuke, Erin O'Donnell, Melvin Caban, Elvis Caban

Back Row (L-R): Brian Gaynair, Frank Sanabria, Stephen Ivelja, Susan Maxwell, Paul Rodriguez

Cast Continued

Ensemble/Someday
    Backup Singer ......DAN'YELLE WILLIAMSON
Felicia ....MONTEGO GLOVER
Huey ....CHAD KIMBALL
Mr. Simmons ....ALLEN FITZPATRICK
Clara/White Mother/Ensemble JENNIFER ALLEN
Buck Wiley/Ensemble/
    Martin Holton ....KEVIN COVERT
Ensemble/Teenager ....HILLARY ELK
Ensemble ....BRYAN FENKART
Ensemble/
    Double Dutch Girl ....BETSY STRUXNESS
Ensemble ....PAUL McGILL
Ensemble ....ANDY MILLS
Perry Como/Ensemble/Frank Dryer ....BRAD BASS
Ensemble ....BRYAN LANGLITZ
Mama ....CASS MORGAN

SWINGS

TYRONE A. JACKSON,
CANDICE MONET McCALL,
JILL MORRISON, SYDNEY MORTON,
JERMAINE R. REMBERT

UNDERSTUDIES

For Mama: JENNIFER ALLEN,
    BETSY STRUXNESS
For Huey: BRAD BASS, BRYAN FENKART
For Felicia: TRACEE BEAZER,
    DAN'YELLE WILLIAMSON
For Gator: RHETT GEORGE, TODRICK HALL,
    JERMAINE R. REMBERT
For Bobby, Delray: RHETT GEORGE,
    JOHN ERIC PARKER
For Mr. Simmons: JOHN JELLISON,
    KEVIN COVERT

DANCE CAPTAIN

JERMAINE R. REMBERT

TIME

The 1950s

BAND

Conductor: KENNY J. SEYMOUR
Associate Conductor: SHELTON BECTON
Keyboard 1: KENNY J. SEYMOUR
Keyboard 2: SHELTON BECTON
Guitars: JOHN PUTNAM
Bass: GEORGE FARMER
Drums: CLAYTON CRADDOCK
Trumpet: NICHOLAS MARCHIONE
Trombone: MIKE DAVIS
Reeds: TOM MURRAY, KEN HITCHCOCK
Music Coordinator: MICHAEL KELLER

Memphis

Chad Kimball
Huey

Montego Glover
Felicia

Derrick Baskin
Gator

J. Bernard Calloway
Delray

James Monroe
Iglehart
Bobby

Allen Fitzpatrick
Mr. Simmons

Cass Morgan
Mama

Jennifer Allen
Ensemble

Brad Bass
Ensemble

Tracee Beazer
Ensemble

Tanya Birl
Ensemble

Sam J Cahn
Ensemble

Kevin Covert
Ensemble

Preston W. Dugger
III
Ensemble

Hillary Elk
Ensemble

Bryan Fenkart
Ensemble

Dionne Figgins
*Ensemble, Assistant
Dance Captain*

Bahiyah Sayyed
Gaines
Ensemble

Rhett George
Ensemble

Todrick Hall
Ensemble

Tyrone A. Jackson
Swing

John Jellison
Ensemble

Bryan Langlitz
Ensemble

Candice Monet
McCall
Swing

Paul McGill
Ensemble

Andy Mills
Ensemble

Jill Morrison
Swing

Sydney Morton
Swing

John Eric Parker
Ensemble

Jermaine R. Rembert
*Swing,
Dance Captain,
Fight Captain*

Betsy Struxness
Ensemble

Dan'yelle Williamson
Ensemble

Joe DiPietro
Book and Co-Lyrics

David Bryan
Music, Co-Lyrics

Christopher Ashley
Director

Memphis

Sergio Trujillo
Choreographer

Christopher Jahnke
*Music Producer/
Music Supervisor*

David Gallo
*Set and
Co-Projections
Design*

Howell Binkley
Lighting Design

Paul Tazewell
Costume Design

Ken Travis
Sound Design

Charles G. LaPointe
Hair and Wig Design

Steve Rankin
Fight Director

Bernard Telsey,
Telsey + Company
Casting

Kelly Devine
*Associate
Choreographer*

Daryl Waters
Co-Orchestrator

Kenny J. Seymour
*Music Director/
Conductor*

August Eriksmoen
Dance Arranger

Michael Keller
Music Coordinator

Joseph DeLuise, Alexandra Paull,
Hillary Blanken, Ana Rose Greene,
Kevin Broomell, Guy Kwan,
Juniper Street Productions
Production Manager

Carl Pasbjerg,
Alchemy Production
Group LLC
*General
Management*

Beatrice Terry
Associate Director

Edgar Godineaux
*Associate
Choreographer*

Randy Adams,
Junkyard Dog
Productions
Producer

Kenny Alhadeff,
Junkyard Dog
Productions
Producer

Sue Frost,
Junkyard Dog
Productions
Producer

Barbara Freitag
Producer

Buddy Freitag
Producer

Marleen Alhadeff
Producer

Jim Blair
Producer

Susan Blair
Producer

Nick Demos,
Demos Bizar
Entertainment
Producer

Tim Kashani,
Apples and Oranges
Productions
Producer

Pamela Winslow
Kashani,
Apples and Oranges
Productions
Producer

Aubrey Dan,
Dancap Productions
Inc.
Producer

Alex Lukianov
Producer

Tony Ponturo
Producer

Lauren Doll
Producer

John Gore,
CEO,
Broadway Across
America
Producer

Memphis

Linda and Bill Potter
Producers

Thomas B. McGrath,
Chairman,
Broadway Across
America
Producer

Patty Baker,
Good Productions
Producer

Kaylin and Scott Union
Producers

Loraine Alterman
Boyle
Producer

Chase Mishkin
Producer

Remmel T. Dickinson
Producer

Pat Halloran,
Memphis Orpheum
Group
Producer

Vijay Vashee
Producer

Sita Vashee
Producer

Ken Clay
Associate Producer

David Armstrong
*Executive Producer/
Artistic Director,
The 5th Avenue
Theatre*

Bernadine Griffin
*Managing Director,
The 5th Avenue
Theatre*

Bill Berry
*Producing Director,
The 5th Avenue
Theatre*

Robert Kelley
*Artistic Director,
TheatreWorks*

Phil Santora
*Managing Director,
TheatreWorks*

James Brown III
Ensemble

Erica Dorfler
*Ensemble/Someday
Backup Singer*

Gregory Haney
Ensemble

Michael McGrath
Mr. Simmons

Vivian Nixon
Ensemble

LaQuet Sharnell
Ensemble/Ethel

Monique Smith
*Ensemble/Someday
Backup Singer/
Double Dutch Girl*

Ephraim M. Sykes
*Ensemble/
Be Black Trio*

Cary Tedder
Ensemble

Daniel J. Watts
*Ensemble/
Be Black Trio*

Charlie Williams
Ensemble

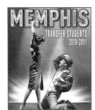

Darius Barnes
Ensemble

Ashley Blanchet
*Ensemble/Someday
Backup Singer*

Felicia Boswell
*Ensemble/Someday
Backup Singer,
Swing*

Robert Hartwell
*Ensemble/
Wailin' Joe/
Reverend Hobson*

Memphis

Tiffany Janene
Howard
*Ensemble/Someday
Backup Singer/
Double Dutch Girl*

Elizabeth Ward Land
*Clara/White Mother/
Ensemble*

Kyle Leland
*Ensemble/
Be Black Trio*

Kevin Massey
Ensemble

David McDonald
*White DJ/Mr. Collins/
White Father/
Gordon Grant/
Ensemble*

Michael McGrath
Mr. Simmons

Monette McKay
Ensemble/Ethel

Nancy Opel
Mama

Justin Patterson
*Buck Wiley/
Ensemble/
Martin Holton*

Jamison Scott
*Perry Como/
Ensemble/
Frank Dryer*

Ephraim Sykes
Ensemble

Daniel J. Watts
Swing

HAIR
(L-R): MaryKay Yezerski-Bondoc, Michele Rutter, Charlene Belmond,
Jameson Eaton

STAGE MANAGEMENT
(Clockwise, from Top Left): Gary Mickelson, Arturo Porazzi, Janet Takami,
Alexis Shorter

CREW
Front Row (L-R): Tommy Maher, Jim Spradling, A.J. Giegerich, Karen Hyman,
Tommy Anderson, Greg Freedman, Sean Pilipski

Back Row (L-R): Mike Maher, John Paull, Joe Pearson, Hank Hale,
Stephen Schrorettnig, Eric Yans, Cassy Givens

WARDROBE
Front Row (L-R): Franc Weinperl, Ryan Moller

Middle Row (L-R): Dora Bonilla, Kyle Wesson, Tasha Cowd, Maggie Horkey,
Maureen George

Back Row (L-R): Charles Van de Craats, Rick Ortiz, Kim Kaldenberg,
Rory Powers

Memphis

Memphis
SCRAPBOOK

Correspondent: Bryan Fenkart, "Ensemble"

Most Exciting Celebrity Visitor: Jason Segel, who ran up to me backstage after a Huey performance, hugged me off the ground and said, "Dude, I don't even KNOW you and I'm f***ing proud of you!"

Special Backstage Rituals: More than I can count, but rest assured, they are all equally superstitious and useless.

Favorite In-Theatre Gathering Place: The Bungalow, clearly! (Authorized personnel only.)

Favorite Off-Site Hangout: I spend an inordinate amount of time scarfing down the Chicken Twister Wraps and a cup of Chicken Rice Soup at Westway Diner. And there's always that emerging after-show gem, Glass House Tavern.

Favorite Snack Foods: Pretzel rods I stole from Stage Management, because they taste like victory.

Mascot: Um. Wailin' Joe?

Favorite Therapy: Mucinex DM. Sold in your local pharmacy, but hand-made by God.

Memorable Ad-Lib: Michael McGrath once inserted the word "bollweevil" in place of "sumbitch" because it was a "clean matinee."

Record Number of Cell Phone Rings, Cell Phone Photos or Texting Incidents During a Performance: I personally have only heard a few here and there. But we've triangulated their location. They won't be bothering us anymore.

Memorable Stage Door Fan Encounter: A girl once asked me to sign her throat so she could sing better.

Web Buzz: I don't think any of us anticipated the caliber of buzz our show would muster, or the momentum it seems to keep gaining. And tell you what, we don't take it for granted either.

Fastest Costume Change: About 10 seconds, after "Radio," into the proposal scene. It sometimes ends with me cursing under my breath. Into a live microphone.

Catchphrases Only the Company Would Recognize: "Man, it's always FIVE!" "Bon Appetit." "Hey, who's in charge of SNOB?"

Sweethearts Within the Company: No comment. And Betsy Struxness will also have no comment.

Orchestra Member Who Played the Most Instruments: Joe! Accordion, flugelhorn and dobro! Did I win?

Orchestra Member Who Played the Most Consecutive Performances Without A Sub: I'm gonna say Clayton Craddock, then you can find out who it really is by seeing who punches me after they read this.

Memorable Directorial Note: "So, tonight we're gonna go back to the old opening."

Company In-Joke: "Football pool!" "It's time for Huey Calhoun's...after-school...playhouse... and...HERE HE IS!"

Understudy Anecdote: After one Huey performance, a man called to me at the stage door, "Chad!" I replied, "Oh, I'm not Chad, I'm his understudy, Bryan." He then proceeded to point to Chad's picture in the Playbill and

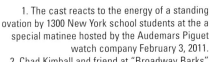

1. The cast reacts to the energy of a standing ovation by 1300 New York school students at the a special matinee hosted by the Audemars Piguet watch company February 3, 2011.
2. Chad Kimball and friend at "Broadway Barks" July 10, 2010..
3. The audience at the conclusion of the February 3 student performance.
4. Composer/lyricist David Bryan and librettist/lyricist Joe DiPietro at the show's first anniversary party.

ask me, "This isn't you?" Oh, sorry sir, MY mistake.

Nicknames: Daniel Watts: D-Watts, Wattage. Sydney Morton: SydMo. Betsy Struxness: The Strux. John Jellison: Double J. Me: Fenk. Montego Glover: Ms. Glover.

Embarrassing Moments: I once went into the proposal scene as Huey without the engagement ring. That's a naked-feeling moment.

Ghostly Encounters Backstage: I can't be

sure, but I think Laurence Olivier once gave me a wet willie.

Coolest Thing About Being in This Show: There are very few things out there anymore that are fully original. Not songs you've heard before, not a movie you've seen before or a book you've read. Just something fresh and satisfying and alive. Also, I get to do my first Broadway show on the very Shubert stage where I saw my first Broadway show when I was a kid, *Crazy for You*.

The Merchant of Venice

First Preview: October 19, 2010. Opened: November 13, 2010. Went on hiatus January 10-31, 2011.
Closed February 20, 2011 after 26 Previews and 73 Performances.

PLAYBILL

Shakespeare's 16th century classic about a wealthy Christian merchant named Antonio. He borrows a great sum from the Jewish moneylender Shylock, whom he had previously vilified for his religion. When Antonio cannot repay the loan, Shylock demands his agreed-upon bond: a pound of Antonio's flesh.

THE COMPANY
(in order of speaking)

Antonio, a Venetian merchant .BYRON JENNINGS
Salerio, his friend..........PETER FRANCIS JAMES
Solanio, his friend.............MATTHEW RAUCH
Bassanio, a lord,
  Antonio's friend...............DAVID HARBOUR
Lorenzo, a gentleman of Venice ..SETH NUMRICH
Gratiano, a gentleman of Venice .JESSE L. MARTIN
Portia, an heiress in Belmont ....LILY RABE
Nerissa, her lady ...MARSHA STEPHANIE BLAKE
Balthasar, servant to Portia ....HERB FOSTER
Shylock, a Jewish moneylender ....AL PACINO
Prince of Morocco,
  suitor to Portia ....ISAIAH JOHNSON
Launcelot Gobbo, servant
  to Shylock......CHRISTOPHER FITZGERALD
Jessica, Shylock's daughter ....HEATHER LIND
Prince of Arragon,
  suitor to Portia ....CHARLES KIMBROUGH
Antonio's Man ....GLENN FLESHLER
Tubal, an associate of Shylock's .RICHARD TOPOL
Duke of Venice ....GERRY BAMMAN
Priest ....BAYLEN THOMAS

Continued on next page

The Playbill Broadway Yearbook 2010-2011

---

⑥ BROADHURST THEATRE
235 West 44th Street
A Shubert Organization Theatre

Philip J. Smith, *Chairman*   **Robert E. Wankel,** *President*

THE PUBLIC THEATER
OSKAR EUSTIS, ARTISTIC DIRECTOR ANDREW D. HAMINGSON, EXECUTIVE DIRECTOR
JEFFREY RICHARDS JERRY FRANKEL
DEBBIE BISNO & EVA PRICE AMY NEDERLANDER JONATHAN FIRST STEWART F. LANE & BONNIE COMLEY
UNIVERSAL PICTURES STAGE PRODUCTIONS MERRITT FORREST BAER THE ARACA GROUP
BROADWAY ACROSS AMERICA JOSEPH & MATTHEW DEITCH JK PRODUCTIONS TERRY ALLEN KRAMER
CATHY CHERNOFF/JAY & CINDY GUTTERMAN MALLORY FACTOR/CHERYL LACHOWICZ
JOEY PARNES EXECUTIVE PRODUCER
and
THE SHUBERT ORGANIZATION
present

AL PACINO
in
The MERCHANT *of* VENICE

by
WILLIAM SHAKESPEARE

with
LILY RABE

DAVID HARBOUR BYRON JENNINGS JESSE L. MARTIN

GERRY BAMMAN MARSHA STEPHANIE BLAKE CHRISTOPHER FITZGERALD
PETER FRANCIS JAMES ISAIAH JOHNSON CHARLES KIMBROUGH HEATHER LIND
SETH NUMRICH MATTHEW RAUCH RICHARD TOPOL

HAPPY ANDERSON LIZA J. BENNETT GLENN FLESHLER LUKE FORBES
HERB FOSTER BRYCE GILL THOMAS MICHAEL HAMMOND JADE HAWK
BETHANY HEINRICH CURT HOSTETTER TIA JAMES
KELSEY KURZ BRIAN KEITH MacDONALD DORIEN MAKHLOGHI
KIM MARTIN-COTTEN BAYLEN THOMAS

SCENIC DESIGN	COSTUME DESIGN	LIGHTING DESIGN	SOUND DESIGN
MARK WENDLAND	JESS GOLDSTEIN	KENNETH POSNER	ACME SOUND PARTNERS
HAIR & WIG DESIGN	MUSIC COMPOSED BY	FIGHT DIRECTOR	CHOREOGRAPHER
CHARLES LaPOINTE	DAN MOSES SCHREIER	THOMAS SCHALL	MIMI LIEBER
PRODUCTION STAGE MANAGER	CASTING	PRESS REPRESENTATIVE	ASSOCIATE PRODUCERS
STEPHEN M. KAUS	JORDAN THALER	CANDI ADAMS	JOY NEWMAN
	HEIDI GRIFFITHS		DAVID SCHUMEISTER

ASSOCIATE PRODUCERS
BARRY EDELSTEIN JEREMY SCOTT BLAUSTEIN ELON RUTBERG
SD WAGNER JOHN JOHNSON

DIRECTED BY
DANIEL SULLIVAN

11/13/10

(L-R): Gerry Bamman (background), Lily Rabe and Al Pacino (foreground) with the company

Photo by Joan Marcus

235

The Merchant of Venice

Jay and Cindy Gutterman
Producer

Joey Parnes
Executive Producer

David Aaron Baker
Gratiano

George Bartenieff
Balthasar, Ensemble

Brian Sgambati
Ensemble

STAFF FOR *THE MERCHANT OF VENICE*

GENERAL MANAGEMENT
Joey Parnes
John Johnson   S.D. Wagner

COMPANY MANAGER
Kim Sellon

FOR THE PUBLIC THEATER
Artistic Director ....Oskar Eustis
Executive Director ....Andrew D. Hamingson
Associate Artistic Director ....Mandy Hackett
General Manager ....Andrea Nellis
Associate Producer ....Maria Goyanes
Director of Production ....Ruth Sternberg
Director of Shakespeare Initiative ....Barry Edelstein
Director of Marketing ....Nella Vera

PRESS REPRESENTATIVES
CANDI ADAMS
Josh Ferri   Julie Danni

Production Stage Manager ....Stephen M. Kaus
Stage Manager ....David Sugarman
Assistant Company Manager ....Christina Huschle
Management Associates ....Kristen Luciani,
                                              Nate Koch
Assistant Director ....Laura Savia
Dialect Coach ....Kate Wilson
Dramaturgy ....Barry Edelstein
Assistant Scenic Designer ....Rachel Nemec
Assistant Scenic Designer ....Jon Collins
Assistant Costume Designers ....China Lee,
                                   Tristan Scott Barton Raines
Associate Lighting Designer ....John Viesta
Associate Sound Designer ....Nick Borisjuk
Assistant to Wig Designer ....Leah Loukas
Dialect Coach ....Kate Wilson

Production Carpenter ....Larry Morley
Production Electrician ....Richard Mortell
Head Electrician ....Jeff Turner
Production Prop Supervisor ....Mike Smanko
Head Props ....Faye Armon
Head Sound ....Mike Farfalla
Wardrobe Supervisor ....Rick Kelly
Mr. Pacino's Dresser ....Emily Merriweather
Dressers ....Gary Biangone, Cat Dee,
                              Mary Ann Lewis-Oberpriller,
                                         Erick Medinilla
Hair Supervisor ....Linda Rice
Assistant Hair Supervisor ....Carole Morales
Production Assistants ....Vanessa Coakley,
                                          Sean M. Thorne

Production Technical Assistant ....Amanda Raymond
Management Interns ....Lauren Hall,
                                         Marissa Schwartz
Assistant Producer ....Michael Crea
Assistant to Jeffrey Richards ....Will Trice
Creative Director,
    Broadway Best Shows ....Andy Drachenberg
Director of Communications,
    Broadway Best Shows ....Joe Byrne
Assistant to Oskar Eustis ....Jesse Alick
Assistant to
    Andrew D. Hamingson ....Rosalind Barbour

Casting Associate ....Amber Wakefield
Casting Assistant ....Kate Murray
Casting Intern ....Carolina Cuervo
Press Intern ....Taleah Griffin

Advertising ....Serino Coyne/
                            Greg Corradetti, Tom Callahan,
                              Robert Jones, Danielle Boyle
Website Design/
    New Media Marketing ....Art Meets Commerce:
                            Jim Glaub, Chip Meyrelles,
                            Laurie Connor, Kevin Keating,
                            Ryan Greer, Crystal Chase
Merchandise ....Randi Grossman/
                                        Max Merchandising
Legal Counsel ....Lazarus & Harris LLP/
                            Scott Lazarus Esq., Robert Harris, Esq.
Public Theater
    Counsel ....Paul, Weiss, Rifkind,
                                      Wharton & Garrison/
                            Charles H. Googe, Jr., Esq. and
                  Carolyn J. Casselman, Esq.; Littler Mendelson, P.C./
                            Gerald T. Hathaway; Dewey & LeBoeuf
Accountants ....Rosenberg, Neuwirth & Kuchner/
                            Mark D' Ambrosi, Patricia A. Pedersen
Banking ....City National Bank/
                            Stephanie Dalton, Michele Gibbons
Insurance ....AON/Albert G. Ruben/
                            George Walden, Claudia B. Kaufman
Payroll ....Castellana Services Inc./
                            Lance Castellana, James Castellana,
                                         Norman Sewell
Production Photographer ....Joan Marcus

RECORDED MUSIC PERFORMED BY
Piano/Conductor ....Rob Berman
Violin ....Suzanne Ornstein
Viola ....Richard Brice
Cello ....Roger Shell
Clarinet ....Lino Gomez
English horn ....Melanie Feld
Bassoon ....Ronald Jannelli

Contractor ....Seymour Red Press

CREDITS
Scenery and automation by Hudson Scenic Studio Inc.
Lighting equipment by PRG Lighting. Sound equipment by
Masque Sound. Men's custom suits by Saint Laurie
Merchant Tailors, NYC. Men's tailoring by Studio Rouge
Inc. Dresses by Eric Winterling Inc., Fritz Masten,
Timberlake Studios Inc. and Roberta Hamelin. Millinery by
Rodney Gordon and Janet Linville. Shoes by Worldtone.
Props by Prism Props. Props construction by Paper Mache
Monkey. Car service by IBA Limousine. Water provided by
Poland Spring. Natural herb cough drops courtesy of Ricola
USA.

SPECIAL THANKS
Julian Christenberry, Jane Pfeffer, Amy Carothers, Louise
Foisy, Barry Rosenberg, Stuart Levy, Ruth Sternberg, Tom
Grady, Kit Ingui and The Icon.

THE SHUBERT ORGANIZATION, INC.
Board of Directors

Philip J. Smith	**Robert E. Wankel**
Chairman	President
Wyche Fowler, Jr.	**John W. Kluge**
Lee J. Seidler	**Michael I. Sovern**

Stuart Subotnick

Elliot Greene	**David Andrews**
Chief Financial	Senior Vice President –
Officer	Shubert Ticketing
Juan Calvo	**John Darby**
Vice President –	Vice President –
Finance	Facilities
Peter Entin	**Charles Flateman**
Vice President –	Vice President –
Theatre Operations	Marketing
Anthony LaMattina	**Brian Mahoney**
Vice President –	Vice President –
Audit & Production Finance	Ticket Sales

D.S. Moynihan
Vice President – Creative Projects

House Manager ....Hugh Barnett

The Merchant of Venice
Scrapbook

Correspondent: Richard Topol, "Tubal"

Opening Night Gifts: Miniature wooden caskets (like the ones in the play) from the producers. Miniature Buddhas from Peter Francis James.

Celebrity Visitors: Meryl Streep. Joe Torre. Robert De Niro, who said about the show, "Good, Good, Fine. Fine." Tony Bennett. Johnny Depp who said, "It was fantastic."

Who Performed the Most Roles in This Show: Bryce Gill.

Actors Who Has Done the Most Shows in His Career: Herb Foster or Dan Sullivan.

Backstage Rituals: Before each entrance Al Pacino touches all the doorknobs in his path, shakes hands with a number of actors and touches whichever actors he is going on stage with.

At intermission Jesse Martin and the women who sing backup with him for the song "Fancy Bred" (Bethany Heinrich, Tia James and Liza Bennett) sing the song twice to warm up—the first time straight ahead, and then a second time based on whatever beat Seth Numrich sets on whatever he uses for a drum that night.

Favorite Moments in the Show: Jessica's leap off the tower into the revelers' arms.

Antonio in the trial scene fiercely condemning Shylock and "his Jewish heart."

In-Theatre Gathering Places: Tia James' dressing room during intermission for "Fancy Bred" rehearsal. The men's ensemble dressing room for Thursday night poker.

Off-Site Hangout: Jesse Martin's apartment for parties.

Favorite Snack Food: "White Trash" (Chex mix, powdered sugar, white chocolate)—but we can't eat it in costume thanks to Happy Anderson spilling coffee on himself *twice*.

Mascot: Marsha Stephanie Blake's baby, Lucia.

Favorite Therapy: Ricola vs lemon drops to make it through the half-hour trial scene without coughing.

Curtain call on opening night (L-R): *Yearbook* correspondent Richard Topol, Isaiah Johnson, Jesse L. Martin, Marsha Stephanie Blake, Al Pacino, Lily Rabe, Byron Jennings, David Harbour, Peter Francis James and Matthew Rauch.

Photo by Joseph Marzullo/WENN

Memorable Ad-Libs: Al Pacino saying "I am NOT pleased" instead of "I am not bound to please you with my answers."

Lily Rabe saying "A WHITE wife makes a heavy husband," instead of "a LIGHT wife."

Cell Phone Photos: About 1000 photos of Al Pacino during the trial scene. About 1147 photos of Al Pacino during the curtain call.

Cell Phone Rings: One night a cell phone gave a musical ring during Launcelot Gobbo's monologue to audience and Chris Fitzgerald (as Gobbo) whistled the tune back. The audience had no idea what was going on.

Memorable Stage Door Fan Encounters: A playwright with a beard on only one side of his face was giving out copies of his plays to the actors.

Someone told Jesse Martin "You are a really good Christian," and handed him rosary beads. One night Al Pacino came out the stage door after the show to bring Tony Bennett backstage and the crowd waiting for autographs went wild. One man jumped the barricade and yelled to Al, "I like your work!" Along the way he accidentally punched David Harbour in the face as he was coming out of the stage door.

Latest Audience Arrival: Because we do Tuesday-Thursday shows at 7 p.m., lots of people show up 45 minutes late. Once, during Gobbo's first scene, about 40 minutes into the show, a woman came to sit in a front row center seat, got her coat caught on one of the stage floor microphones, and kept saying "I'm stuck" loudly enough that the mike picked it up and the whole audience could hear.

Fastest Costume Changes: Heather Lind on stage disguises herself as a boy to run away with Lorenzo.

Jesse Martin AFTER the show changes into street clothes and gets out of the building before the fans can swamp him.

Busiest Day at the Box Office: Probably the first day tickets went on sale. But ours is busy every day.

Heaviest Costume: Isaiah Johnson as the

Prince of Morocco, complete with turban.

Who Wore the Least: Heather Lind as Jessica in the pool during the Belmont scene.

Company Catchphrases: "Fancy Bred." "I love a pinky ring." "I did dream of moneybags last night."

Understudy Anecdote: After first understudy rehearsal Kim Martin-Cotten went to a Bikram Yoga class, telling husband Jacques she'd meet him for dinner. Came out of class at 6 PM and her groovy 60-year-old yoga teacher said, "You're on tonight." Kim: "What?" Yoga Teacher: "You're going on." Kim: "That's not possible." Yoga Teacher: "It is. The theatre was here looking for you." Kim threw her clothes on, got to the theatre and having rehearsed only half of the play only once, proceeded to give a flawless and inspired performance of Portia, one of the great female roles in Shakespeare, opposite Al Pacino!

Embarrassing Moments: Byron Jennings entering 25 seconds late in the carnival scene with his reading glasses on because he forgot his entrance and was sitting in his dressing room reading.

David Harbour slipping on the water onstage and falling flat on his ass during the curtain call. Rich Topol slipping on the water onstage (the night before Harbour's wipeout) and falling flat on his ass, almost knocking down Pacino at the end of the Baptism scene.

New Tradition Started: After first performance all Equity members making their Broadway debuts grabbed a buddy with Broadway experience who had to buy them drinks all night. We had almost a dozen newbies christened in this show.

Opening Night Letter: Emily Mann, artistic director of McCarter Theatre, sent a lovely note praising the show and the cast, especially remarking on how great an AMERICAN Shakespeare production we had created.

Coolest Thing about Being in This Show: Al Pacino! Also, a seven-show week and four days off in a row every week, thanks to Al Pacino!

Million Dollar Quartet

First Preview: March 13, 2010. Opened: April 11, 2010.
Still running as of May 31, 2011.

A recreation of the legendary night in 1956 when four country music legends–Elvis Presley, Carl Perkins, Johnny Cash and Jerry Lee Lewis–jammed together for their "discoverer," Sam Phillips, at Sun Records in Memphis, Tennessee, the label that gave the four of them their respective starts. The score features a treasury of their hit songs.

CAST
(in order of appearance)

Carl Perkins	ROBERT BRITTON LYONS
Johnny Cash	LANCE GUEST
Jerry Lee Lewis	LEVI KREIS
Elvis Presley	EDDIE CLENDENING
Jay Perkins (Bass Player)	COREY KAISER
Fluke (Drummer)	LARRY LELLI
Sam Phillips	HUNTER FOSTER
Dyanne	ELIZABETH STANLEY

UNDERSTUDIES

For Johnny Cash, Sam Phillips:
CHRISTOPHER RYAN GRANT
For Elvis Presley, Carl Perkins:
ERIK HAYDEN
For Jerry Lee Lewis, Carl Perkins:
JARED MASON
For Dyanne:
VICTORIA MATLOCK
For Sam Phillips:
JAMES MOYE

Continued on next page

⇒N⇐ NEDERLANDER THEATRE
UNDER THE DIRECTION OF
JAMES M. NEDERLANDER AND JAMES L. NEDERLANDER

RELEVANT THEATRICALS, JOHN COSSETTE PRODUCTIONS, AMERICAN POP ANTHOLOGY,
BROADWAY ACROSS AMERICA AND JAMES L. NEDERLANDER

PRESENT

MILLION DOLLAR QUARTET

BOOK BY COLIN ESCOTT & FLOYD MUTRUX

ORIGINAL CONCEPT AND DIRECTION BY FLOYD MUTRUX

INSPIRED BY
ELVIS PRESLEY, JOHNNY CASH, JERRY LEE LEWIS AND CARL PERKINS

FEATURING
EDDIE CLENDENING   LANCE GUEST   LEVI KREIS   ROBERT BRITTON LYONS

WITH
ELIZABETH STANLEY

AND
HUNTER FOSTER

SCENIC DESIGN	COSTUME DESIGN	LIGHTING DESIGN	SOUND DESIGN
DEREK McLANE	JANE GREENWOOD	HOWELL BINKLEY	KAI HARADA

HAIR AND WIG DESIGN	ASSOCIATE MUSIC SUPERVISOR	CASTING
TOM WATSON	AUGUST ERIKSMOEN	TELSEY + COMPANY

MARKETING DIRECTOR	PRESS REPRESENTATION	MARKETING
CAROL CHIAVETTA	BONEAU/BRYAN-BROWN	TYPE A MARKETING

PRODUCTION STAGE MANAGER	PRODUCTION MANAGER	GENERAL MANAGEMENT
ROBERT WITHEROW	JUNIPER STREET PRODUCTIONS	ALAN WASSER · ALLAN WILLIAMS

MUSICAL ARRANGEMENTS AND SUPERVISION
CHUCK MEAD

DIRECTED BY
ERIC SCHAEFFER

DEVELOPED AND PRODUCED AT VILLAGE THEATRE, ISSAQUAH, WASHINGTON
ROBB HUNT, PRODUCER · STEVE TOMKINS, ARTISTIC DIRECTOR

ORIGINALLY PRESENTED BY SEASIDE MUSIC THEATER
TIPPIN DAVIDSON, PRODUCER
LESTER MALIZIA, ARTISTIC DIRECTOR

10/1/10

(L-R): Hunter Foster, Levi Kreis,
Robert Britton Lyons, Eddie Clendening
and Lance Guest

Photo by Joan Marcus

Million Dollar Quartet

MUSICAL NUMBERS

"Blue Suede Shoes" .... COMPANY
"Real Wild Child" .... JERRY LEE LEWIS
"Matchbox" .... CARL PERKINS
"Who Do You Love?" .... CARL PERKINS
"Folsom Prison Blues" .... JOHNNY CASH
"Fever" .... DYANNE
"Memories Are Made of This" .... ELVIS PRESLEY
"That's All Right" .... ELVIS PRESLEY
"Brown Eyed Handsome Man" .... COMPANY
"Down by the Riverside" .... COMPANY
"Sixteen Tons" .... JOHNNY CASH
"My Babe" .... CARL PERKINS
"Long Tall Sally" .... ELVIS PRESLEY
"Peace in the Valley" .... COMPANY
"I Walk the Line" .... JOHNNY CASH
"I Hear You Knocking" .... DYANNE
"Party" .... CARL PERKINS & COMPANY
"Great Balls of Fire" .... JERRY LEE LEWIS
"Down by the Riverside" (Reprise) .... COMPANY
"Hound Dog" .... ELVIS PRESLEY
"Riders in the Sky" .... JOHNNY CASH
"See You Later Alligator" .... CARL PERKINS
"Whole Lotta Shakin' Goin' On" .... JERRY LEE LEWIS

Cast Continued

Production Stage Manager:
ROBERT WITHEROW
Assistant Stage Managers:
CAROLYN KELSON, ERIK HAYDEN

TIME: December 4, 1956
PLACE: Sun Records, Memphis

Additional arrangements by LEVI KREIS

(L-R): Levi Kreis and Robert Britton Lyons

Photo by Joan Marcus

Eddie Clendening
Elvis Presley

Lance Guest
Johnny Cash

Levi Kreis
Jerry Lee Lewis

Robert Britton Lyons
Carl Perkins

Elizabeth Stanley
Dyanne

Hunter Foster
Sam Phillips

Christopher Ryan Grant
*u/s Johnny Cash,
u/s Sam Phillips*

Erik Hayden
*u/s Elvis Presley,
u/s Carl Perkins,
Assistant Stage
Manager*

Jared Mason
*u/s Jerry Lee Lewis,
u/s Carl Perkins*

Victoria Matlock
u/s Dyanne

James Moye
u/s Sam Phillips

Corey Kaiser
*Jay Perkins,
Bass Player*

Larry Lelli
Fluke, Drummer

Eric Schaeffer
Director

Million Dollar Quartet

Colin Escott
Co-Author

Floyd Mutrux
*Co-Author,
Original Concept
and Direction*

Derek McLane
Scenic Design

Howell Binkley
Lighting Design

Jane Greenwood
Costume Design

Kai Harada
Sound Design

Chuck Mead
*Musical
Arrangements and
Supervision*

Michael Keller
Music Contractor

Tom Watson
Hair and Wig Design

August Eriksmoen
*Associate Music
Supervisor*

David Ruttura
Assistant Director

Bernard Telsey,
Telsey + Company
Casting

Alan Wasser
*General
Management*

Allan Williams
*General
Management*

Joseph DeLuise, Alexandra Paull,
Hillary Blanken, Ana Rose Greene,
Kevin Broomell, Guy Kwan,
Juniper Street Productions
Production Manager

Gigi Pritzker,
Relevant Theatricals
Producer

Ted Rawlins,
Relevant Theatricals
Producer

John Cossette
Productions
Producer

John Gore,
CEO,
Broadway Across
America
Producer

Thomas B. McGrath,
Chairman,
Broadway Across
America
Producer

James L.
Nederlander
Producer

David Abeles
Jerry Lee Lewis

Steve Benoit
u/s Elvis Presley

BOX OFFICE
(L-R): Keshave Sattaur, Anne Huston, Augie Pugliese

Nicolette Hart
u/s Dyanne

Dan Mills
u/s Carl Perkins

Randy Redd
u/s Jerry Lee Lewis

Billy Woodward
*u/s Elvis Presley,
Johnny Cash*

Million Dollar Quartet

Photos by Brian Mapp

CREW
(L-R): Robert Witherow, Johnny Van, Joe Ferreri Jr., Billy Wright Jr., Patrick Pummill, Aaron Straus

WARDROBE & HAIR
Ryan Rossetto, Shanah-Ann Kendall, Francine Schwartz-Buryiak, Aughra Moon

FRONT OF HOUSE STAFF
Front Row (L-R): Louise Angelino, Veronica Figaroa, Ralph Hendrix, Iris Cortes, Elena Mavoides, Renee Fleetwood
Middle Row (L-R): John Rowe, Austin Presanda, Brian Baeza, Erin
Back Row (L-R): Katie Spillane, Marlon Pichardo, Kyle Luker, Mike Rios

---

STAFF FOR *MILLION DOLLAR QUARTET*

GENERAL MANAGEMENT
ALAN WASSER ASSOCIATES
Alan Wasser   Allan Williams
Mark Shacket   Dawn Kusinski

COMPANY MANAGER
Jolie Gabler

GENERAL PRESS REPRESENTATIVE
BONEAU/BRYAN-BROWN
Adrian Bryan-Brown   Aaron Meier   Amy Kass

CASTING
TELSEY + COMPANY
Bernie Telsey CSA, Will Cantler CSA, David Vaccari CSA,
Bethany Knox CSA, Craig Burns CSA,
Tiffany Little Canfield CSA, Rachel Hoffman CSA,
Carrie Rosson CSA, Justin Huff CSA, Bess Fifer CSA,
Patrick Goodwin CSA, Abbie Brady-Dalton

Million Dollar Quartet

PRODUCTION MANAGEMENT
Juniper Street Productions
Hillary Blanken   Kevin Broomell
Guy Kwan   Ana Rose Greene   Sue Semaan

ASSISTANT DIRECTOR
David Ruttura

**ASSOCIATE PRODUCERS FOR
BROADWAY ACROSS AMERICA**
Jennifer Costello   Sara Skolnick

UK CONSULTING PRODUCERS
Joseph Smith/Michael McCabe

JAPAN CONSULTING PRODUCER
TBS Services, Inc.

Production Stage Manager ....Robert Witherow
Stage Manager ....Carolyn Kelson
Associate Set Designer ....Shoko Kambara
Associate Costume Designer ....Moria Clinton
Associate Lighting Designer ....Ryan O'Gara
Assistant Lighting Designers ....Amanda Zieve, Sean Beach
Music Contractor ....Michael Keller
Production Carpenter ....Todd Frank
Advance Carpenter ....John Riggins
Automation Carpenter ....Scott "Gus" Poitras
Production Electricians ..James J. Fedigan, Randall Zaibek
Head Electrician ....Dan Coey
Production Sound Engineer ....Patrick Pummill
Production Properties Supervisor ....Will Sweeney
Moving Light Programmer ....David Arch
Wardrobe Supervisor ....Ryan Rossetto
Dresser ....Francine Buryiak
Stitcher/Dayworker ....Aughra Taylor Moon
Hair & Wig Supervisor ....Shanah-Ann Kendall
Guitars provided by ....Gibson Guitar Corporation
Bass provided by ....Engelhardt-Link
Drums provided by ....Yamaha Corporation of America
Drum Heads provided by ....Remo Drumheads
Cymbals provided by ....Sabian Cymbals
Makeup by ....M•A•C Cosmetics
Makeup Consultant ....Ashley Ryan
Technical Production Assistants ....Alexandra Paull,
Steve Chazaro, Jennie Bownan
Legal Counsel ....Levine Plotkin & Menin, LLP/
Loren H. Plotkin, Cris Criswell
Loeb & Loeb LLP/Douglas Mirell
Accountant ....Rosenberg, Neuwirth &
Kuchner, CPAs/Christopher Cacace,
Marina Flom, Kirill Baytalskiy
Advertising ....Spotco/Drew Hodges, Jim Edwards,
Tom Greenwald, Stephen Sosnowski,
Meghan Ownbey
Marketing ....Carol Chiavetta, Elizabeth Kandel
Type A/Anne Rippey,
John McCoy, Robin Steinthal
Website Design ....Spotco/
Sara Fitzpatrick, Matt Wilstein, Stephen Santore
Payroll Services ....Castellana Services, Inc.
Production Photographer ....Joan Marcus
Management Associate ....Mark Barna
General Management Office ....Christopher Betz,
Jake Hirzel, Jennifer O'Connor,
Aurora Segura

Opening Night Coordination ....The Lawrence Company/
Michael Lawrence
Banking ....Signature Bank, Barbara Von Borstel,
Margaret Monigan, Mary Ann Fanelli
Insurance ....DeWitt Stern Group, Inc./
Peter Shoemaker, Cathy Dumancela
Rehearsed at ....New 42nd Street Studios
Theatre Displays ....King Displays
Merchandising ....Creative Goods Merchandise/
Pete Milano, Jennifer Alam

Tour Bookings ....The Booking Group/
Meredith Blair

SPECIAL THANKS

John R. Cash Revocable Trust. Johnny Cash is a registered trademark of John R. Cash Revocable Trust. Image and likeness of Johnny Cash used with permission.
Jerry Lee Lewis ™, The Killer ™ and the image and likeness of Jerry Lee Lewis are used with permission. Courtesy Pont Neuf, Inc.
Carl Perkins Enterprises. Image and likeness of Carl Perkins used with permission.
Elvis Presley Enterprises, Inc. Elvis Presley is a registered trademark of EPE, Inc. Image and likeness of Elvis Presley used with permission.

CREDITS

Scenery and scenic effects built and electrified by PRG Scenic Technologies, New Windsor, NY. Scenery painted by Scenic Art Studios, Cornwall, NY. Costumes built by Eric Winterling, Inc. Show control and scenic motion control featuring Stage Command Systems® by PRG Scenic Technologies, New Windsor, NY. Lighting equipment provided by PRG Lighting, North Bergen, NJ. Sound equipment provided by PRG Audio, Mt. Vernon, NY. Music license consulting by Jill Meyers.

MUSIC COPYRIGHTS

"Blue Suede Shoes" (Carl Perkins), ©MPL Music Publishing Inc. All rights reserved. Used by permission of Wren Music Co. o/b/o Carl Perkins Music Inc. "Real Wild Child" (John Greenan, John O'Keefe, David Owens), ©MPL Music Publishing Inc. All rights reserved. Used by permission of Wren Music Co. "Matchbox" (Carl Perkins), ©MPL Music Publishing Inc. All rights reserved. Used by permission of Wren Music Co. o/b/o Carl Perkins Music Inc. "Who Do You Love?" (Ellas McDaniel), ©ARC Music Corp. All rights reserved. Used by permission. "Folsom Prison Blues" written by John R. Cash. Published by House of Cash, Inc. Administered by Bug Music Inc. All rights reserved. Used by permission. "Fever" (John Davenport, Eddie Cooley), ©Carlin America Music/Windswept Pacific Music Publishing. Published by Fort Knox Music, Inc. All rights reserved. Used by permission. "Memories Are Made of This" (Richard Dehr, Terry Gilkyson, Frank Miller), ©EMI Blackwood Music, Inc. (BMI). All rights reserved. Used by permission. "That's All Right" (Arthur Crudup), ©1947 (renewed). Unichappell Music Inc. (BMI) and Crudup Music (BMI). All rights administered by Unichappell Music Inc. All rights reserved. Used by permission. "Brown Eyed Handsome Man" (Chuck Berry), ©Arc Music Corp. All rights reserved. Used by permission. "Down by the Riverside" (Traditional; arranged by Chuck Mead), ©Zoilink Music. All rights administered by Coburn Music. All rights reserved. Used by permission. "Sixteen Tons"

(Merle Travis), ©Merle's Girls Music. All rights reserved. Used by permission. "My Babe" (Willie Dixon), ©Bug Music, Inc. o/b/o Hoochie Coochie Music (BMI). All rights reserved. Used by permission. "Long Tall Sally" (Robert Blackwell, Enotris Johnson, Richard Penniman), ©Sony/ATV Music Publishing LLC. All rights reserved. Used by permission. "(There Will Be) Peace in the Valley for Me" (Thomas A. Dorsey), ©(renewed) 1939 Warner-Tamerlane Publishing Corp. (BMI). All rights reserved. Used by permission. "I Walk the Line" written by John R. Cash. Published by House of Cash, Inc. Administered by Bug Music Inc. All rights reserved. Used by permission. "I Hear You Knocking" (Dave Bartholomew, Pearl King), ©EMI Unart Catalog Inc. All rights reserved. Used by permission. "Party" (Jessie Mae Robinson), ©MPL Music Publishing Inc. All rights reserved. Used by permission. "Great Balls of Fire" (Otis Blackwell, Jack Hammer), ©1957 (renewed), Unichappell Music Inc. (BMI), Mijac Music (BMI), Chappell & Co., Inc. (ASCAP) and Mystical Light Music (ASCAP). All rights reserved on behalf of itself and Mijac Music, administered by Unichappell Music Inc. All rights reserved on behalf of itself and Mystical Light Music, administered by Chappell & Co., Inc. All rights reserved. Used by permission. "Hound Dog" (Jerry Leiber and Mike Stoller). Published by Sony/ATV Songs LLC. Copyright 1953 Sony/ATV Music Publishing LLC. All rights administered by Sony/ATV Music Publishing LLC, 8 Music Square West, Nashville TN 37203. All rights reserved. Used by permission. "Riders in the Sky" (Stan Jones), ©MPL Music Publishing Inc. All rights reserved. Used by permission of Edwin H. Morris & Company. "See You Later Alligator" (Robert Guidry), ©]Arc Music Corp. All rights reserved. Used by permission. "Whole Lotta Shakin' Goin' On" (Curly Williams), ©1997 N'Mani Entertainment Co. (ASCAP). All rights reserved. Used by permission.

To learn more about the production,
please visit www.MillionDollarQuartetLive.com
Find us on Facebook.
Follow us on Twitter @MillionDQuartet

NEDERLANDER

Chairman	**James M. Nederlander**
President	**James L. Nederlander**

Executive Vice President
Nick Scandalios

Vice President	Senior Vice President
Corporate Development	Labor Relations
Charlene S. Nederlander	**Herschel Waxman**

Vice President	Chief Financial Officer
Jim Boese	**Freida Sawyer Belviso**

STAFF FOR THE NEDERLANDER THEATRE

House Manager ....Austin Nathaniel
Treasurer ....Anthony Giannone
Assistant Treasurer ....Keshave Sattaur
House Carpenter ....Joseph Ferreri Sr.
Flyman ....Joseph Ferreri Jr.
House Electrician ....Richard Beck
House Properties ....William Wright

Million Dollar Quartet
SCRAPBOOK

Correspondent: Ryan Rossetto, Wardrobe Supervisor

Opening Night Gifts: The cast got iPads and iPods and the crew got a fancy messenger bag!

Most Exciting Celebrity Visitors and What They Did/Said: The real Jerry Lee Lewis came, Bill Clinton came the same night. Jerry Lee has a loaded gun in his jacket. The Secret Service was not amused! Also, the ghost of Elvis came and sat on everyone's toilet.

"Carols for a Cure" Carol: "Run Run Rudolph." They liked it so much they added it to the show! So that, combined with the "Gypsy of the Year" collection speech made the intermissionless show even longer!

Which Actor Performed the Most Roles in This Show: Tom Hanks played all the roles at one point or another.

Special Backstage Rituals: "Places" at our show is sort of a guideline. People may start to get dressed at "places," show up to the theatre, the company manager will take care of business at "places" that could have been taken care of earlier, people decide they need to go home, order from Schnippers' et cetera....

Favorite Moment During Each Performance (On Stage or Off): Trying to decipher the lyrics that Levi Kreis is singing.

Favorite Gathering Place: Bar 41 next door.

Mascot: Ace of Base, there is a shrine to them hidden on the set inside the recording studio.

Embarrassing Moment: One night a woman in the front row was giving her boyfriend a handjob. Yes, seriously! "Whole Lot of Shakin' Goin' On" had new meaning.

Record Number of Cell Phone Rings, Cell Phone Photos, Tweeting or Texting Incidents During a Performance: There are hundreds every night. No one bothers to stop anyone anymore.

What Did You Think of the Web Buzz on Your Show: It was pretty cool!

Memorable Press Encounter: They had a cereal dispenser at the Don Imus show!

Memorable Stage Door Fan Encounter: There was a stalker who snuck into the building. She's not allowed in the building anymore. She's pretty.

Latest Audience Arrival: Our show is an hour and 40 minutes long. A couple once arrived at 9:15 for an 8 o'clock curtain.

Fastest Costume Change: no one changes costumes in our show, thank God, because that would just be one more thing for them to complain about!

Who Wore the Least: Probably the cast of *Hair*.

Catchphrases Only the Company Would Recognize: "Oh Mr. Phillips!" and "Powerfull!"

Best In-House Parody Lyrics: "Come Put Your Cock In" for "I Hear You Knocking."

Memorable Directorial Note: "If we change her shoes it will fix everything!"

Company In-Jokes: Johnny Cash, a cigarette and Victoria Matlock's wig....

Company Legend: Ryan Rossetto

1. At a backstage party celebrating the show's anniversary (L-R):
Jared Wayne Mason, Corey Kaiser, Victoria Matlock, Eddie Clendening, Marilyn Evans Riehl, Elizabeth Stanley, James Moye, Lance Guest, Erik Hayden, Christopher Ryan Grant, Don Peretz and Billy Woodard.
2. A special jam session celebrating the final guest performance of Lee Rocker (C) January 30, 2011.
3. Levi Kreis (top), who plays Jerry Lee Lewis in the show, jams on an encore with the the real-life Jerry Lee Lewis September 9, 2010.

Understudy Anecdote: "Oh, do they still do that? I haven't watched the show in months!"

Nickname: *M$Q*.

Sweethearts Within the Company: In the first year of our run there were six divorces in the company, one quick hookup and a rebound relationship that lasted a few months.

Ghostly Encounters Backstage: Sadly none, not even Lena Horne, but if you listen quietly you can still hear Des McAnuff trying to fix *Guys and Dolls*.

The Motherf**ker With the Hat

First Preview: March 15, 2011. Opened: April 11, 2011.
Still running as of May 31, 2011.

PLAYBILL®

Jackie, an emotional con just released from prison, is working his way through a 12-step drug and alcohol program with the help of his sponsor, Ralphie D. But Jackie's recovery (and parole) are jeopardized when he finds a man's hat in his addict girlfriend's apartment and he sets out to find and punish the hat's owner with the help of his Cousin Julio. But Jackie discovers that life on the Outside can be full of complications and double- and triple-crosses.

CAST

(in order of appearance)

Veronica .... ELIZABETH RODRIGUEZ
Jackie .... BOBBY CANNAVALE
Ralph D. .... CHRIS ROCK
Victoria .... ANNABELLA SCIORRA
Cousin Julio .... YUL VÁZQUEZ

New York City, present day

UNDERSTUDIES

For Veronica, Victoria:
ROSAL COLON
For Ralph D.:
RON CEPHAS JONES
For Jackie, Cousin Julio:
ALFREDO NARCISO

---

⑧ GERALD SCHOENFELD THEATRE

236 West 45th Street
A Shubert Organization Theatre

Philip J. Smith, *Chairman*   Robert E. Wankel, *President*

SCOTT RUDIN   STUART THOMPSON
PUBLIC THEATER PRODUCTIONS   LABYRINTH THEATER COMPANY
FABULA MEDIA PARTNERS LLC   JEAN DOUMANIAN   RUTH HENDEL
CARL MOELLENBERG   JON B. PLATT   TULCHIN BARTNER/JAMIE DE ROY

present

THE MOTHERF**KER WITH THE HAT

by

STEPHEN ADLY GUIRGIS

BOBBY   CHRIS   ELIZABETH   ANNABELLA   YUL
CANNAVALE   ROCK   RODRIGUEZ   SCIORRA   VÁZQUEZ

Scenic Design	Costume Design	Lighting Design	Sound Design
TODD ROSENTHAL	MIMI O'DONNELL	DONALD HOLDER	ACME SOUND PARTNERS

Original Music by	Casting	Production Stage Manager
TERENCE BLANCHARD	JORDAN THALER & HEIDI GRIFFITHS	CHARLES MEANS

Production Management	Press Representative	General Management
AURORA PRODUCTIONS	BONEAU/BRYAN-BROWN	STP/MARSHALL B. PURDY

Directed by

ANNA D. SHAPIRO

THE MOTHERF**KER WITH THE HAT was developed at the Ojai Playwrights Conference and at LAByrinth Theater Company. The Producers wish to express their appreciation to Theatre Development Fund for its support of this production.

4/11/11

(L-R): Bobby Cannavale and Chris Rock

Photo by Joan Marcus

The Motherf**ker With the Hat

Bobby Cannavale
Jackie

Chris Rock
Ralph D.

Elizabeth Rodriguez
Veronica

Annabella Sciorra
Victoria

Yul Vázquez
Cousin Julio

Rosal Colon
*u/s Veronica,
Victoria*

Ron Cephas Jones
u/s Ralph D.

Alfredo Narciso
*u/s Jackie,
Cousin Julio*

Stephen Adly Guirgis
Playwright

Anna D. Shapiro
Director

Todd Rosenthal
Scenic Design

Mimi O'Donnell
Costume Design

Donald Holder
Lighting Design

Terence Blanchard
Composer

Sten Severson, Tom Clark, Mark Menard and Nevin Steinberg,
Acme Sound Partners
Sound Design

Heidi Griffiths and
Jordan Thaler
Casting

Scott Rudin
Producer

Stuart Thompson
Producer

Oskar Eustis,
Artistic Director,
Public Theater
Productions
Producer

Annabella
Sciorra

Photo by Joan Marcus

Joey Parnes,
Executive Director,
Public Theater
Productions
Producer

Danny Feldman,
Managing Director,
LAByrinth Theater
Company
Producer

Chip Meyrelles,
Fabula Media
Partners
Producer

Ken Greiner,
Fabula Media
Partners
Producer

Jean Doumanian
Producer

Ruth Hendel
Producer

Carl Moellenberg
Producer

Jon B. Platt
Producer

Jamie deRoy
Producer

The Motherf**ker With The Hat

SCRAPBOOK

Correspondents: Antonia Gianino, Mike Farfalla and Charles Means.

Memorable Opening Night Event: Justin's (light board operator) son being born.

Opening Night Gifts: *MFWTH* hoodie from Yul and bound *MFWTH* script from the producers.

Most Exciting Celebrity Visitor: Oprah.

Special Backstage Ritual: The Mofo's meeting at five-minute call.

Favorite Moment During Each Performance: "Wow."

Favorite In-Theatre Gathering Place: Stage left by the calling desk.

Favorite Off-Site Hangouts: Bar Centrale, Bowling at Bowlmore between shows.

Favorite Snack Food: Heath bars.

Mascot: Little fuzzy bear that grips and shit.

Favorite Therapy: Schnipper's.

Most Memorable Ad-Libs: "I love you, Chris Rock." "Line." "Moralistic."

Memorable Press Encounter: Michael Riedel's column in the *Post* the day we started press previews.

Latest Audience Arrival: Forty minutes late on a 90-minute show!

Fastest Costume Change: Bobby into Scene 6 —10 seconds.

Busiest Day at the Box Office: The day after opening.

Who Wore the Heaviest/Hottest Costume: Bobby's blue jacket.

Who Wore the Least: Elizabeth.

Catchphrase Only the Company Would Recognize: "I'm Chuck and I don't give a f**k."

Memorable Directorial Note: All of Anna's notes are memorable.

Company In-Joke: High Five.

Nicknames: "Chrisser," "Bob," "Mofo's."

Sweethearts Within the Company: MF + CM.

Embarrassing Moment: The Mofo hat left on stage after Scene 1 the night the *New York Times* was in the house.

Ghostly Encounters Backstage: A ghost in Bobby's dressing room keeps turning on the hot water.

Coolest Thing About Being in This Show: The title.

2010-2011 AWARDS

DRAMA DESK AWARD
Outstanding Actor in a Play
(Bobby Cannavale)

OUTER CRITICS CIRCLE AWARD
Outstanding Featured Actress in a Play
(Elizabeth Rodriguez)

THEATRE WORLD AWARD
Lunt-Fontanne Award
for Ensemble Excellence
(Bobby Cannavale, Chris Rock, Annabella Sciorra, Elizabeth Rodriguez and Yul Vázquez)

Mrs. Warren's Profession

First Preview: September 3, 2010. Opened: October 3, 2010.
Closed November 28, 2010 after 35 Previews and 65 Performances.

PLAYBILL

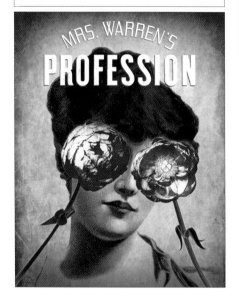

A proper young student is shocked to discover that the source of her family's fortune is a pair of highly profitable brothels employing young ladies not that different from herself. A revival of Socialist playwright George Bernard Shaw's examination of Great Britain's hypocritical attitudes towards the world's oldest capitalistic business.

CAST

(in order of appearance)

Vivie Warren .... Sally Hawkins
Mr. Praed .... Edward Hibbert
Mrs. Kitty Warren .... Cherry Jones
Sir George Crofts .... Mark Harelik
Frank Gardner .... Adam Driver
Reverend Samuel Gardner .... Michael Siberry

Time: Late Summer   **Place:** England

Act I: Wednesday afternoon in a cottage garden
near Haslemere, Surrey
Act II: Inside the cottage around nightfall
Act III: Late next morning in
a rectory garden nearby
Act IV: Two days later in Honoria Fraser's chambers,
Chancery Lane, London

UNDERSTUDIES/STANDBYS

For Vivie Warren: STEPHANIE JANSSEN
For Mrs. Kitty Warren: CHARLOTTE MAIER
For Mr. Praed, Sir George Crofts,
Reverend Samuel Gardner: PETER BRADBURY
For Frank Gardner: CARY DONALDSON

Continued on next page

AMERICAN AIRLINES THEATRE

ROUNDABOUTTHEATRECOMPANY

Todd Haimes, Artistic Director
Harold Wolpert, Managing Director
Julia C. Levy, Executive Director

Presents

Cherry Jones   Sally Hawkins

in

MRS. WARREN'S
PROFESSION

By
George Bernard Shaw

with

Adam Driver Mark Harelik Edward Hibbert Michael Siberry

Set Design Scott Pask	*Costume Design* Catherine Zuber	*Lighting Design* Kenneth Posner	*Original Music and Sound Design* David Van Tieghem
Hair and Wig Design Tom Watson	*Dialect Consultant* Elizabeth Smith	*Production Stage Manager* James FitzSimmons	*Production Management* Aurora Productions

Casting by Jim Carnahan, C.S.A. & Carrie Gardner, C.S.A.	*General Manager* Rebecca Habel	*Press Representative* Boneau/Bryan-Brown

Director of Marketing and Sales Promotion David B. Steffen	*Director of Development* Lynne Gugenheim Gregory	*Founding Director* Gene Feist	*Associate Artistic Director* Scott Ellis

Directed by
Doug Hughes

Lead support provided by Roundabout's Play Production Fund Partners: Beth and Ravenel Curry
Roundabout Theatre Company is a member of the League of Resident Theatres.
www.roundabouttheatre.org

10/3/10

(L-R): Sally Hawkins,
Cherry Jones

Photo by Joan Marcus

Mrs. Warren's Profession

STAGE MANAGEMENT
(L-R): James FitzSimmons, Bryce McDonald, Morgan Holbrook

BOX OFFICE
(L-R): Ted Osborne, Solangel Bido, Mead Margulies

WARDROBE
(L-R): Kat Martin, Susan Fallon, Lauren Gallitelli

Cast Continued

Production Stage Manager:
JAMES FITZSIMMONS
Stage Manager: BRYCE MCDONALD

Sally Hawkins is appearing with the permission of
Actors' Equity Association.

Photos by Brian Mapp

Cherry Jones
Mrs. Kitty Warren

Sally Hawkins
Vivie Warren

Adam Driver
Frank Gardner

Mark Harelik
Sir George Crofts

Edward Hibbert
Mr. Praed

Michael Siberry
Reverend Samuel Gardner

Peter Bradbury
u/s Praed, Sir George Crofts, Reverend Gardner

Cary Donaldson
u/s Frank Gardner

Stephanie Janssen
Standby Vivie Warren

Charlotte Maier
Standby Mrs. Kitty Warren

George Bernard Shaw
Playwright

Doug Hughes
Director

Scott Pask
Set Designer

Catherine Zuber
Costume Designer

Kenneth Posner
Lighting Designer

Tom Watson
Hair and Wig Design

Elizabeth Smith
Dialect Consultant

Jim Carnahan
Casting

Gene Feist
Founding Director, Roundabout Theatre Company

Todd Haimes
Artistic Director, Roundabout Theatre Company

Mrs. Warren's Profession

Photos by Brian Mapp

FRONT OF HOUSE STAFF
Front Row (L-R): Crystal Suarez,
Taylor Martin

Back Row (L-R): Ilia Diaz,
Christopher Busch

CREW
Front Row (L-R): Sarah K. Conyers, Robert W. Dowling II, Mike Allen,
Christopher Ford

Middle Row (L-R): Jennifer Pesce-Fagant

Back Row (L-R): Brian Maiuri, Richard Holst, Dann Wojnar

HAIR AND WIG SUPERVISOR
Manuela LaPorte

ROUNDABOUT THEATRE COMPANY STAFF
ARTISTIC DIRECTOR ....TODD HAIMES
MANAGING DIRECTOR ....HAROLD WOLPERT
EXECUTIVE DIRECTOR ....JULIA C. LEVY
ASSOCIATE ARTISTIC DIRECTOR ..SCOTT ELLIS

ARTISTIC STAFF
DIRECTOR OF ARTISTIC DEVELOPMENT/
 DIRECTOR OF CASTING ....Jim Carnahan
Artistic Consultant ....Robyn Goodman
Resident Director ....Doug Hughes
Associate Artists ....Mark Brokaw, Scott Elliott,
 Bill Irwin, Joe Mantello,
 Kathleen Marshall, Theresa Rebeck
Literary Manager ....Jill Rafson
Casting Director ....Carrie Gardner
Casting Associate ....Kate Boka
Casting Associate ....Stephen Kopel
Artistic Assistant ....Amy Ashton
Literary Associate ....Josh Fiedler
The Blanche and Irving Laurie Foundation
 Theatre Visions Fund Commissions ....Stephen Karam,
 Nathan Louis Jackson
Educational Foundation of
 America Commissions ....Bekah Brunstetter,
 Lydia Diamond, Diana Fithian,
 Julie Marie Myatt
New York State Council
 on the Arts Commission ....Nathan Louis Jackson
Roundabout Commissions ....Steven Levenson,
 Matthew Lopez, Kim Rosenstock
Casting Interns ....Kyle Bosley, Jillian Cimini,
 Erin Drake, Andrew Femenella,
 Lauren Lewis, Quinn Meyers
Script Readers ....Jay Cohen, Ben Izzo,
 Nicholas Stimler

Artistic Intern ....Alexis Roblan

EDUCATION STAFF
EDUCATION DIRECTOR ....Greg McCaslin
Associate Education Director ....Jennifer DiBella
Education Associate
 for Theatre-Based Programs ....Sarah Malone
Education Program Associate ....Aliza Greenberg
Education Dramaturg ....Ted Sod
Teaching Artists ....Cynthia Babak, Victor Barbella,
 Grace Bell, LaTonya Borsay,
 Mark Bruckner, Joe Clancy, Vanessa Davis,
 Joe Doran, Elizabeth Dunn-Ruiz,
 Carrie Ellman-Larsen, Kevin Free,
 Tony Freeman, Deanna Frieman,
 Natalie Gold, Sheri Graubert,
 Matthew A.J. Gregory, Melissa Gregus,
 Adam Gwon, Devin Haqq,
 Carrie Heitman, Karla Hendrick,
 Jim Jack, Jason Jacobs, Lisa Renee Jordan,
 Jamie Kalama, Alvin Keith,
 Tami Mansfield, Erin McCready, Kyle McGinley,
 Andrew Ondrejcak, Meghan O'Neill,
 Laura Poe, Nicole Press, Jennifer Rathbone,
 Leah Reddy, Amanda Rehbein,
 Bernita Robinson, Christopher Rummel,
 Cassy Rush, Nick Simone, Heidi Stallings,
 Daniel Sullivan, Carl Tallent, Vickie Tanner,
 Jolie Tong, Cristina Vaccaro, Jennifer Varbalow,
 Leese Walker, Eric Wallach, Michael Warner,
 Christina Watanabe, Gail Winar,
 Conwell Worthington, III
Teaching Artist Emeritus ....Reneé Flemings
Teaching Artist Apprentices ....Carrie Ellman-Larsen,
 Deanna Frieman, Meghan O'Neill
Education Intern ....Erin Monahan

ADMINISTRATIVE STAFF
GENERAL MANAGER......................Sydney Beers
Associate Managing Director ....Greg Backstrom
General Manager,
 American Airlines Theatre ....Rebecca Habel
General Manager,
 Steinberg Center ....Rachel E. Ayers
Human Resources Manager ....Stephen Deutsch
Operations Manager ....Valerie D. Simmons
Associate General Manager ....Maggie Cantrick
Office Manager ....Scott Kelly
Management Associate ....Jill K. Boyd
Archivist ....Tiffany Nixon
Receptionists ....Dee Beider, Raquel Castillo,
 Elisa Papa, Allison Patrick,
 Monica Sidorchuk
Messenger ....Darnell Franklin
Management Intern ....Elizabeth Johnstone
Archives Intern ....Matthew Kagen

FINANCE STAFF
DIRECTOR OF FINANCE.................Susan Neiman
Payroll Director ....John LaBarbera
Accounts Payable Manager ....Frank Surdi
Payroll Benefits Administrator ....Yonit Kafka
Manager Financial Reporting ....Joshua Cohen
Business Office Assistant ....Jackie Verbitski
Business Intern ....Maurice Blackman

DEVELOPMENT STAFF
DIRECTOR OF
 DEVELOPMENT ....Lynne Gugenheim Gregory
Director, Institutional Giving..................Liz S. Alsina
Director, Special Events ....Steve Schaeffer
Associate Director, Individual Giving ....Tyler Ennis
Manager, Telefundraising ....Gavin Brown

Mrs. Warren's Profession

Manager, Corporate Relations .... Roxana Petzold
Manager, Donor Information Systems .... Lise Speidel
Associate Manager, Patron Programs .... Marisa Perry
Patron Services Associate .... Joseph Foster
Assistant to the Executive Director .... Nicole Tingir
Assistant to the Director of Development .... Liz Malta
Institutional Giving Assistant .... Brett Barbour
Development Assistant .... Martin Giannini
Special Events Assistant .... Amy Rosenfield
Development Interns .... Emma Acciani,
Sophia Hinshelwood

INFORMATION TECHNOLOGY STAFF
IT DIRECTOR .... Antonio Palumbo
IT Associate .... Dylan Norden
IT Associate .... Jim Roma
DIRECTOR DATABASE
OPERATIONS .... Wendy Hutton
Database Administrator/Programmer .... Revanth Anne

MARKETING STAFF
DIRECTOR OF MARKETING
AND SALES PROMOTION .... David B. Steffen
Associate Director of Marketing .... Tom O'Connor
Senior Marketing Manager .... Shannon Marcotte
Digital Marketing Manager .... Lauren Brender
Website Consultant .... Keith Powell Beyland
Director of Telesales
Special Promotions .... Marco Frezza
Telesales Manager .... Patrick Pastor
Marketing Intern .... Bradley Sanchez

TICKET SERVICES STAFF
Director of Sales Operations .... Charlie Garbowski, Jr.
Ticket Services Manager .... Ellen Holt
Acting Subscription Manager .... Bill Klemm
Box Office Managers .... Edward P. Osborne,
Jaime Perlman, Krystin MacRitchie,
Nicole Nicholson
Group Sales Manager .... Jeff Monteith
Assistant Box Office Managers .... Robert Morgan,
Andrew Clements, Scott Falkowski,
Catherine Fitzpatrick
Assistant Ticket Services Managers .... Robert Kane,
Lindsay Ericson
Acting Assistant Ticket Services
Manager .... Jessica Pruett-Barnett
Customer Services Coordinator .... Thomas Walsh
Ticket Services .... Solangel Bido, Arianna Boykins,
Lauren Cartelli, Joseph Clark,
Nisha Dhruna, Adam Elsberry,
Joseph Gallina, James Graham,
Kara Harrington, Tova Heller,
Nicki Ishmael, Kate Longosky,
Michelle Maccarone, Elisa Mala,
Mead Margulies, Laura Marshall,
Chuck Migliaccio, Carlos Morris,
Bekah Nutt, Hillary Parker,
Kaia Rafoss, Josh Rozett,
Ben Schneider, Kenneth Senn,
Heather Siebert, Nalane Singh,
Lillian Soto, Ron Tobia,
Hannah Weitzman
Ticket Services Intern .... Lindsay Hoffman

SERVICES
Counsel .... Paul, Weiss,
Rifkind, Wharton and Garrison LLP,
Charles H. Googe Jr., Carol M. Kaplan
Counsel .... Rosenberg & Estis
Counsel .... Andrew Lance,
Gibson, Dunn, & Crutcher, LLP
Counsel .... Harry H. Weintraub,
Glick and Weintraub, P.C.
Counsel .... Stroock & Stroock & Lavan LLP
Counsel .... Daniel S. Dokos,
Weil, Gotshal & Manges LLP
Immigration Counsel .... Mark D. Koestler and
Theodore Ruthizer
Counsel .... Claudia Wagner/
Manatt, Phelps & Phillips, LLP
House Physicians .... Dr. Theodore Tyberg,
Dr. Lawrence Katz
House Dentist .... Neil Kanner, D.M.D.
Insurance .... DeWitt Stern Group, Inc.
Accountant .... Lutz & Carr CPAs, LLP
Advertising .... Spotco/
Drew Hodges, Jim Edwards,
Tom Greenwald, Kyle Hall,
Cory Spinney
Interactive Marketing .... Situation Interactive/
Damian Bazadona, John Lanasa,
Eric Bornemann, Randi Fields
Events Photography .... Anita and Steve Shevett
Production Photographer .... Carol Rosegg
Theatre Displays .... King Displays, Wayne Sapper
Lobby Refreshments .... Sweet Concessions
Merchandising .... Spotco Merch/
James Decker

MANAGING DIRECTOR
EMERITUS .... Ellen Richard

Roundabout Theatre Company
231 West 39th Street, New York, NY 10018
(212) 719-9393.

GENERAL PRESS REPRESENTATIVES
BONEAU/BRYAN-BROWN
Adrian Bryan-Brown
Matt Polk   Jessica Johnson   Amy Kass

STAFF FOR *MRS. WARREN'S PROFESSION*
Company Manager .... Carly DiFulvio
Production Stage Manager .... James FitzSimmons
Stage Manager .... Bryce McDonald
Production Management by ..... Aurora Productions Inc./
Gene O'Donovan, W. Benjamin Heller II,
Stephanie Sherline, Jarid Sumner,
Liza Luxenberg, Ryan Stanisz,
Jason Margolis, Melissa Mazdra
Assistant Director .... Alexander Greenfield
Associate Scenic Designer .... Frank McCullough
Assistant Scenic Designers .... Lauren Alvarez,
Jeff Hinchee
Assistant Costume Designer .... Nicole Moody
Assistant to the Costume Designer .... Ryan Park
Assistant Lighting Designer .... Peter Hoerburger
Associate Sound Designer .... Brandon Wolcott
Additional Dialect Coaching .... Deborah Hecht
Production Properties Supervisor .... Peter Sarafin

PRODUCTION
Production Carpenter .... Glenn Merwede
Production Electrician .... Brian Maiuri
Running Properties .... Robert W. Dowling II
Sound Operator .... Dann Wojnar
Flyman .... Mike Allen
Automation Operator .... Richard Holst
Stagehand/Props .... Jennifer Fagant
Wardrobe Supervisor .... Susan J. Fallon
Dressers .... Cathy Cline, Kat Martin
Wardrobe Dayworker .... Lauren Gallitelli
Hair and Wig Supervisor .... Manuela LaPorte
Production Assistant .... Morgan R. Holbrook
Rehearsal PA .... James Steele
IA Apprentice .... Sarah K. Conyers
Assistant to Mr. Posner .... Jelani Eastmond
Scenery Fabrication, Show Control &
Scenic Motion Control by .... Scenic Technologies,
a Division of Production Resource Group, LLC
Scenery Fabrication by .... Great Lakes Scenic Studios,
Burlington, Ontario
Scenery Fabrication by .... Showman Fabricators, Inc.,
Long Island City, NY
Lighting Equipment provided by .... PRG Lighting,
a division of Production Resource Group, LLC
Sound provided by .... Sound Associates
Costumes constructed by .... EuroCo Costumes,
Arnold Levine, Angels the Costumiers,
Brian Hemesath
Partners Desk built by .... Craig Grigg
Arts and Crafts Writing Desk built by .... Chris Elliott
Garden Statue built by .... Scenic Technologies,
a Division of Production Resource Group, LLC
Prop Lighting Wiring .... Garin Marshall

M•A•C Cosmetics
Official Makeup of Roundabout Theatre Company

To learn more about Roundabout Theatre Company,
please visit roundabouttheatre.org
Find us on Facebook.

AMERICAN AIRLINES THEATRE STAFF
Company Manager .... Carly DiFulvio
House Carpenter .... Glenn Merwede
House Electrician .... Brian Maiuri
House Properties .... Robert W. Dowling II
House Sound .... Dann Wojnar
IA Apprentice .... Sarah K. Conyers
Wardrobe Supervisor .... Susan J. Fallon
Box Office Manager .... Ted Osborne
Assistant Box Office .... Robert Morgan
House Manager .... Stephen Ryan
Associate House Manager .... Zipporah Aguasvivas
Head Usher .... Ilia Diaz
House Staff .... Anne Ezell, Denise Furbert,
Edlyn Gonzalez, Lee Henry,
Paul Krasner, Rebecca Knell,
Taylor Martin, Joaquin Melendez,
Ariana Murphy, Argenis Peguero,
Celia Perez, Fatimah Robinson,
Crystal Suarez, Adam Wier
Security .... Julious Russell
Additional Security provided by .... Gotham Security
Maintenance .... Jerry Hobbs, Daniel Pellew,
Willie Philips, Magali Western
Lobby Refreshments .... Sweet Concessions

Mrs. Warren's Profession
SCRAPBOOK

Correspondent: Bryce McDonald, Stage Manager

Memorable Opening Night Letters, Faxes or Notes: We didn't get as many as when we opened Off-Broadway, but we got some really nice ones from *Next to Normal; Promises, Promises* and *Pitmen Painters*. We also got lots of shout-outs to Cherry Jones and Edward Hibbert because people knew them from their many other shows.

Opening Night Gifts: There was a lot of wine and other beverages given out. Who does not love a good bottle of wine?

Most Exciting Celebrity Visitors: Cherry and Edward have a lot of famous friends, but they come to see the show and then they will go and wait at Bar Centrale. We don't have a big flood backstage. Sweet Marian Seldes was here on opening night and was so gracious to everyone. Marian told Cherry, "I believe that Cherry Jones is the future of the American stage."

Who Has Done the Most Shows in Their Career: Edward Hibbert, I believe.

Special Backstage Ritual: Coffee is a big ritual on this show. Cherry and Edward like it to be ready at 6:35 and production assistant Morgan Holbrook makes them a custom blend of two different coffees.

Favorite Moment During Each Performance (On Stage or Off): The end of Act I Scene 1. When the curtain comes down we have be ready to go into a huge scenery shift. Cherry must exit stage left for a big costume change and there is under a minute until the next scene. Everyone else runs stage right. Adam Driver charges through like a madman and we do a high five.

Favorite In-Theatre Gathering Place: Edward Hibbert's dressing room, known as "Praeddy's Place" (his name in the show is Praed). Edward can hold court with the best of them. He receives guests in his dressing room like a prince. We do talkbacks with the audience on certain nights, after which we hang out in Edward's dressing room for little dinners if there is extra food and wine. He sometimes hosts a Prosecco party and we sit on his couch and share wine and stories.

Favorite Off-Site Hangout: We sometimes go to Bar Centrale but our everyday meeting place is Rosie O'Grady's on 46th Street on the wrong side of Broadway. They're very good to us. People don't know this gem of a bar is there. They have a jukebox upstairs and they keep the kitchen open late for us. It's like a private cast party. There's a group from Fox News that leaves about 10 p.m. We come in about 10:30 and have the bar for the rest of the night. The TV plays sports, but you can turn it to something else if you want. You can sit by the window and look out at the Times Square crowd. It's so laid back.

Internet Buzz on the Show: It's been fairly positive, but I always think it could be more positive. In general we all try to stay away from it so that no negativity gets through.

1. (L-R) Sally Hawkins, Edward Hibbert and Cherry Jones at the opening night party at the American Airlines Theatre.
2. (L-R): Adam Driver, Edward Hibbert, Sally Hawkins, Cherry Jones, Mark Harelik and Michael Siberry take bows on opening night.

Favorite Snack Food: We are the candy eatingest bunch I've ever seen. We go through it like mad: Snickers, Milky Ways, Nerds, Sweettarts. If it's chocolate and you put it out at 6:30, by 7:15 it will be gone, and it's like, "Where's the candy?"

Favorite Therapies: Ricola and Altoids are our therapy right now. It's all about the throat.

Memorable Ad-Lib: None. Shaw's language has such a rhythm that you can't really change it. If you walk through the dressing room area you can hear the actors run through the entire show before the curtain each night. It's like vocal warmups, but they're doing it to Shaw.

Cell Phone Incidents During a Performance: We've had the dreaded cell phones a lot—usually at least one a night. The worst was during the very exciting coup de gras scene at the end of the show: very emotional and heightened and pivotal. On this night a woman let her phone ring four separate times and refused to acknowledge it or turn it off. It sounded like an old home phone, as loud as loud could be. But she just let it ring and ring!

Who Wore the Heaviest/Hottest Costume: It might be Cherry. Cathy Zuber is such a brilliant designer. Her clothes are very much of that period, the late 19th century, so Cherry had a lot of layers over a corset. But no one complained, including the men who were in three-piece suits. We also kept the theatre at a good cool temperature.

Nickname: Edward calls Cherry "Cher."

Coolest Thing About Being in This Show: Cherry Jones!

Next to Normal

First Preview: March 27, 2009. Opened: April 15, 2009.
Closed January 16, 2011 after 21 Previews and 733 Performances.

PLAYBILL®

This Pulitzer Prize-winning musical presents a portrait of a woman who is coping with a mental illness that is gradually destroying her sanity, her marriage and her family life, and which responds erratically to treatment.

CAST
(in alphabetical order)

Henry	ADAM CHANLER-BERAT
Dan	JASON DANIELEY
Natalie	MEGHANN FAHY
Dr. Madden/Dr. Fine	LOUIS HOBSON
Gabe	KYLE DEAN MASSEY
Diana	MARIN MAZZIE

UNDERSTUDIES and STANDBYS

Standby for Diana: KATHY VOYTKO
Standby for Dan: MICHAEL BERRY
Understudy for Dr. Madden/Dr. Fine:
MICHAEL BERRY
For Natalie: MacKENZIE MAUZY,
EMMA HUNTON
For Gabe, Henry: BRIAN CRUM

DANCE CAPTAIN

BRIAN CRUM

BAND

Conductor/Piano: CHARLIE ALTERMAN
Violin/Keyboard: YUIKO KAMAKARI
Cello: ALISA HORN
Guitars: ERIC B. DAVIS
Bass: MICHAEL BLANCO

Continued on next page

⊛ BOOTH THEATRE
222 West 45th Street
A Shubert Organization Theatre

Philip J. Smith, *Chairman*   Robert E. Wankel, *President*

DAVID STONE
JAMES L. NEDERLANDER   BARBARA WHITMAN   PATRICK CATULLO
SECOND STAGE THEATRE
Carole Rothman   Ellen Richard

present

MARIN MAZZIE   JASON DANIELEY

next to normal

music by
TOM KITT

book and lyrics by
BRIAN YORKEY

also starring

KYLE DEAN MASSEY
MEGHANN FAHY
ADAM CHANLER-BERAT   LOUIS HOBSON

MICHAEL BERRY   BRIAN CRUM   EMMA HUNTON
MacKENZIE MAUZY   KATHY VOYTKO

set design by	costume design by	lighting design by	sound design by
MARK WENDLAND	**JEFF MAHSHIE**	**KEVIN ADAMS**	**BRIAN RONAN**

orchestrations by
MICHAEL STAROBIN and TOM KITT

vocal arrangements	music director	music coordinator
ANNMARIE MILAZZO	**CHARLIE ALTERMAN**	**MICHAEL KELLER**

casting	press representative
TELSEY + COMPANY	**THE HARTMAN GROUP**

production stage manager	technical supervisor	general management
JUDITH SCHOENFELD	**LARRY MORLEY**	**321 THEATRICAL MANAGEMENT**

musical staging by
SERGIO TRUJILLO

directed by
MICHAEL GREIF

The World Premiere of **next to normal** was presented by Second Stage Theatre on February 13, 2008.
next to normal was subsequently presented at Arena Stage, Washington D.C. in November 2008.
The producers wish to express their appreciation to Theatre Development Fund for its support of this production.
Original Broadway Cast Recording on GHOSTLIGHT RECORDS

(L-R): Kyle Dean Massey,
Marin Mazzie and
Jason Danieley

Photo by Joan Marcus

Next to Normal

Cast Continued

Drums/Percussion: SHANNON FORD
Drum and Additional Percussion Arrangements by
DAMIEN BASSMAN

Additional Guitar Arrangements by
MICHAEL AARONS

Music Coordinator: MICHAEL KELLER
Copyist: EMILY GRISHMAN MUSIC
PREPARATION

Photo by Joan Marcus

(L-R): Kyle Dean Massey, Jason Danieley, Adam Chanler-Berat and Meghann Fahy

Marin Mazzie
Diana

Jason Danieley
Dan

Kyle Dean Massey
Gabe

Meghann Fahy
Natalie

Adam Chanler-Berat
Henry

Louis Hobson
Dr. Madden/Dr. Fine

Michael Berry
Standby for Dan

Brian Crum
*u/s Gabe, Henry,
Dance Captain*

Emma Hunton
u/s Natalie

MacKenzie Mauzy
u/s Natalie

Kathy Voytko
Standby for Diana

Tom Kitt
*Composer/
Co-Orchestrator*

Brian Yorkey
Librettist/Lyricist

Michael Greif
Director

Sergio Trujillo
Musical Staging

Mark Wendland
Set Design

Jeff Mahshie
Costume Design

Kevin Adams
Lighting Design

Brian Ronan
Sound Design

Charlie Alterman
Musical Director

Michael Starobin
Co-Orchestrator

AnnMarie Milazzo
Vocal Arrangements

Michael Keller
Music Coordinator

Bernard Telsey,
Telsey + Company
Casting

Marcia Goldberg, Nancy Nagel Gibbs and
Nina Essman,
321 Theatrical Management
General Management

Laura Pietropinto
Assistant Director

Dontee Kiehn
*Associate
Choreographer*

Next to Normal

David Stone
Producer

James L.
Nederlander
Producer

Barbara Whitman
Producer

Patrick Catullo
Producer

Carole Rothman,
Artistic Director,
Second Stage
Theatre
Producer

Jennifer Damiano
Natalie

Brian d'Arcy James
Dan

Curt Hansen
u/s Gabe

Adam Kantor
u/s Henry

Michael McElroy
*u/s Dr. Madden/
Dr. Fine*

Jessica Phillips
*Dance Captain,
Standby for Diana*

Alice Ripley
Diana

Asa Somers
*u/s Dan, Dr. Madden/
Dr. Fine*

Adam Kantor
u/s Henry

Catherine Porter
Standby for Diana

BAND
Hiroko Taguchi
(Violin/Synth sub),
Yuiko Kamakari
(Violin/Synth),
Eric Davis (Guitar),
Charlie Alterman
(Piano/Conductor),
Michael Blanco
(Bass),
Alisa Horn (Cello),
Shannon Ford
(Drums/Percussion)

Next to Normal

SCRAPBOOK

Correspondent: Meghann Fahy, "Natalie"

Most Exciting Celebrity Visitors: We've had everyone from Bill Clinton to Barbra Streisand, but my favorite celebrity visitor was Mariska Hargitay from "Law and Order: SVU." She said she wanted me on the show. I'm still waiting....

Favorite Part of Each Performance: I love Act II. From "Why Stay/ A Promise" through the end of the show is my favorite part.

Favorite Off-Site Hangout: Kodama. Best sushi ever.

Favorite Snack Food: Anything on the snack shelf (the windowsill outside of the SM office).

Mascot: Marin and Jason's miniature schnauzer, Oscar.

Favorite Therapies: Throat Coat Tea, Entertainer's Secret, Grether's Pastilles and swearing a lot during the show.

Memorable Ad-Lib: Whenever Louis forgets a line he stays in character and just says "uhh...uh...uh...."

Memorable Stage Door Fan Encounter: It's really special when people share stories of how they identify with the show and how it's affected their lives. And people who have gotten *Next to Normal* tattoos.

Fastest Costume Change: During "Just Another Day," changing from my PJ's to my outfit for school. I only have till the end of Dan's verse.

Catchphrase Only the Company Would Recognize: "Hello, please."

Sweetheart Within the Company: Jason Danieley: Every Tuesday he brings candy around to every member of the company.

Memorable Directorial Note: "Clubs are to get sexual."

Company Legend: Alice Ripley

Understudy Anecdote: I once had to go on during the middle of Act II when I was an understudy because Jenn Damiano got hit by a moving set piece.

Embarrassing Moment: At the top of Act II during the scene before "Wish I Were Here" Adam and I pull on each other. Once when he let go of me I had a lot of momentum going the opposite direction. I was tripping for an unreasonable amount of time and then eventually fell on my face. The "Oooooh!" from the audience was audible.

Coolest Thing About Being in This Show: Helping to tell the story, and to be a part of something so profound and fulfilling.

Photo by Brian Mapp

CREW

Front Row (L-R): Robert Witherow, Sally E. Sibson, Sara Jayne Darneille, Christopher Sloan, Susan Goulet, Judith Schoenfeld

Back Row (L-R): Vangeli Kaseluris, Jenny Scheer-Montgomery, Kyle LaColla, Elizabeth Berkeley, Angelo Grasso, Kenneth McDonough, Timmy McWilliams

---

STAFF FOR *NEXT TO NORMAL*

GENERAL MANAGEMENT
321 THEATRICAL MANAGEMENT
Nina Essman   Nancy Nagel Gibbs
Marcia Goldberg

CASTING
TELSEY + COMPANY
Bernie Telsey CSA, Will Cantler CSA, David Vaccari CSA,
Bethany Knox CSA, Craig Burns CSA,
Tiffany Little Canfield CSA, Rachel Hoffman CSA,
Carrie Rosson CSA, Justin Huff CSA, Bess Fifer CSA,

Patrick Goodwin, Abbie Brady-Dalton

GENERAL PRESS REPRESENTATIVE
THE HARTMAN GROUP
Michael Hartman
Tom D'Ambrosio   Michelle Bergmann

Next to Normal

TECHNICAL SUPERVISOR .... Larry Morley

COMPANY MANAGER .... Lisa Koch Rao

PRODUCTION STAGE MANAGER .. Judith Schoenfeld
Stage Manager .... Shawn Pennington
Assistant Stage Manager .... Sally E. Sibson
Assistant Director .... Laura Pietropinto
Associate Choreographer .... Dontee Kiehn
Assistant Music Director .... Mat Eisenstein
Associate Lighting Designer .... Joel E. Silver
Associate Sound Designer .... David Stollings
Assistant Scenic Designer .... Rachel Nemec
Assistant Lighting Designers .... Paul Toben,
Aaron Sporer
Lighting Programmer .... Michael Pitzer
Scenic Design Assistants .... Jonathan Collins,
Shoko Kambara
Associate Technical Supervisor .... Bradley Thompson
Dance Captain .... Brian Crum
Assistant to Mr. Kitt and Mr. Yorkey .... Brandon Ivie
Production Carpenter .... Bill Craven
Production Electrician .... Richard Mortell
Production Audio .... Mike Farfalla
Carpenter .... Kenneth McDonough
Flyman .... Ed White
Electrician .... Susan Goulet
Props .... James Keane
Sound Engineer .... Beth Berkeley
Asst. Sound Engineer .... Elspeth Appleby
Wardrobe Supervisor .... Kyle LaColla
Dressers .... Sara Jayne Darneille,
Vangeli Kaseluris
Music Preparation .... Emily Grishman/
Emily Grishman Music Preparation Inc.
Assistant to Mr. Stone .... Aaron Glick
Assts. to the
General Managers .... Mattea Cogliano-Benedict,
Petrina Moritz
Management Associate .... Kate Elliott
Production Assistant .... Stuart Shefter
Advertising .... Serino Coyne Inc./
Greg Corradetti, Joaquin Esteva
Interactive Marketing .... Situation Interactive
Merchandising .... The Araca Group
Legal Counsel .... Schreck, Rose and Dapello/
Nancy Rose, David Berlin
Director of Finance .... John DiMeglio
Accountant .... FK Partners CPA's LLP/
Robert Fried
Banking .... JPMorgan Chase/
Stefanie Boger, Salvatore Romano
Insurance .... AON/Albert G. Ruben Insurance/
Claudia Kaufman, Susan Weiss
Payroll Service .... Castellana Services Inc.
Production Photography .... Joan Marcus

Group Sales: Shubert Group Sales
800-432-7780

321 THEATRICAL MANAGEMENT
Roeya Banuazizi, Bob Brinkerhoff, Amy Merlino Coey, Eric
Cornell, Tara Geesaman, Margie McGlone, Alex Owen, Kat
Ramsburg, Susan Sampliner, Greg Schaffert, Ken Silverman

Earlier development of *Next to Normal*
was made possible by:

THE JONATHAN LARSON FOUNDATION

THE NEW YORK MUSIC THEATRE FESTIVAL
Isaac Robert Hurwitz, Executive Producer

VILLAGE THEATRE
Issaquah, Washington
Robb Hunt, Executive Producer/
Steve Tomkins, Artistic Director

SECOND STAGE THEATRE
Artistic Director .... Carole Rothman
Executive Director .... Casey Reitz
Associate Artistic Director .... Christopher Burney
Production Manager .... Jeff Wild
Technical Director .... Robert Mahon
Director of Finance .... Janice B. Cwill
General Manager .... Don-Scott Cooper
Literary Manager .... Sarah Steele
Director of Marketing .... Laura DiLorenzo
Ticket Services Manager .... Greg Turne

SECOND STAGE THEATRE BOARD OF TRUSTEES
Anthony C.M. Kiser, *Chairman Emeritus*
Stephen C. Sherrill, *Chairman*
Hamilton E. James (*President*), Suzanne Davidson
(*Treasurer*), Mary Moran (*Secretary*), David A. Ackert,
Elizabeth C. Berens, Elizabeth H. Berger, Tavener Holmes
Berry, Susan Braddock, Jeffrey H. Bunzel, Sally D. Clement,
Lawrence G. Creel, Judy Davis, Carla Emil, Frances D.
Fergusson, Wendy Evans Joseph, Steven B. Klinsky, Terry
Lindsay, George S. Loening, Patti LuPone, Timothy J.
McClimon, Anne McMillen, John Partilla, Bambi Putnam,
Kirk A. Radke, Lynne Randall, Donna Rosen, Michael
Rothfeld, Carole Rothman, Joshua Ruch, Nathan E. Saint-
Amand, Didi Schafer, John Schmidt, Michael E. Singer,
John M. Sullivan, Jr., Ann Tenenbaum, James E. Thomas,
Nancy Walker, Candace Weir

The development of *Next to Normal* at Second Stage Theatre
was supported by the Edgerton Foundation, the Jonathan
Larson Foundation, the National Endowment for the Arts
and the New York City Department of Cultural Affairs.

ARENA STAGE
Artistic Director .... Molly Smith
Managing Director .... Edgar Dobie
Director of Communications .... Chad M. Bauman
Director of Finance and
Administration .... Joe Berardelli
Associate Artistic Director .... David Dower
Technical Director .... Jim Glendinning
Production Manager .... Carey Lawless
Director of Community
Engagement .... Anita Maynard-Losh
Chief Development Officer .... Carmel Owen

ARENA STAGE BOARD
Chair: Mark Shugoll. Vice Chairs: Guy Bergquist, Michele
G. Berman, Susan Haas Bralove, John M. Derrick Jr., Terry
R. Peel, Les Silverman. Secretary: Ronald A. Paul, M.D.
Treasurer: Hubert M. Schlosberg. Andrew R. Ammerman,
Ashok Bajaj, Steven R. Bralove, David S. Broder, Donald de
Laski, Nancy de Laski, Gina H. Despres, Wendy L. Farrow,
Nancy M. Folger, Ellen K. Harrison, Fruzsina Harsanyi,
Joseph H. Jarboe, Margot Kelly, W. Buford Lewis, B.

Thomas Mansbach, Beverly Perry, William S. Sessions,
David E. Shiffrin, Molly Smith, Richard W. Snowdon,
Roderic L. Woodson. Honorary Board: Susan Clampitt,
Allan D. Cors, Fred Grandy, Priscilla Dewey Houghton,
Judy Lansing Kovler, David O. Maxwell, Joan P. Maxwell,
Stacey J. Mobley, Judy Lynn Prince, Beth Newburger
Schwartz, Margaret Tomlinson. Life Trustees: Norman
Bernstein, Zelda Fichandler, J. Burke Knapp, Dr. Jaylee M.
Mead, Lee G. Rubenstein. Emeritus: Joan & Peter Andrews,
Arlene Kogod, Jonathan M. Weisgall

Official Opening Night Party at
THE EDISON BALLROOM

CREDITS
Scenery constructed by Daedalus Design and Production
Inc. Show control and scenic motion control featuring Stage
Command System ®by PRG Scenic Technologies. Lighting
equipment by PRG Lighting. Sound equipment by PRG
Audio. Additional wardrobe provided by Juliana Margulies
and Jessica Weinstein. Prop body by Den Design Studio.
Wig for prop body by J. Jared Janas.

SPECIAL THANKS
The authors would like to thank the following for their
invaluable medical expertise: Dr. Anthony Pietropinto,
MD., Dr. Nancy Elman, PhD., Dr. Quentin Van Meter,
MD.

Piano provided by Steinway & Sons

www.NextToNormal.com

 THE SHUBERT ORGANIZATION, INC.
Board of Directors

House Manager .... Laurel Ann Wilson

The Normal Heart

First Preview: April 19, 2011. Opened: April 27, 2011.
Still running as of May 31, 2011.

PLAYBILL

A revival of Larry Kramer's drama set in the earliest days of the AIDS epidemic, about a crusader who mounts a frustrating campaign to get government, media and the gay community to take the threat seriously.

CAST

(in order of appearance)

Craig Donner	LUKE MACFARLANE
Mickey Marcus	PATRICK BREEN
Ned Weeks	JOE MANTELLO
David	WAYNE ALAN WILCOX
Dr. Emma Brookner	ELLEN BARKIN
Bruce Niles	LEE PACE
Felix Turner	JOHN BENJAMIN HICKEY
Ben Weeks	MARK HARELIK
Tommy Boatwright	JIM PARSONS
Hiram Keebler	RICHARD TOPOL
Grady	LUKE MACFARLANE
Examining Doctor	RICHARD TOPOL

UNDERSTUDIES AND STANDBYS

Alternate for Felix Turner:
WAYNE ALAN WILCOX
Understudy for Dr. Emma Brookner:
JORDAN BAKER
Understudy for Ned Weeks, Ben Weeks, Mickey Marcus, Hiram Keebler/Examining Doctor:
JON LEVENSON
Understudy for Craig Donner/Grady, Bruce Niles, Tommy Boatwright, David:
LEE AARON ROSEN

The action of this play takes place between July, 1981, and May, 1984 in New York City.

GOLDEN THEATRE
A Shubert Organization Theatre
Philip J. Smith, *Chairman*   Robert E. Wankel, *President*

DARYL ROTH
PAUL BOSKIND AND MARTIAN ENTERTAINMENT

IN ASSOCIATION WITH
GREGORY RAE   JAYNE BARON SHERMAN/ALEXANDER FRASER
PRESENT

LARRY KRAMER'S

THE NORMAL HEART

STARRING

ELLEN BARKIN   PATRICK BREEN   MARK HARELIK   JOHN BENJAMIN HICKEY
LUKE MACFARLANE   JOE MANTELLO   LEE PACE
JIM PARSONS   RICHARD TOPOL   WAYNE ALAN WILCOX

SCENIC DESIGN	COSTUME DESIGN	LIGHTING DESIGN
DAVID ROCKWELL	MARTIN PAKLEDINAZ	DAVID WEINER

PROJECTION DESIGN	ORIGINAL MUSIC AND SOUND DESIGN
BATWIN + ROBIN PRODUCTIONS, INC.	DAVID VAN TIEGHEM

CASTING	TECHNICAL SUPERVISOR	PRODUCTION STAGE MANAGER
TELSEY + COMPANY	PETER FULBRIGHT	KAREN ARMSTRONG

PRESS REPRESENTATIVE	MARKETING	GENERAL MANAGEMENT
O&M CO.	SERINO COYNE	101 PRODUCTIONS, LTD.

DIRECTED BY
JOEL GREY & GEORGE C. WOLFE

The producers wish to express their appreciation to Theatre Development Fund
for its support of this production.

4/27/11

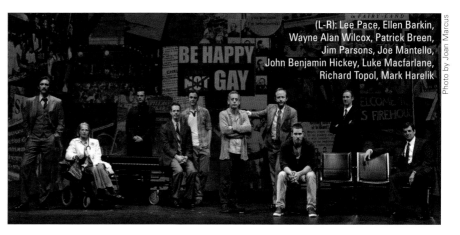

(L-R): Lee Pace, Ellen Barkin, Wayne Alan Wilcox, Patrick Breen, Jim Parsons, Joe Mantello, John Benjamin Hickey, Luke Macfarlane, Richard Topol, Mark Harelik

Photo by Joan Marcus

The Pee-wee Herman Show

First Preview: October 26, 2010. Opened: November 11, 2010.
Closed January 2, 2011 after 18 Previews and 62 Performances.

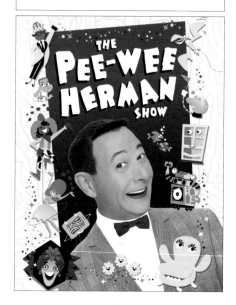

A recreation of the brightly-colored, surreal world of Pee-wee Herman (alter ego of Paul Reubens), originated on stage in the 1980s, and adapted as a free-form kids' TV series (1986-1990).

CAST

(in order of appearance)

Pee-wee Herman ....PAUL REUBENS
Mailman Mike ....JOHN MOODY
Bear ....DREW POWELL
Jambi ....JOHN PARAGON
Sergio ....JESSE GARCIA
Cowboy Curtis..........................PHIL LaMARR
Miss Yvonne ....LYNNE MARIE STEWART
King of Cartoons ....LANCE ROBERTS
Firefighter ....JOSH MEYERS
Voices ....LEXY FRIDELL, JOSH MEYERS,
JOHN PARAGON, DREW POWELL,
LANCE ROBERTS

PUPPETEERS

OLIVER DALZELL, HALEY JENKINS,
MATT LEABO, ERIC NOVAK,
ADAM PAGDON, JESSICA SCOTT,
AMANDA VILLALOBOS, CHRIS DE VILLE

UNDERSTUDIES

For Miss Yvonne:
LEXY FRIDELL
For Cowboy Curtis, Sergio,
King of Cartoons, Bear, Voices:
CAESAR SAMAYOA
For Jambi, Mailman Mike, Firefighter:
DREW POWELL

STEPHEN SONDHEIM THEATRE

SCOTT SANDERS PRODUCTIONS
Adam S. Gordon   Allan S. Gordon   Élan V. McAllister
Roy Miller   Carol Fineman
Scott Zeilinger Productions/Radio Mouse Entertainment
StylesFour Productions/Randy Donaldson/Tim Laczynski

Present

THE PEE-WEE HERMAN SHOW

Production created and conceived by Paul Reubens

Written by
Paul Reubens and Bill Steinkellner
Additional material by John Paragon

Music by Jay Cotton

Starring
Paul Reubens

Lynne Marie Stewart   Phil LaMarr
Lexy Fridell   Jesse Garcia   Josh Meyers   John Moody
John Paragon   Drew Powell   Lance Roberts   Caesar Samayoa

Oliver Dalzell   Haley Jenkins   Matt Leabo   Eric Novak
Adam Pagdon   Jessica Scott   Amanda Villalobos   Chris de Ville

Scenic Design	Costume Design	Lighting Design	Sound Design
David Korins	Ann Closs-Farley	Jeff Croiter	M.L. Dogg
Puppetry	Projection Design	Technical Supervisor	Design Consultant
Basil Twist	Jake Pinholster	Larry Morley/Sam Ellis	Jimmy Cuomo

Cartoon & Film Consultant   Make-up/Hair/Wig Design
Prudence Fenton   Ve Neill

Press Representatives	Marketing/Promotions	Key Art	Advertising
The Hartman Group / ID	TEAM Services	Mixed Business Group	SpotCo

Associate Producers	Production Stage Manager	General Management
Jared Geller	Lois L. Griffing	Richards/Climan, Inc.
David J. Foster		
Anne Caruso		

Associate Producer
Kelly Bush

Directed by
Alex Timbers

Based on the original *The Pee-wee Herman Show* by Paul Reubens, Bill Steinkellner, Phil Hartman, John Paragon,
Edie McClurg, John Moody, Lynne Marie Stewart, Ivan Flores, Brian Seff, Monica Ganas, Tito Larriva
Playhouse design is based on the original "Pee-wee's Playhouse" production design by Gary Panter
Make-up and hair designs based on the original "Pee-wee's Playhouse"

11/11/10

Photo by Joan Marcus

(L-R): Paul Reubens and
Lynne Marie Stewart

The Pee-wee Herman Show

Paul Reubens
*Pee-wee Herman,
Playwright*

Lynne Marie Stewart
Miss Yvonne

Phil LaMarr
Cowboy Curtis

Lexy Fridell
*Chairry, Magic
Screen, Ginger, Fish,
Flowers*

Jesse Garcia
Sergio

Josh Meyers
*Firefighter, Conky,
Clocky, Fish, Randy,
Shamwow*

John Moody
Mailman Mike

John Paragon
*Jambi, Pterri,
Additional Material*

Drew Powell
*Bear, Mr. Window,
Randy, Flowers*

Lance Roberts
*King of Cartoons,
Globey,
Mr. Knucklehead,
Flowers*

Caesar Samayoa
*u/s Cowboy Curtis,
Sergio, King of
Cartoons, Bear,
Voices*

Oliver Dalzell
Puppeteer

Haley Jenkins
Puppeteer

Matt Leabo
Puppeteer

Eric Novak
Puppeteer

Adam Pagdon
*Puppeteer,
Puppet Captain*

Jessica Scott
Puppeteer

Amanda Villalobos
Puppeteer

Chris de Ville
Puppeteer

Alex Timbers
Director

David Korins
Scenic Design

Ann Closs-Farley
Costume Design

Jeff Croiter
Lighting Design

Basil Twist
Puppetry

Wendy Seyb
Choreographer

Jimmy Cuomo
Design Consultant

Prudence Fenton
*Cartoon and Film
Consultant*

Ian Unterman
Associate Director

David R. Richards and Tamar Haimes,
Richards/Climan, Inc.
General Manager

Scott Sanders
Productions
Lead Producer

Allan S. Gordon
Producer

Élan V. McAllister
Producer

Roy Miller
Producer

Scott Zeilinger
Productions
Producer

The Pee-wee Herman Show

Jason E. Grossman,
Radio Mouse
Entertainment
Producer

M. Kilburg Reedy,
Radio Mouse
Entertainment
Producer

John Styles,
StylesFour
Productions
Producer

Dave Clemmons,
StylesFour
Productions
Producer

Jason Styles,
StylesFour
Productions
Producer

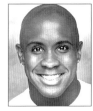

Randy Donaldson
Producer

David J. Foster
Associate Producer

Lute Ramblin Breuer
Puppeteer

STAFF FOR *THE PEE-WEE HERMAN SHOW*

GENERAL MANAGEMENT
RICHARDS/CLIMAN, INC.

DAVID R. RICHARDS   TAMAR HAIMES
Michael Sag   Kyle Bonder
Cesar Hawas   Julianna Slaten

COMPANY MANAGER
Doug Gaeta

GENERAL PRESS REPRESENTATIVES
THE HARTMAN GROUP
Michael Hartman
Tom D'Ambrosio   Michelle Bergmann

ID
Carrie Byalick   Liz Mahoney   Molly Kawachi
Natalie Lent

MARKETING
TEAM SERVICES MARKETING & PROMOTION
Bonnie Werth
James McCune

PRODUCTION
STAGE MANAGER .... **LOIS L. GRIFFING**
Stage Manager .... James D. Latus
Puppet Captain .... Adam Pagdon
Choreography .... Wendy Seyb
L.A. Production Casting .... Bruce H. Neuberg, CSA
NY Casting .... Carrie Gardner, CSA
Associate Director .... Ian Unterman
Assistant Director .... Jeremy Bloom
Associate Scenic Designer .... Rod Lemmond
Assistant Costume Designer .... Kharen Zeunert
Associate Lighting Designer .... Grant W.S. Yaeger
Sound System Designer .... Cody Spencer
Production Sound Engineer .... Francis Elers
Deck Sound .... Jocelyn Smith
Associate Projection Designer .... Daniel Brodie

Assistant Projection Designers .... Price Johnston,
                                           Micah Stieglitz
Production Carpenter .... John J. Tutalo
Production Electrician .... Cletus Karamon
Production Props .... Neil Rosenberg
Audio Effects Operator .... Joshua Maszle
Puppet Consultant .... Sean Johnson, Swazzle Inc.
Miss Yvonne Wig Designer .... Steven Perfidia
Wardrobe Supervisor .... Melissa Crawford
Dresser .... Lauren Oppelt
Make-up/Hair/Wig Supervisor .... Cristina Waltz
Assistants to Paul Reubens .... Allison Berry,
                                              Sarah Sahin
Management for Paul Reubens .... Kelly Bush,
                                          Vie Entertainment
Management Associate for
   Paul Reubens .... Kristina Sorensen,
                                          Vie Entertainment
Merchandising for Paul Reubens .... Beth Goss
Broadway Merchandise .... Pete Milano,
                                            Creative Goods
Attorney for Paul Reubens .... John LaViolette
Business Manager for Paul Reubens .... Robert Philpott
Business Affairs for
   Paul Reubens .... Melody Silverman
Assistant to Scott Sanders .... Jason Grossman
Production Assistants .... Megan J. Alvord,
                                 Stephanie Ward, Alex Hilhorst
Key Art .... Mixed Business Group/
                             Marc Balet, Mark Cline, Ryan Cox
Advertising .... SpotCo./
                                  Drew Hodges, Jim Edwards,
                                 Tom McCann, Josh Fraenkel
Banking .... City National Bank/
                                          Michele Gibbons
Accountant .... Fried & Kowgios, CPA's LLP/
                                          Robert Fried, CPA
Comptroller .... Elliott Aronstam
Insurance .... DeWitt Stern Group Inc./
                             Anthony Pittari, Joseph Bower
Legal Counsel .... Davis Wright Tremaine LLP/
                                        M. Graham Coleman
Payroll .... CSI/Lance Castellana
Opening Night Coordinator ..... The Lawrence Company/
                                          Michael Lawrence

"Penny" cartoon created for CBS's "Pee-wee's Playhouse"
©Paul Reubens, used courtesy of "Pee-wee's Playhouse."
Animation supervision by Prudence Fenton. Animation by
Aardmans, Nick Park, Richard Goleszowski. Direction by
Peter Lord, David Sproxton.

CREDITS

Scenery constructed by Daedalus Design & Production.
Lighting and audio equipment from Production Resource
Group. Video projection system provided by Scharff
Weisberg Inc. Puppets created by Chiodo Bros. Productions,
Inc. (Charles Chiodo, Stephen Chiodo, Edward Chiodo).
Select puppets built by Tandem Otter Productions. Cranes
supplied by Chapman/Leonard Studio. Costume
construction by Vito Leanza, Johnathan Behr, Angela
Wood, Alex in Wonderland, Kharen Zuenert, Mark
Crowell, Cyndee Fox-Hidde, Kyle Tadoulatif, Hollywood
Wigs and John Burton. Show clearances and permissions by
License It. "Tequila" written by Chuck Rio, published by
EMI Longitude Music (BMI), Universal Music Publishing
(BMI), performed by The Champs. *The Pee-wee Herman
Show* would like to thank the following companies and
products for permissions: The Bedazzler™, Bumpits™,
ShamWow™, Chia Pet™, The Clapper™, Doublemint
Gum™, Meow Mix™, Smart For Life™, "Eat Cookies,
Lose Weight." Makeup provided by M•A•C.

SPECIAL THANKS
John Koch, Josh Meyers, Phil Rosenthal & Paul Rust.
Foursquare/Dennis Crowley & Naveen Selvadurai. Jared
Geller.

STEPHEN SONDHEIM THEATRE
SYDNEY BEERS   GREG BACKSTROM
General Manager   Associate Managing Director
VALERIE SIMMONS
Operations Manager

STAFF FOR
THE STEPHEN SONDHEIM THEATRE
House Manager .... Johannah-Joy G. Magyawe
Treasurer .... Jaime Perlman
House Carpenter .... Steve Beers
House Electrician .... Josh Weitzman
House Properties .... Andrew Forste
Assistant Treasurers .... Andrew Clements,
                            Carlos Morris, Ronnie Tobias
Engineer .... Deosarran
Security .... Gotham Security
Maintenance .... C+W Cleaning Services Inc.
Lobby Refreshments by .... Sweet Concessions

(L-R): John Paragon
and Paul Reubens

Photo by Joan Marcus

The Pee-wee Herman Show

THE CAST AND STAFF OF THE ORIGINAL
THE PEE-WEE HERMAN SHOW

The original production of
The Pee-wee Herman Show
premiered at the Groundlings Theatre on
February 7, 1981 at midnight.

CAST OF CHARACTERS

(in order of appearance)

Pee-wee Herman	PAUL REUBENS
Mailman Mike	JOHN MOODY
Hammy	TITO LARRIVA
Susan	NICOLE PANTER
Mrs. Jelly Donut	MONICA GANAS
Mr. Jelly Donut	BRIAN SEFF
Jambi the Genie	JOHN PARAGON
Kap'n. Karl	PHIL HARTMANN
Miss Yvonne	LYNNE STEWART
Hermit Hattie	EDIE McCLURG
Salvador Sanchez	IVAN FLORES

Technical Director	Mark Beam
Audio Engineer	Joey Wolpert
Set Construction, Crew Chief	Steve Ralph
Stage Manager	Steve Carmendy
Assistant Stage Manager	Alex Rodriguez
Properties & Set Decoration	Leslie Williams
Puppet Construction	Tim Guyer and Chuck Morelli
Follow-Spot and Projector	Jason Goodman
Lights Operated By	Paul Gadson

VOICES

Clocky	Edie McClurg
Pterry-Dactyl	John Paragon
Monsieur LeCroq	Phil Hartmann

UNDERSTUDIES

JOAN LEIZMAN, STEVE CARMENDY,
MARK BEAM

Produced by
BETSY HEIMANN and CHUCK MINSKY
Directed by
PAUL REUBENS and BILL STEINKELLNER
Production Design, Art Direction, Puppets
and Poster Art by
GARY PANTER
Costume Design by
BETSY HEIMANN
Make-up and Hair Design by
VE NEILL

Puppet Operators	Tim Guyer, Phil Hartmann, Edie McClurg, Chuck Morelli, Gary Panter, John Paragon, Rick Potts, Leslie Williams
Technical Staff	Kathy Clark, Paul Gadson, Jason Goodman, Tim Guyer, Chuck Morelli, Guy Pohlman, Laura Petticord, Rick Potts, Alex Rodriguez, John Stark, Tom Willard, Joan Wolpert
Publicity Consultant	Agee, Stevens & Acree, Inc./ Robert Olive, Account Executive

Lighting Design by
BARBARA LING
Writing Supervised by
BILL STEINKELLNER AND PAUL REUBENS
Written by
PAUL REUBENS, BILL STEINKELLNER,
PHIL HARTMANN, JOHN PARAGON,
EDIE McCLURG, JOHN MOODY,
LYNNE STEWART, IVAN FLORES, BRIAN SEFF,
MONICA GANAS, and TITO LARRIVA
Music Composed and Arranged by
JAY COTTON
Executive in Charge of Production
DAWNA KAUFMANN
Executive Producer
PAUL REUBENS

This show is dedicated to my parents for their love and support. — Paul Reubens

The Pee-wee Herman Orchestra
and Chorale ...... Eric Bikales, Carrie Brown,
Stacy Brown, Jay Cotton, David Dial,
Marcia Dickstein, Cindy Fee, Ivan Flores,
John Gilles, Jenji Kohan, Jeff McLane,
Wayland Pickard, Mark Pierson,
John Paragon, Planet Swann, B.J. Ward,
Robert Williams

(L-R): Paul Reubens (center) and company

Photo by Joan Marcus

The Pee-wee Herman Show
SCRAPBOOK

Correspondent: Drew Powell, "Bear," "Voice"

Opening Night Gifts: There were many thoughtful gifts but the one that I used the most were the "iPhone-accessible" gloves from Scott Sanders. They have removable tips on the forefinger and thumb so I can use the touchscreen on my phone without removing my gloves. Coming from LA, I didn't even OWN a pair of gloves!

Most Exciting Celebrity Visitors: We had a lot of celebrities come through the Playhouse: Prince, Paul Simon, Natalie Portman, Elvis Costello and Diana Krall, Michael Moore, the cast and writers of "Saturday Night Live" and "The Daily Show"—and that's just to name a few. But probably the best was David Bowie. My wife's a big fan and I was the only one to get a photo with him to give to her. He and Iman brought their two girls and had a great time.

Actor Who Performed the Most Roles in This Show: Many of us played multiple roles with the puppet voices and the on stage characters.

Special Backstage Ritual: Before every show we had the obligatory group circle. However ours generally lasted up to 10 minutes or more and our chants got more elaborate every night! I'm not at liberty to divulge the contents of the chants on the grounds that it might incriminate all of us....

Favorite Moment During Each Performance: I love John Moody's (Mailman Mike's) goofy over-the-top stance right before the Mekalekahi scene! Priceless....

Favorite In-Theatre Gathering Place: I have to believe that we had the greatest post show/dressing room hangout in Broadway history. One of the men's dressing rooms was turned into "The Bumpit Lounge" and was completely decorated in Christmas finery! There were lights, a tree, garland, more lights, a fake fireplace, lots more lights, and Christmas cards from Pee-wee fans across the world (hundreds!). We always had a stocked fridge and were even sponsored by Ketel One vodka and Red Bull and Buffalo Trace bourbon. We would stay there carrying on and jamming with guitar and ukulele until midnight or later. Definitely one of the best parts of the whole experience!

Favorite Off-Site Hangout: When they kicked us out of The Bumpit Lounge we usually made our way across the street to BXL or Un Deux Trois on 44th Street.

Favorite Snack Food: Our Stage Manager James Latus baked amazing cakes for people's birthdays. We tried to figure a way to have a birthday every day. Amazing!

Mascot: I played a Bear which very much looked like a mascot and with all of the other puppets around you could say we were full of mascots. I do seem to recall a stuffed monkey that would find its way into different places every night.

Favorite Therapy: Massage. And also massage. Did I mention massage?

Most Memorable Ad-Lib: Josh Meyers had to do some serious improvising when the puppet he was voicing (Randy) got tangled up and was essentially hanging sideways. One of the things he said was, "Don't worry, this ain't as painful as it looks!" That got a big laugh from the audience and from the cast and crew backstage.

Who Wore the Heaviest/Hottest Costume: I win (lose?) that prize. I was in a full Bear costume which was thick and heavy with a massive bear head. Thank goodness they kept the theatre a nice and chilly 58 degrees!

1. Cast member Lance Roberts arrives at the opening night party at Bryant Park Grill.
2. *Yearbook* correspondent Drew Powell.
3. Paul Reubens mugs for the press with a young fan at the premiere.
4. Author/star Reubens arrives at the theatre in his Pee-wee Herman persona.
5. Cast member Lexy Fridell.

Who Wore the Least: John Moody (Mailman Mike) had to wear shorts in that ice box!

Catchphrases Only the Company Would Recognize: "Meet you at The Bumpit." "Lute into Conky." "Is that a euphemism for something?" "I love that story."" "Viva zacapa!"

Embarrassing Moments: One night on my exit after Pee-wee yells "Get Out!" I turned to run out and fell on my face. The audience thought it was part of the gag but all I could think was "Please don't let the (bear) head come off," as I literally crawled off the stage.

The People in the Picture

First Preview: April 1, 2011. Opened: April 28, 2011.
Still running as of May 31, 2011.

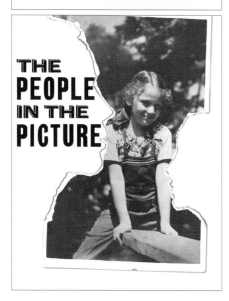

This original musical jumps back and forth in time from the 1930s and 1940s to the 1970s in telling the story of Raisel, a Jewish star of Polish stage and screen, who survives the Holocaust and tries to pass on her heritage to her young granddaughter. She is helped in telling her story by the ghosts of her old Polish theatre troupe—the "people in the picture" of the title. Along the way they reveal a terrible secret of how far Raisel went to save her daughter's life.

CAST

(in order of appearance)

Doovie Feldman	HAL ROBINSON
Moishe Rosenwald	ALEXANDER GEMIGNANI
Chayesel Fisher	JOYCE VAN PATTEN
Yossie Pinsker	CHIP ZIEN
Avram Krinsky	LEWIS J. STADLEN
Chaim Bradovsky	CHRISTOPHER INNVAR
Jenny	RACHEL RESHEFF
Bubbie/Raisel	DONNA MURPHY
Red	NICOLE PARKER
Hoodlums	JEREMY DAVIS, JEFFREY SCHECTER
Hollywood Girls	EMILEE DUPRÉ, SHANNON LEWIS, JESSICA LEA PATTY, MEGAN REINKING
Rabbi Velvel	HAL ROBINSON
Dobrisch	MEGAN REINKING
Dr. Goldblum	LOUIS HOBSON
Young Red	ANDIE MECHANIC
Jerzy	PAUL ANTHONY STEWART
Rachel	MAYA GOLDMAN

Continued on next page

STUDIO 54

ROUNDABOUTTHEATRECOMPANY

Todd Haimes, Artistic Director
Harold Wolpert, Managing Director
Julia C. Levy, Executive Director

In association with

Tracy Aron   Al Parinello   Stefany Bergson

Present

Donna Murphy

in

THE PEOPLE IN THE PICTURE

Book & Lyrics by
Iris Rainer Dart

Music by
Mike Stoller & Artie Butler

with

Alexander Gemignani   Christopher Innvar   Nicole Parker
Rachel Resheff   Hal Robinson   Lewis J. Stadlen   Joyce Van Patten   Chip Zien

Brad Bradley   Rachel Bress   Jeremy Davis   Emilee Dupré   Maya Goldman
Louis Hobson   Shannon Lewis   Andie Mechanic   Jessica Lea Patty   Megan Reinking
Jeffrey Schecter   Paul Anthony Stewart   Lori Wilner   Stuart Zagnit

Set Design	Costume Design	Lighting Design	Sound Design	Projection Design
Riccardo Hernández	Ann Hould-Ward	James F. Ingalls	Dan Moses Schreier	Elaine J. McCarthy

Hair & Wig Design	Makeup Design	Orchestrations	Dance Music Arrangements	Dialect Coach	Fight Director
Paul Huntley	Angelina Avallone	Michael Starobin	Alex Lacamoire	Kate Wilson	Rick Sordelet

Production Stage Manager	Production Management	Casting	General Manager	Executive Producer
Peter Wolf	Aurora Productions	Jim Carnahan, C.S.A. & Stephen Kopel	Rebecca Habel	Sydney Beers

Press Representative	Director of Marketing & Sales Promotion	Director of Development	Founding Director	Associate Artistic Director
Boneau-Bryan/Brown	David B. Steffen	Lynne Gugenheim Gregory	Gene Feist	Scott Ellis

Musical Direction by
Paul Gemignani

Musical Staging by
Andy Blankenbuehler

Directed by
Leonard Foglia

Roundabout Theatre Company is a member of the League of Resident Theatres.
www.roundabouttheatre.org

4/28/11

(L-R): Donna Murphy, Rachel Resheff

Photo by Joan Marcus

The People in the Picture

MUSICAL NUMBERS

ACT I

"Prologue"	Orchestra
*"Bread and Theatre"	Raisel, The Warsaw Gang and the Company
*"Matryoshka"	Bubbie and Jenny
*"Matryoshka" (Reprise)	Red
*"Before We Lose the Light/The Dybbuk"	Raisel, The Warsaw Gang and the Company
***"Remember Who You Are"	Yossie Pinsker, Avram Krinsky
*"Hollywood Girls"	Chaim Bradovsky, Raisel and the Company
***"Remember Who You Are" (Reprise)	Avram Krinsky, Yossie Pinsker, Raisel, Moishe Rosenwald, Chaim Bradovsky, Chayesel Fisher
*"And God Laughs"	Moishe Rosenwald, Raisel, Rabbi Velvel
†"Oyfen Pripitchik"	Raisel, Dobrisch
*"Red's Dilemma"	Red
*"For This"	Bubbie, Red, Jenny
†"Oyfen Pripitchik" (Reprise)	Jenny, Avram Krinsky, Chayesel Fisher, Moishe Rosenwald and the Company

ACT II

"Prologue"	Orchestra
***"We Were Here"	Raisel, Moishe Rosenwald, Chayesel Fisher, Avram Krinsky and the Company
*"Now and Then"	Red
***"Ich, Uch, Feh"	Raisel and the Company
*"Selective Memory"	Raisel
***"Saying Goodbye"	Raisel, Dobrisch, Red, Young Red
*"Child of My Child"	Bubbie
***"Remember Who You Are" (Reprise)	Bubbie
"Bread and Theatre"/"We Were Here" (Finale)	Raisel and The Warsaw Gang

* Music by Mike Stoller
** Music by Artie Butler
† Music & Lyrics by Mark Warshavsky (1845-1907)

Cast Continued

SWINGS
BRAD BRADLEY, RACHEL BRESS

DANCE CAPTAIN
RACHEL BRESS

UNDERSTUDIES
For Bubbie/Raisel, Chayesel Fisher: LORI WILNER
For Red: JESSICA LEA PATTY
For Jenny, Young Red: MAYA GOLDMAN
For Moishe Rosenwald: LOUIS HOBSON
For Doovie Feldman, Rabbi Velvel, Avram Krinsky: STUART ZAGNIT
For Yossie Pinsker: JEFFREY SCHECTER
For Dr. Goldblum, Jerzy: BRAD BRADLEY
For Dobrisch: EMILEE DUPRÉ
For Rachel: ANDIE MECHANIC

TIME AND PLACE
New York City 1977 and
Warsaw, Poland 1935-1946

Production Stage Manager: PETER WOLF
Stage Manager: BRIAN BOGIN

ORCHESTRA
Musical Director: PAUL GEMIGNANI
Associate Conductor: MARK MITCHELL
2nd Associate Conductor: LARRY LELLI
1st Violin, Concertmaster: SYLVIA D'AVANZO
Cello: DEB ASSAEL-MIGLIORI
Oboe, EH, FL Clarinet, Tenor: STEVE LYON
Clarinet, Bass Clarinet, Bassoon, Baritone: DON McGEEN
Flute, Piccolo, Alto Sax, Soprano Sax: GREG THYMIUS
Trumpet 1, Piccolo Trumpet, Flugal Horn, Cornet: DOMINIC DERASSE
Trombone, Euphonium, House Contractor: BRUCE EIDEM
Trumpet 2, Flugal Horn, Librarian: PHIL GRANGER
Synth, Accordion: RANDY COHEN
Synth: MARK MITCHELL
Drummer, Small Percussion: LARRY LELLI
Bass: JOHN BEAL
Music Copying: EMILY GRISHMAN MUSIC PREPARATION/KATHARINE EDMONDS, EMILY GRISHMAN

(L-R): Alexander Gemignani, Chip Zien, Donna Murphy, Joyce Van Patten, Lewis J. Stadlen

Photo by Joan Marcus

The People in the Picture

Donna Murphy
Bubbie/Raisel

Alexander Gemignani
Moishe Rosenwald

Christopher Innvar
Chaim Bradovsky

Nicole Parker
Red

Rachel Resheff
Jenny

Hal Robinson
*Doovie Feldman,
Rabbi Velvel*

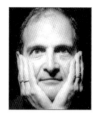
Lewis J. Stadlen
Avram Krinsky

Joyce Van Patten
Chayesel Fisher

Chip Zien
Yossie Pinsker

Brad Bradley
Swing

Rachel Bress
*Associate Musical
Staging, Swing,
Dance Captain*

Jeremy Davis
Hoodlum

Emilee Dupré
Hollywood Girl

Maya Goldman
Rachel

Louis Hobson
Doctor Goldblum

Shannon Lewis
Hollywood Girl

Andie Mechanic
Young Red

Jessica Lea Patty
Hollywood Girl

Megan Reinking
*Dobrisch,
Hollywood Girl*

Jeffrey "Shecky"
Schecter
Hoodlum

Paul Anthony
Stewart
Jerzy

Lori Wilner
*u/s Bubbie/Raisel,
Chayesel Fisher*

Stuart Zagnit
*u/s Doovie Feldman,
Rabbi Velvel,
Avram Krinsky*

Iris Rainer Dart
Book & Lyrics

Mike Stoller
Music

Artie Butler
Music

Leonard Foglia
Director

Andy
Blankenbuehler
Musical Staging

Paul Gemignani
Musical Director

Ann Hould-Ward
Costume Design

Dan Moses Schreier
Sound Design

Elaine J. McCarthy
Projection Design

Paul Huntley
Hair & Wig Design

Angelina Avallone
Makeup Design

Michael Starobin
Orchestrations

The People in the Picture

Alex Lacamoire
Dance Music Arrangements

Kate Wilson
Dialect Coach

Rick Sordelet
Fight Director

Cat Williams
Assistant Director

Jim Carnahan
Casting Director

Tracy Aron

Al Parinello

Stefany Bergson

Gene Feist
Founding Director, Roundabout Theatre Company

Todd Haimes
Artistic Director, Roundabout Theatre Company

Amanda Lea LaVergne
Swing

STAGE AND COMPANY MANAGEMENT AND PRODUCTION ASSISTANTS
(L-R): Jenn McNeil, Rachel Miller Davis, Brian Bogin, Laura Stuart, Peter Wolf, Karl Baudendistel

BOX OFFICE
(L-R): Joseph Clark, Kara Harrington, Benjamin Schneider

Photos by Brian Mapp

CREW
Front Row (L-R): Dan Hoffman, Paul Coltoff, Lawrence Jennino, Mike Widmer

Middle Row (L-R): Erin Mary Delaney, Rebecca O'Neill, Susanne Poulin, Barb Bartel

Back Row (L-R): Cory Verkuilen, Steve Jones, John Wooding, Scott Anderson

The People in the Picture

ROUNDABOUT THEATRE COMPANY STAFF
ARTISTIC DIRECTOR .... TODD HAIMES
MANAGING DIRECTOR .... HAROLD WOLPERT
EXECUTIVE DIRECTOR .... JULIA C. LEVY
ASSOCIATE ARTISTIC DIRECTOR ...SCOTT ELLIS

ARTISTIC STAFF
DIRECTOR OF ARTISTIC DEVELOPMENT/
  DIRECTOR OF CASTING ....Jim Carnahan
Artistic Consultant ....Robyn Goodman
Resident Director ....Doug Hughes
Associate Artists ....Mark Brokaw, Scott Elliott,
    Sam Gold, Bill Irwin, Joe Mantello,
    Kathleen Marshall, Theresa Rebeck
Literary Manager ....Jill Rafson
Casting Director ....Carrie Gardner
Casting Associate ....Kate Boka
Casting Associate ....Stephen Kopel
Casting Assistant ....Jillian Cimini
Artistic Assistant ....Amy Ashton
Literary Associate ....Josh Fiedler
The Blanche and Irving Laurie Foundation
  Theatre Visions Fund Commissions ....Stephen Karam,
    Nathan Louis Jackson
Educational Foundation of
  America Commissions ....Bekah Brunstetter,
    Lydia Diamond, Diana Fithian,
    Julie Marie Myatt
New York State Council
  on the Arts Commission ....Nathan Louis Jackson
Roundabout Commissions ....Steven Levenson,
    Matthew Lopez, Kim Rosenstock
Casting Interns ....Devon Caraway, Kyle Eberlein,
    Jonny Lang, Aaron Quinn
Script Readers..........................Jay Cohen, Ben Izzo,
    Alexis Roblan, Nicholas Stimler
Artistic Intern ....Becky Bicks

EDUCATION STAFF
EDUCATION DIRECTOR ....Greg McCaslin
Associate Education Director ....Jennifer DiBella
Education Program Associates ....Aliza Greenberg,
Sarah Malone
Education Assistant ....Holly Sansom
Education Dramaturg ....Ted Sod
Teaching Artists ....Cynthia Babak, Victor Barbella,
    Grace Bell, LaTonya Borsay, Mark Bruckner,
    Joe Clancy, Vanessa Davis-Cohen, Joe Doran,
    Jimena Duca, Elizabeth Dunn-Ruiz,
    Carrie Ellman-Larsen, Deanna Frieman,
    Natalie Gold, Sheri Graubert, Benton Greene,
    Melissa Gregus, Adam Gwon, Devin Haqq,
    Carrie Heitman, Karla Hendrick, Mary Hunt,
    Jason Jacobs, Lisa Renee Jordan, Jamie Kalama,
    Alvin Keith, Tami Mansfield, Erin McCready,
    Kyle McGinley, Nick Moore, Andrew Ondrejcak,
    Meghan O'Neill, Laura Poe, Nicole Press,
    Jennifer Rathbone, Leah Reddy, Cassy Rush,
    Nick Simone, Joe Skowronski, Heidi Stallings,
    Daniel Sullivan, Carl Tallent, Vickie Tanner,
    Jolie Tong, Larine Towler, Cristina Vaccaro,
    Jennifer Varbalow, Leese Walker, Eric Wallach,
    Michael Warner, Christina Watanabe,
    Gail Winar, Chad Yarborough
Teaching Artist Emeritus ....Reneé Flemings
Education Intern ....Erin Monahan

FRONT OF HOUSE STAFF
Front Row (L-R): Linda Gjonbalaj, Diana Trent, LaConya Robinson, Victor Rosa

Middle Row (L-R): Essence Mason, Nicole Ramirez, Valerie Simmons, Samantha Rivera

Back Row (L-R): Alvin Vega, Jason Battle, Willema Robinson, Felisha Whatts

EXECUTIVE ADMINISTRATIVE STAFF
ASSOCIATE MANAGING
  DIRECTOR ....Greg Backstrom
Assistant Managing Director ....Jill Boyd
Assistant to the Managing Director . ...Zachary Baer
Assistant to the Executive Director ....Nicole Tingir

MANAGEMENT/ADMINISTRATIVE STAFF
GENERAL MANAGER ....Sydney Beers
General Manager,
  American Airlines Theatre ....Rebecca Habel
General Manager, Steinberg Center ....Rachel E. Ayers
Human Resources Director ....Stephen Deutsch
Operations Manager ....Valerie D. Simmons
Associate General Manager ....Maggie Cantrick
Office Manager ....Scott Kelly
Archivist ....Tiffany Nixon
Receptionists ....Dee Beider, Emily Frohnhoefer,
    Elisa Papa, Allison Patrick
Messenger ....Darnell Franklin
Management Intern ....Catherine Moreton
Archives Intern ....Carina Don

FINANCE STAFF
DIRECTOR OF FINANCE.................Susan Neiman
Payroll Director ....John LaBarbera
Accounts Payable Manager ....Frank Surdi
Payroll Benefits Administrator ....Yonit Kafka
Manager Financial Reporting ....Joshua Cohen
Business Office Assistant ....Jackie Verbitski
Business Interns..........Nicholas Barbato, Ayla Schermer

DEVELOPMENT STAFF
DIRECTOR OF
  DEVELOPMENT ....Lynne Gugenheim Gregory

Assistant to the Director of Development ....Liz Malta
Director, Institutional Giving ....Liz S. Alsina
Director, Individual Giving ....Christopher Nave
Director, Special Events ....Steve Schaeffer
Associate Director, Individual Giving ....Tyler Ennis
Manager, Telefundraising ....Gavin Brown
Manager, Corporate Relations ....Sohyun Kim
Manager, Donor Information Systems ....Lise Speidel
Associate Manager, Patron Programs ....Marisa Perry
Patron Services Associate ....Joseph Foster
Institutional Giving Assistant ....Brett Barbour
Development Assistant ....Martin Giannini
Individual Giving Assistant ....Sophia Hinshelwood
Special Events Assistant ....Amy Rosenfield
Development Interns .....Bethany Nothstein, Sara Valencia

INFORMATION TECHNOLOGY STAFF
IT DIRECTOR ....Antonio Palumbo
IT Associates ....Jim Roma, Cary Kim
DIRECTOR DATABASE
  OPERATIONS ....Wendy Hutton
Database Administrator/Programmer ....Revanth Anne

MARKETING STAFF
DIRECTOR OF MARKETING
  AND SALES PROMOTION ....David B. Steffen
Associate Director of Marketing ....Tom O'Connor
Senior Marketing Manager ....Shannon Marcotte
Marketing Associate...............................Eric Emch
Marketing Assistant ....Bradley Sanchez
Website Consultant ....Keith Powell Beyland
Director of Telesales Special Promotions ......Marco Frezza
Telesales Manager ....Patrick Pastor
Marketing Interns ....J. Samuel Horvath,
    Claire-Marine Sarner

The People in the Picture

The People in the Picture
SCRAPBOOK

Correspondent: Shannon Lewis, "Hollywood Girl"

Company In-Joke: Horses. We rehearsed at the Roundabout studio near Sixth Avenue, which was different from what we were used to. You feel like you're in your own little bubble, like you're out in the wilderness. We started referring to the rooms as stables and referred to ourselves as thoroughbreds or workhorses. When Andy Blankenbuehler tried to round us up, we would neigh. It became a whole thing.

Opening Night Party/Gifts: It was held at the Marriott Marquis ballroom, and there were a lot of horse references and horse-related personal gifts to each other. There was also some beautiful cards and artwork devoted to survivors of the Warsaw ghetto and the pictures we talk about so much in our show. Some people made paintings of their own that were related directly to the show. Some people made donations to organization like that as well.

Most Exciting Celebrity Visitors: We've seen Bette Midler who was in one of the first workshops of the show. We also saw Sarah Jessica Parker and Matthew Broderick.

Actors Who Performed the Most Roles in This Show: Jeffrey Schecter and Jeremy Davis play hoodlums and all types of characters throughout the show. Donna goes back and forth between her own character and various characters in movies, so she might actually win that title.

Who Has Done the Most Shows in Their Career: We have some pretty heavy hitters in this cast. Lewis J. Stadlen, Chip Zien and Joyce Van Patten have done more than anybody in terms of plays and things.

Mascot: It would be a horse, if there was one.

Special Backstage Rituals: Chip Zien loves to tell jokes and stories to us just before he goes on and gets us laughing hysterically. He sometimes forgets to put his prop money in his pockets because he's too busy telling jokes. We dancers warm up in the house on our own. There's always a fight call on stage at half-hour.

Favorite Moment During Each Performance: I really love dancing that Act II ballet with Jeremy Davis. It's a moment in the show when the story is truly told through dance, and it is so beautifully choreographed. I love to do that every night.

Favorite In-Theatre Gathering Place: At Studio 54 the greenroom is a hallway under the stage. Everybody is always down there totally rocking out all the time. There's a lot of laughter and a lot of food. You can barely get through with all the feet in the way. We call it the green hallway.

Favorite Off-Site Hangout: We've gone out a few times but it's always different. Usually we're too exhausted. Instead, each Sunday night, the boys and girls gather in the dressing room and have tequila or champagne to celebrate getting through another week.

Favorite Snack Food: I make these little trail

(L-R): Rachel Resheff, Donna Murphy, Nicole Parker and Christopher Innvar on opening night.

mix concoctions. I go to Trader Joe's and buy loose nuts and fruit and put it in a bowl and we all love it. We should market it: *People in the Picture* Trail Mix.

Favorite Therapies: We love our physical therapy and have lots and lots of Ricolas backstage. Some people can't do the show without a Ricola, so that's important. Donna uses blackcurrent pastilles that she has on hand all the time.

Most Memorable Ad-Lib: Our show went through many changes in previews. Chip Zien and Lewis Stadlen had a comedy song together and they would laugh and ad-lib their way through it, which only made the audience love them more. I always thought it was funnier the way they did it than the way it was written. But it got cut.

What Did You Think of the Web Buzz on Your Show: When you're in the process of creating a new show you tend not to read what people say on the message boards because you are changing so many things. I know they did a campaign for our show, with people posting pictures from their own families. It was a nice campaign that helped people make the story personal.

Memorable Stage Door Fan Encounters: People tend to be very emotional after our show. It touches people deeply and sometimes they are still crying when we come out of the stage door.

Fastest Costume Change: The majority happen with Donna right on stage with the rest of us acting as her dressers. She would have to change from an elderly American grandma to a young, gorgeous Polish movie star in ten seconds or less.

Who Wore the Heaviest/Hottest Costume: Donna, who has to wear her harness to fly in the opening number.

Who Wore the Least: This is the most dressed in a show I've ever been; I've never had this many clothes on in a show in my life.

Catchphrase Only the Company Would Recognize: "Neigh-gh-gh-gh."

Best In-House Parody Lyrics: We had a great number called "Before We Lose the Light"

which went through many different incarnations before it was finally cut. We called it "Before We Lose Our Minds."

One of the best opening night gifts we got was a fully produced version of a song parody we did. There is a tender moment in Act II when one character sings about how "You were a baby...your life began inside of me...you are my treasure girl." We turned this beautiful ballad into a ridiculous rap song complete with horse sounds in the background. Dance arranger Alex Lacamoire found out about it and did a fully-produced version that could have been uploaded to iTunes.

Understudy Anecdote: One of our older male character actors became ill during a preview, so Stuart Zagnit got thrown into the show with barely an understudy rehearsal. It was "shove with love." He said, "Just push me where I need to go," so we pushed him into spotlight, and he did an incredible job.

Nickname: Jeff Schecter looks like Jiminy Cricket in one of his outfits, so we call him "Jimmy the Cricket," like he's a New Jersey mob guy.

Sweethearts Within the Company: One of our young child stars Rachel Resheff, has a crush on Daniel Radcliffe over at *How To Succeed*. She got a signed picture from him at the stage door and has decided that they are now getting married.

Embarrassing Moment: One of swings went on and her skirt came undone and was down around her ankles.

Ghostly Encounters Backstage: Studio 54 is haunted by the ghosts of drugs past. We sometimes go down to the old VIP suite for PT and try to imagine what kind of debauchery happened in that room.

Superstition: Someone whistled once and I made them go outside and come back in to clear the air.

Coolest Thing About Being in This Show: What's really rewarding is looking out during the bows and seeing a lot of teary-eyed people, which shows they really cared about the characters—something you don't get very often in musical comedy. It's a nice moment.

The Phantom of the Opera

First Preview: January 9, 1988. Opened: January 26, 1988.
Still running as of May 31, 2011.

PLAYBILL

The dashing Raoul is in love with Christine Daaé, a pretty soprano in the chorus of the Paris Opera. But Raoul discovers that she is under the spell of the legendary Phantom of the Opera, a disfigured musical genius who haunts the endless grottos beneath the ancient opera house. The obsessed Phantom demands that Christine be elevated to star and that the company produce an unplayable opera he has written. When his commands are not obeyed the Phantom becomes violent, even murderous. Raoul strives ever more desperately to free Christine from his clutches. As a torch-wielding mob closes in on his lair, the Phantom makes one last bid for Christine's love.

CAST

The Phantom of the Opera	HUGH PANARO
Christine Daaé	SARA JEAN FORD
Christine Daaé	MARNI RAAB
(Mon. & Thurs. performances)	
Raoul, Vicomte de Chagny	RYAN SILVERMAN
Carlotta Giudicelli	PATRICIA PHILLIPS
Monsieur André	GEORGE LEE ANDREWS
Monsieur Firmin	JAMES ROMICK
(Mon.–Wed. performances)	
Monsieur Firmin	JOHN KUETHER
(Thurs.–Sat. performances)	
Madame Giry	CRISTIN J. HUBBARD
Ubaldo Piangi	EVAN HARRINGTON
Meg Giry	HEATHER McFADDEN
Monsieur Reyer/	
Hairdresser ("Il Muto")	KYLE BARISICH
Auctioneer/	
Don Attilio ("Il Muto")	JOHN KUETHER
Jeweler ("Il Muto")	FRANK MASTRONE
Monsieur Lefèvre/Firechief	KENNETH KANTOR

⑥ MAJESTIC THEATRE

247 West 44th Street
A Shubert Organization Theatre

Philip J. Smith, *Chairman*   Robert E. Wankel, *President*

CAMERON MACKINTOSH and
THE REALLY USEFUL THEATRE COMPANY, INC.

present

The
PHANTOM
of the
OPERA.

starring

HUGH PANARO
SARA JEAN FORD
RYAN SILVERMAN

GEORGE LEE ANDREWS   DAVID CRYER   PATRICIA PHILLIPS
CRISTIN J. HUBBARD   EVAN HARRINGTON   HEATHER McFADDEN

At certain performances
MARNI RAAB
plays the role of "Christine"

Music by
ANDREW LLOYD WEBBER

Lyrics by **CHARLES HART**

Additional lyrics by **RICHARD STILGOE**
Book by **RICHARD STILGOE & ANDREW LLOYD WEBBER**

Based on the novel 'Le Fantôme de L'Opéra' by **GASTON LEROUX**

Production Design by **MARIA BJÖRNSON**   Lighting by **ANDREW BRIDGE**
Sound Design by **MICK POTTER**   Original Sound Design by **MARTIN LEVAN**
Musical Supervision & Direction **DAVID CADDICK**   Musical Director **KRISTEN BLODGETTE**
Production Supervisor **PETER von MAYRHAUSER**
Orchestrations by **DAVID CULLEN & ANDREW LLOYD WEBBER**
Casting by **TARA RUBIN CASTING**   Original Casting by **JOHNSON-LIFF ASSOCIATES**
General Management **ALAN WASSER ASSOCIATES**

Musical Staging & Choreography by **GILLIAN LYNNE**

Directed by **HAROLD PRINCE**

10/1/10

Joseph Buquet	RICHARD POOLE
Passarino	
("Don Juan Triumphant")	JEREMY STOLLE
Slave Master ("Hannibal")	JAMES ZANDER
Solo Dancer ("Il Muto")	MYKAL D. LAURY, II
Page ("Don Juan Triumphant")	KIMILEE BRYANT
Porter/Fireman	CHRIS BOHANNON
Spanish Lady	
("Don Juan Triumphant")	MELANIE FIELD
Wardrobe Mistress/Confidante	
("Il Muto")	MICHELE McCONNELL
Princess ("Hannibal")	SUSAN OWEN
Madame Firmin	KRIS KOOP
Innkeeper's Wife	
("Don Juan Triumphant")	MARY ILLES

Continued on next page

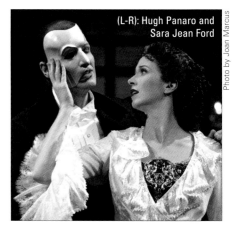

(L-R): Hugh Panaro and Sara Jean Ford

Photo by Joan Marcus

The Phantom of the Opera

MUSICAL NUMBERS

PROLOGUE
The stage of the Paris Opéra House, 1911

OVERTURE

ACT ONE—PARIS, LATE NINETEENTH CENTURY

Scene 1—The dress rehearsal of "Hannibal"
"Think of Me" ....Carlotta, Christine, Raoul
Scene 2—After the Gala
"Angel of Music" ....Christine and Meg
Scene 3—Christine's dressing room
"Little Lotte/The Mirror" (Angel of Music) ....Raoul, Christine, Phantom
Scene 4—The Labyrinth underground
"The Phantom of the Opera" ....Phantom and Christine
Scene 5—Beyond the lake
"The Music of the Night" ....Phantom
Scene 6—Beyond the lake, the next morning
"I Remember/Stranger Than You Dreamt It" ....Christine and Phantom
Scene 7—Backstage
"Magical Lasso" ....Buquet, Meg, Madame Giry and Ballet Girls
Scene 8—The Managers' office
"Notes/Prima Donna" ....Firmin, André, Raoul, Carlotta, Giry, Meg,
Piangi and Phantom
Scene 9—A performance of "Il Muto"
"Poor Fool, He Makes Me Laugh" ....Carlotta and Company
Scene 10—The roof of the Opéra House
"Why Have You Brought Me Here/Raoul, I've Been There" ....Raoul and Christine
"All I Ask of You" ....Raoul and Christine
"All I Ask of You" (Reprise) ....Phantom

ENTR'ACTE

ACT TWO—SIX MONTHS LATER

Scene 1—The staircase of the Opéra House, New Year's Eve
"Masquerade/Why So Silent" ....Full Company
Scene 2—Backstage
Scene 3—The Managers' office
"Notes/Twisted Every Way" ....André, Firmin, Carlotta, Piangi, Raoul,
Christine, Giry and Phantom
Scene 4—A rehearsal for "Don Juan Triumphant"
Scene 5—A graveyard in Perros
"Wishing You Were Somehow Here Again" ....Christine
"Wandering Child/Bravo, Bravo" ....Phantom, Christine and Raoul
Scene 6—The Opéra House stage before the Premiere
Scene 7—"Don Juan Triumphant"
"The Point of No Return" ....Phantom and Christine
Scene 8—The Labyrinth underground
"Down Once More/Track Down This Murderer" ....Full Company
Scene 9—Beyond the lake

Cast Continued

Marksman ....PAUL A. SCHAEFER
The Ballet Chorus of
the Opéra Populaire ....KARA KLEIN,
GIANNA LOUNGWAY, MABEL MODRONO,
AUBREY MORGAN, JESSICA RADETSKY,
CARLY BLAKE SEBOUHIAN
Ballet Swing ....LAURIE V. LANGDON
Swings ....SCOTT MIKITA, JAMES ROMICK,
KRISTIE DALE SANDERS, JIM WEITZER

UNDERSTUDIES
For the Phantom: JAMES ROMICK,
PAUL A. SCHAEFER, JEREMY STOLLE
For Christine: KIMILEE BRYANT,
SUSAN OWEN
For Raoul: KYLE BARISICH, JAMES ROMICK,
PAUL A. SCHAEFER, JEREMY STOLLE,
JIM WEITZER
For Firmin: KENNETH KANTOR,
JOHN KUETHER, JAMES ROMICK
For André: FRANK MASTRONE,
SCOTT MIKITA, RICHARD POOLE,
JAMES ROMICK
For Carlotta: KIMILEE BRYANT, KRIS KOOP,
MICHELE McCONNELL
For Mme. Giry: KIMILEE BRYANT,
MARY ILLES, KRIS KOOP
For Piangi: CHRIS BOHANNON,
FRANK MASTRONE, JEREMY STOLLE
For Meg Giry: KARA KLEIN,
CARLY BLAKE SEBOUHIAN
For Slave Master, Solo Dancer ("Il Muto"): KFIR,
MYKAL D. LAURY, II
Dance Captain: LAURIE V. LANGDON
Assistant Dance Captain: HEATHER McFADDEN

ORCHESTRA
Conductors: DAVID CADDICK,
KRISTEN BLODGETTE, DAVID LAI,
TIM STELLA, NORMAN WEISS
Violins: JOYCE HAMMANN (Concert Master),
CLAIRE CHAN, KURT COBLE,
JAN MULLEN, KAREN MILNE,
SUZANNE GILMAN
Violas: VERONICA SALAS,
DEBRA SHUFELT-DINE
Cellos: TED ACKERMAN, KARL BENNION
Bass: MELISSA SLOCUM
Harp: HENRY FANELLI
Flute: SHERYL HENZE
Flute/Clarinet: ED MATTHEW
Oboe: MELANIE FELD
Clarinet: MATTHEW GOODMAN
Bassoon: ATSUKO SATO
Trumpets: LOWELL HERSHEY,
FRANCIS BONNY
Bass Trombone: WILLIAM WHITAKER
French Horns: DANIEL CULPEPPER,
PETER REIT, DAVID SMITH
Percussion: ERIC COHEN, JAN HAGIWARA
Keyboards: TIM STELLA, NORMAN WEISS

The Phantom of the Opera

Hugh Panaro
The Phantom of the Opera

Sara Jean Ford
Christine Daaé

Ryan Silverman
Raoul, Vicomte de Chagny

George Lee Andrews
Monsieur André

David Cryer
Monsieur Firmin

Patricia Phillips
Carlotta Giudicelli

Cristin J. Hubbard
Madame Giry

Evan Harrington
Ubaldo Piangi

Heather McFadden
Meg Giry/Assistant Dance Captain

Marni Raab
Christine Daaé at certain performances

Kyle Barisich
Monsieur Reyer/ Hairdresser

Chris Bohannon
Porter/Fireman

Kimilee Bryant
Page

Melanie Field
Spanish Lady

Mary Illes
Innkeeper's Wife

Kenneth Kantor
Monsieur Lefèvre/ Firechief

Kara Klein
Ballet Chorus

Kris Koop
Madame Firmin

John Kuether
Auctioneer/ Don Attilio & Monsieur Firmin at certain performances

Laurie V. Langdon
Dance Captain/ Ballet Swing

Mykal D. Laury, II
Solo Dancer

Sarah Anne Lewis
Swing

Gianna Loungway
Ballet Chorus

Frank Mastrone
Jeweler

Michele McConnell
Wardrobe Mistress/ Confidante

Scott Mikita
Swing

Mabel Modrono
Ballet Chorus

Aubrey Morgan
Ballet Chorus

Susan Owen
Princess

Richard Poole
Joseph Buquet

Jessica Radetsky
Ballet Chorus

James Romick
Swing & Monsieur Firmin at certain performances

Kristie Dale Sanders
Swing

Paul A. Schaefer
Marksman

Carly Blake Sebouhian
Ballet Chorus

The Phantom of the Opera

Jeremy Stolle
Passarino

Jim Weitzer
Swing

James Zander
Slave Master

Andrew Lloyd Webber
Composer/Book/Co-Orchestrator

Harold Prince
Director

Charles Hart
Lyrics

Richard Stilgoe
Book and Additional Lyrics

Gillian Lynne
Musical Staging and Choreography

Maria Björnson
Production Design

Andrew Bridge
Lighting Designer

Mick Potter
Sound Designer

Martin Levan
Original Sound Designer

David Cullen
Co-Orchestrator

David Caddick
Musical Supervision and Direction

Kristen Blodgette
Associate Musical Supervisor/Musical Director

Peter von Mayrhauser
Production Supervisor

Denny Berry
Production Dance Supervisor

Jake Bell
Technical Production Manager

Craig Jacobs
Production Stage Manager

Bethe Ward
Stage Manager from the beginning

David Lai
Conductor

Vincent Liff and Geoffrey Johnson, Johnson-Liff Associates
Original Casting

Tara Rubin Casting
Casting

Alan Wasser Associates
General Management

Cameron Mackintosh
Producer

Emily Adonna
The Ballet Chorus of the Opéra Populaire

Polly Baird
Meg Giry at certain performances, The Ballet Chorus of the Opéra Populaire

Erin Brooke Burton
The Ballet Chorus of the Opéra Populaire

John Cudia
The Phantom of the Opera

Julie Hanson
Princess ("Hannibal")

Jessy Hendrickson
Ballet Swing, The Ballet Chorus of the Opéra Populaire

Ted Keegan
Monsieur André, Monsieur Reyer/Hairdresser ("Il Muto")

Greg Mills
Monsieur Reyer/Hairdresser ("Il Muto")

The Phantom of the Opera

Janet Saia
Swing

Julie Schmidt
*Innkeeper's Wife,
Madame Firmin,
Princess, Swing,
Wardrobe Mistress/
Confidante*

Stephen Tewksbury
*The Phantom of the
Opera at certain
performances,
Swing*

Dianna Warren
*The Ballet Chorus of
the Opéra Populaire*

Jennifer Hope Wills
Christine Daaé

2010-2011
TRANSFER
STUDENTS

Dara Adler
*Ballet Swing,
Dance Captain*

Polly Baird
*Meg Giry at certain
performances,
The Ballet Chorus of
the Opéra Populaire*

Harlan Bengel
*Slave Master
("Hannibal"),
Solo Dancer
("Il Muto")*

Sean A. Carmon
*Solo Dancer
("Il Muto")*

Marilyn Caskey
*Madame Giry
at certain
performances*

Paloma Garcia-Lee
*Meg Giry at certain
performances,
The Ballet Chorus of
the Opéra Populaire*

Joelle Gates
*Ballet Swing,
Dance Captain*

Kelly Jeanne Grant
*Innkeeper's Wife,
Spanish Lady, Swing,
Wardrobe Mistress/
Confidante*

Nancy Hess
Madame Giry

Satomi Hofman
*Carlotta Giudicelli,
Spanish Lady ("Don
Juan Triumphant")*

Rebecca Judd
Madame Firmin

Peter Lockyer
Jeweler ("Il Muto")

Sean MacLaughlin
*Raoul, Vicomte de
Chagny*

Liz McCartney
Carlotta Giudicelli

Greg Mills
*Monsieur Reyer/
Hairdresser, Raoul,
Vicomte de Chagny
at certain
performances, Swing*

Janet Saia
*Madame Giry
at certain
performances,
Swing*

Carrington Vilmont
*Monsieur Reyer/
Hairdresser
("Il Muto")*

(L-R): Evan Harrington and Liz McCartney with a cake celebrating the show's 23rd anniversary on Broadway.

Photo by Joseph Marzullo/WENN

Elizabeth Welch
*Christine Daaé at
certain
performances,
Princess
("Hannibal")*

The Phantom of the Opera

Staff for *THE PHANTOM OF THE OPERA*

General Manager
ALAN WASSER ASSOCIATES
Alan Wasser   Allan Williams

General Press Representative
THE PUBLICITY OFFICE
Marc Thibodeau   Michael S. Borowski
Jeremy Shaffer   Matt Fasano

Assistant to Mr. Prince
RUTH MITCHELL

Production Supervisor
PETER von MAYRHAUSER

Production Dance Supervisor
DENNY BERRY

Associate Musical Supervisor
KRISTEN BLODGETTE

Casting
TARA RUBIN CASTING

Technical Production Manager ....JAKE BELL
Company Manager ....STEVE GREER
Production Stage Manager ....CRAIG JACOBS
Stage Managers ....Bethe Ward, Brendan Smith
Assistant Company Manager ....Katherine McNamee

U.S. Design Staff
Associate Scenic Designer ....DANA KENN
Associate Costume Designer ....SAM FLEMING
Associate Lighting Designer ....DEBRA DUMAS
Associate Sound Designer ....PAUL GATEHOUSE
Sculptures Consultant ....Stephen Pyle
Pro Tools Programmer ....Lee McCutcheon

Casting Associates ....Dale Brown, Eric Woodall, CSA;
            Laura Schutzel, CSA; Merri Sugarman, CSA
Casting Assistants ....Paige Blansfield, Kaitlin Shaw
Dance Captain ....Laurie V. Langdon
Production Carpenter ....Joseph Patria
Production Electrician ....Robert Fehribach
Production Propertyman ....Timothy Abel
Production Sound Engineer ....Garth Helm
Production Wig Supervisor ....Leone Gagliardi
Production Make-up Supervisor ....Thelma Pollard
Assistant Make-up Supervisors ....Magdalena Kolodziej,
            Pearleta N. Price, Shazia J. Saleem
Head Carpenter ....Russell Tiberio III
Automation Carpenters ..Santos Sanchez, Michael Girman
Assistant Carpenter ....Giancarlo Cottignoli
Flyman ....Daryl Miller
Head Electrician ....Alan Lampel
Assistant Electrician ....JR Beket
Head Props ....Matthew Mezick
Asst. Props./Boat Captain ....Joe Caruso
Sound Operator ....Paul Verity
Wardrobe Supervisor ....Julie Ratcliffe
Assistant Wardrobe Supervisor ....Robert Strong Miller
Hair Supervisor ....Leone Gagliardi
Hairdressers ....Charise Champion, Isabelle Decauwert,
            Jameson Eaton, Erika Smith

Conductor ....David Lai
Associate Conductor ....Tim Stella
Assistant Conductor ....Norman Weiss
Musical Preparation
    Supervisor (U.S.) ....Chelsea Music Service, Inc
Synthesizer Consultant ....Stuart Andrews

Assistants to the Gen. Mgr. ....Hilary Ackerman,
            Jake Hirzel, Jennifer O'Connor

Legal Counsel ....F. Richard Pappas
Accounting ....Rosenberg, Neuwirth and Kutchner
            Christopher A. Cacace
Logo Design and Graphics ....Dewynters Plc London
Merchandising ....Dewynters Advertising Inc
Advertising ....Serino Coyne Inc.,
            Greg Corradetti, Andrea Prince
Marketing Direction ....Type A Marketing
            Anne Rippey
Displays ....King Displays, Wayne Sapper
Insurance (U.S.) ....DeWitt Stern Group
            Peter K. Shoemaker
Insurance (U.K.) ....Walton & Parkinson Limited
            Richard Walton
Banking ....Signature Bank/
            Barbara von Borstel
Payroll Service ....Castellana Services, Inc.

Original Production Photographer ....Clive Barda
Additional Photography ....Joan Marcus,
            Bob Marshak, Peter Cunningham
House Manager ....Peter Kulok

CREDITS AND ACKNOWLEDGMENTS
Scenic construction and boat automation by
Hudson Scenic Studios.
Scenery automation by Jeremiah J. Harris Associates,
Inc./East Coast Theatre Supply, Inc. Scenery painted by
Nolan Scenery Studios. Set and hand properties by McHugh
Rollins Associates, Inc. Sculptural elements by Costume
Armour. "Opera Ball" newell post statues and elephant by
Nino Novellino of Costume Armour. Proscenium sculptures
by Stephen Pyle. Draperies by I. Weiss and Sons, Inc. Soft
goods provided by Quartet Theatrical Draperies. Safety
systems by Foy Lighting equipment and special lighting
effects by Four Star Lighting, Inc. Sound equipment and
technical service provided by Masque Sound and Recording
Corp. Special effects designed and executed by Theatre
Magic, Inc., Richard Huggins, President. Costumes
executed by Barbara Matera, Ltd. Costumes for "Hannibal"
and "Masquerade" executed by Parsons/
Meares, Ltd. Men's costumes by Vincent Costumes, Inc.
Costume crafts for "Hannibal" and "Masquerade" by Janet
Harper and Frederick Nihda. Fabric painting by Mary
Macy. Additional costumes by Carelli Costumes, Inc.
Costume accessories by Barak Stribling. Hats by Woody
Shelp. Millinery and masks by Rodney Gordon. Footwear
by Sharlot Battin of Montana Leatherworks, Ltd. Shoes by
JC Theatrical and Costume Footwear and Taffy's N.Y.
Jewelry by Miriam Haskell Jewels. Eyeglasses by H.L. Purdy.
Wigs by The Wig Party. Garcia y Vega cigars used. Makeup
consultant Kris Evans. Emer'gen-C super energy booster
provided by Alacer Corp.

Champagne courtesy of
Champagne G.H. Mumm

Furs by Christie Bros.

Shoes supplied by Peter Fox Limited

"The Phantom" character make-up created and
designed by Christopher Tucker

Magic Consultant—Paul Daniels

CAMERON MACKINTOSH, INC.
Managing Director ....Nicholas Allott
Production Associate ....Shidan Majidi

THE REALLY USEFUL COMPANY INC
Public Relations ....BROWN LLOYD JAMES/
            PETER BROWN

THE REALLY USEFUL GROUP
Directors ....LORD LLOYD WEBBER
            LADY LLOYD WEBBER
            ANDRÉ PTASZYNSKI
            JONATHAN HULL
            HOWARD WITTS
            MARK WORDSWORTH

Performance rights to *The Phantom of the Opera*
are licensed by R&H Theatricals:
www.rnhtheatricals.com

To learn more about the production,
please visit
www.PhantomBroadway.com
Find us on Facebook: The Phantom of the Opera

 **THE SHUBERT ORGANIZATION, INC.**
Board of Directors

The Phantom of the Opera

SCRAPBOOK

Correspondent: Kris Koop Ouellette, "Madame Firmin," understudy "Carlotta," "Madame Giry"

Celebrity Visitors This Year: Carrie Underwood; the entire cast of *That Championship Season*; Cloris Leachman! George Lee Andrews makes us giggle by inventing a very important guest visitor in our audience for every performance. He makes sure to provide proper spelling to me, who faithfully keeps record. Memorizing the names has become our favorite anti-Alzheimer's regimen. Favorites include: Mimee Moomoux Peepi Poopuu, Annagazander Binnaclebatt, and Cecily Sisslesasselsossly.

Backstage Rituals: George Lee Andrews, who has been with the *Phantom* company on Broadway since the show opened 23 years ago, performs a rather elaborate improvised comic dance for the Prop Department Head Tim Higgins and Jon DeVerna, also of Props, immediately prior to his stage left entrance for a crossover scene. The space is tight, but George works his silly magic and almost always puts a button on the number with a nice juicy "raspberry." George also recites Irish poetry—memorized—over the PA system every St. Patrick's Day.

Therapy: Joe Caruso gives the best 30-second shoulder rub immediately prior to our *Hannibal* entrance. (Even with two cracked ribs, this man brings the love!) Many *Phantom* folk enjoy hitting the gym hard, and then TALKING ABOUT IT for the rest of the day. Raoul Bar is a destination—a goal, even—a chance to celebrate another week of surprises. Matt Mezick and Kelly Jeanne Grant are marathoners, raising money for favorite charities as they run. Kelly even started a running group while on the *Phantom* tour.

Make a Little Broadway History Anyone?: Our beautiful, calm Christine, Sara Jean Ford, was serving as a juror on the "most boring civil trial in America" when her cell rang with a frantic call. Would Sara be available to appear in the role of Petra in Broadway's *A Little Night Music*, a role she had understudied months prior, yet never performed. Reminding the Stage Manager that she had left the *ALNM* company quite a while ago to star in *Phantom* on Broadway, Sara was assured that this was no joke. A perfect storm had occurred: the actress playing Petra and both of her understudies were out. Sara instantly agreed that if *Phantom* could excuse her, she would do it! She then began reviewing her lines and the limited blocking she knew. The session broke and just a short commute later, she stood on stage of the Walter Kerr Theatre with "that amazing cast." She used her yoga breathing and her acting training (and New Year's Resolution) to "be in the moment" and make her stunningly successful Broadway bow as Petra.

Who Wears the Least/Most: We have a curious combination of players here—tiny ballerinas with zero body fat, and the rest of us. Small, Medium and Extra-Large opera singers

(L-R): Director Hal Prince, Hugh Panaro and Sara Jean Ford celebrate the show's 23rd anniversary on Broadway January 26, 2011 with the cutting of a cake on stage.

with, let's just say it, PLENTY of body fat. The Teeny Ballerini wear the least, of course. Bare arms, nearly bare legs, short skirts. Those of us who could maybe stand to lose a few pounds are draped in heavy dresses, luxurious furs, and hats upon hats. Trying to keep a "comfortable" temperature around here makes for true madness. It is not uncommon to see an opera singer standing outside in the freezing cold, nor a ballerina wearing her down coat, leg warmers and moon boots, just offstage, prior to an entrance.

Catchphrases Only the Company Would Recognize: "Save your voice—protect your instrument—better mark it…" said before *Don Juan* after a certain Prima Donna left the performance before Act II for the third time, complaining that the sound mix had caused her to blow out her voice.

Richard Poole's "involuntary Chinese splits."

Memorable Directorial Notes: Denny Berry: "Throw up the magic on TAKE." Frank Mastrone: "Where do we THROW UP the magic??"

DB: "TAAAAAAAAAAAAAAKE!!!!!!!!!!"

At another rehearsal…

DB: (after a note session directed to another cast member) "Did you get that, Frank?" FM: "Every word." DB: "I wanted to make sure you weren't dozing off…" FM: "I would hear your voice in my dreams."

"Hear the silence of the lambs," Hal Prince, misquoting "Here the sire may serve the dam" from *Don Juan*.

"Where's my Meg? That was just terrible. That scene just went dead. Make up a line or SOMETHING." —Hal Prince

"I don't know what it was—I don't even know how to describe it. I want to tell you so you can fix it, but I don't have words." —Denny Berry

"The word GUESTS…. Make the final STS… like the sound of a spray bottle. STS. STS. STS." —Kristen Blodgette, indicating said spraying action with her finger.

Biggest Bloopers of 2010/2011: Our show runs with such well-maintained technical and artistic precision, it is extremely rare when we must stop a performance due to a technical difficulty. Recently, five candelabra were bent when the trap doors closed upon them. We had to hold the show for 13 minutes while our carpentry crew worked furiously to get the damaged pieces to descend. An announcement was made to the audience that we would be taking an unscheduled intermission. The audience was so supportive, they cheered when we resumed, then laughed uproariously when, a few minutes back into our performance as Joseph Buquet's hanging causes a delay in the performance of *Il Muto*. M. Firmin announced that the "play will continue in ten minutes time…" Art imitating life!

At a different performance, our pianola began playing on cue, but stopped after just a few notes. The conductor cued the pit pianist, Norman Weiss, to take over, but his keyboard tapped into a bad patch and it sounded like goat-murder. An offstage actor very loudly said, "Holy crap!" just before the ensemble sang our atonal tune a capella. Yet, we were perfectly pitched, which isn't easy to accomplish when performing atonally. We are operatic bad-asses!

In-Theatre Hangouts: There are many, as space is tight. Hugh Panaro's dressing room has maintained the lively gatherings that John Cudia's dressing room previously held. Not nearly big enough for all the visitors, lots of guests hit the floor. The guest who unfailingly gets top priority is Soot, Hugh's beautiful dog. Soot is a good boy, and if Soot wants the couch, not a soul in the building would deny him. Raoul Bar is so popular a hangout that our neighbors, Chris Noth, Kiefer Sutherland, Jason Patric, Jim Gaffigan and Brian Cox stopped by and shared a few laughs and a few drinks after wrapping rehearsal one night. The Stage Manager's office is cramped with actual equipment: computers, printers, copier, fax

The Phantom of the Opera
SCRAPBOOK

machine—and stuffed beyond the gills with merchandise we are preparing to sell for our beloved BC/EFA. Still, we manage to squeeze in, sit on the mini-fridge and chomp down on a bite-size Snickers (or Butterfinger, if you can get there before Andrew Nelson...or Ken Kantor, or just about anyone who sorts through the stash and steals them all). Our Green Room is a row of truly despicable chairs next to a pay phone. It's so cramped, we hang the receiver upside-down so the cord doesn't hit anyone in the face. The Hair Room has become quite the draw because of its offering of sweets, pretzels and always a jar of peanut butter. Dick Miller frequently provides deli snacks and sports on TV, so his space (still painted pink after a practical joke was played) is a real happy place to hang. Thanks to the iPhone, wherever we are, we all sit and chat while playing word games or Angry Birds or watching YouTube videos. We are still connected, but a little less face-to-face.

Off-Site Hangout: Marni Raab organizes a weekly event devoted to quenching our thirst at a wider and wider selection of pubs and clubs in the neighborhood. Southern Hospitality, Nizza, The Russian Vodka Bar, Angus McIndoe, The Rum House, Landmarc, Hourglass Tavern are all tops on the list. Great company, great food & drink, and great service!

Wardrobe Achievement: I would like to draw attention to the artistry and painstaking attention to detail required for the creation of a new masterpiece for our show. This summer, the Eric Winterling Studio hosted our Costume Head Sam Fleming, her right-hand gal Julie Ratcliffe, and my own true self to outfit me with a brand new costume for my new role as Mme. Firmin. I was quickly suited in a white muslin mock-up that any bride in her right mind would be proud to wear on the big day. (Gorgeous, and just the stunt double for what was to come!) Consulting with the original renderings of Costume and Set Designer, Maria Björnson, Sam and Eric brought out swatches of gorgeous fabrics and sort of flapped them over the muslin dress. Watching their very talented eyes make mixes and matches was fascinating, and though I couldn't see how this acid green and brown swatch would EVER go with the Monet-like violet and lilac watercolor print, I knew to trust what they were doing. Weeks later, I was called in for a fitting. This gorgeous confection was revealed and I nearly wept. As they dropped me into it, and it onto me, I realized what couture really is. This dress fit me better than my own skin on most mornings. And so gorgeous! Soooo stunningly beautiful! The buttons and trim were done in the acid green and it highlighted the softer hues of the Monet-like fabric. The structure of the dress gave me an hourglass figure that even I envy, and I am told that the ruffles at the base of the dress took 40 hours to sew. (I made a blind nun joke, but nobody heard. They were too consumed with the perfection of this dress.) I get to wear it in two scenes in the show,

(L-R): David Cryer and original cast member George Lee Andrews (who play Mssrs. Firmin and André) backstage July 9, 2010.

though I sport the matching hat in only one. I suggested we ride the hat in Macy's Thanksgiving Day Parade—not a comment on its size, but its stellar beauty. I will never tire of this dress and hat, and I thank the amazing people at Winterling, as well as Sam Fleming for having the vision to create this work of art!

Sweethearts: Sean MacLaughlin went and married his Monkey! Seriously. Actress Elaine Matthews, who danced the role of the Monkey in the Masquerade scene on tour, said "I do!" at their New Year's Eve wedding this past December. The couple met on the tour and dated for a year before Sean popped the question in a very memorable way. Because they had recently bought an apartment, Sean decided to buy a kitschy ring rather than spending his last cash on a much more expensive engagement ring. He had his eye on a golden Mickey Mouse ring with a QZ stone at Disney's Hollywood Studios, but the two were having so much fun, he couldn't get a moment alone to purchase it. So, Sean did the only logical thing. He picked a fight with Elaine, causing her to storm off. Later, when the couple rejoined at their car, Sean kept up the act, swinging the bag that held the ring and taunting her. She asked to see what it was, and when he didn't hand it over, she grabbed it from him to see what was inside. With the ring in her hands, Sean popped the question and Elaine instantly started crying tears of joy. Wouldn't it be nice if every argument ended like that? They really, really GET each other, and we wish them a lifetime of happiness.

Another Amazing Couple: Wig Stylist Erika Smith and Props Department Dennis Abberton recently became engaged. We are all in love with this couple and everyone had reason to celebrate when the engagement was announced. Dennis found an antique ring that somehow COMPLETELY captures Erika's brilliant spirit...perfect! The big day will be in September 2011, and we hope their gorgeous

dog, Hudson, will be in the ceremony! Best, warm wishes to the happy couple.

Mascot: We have many babies on the way, but one little charmer has stolen all of our hearts. Cameron Joseph Saia, son of Janet and Bennet Saia, has a smile that melts even the hardest of hearts. Every time he visits the building, we all put down whatever we are doing and just try to get close to this little light, bright spirit. Even when he is cranky-pants, which is rare, he's adorable. Janet named Cameron in honor of our beloved Cameron Mackintosh, since most of her lovely career has been performing in his musicals. WE LOVE CAMERON!!!!

Memorable Ad-Lib: Kenneth M. Kantor, aka, MR. "OOPS, I DID IT AGAIN," once again rises to the top of this category. Ken is one stellar talent, but on occasion, Ken 'mis-remembers' his lines. This may be because Ken NEVER misses a performance, and he is SOOOOOOOOOOOO OOOOOLD (tee hee hee), and just by the law of averages, is bound to make a mistake here or there. But let's get on with it! On the deadline date—yes, the deadline had arrived—for last year's *Playbill Yearbook*, I mentioned that Ken had better hurry if he was going to be memorialized in print. And we LAUGHED and LAUGHED, and then I saw a terrible look cross his face. I had jinxed him. Moments later, Ken was making his entrance as Don Attilio, a feature role he understudies. He waddled out as directed and began the scene. But instead of singing: "I suspect my young bride has been untrue to me. I SHALL NOT LEAVE, BUT SHALL HIDE OVER THERE TO OBSERVE HER," Ken sang a patter song of his own creation: "I suspect my young bride has been untrue to me. I shall MEND AND REPEND HER, AND GO OVER THERE AND TRY TO OBSERVE HER." (Personally, I swore he said, "BEND AND UPEND HER." but that's where my brain goes, so....) We also have a castmate who swears Ken sang: "AND GO OVER THERE AND SING MY LOW NOTE." Whatever he sang, he pretty much crapped his pants and we all peed a little!

At a recent rehearsal, the ballet corps broke into a tap dance during the *Il Muto* ballet to see if Denny Berry had indeed "worked on getting a sense of humor" as she had teasingly promised the day before. Denny howled and we all cheered. Nice work EVERYONE!!!

Thirty Seconds with Hugh Panaro: Favorite Celebrity Visitor: Cloris Leachman. Special Backstage Ritual: "Must have dark chocolate before every show!!!" Favorite Therapy: "Organic Cucumber Vodka Monday nights after the show!!!!" Off-site Hangout: "Rio & You sushi and sake!!!!" Mascot: "Soot, of course!!"

A Special Note of Thanks: To Nancy Takei, a wonderful woman who attends every single Wednesday matinee performance of *Phantom*. She rushes from her seat during BC/EFA collections to join us behind the Bar to help us sell our posters, bags, luggage tags and pins. She is our angel! Thank you, sweet Nancy!!!!

The Pitmen Painters

First Preview: September 14, 2010. Opened: September 30, 2010.
Closed December 12, 2010 after 18 Previews and 86 Performances.

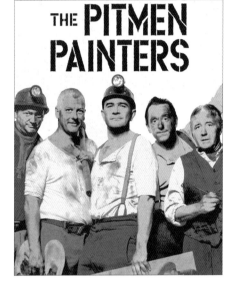

Based on the true story of a group of British miners ("pitmen") who take an art class and wind up becoming famous artists themselves.

CAST
(in alphabetical order)

Oliver Kilbourn ....CHRISTOPHER CONNEL
Harry Wilson ....MICHAEL HODGSON
Robert Lyon ....IAN KELLY
Young Lad/Ben Nicholson .....BRIAN LONSDALE
Susan Parks ....LISA McGRILLIS
George Brown ....DEKA WALMSLEY
Jimmy Floyd ....DAVID WHITAKER
Helen Sutherland ....PHILLIPPA WILSON

The action takes place in Ashington,
Northumberland, Newcastle upon Tyne,
London and Edinburgh between 1934 and 1947.

Stage Manager.............ELIZABETH MOLONEY

UNDERSTUDIES
For Oliver Kilbourn/Harry Wilson/
Young Lad/George Brown/Jimmy Floyd:
TREVOR FOX
For Robert Lyon/Ben Nicholson:
JACK KOENIG
For Susan Parks/Helen Sutherland:
CHRISTA SCOTT-REED

The Actors in *The Pitmen Painters* are appearing with the permission of Actors' Equity Association.

MANHATTAN THEATRE CLUB
SAMUEL J. FRIEDMAN THEATRE

ARTISTIC DIRECTOR
LYNNE MEADOW

EXECUTIVE PRODUCER
BARRY GROVE

BY SPECIAL ARRANGEMENT WITH
BOB BOYETT

PRESENTS

LIVE THEATRE, NEWCASTLE/NATIONAL THEATRE OF GREAT BRITAIN'S

CO-PRODUCTION OF

THE PITMEN PAINTERS

BY
LEE HALL

INSPIRED BY A BOOK BY
WILLIAM FEAVER

WITH

**CHRISTOPHER CONNEL   MICHAEL HODGSON   IAN KELLY
BRIAN LONSDALE   LISA McGRILLIS   DEKA WALMSLEY
DAVID WHITAKER   PHILLIPPA WILSON**

SCENIC & COSTUME DESIGN
GARY McCANN

LIGHTING DESIGN
DOUGLAS KUHRT

SOUND DESIGN
MARTIN HODGSON

PRODUCTION STAGE MANAGER
CHARLES MEANS

DIRECTED BY
MAX ROBERTS

GENERAL MANAGER
FLORIE SEERY

ASSOCIATE ARTISTIC DIRECTOR
MANDY GREENFIELD

DIRECTOR OF ARTISTIC DEVELOPMENT
JERRY PATCH

DIRECTOR OF MARKETING
DEBRA WAXMAN-PILLA

PRESS REPRESENTATIVE
BONEAU/BRYAN-BROWN

PRODUCTION MANAGER
KURT GARDNER

DIRECTOR OF CASTING
NANCY PICCIONE

ARTISTIC LINE PRODUCER
LISA McNULTY

DIRECTOR OF DEVELOPMENT
LYNNE RANDALL

9/30/10

Sitting (L-R): Phillippa Wilson, Brian Lonsdale
Standing (L-R): David Whitaker, Michael Hodgson, Ian Kelly, Deka Walmsley, Christopher Connel

The Pitmen Painters

Christopher Connel
Oliver Kilbourn

Michael Hodgson
Harry Wilson

Ian Kelly
Robert Lyon

Brian Lonsdale
Young Lad/
Ben Nicholson

Lisa McGrillis
Susan Parks

Deka Walmsley
George Brown

David Whitaker
Jimmy Floyd

Phillippa Wilson
Helen Sutherland

Trevor Fox
u/s Oliver Kilbourn/
Harry Wilson/Young
Lad/George Brown/
Jimmy Floyd

Jack Koenig
u/s Robert Lyon/
Ben Nicholson

Christa Scott-Reed
u/s Susan Parks/
Helen Sutherland

Lee Hall
Playwright

Max Roberts
Director

Gary McCann
Scenic & Costume
Design

Douglas Kuhrt
Lighting Design

Lynne Meadow
Artistic Director,
Manhattan Theatre
Club, Inc.

Barry Grove
Executive Producer,
Manhattan Theatre
Club, Inc.

Bob Boyett

John Curless
u/s Oliver Kilbourn/
Young Lad

FRONT OF HOUSE STAFF
Front Row (L-R): Christine Snyder, Patricia Polhill, Wendy Wright, Bridget Leak
Back Row (L-R): John Wyffels, Roger Darbasie, Ed Brashear, Jim Joseph, Richard Ponce

The Pitmen Painters

STAGE MANAGEMENT
(L-R): Charles Means (Production Stage Manager), Elizabeth Moloney (Stage Manager), Sara Gunter (UK Stage Manager), Melissa Miller (Production Assistant), Seth Shepsle.

BOX OFFICE
(L-R): Jeff Davis, David Dillon

CAST AND CREW
Front Row (L-R): Michael Hodgson, Brian Lonsdale, Elizabeth Moloney, Christa Scott-Reed, Charles Means
Middle Row (L-R): Robin Baxter, Deka Walmsley, Trevor Fox, Lisa McGrillis, Jackie Gehrt, Tom Sharkey
Back Row (L-R): David Whitaker, Jason Dodds, Phillippa Wilson, Tim Walters, Ian Kelly, Lou Shapiro, Jeff Dodson, Peggie Kurz, Christopher Connel, Sam Patt, John Curless

The Pitmen Painters

The Pitmen Painters
SCRAPBOOK

Correspondent: Phillippa Wilson, "Helen Sutherland"

Memorable Opening Night Letter, Fax or Note: One from my mum which said "Completely totally proud of You" on the front!! I was quite emotional.

Opening Night Gifts: A brilliant Hoody from MTC with University of Ashington on the front and "*Pitmen Painters*" and all the dates on the back. I shall wear it proudly!!!!

Most Exciting Celebrity Visitor: Probably Zach Levi of "Chuck," *Tangled* and *Alvin and the Chipmunks 2* fame. He came back after and loved the show and was incredibly sweet with my 7-year-old daughter Daisy who has a total crush on him, as do I!!

Actors Who Performed the Most Roles in This Show: Brian Lonsdale, who has two parts, and Trevor Fox, who understudies all five Pitmen.

Who Has Done the Most Shows in Their Career: Davey Whitaker.

Special Backstage Rituals: Before every show, we sing the miners' hymn "Gresford" as a vocal warmup onstage. Preshow Joke time with Deka Walmsley (especially the one about the camp Christian gladiators).

Favorite Moments During Each Performance: If the audience are with us and laughing loudly, every moment.

The guys "counting Geordies" during the pre-show announcement.

Giving the V-sign to Brian backstage whenever possible.

Favorite In-Theatre Gathering Place: The boys come into the girls' dressing room quite a lot funnily enough, sometimes to borrow makeup!! No names....

Favorite Off-Site Hangouts: The Glasshouse Tavern over the road from the theatre. The staff are lovely!!! Leicester Square Wagamamas and the National Theatre Canteen.

Favorite Snack Food: All American food!!! Tootsie rolls, candy corn.

Mascot: Daisy the Deputy Assistant Stage Manager.

Favorite Therapy: Stella Artois. Altoids. Tea and Jaffa Cakes.

Memorable Press Encounter: Being in *The New York Times* and getting a good review was something I won't forget in a hurry.

Memorable Stage Door Fan Encounter: They've all been delightful and very appreciative!!

Internet Buzz: I had Google alerts on my computer and was quite amazed as to how much buzz there was!!! Also Joan Rivers had said on Twitter that she was heading home from Las Vegas to see her dogs and *The Pitmen Painters*. Sadly she cancelled!! Gutted!!

Fastest Costume Change: I was Skyping with some friends when I heard my call to go on for the second half and I was in a state of undress. I went on stage with a loudly beating heart that night!! An actor prepares!!!!

Who Wore the Heaviest/Hottest Costumes:

1. Bows following the opening night on Broadway. (L-R): Christopher Connel, Michael Hodgson, Phillippa Wilson (*Yearbook* correspondent) and Brian Lonsdale.
2. Ian Kelly grins at the audience reaction during curtain calls at the Broadway premiere.
3. (L-R): Ian Kelly, Phillippa Wilson, Chris Connel, Brian Lonsdale, David Whitaker, Lisa McGrillis, Deka Walmsley, Michael Hodgson. The last night of the UK Tour.

All the boys are in heavy woolen three-piece suits. I have the most costumes and changes though!!

Who Wore the Least: Lisa McGrillis, wearing only a drape. Which she drops to the floor.

Catchphrases Only the Company Would Recognize: "Ye de de art divvint ya?" "Nothing queer about old Carruthers!"

Memorable Directorial Note: Act better!

Company In-Jokes: Funday Sunday. Al-a-toids and Small-a-toids.

Nicknames: "The Captain." "Ian Kelly" off the Tele.

Sweethearts Within the Company: None, we can't stand each other (joke!!). Michael Hodgson and the Tin of Candy in the stage management office.

Coolest Thing About Being in This Show: It's just the most wonderful show and company I've ever worked with and just being here on Broadway doing it is sooooo cool.

Also: On the first day of rehearsals in Newcastle back in 2007, someone opened the door of the rehearsal room and some pigeons decided to join us and spent the whole day flapping around and look at us now!!!

Priscilla Queen of the Desert

First Preview: February 28, 2011. Opened: March 20, 2011.
Still running as of May 31, 2011.

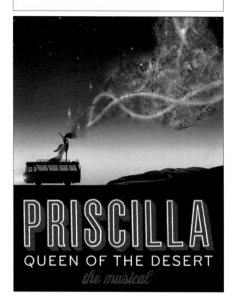

PRISCILLA
QUEEN OF THE DESERT
the musical

Three drag queens go on an epic adventure through the dusty Outback of Australia in a tricked-out bus named Priscilla. They believe they are headed to do a show in a distant city, but one of them has a hidden goal—to be reunited with his son. Based on a popular film, this musical uses pop songs of the 1970s and 1980s to tell its story.

CAST
(in order of appearance)

Divas	JACQUELINE B. ARNOLD, ANASTACIA McCLESKEY, ASHLEY SPENCER
Tick (Mitzi)	WILL SWENSON
Miss Understanding	NATHAN LEE GRAHAM
Marion	JESSICA PHILLIPS
Benji	LUKE MANNIKUS, ASHTON WOERZ
Farrah/Young Bernadette	STEVE SCHEPIS
Bernadette	TONY SHELDON
Adam (Felicia)	NICK ADAMS
Shirley	KEALA SETTLE
Jimmy	JAMES BROWN III
Bob	C. DAVID JOHNSON
Cynthia	J. ELAINE MARCOS
Frank	MIKE McGOWAN
Ensemble	THOM ALLISON, JACQUELINE B. ARNOLD, JAMES BROWN III, KYLE BROWN, NATHAN LEE GRAHAM, GAVIN LODGE, J. ELAINE MARCOS, ANASTACIA McCLESKEY, MIKE McGOWAN, JEFF METZLER, JESSICA PHILLIPS, STEVE SCHEPIS, KEALA SETTLE, ASHLEY SPENCER,

Continued on next page

⇥N⇤ PALACE THEATRE
UNDER THE DIRECTION OF
STEWART F. LANE, JAMES M. NEDERLANDER AND JAMES L. NEDERLANDER

Bette Midler; James L. Nederlander; Garry McQuinn; Liz Koops; Michael Hamlyn; Allan Scott; Roy Furman/Richard Willis; Terry Allen Kramer; Terri and Timothy Childs; Ken Greiner; Ruth Hendel; Chugg Entertainment; Michael Buckley; Stewart F. Lane/Bonnie Comley; Bruce Davey; Thierry Suc /TS3; Bartner/Jenkins; Broadway Across America/H. Koenigsberg; M. Lerner/D. Bisno/K. Seidel/R. Gold; Paul Boskind and Martian Entertainment/Spirtas-Mauro Productions/MAS Music Arts & Show; and David Mirvish

In association with MGM ON STAGE
Darcie Denkert and Dean Stolber
Present

PRISCILLA
QUEEN OF THE DESERT
the musical

Book by
STEPHAN ELLIOTT & ALLAN SCOTT
Based on the Latent Image/ Specific Films Motion Picture
Distributed by Metro-Goldwyn-Mayer Inc.

Starring

WILL SWENSON	TONY SHELDON	NICK ADAMS	C. DAVID JOHNSON

with
JAMES BROWN III   NATHAN LEE GRAHAM   J. ELAINE MARCOS   MIKE McGOWAN   JESSICA PHILLIPS   STEVE SCHEPIS   KEALA SETTLE
and
JACQUELINE B. ARNOLD   ANASTACIA MCCLESKEY   ASHLEY SPENCER

THOM ALLISON   KYLE BROWN   JOSHUA BUSCHER   GAVIN LODGE   LUKE MANNIKUS   ELLYN MARIE MARSH   JEFF METZLER
ERIC SCIOTTO   AMAKER SMITH   ESTHER STILWELL   BRYAN WEST   TAD WILSON   ASHTON WOERZ

Bus Concept & Production Design BRIAN THOMSON	*Costume Design* TIM CHAPPEL & LIZZY GARDINER	*Lighting Design* NICK SCHLIEPER	*Sound Design* JONATHAN DEANS & PETER FITZGERALD
Orchestrations STEPHEN "SPUD" MURPHY & CHARLIE HULL	*Musical Coordinator* JOHN MILLER	*Music Director* JEFFREY KLITZ	*Developed for the Stage By* SIMON PHILLIPS
Casting TELSEY · COMPANY	*Press Representative* BONEAU/BRYAN-BROWN	*Advertising* SPOTCO	*Director of Marketing* NICK PRAMIK
Technical Supervisor DAVID BENKEN	*Production Stage Manager* DAVID HYSLOP	*Flying By* FOY	*Makeup Design* CASSIE HANLON
Associate Director DEAN BRYANT	*Associate Choreographer* ANDREW HALLSWORTH		*Associate Producer* KEN SUNSHINE

General Manager
B.J. HOLT

Executive Producer
ALECIA PARKER

Production Supervised by
JERRY MITCHELL

Music Supervision & Arrangements
STEPHEN "SPUD" MURPHY

Choreographer
ROSS COLEMAN

Director
SIMON PHILLIPS

The original motion picture was written by Stephan Elliott, produced by Al Clark and Michael Hamlyn, executive producer Rebel Penfold-Russell and was financed with the assistance of the Film Finance Corporation of Australia Limited and the New South Wales Film and Television Office.

3/20/11

(L-R): Will Swenson, Nick Adams, Tony Sheldon and the cast

Photo by Joan Marcus

Priscilla Queen of the Desert

MUSICAL NUMBERS

Music composer and publisher information at www.PriscillaOnBroadway.com.

ACT I

DOWNTOWN SYDNEY
The Overture
"It's Raining Men" .... The Divas, Tick and Company
"What's Love Got to Do With It?" .... Miss Understanding
"I Say a Little Prayer" .... Tick
"Don't Leave Me This Way" .... Bernadette, Tick and Company
"Material Girl" .... Felicia and the Boys
"Go West" .... Bernadette, Tick, Adam and Company

THE BLACK STUMP
"Holiday/Like a Virgin" .... Adam, Tick, Bernadette
"I Say a Little Prayer" (reprise) .... Tick and the Divas

BROKEN HILL
"I Love the Nightlife" .... Shirley, Bernadette, Mitzi, Felicia and Company
"True Colors" .... Bernadette, Mitzi, Felicia

THE ROAD TO NOWHERE
"Sempre Libre" .... Felicia and the Divas

THE MIDDLE OF NOWHERE
"Color My World" .... Adam, Tick, Bernadette and Company
"I Will Survive" .... Bernadette, Felicia, Mitzi, Jimmy and Company

ACT II

WOOP WOOP
"Thank God I'm a Country Boy" .... The Company
"A Fine Romance" .... Young Bernadette and Les Girls
"Thank God I'm a Country Boy" (reprise) .... The Company
"Shake Your Groove Thing" .... Mitzi, Bernadette, Felicia and the Divas
"Pop Muzik" .... Cynthia and Company
"A Fine Romance" (reprise) .... Bob

THE BACK BEYOND
"Girls Just Wanna Have Fun" .... Adam and the Divas

COOBER PEDY
"Hot Stuff" .... Felicia, the Divas and Bernadette
"MacArthur Park" .... Bernadette, Tick, the Divas and Company

ALICE SPRINGS
"Boogie Wonderland" .... The Company
"The Floor Show" .... Mitzi, Bernadette, Felicia and Company
"Always on My Mind" .... Tick, Benji
"Like a Prayer" .... Felicia and Company
"We Belong" .... Felicia, Mitzi, Bernadette and Company
"Finally Medley" .... The Company

The Company

Photo by Joan Marcus

Cast Continued

BRYAN WEST, TAD WILSON

Dance Captain: ERIC SCIOTTO
Assistant Dance Captain: JOSHUA BUSCHER

Tony Sheldon is appearing with the permission of
Actors' Equity Association.

UNDERSTUDIES
Swings:
JOSHUA BUSCHER, ELLYN MARIE MARSH,
ERIC SCIOTTO, AMAKER SMITH,
ESTHER STILWELL

For Divas, Marion, Shirley, Cynthia:
ELLYN MARIE MARSH, ESTHER STILWELL
For Tick (Mitzi):
GAVIN LODGE, ERIC SCIOTTO
For Miss Understanding:
THOM ALLISON, JAMES BROWN III
For Benji:
LUKE MANNIKUS, ASHTON WOERZ
For Farrah/Young Bernadette:
JOSHUA BUSCHER, JEFF METZLER
For Bernadette:
THOM ALLISON, GAVIN LODGE
For Adam (Felicia):
STEVE SCHEPIS, BRYAN WEST
For Jimmy:
THOM ALLISON, AMAKER SMITH
For Bob:
MIKE McGOWAN, TAD WILSON
For Frank:
KYLE BROWN, GAVIN LODGE

ORCHESTRA
Conductor:
JEFFREY KLITZ
Associate Conductor:
JEFF MARDER
Woodwinds:
DAVID MANN
Guitar:
ED HAMILTON
Trumpet:
BARRY DANIELIAN
Trombone:
MICHAEL DAVIS
Bass:
LUICO HOPPER
Drums:
WARREN ODZE
Percussion:
ROGER SQUITERO
Music Coordinator:
JOHN MILLER

Priscilla Queen of the Desert

Will Swenson
Tick/Mitzi

Tony Sheldon
Bernadette

Nick Adams
Adam/Felicia

C. David Johnson
Bob

Jacqueline B. Arnold
Diva

Anastacia
McCleskey
Diva

Ashley Spencer
Diva

James Brown III
Jimmy

Nathan Lee Graham
Miss Understanding

J. Elaine Marcos
Cynthia

Mike McGowan
Frank

Jessica Phillips
Marion

Steve Schepis
Farrah/
Young Bernadette

Keala Settle
Shirley

Thom Allison
Ensemble

Kyle Brown
Ensemble

Joshua Buscher
Swing,
Asst. Dance Captain

Gavin Lodge
Ensemble

Luke Mannikus
Benji

Ellyn Marie Marsh
Swing

Jeff Metzler
Ensemble

Eric Sciotto
Swing,
Dance Captain

Amaker Smith
Swing

Esther Stilwell
Swing

Bryan West
Ensemble

Tad Wilson
Ensemble

Ashton Woerz
Benji

Simon Phillips
Director

Jerry Mitchell
Production
Supervisor

Tim Chappel
Costume Design

Lizzy Gardiner
Costume Design

Jonathan Deans
Sound Design

Jeffrey Klitz
Music Director

John Miller
Music Coordinator

Bernard Telsey,
Telsey + Company
Casting

Priscilla Queen of the Desert

Dean Bryant
Associate Director

David Benken
Technical Supervisor

Alecia Parker
Executive Producer

Bette Midler
Producer

James L.
Nederlander
Producer

Garry McQuinn
Producer

Llz Koops
Producer

Roy Furman
Producer

Richard Willis
Producer

Terry Allen Kramer
Producer

Timothy Childs
Producer

Ken Greiner
Producer

Ruth Hendel
Producer

Michael Chugg
Producer

Stewart F. Lane/Bonnie Comley
Producers

John Gore,
Broadway Across
America
Producer

Thomas B. McGrath,
Broadway Across
America
Producer

Myla Lerner
Producer

Debbie Bisno
Producer

Kit Seidel
Producer

Rebecca Gold
Producer

Paul Boskind and
Martian
Entertainment
Producer

Carl D. White,
Martian
Entertainment LLC
Producer

Kevin Spirtas,
Spirtas-Mauro
Productions
Producer

Scott Mauro,
Spirtas-Mauro
Productions
Producer

Photo by Brian Mapp

COMPANY MANAGEMENT & STAGE MANAGEMENT
Standing (L-R): Thom Clay, Glynn David Turner, Mahlon Kruse, David Hyslop

Seated (L-R): Tammie Ward and Megan Schneid

Priscilla Queen of the Desert

HAIR/MAKE UP DEPARTMENT
(L-R): Mitch Hale, Jacqueline Bensaid, Hagen Linss,
John "Jack" Curtin

Photos by Brian Mapp

EVENING DOORMAN
Freddy Quinones

WARDROBE DEPARTMENT
Seated (L-R): Emily Ockenfels, Del Miskie,
Sara Darneille, Laura Horner

Middle Row (L-R): Danny Foss, Pam Hughes,
Amy Micallef

Back Row (L-R): Keith Shaw, Laura Ellington,
Jennifer Jefferson, Herb Ouellette,
Vangeli Kaseluris, Thomas Sharkey,
Meghan Carsella, James Roy, Megan Bowers

CREW
Standing (L-R): Steve Henshaw, Jerry Marshall,
Patrick Eviston, Jamie Leonard, Roy Frank

Kneeling (L-R): James Cariot, Brian Penney,
Michael Shepp Jr., Jesse Hancox

Promises, Promises

First Preview: March 28, 2010. Opened: April 25, 2010.
Closed January 2, 2011 after 30 Previews and 289 Performances.

PLAYBILL

A 1960's morality tale about Chuck Baxter, an ambitious young insurance company clerk who hopes to speed his rise in the company by lending out his apartment to high-ranking executives for their extramarital affairs. Baxter hopes his quick promotions will impress Fran Kubelik, a pretty coworker he likes. But fate has a surprise in store.

CAST

(in order of appearance)

Chuck Baxter	SEAN HAYES
J.D. Sheldrake	TONY GOLDWYN
Fran Kubelik	KRISTIN CHENOWETH
Eddie Roth	KEITH KÜHL
Mr. Dobitch	BROOKS ASHMANSKAS
Sylvia Gilhooley, Nurse, Miss Polansky	MEGAN SIKORA
Mike Kirkeby	PETER BENSON
Ginger, Miss Della Hoya, Lum Ding Hostess	CAMERON ADAMS
Mr. Eichelberger	SEÁN MARTIN HINGSTON
Vivien, Miss Wong	MAYUMI MIGUEL
Dr. Dreyfuss	DICK LATESSA
Jesse Vanderhof	KEN LAND
Miss Kreplinski, Helen Sheldrake	ASHLEY AMBER
Company Doctor, Karl Kubelik	BRIAN O'BRIEN
Miss Olson	HELEN ANKER
Kathy, Orchestra Voice	SARAH JANE EVERMAN
Patsy, Orchestra Voice	KRISTEN BETH WILLIAMS

Continued on next page

☺ BROADWAY THEATRE

1681 Broadway
A Shubert Organization Theatre

Philip J. Smith, *Chairman*   Robert E. Wankel, *President*

BROADWAY ACROSS AMERICA   CRAIG ZADAN   NEIL MERON
THE WEINSTEIN COMPANY / TERRY ALLEN KRAMER   CANDY SPELLING   PAT ADDISS
BERNIE ABRAMS / MICHAEL SPEYER   TAKONKIET VIRAVAN / SCENARIO THAILAND
NORTON & ELAYNE HERRICK / BARRY & FRAN WEISSLER / TBS SERVICE / LAUREL OZTEMEL

SEAN HAYES   KRISTIN CHENOWETH

The Musical Comedy

Book by   Music by   Lyrics by
NEIL SIMON   BURT BACHARACH   HAL DAVID

Based on the screenplay "The Apartment" by BILLY WILDER *and* I. A. L. DIAMOND
By arrangement with MGM ON STAGE

TONY GOLDWYN

DICK LATESSA
and
MOLLY SHANNON

BROOKS ASHMANSKAS   HELEN ANKER   PETER BENSON   SEÁN MARTIN HINGSTON   KEN LAND

CAMERON ADAMS   ASHLEY AMBER   WENDI BERGAMINI   NIKKI RENEE DANIELS   MARGOT DE LA BARRE
SIMONE DE LA RUE   SARAH JANE EVERMAN   KEITH KÜHL   MARTY LAWSON   IAN LIBERTO   MAYUMI MIGUEL
BRIAN O'BRIEN   SARAH O'GLEBY   ADAM PERRY   MEGAN SIKORA   MATT WALL
RYAN WATKINSON   KRISTEN BETH WILLIAMS

Scenic Design by **SCOTT PASK**	Costume Design by **BRUCE PASK**	Lighting Design by **DONALD HOLDER**	Sound Design by **BRIAN RONAN**
Hair and Wig Design by **TOM WATSON**	Music Coordinator **HOWARD JOINES**		Dance Music Arranger **DAVID CHASE**
Casting by **TARA RUBIN CASTING**	Production Stage Manager **MICHAEL J. PASSARO**		Associate Director / Choreographer **CHRISTOPHER BAILEY**
Production Manager **JUNIPER STREET PRODUCTIONS**	Press Representative **THE HARTMAN GROUP**		Marketing **TYPE A MARKETING ANNE RIPPEY**
General Management **ALAN WASSER - ALLAN WILLIAMS MARK SHACKET**	Associate Producers **MICHAEL MCCABE / JOSEPH SMITH STAGE VENTURES 2009 NO. 2 LIMITED PARTNERSHIP**		Executive Producer **BETH WILLIAMS**

Music Director
PHIL RENO

Orchestrations by
JONATHAN TUNICK

Directed *and* Choreographed by
ROB ASHFORD

10/11/10

(L-R): Sean Hayes and Kristin Chenoweth

Photo by Joan Marcus

Promises, Promises

MUSICAL NUMBERS

Manhattan, 1962

ACT I

"Half As Big As Life"	Chuck
"Grapes of Roth"	Chuck, Bar Patrons
"Upstairs"	Chuck
"You'll Think of Someone"	Fran, Chuck
"Our Little Secret"	Chuck, Sheldrake
"I Say a Little Prayer"	Fran, Girls
"She Likes Basketball"	Chuck
"Knowing When to Leave"	Fran
"Where Can You Take a Girl?"	Dobitch, Kirkeby, Eichelberger, Vanderhof
"Wanting Things"	Sheldrake
"Turkey Lurkey Time"	Miss Polansky, Miss Wong, Miss Della Hoya and the Employees of Consolidated Life
"A House Is Not a Home"	Fran

ACT II

"A Fact Can Be a Beautiful Thing"	Chuck, Marge, Bar Patrons
"Whoever You Are"	Fran
"Christmas Day"	Sheldrake, Mrs. Sheldrake, Party Guests
"A House Is Not a Home" (Reprise)	Chuck
"A Young Pretty Girl Like You"	Chuck, Dr. Dreyfuss
"I'll Never Fall in Love Again"	Fran, Chuck
"Promises, Promises"	Chuck
"I'll Never Fall in Love Again" (Reprise)	Fran, Chuck

ORCHESTRA

Conductor: PHIL RENO
Associate Conductor: MAT EISENSTEIN
Music Coordinator: HOWARD JOINES
Reeds: LES SCOTT, JAMES ERCOLE,
   KENNETH DYBISZ,
   JACQUELINE HENDERSON
Trumpets: DAVID TRIGG, DAN URNESS,
   BARRY DANIELIAN
Trombone: JASON JACKSON
Drums: PERRY CAVARI
Bass: MICHAEL KUENNEN
Guitar: ED HAMILTON
Percussion: BILL HAYES
Concertmaster: RICK DOLAN
Violin: ELIZABETH LIM-DUTTON
Viola: LIUH-WEN TING
Cello: LAURA BONTRAGER
Keyboard 1: MATTHEW PERRI
Keyboard 2/Associate Conductor:
   MAT EISENSTEIN
Synthesizer Programmer: BRUCE SAMUELS
Music Copying:
   EMILY GRISHMAN MUSIC PREPARATION
   – KATHARINE EDMONDS/
   EMILY GRISHMAN

(L-R): Sean Hayes and Molly Shannon

Photo by Joan Marcus

The Playbill Broadway Yearbook 2010-2011

Cast Continued

Barbara,
   Orchestra Voice ....NIKKI RENEE DANIELS
Sharon,
   Orchestra Voice .... MARGOT DE LA BARRE
Night Watchman,
   New Young Executive .....RYAN WATKINSON
Lum Ding Waiter ....MARTY LAWSON
Eugene ....ADAM PERRY
Marge MacDougall ....MOLLY SHANNON

SWINGS

WENDI BERGAMINI, SIMONE DE LA RUE,
IAN LIBERTO, SARAH O'GLEBY, MATT WALL

UNDERSTUDIES

For Chuck Baxter: MATT WALL
For Fran Kubelik: SARAH JANE EVERMAN,
   MEGAN SIKORA
For J.D. Sheldrake: KEN LAND,
   BRIAN O'BRIEN
For Dr. Dreyfuss: KEN LAND
For Marge MacDougall: MEGAN SIKORA,
   KRISTEN BETH WILLIAMS
For Mr. Dobitch, Vanderhof: BRIAN O'BRIEN,
   MATT WALL
For Eichelberger, Mike Kirkeby:
   MARTY LAWSON, MATT WALL,
   RYAN WATKINSON
For Karl Kubelik: IAN LIBERTO, MATT WALL,
   RYAN WATKINSON
For Night Watchman, Lum Ding Waiter, Company
   Doctor, New Young Executive: IAN LIBERTO,
   MATT WALL
For Miss Olson, Miss Polansky: ASHLEY AMBER,
   WENDI BERGAMINI, SARAH O'GLEBY
For Miss Della Hoya, Ginger, Miss Wong, Vivian,
   Miss Kreplinski, Helen Sheldrake, Sylvia
   Gilhooley, Nurse, Lum Ding Hostess, Orchestra
   Voices: WENDI BERGAMINI, SARAH
   O'GLEBY

Dance Captain: SARAH O'GLEBY
Assistant Dance Captain: MATT WALL

Promises, Promises

Sean Hayes
Chuck Baxter

Kristin Chenoweth
Fran Kubelik

Tony Goldwyn
J.D. Sheldrake

Molly Shannon
Marge MacDougall

Dick Latessa
Dr. Dreyfuss

Brooks Ashmanskas
Mr. Dobitch

Helen Anker
Miss Olson

Peter Benson
Mike Kirkeby

Seán Martin
Hingston
Mr. Eichelberger

Ken Land
Jesse Vanderhof

Cameron Adams
*Miss Della Hoya,
Ginger,
Lum Ding Hostess*

Ashley Amber
*Miss Kreplinski,
Helen Sheldrake*

Wendi Bergamini
Swing

Nikki Renee Daniels
*Barbara,
Orchestra Voice*

Margot de La Barre
*Sharon,
Orchestra Voice*

Simone De La Rue
Swing

Sarah Jane Everman
*Kathy,
Orchestra Voice*

Keith Kühl
Eddie Roth

Marty Lawson
Lum Ding Waiter

Ian Liberto
Swing

Mayumi Miguel
Miss Wong, Vivien

Brian O'Brien
*Company Doctor,
Karl Kubelik*

Sarah O'Gleby
*Swing,
Dance Captain*

Adam Perry
Eugene

Megan Sikora
*Miss Polansky,
Sylvia Gilhooley,
Nurse*

Matt Wall
*Swing, Assistant
Dance Captain*

Ryan Watkinson
*Night Watchman,
New Young
Executive*

Kristen Beth
Williams
*Patsy,
Orchestra Voice*

Neil Simon
Book

Burt Bacharach
Music

Hal David
Lyricist

Rob Ashford
*Director/
Choreographer*

Phil Reno
Music Director

Scott Pask
Scenic Design

Bruce Pask
Costume Design

Promises, Promises

Donald Holder
Lighting Design

Brian Ronan
Sound Design

Tom Watson
Hair and Wig Design

Thomas Schall
Fight Director

Jonathan Tunick
Orchestrations

David Chase
*Dance Music
Arranger*

Howard Joines
Music Coordinator

Joseph DeLuise, Alexandra Paull,
Hillary Blanken, Ana Rose Greene,
Kevin Broomell, Guy Kwan,
Juniper Street Productions
Production Manager

Tara Rubin Casting
Casting

Alan Wasser
*General
Management*

Allan Williams
*General
Management*

John Gore,
CEO,
Broadway Across
America
Producer

Thomas B. McGrath,
Chairman
Broadway Across
America
Producer

Craig Zadan and Neil Meron
Producers

Candy Spelling
Producer

Pat Flicker Addiss
Producer

Bob Weinstein,
The Weinstein
Company
Producer

Harvey Weinstein,
The Weinstein
Company
Producer

Terry Allen Kramer
Producer

Bernard Abrams
Producer

Michael Speyer
Producer

Norton Herrick
Producer

Barry & Fran Weissler
Producers

Beth Williams
Executive Producer

Nathan Balser
Swing

Katie Finneran
Marge MacDougall

Chelsea Krombach
*Sharon,
Orchestra Voice*

Matt Loehr
Lum Ding Waiter

Matthew Steffens
Swing

Chelsea Krombach
*Sharon,
Orchestra Voice*

Promises, Promises

ORCHESTRA
Front Row (L-R): Phil Reno, Rick Dolan, Jackie Henderson, Mat Eisenstein

Back Row (L-R): Barry Danielian, Joe Choroszewski, Richard Brice, Mike Kuennen, Les Scott, Jimmy Ercole, Ken Dybisz, Matt Perri, Ed Hamilton

WARDROBE
Front Row (L-R): Jay Woods, Barry Hoff, Dolly Williams, Eugene Nicks, Veneda Truesdale

Back Row (L-R): Brendan Cooper, Christel Murdock, Melanie McClintock, Shana Albery, Fred Castner, Michael Harrell

STAGE DOOR
Ellsworth Butts

WIG/HAIR DEPARTMENT
Joshua First, Carmel Vargyas, Tom Augustine

COMPANY MANAGEMENT AND STAGE MANAGEMENT
Front Row: Cathy Kwon

Back Row (L-R): Penny Daulton, Alex Lyu Volckhausen, Michael J. Passaro, Pat Sosnow, Shannon Hammons

Promises, Promises

Photos by Brian Mapp

STAGE CREW
Front Row (L-R): Mike Bernstein, Devin Biggart, Rick DalCortivo, Rick DalCortivo Jr, Peter Becker

Back Row (L-R): Charles Rasmussen, George Milne, Scott "Gus" Poitras, Alan Grudzinski, Tommy Cole, Mike Farfalla, Chris Sloan, Tyler Ricci, Mike Cornell

BOX OFFICE
(L-R): James Toguville, Debbie Giarratano

FRONT OF HOUSE STAFF
Front Row (L-R) Dom Giovanni, Ismeal Tirado, Isaac Trujillo, Michael S. R. Harris, Casey Ademick, Brook Bokun, Lori Bokun

Middle Row (L-R): William Phelan, Barbara Arias, Andie (Infra-Red), Ulises Santiago, Tiffany Murphy, Lisa Maisonet, Mario Carillo, Jorge Colon, Svetlana Pinkhas

Back Row (L-R): Mattie Robinson, John Hall, Andrew Sanford, Mae Park, Sean Lanigan, Ron (Security), Jerry Gallagher, Tony (Security), Kathleen Powell, Selene Nelson

---

STAFF FOR *PROMISES, PROMISES*

GENERAL MANAGEMENT
ALAN WASSER ASSOCIATES
Alan Wasser   Allan Williams
Mark Shacket

GENERAL PRESS REPRESENTATIVE
THE HARTMAN GROUP
Michael Hartman
Wayne Wolfe   Matt Ross

COMPANY MANAGER
Penelope Daulton

CASTING
TARA RUBIN CASTING
Tara Rubin CSA, Merri Sugarman CSA,
Eric Woodall CSA, Laura Schutzel CSA, Dale Brown CSA,
Paige Blansfield, Kaitlin Shaw

PRODUCTION MANAGEMENT
JUNIPER STREET PRODUCTIONS
Hillary Blanken Guy Kwan
Kevin Broomell   Ana Rose Greene

FIGHT DIRECTOR
Thomas Schall

Production Stage Manager	Michael J. Passaro
Stage Manager	Pat Sosnow
Assistant Stage Manager	Jim Athens
Assistant Company Manager	Cathy Kwon
Assistant Director	Stephen Sposito
SDC Ockrent Directing Fellow	Gregg Wiggans
Dance Captain	Sarah O'Gleby
Assistant Dance Captain	Matt Wall
Associate Scenic Designer	Orit Jacoby Carroll
Assistant Scenic Designer	Lauren Alvarez
Assistant to the Scenic Designer	G. Warren Stiles
Associate Costume Designer	Matthew Pachtman
Assistant Costume Designer	Katie Irish
Assistant to the Costume Designer	Jessica Pabst

Promises, Promises

Costume Shopper ....Amanda Bujak
Associate Lighting Designer ....Karen Spahn
Associate Lighting Designer ....Carolyn Wong
Assistant to the Lighting Designer ...R. Christopher Stokes
Associate Sound Designer ....Joanna Staub
Moving Lighting Programmer ....Richard Tyndall
Make-up Design ....Ashley Ryan
Technical Director ....Fred Gallo
Head Carpenter ....Scott "Gus" Poitras
Flyman ....Joel DeRuyter
Automation Carpenter ....Hugh Hardyman
Assistant Carpenters ....Alan Grudzinski,
Devin Biggart
Production Electricians ....Randall Zaibek,
James Fedigan
Head Electrician ....Michael Cornell
Production Properties Supervisor ....Tim Abel
Head Properties Supervisor ....Mike Bernstein
Production Sound Engineer ....Christopher Sloan
Deck Audio ....Jason McKenna
Advance Audio ....Jason McKenna
Wardrobe Supervisor ....Dolly Williams
Assistant Wardrobe Supervisor ....Fred Castner
Dresser to Mr. Hayes ....Barry Hoff
Dresser to Ms. Chenoweth ....Jay Woods
Dressers ....Shana Albery, Brendan Cooper,
Michael Harrell, Melanie McClintock,
Jess McGovney, Virginia Neininger,
Eugene Nicks, Emily Ockenfels,
Veneda Truesdale
Hair Supervisor ....Thomas Augustine
Assistant Hair Supervisor ....Joshua First
Hair Dresser ....Joshua Gericke
House Carpenter ....Charles Rasmussen
House Electrician ....George D. Milne
House Properties ....Rick DalCortivo
House Flyman ....Thomas Cole Jr.
Music Coordinator ....Howard Joines
Music Copying ......Emily Grishman Music Preparation –
Katharine Edmonds / Emily Grishman
Advertising ....Serino Coyne/Nancy Coyne,
Sandy Block, Greg Corradetti,
Robert Jones, Danielle Boyle
Marketing ....Type A Marketing/
Anne Rippey, Elyce Henkin,
Sarah Ziering
Website Design &
Internet Marketing ....Art Meets Commerce/
Jim Glaub, Laurie Connor,
Kevin Keating, Chip Meyrelles,
Whitney Manalio Creighton, Mark Seeley
Theatre Displays ....King Displays
Legal Counsel ....Levine Plotkin & Menin LLP/
Loren Plotkin, Esq.;
Susan Mindell, Cris Criswell, Conrad Rippy
Accounting ....Rosenberg, Neuwirth & Kuchner/
Chris Cacace, Marina Flom,
Kirill Baytalskiy
Assistant to Ms. Chenoweth ....Julie Trussell
General Management Associates ....Aaron Lustbader,
Lane Marsh, Thom Mitchell
General Management Office ....Mark Barna,
Christopher Betz, Jake Hirzel,
Dawn Kusinski, Patty Montesi,
Jennifer O'Connor
Production Photographer ....Joan Marcus

Technical Production Assistant ....Alexandra Paull
Production Assistants ....John Ferry,
Shannon Hammons, Libby Unsworth
Physical Therapist ....Encore Physical Therapy PC
Orthopaedist ....David S. Weiss, M.D.
Insurance ....Ventura Insurance Brokerage/
Christine Sadofsky
Banking ....Signature Bank/Barbara von Borstel,
Margaret Monigan, Mary Ann Fanelli,
Janett Urena
Payroll ....Castellana Services, Inc.
Opening Night Coordination ....The Lawrence Company/
Michael P. Lawrence
Specialty Promotional
Partners ....The Sponsor Company/
Keith Hurd, Christopher Raphael
Group Sales ....Telecharge.com Group Sales/
800-432-7780
TTY: 888-889-TKTS (8587)
Transportation ...........................I.B.A. Limousine,
Carmine Lucariello Inc., Get Services

CREDITS AND ACKNOWLEDGEMENTS

Show control and scenic motion control featuring stage command systems by Scenic Technologies, a division of Production Resource Group, LLC, New Windsor, NY. Scenic elements constructed by Global Scenic Services, Inc., Bridgeport, CT. Engineering review by McLaren Engineering Group, West Nyack, NY. Audio equipment from PRG Audio, Mount Vernon, NY. Lighting equipment from PRG Lighting, North Bergen, NJ. Props built by The Spoon Group, Rahway, NJ, and Cigarbox Studios, Newburgh, NY. Soft goods built by I. Weiss and Sons, Inc., Long Island City, NY. Costumes by Euroco Costumes, Inc.; Gayle Palmieri; House of Savoia; Jennifer Love Costumes; Katrina Patterns; Maria Ficalora Knitwear, Ltd.; Tricorne, Inc. Custom shirting by Brooks Brothers. Fur by Fur & Furgery. Millinery by Lynne Mackey Studios, Inc. Gloves by Daniel Storto. Custom fabric dyeing & painting by Gene Mignola, Inc. Custom footwear by J.C. Theatrical, LaDuca Shoes, Worldtone Dance. Leather jacket provided by Schott, Inc.; Harris tweed fabrics supplied by HTT (manufacturing), Carloway Mills, Scotland. Mr. Hayes' wristwatch provided by Hamilton Watch. Special thanks to Bra*Tenders for hosiery & undergarments.

SPECIAL THANKS

Autumn Olive, Ava Lounge, Brooks Brothers, Jennifer Costello, Jim David, Dream Hotel, Ben Famiglietti, Florsheim, Holland & Sherry Fabrics, Ilene Chazanof, Imogene & Willie, Kaufman's Army Navy, Scott Mauro, Erin McMurrough, NY Vintage, Serafina Broadway, Michelle Singer, Kevin Spirtas, David Stern, Dean Stolber and Darcie Denkert, Adam Waring, Chad Woerner

Makeup provided by M•A•C Cosmetics

Certain scenery and scenic effects built, painted and electrified by Show Motion, Inc., Norwalk, Connecticut.

Rehearsed at the New 42nd Street Studios

Souvenir Merchandise designed and created by The Araca Group

www.PromisesPromisesBroadway.com

THE SHUBERT ORGANIZATION, INC.
Board of Directors

Theatre Manager ....Michael S. R. Harris

Photo by Joan Marcus

Tony Goldwyn

Promises, Promises
SCRAPBOOK

Correspondent: Kristen Beth Williams, "Patsy," Orchestra Voice

Most Vivid Memories of the Final Performance: Our final performance was off the charts! The audience was amazing; it was almost like Opening Night all over again! The response at the end of the opening number was overwhelming, and it really let us know 1) how much the fans loved our show, and 2) what to expect for the duration of the show.

The best and probably most emotional part of the last show came at the very end. After Fran (Kristin Chenoweth) comes back to the apartment, and she and Chuck (Sean Hayes) sing a final reprise of "I'll Never Fall in Love Again," Chuck says, "I love you, Miss Kubelik." Just as he was about to say that line, it hit him. As he stood there, looking at Kristin, unable to say that line because his emotions had gotten the best of him, the audience went wild! The entire cast was in the wings, watching him, watching Kristin, holding hands, some crying, all one hundred percent with Sean...and when he said, "I love you, Miss Kubelik," I can't speak for the audience, but I don't think there was a dry eye backstage!

Memorable Quote from Farewell Stage Speech: Kristin Chenoweth: "You know, I've been on Broadway a few times...[audience laughs]...but this cast...I mean, Sean Hayes...." Sean Hayes: "Is right here."

Memorable Note, Fax or Fan Letter in the Final Weeks: We had letters and texts from several cast members who had left the show before the final performance wishing us all the best for the last show, and Kristin Chenoweth received a gift from one of her many fans almost every day for the last two weeks of the show, including a cake, boxes of cake-pops, flowers, and a hand-made bag covered in pictures of her (Chenoweth) on one side and her dog (Maddy) on the other—which was filled with candy!!

Farewell Parties and Gift: Sean, Kristin and Tony Goldwyn threw a holiday party two weeks before closing night. It was a great way to let loose before the hectic holiday schedule set in. Closing Night party was at Pigalle! What a fabulous place for an event like that, lots of space, great food...and Scott Icenogle created a "farewell video," chronicling the entire journey of the show from the first rehearsal to the last performance, that had us all laughing till we cried and crying till we laughed!

Most Exciting Celebrity Visitors: Matt Damon and his lovely wife came to our show, and when they came backstage, Matt revealed he was wearing a t-shirt Sean Hayes had made for him when Matt was a guest star on "Will & Grace"!

Special Backstage Rituals: Oh, you know...your general warm-ups...stretches, some light yoga, some improv dance, "popcorn" at "5," the night's song from Brooks Ashmanskas, a stomp routine.... What? Doesn't everyone do that backstage?

And every Saturday night, our amazing Stage Manager Michael Passaro (and the whole SM team) would pick a song to play for the "half-hour" announcement. Why? Because "It's

1. Leading lady Kristin Chenoweth cuts a special *Promises, Promises*-themed birthday cake prepared for her by the cast.
2. Leading man Sean Hayes takes part in Broadway Barks: The 12th Annual Dog and Cat Adopt-a-thon held in Shubert Alley.

Saturday Night on BROADWAY!!!"

Favorite Moments During the Final Weeks: During the last three weeks of the show, we had three people leave our company. So, of course, we had to throw a party (or two). Each party had a theme.

British Party: For one of our Brits, Helen Anker...full of British food, British sayings, and some remarkable fake British accents.

Trash Party: For the fabulous Ashley Amber and Josh First. Who doesn't need a ton of comfort food every now and then? Complete with mac and cheese, man-wiches, Velveeta and Rotel, and Frito pie!

Left-over Party: Clean out the fridge, it's our last "Saturday Night on Broadway!"

Favorite In-Theatre Gathering Place: The fourth floor landing, just outside the male ensemble's dressing room. This area got decorated for every holiday from Halloween to Christmas and was also home to an over-sized bean bag (see "Mascot").

Mascot: Jabba (an over-sized bean bag that was given to Kristin Chenoweth as a gift for her dressing room. It didn't fit, so she gave it to the ensemble! Perfect for between-show naps!)

Favorite Off-Site Hangouts: McGee's, Stecchino and Serafina.

Favorite Snack Foods: Peanut-butter filled pretzels, chips, pizza, wings, cake pops.

Favorite Therapies: Rub-a-Dub on 52nd between Eighth and Ninth Avenues (feet, backs, necks).

Ricola (for the girls in "The Cage").

Tiger Balm (for the dancers).

Altoids and Purell (for multiple herbal cigarettes during the show).

Physical Therapy (a necessity for all!!!).

Memorable Ad-Libs: During Ellen DeGeneres' cameo appearance as "the nurse," both Sean and Kristin had a couple great ad-libs:

Ellen: (in a slightly British, very elongated voice) "If you would please...sit down...sir...."

Sean: "You sound like a ghost."

Ellen: "I am...emoting to you sir...so...if you would please...have a seat...."

(Later in the scene)

Ellen: "Baxter!..Sheldrake will see...Mr.

Photos by Joseph Marzullo/WENN

Promises, Promises
SCRAPBOOK

1. Male quartet at curtain call (L-R): Ken Land, Brooks Ashmanskas, Seán Martin Hingston and Peter Benson.
2. (L-R): Kristin Chenoweth, Molly Shannon and Sean Hayes take bows on Shannon's first night in the role of Marge MacDougall.

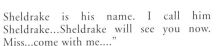

Sheldrake is his name. I call him Sheldrake...Sheldrake will see you now. Miss...come with me...."
Kristin: "You're new here, aren't you?"
We also had a memorable ad-lib when we discovered a girl sleeping in the front row. She was asleep at the top of the overture, and 30 minutes in, she was still asleep! Sean Hayes, having the liberty to talk to the audience because it's written into the script, came up with a brilliant line! Both of our stars were amazing at coming up with witty ad libs whenever anything would go wrong!
The actual line is:
(after Fran exits)
Chuck: (to audience) "I really didn't expect her to go anyway."
Fran: (re-entering) "What time does the game begin?"
The ad-lib:
(after Fran exits)
Sean: (to audience) "I really didn't expect her to go anyway...and I also didn't expect to see someone sleeping in the front row!"
(audience roars with laughter)
Kristin: (re-entering) "It's entertaining, isn't it Chuck?" (audience laughs) "What time does the game begin?"
Sean: (says entire original line)
Kristin: "I can meet you at the entrance about nine."
Sean: "Nine?! Nine is the perfect time. You don't run into all those early rushers who want to see everything!"
Kristin: "I'll see you at nine...and I won't be asleep." (exit)
Note: The girl slept through the entire first act!!!
Record Number of Cell Phone Rings or Cell Phone Photos During a Performance: We didn't have a lot of cell phone rings or photos taken during the show. There were a lot of pictures taken at curtain call, but our audiences were very polite about it during the show.
Memorable Stage Door Fan Encounters: At one performance in September sometime, there was a

girl dressed as Marge MacDougal, waiting at the stage door—complete with a red wig and an "owl" coat. She didn't attend the performance that afternoon, but she was definitely a fan of the show! Also, we had one young fan, Joscelyn Poll, who saw the show 10 times, I believe. It's amazing when people have that kind of love and attachment to a show and its cast!
What Did You Think of the Web Buzz on Your Show: We loved it! The fans really kept us alive, I think! We didn't get entirely favorable reviews, but our audiences LOVED the show!
The four singer-girls, Nikki Renee Daniels, Sarah Jane Everman, Chelsea Krombach and myself, started writing and singing jingles... "etiquette jingles," we called them. They came about from the amount of time we spent together in our singing booth, and when our press department sent around a couple of "flip" cameras to film the goings-on backstage, "Lessons From the Cage" was born! Check us out. We're still on YouTube!
Fastest Costume Change: The entire women's ensemble had a change out of "Wanting Things" into "Turkey Lurkey": 8 women. 8 dressers. 8 wigs to change. 3 people in the hair department. 1 scene to get changed and preset on the staircase. 45 seconds.
Catchphrase Only the Company Would Recognize: [sung] Clancy's Bar & Grill (take your top off).
Sweethearts Within the Company: Our Associate Director/Choreographer Chris Bailey and our Swing/Dance Captain Sarah O'Gleby have been sweethearts for several years!
Orchestra Members Who Played the Most Instruments: Bill Hayes (percussion) played the tympani, vibes, glockenspiel, xylophone, triangle, and scraper. James Ercole (reeds) played the flute, piccolo, alto flute, alto saxophone, and the clarinet.
Which Orchestra Member Who Played the Most Consecutive Performances Without a Sub: Joe Choroszewski, our drummer.
Best In-House Parody Lyrics: [To Chuck's

Theme, "Half As Big As Life"] Worry, Sheldrake! Sheldrake, Worry!! (It's much more effective when sung by our four executives, Ken Land, Brooks Ashmanskas, Peter Benson, and Seán Martin Hingston!)
Also: Not parody lyrics to a song, but a song to a few of Sheldrake's (Tony Goldwyn) lines:
Line: "Tommy's got a cold." (sung to the tune of Aerosmith's "Janie's Got a Gun").
Line: "No one. NO ONE means anything to me anymore, except you!" (Alicia Keys' "No One").
Memorable Directorial Notes: Rob Ashford uses some fantastic metaphors to describe the feeling and pace of certain aspects of the show. He talked about the "Manhattan energy" he wanted for the pace of life in the office building. For "Turkey Lurkey," it was "dancing on the edge of the world" and "Bacchanal." All I have to say is, give an actor an inch....
Company In-Jokes: "I'm in trouble"—Brooks Ashmanskas
"Worry"—Brooks Ashmanskas
Embarrassing Moment: One night during the overture, the scrim didn't fly out when it was supposed to (computer glitch). We had no contingency plan for this circumstance, so, long story short, we felt, and looked, like a bunch of bumper cars wheeling around in our task chairs. Everyone was running around, trying to get their chairs in the right places and get to their partners for lifts because the show must go on, right?! Mortifying!!!!
Coolest Thing About Being in This Show: For me, this show was the perfect "Broadway Debut" experience. So many actors make their Broadway debut as a replacement in a show that's already running. I am so very fortunate that my first Broadway experience encompassed every aspect of opening a show, from the original casting process to the first rehearsal, from recording the cast album to performing on the Tony Awards...with this group of people, from our stars and producers to the creative team, to the cast and the orchestra and the entire crew. What an amazing group of people!

Photos by Joseph Marzullo/WENN

Race

First Preview: November 17, 2009. Opened: December 6, 2009.
Closed August 21, 2010 after 23 Previews and 297 Performances.

PLAYBILL

RACE

Two veteran attorneys and a newcomer (one of them white; two black) are forced to confront their attitudes toward racial prejudice when they are asked to defend a white businessman accused of a sex crime against a black woman.

CAST

(in order of appearance)

Jack Lawson .... EDDIE IZZARD
Henry Brown .... DENNIS HAYSBERT
Susan .... AFTON C. WILLIAMSON
Charles Strickland .... RICHARD THOMAS

UNDERSTUDIES/STANDBYS

For Jack Lawson, Charles Strickland:
JORDAN LAGE

For Susan:
KARI NICOLLE

For Henry Brown:
RAY ANTHONY THOMAS

⊛ ETHEL BARRYMORE THEATRE
243 West 47th Street
A Shubert Organization Theatre
Philip J. Smith, *Chairman*   **Robert E. Wankel,** *President*

Jeffrey Richards   Jerry Frankel   Jam Theatricals
JK Productions   Peggy Hill & Nicholas Quinn Rosenkranz   Scott M. Delman
Terry Allen Kramer/James L. Nederlander   Swinsky Deitch
Bat-Barry Productions   Ronald Frankel   James Fuld Jr.
Kathleen K. Johnson   Terry Schnuck   The Weinstein Company
Marc Frankel   Jay & Cindy Gutterman/Stewart Mercer

present

Eddie Izzard   Dennis Haysbert   Afton C. Williamson

and

Richard Thomas

in

RACE

Written and Directed by
David Mamet

Scenic Design	Costume Design	Lighting Design
Santo Loquasto	**Tom Broecker**	**Brian MacDevitt**

Production Stage Manager	Casting	Technical Supervision	Company Manager
Matthew Silver	**Telsey + Company**	**Hudson Theatrical Associates**	**Bruce Klinger**

Press Representative	Associate Producer	General Management
Jeffrey Richards Associates Irene Gandy/Alana Karpoff	**Jeremy Scott Blaustein**	**Richards/Climan, Inc.**

The Producers wish to express their appreciation to the Theatre Development Fund for its support of this production.

8/21/10

(L-R): Eddie Izzard, Dennis Haysbert and Richard Thomas.

Photo by Carol Rosegg

Continued on next page

Race

Eddie Izzard
Jack Lawson

Dennis Haysbert
Henry Brown

Afton C. Williamson
Susan

Richard Thomas
Charles Strickland

Jordan Lage
u/s Jack, Charles

Kari Nicolle
u/s Susan

Ray Anthony Thomas
u/s Henry

David Mamet
Playwright/Director

Santo Loquasto
Scenic Design

Brian MacDevitt
Lighting Design

Bernard Telsey,
Telsey + Company
Casting

Sharon Bialy and Sherry Thomas
West Coast Casting

Neil A. Mazzella/
Hudson Theatrical
Associates
*Technical
Supervision*

David R. Richards
and Tamar Haimes,
Richards/Climan Inc.
General Manager

Jeffrey Richards
Producer

Jerry Frankel
Producer

Arny Granat,
Jam Theatricals
Producer

Steve Traxler,
Jam Theatricals
Producer

Peggy Hill
Producer

Nicholas Quinn
Rosenkranz
Producer

Terry Allen Kramer
Producer

James L.
Nederlander
Producer

Mort Swinsky
Producer

Joseph Deitch
Producer

Barry Weisbord,
Bat-Barry
Productions
Producer

James Fuld Jr.
Producer

Terry Schnuck
Producer

Bob Weinstein,
The Weinstein
Company
Producer

Harvey Weinstein,
The Weinstein
Company
Producer

Jay and Cindy Gutterman
Producer

Jeremy Scott
Blaustein
Associate Producer

Race

ALUMNI
2010-2011

David Alan Grier
Henry Brown

James Spader
Jack Lawson

Kerry Washington
Susan

Photos by Brian Mapp

FRONT OF HOUSE STAFF
Front Row (L-R): Pamela Gittlitz (Usher),
Dan Landon (House Manager), Aileen Kilburn
(Usher)

Back Row (L-R): Dexter Luke (Head Usher),
John Cashman (Usher), John Barbaretti
(Ticket Taker)

CREW
Sitting (L-R): Jillian Oliver (Stage Manager),
Sandy Binion (Wardrobe Supervisor)

Standing (L-R): Victor Verdejo (House Carpenter),
Matthew Silver (Production Stage Manager),
Phillip Feller (House Props), Bruce Klinger
(Company Manager), Al Galvez (Flyman),
David Marques (Dresser)

Not pictured: John Randolph Ferry
(Production Assistant)

Race

BOX OFFICE
(L-R): Chuck Loesche, Diane Heatherington,
Steve Deluca

STAFF FOR *RACE*

GENERAL MANAGEMENT
RICHARDS/CLIMAN, INC.
David R. Richards   Tamar Haimes

COMPANY MANAGER
BRUCE KLINGER

GENERAL PRESS REPRESENTATIVE
JEFFREY RICHARDS ASSOCIATES
IRENE GANDY/ALANA KARPOFF
Elon Rutberg   Diana Rissetto

CASTING
TELSEY + COMPANY
Bernie Telsey CSA, Will Cantler CSA, David Vaccari CSA,
Bethany Knox CSA, Craig Burns CSA,
Tiffany Little Canfield CSA, Rachel Hoffman CSA,
Carrie Rosson CSA, Justin Huff CSA, Bess Fifer CSA,
Patrick Goodwin CSA, Abbie Brady-Dalton

WEST COAST CASTING
Sharon Bialy & Sherry Thomas, C.S.A.

PRODUCTION MANAGEMENT
HUDSON THEATRICAL ASSOCIATES
Neil Mazzella   Sam Ellis   Irene Wang

PRODUCTION
STAGE MANAGER ....MATTHEW SILVER
Stage Manager ....Jillian M. Oliver
Assistant to the Director ....Justin Fair
Associate Scenic Designer ....Jenny Sawyers
Associate Costume Designer ....David Withrow
Associate Lighting Designer ....Driscoll Otto
Associate General Manager ....Michael Sag
General Management Associate ....Jeromy Smith
General Management Assistant ....Cesar Hawas
Production Assistant ....John Ferry
Production Carpenter ....Don Oberpriller

Production Electrician ....Jimmy Maloney
Production Props ....Kathy Fabian/Propstar
Wardrobe Supervisor ....Rob Bevenger
Dresser ....Sandy Binion
Associate Props Coordinator ....Carrie Mossman
Props Assistants ....Tim Ferro, Sarah Bird
Assistant to Mr. Mamet ....Pam Susemiehl
Assistant to Mr. Traxler ....Brandi Preston
Assistants to Mr. Richards ....Michael Crea, Will Trice
Advertising ....Serino Coyne, Inc./
Greg Corradetti, Tom Callahan,
Robert Jones, Danielle Boyle
Interactive Marketing
Agency ....Situation Marketing/
Damian Bazadona, John Lanasa,
Miriam Naggar
Website ....Robert J. Saferstein
Banking ....City National Bank/Michele Gibbons
Accountants ....Fried & Kowgios, CPA's LLP/
Robert Fried, CPA
Comptroller ....Elliott Aronstam, CPA
Legal Counsel ....Lazarus & Harris LLP./
Scott R. Lazarus, Esq.,
Robert C. Harris, Esq.
Insurance ....DeWitt Stern Group Inc./
Jolyon F. Stern, Joseph Bower
Payroll ....CSI/Lance Castellana
Production Photographers ....Brigitte Lacombe,
Robert J. Saferstein
Company Mascots ....Skye, Franco, Josie, Mecca
Opening Night Sponsor ....Movado

CREDITS
Scenery constructed by Hudson Scenic Studios, Lighting
equipment from PRG Lighting. Flame treatment by
Turning Star Inc. Richard Thomas' suit and overcoat from
Hugo Boss.

SPECIAL THANKS
Shelby Steele, Stan Coleman, Rabbi Mordecai Finley,
Cynthia Silver, The Atlantic Theater Company, Jennifer

Brennan, Peter Johnson, The Law Book Exchange,
Anything But Costumes

www.RaceOnBroadway.com
www.BroadwaysBestShows.com

 THE SHUBERT ORGANIZATION, INC.
Board of Directors

Philip J. Smith
Chairman

Robert E. Wankel
President

Wyche Fowler, Jr.

John W. Kluge

Lee J. Seidler

Michael I. Sovern

Stuart Subotnick

Elliot Greene
Chief Financial
Officer

David Andrews
Senior Vice President
Shubert Ticketing

Juan Calvo
Vice President
and Controller

John Darby
Vice President –
Facilities

Peter Entin
Vice President –
Theatre Operations

Charles Flateman
Vice President –
Marketing

Anthony LaMattina
Vice President –
Audit & Production Finance

Brian Mahoney
Vice President –
Ticket Sales

D.S. Moynihan
Vice President – Creative Projects

Staff for The Ethel Barrymore
House Manager ....Dan Landon

Race
SCRAPBOOK

Photos by Joseph Marzullo/WENN

RACE

BARRYMORE

EDDIE IZZARD
DENNIS HAYSBERT
AFTON C. WILLIAMSON
AND
RICHARD THOMAS

RACE

WRITTEN AND
DIRECTED BY DAVID MAMET

"PROVOCATIVE
AND PROFANE!"

**At the Final Performance,
August 21, 2010**

1. Backstage on closing night
(L-R): Michael Friedman,
Dennis Haysbert,
Afton C. Williamson,
playwright David Mamet
and Richard Thomas.
2. Eddie Izzard applauds
his fellow cast members.
3. Mamet with director Neil Pepe
backstage at the Barrymore.
4. Thomas and Williamson.
5. Haysbert at final curtain call.
6. Marquee of the Ethel Barrymore
Theatre late in the show's run.
7. The final bow.

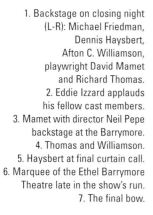

Rain: A Tribute to The Beatles on Broadway

First Preview: October 19, 2010. Opened: October 26, 2010. Played at the Neil Simon Theatre through January 15, 2011, then reopened at the Brooks Atkinson Theatre February 8, 2011. Still running as of May 31, 2011.

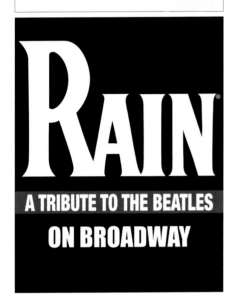

The Fab Four live again in a never-never concert featuring many of the band's greatest hits.

MUSICIANS

STEVE LANDES ....Vocals, Rhythm Guitar, Piano, Harmonica
JOEY CURATOLO ....Vocals, Bass, Piano, Guitar
JOE BITHORN ....Vocals, Lead Guitar, Guitar Synth, Sitar
RALPH CASTELLI ....Drums, Percussion, Vocals
MARK BEYER ....Keyboard, Percussion

AT CERTAIN PERFORMANCES

GRAHAM ALEXANDER ....Vocals, Bass, Piano, Guitar
JOE BOLOGNA ....Drums, Percussion, Vocals
DOUGLAS COX ....Drums, Percussion, Vocals
JIM IRIZARRY ....Vocals, Rhythm Guitar, Piano, Harmonica
DAVID LEON ....Vocals, Rhythm Guitar, Piano, Harmonica
MARK LEWIS ....Keyboard, Percussion
JIMMY POU ......Vocals, Lead Guitar, Guitar Synth
MAC RUFFING ....Vocals, Bass, Piano, Guitar
CHRIS SMALLWOOD ....Keyboard, Percussion
TOM TEELEY ....Vocals, Lead Guitar, Guitar Synth, Sitar

NEIL SIMON THEATRE
UNDER THE DIRECTION OF JAMES M. NEDERLANDER AND JAMES L. NEDERLANDER

Annerin Productions, Magic Arts & Entertainment/NewSpace/Tix Productions
Nederlander Presentations, Inc. and RAIN

Present

Starring

STEVE LANDES
JOEY CURATOLO
JOE BITHORN
RALPH CASTELLI

Scenic Design	Video Design	Lighting Design	Sound Design
Scott Christensen	Darren McCaulley	Stephan Gotschel	Abe Jacob
Todd Skinner	Mathieu St-Arnaud		

General Management	Band Management	Production Supervisor	Press Representative	Marketing Director
NIKO Companies	Mark Lewis	Theatrical Services, Inc.	Merle Frimark	Bruce Granath
& Steve Boulay		Artie Siccardi		
		Pat Sullivan		

10/26/10

Rain: A Tribute to The Beatles on Broadway

Steve Landes
Vocals, Rhythm Guitar, Harmonica, Piano

Joey Curatolo
Vocals, Bass, Piano, Guitar

Joe Bithorn
Vocals, Lead Guitar, Guitar Synth, Sitar

Ralph Castelli
Drums, Percussion, Vocals

Mark Beyer
Keyboards, Percussion

Mark Lewis
Founder, Manager, Original Keyboardist

Graham Alexander
Vocals, Bass, Piano, Guitar

Joe Bologna
Drums, Percussion, Vocals

Douglas Cox
Drums, Percussion, Vocals

Jim Irizarry
Vocals, Rhythm Guitar, Piano, Harmonica

David Leon
Vocals, Rhythm Guitar, Piano, Harmonica

Jimmy Pou
Vocals, Lead Guitar, Guitar Synth

Mac Ruffing
Vocals, Bass, Piano, Guitar

Chris Smallwood
Keyboard, Percussion

Tom Teeley
Vocals, Lead Guitar, Guitar Synth, Sitar

James M. Nederlander,
Nederlander Presentations, Inc.
Producer

James L. Nederlander,
Nederlander Presentations, Inc.
Producer

Manny Kladitis,
Niko Companies, Ltd.
General Management

Arthur Siccardi
Theatrical Services
Production Supervisor

2010-2011 AWARD

DRAMA DESK AWARD
Outstanding Revue

BOX OFFICE
(L-R): Guy Bentley, Erich Stollberger

Photos by Brian Mapp

RAIN
2010-2011
TRANSFER STUDENTS

John Korba
Keyboard, Percussion

Ardy Sarraf
Vocals, Bass, Piano, Guitar

STAGE DOOR STAFF
Errolyn Rosa (Stage Door), Roxanne Mosaphir (Stage Door), Dawn Edmonds (Elevator Operator)

Rain: A Tribute to The Beatles on Broadway

Photos by Brian Mapp

FRONT OF HOUSE STAFF
Front Row (L-R): Michelle Schechter (Usher), Dana Diaz (Ticket Taker), Joanne DeCicco, Megan Frazier, Grace Darbasie, Marilyn Christie (Ushers), Christopher Langdon (Ticket Taker)

Middle Row (L-R): Eshautine King, Michelle Smith, Maria Collado, Jean Manso, Deborah Ryan, Eddie Cuevas, Kaitlyn Spillane, Christine Bentley, Frank Clark (Ushers)

Back Row (L-R): Ryan Goodale, Jen King, Mike D'arcy (Merchandise); Jose Lopez (Porter), Steven Ouellette (House Manager), Angel Diaz (Head Usher), Jane Publik, Evelyn Gutierrez, Marisol Olavarrio, Evelyn Olivero, Kim Raccioppi (Ushers)

CREW
Kneeling (L-R): Sean Farrugia (Carpenter), Bill Teeley (Guitar Tech), Mitchell Christenson (Electrics), Stephen Vessa (Electrics), John Kelly (Electrics), Arthur Lutz (Electrics)

Standing (L-R): Jim vanBergen (Production Sound Operator), Max Reed (Carpenter), John Gordon (House Carpenter), Sean McGrath (Carpenter), Doug McNeill (Flyman), Mike Bennet (Carpenter), Brandon Epperson (Video Technician), Jens McVoy (Electrics), Danny Viscardo (House Propman), Michael Cornell (Show Electrician), James Travers, Sr (House Electrician), Craig Van Tassel (Monitor Mixer)

Drums: Lurie Horns Pfeffer (PSM)

Rain: A Tribute to The Beatles on Broadway

STAFF FOR
*RAIN: A TRIBUTE TO THE BEATLES
ON BROADWAY*

GENERAL MANAGEMENT
NIKO COMPANIES
Manny Kladitis
David Loughner   Jason T. Vanderwoude

NEW SPACE ENTERTAINMENT
Steve Boulay

PRESS/MARKETING REPRESENTATIVE
MERLE FRIMARK ASSOCIATES

PRODUCTION MANAGER
Scott Christensen

COMPANY MANAGER
Jesse White

PRODUCTION STAGE MANAGER
Lurie Horns Pfeffer

Costume Coordinators ....Robin Robinson, Russ Lease
Assistant to Mr. Jacob ....Joshua D. Reid
Production Sound Operator ....Jim vanBergen
Monitor Mixer ....Craig Van Tassel
Sound System Consultants ....Acme Sound Partners
Video Technician ....Brandon Epperson
Show Electrician/Board Operator ....Michael Cornell
Electric Advisor ....Jimmy Fedigan
Wardrobe Supervisor ....Allison Goodsell
Backline ....Ted Pallas
Graphic Design ....Gary Hewitt, Wedge.a&d
Media Design ....Paul J. Toth, AdvanceHD.com
Press Associates ....Amy Katz, Twilla Duncan
Advertising ....SpotCo/
Drew Hodges, Jim Edwards,
Tom Greenwald, Stephen Sosnowski,
Meghan Ownbey
Interactive/Online Marketing Strategy ....SpotCo/
Sara Fitzpatrick, Matt Wilstein,
Stephen Santore, Marc Mettler
Marketing and Partnerships ....SpotCo/Nick Pramik
Exclusive Tour Direction ....The Road Company/
Stephen Lindsay, Brett Sirota,
Magaly Barone, Shawn Willett,
Justin Pifer, Jenny Kirlin, Kate Anderson
Merchandising Consultant ....Kim Valentine
Merchandise Art Design ....Sheffield Abella
Payroll ....Castellana Services, Inc.
Production Photographers ....Joan Marcus,
Cylla von Tiedemann

STAFF FOR ANNERIN PRODUCTIONS
Chief Executive Officer/Producer ....Jeff Parry
Chief Operating Officer ....Ralph Schmidtke
Chief Financial Officer ....Stu Peterson
Production Manager ....Scott Christensen
Production Assistant ....Jenna DeBoice
Administration ....Kate McConney

**STAFF FOR
MAGIC ARTS & ENTERTAINMENT/NEW SPACE/
TIX PRODUCTIONS**

President ....John W. Ballard
Producer ....Lee D. Marshall
Producer ....Joe Marsh
Chief Operating Officer ....Steve Boulay
Marketing Director ....Bruce Granath
Operations Manager ....Mary Ann Porcaro
Controller ....Patty Vartenuk
Marketing Associate ....Elizabeth Randau
General Manager ....Dave Stinson
Box Office Manager ....Rachelle Tuten
Accounting ....Sandy Winchester, David Rooker

SPECIAL THANKS
To John, Paul, George and Ringo,
without whom we wouldn't be here.
Thank you to our families, friends and fans for all their
love and support throughout the years.
Jerry Hoban as Ed Sullivan
Mr. Sid Bernstein
Casey Leonard
Merle Frimark
Frieda Kelly
Höfner Guitars/Thomas Jordan
Shea Stadium photos courtesy of Tony Griffin.
SONY/ATV MUSIC PUBLISHING: Martin Bandier,
Peter Brodsky, Jimmy Asci.
The *Rain* touring road crew for all their hard work and
dedication: Brett Wolf, Daniel Conley,
Aran Whittemore, Sean Goodman, Andy Broughton,
Dan Hamilton, Russ Wood, Lance Stadnyk,
Sky Lebreton, Alex Spence, Joel Weiss,
Marc-André Gelinas, Dominic Pelletier, Roger Taillefer,
Eric Dazmarczyk, Greg Clinton, Byron Runka,
Wayne Carey, Joe Traylor; Tour Tech East:
Frank Di Casta; Truck 'n Roll: Ghislain Arsenault;
Hal-Joe Custom Coaches: Joe Banford;
Imex Import and Export: Dave McKay:
Inframe Designs: Alex Nadon, Martin Kelly,
Dorothy McAuley, Joanne Osbaldeston;
Thomas Gordon, recording engineer @Imirage Sound
Lab, Dr. Lawrence Davis, owner.
And the late Jim Riddle.

CREDITS
Joey Curatolo and Steve Landes are endorsed by Epiphone.
Joey Curatolo is endorsed by Höfner & Martin guitars.
Ralph Castelli is endorsed by Ludwig Drums, Zildjian
Cymbals, Vic Firth Drumsticks, Evans Drumheads.
Pyramid Strings. Dean Markley Strings. Dan Dean/Dan
Dean Productions for his Solo Strings Advanced. Muse
Research. Guitars supplied by Gibson Guitars. Loudspeaker
systems by Meyer Sound Labs. Sound and video equipment
by Sound Associates. Main sound console by DiGiCo.
Bluthner Pianos. Rivera Amplifiers. TC Electronic. Visual
Sound. Lighting Supplier – Christie Lites. Hudson Scenic
and Production, Canada.

MUSIC CREDITS
"All My Lovin'," "This Boy," "I Want to Hold Your Hand,"
"I Saw Her Standing There," "A Hard Day's Night," "I'm
Happy Just to Dance With You," "Yesterday," "Help!," "Day
Tripper," "Sgt. Pepper," "With a Little Help From My
Friends," "Eleanor Rigby," "Strawberry Fields," "When I'm
64," "A Day in the Life," "Hello Goodbye," "I Am the
Walrus," "Girl," "Norwegian Wood," "We Can Work It
Out," "Blackbird," "Mother Nature's Son," "I've Just Seen a

Face," "And I Love Her." "Rocky Raccoon," "Come
Together," "Get Back," "Revolution," "The End," "Let It
Be," "Hey Jude," "All You Need Is Love" written by John
Lennon and Paul McCartney, ©Sony/ATV Music
Publishing LLC. "Twist and Shout" written by Bert Berns
and Phil Medley, ©Sony/ATV Music Publishing LLC and
Sloopy II Music. "While My Guitar Gently Weeps" written
by George Harrison, ©Wixen Music Publishing as agent for
Harrisongs Ltd.

www.raintribute.com

NEDERLANDER

Chairman ....James M. Nederlander
President ....James L. Nederlander

Executive Vice President
Nick Scandalios

Vice President	Senior Vice President
Corporate Development	Labor Relations
Charlene S. Nederlander	**Herschel Waxman**

| Vice President | Chief Financial Officer |
| **Jim Boese** | **Freida Sawyer Belviso** |

STAFF FOR THE NEIL SIMON THEATRE
Theatre Manager ....Steve Ouellette
Treasurer ....Eddie Waxman
Associate Treasurer ....Marc Needleman
House Carpenter ....John Gordon
Flyman ....Douglas McNeill
House Electrician ....James Travers, Sr.
House Propman ....Danny Viscardo
House Engineer ....John Astras

(L-R): Joe Bithorn,
Steve Landes

Rain: A Tribute to The Beatles on Broadway
SCRAPBOOK

1. Backstage on opening night (L-R) Joey Curatolo as Paul McCartney, Joe Bithorn as George Harrison, real-life John Lennon girlfriend May Pang, Ralph Castelli as Ringo Starr and Steve Landes as Lennon.
2. (L-R): Castelli, Bithorn and Landes play the encore.
3. Real-life promoter and producer Sid Bernstein, who brought the Beatles to the U.S., at premiere.
4. Moody shot of Landes at premiere.

Correspondents: Steve Landes, "John Lennon" and Joey Curatolo "Paul McCartney"
Memorable Opening Night Letter, Fax or Note: Receiving the "Happy opening night" letters from so many of the other shows on Broadway was fantastic!
Opening Night Gifts: Champagne, flowers, and a custom-made *Rain* poster from our producers that had the headline, "An overnight success—after 30 years on the road!!" We loved it all!
Most Exciting Celebrity Visitors: There are many! It was a thrill for us to actually meet the legendary Chita Rivera, who said she loved the show so much she wants to come back and sit in the second row and scream! Sid Bernstein, the famed impresario who presented The Beatles at Shea Stadium and Carnegie Hall said he loves being transported back to those great

times in the '60s. Famed radio personality Cousin Brucie (currently on Sirius/XM radio, who was also known as the Fifth Beatle back in the day) came to the show, and said it was like he was "with the boys again!" We truly enjoyed meeting a number of people who worked closely with The Beatles like Nat Weiss (Brian Epstein's NY partner) and May Pang (who raved). Nat marveled at our "harmonies" and how difficult that is to replicate and told us stories about his days with Epstein. Phil Collen, the guitarist from the band Def Leppard, said he was "blown away!"
Who Has Done the Most Shows in Their Career: Joey, Joe, and Ralph have been in the group the longest, and have probably each done thousands of shows.
Special Backstage Rituals: Our sound checks before the show when we jam on whatever

Beatles (and others) songs we want to, hot tea, stretching, and all around madness...lol…
Favorite Moment During Each Performance (On Stage or Off): When the audience sings along to "Hey Jude" and seeing three generations of Beatles fans singing the song together.
Favorite In-Theatre Gathering Place: On stage just before the show starts, and the greenroom (where the food is!).
Favorite Off-Site Hangouts: Starbucks, Cosmic Diner, Chez Josephine
Favorite Snack Food: Pizza, Tootsie Rolls from the "Candy Lady"'s candy bag.
Favorite Therapies: Hall's Vitamin C Drops, Twinings Earl Grey tea, Throat-Coat tea, and lots of Advil!
Most Memorable Ad-Lib: Joey: My "Yesterday" guitar was broken for some reason and I had to pick up another guitar. The "Yesterday" guitar is tuned down a whole step, so upon reaching for the next guitar, I had to transpose the song on the fly in front of the audience. Talk about nerves....
Record Number of Cell Phone Rings, Cell Phone Photos, Tweeting or Texting Incidents During a Performance: Probably only two or three. Our show is too loud to hear such things!
Web Buzz on the Show: Outstanding!! The fans and the Broadway community were very gracious as we settled into the Neil Simon Theatre.
Memorable Press Encounter: Taping a segment for the Thanksgiving Day Parade on CBS when we recreated The Beatles' famous 1969 rooftop concert. We were on the roof of a 22-story residential building near the U.N. which had fantastic views of the river and the New York skyline! The weather was sunny and warm and so perfect. We sang "Get Back" just as The Beatles did so many years ago. It was thrilling to be able to recreate this.
Memorable Stage Door Fan Encounter: Ed Sullivan's granddaughter was at the Stage Door one night, and had some great stories about him and his show.
Latest Audience Arrival: During "Sgt. Pepper," about 15 minutes before the end of Act I.
Fastest Costume Changes: Steve: I have to make a complete costume change from John's hippie look of shag hair, paisley shirt, satin robe, bellbottoms, and love beads, to his "Abbey Road" white suit, white shirt, talisman necklace, and long hair in about a minute and a half.
Busiest Day at the Box Office: Saturday nights are always the most "Rock 'n' Roll"!
Who Wore the Least: Everyone is always fully dressed, but the trousers are very tiiiiight.
Catchphrases Only the Company Would Recognize: "BIG!"
Company In-Jokes: "Taters!"
Coolest Thing About Being in This Show: Being able to bring this music to generations, and having the time of our lives in a family/brotherhood style.

Rock of Ages

First Preview: March 17, 2009. Opened: April 7, 2009 at the Brooks Atkinson Theatre. Re-opened at the Helen Hayes Theatre on March 24, 2011 after a 10-week hiatus. Still running as of May 31, 2011.

Drew and Sherrie are two starry-eyed kids who arrive in Los Angeles with dreams of becoming long-haired head-banging rock stars, but they have to learn a lot about life—and help save a rock club destined for the wrecker's ball—before their dreams can come true. This musical has an original story but a score of classic 1980s rock hits.

CAST
(in order of appearance)

Lonny	MITCHELL JARVIS
Justice	MICHELE MAIS
Dennis	ADAM DANNHEISSER
Drew	DAN DOMENECH
Sherrie	REBECCA FAULKENBERRY
Father	MiG AYESA
Mother	MICHELE MAIS
Regina	JOSEPHINE ROSE ROBERTS
Mayor	ANDRE WARD
Hertz	PAUL SCHOEFFLER
Franz	CODY SCOTT LANCASTER
Stacee Jaxx	MiG AYESA
Waitress #1	ERICKA HUNTER
Reporter	EMILY WILLIAMS
Ja'Keith Gill	ANDRE WARD
Record Company Men	MITCHELL JARVIS/ ADAM DANNHEISSER
Sleazy Producer	JEREMY WOODARD
Joey Primo	JEREMY WOODARD
Candi	JOSEPHINE ROSE ROBERTS
Strip Club DJ	ANDRE WARD
Young Groupie	TESSA ALVES

Continued on next page

THE HELEN HAYES THEATRE

MARTIN MARKINSON   DONALD TICK

MATTHEW WEAVER   CARL LEVIN   JEFF DAVIS   BARRY HABIB   SCOTT PRISAND
MICHAEL COHL   REAGAN SILBER   S2BN ENTERTAINMENT   RELATIVITY MEDIA

in association with

JANET BILLIG RICH   HILLARY WEAVER
CORNER STORE FUND   RYAN KAVANAUGH   TONI HABIB
PAULA DAVIS   SIMON AND STEFANY BERGSON/JENNIFER MALONEY   CHARLES ROLECEK
SUSANNE BROOK   CRAIG COZZA   ISRAEL WOLFSON   SARA MERCER   JAYSON RAITT   MAX GOTTLIEB
MICHAEL MINARIK   DAVID KAUFMAN/JAY FRANKS   MICHAEL WITTLIN   PROSPECT PICTURES
LAURA SMITH/BILL BODNAR   WIN SHERIDAN   HAPPY WALTERS   MICHELE CARO   NEIL CANELL/JAY CANELL   MARIANO TOLENTINO
MARC BELL and THE ARACA GROUP

present

ROCK OF AGES

book by
CHRIS D'ARIENZO

starring

REBECCA FAULKENBERRY   DAN DOMENECH   ADAM DANNHEISSER   CODY SCOTT LANCASTER
MICHELE MAIS   JOSEPHINE ROSE ROBERTS   PAUL SCHOEFFLER   *with* MITCHELL JARVIS *and* MiG AYESA

TESSA ALVES   JENIFER FOOTE   ERICKA HUNTER   TONY LePAGE   MICHAEL MINARIK
CASSIE SILVA   ANDRE WARD   EMILY WILLIAMS   JEREMY WOODARD

scenery based on an original design by BEOWULF BORITT	*costume design* GREGORY GALE	*lighting design* JASON LYONS	*sound design* PETER HYLENSKI	*projection design* ZAK BOROVAY

hair/wig design TOM WATSON	*make-up design* ANGELINA AVALLONE	*casting* TELSEY + COMPANY	*production stage manager* ADAM JOHN HUNTER

associate choreographer ROBERT TATAD	*associate producer* DAVID GIBBS

general management ROY GABAY	*press representative* THE HARTMAN GROUP	*advertising & marketing* aka	*technical supervisor* TECH PRODUCTION SERVICES

music director HENRY ARONSON	*music coordinator* JOHN MILLER	*original arrangements* DAVID GIBBS

music supervision, arrangements & orchestrations by
ETHAN POPP

choreographed by
KELLY DEVINE

directed by
KRISTIN HANGGI

3/24/11

(L-R): Mitchell Jarvis, Adam Dannheisser, Dan Domenech

Photo by Paul Kolnik

Rock of Ages

Cast Continued

THE ENSEMBLE
TESSA ALVES, ERICKA HUNTER,
ANDRE WARD, EMILY WILLIAMS,
JEREMY WOODARD

OFFSTAGE VOICES
TONY LePAGE, CASSIE SILVA

UNDERSTUDIES
For Sherrie: TESSA ALVES, ERICKA HUNTER
For Drew/Franz, Stacee Jaxx: TONY LePAGE,
 JEREMY WOODARD
For Lonny/Dennis/Hertz: TONY LePAGE,
 MICHAEL MINARIK
For Regina: JENIFER FOOTE, CASSIE SILVA
For Justice: TESSA ALVES, JENIFER FOOTE

SWINGS
JENIFER FOOTE, TONY LePAGE,
MICHAEL MINARIK, CASSIE SILVA

DANCE CAPTAIN
JENIFER FOOTE

BAND
Conductor/Keyboard: HENRY ARONSON
Guitar 1: JOEL HOEKSTRA
Guitar 2: TOMMY KESSLER
Drums: JON WEBER
Bass: WINSTON ROYE

Synthesizer Programming: RANDY COHEN
Music Coordinator: JOHN MILLER
Copyist: FIREFLY MUSIC SERVICE/
BRIAN ALLAN HOBBS

HEAD DOORMAN
Ernest Paylor

STAGE MANAGEMENT
(L-R): Shelley Miles, Justin Scribner,
Matthew DiCarlo, Adam John Hunter

Rebecca
Faulkenberry
Sherrie

Dan Domenech
Drew

MiG Ayesa
Stacee Jaxx/Father

Mitchell Jarvis
Lonny

Adam Dannheisser
Dennis

Cody Scott Lancaster
Franz

Michele Mais
Justice/Mother

Josephine Rose
Roberts
Regina/Candi

Paul Schoeffler
Hertz

Tessa Alves
Ensemble

Jenifer Foote
Swing

Ericka Hunter
Ensemble

Tony LePage
Swing

Michael Minarik
Swing

Cassie Silva
Swing

Andre Ward
Ensemble

Emily Williams
Ensemble

Jeremy Woodard
Ensemble

Chris D'Arienzo
Book

Kristin Hanggi
Director

Rock of Ages

Kelly Devine
Choreographer

Beowulf Boritt
*Original Scenery
Design*

Gregory Gale
Costume Design

Jason Lyons
Lighting Design

Peter Hylenski
Sound Designer

Zachary Borovay
Projection Designer

Tom Watson
Hair and Wig Design

Angelina Avallone
Make-up Design

Peter Fulbright/
Tech Production
Services
Technical Supervisor

Ethan Popp
*Music Supervisor,
Arranger,
Orchestrator*

John Miller
Music Coordinator

Bernard Telsey,
Telsey + Company
Casting

Robert Tatad
*Associate
Choreographer*

Roy Gabay
General Manager

Matthew Weaver
Producer

Barry Habib
Producer

Scott Prisand
Producer

Michael Cohl
Producer

Ryan Kavanaugh,
Relativity Media, LLC
Producer

Toni Habib
Producer

Stefany Bergson
Producer

Jennifer Maloney
Producer

Jayson Raitt
Producer

Bill Bodnar
Producer

Mariano Tolentino
Producer

Marc Bell
Producer

Michael Rego, Hank Unger and
Matthew Rego,
The Araca Group
Producer

James Carpinello
Father, Stacee Jaxx

Jay Klaitz
*Lonny, Record
Company Man*

Constantine Maroulis
Drew

Ralph Meitzler
Swing

Lauren Molina
Candi, Regina

Julie Nelson
*Ensemble,
Young Groupie*

Rock of Ages

Geoff Packard
Swing

Emily Padgett
Sherrie

Angel Reed
*Ensemble,
Young Groupie*

Justin Matthew
Sargent
Swing

Dee Snider
*Dennis, Record
Company Man*

Derek St. Pierre
Franz

Matthew Stocke
*Offstage Voice,
Strip Club DJ*

Sarrah Strimel
Ensemble, Reporter

Joey Taranto
Drew

Becca Tobin
*Offstage Voice,
Swing*

Katie Webber
*Ensemble,
Waitress #1*

Valerie Stanois
*Dance Captain,
Swing*

FRONT OF HOUSE STAFF
Front Row (L-R): Tyler Biancamano, Katherine Angulo, Stephanie Usis, Berd Vaval, Linda Maley, Margaret Flanagan, Jackie Munoz, Kim DeAndrade

Back Row (L-R): Shani Colleen Murfin, Helene Waldemarson, Emanuel Grantham, Mia Fantaci, Robin Mates, Natasha Thomas, Brian Spears, Chiyo Sakai, Ron Johnson, Susan Myerberg (General Manager), Alan R. Markinson (House Mgr.), Ronald Hornsby, John Biancamano

CREW
From Top of Steps (L-R): Stacey Haynes, Kat Ventura, Mikey Goodmark, Wendall Goings, Tim Hanlon, Thom Carlson, Doug Purcell, Joe Beck

Behind the Bar (L-R): Matt Nieski, Bob Etter, Paul Delcioppo

Photos by Brian Mapp

STAFF FOR *ROCK OF AGES*

GENERAL MANAGEMENT
ROY GABAY PRODUCTIONS
Roy Gabay   Mandy Tate
Bruce Kagel   Megan Savage

COMPANY MANAGER
Daniel Kuncy
Associate Company Manager .... Chris Aniello

GENERAL PRESS REPRESENTATIVE
THE HARTMAN GROUP
Michael Hartman
Leslie Papa   Alyssa Hart

CASTING
TELSEY + COMPANY
Bernie Telsey CSA, Will Cantler CSA, David Vaccari CSA,
Bethany Knox CSA,
Craig Burns CSA, Tiffany Little Canfield CSA,
Rachel Hoffman CSA, Justin Huff CSA,
Patrick Goodwin CSA, Abbie Brady-Dalton CSA,
David Morris, Cesar A. Rocha

TECHNICAL SUPERVISOR
TECH PRODUCTION SERVICES
Peter Fulbright
Colleen Houlehen   Mary Duff
Kaitlyn Anderson

Associate Director/
   Production Stage Manager .... Adam John Hunter
Stage Manager .... Matthew DiCarlo
Assistant Stage Manager .... Justin Scribner
Production Manager .... Peter Fulbright
Production Management Associate ...... Colleen Houlehen
Associate Scenic Designer .... Jo Winiarski
Assistant Scenic Designers .... Maiko Chii,
                    Alexis Distler, Buist Bickley
Associate Costume Designer .... Karl Ruckdeschel
Assistant Costume Designers .... Julia Broer,
                       Colleen Kesterson
Associate Lighting Designer .... Grant Wilcoxen
Assistant Lighting Designer .... Sean Beach
Assistant Lighting Designer .... Driscoll Otto

Rock of Ages

Assistant to Mr. Lyons ....Zach Pizza
Moving Light Programmer ....Marc Polimeni
Associate Sound Designer ....Keith Caggiano
Assistant Sound Designer ....Drew Levy
Associate Projection Designer ....Daniel Brodie
Assistant Projection Designer ....Austin Switser
Associate Choreographer ....Robert Tatad
Creative Advisor ....Wendy Goldberg
Production Carpenter ....Doug Purcell
Advance Production Carpenter ....Brian Munroe
Production Electrician ....Joseph Beck
Production Sound ....Phil Lojo
Head Mixer ....Robert Etter
Head Propman ....Roger Keller
Wardrobe Supervisor ....Wendall Goings
Dressers ....Michael Goodmark, Timothy Hanlon,
                                                  Stacey Haynes
Stitcher/Laundry ....Pierre Parisi
Daywork/Band Dresser ....Thom Carlson
Hair & Wig Supervisor ....Barry Lee Moe
Production Assistant ....Shelley Miles
Production Intern ....Ashley Zednick
Script Supervisor ....Justin Mabardi
Executive for
    Corner Store Entertainment ....Tom Pelligrini
Production Associate ....Rebecca Breithaupt
Assistant to Mr. Levin ....Alexandra Bisker
Music Director/Conductor ....Henry Aronson
Music Coordinator ....John Miller
Assistant to John Miller ....Nichole Jennino
Production Vocal Coach ....Liz Caplan
Synthesizer Programmer ....Randy Cohen
Music Copying/
    Music Preparation ....Anixter Rice Music Service
Advertising & Marketing ....aka/
                                              Scott A. Moore, Liz Furze,
                                          Clint Bond Jr., Melissa Marano,
                                          Adam Jay, Joshua Lee Poole, Janette Roush,
                                          Jessica Albano-English, Jacob Matsumiya
Internet Marketing and Strategy 87AM/
                                          Adam Cunningham, Lisa Egan,
                                                  Alexandra Bisker
Press Associates ....Michelle Bergmann,
                                          Nicole Capatasto, Tom D'Ambrosio,
                                          Juliana Hannett, Bethany Larsen,
                                          Emily McGill, Matt Ross,
                                          Frances White, Wayne Wolfe
Production Photography ....Joan Marcus
Insurance ....Ventura Insurance Brokerage/
                                                  Tick and Co.
Legal Counsel ....Sendroff and Baruch, LLP/
                                                  Jason Baruch
Banking ....City National Bank
Payroll Service ....Checks and Balances
Accounting ....Fried & Kowgios Partners, CPAs, LLP
Bookkeeper ....Galbraith & Company
Additional New York
    Rehearsal ....Manhattan Theatre Club
Group Sales ....Broadway Inbound

CREDITS AND ACKNOWLEDGEMENTS

Avalon Salon & Day Spa, Gibson, Ernie Ball, Baldwin Piano, Vic Firth, Vans and The Spoon Group. Audio and video provided by PRG Secaucus. Scenery and automation by Showmotion, Inc., Milford, CT. Lighting equipment from Hudson/Christie Lighting, Mimi Bilinski. Costumes constructed by Jennifer Love Costumes. Custom leatherwear by www.rawhides.com. Shoes and boots constructed by T.O. Dey and Worldtone. Fabric painting and costume crafts by Jeffrey Fender. Hosiery and undergarments by Bra*Tenders. Keyboards by Yamaha. Additional scenery by Daddy-O. Dany Margolies

---

A special thanks to Trash and Vaudeville
for the rock 'n' roll gear.

MUSIC CREDITS

"Anyway You Want It" written by Steve Perry and Neal Schon. © Published by Lacey Boulevard Music and Weed High Nightmare Music.
"Beaver Hunt" written by David Gibbs and Chris Hardwick. Published by Feed the Pony Songs and Fish Ladder, Inc. (BMI).
"Can't Fight This Feeling" written by Kevin Cronin. © Published by Fate Music (ASCAP).
"Cum on Feel the Noize" written by Neville Holder and James Lea. © Barn Publishing (Slade) Ltd.
"Don't Stop Believin'" written by Jonathan Cain, Stephen Ray Perry, Neal J. Schon © Published by Weed High Nightmare Music and Lacey Boulevard Music.
"Every Rose Has Its Thorn" written by Bobby Dall, Bruce Anthony Johannesson, Bret Michaels, Rikki Rocket. © All rights owned or administered by Universal Music-Z Songs on behalf of Cyanide Publ./BMI. Used by permission.
"The Final Countdown" written by Joey Tempest. © Screen Gems-EMI Music Inc.
"Harden My Heart" written by Marvin Webster Ross. © 1980 WB Music Corp. (ASCAP), Narrow Dude Music (ASCAP) and Bonnie Bee Good Music. All rights administered by WB Music Corp. All rights reserved. Used by permission.
"Heat of the Moment" written by Geoffrey Downes and John K. Wetton. © 1982 WB Music Corp. (ASCAP), Almond Legg Music Corp (ASCAP) and Pallan Music. All rights on behalf of itself and Almond Legg Music Corp. administered by WB Music Corp. All rights reserved. Used by permission.
"Heaven" written by Jani Lane, Erik Turner, Jerry Dixon, Steven Sweet and Joey Allen ©.
"Here I Go Again" written by David Coverdale and Bernard Marsden. © 1982 C.C. Songs Ltd. (PRS) and Seabreeze Music Ltd. Administered by WB Music Corp. (ASCAP). All rights reserved. Used by permission.
"High Enough" written by Jack Blades, Ted Nugent and Tommy R. Shaw. © Published by Bicycle Music Company, Broadhead Publishing and Wixen Music.
"Hit Me With Your Best Shot" written by E. Schwartz. © Sony/ATV Tunes LLC/ASCAP.
"I Hate Myself for Loving You" written by Desmond Child and Joan Jett. © All rights owned or administered by Universal-PolyGram Int. Publ., Inc./ASCAP. Used by permission.
"I Wanna Rock" written by Daniel Dee Snider. © All rights owned or administered by Universal Music-Z Melodies on behalf of Snidest Music/SESAC. Used by permission.
"I Want to Know What Love Is" written by Michael Leslie Jones. © Published by Somerset Songs Publishing, Inc.
"Just Like Paradise" written by David Lee Roth and Brett Tuggle. © Diamond Dave Music c/o RS Plane Music.
"Keep on Lovin' You" written by Kevin Cronin. © Published by Fate Music (ASCAP).
"Kiss Me Deadly" written by Mick Smiley. © Published by The Twin Towers Co. and Mike Chapman Publishing Enterprises.

"More Than Words" written by Nuno Bettencourt and Gary F. Cherone. © All rights owned or administered by Almo Music Corp. on behalf of Color Me Blind Music/ASCAP. Used by permission.
"Nothin' But a Good Time" written by Bobby Dall, Bruce Anthony Johannesson, Bret Michaels, Rikki Rocket. © All rights owned or administered by Universal Music-Z Songs on behalf of Cyanide Publ./BMI. Used by permission.
"Oh Sherrie" written by Steve Perry, Randy Goodrum, Bill Cuomo, Craig Krampf. © Published by Street Talk Tunes, April Music Inc & Random Notes, Pants Down Music and Phosphene Music.
"Renegade" written by Tommy Shaw. © All rights owned or administered by Almo Music Corp. on behalf of itself and Stygian Songs /ASCAP. Used by permission.
"The Search Is Over" written by Frank Sullivan and Jim Peterik. © Published by Ensign Music LLC (BMI). Used by permission. All rights reserved.
"Shadows of the Night" written by D.L. Byron. © Zen Archer/ASCAP.
"Sister Christian" written by Kelly Keagy. © Published by Bicycle Music Company.
"To Be With You" written by David Grahame and Eric Martin. ©EMI April Music, Inc. obo itself, Dog Turner Music and Eric Martin Songs (ASCAP).
"Too Much Time on My Hands" written by Tommy Shaw. © Stygian Songs/ASCAP.
"Waiting for a Girl Like You" written by Michael Leslie Jones and Louis Gramattico. © Published by Somerset Songs Publishing, Inc.
"Wanted Dead or Alive" written by Jon Bon Jovi and Richard S. Sambora. © All rights owned or administered by Universal-Polygram Int. Publ., Inc. on behalf of itself and Bon Jovi Publishing/ASCAP. Used by permission.
"We Built This City" written by Dennis Lambert, Martin George Page, Bernie Taupin and Peter Wolf. © All rights owned or administered by Universal-Polygram Int. Publ., Inc. on behalf of Little Mole Music Inc./ASCAP. Used by permission.
"We're Not Gonna Take It" written by Daniel Dee Snider. © All rights owned or administered by Universal Music-Z Melodies on behalf of Snidest Music/SESAC. Used by permission.

THE HELEN HAYES THEATRE STAFF

Owned and Operated by Little Theatre Group LLC
Martin Markinson and Donald Tick

General Manager and Counsel ....Susan S. Myerberg
House Manager ....Alan R. Markinson
Engineer ....Hector Angulo
Treasurer ....David Heveran
Assoc. Gen. Manager ....Sharon Fallon
Assistant Treasurer ....Chuck Stuis
Head Ushers ....Linda Maley, Berd Vaval,
                                                  John Biancamano
Stage Door ....Robert Seymour, Jonathan Angulo,
                                                  Luis Muniz
Accountant ....Chen-Win Hsu, CPA, PC
Intern ....Jacqueline Munoz

Helen Hayes Theatre is a proud member of the Broadway
Green Alliance.

Rock of Ages
SCRAPBOOK

Correspondent: Rebecca Faulkenberry "Sherrie"

Memorable Fan Letter: I had this beautiful 11-year-old girl write on my fan page and tell me I should keep doing what I was doing because it was a gift, and when I responded with my thanks and noted that I was not going to reveal MY age, she said I looked very young! And kids don't lie! Right?!

Parties: On tour we always had an array of birthday cakes and communal "load out night" shots (yes, of the alcoholic nature). I've been in the Broadway cast for only about three weeks now and we've had only one celebratory event so far. However it was a good one: Andre is getting married—he left for the wedding yesterday!

Actor Who Performed the Most Roles in This Show: Our cast stays VERY busy the whole show as we have such a small ensemble—three ladies and two boys, who are brilliant! However, if we're talking about performing the most roles, we have a super swing at the moment—Tony LePage, and he understudies every single male in the show...that's eight parts! Do you know how many different harmonies that is to learn?!

Actor Who Has Done the Most Shows: It would have to be Maisey who plays Justice. She has been with the show since its inception in LA and I remember hearing how she literally has never missed a show since she started! That's about five years' worth of shows!

Special Backstage Ritual: I enter at the end of the opening number, and while the last big dance break is happening onstage, I have my own little dance party offstage left. I've done the show about 7 months now combining tour and Broadway, and I've never missed it. And this is full-out dancing—Barry our wig stylist waits to brush me out until I'm finished since I get my hair all awry with my air guitar and drum solos —it's all happening off stage left :-) Gets me energized and ready to head-bang for two and a half hours!

Favorite Moments: Onstage—I love the end of "Harden My Heart" and "Here I Go Again." And "Don't Stop Believin'" is always pretty awesome to see how energized the audience is. Offstage—Different every night. A lot of funny things can happen in those quick changes.

Favorite In-Theatre Gathering Place: The Helen Hayes has a pretty small backstage/dressing room area, so we can literally talk to everyone through the walls sitting in our own dressing room. So the entire dressing room area is like an already-made gathering place.

Favorite Snack Foods: On tour, Tami our wig supervisor got me addicted to ginger chews! You can get them in different flavors too— coffee, red apple, peanut butter—they're delicious. Also, Green Symphony on 43rd makes these oat cookies I'm addicted to. They're like little mounds of goodness.

Yearbook Correspondent Rebecca Faulkenberry (second from left) with members of the tour ensemble at her last performance before leaving for the Broadway company.

Favorite Off-Site Hangout: Angus McIndoe is very convenient as it's right next to us, and has all the food and drinks you may need. However, I know that a lot of our old Broadway cast have a special place in their hearts for the Glass House Tavern as they were next door at the Brooks Atkinson Theatre for so long.

Mascot: I guess that would have to be our llama from Uruguay. And when MiG (our Stacee Jaxx, who was also on tour with me) and I were in Boston, we met a girl from Uruguay who was called Kendra, so we fondly refer to our llama as Kendra—although that might just be between him and me, huh?

Favorite Therapies: I always have Throat-Coat Tea (has to be with honey though) during the show, and I like Olbas pastilles, Vocalzones (they're British), and there's something else I'm not going to be able to spell, but phonetically sounds like "paper cow" that you can get at any Chinese Medicine store, which is gorgeous! Gym and all of that is a must—but my special treat, which is expensive so doesn't happen very often but cures many ailments from wearing heels eight shows a week—is a full body deep tissue massage. I enjoy few things more!

Memorable Stage Door Fan Encounter: When I was in Columbus a fan asked me my favorite color, which is green, and then a few days later came back with a bouquet of flowers that was pretty much based with green flowers...which are hard to come by. And were mainly white flowers that had been dyed...but the sentiment was flattering!

Superstitions That Turned Out To Be True: I don't really have any superstitions myself— but I share a dressing room with Maisey (Justice) and she is very strict about superstitions in the theatre! And it's also infiltrated into Josie (Regina)...so I'm sure in a month or two I'll be on the band wagon as well.

Fastest Costume Change: Our ladies have some pretty quick ones, but I've also got a really fast one where I finish "Harden My Heart," run off stage and change wig, shoes and costume in about a four-line monologue to come on and begin the next song. It's all very choreographed and takes about three people and another stage manager supervising to get it done.

Heaviest/Hottest Costume: A lot of the boys' coats are surprisingly heavy—they're thick leather with fringe or studs.

Who Wore the Least: That's an impossible question for *Rock of Ages*. Ha, we couldn't wear any less without being a nudie show.

Orchestra Member Who Played the Most Instruments: I think most of our band doubles and and triples. I know both of our guitarists are switching between guitars whether it's acoustic, 12-string, etc.... Yeah, a lot of that goes on.

Tales From the Put-in: I don't remember our Broadway put-in, except that we did it in two days. Insanity. But we did it :-)

Nickname: "Titty Disco Ball" was the name assigned to my character "Sherrie Christian" when she became a stripper. We use a lot of body glitter in this show.

Embarrassing Moment: I forget what city it was in, but I was following Stacee Jaxx down the stairs and missed the bottom stair and face planted right into center stage. And then had to continue the scene after peeling myself off the floor. That was embarrassing.

Coolest Thing About Being in This Show: Getting to rock out and belt away every evening, with audiences that are in some euphoric 80's vibe on their feet dancing and singing!

Who Heads Your Fan Club: Myself :-) It's just a fan page on Facebook, but it has been a really great way to respond to people and give my appreciation to them for coming out, seeing the show, and saying lovely things!

The Scottsboro Boys
SCRAPBOOK

Correspondent: Colman Domingo, "Mr. Bones"

Opening Night: Most of our cast had been doing the show since January 2010, first Off-Broadway at the Vineyard Theatre, and then at the Guthrie Theatre. We truly became a family and missed each other when we were apart. Opening night on Broadway was the cherry on top, and a big family affair.

Backstage Ritual: Before each performance we come together downstairs and sing uplifting and inspirational songs. Wardrobe sometimes joins us. We then share some inspirational words, and go into a prayer. What we say varies from day to day depending on the energy that day, and what happens that day to bring our hearts, minds, voices and bodies together. We have to be so open and generous in front of an audience so we can get to them. Sometimes it's like a church revival downstairs before we even get to the stage.

Most Exciting Celebrity Visitors: Denzel Washington, Halle Berry, Whoopi Goldberg, former NAACP chairman Julian Bond, Vanessa Williams, America Ferrara, Bebe Winans and Lee Daniels. When Whoopi heard we had protesters she said she was very disappointed. It reminded her of the opening of the film *The Color Purple* when groups protested that Steven Spielberg was directing an African-American piece. The film was praised with nominations, but then shut out because of the controversy. The protests against our show were so unfounded. Telling this story like a minstrel show was a creative decision and we supported it. Susan Stroman told us, "Keep your heads up,

(L-R): Librettist David Thompson, director/choreographer Susan Stroman, composer John Kander at the cast party on opening night.

don't let your heads slump. The moment they slump and people think there's something wrong with what you're doing, the protesters

---

The Scottsboro Boys
SCRAPBOOK

will have won." She was very inspiring in that way. We made sure to hold our heads high.

Who Got the Gypsy Robe: JC Montgomery. He added the logo of *Scottsboro Boys* in LED lights.

Actor Who Performed the Most Roles in This Show: Me: "Sheriff," "Mr. Bones," "Lawyer Bones,""Guard," "Attorney General," "Clerk," the voice of the Cat, offstage voice of George Wallace Sr., "Showgirl."

Actor Who Has Done the Most Shows in Their Career: John Cullum.

Favorite Moment During Each Performance: The entire backstge crew and cast make sure we honor that moment the first time Rosa Park speaks. That's the moment everything stops. We wait to hear that bass drum. It's a beautiful moment. We make sure everything is completely silent for that line.

Favorite In-Theatre Gathering Place: The greenroom right behind the orchestra under the stage.

Favorite Off-Site Hangouts: We would get together at Café Un Deux Trois and Famous Dave's Barbecue; also Sharon Washington's apartment. Or, when it was warm, my terrace.

Favorite Snack Food: Red velvet cake.

Favorite Therapy: Mr. Margolin, our chiropractor.

Memorable Ad-Lib: When I was playing Lawyer Bones I broke my cane. It fell apart when I banged it on the floor. I just said, "Oh hell...."

Cell Phone Rings, Photos or Texting Incidents During a Performance: We didn't have too much of a problem. We had a much bigger problem with food. Our audience liked to bring food in. One night someone in the front row was eating a bag of chips really loudly. We had to break the fourth wall and say "Shhhh!"

What Did You Think of the Web Buzz on Your Show: John Cullum said that in all his years he was never in anything that caused so much controversy. It seemed like everyone wanted to have a voice about this piece and they were Twittering, texting and emailing each other—and us—about what they thought. People were starting blogs just to engage in discussion. The show walked a fine line; that was its intention. That's what made it so successful. It created a dialogue about race.

Memorable Press Encounter: The *Amsterdam News* reporter sent to interview me didn't take the time to find out who I was or what race I was. I could tell from the questions that she was assuming we were white men in blackface playing the Scottsboro Boys. All you have to do is Google me and you'd know I'm a black man.

Memorable Stage Door Fan Encounters: Never before in my career have I experienced people's need to embrace you. People would open their arms and hug you and say "Thank you." In Minneapolis an elderly white woman told one of our cast member, "I feel so horrified and embarrassed that this happened. And I feel so horrified that I didn't know it happened." People are always very emotional after this show.

Curtain call on opening night (L-R): Sharon Washington, *Yearbook* correspondent Colman Domingo, Joshua Henry, Forrest McClendon, John Cullum and Josh Breckenridge.

Some fans can't speak. Usually I say, "It's OK. I understand," and I sign their Playbill or take a picture with them and you can see the tears welling up in their eyes. They say they feel like they've been punched in the stomach. and yet they're standing there with so much love and compassion for you.

Fastest Costume Change: Me, from Lawyer Bones back into the Sheriff, seven seconds.

Who Wore the Heaviest/Hottest Costume: Forrest McClendon and I were underdressed in sometimes as many as four layers, all wool.

Who Wore the Least: At some point all nine Scottsboro Boys have to go down to dance belts and boxers.

Catchphrases Only the Company Would Recognize: "If you're gonna tell it, tell it right." "It's just cake, It ain't freedom."

Which Orchestra Member Played the Most Instruments: Percussionist Bruce Doctor played most instruments. That reminds me: I'll never forget our conductor Paul Masse. He would laugh so hard whenever something would go awry. And we would just see his head, sticking up over the edge of the stage, laughing.

Memorable Directorial Note: "Full out, with great conviction."

Understudy Anecdote: Unfortunately I thought we had a 3 p.m. matinee one Wednesday. Luckily my understudy, J.C. Montgomery, had breakfast with the cast and went with them to the theatre. It turns out we had a 1 p.m. student matinee that day and when I didn't show up, J.C. had to go on with twenty minutes' notice. He probably still wants to kill me for that.

Nicknames: We call Derrick Cobey "Millicent" because his backstage persona is this annoying little girl named Millicent.

Embarrassing Moment: One night I discovered that I had my zipper down during "Financial Advice." When I was shoving "Jew money" into my pants, I discovered that I had left my pants fully open.

Ghostly Encounters Backstage: We didn't see any, but we could feel them. On the Friday night of our last weekend things were happening backstage and onstage with the lights and the computer equipment. We definitely felt we were in the presence of some ghosts.

Coolest Thing About Being in This Show: Being in the company of so many talented African-American men in one show. That's rare for us. The idea that there are twelve men and one woman, all African-American, all triple-threats, was very special and very cool. Everyone felt honored. There was no sense of competitiveness. We were full of admiration for each other and for their gifts.

The Final Performance, December 12, 2010: That whole day, both shows, everyone's emotions were up and down. There were moments that were like a fraternity party. Even fifteen minutes to places we were signing each other's programs and window cards, all making sure we were taking care of each other in that way. Susan Stroman and John Kander were running around signing posters. It was so beautiful that everyone was there including the whole design team.

During the final performance, more than anything, we felt the audience's appreciation that this piece had been done. John Kander spoke on stage at the end with Susan Stroman and David Thompson, and then when our assistant choreographer came out with champagne and there were toasts to Fred Ebb and the Scottsboro Boys themselves. It just seemed to me like the classiest closing night ever.

I try not to get too emotional, but I couldn't help it. I just burst into tears. I thought, who knows if this will happen again? I knew in that moment that I was living in history. It was a historic moment and I wanted to take it in and not rush it. I wanted to look into everyone's eyes. I watched Jeremy Gumbs embracing John Kander and I recognized that we were all better for having done this show. Better as performers and better as artists and better as activists. It was beautiful to see.

Many of us originated these roles. We enjoy the ownership of that. Like the original performers in *Cabaret* and *Chicago*, our names are etched into a script that is going to live on beyond December 12.

We had this little family. It was not a big splashy musical where there are so many producers you don't even know who they are. Ours was a small musical and those of us who worked on it were a family.

Sister Act

First Preview: March 24, 2011. Opened: April 20, 2011.
Still running as of May 31, 2011.

A musical comedy adaptation of the 1992 film of the same title, about a nightclub singer on the run from the mob who transforms the lives of a convent full of nuns when she hides out among them.

CAST
(in order of appearance)

Deloris Van Cartier	PATINA MILLER
Michelle	RASHIDRA SCOTT
Tina	ALÉNA WATTERS
Curtis Jackson	KINGSLEY LEGGS
Joey	JOHN TREACY EGAN
Pablo	CAESAR SAMAYOA
TJ	DEMOND GREEN
Eddie Souther	CHESTER GREGORY
Mother Superior	VICTORIA CLARK
Monsignor O'Hara	FRED APPLEGATE
Mary Robert	MARLA MINDELLE
Mary Patrick	SARAH BOLT
Mary Lazarus	AUDRIE NEENAN

ENSEMBLE
JENNIFER ALLEN, CHARL BROWN,
HOLLY DAVIS, CHRISTINA DeCICCO,
MADELEINE DOHERTY, ALAN H. GREEN,
BLAKE HAMMOND, WENDY JAMES,
KEVIN LIGON, MARISSA PERRY,
CORBIN REID, RASHIDRA SCOTT,
JENNIFER SIMARD, LAEL VAN KEUREN,
ROBERTA B. WALL, ALÉNA WATTERS

Continued on next page

 BROADWAY THEATRE
1681 Broadway
A Shubert Organization Theatre

Philip J. Smith, *Chairman*   Robert E. Wankel, *President*

WHOOPI GOLDBERG & STAGE ENTERTAINMENT
IN ASSOCIATION WITH
THE SHUBERT ORGANIZATION AND DISNEY THEATRICAL PRODUCTIONS

PRESENT

MUSIC
ALAN MENKEN

LYRICS
GLENN SLATER

BOOK
**CHERI STEINKELLNER
& BILL STEINKELLNER**

ADDITIONAL BOOK MATERIAL
DOUGLAS CARTER BEANE

BASED ON THE TOUCHSTONE PICTURES MOTION PICTURE "SISTER ACT" WRITTEN BY JOSEPH HOWARD

STARRING
PATINA MILLER   VICTORIA CLARK

WITH
**FRED APPLEGATE   SARAH BOLT   JOHN TREACY EGAN   DEMOND GREEN   CHESTER GREGORY
KINGSLEY LEGGS   MARLA MINDELLE   AUDRIE NEENAN   CAESAR SAMAYOA**

JENNIFER ALLEN   NATALIE BRADSHAW   CHARL BROWN   CHRISTINA DeCICCO   HOLLY DAVIS   MADELEINE DOHERTY
ALAN H. GREEN   BLAKE HAMMOND   WENDY JAMES   CARRIE A. JOHNSON   KEVIN LIGON
LOUISE MADISON   MARISSA PERRY   ERNIE PRUNEDA   CORBIN REID   LANCE ROBERTS   RASHIDRA SCOTT
JENNIFER SIMARD   LAEL VAN KEUREN   ROBERTA B. WALL   ALÉNA WATTERS

SET DESIGN	COSTUME DESIGN	LIGHTING DESIGN	SOUND DESIGN
KLARA ZIEGLEROVA	**LEZ BROTHERSTON**	**NATASHA KATZ**	**JOHN SHIVERS**

CASTING	WIG AND HAIR DESIGN	PRODUCTION MANAGEMENT	PRODUCTION SUPERVISOR
TELSEY + COMPANY	**DAVID BRIAN BROWN**	**AURORA PRODUCTIONS**	**STEVEN BECKLER**

ORCHESTRATIONS	DANCE ARRANGER	MUSIC DIRECTOR	MUSIC COORDINATOR
DOUG BESTERMAN	**MARK HUMMEL**	**BRENT-ALAN HUFFMAN**	**JOHN MILLER**

MUSIC SUPERVISOR, VOCAL AND INCIDENTAL MUSIC ARRANGEMENTS
MICHAEL KOSARIN

ORIGINAL PRODUCTION DEVELOPED IN ASSOCIATION WITH PETER SCHNEIDER & MICHAEL RENO

ASSOCIATE PRODUCER FOR WHOOP INC.	PRESS	DIRECTOR OF CREATIVE DEVELOPMENT	GENERAL MANAGER	EXECUTIVE PRODUCER
TOM LEONARDIS	**THE HARTMAN GROUP**	**ULRIKE BURGER-BRUJIS**	**321 THEATRICAL MANAGEMENT**	**BEVERLEY D. MAC KEEN**

PRODUCERS
WHOOPI GOLDBERG, JOOP VAN DEN ENDE, BILL TAYLOR & REBECCA QUIGLEY

CHOREOGRAPHER
ANTHONY VAN LAAST

DIRECTOR
JERRY ZAKS

ORIGINALLY PRODUCED BY PASADENA PLAYHOUSE, PASADENA, CA AND ALLIANCE THEATRE, ATLANTA, GA.

4/20/11

Patina Miller (center)
and company

Photo by Joan Marcus

Sister Act

MUSICAL NUMBERS

ACT ONE

"Take Me to Heaven" .... Deloris, Michelle, Tina
"Fabulous, Baby!" .... Deloris, Michelle, Tina
"Here Within These Walls" .... Mother Superior, Deloris
"It's Good to Be a Nun" .... Deloris, Mary Patrick, Mary Robert, Mary Lazarus, Nuns
"When I Find My Baby" .... Curtis, Joey, Pablo, TJ
"I Could Be That Guy" .... Eddie, Bums
"Raise Your Voice" .... Deloris, Mary Patrick, Mary Robert, Mary Lazarus, Nuns
"Take Me to Heaven" (Reprise) .... Deloris, Mary Patrick, Mary Robert, Mary Lazarus, Nuns

ACT TWO

"Sunday Morning Fever" .... Deloris, Mother Superior, Monsignor O'Hara, Eddie,
Mary Patrick, Mary Robert, Mary Lazarus, Nuns, Workers
"Lady in the Long Black Dress" .... Joey, Pablo, TJ
"Haven't Got a Prayer" .... Mother Superior
"Bless Our Show" .... Deloris, Mary Patrick, Mary Robert, Mary Lazarus, Nuns
"The Life I Never Led" .... Mary Robert
"Fabulous, Baby!" (Reprise) .... Deloris, Eddie, Nuns, Fantasy Dancers
"Sister Act" .... Deloris
"When I Find My Baby" (Reprise) .... Curtis
"The Life I Never Led" (Reprise) .... Mary Robert
"Sister Act" (Reprise) .... Deloris, Mother Superior, Mary Patrick,
Mary Robert, Mary Lazarus, Nuns
"Spread the Love Around" .... The Company

(L-R front): Sarah Bolt, Marla Mindelle, Patina Miller

ORCHESTRA

Conductor:
MICHAEL KOSARIN
Associate Conductor:
BRENT-ALAN HUFFMAN
Assistant Conductor:
ARON ACCURSO
Concert Master:
SUZANNE ORNSTEIN
Violins:
MINEKO YAJIMA, ERIC DeGIOIA,
KRISTINA MUSSER
Cello:
ROGER SHELL
Woodwinds:
ANDREW STERMAN, MARC PHANEUF,
JACQUELINE HENDERSON

Trumpets:
CRAIG JOHNSON, SCOTT HARRELL
Trombones:
GARY GRIMALDI, JEFF NELSON
Guitar:
JOHN BENTHAL
Bass:
DICK SARPOLA
Drums:
RICH MERCURIO
Percussion:
MICHAEL ENGLANDER
Keyboards:
BRENT-ALAN HUFFMAN, ARON ACCURSO
Musical Coordinator:
JOHN MILLER

Cast Continued

SWINGS
NATALIE BRADSHAW, CARRIE A. JOHNSON,
LOUISE MADISON, ERNIE PRUNEDA,
LANCE ROBERTS

DANCE CAPTAIN
LOUISE MADISON

UNDERSTUDIES
For Deloris:
CORBIN REID, RASHIDRA SCOTT
For Mother Superior:
JENNIFER ALLEN, WENDY JAMES
For Curtis:
ALAN H. GREEN, LANCE ROBERTS
For Mary Robert:
CHRISTINA DeCICCO, LAEL VAN KEUREN
For Mary Patrick:
HOLLY DAVIS, MARISSA PERRY
For Mary Lazarus:
JENNIFER ALLEN, ROBERTA B. WALL
For Eddie:
CHARL BROWN, ERNIE PRUNEDA
For Monsignor O'Hara, Joey:
BLAKE HAMMOND, KEVIN LIGON
For Pablo, TJ:
CHARL BROWN, ERNIE PRUNEDA
For Michelle, Tina:
CORBIN REID, LAEL VAN KEUREN

Photo courtsey Frances White

STAGE DOOR
Fernando Sepulveda

Photo by Brian Mapp

STAGE DOOR
Donald L. Sullivan

Sister Act

Patina Miller
Deloris Van Cartier

Victoria Clark
Mother Superior

Fred Applegate
Monsignor O'Hara

Sarah Bolt
Mary Patrick

John Treacy Egan
Joey

Demond Green
TJ

Chester Gregory
Eddie Souther

Kingsley Leggs
Curtis Jackson

Marla Mindelle
Mary Robert

Audrie Neenan
Mary Lazarus

Caesar Samayoa
Pablo

Jennifer Allen
Ensemble

Natalie Bradshaw
Swing

Charl Brown
Ensemble

Christina DeCicco
Ensemble

Holly Davis
Ensemble

Madeleine Doherty
Ensemble

Alan H. Green
Ensemble

Blake Hammond
Ensemble

Wendy James
Ensemble

Carrie A. Johnson
Swing

Kevin Ligon
Ensemble

Louise Madison
*Swing,
Dance Captain*

Marissa Perry
Ensemble

Ernie Pruneda
Swing

Corbin Reid
Ensemble

Lance Roberts
Swing

Rashidra Scott
Ensemble

Jennifer Simard
Ensemble

Lael Van Keuren
Ensemble

Roberta Wall
Ensemble

Aléna Watters
Ensemble

Alan Menken
Composer

Glenn Slater
Lyrics

Cheri Steinkellner
Book

Sister Act

Bill Steinkellner
Book

Douglas Carter Beane
Additional Book Material

Jerry Zaks
Director

Anthony Van Laast
Choreography

Klara Zieglerova
Set Design

Lez Brotherston
Costume Design

Natasha Katz
Lighting Design

John Shivers
Sound Design

Bernard Telsey, Telsey + Company
Casting

David Brian Brown
Wig & Hair Design

Steven Beckler
Production Supervisor

Marcia Goldberg, Nancy Nagel Gibbs and Nina Essman, 321 Theatrical Management
General Management

Michael Kosarin
Music Supervisor/ Vocal and Incidental Music Arranger/ Conductor

Doug Besterman
Orchestrations

Mark Hummel
Dance Music

John Miller
Music Coordinator

Whoopi Goldberg
Producer

Philip J. Smith, Chairman, The Shubert Organization
Producer

Robert E. Wankel, President, The Shubert Organization
Producer

Joop van den Ende
Producer

Bill Taylor
Producer

Rebecca Quigley
Producer

Susan V. Booth, Artistic Director, Alliance Theatre
Original Production

COMPANY MANAGEMENT (L-R): Rebecca Petersen, Roeya Banuazizi, Eric Cornell

Photo by Brian Mapp

Sheldon Epps, Artistic Director, The Pasadena Playhouse
Original Production

2010-2011 AWARDS

THEATRE WORLD AWARD
Outstanding Broadway or
Off-Broadway Debut
(Patina Miller)

DRAMA LEAGUE AWARD
Unique Contribution to the Theatre
(Whoopi Goldberg)

STAGE MANAGEMENT (L-R): Steven Beckler, Mary MacLeod, Jason Trubitt

Photo courtesy *Sister Act* Stage Managers

Sister Act

ORCHESTRA
Front Row (L-R): Michael Kosarin (Music Supervisor, Arranger & Principal Conductor), Doug Besterman (Orchestrator), Aron Accurso (Assistant Conductor/Keyboard), Mike Englander (Percussion), Brent-Alan Huffman (Associate Conductor/Keyboard), Eric DeGioia (Violin), Suzanne Ornstein (Concertmaster), John Miller (Music Coordinator)

Middle Row (L-R): Roger Shell (Cello), Kristina Musser (Violin), Mineko Yajima (Violin), Jackie Henderson (Woodwinds), Gary Grimaldi (Trombone), Andrew Sterman (Woodwinds), Jeff Nelson (Bass Trombone), Brendan Whiting (Music Intern)

Back Row (L-R): Scott Harrell (Trumpet), John Benthal (Guitar), Craig Johnson (Trumpet), Don Rice (Copyist), Rich Mercurio (Drums), Marc Phaneuf (Woodwinds), Dick Sarpola (Bass)

Photo by Colleen Croft

Photo by Brian Mapp

CREW
Front Row (L-R): Paul Davila, Steve Schroettnig, Anmaree Rodibaugh, Brian Schweppe, Gene Syzmanski

Middle Row (L-R): Rick DalCortivo, Pitsch Karrer, Dominic Intagliato

Back Row (L-R): Fran Rapp, Jeremy Wahlers, Declan McNeil, Justin McClintock, Tommy Cole, Richard DalCortivo, Jr., Peter Becker, Patrick Shea, Jim Ernest

FRONT OF HOUSE STAFF
(Top-Bottom):
Svetlana Pinkhas, Tiffany Murphy, Ismeal Tirado, Nathaniel Wright, Jonathan Rodriguez, Lisa Maisonet, Mario Carrillo, Karen Banyai, John Hall, Mattie Robinson, William Phalen, Mae Park, Ulises Santiago, Jorge Colon, Lori Bokun, Selene Nelson, Michael Harris

Photo by Brian Mapp

Sister Act

Sister Act
SCRAPBOOK

Correspondents: John Treacy Egan, "Joey"; and Marissa Perry, Ensemble

Parties and/or Gifts: We had some terrific parties thrown by our producer Joop van den Ende. He threw us a party after the first (Sardi's) and last (Gallagher's) preview, not to mention a huge opening night party (Gotham Hall).

The best opening night gift was from Holly Davis and Steve Bebout—they gave us really cool baseball hats that say "Queen of Angels" (the name of the church in the show).

Most Exciting Celebrity Visitors: Aretha Franklin came and sent flowers to a couple of the cast members. And, of course, Whoopi Goldberg and her famous quote to us, "ya'll shat gold!"

Actor Who Performed the Most Roles in This Show: Blake Hammond. He plays six.

Actor Who Has Done the Most Shows: Kevin Ligon was our cast member to receive the Gypsy Robe. He has been in seven Broadway productions. His first was *The Secret Garden*. Then of course there are the veterans: Victoria Clark, Jen Allen, Fred Applegate.

Special Backstage Rituals: Prayer circle at places, yelling out the window on Saturday nights, Vicki Clark's nun sperm dance, Patina Miller and Mary MacLeod dance before bar scene, Fantasy dancers surprise scene for Chester Gregory after apartment scene, Kevin Ligon gets his ass slapped before the fantasy dancer number.

Favorite Moment During Each Performance: The finale is awesome, we love seeing the audience up on their feet, singing and dancing along with us.

Mascot: Tzi Tzi Jenkins (Aléna Watters' alter ego) and Tiny the stuffed Penguin (who was cut from the show in previews). He now lives on the fifth floor.

Favorite Therapy: Jeremy, our physical therapist.

Memorable Ad-Libs: We always love when a gun does or doesn't go off in the right place. One night, eight lines were cut when a gun pointed at Blake Hammond went off prematurely. When the gun went off, he just had to fall over and die.

Web Buzz: I think our show caught Broadway by surprise. People are so responsive and seem to be having an amazing time. I've heard people say they didn't realize how funny it would be, and how they didn't expect to jump up and dance at the curtain call.

Latest Audience Arrivals: Tuesday audience members who don't realize that the 7 p.m. show doesn't start at 8 p.m.

Fastest Costume Change: This would be Chester Gregory who has on two tear-away suits that are pulled off during his number "I Could Be That Guy." Luckily he has one more suit on underneath.

Heaviest/Hottest Costumes: The Nuns' finale costumes.

Who Wore the Least: At one point a drag character has her dress, wig, and falsies torn off on stage, leaving the very handsome Charl

1. The cast and crew gather on the stage for the opening night Gypsy Robe ceremony. Recipient was Kevin Ligon (center, in robe).
2. (L-R): Production Supervisor Steven Beckler and Director Jerry Zaks give notes.
3. "Funky Nuns" horse around backstage (clockwise from top left): Demond Green, Audrie Neenan, *Yearbook* Correspondent John Treacy Egan, Caesar Samayoa, Marla Mindelle and Patina Miller.
4. (Reclining): Victoria Clark relaxes backstage with (Seated, L-R): Caesar Samayoa, Fred Applegate and John Treacy Egan.

Brown standing shirtless in boots and shorts center stage.

Sweethearts Within the Company: Jerry Zaks and the entire cast. We love him.

Memorable Directorial Note: Jerry Zaks told us to take no direction from anyone except the choreographer, the musical director or himself. As he put it: "If anyone gives you direction, tell them that your director told you to tell them to F*CK OFF!" He also said, "Plant your feet, look the other guy in the eye and tell the truth."

Nicknames: Marissa Perry—"Italian stallion"/ "Smurf." Corbin Reid —"Sister Mary Saunter." Patina Miller—"Pateetress Milltress." Aléna Watters—"Sass"/"Tzi Tzi." Lael van Keuren— "Lael as in sale"/"Leechie Jenkins." Carrie

Johnson—"Propecia Rose." The Fantasy Dancers—"Lamar and Leroy Johnson" (no relation), "Chaz Matthews," "Flip Carsen," "Cookie," "Coco," "Cupcake," "Bambi." Christina DeCicco—"Sister Mary Marinara." Wendy James—"Wanda Valdez." Vicki Clark— "Loretta Jenkins." Jen Simard—"Simart." Charl Brown—"Kiki Kardashian." Jerry Zaks— "Original J.Z."

Embarrassing Moments: Holly Davis falls exiting stage after chase and crawls to safety in wing. Jen Simard enters stage early during climax of play with Vicki Clark.

Coolest Thing About Being in This Show: The cast really enjoys each other, and it's such a joyful show.

South Pacific

Cast Continued

For Luther Billis: NICK MAYO,
   GEORGE MERRICK
For Stewpot: MICHAEL ARNOLD,
   TODD CERVERIS
For Lt. Joseph Cable: TAYLOR FREY,
   ROBERT LENZI, PETER LOCKYER
For Capt. George Brackett: ERIC ANDERSON,
   TODD CERVERIS
For Professor: GEORGE MERRICK,
   JASON MICHAEL SNOW
For Cmdr. William Harbison: ROB GALLAGHER,
   GEORGE MERRICK
For Bob McCaffrey, Yeoman Herbert Quale:
   GEORGE PSOMAS, GREG RODERICK
For Ensign Dinah Murphy: JULIE FOLDESI,
   GARRETT LONG
For Lt. Eustis Carmichael, Lt. Buzz Adams:
   TAYLOR FREY, NICK MAYO

ORCHESTRA

Conductor: TED SPERLING
Associate Conductor: CHARLES DU CHATEAU

Violins: BELINDA WHITNEY (Concertmaster),
   KARL KAWAHARA,
   KATHERINE LIVOLSI-LANDAU,
   JAMES TSAO, LISA MATRICARDI,
   RENA ISBIN, MICHAEL NICHOLAS,
   LOUISE OWEN
Violas: KENJI BUNCH, DAVID CRESWELL
Cellos: PETER SACHON, CARYL PAISNER,
   CHARLES DU CHATEAU
Bass: LISA STOKES-CHIN
Flute/Piccolo: LIZ MANN
Clarinet: TODD PALMER, SHARI HOFFMAN
Oboe/English Horn: KELLY PERAL
Bassoon: DAMIAN PRIMIS
French Horns: MICHAEL ATKINSON,
   ROBERT CARLISLE, DANIEL GRABOIS
Trumpets: DOMINIC DERASSE,
   GARETH FLOWERS, WAYNE DUMAINE
Trombones: MARK PATTERSON,
   NATE MAYLAND
Tuba: ANDREW RODGERS
Harp: GRACE PARADISE
Drums/Percussion: BILL LANHAM

Music Coordinator: DAVID LAI

Richard Rodgers' music is being presented in the 30-player orchestration created for the original production. The scores and orchestral parts were restored by The Rodgers & Hammerstein Organization using all existing material, including manuscripts (Rodgers, Trude Rittmann), the full orchestral scores (Robert Russell Bennett) and the individual instrumental parts played by the original orchestra.

Kelli O'Hara
Ensign Nellie Forbush

Paulo Szot
Emile de Becque

Danny Burstein
Luther Billis

Loretta Ables Sayre
Bloody Mary

Andrew Samonsky
Lt. Joseph Cable

Eric Anderson
Stewpot

Sean Cullen
Cmdr. William Harbison

Christian Delcroix
Professor

Luka Kain
Jerome

Li Jun Li
Liat

Laurissa Romain
Ngana

Skipp Sudduth
Capt. George Brackett

Michael Arnold
Johnny Noonan

Craig Bennett
Thomas Hassinger

Christian Carter
Kenneth Johnson

Todd Cerveris
Morton Wise

Helmar Augustus Cooper
Henry

Margot De La Barre
Ensign Connie Walewska/Asst. Dance Captain

Laura Marie Duncan
Ensign Dinah Murphy

Julie Foldesi
Swing

South Pacific

Taylor Frey
Petty Officer
Hamilton Steeves

Rob Gallagher
Ensemble

Maryann Hu
Bloody Mary's
Assistant

Lamae
Bloody Mary's
Assistant

Robert Lenzi
Billy Whitmore

Peter Lockyer
Ensemble

Garrett Long
Ensign Sue Yaeger

Nick Mayo
Richard West

Liz McCartney
Lt. Genevieve
Marshall

George Merrick
Lt. Buzz Adams

William Michals
Understudy for Emile
de Becque

Marla Mindelle
Ensign Cora MacRae

Kimber Monroe
Bloody Mary's
Assistant

Alfie Parker, Jr.
Tom O'Brien

George Psomas
Swing/
Dance Captain

Greg Roderick
Swing

Samantha Shafer
Ensign Janet
MacGregor

Jason Michael Snow
Yeoman Herbert
Quale

Jerold E. Solomon
James Hayes

Correy West
Swing

Joshua Logan
Co-Author
(1908-1988)

Richard Rodgers
Music
(1902-1979)

Oscar Hammerstein II
Lyrics and Co-Author
(1895-1960)

James A. Michener
Author, Tales of the
South Pacific
(1907-1997)

Barlett Sher
Director

Christopher Gattelli
Musical Staging

Ted Sperling
Music Direction

Michael Yeargan
Sets

Catherine Zuber
Costumes

Donald Holder
Lighting

Scott Lehrer
Sound

Robert Russell
Bennett
Orchestrations
(1894-1981)

Trude Rittmann
Dance and Incidental
Music Arrangements
(1908-2005)

David Lai
Music Coordinator

Bernard Telsey,
Telsey + Company
Casting

South Pacific

Bob Boyett

André Bishop and Bernard Gersten,
Lincoln Center Theater
Producer

Laura Osnes sings "I'm
Gonna Wash That Man
Right Outa My Hair"

Photo by Joan Marcus

Becca Ayers
*Understudy for
Ensign Dinah Murphy*

Christopher Carl
*Understudy for Emile
de Becque*

Deborah Lew
*Bloody Mary's
Assistant, Ensemble*

Laura Osnes
*Ensign Nellie
Forbush*

Sarah Solie
Ensign Dinah Murphy

STAGE MANAGEMENT
(L-R): Andrea O. Saraffian (ASM), Rolt Smith (PSM) and Dana
Williams (ASM)

Photos by Brian Mapp

FRONT OF HOUSE STAFF
Front Row (L-R): Paula Gallo, Amy Yedowitz, Ann Danilovics, Susan Lehman,
Officer Steve Spear

Middle Row (L-R): Ruby Jaggernauth, Margie Blair, Jeff Goldstein

Back Row (L-R): Beatrice Gilliard, Nick Andors

South Pacific

HAIR CREW
(L-R): John McNulty, Carrie Rohm (Hair Supervisor), and Isaac Grnya

Photos by Brian Mapp

COSTUME CREW
Front Row (L-R): Linda McAllister, Tamara Kopko, Mark Klein

Back Row (L-R): Stacia Williams, Liam O'Brien, Patti Luther, Lynn Bowling (Wardrobe Supervisor)

Not Pictured: James Nadeaux, Leo Namba, Chuck ReCar

RUNNING CREW
Kneeling (L-R): Bruce Rubin (Electrician/Board Operator), Andrew Belits (Carpenter), Mark Dignam (Props), Rudy Wood (Props), John Weingart (Production Flyman), Jeff Ward (Follow Spot Operator), John Ross (Props), Kristina Clark (Electrics), Julia Rubin (Sound Deck), Fred Bredenbeck (Carpenter)

Standing (L-R): Charles Rausenberger (Props), Bill Nagle (Production Carpenter), Paul Gruen (Flyman), Greg Cushna (Flyman), Ray Skillin (Deck Carpenter), Matt Altman (Follow Spot), Joe Pizzuto (Follow Spot), Pat Merryman (Production Electrician), Juan Bustamante (Deck Automation), John Howie (Carpenter), Bill Burke (Deck Automation), Frank Linn (Electrician/Automation Tech), Nick Irons (Follow Spot), Marc Salzberg (Production Soundman), Gary Simon (Sound Deck)

Not Pictured: Karl Rausenberger (Production Propman), Kevin McNeil (Flyman), Takuda Moody (Sound Deck)

South Pacific

LINCOLN CENTER THEATER

ANDRÉ BISHOP	BERNARD GERSTEN
ARTISTIC DIRECTOR	EXECUTIVE PRODUCER

ADMINISTRATIVE STAFF

GENERAL MANAGER ....ADAM SIEGEL
   Associate General Manager ....Jessica Niebanck
   General Management Assistant ....Meghan Lantzy
   Facilities Manager ....Alex Mustelier
   Associate Facilities Manager ....Michael Assalone
GENERAL PRESS AGENT ....PHILIP RINALDI
   Press Associate ....Barbara Carroll
PRODUCTION MANAGER ....JEFF HAMLIN
   Associate Production Manager ....Paul Smithyman
DIRECTOR OF
   DEVELOPMENT ....HATTIE K. JUTAGIR
   Associate Director of Development ......Rachel Norton
   Manager of Special Events and
     Young Patron Program ....Karin Schall
   Grants Writer ....Neal Brilliant
   Manager, Patron Program ....Sheilaja Rao
   Assistant to the
     Director of Development ....Raelyn R. Lagerstrom
   Development Associate/Special Events &
     Young Patrons Program ....Jennifer H. Rosenbluth
   Development Assistant/
     Individual Giving ....Sydney Rais-Sherman
DIRECTOR OF FINANCE.........DAVID S. BROWN
   Controller ....Susan Knox
   Systems Manager ....Stacy Valentine
   Finance Assistant ....Kristen Parker
DIRECTOR OF MARKETING .LINDA MASON ROSS
   Marketing Associate ....Ashley M. Dunn
   Marketing Assistant ....John Casavant
DIRECTOR OF EDUCATION ....KATI KOERNER
   Associate Director of Education ....Alexandra Lopez
Assistant to the Executive Producer ......Barbara Hourigan
Office Manager ....Brian Hashimoto
Office Assistant ....Rhonda Lipscomb
Messenger ....Esau Burgess
Reception ....Brenden Rogers, Michelle Metcalf

ARTISTIC STAFF

ASSOCIATE DIRECTORS ......GRACIELA DANIELE,
                      NICHOLAS HYTNER,
                      JACK O'BRIEN,
                      SUSAN STROMAN,
                      DANIEL SULLIVAN
RESIDENT DIRECTOR ....BARTLETT SHER
DRAMATURG and DIRECTOR,
   LCT DIRECTORS LAB ....ANNE CATTANEO
CASTING DIRECTOR ....DANIEL SWEE, CSA
MUSICAL THEATER
   ASSOCIATE PRODUCER ....IRA WEITZMAN
DIRECTOR OF LCT3 ....PAIGE EVANS
Artistic Administrator ....Julia Judge
Casting Associate ....Camille Hickman
Lab Assistant ....Kate Marvin

HOUSE STAFF

HOUSE MANAGER.............RHEBA FLEGELMAN
Production Carpenter........................William Nagle
Production Electrician ....Patrick Merryman
Production Propertyman ....Karl Rausenberger
Production Flyman ....John Weingart
House Technician ....Linda Heard
Chief Usher .... M.L. Pollock

Box Office Treasurer ....Fred Bonis
Assistant Treasurer ....Robert A. Belkin

SPECIAL SERVICES

Advertising ....Serino-Coyne/Jim Russek
        Roger Micone, Becca Goland-Van Ryn
Principal Poster Artist ....James McMullan
Poster Art for *Rodgers & Hammerstein's*
   South Pacific ....James McMullan
Counsel ....Peter L. Felcher, Esq.;
                Charles H. Googe, Esq.;
             and Carol Kaplan, Esq. of
      Paul, Weiss, Rifkind, Wharton & Garrison
Immigration Counsel ....Theodore Ruthizer, Esq.;
                Mark D. Koestler, Esq.
   of Kramer, Levin, Naftalis & Frankel LLP
Labor Counsel ....Michael F. McGahan, Esq.
      of Epstein, Becker & Green, P.C.
Auditor...........................Frederick Martens, C.P.A.
               Lutz & Carr, L.L.P.
Insurance ....Jennifer Brown of DeWitt Stern Group
Photographer ....Joan Marcus
Video Services .....Fresh Produce Productions/Frank Basile
Travel ....Tygon Tours
Consulting Architect ....Hugh Hardy,
      H3 Hardy Collaboration Architecture
Construction Manager ....Yorke Construction
Payroll Service ....Castellana Services, Inc.
Merchandising ....Marquee Merchandise, LLC/
                    Matt Murphy
Lobby Refreshments ....Sweet Concessions

STAFF FOR
RODGERS & HAMMERSTEIN'S SOUTH PACIFIC

COMPANY MANAGER ....MATTHEW MARKOFF
Associate Company Manager ...Jessica Perlmeter Cochrane
Assistant Company Manager ....Daniel Hoyos
Assistant Director ....Sarna Lapine
Associate Choreographer ....Joe Langworth
Associate Set Designer ....Lawrence King
Assistant Set Designer ....Mikiko Suzuki
Assistant Costume Designers ....Holly Cain,
             David Newell, Court Watson
Associate Lighting Designer ....Karen Spahn
Assistant Lighting Designer ....Caroline Chao
Automated Light Programmer ....Victor Seastone
Associate Sound Designer ....Leon Rothenberg
Assistant Sound Designer ....Bridget O'Connor
Music Copyist ....Emily Grishman Music Preparation/
        Emily Grishman, Katharine Edmonds
Production Soundman ....Marc Salzberg
Wig and Hair Design .... Tom Watson
Make-up Designer ....Cookie Jordan
Properties Coordinator ....Kathy Fabian
Associate Props Coordinators ....Rose A.C. Howard,
       Carrie Mossman, and Propstar Associates
Prop Scenic Artist ....Curt Tomczyk
Wardrobe Supervisor ....Lynn Bowling
Dressers ....Mark Klein, Tamara Kopko, Patti Luther,
      Linda McAllister, James Nadeaux, Leo Namba,
      Liam O'Brien, Chuck ReCar, Stacia Williams
Hair Supervisor ....Carrie Rohm
Hair Assistants ....Isaac Grnya, John McNulty
Production Assistant ....Brandon Kahn
Children's Guardian ....Vanessa Brown
Children's Tutoring ....On Location Education
Costume Shopper ....Nicole Moody

Electronic Percussion Programming ....Randy Cohen
Rehearsal Pianist ....Jonathan Rose

Vocal Coach ....Deborah Hecht

Telsey + Company

Bernie Telsey CSA, Will Cantler CSA, David Vaccari CSA,
Bethany Knox CSA, Craig Burns CSA,
Tiffany Little Canfield CSA, Rachel Hoffman CSA,
Carrie Rosson CSA, Justin Huff CSA, Bess Fifer CSA,
Patrick Goodwin, Abbie Brady-Dalton

FOR THE RODGERS & HAMMERSTEIN ORGANIZATION

President & Executive Director .... Ted Chapin
Senior Vice President & General Manager ...... Bill Gaden
Senior Vice President &
   General Counsel ....Victoria G. Traube
Senior Vice President/Communications .... Bert Fink
Director of Music ....Bruce Pomahac

Performance rights to *South Pacific* are licensed by
R&H Theatricals: www.rnhtheatricals.com

For help with Michener matters, thanks to Selma Luttinger, Shirley Soenksen at the University of Northern Colorado, Alice Birney (Manuscript Division) and Mark Eden Horowitz (Music Division) of the Library of Congress, and the Vice President's Office at Swarthmore College.

The producers wish to thank the Naval Historical Center; the Navy Medical Department; the CEC/Seabee Historical Foundation; the Intrepid Sea, Air and Space Museum; the New York City Marines; Major Seth Lapine, USMC; Dr. Regina Anna Sekinger, Ph.D; and Katie McGerr for their invaluable assistance with the military research for this production.

CREDITS

Scenery construction by Hudson Scenic Studio, Inc. Show control and scenic motion control featuring Stage Command Systems® by PRG Scenic Technologies, a division of Production Resource Group, LLC, New Windsor, NY. Scenery fabrication by PRG Scenic Technologies, a division of Production Resource Group, LLC, New Windsor, NY. Costumes by Jennifer Love Costumes; Angels the Costumiers; Parsons-Meares, Ltd.; Euro Co. Costumes; and John Cowles. Men's tailoring by Brian Hemesath and Edward Dawson. Millinery by Rodney Gordon, Inc. and Arnold S. Levine, Inc. Fabric painting and distressing by Jeffrey Fender. Fabric painting by Gene Mignola, Inc. Undergarments and hosiery by Bra*Tenders. Tattoos by Louie Zakarian. Sound equipment by Masque Sound. Lighting equipment from PRG Lighting. Specialty props construction by Costume Armour. Specific military props and accessories provided by Jim Korn & Kaufman's Army Navy. Special thanks to Frank Cwiklik at Metropolis Collectibles, South Sea Rattan Collections and Carris Reels. Cymbals provided courtesy of Paiste America Inc. Drumheads provided by Remo Inc. Drum sticks and mallets provided by Vic Firth Inc. Natural herb cough drops courtesy of Ricola USA, Inc. Emergen-C is the official health and energy drink of South Pacific.

Visit www.SouthPacificMusical.com

South Pacific
SCRAPBOOK

Photos by Joseph Marzullo/WENN

The Final Performance, August 22, 2010
1. Curtain call on closing night.
2. Paulo Szot and Kelli O'Hara in a backstage clinch.
3. Danny Burstein takes his bow.
4. Music Director and conductor Ted Sperling.
5. Loretta Ables Sayre and Li Jun Li.
6. The cast applauds Bernard Gersten, executive producer of Lincoln Center Theater.
7. Luka Kain and Laurissa Romain.
8. LCT Artistic Director André Bishop (with microphone) salutes the real military personnel on whom the show was based.

Spider-Man Turn Off the Dark

First Preview: November 28, 2010.
Still previewing as of May 31, 2011.

PLAYBILL

Given extraordinary powers by the bite of a genetically enhanced spider, Peter Parker resolves to do battle with the forces of evil as Spider-Man in this musical based on the comic book character of the same name. The show achieved wide notoriety for its cost, its special effects, the unusual number of injuries among members of its cast, and for playing the most previews of any Broadway show in history.

CAST

(in order of appearance)

Mary Jane Watson .... JENNIFER DAMIANO
Peter Parker/Spider-Man .... REEVE CARNEY
Geek Chorus
   Jimmy-6 .... GIDEON GLICK
   Professor Cobwell ... JONATHAN SCHWARTZ
   Grim Hunter .... MAT DEVINE
   Miss Arrow .... ALICE LEE
Arachne .... T.V. CARPIO
Classics Teacher .... ISABEL KEATING
The Bullies
   Flash .... MATT CAPLAN
   Boyle .... DWAYNE CLARK
   Kong .... LUTHER CREEK
   Meeks .... JOSHUA KOBAK
Uncle Ben .... KEN MARKS
Aunt May .... ISABEL KEATING
MJ's Father .... JEB BROWN
Norman Osborn/
   The Green Goblin .... PATRICK PAGE
Emily Osborn .... LAURA BETH WELLS
J. Jonah Jameson .... MICHAEL MULHEREN
Continued on next page

FOXWOODS THEATRE
A LIVE NATION VENUE

Michael Cohl & Jeremiah J. Harris
Land Line Productions, Hello Entertainment/David Garfinkle/Tony Adams, Sony Pictures Entertainment
Norton Herrick and Herrick Entertainment, Billy Rovzar & Fernando Rovzar, Stephen Bronfman
Jeffrey B. Hecktman, Omneity Entertainment/Richard G. Weinberg
James L. Nederlander, Terry Allen Kramer, S2BN Entertainment, Jam Theatricals
The Mayerson/Gould/Hauser/Tysoe Group, Patricia Lambrecht, and Paul McGuinness

by arrangement with
Marvel Entertainment

Present

SPIDER-MAN TURN OFF THE DARK

Music and Lyrics by
Bono and The Edge

Book by
Julie Taymor and Glen Berger

Starring

Reeve Carney   Jennifer Damiano   T.V. Carpio   Patrick Page

Featuring

Michael Mulheren Ken Marks Isabel Keating Jeb Brown
Mat Devine Gideon Glick Alice Lee Jonathan Schwartz
Matthew James Thomas Laura Beth Wells Matt Caplan Dwayne Clark Luther Creek

with

Kevin Aubin Gerald Avery Collin Baja Marcus Bellamy Emmanuel Brown Daniel Curry Erin Elliott Craig Henningsen
Dana Marie Ingraham Ayo Jackson Joshua Kobak Heather Lang Ari Loeb Natalie Lomonte Kevin C. Loomis Kristen Martin Jodi McFadden
Kristen Faith Oei America Olivo Jennifer Christine Perry Kyle Post Brandon Rubendall Sean Samuels Dollar Tan Christopher W. Tierney

Scenic Design	Lighting Design	Costume Design	Sound Design
George Tsypin	Donald Holder	Eiko Ishioka	Jonathan Deans

Projection Design	Mask Design	Hair Design	Make-up Design
Kyle Cooper	Julie Taymor	Campbell Young Associates Luc Verschueren	Judy Chin

Aerial Design	Aerial Rigging Design	Projection Coordinator / Additional Content Design
Scott Rogers	Jaque Paquin	Howard Werner

Arrangements & Orchestrations	Music Supervision	Music Direction
David Campbell	Teese Gohl	Kimberly Grigsby

Music Coordinator	Vocal Arrangements	Additional Arrangements / Vocal Arrangements
Antoine Silverman	David Campbell, Teese Gohl, Kimberly Grigsby	Dawn Kenny Rori Coleman

Associate Scenic Design	Resident Director	Resident Choreographer	Production Stage Managers
Rob Bissinger	Keith Batten	Cherice Barton	C. Randall White & Kathleen E. Purvis

Casting Director	Marketing Director	Marketing	Associate Producer
Telsey + Company	Len Gill	Keith Hurd	Anne Tanaka

Press Representation	Production Management	General Management	Executive Producers
O & M Co.	Juniper Street Productions & MB Productions	Alan Wasser - Allan Williams Aaron Lustbader	Glenn Orsher Martin McCallum Adam Silberman

Choreography and Aerial Choreography by
Daniel Ezralow

Directed by
Julie Taymor

3/15/11

(L-R): Patrick Page and Reeve Carney

Photo by Jacob Cohl

Spider-Man Turn Off the Dark

MUSICAL NUMBERS

ACT 1

"Splash Page" ....Citizens
"Behold and Wonder" ....Arachne, Miss Arrow, Weavers
"Bullying by Numbers" ....Bullies, High School Girls
"No More" ....Peter, Mary Jane
"D.I.Y. World" ....Osborn, Emily, High School Students, Lab Assistants
"Bouncing Off the Walls" ....Peter, Geek Chorus
"Rise Above" ....Peter, Arachne, Citizens
"Pull the Trigger" ....Osborn, Military Generals, Soldiers
"Picture This" ....Peter, Mary Jane, Osborn, Emily
"I'll Take Manhattan" ....The Green Goblin

ACT 2

"Spider-Man Rising" ....Busker, Citizens
"Turn Off the Dark" ....Arachne
"Walk Away" ....Peter, Mary Jane, Geek Chorus
"Think Again" ....Arachne, Furies
"Sinistereo" ....Jeb Brown, Dwayne Clark, Luther Creek
"Deeply Furious" ....Arachne, Furies
"If the World Should End" ....Mary Jane
"The Boy Falls From the Sky" ....Peter

Cast Continued

Hero Flyer ....JOSHUA KOBAK
Green Goblin Flyer ....COLLIN BAJA
Swarm Exterminator Flyer .CRAIG HENNINGSEN
Purse Snatcher ....SEAN SAMUELS
Busker ....DWAYNE CLARK
The Sinister Six
    Carnage ....COLLIN BAJA
    Kraven the Hunter ....JOSHUA KOBAK
    The Lizard ....BRANDON RUBENDALL
    Electro ....EMMANUEL BROWN
    Swiss Miss ....SEAN SAMUELS
    Swarm ....GERALD AVERY

Citizens, Weavers, Students, Lab Assistants,
    Reporters, Generals, Spider-Men,
    Secretaries, Soldiers, Furies .....GERALD AVERY,
        COLLIN BAJA, MARCUS BELLAMY,
        EMMANUEL BROWN, JEB BROWN,
        MATT CAPLAN, DWAYNE CLARK,
        LUTHER CREEK, CRAIG HENNINGSEN,
        DANA MARIE INGRAHAM, AYO JACKSON,
        ISABEL KEATING, JOSHUA KOBAK,
        HEATHER LANG, NATALIE LOMONTE,
        KEN MARKS, KRISTEN MARTIN,
        JODI McFADDEN, KRISTEN FAITH OEI,
        JENNIFER CHRISTINE PERRY,
        BRANDON RUBENDALL, SEAN SAMUELS,
        DOLLAR TAN, CHRISTOPHER W. TIERNEY,
            LAURA BETH WELLS
Ensemble Aerialists ....KEVIN AUBIN,

GERALD AVERY, COLLIN BAJA,
MARCUS BELLAMY, LUTHER CREEK,
DANIEL CURRY, ERIN ELLIOTT,
CRAIG HENNINGSEN,
DANA MARIE INGRAHAM, AYO JACKSON,
JOSHUA KOBAK, HEATHER LANG,
ARI LOEB, NATALIE LOMONTE,
KRISTEN MARTIN, JODI McFADDEN,
KRISTEN FAITH OEI,
JENNIFER CHRISTINE PERRY,
BRANDON RUBENDALL, SEAN SAMUELS,
CHRISTOPHER W. TIERNEY

At certain performances, the role of Peter
Parker/Spider-Man will be played by
MATTHEW JAMES THOMAS

UNDERSTUDIES

For Peter Parker/Spider-Man: MATT CAPLAN
For Mary Jane Watson: KRISTEN MARTIN
For Jimmy-6, Professor Cobwell, Grim Hunter:
    KYLE POST, MATTHEW JAMES THOMAS
For Miss Arrow: KRISTEN MARTIN
For Arachne: JODI McFADDEN,
    AMERÍCA OLIVO
For Norman Osborn/The Green Goblin:
    JEB BROWN
For J. Jonah Jameson: KEVIN C. LOOMIS,
    KEN MARKS
For Flash, Boyle, Kong, Meeks: KYLE POST

For Uncle Ben: KEVIN C. LOOMIS
For Aunt May: AMERÍCA OLIVO,
    LAURA BETH WELLS
For MJ's father:
    LUTHER CREEK, KEVIN C. LOOMIS
For Emily Osborn: AMERÍCA OLIVO
For Busker: KYLE POST, SEAN SAMUELS
For The Lizard, Carnage, Swiss Miss:
    KEVIN AUBIN, DANIEL CURRY
For Kraven the Hunter: KEVIN AUBIN,
    DANIEL CURRY, ARI LOEB
For Electro: ARI LOEB, DOLLAR TAN
For Swarm: MARCUS BELLAMY, ARI LOEB

Dance Captains: ERIN ELLIOTT, ARI LOEB
Assistant Dance Captain: MARCUS BELLAMY

SWINGS

KEVIN AUBIN, DANIEL CURRY,
ERIN ELLIOTT, ARI LOEB,
KEVIN C. LOOMIS, AMERÍCA OLIVO,
KYLE POST

Matthew James Thomas is appearing with the
permission of Actors' Equity Association.

ORCHESTRA

Conductor: KIMBERLY GRIGSBY
Associate Conductor: CHARLES duCHATEAU
Guitars: ZANE CARNEY (onstage), MATT BECK,
    BEN BUTLER
Basses: AIDEN MOORE (onstage),
    RICHARD HAMMOND
Drums: JON EPCAR
Keyboards: BILLY JAY STEIN,
    CHARLES duCHATEAU
Percussion: JOHN CLANCY
Hammered Dulcimer/Percussion: BILL RUYLE
Concertmaster: ANTOINE SILVERMAN
Viola/Violin: CHRISTOPHER CARDONA
Cello: ANJA WOOD
Trumpets: DON DOWNS, TONY KADLECK
French Horn: THERESA MacDONNELL
Trombone/Tuba: MARCUS ROJAS
Reeds: AARON HEICK

Electronic Music Design: BILLY JAY STEIN
Music Coordination: ANTOINE SILVERMAN
Music Copying Supervisor: STEVEN M. ALPER
Music Copyists: BETTIE ROSS,
    RUSSELL ANIXTER, STEVEN COHEN,
    JODY JAROWEY, DON RICE,
    ROY WILLIAMS, DAVID WOLFSON
Piano Vocal Score Coordination: MARK BAECHLE

Spider-Man Turn Off the Dark

Reeve Carney
Peter Parker/
Spider-Man

Jennifer Damiano
Mary Jane Watson

T.V. Carpio
Arachne

Patrick Page
Norman Osborn/
The Green Goblin

Michael Mulheren
J. Jonah Jameson

Ken Marks
Uncle Ben, Ensemble

Isabel Keating
Aunt May,
Classics Teacher

Jeb Brown
MJ's Father,
Ensemble

Mat Devine
Grim Hunter

Gideon Glick
Jimmy-6

Alice Lee
Miss Arrow

Jonathan Schwartz
Professor Cobwell

Matthew James
Thomas
Peter Parker/
Spider-Man
Alternate

Laura Beth Wells
Emily Osborn,
Ensemble

Matt Caplan
Flash, Ensemble

Dwayne Clark
Boyle, Busker,
Ensemble

Luther Creek
Kong, Ensemble

Kevin Aubin
Swing

Gerald Avery
Swarm, Ensemble

Collin Baja
Carnage, Ensemble

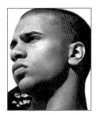
Marcus Bellamy
Assistant Dance
Captain, Ensemble

Emmanuel Brown
Electro, Ensemble

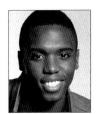
Daniel Curry
Swing

Erin Elliott
Dance Captain,
Swing

Craig Henningsen
Ensemble

Dana Marie
Ingraham
Ensemble

Ayo Jackson
Ensemble

Joshua Kobak
Ensemble

Heather Lang
Ensemble

Ari Loeb
Dance Captain,
Swing

Natalie Lomonte
Ensemble

Kevin C. Loomis
Swing

Kristen Martin
Ensemble

Jodi McFadden
Ensemble

Kristen Faith Oei
Ensemble

Spider-Man Turn Off the Dark

América Olivo
Swing

Jennifer Christine
Perry
Ensemble

Kyle Post
Swing

Brandon Rubendall
The Lizard, Ensemble

Sean Samuels
*Swiss Miss,
Ensemble*

Dollar Tan
Ensemble

Christopher W.
Tierney
Ensemble

Julie Taymor
*Co-Book Writer,
Director,
Mask Designer*

Bono
Music & Lyrics

The Edge
Music & Lyrics

Glen Berger
Co-Book Writer

Daniel Ezralow
*Choreographer,
Aerial
Choreographer*

George Tsypin
Scenic Designer

Donald Holder
Lighting Designer

Eiko Ishioka
Costume Designer

Jonathan Deans
Sound Designer

Kyle Cooper
Projections Designer

Luc Verschueren,
Campbell Young
Associates
Hair Designers

Scott Rogers
Aerial Designer

Jaque Paquin
*Aerial Rigging
Designer*

Howard Werner
*Projection
Coordinator/
Additional Content
Design*

Rob Bissinger
*Associate Scenic
Designer*

Keith Batten
Resident Director

Cherice Barton
*Resident
Choreographer*

David Campbell
*Arrangements and
Orchestrations,
Vocal Arrangements*

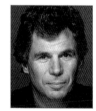

Teese Gohl
Music Supervisor

Kimberly Grigsby
Music Director

Rori Coleman
*Additional
Arrangements/
Vocal Arrangements*

Dawn Kenny
*Additional
Arrangements/
Vocal Arrangements*

Billy Jay Stein
*Electronic Music
Designer*

Bernard Telsey,
Telsey + Company
Casting

Joseph DeLuise, Alexandra Paull,
Hillary Blanken, Ana Rose Greene,
Kevin Broomell, Guy Kwan,
Juniper Street Productions
Production Management

Mike Bauder,
MB Productions
*Production
Management*

Alan Wasser
General Manager

Spider-Man Turn Off the Dark

Allan Williams
General Manager

Michael Cohl
Producer

Jeremiah J. Harris
Producer

David Garfinkle,
CEO,
Hello Entertainment
Producer

Norton Herrick
Producer

Jeffrey B. Hecktman
Producer

James L.
Nederlander
Producer

Terry Allen Kramer
Producer

Arny Granat,
Jam Theatricals
Producer

Steve Traxler,
Jam Theatricals
Producer

Frederic H.
Mayerson,
The Mayerson/
Gould/Hauser/
Tysoe Group
Producer

James M. Gould,
The Mayerson/
Gould/Hauser/
Tysoe Group
Producer

Ron Tysoe,
The Mayerson/
Gould/Hauser/
Tysoe Group
Producer

Glenn Orsher
Executive Producer

Adam Silberman
Executive Producer

Daniel Case
*Ensemble Aerialist,
Swing*

Natalie Mendoza
Arachne

Roberto Aguirre-
Sacasa
Co-Book Writer

Philip Wm. McKinley
Creative Consultant

Chase Brock
*Additional
Choreography*

Stephen Howard
Executive Producer

BOX OFFICE STAFF
(L-R): Augie Pugliese and Jimmy Smith

Not pictured: Spencer Taustine, Michelle
Smith, Lorraine Lester, John Dunn, Carol
Nipoti, Fran Oestricher, Karen Winer

HAIR, MAKEUP AND WARDROBE
Front Row (L-R): Michael D. Hannah, Diana Calderazzo, Alejandra Rubinos, Rachel Garrett, Leslie Moulton, Jack Scott
Second Row (L-R): Lyle Jones, Sonya Wysocki, Jackie Freeman, Lacie Pulido, Ron Tagert
Third Row (L-R): Carrie Kamerer, Dana Burkart, Kyle Stewart, Bobby Belopede, Cheryl Widner, Michael Piscitelli
Fourth Row (L-R): Angela Johnson, Arlene Watson, Therese Ducey
Fifth Row (L-R): John James, Tiffany Hicks, Christel Murdock, Daniel Mura, Brian Hennings, Kyle O'Connor

Spider-Man Turn Off the Dark

CREW

Front Row: Tommy Galinski, Andy Elman, Mike Norris, Pat O'Connor, John Gibson, Valerie Spradling, Kevin Keane, Dan Hochstine

Middle Row: John Eckert, Kris Keene, Joe Harris, Matty Lynch, Tim Abel, John Warburton, John Harris, Sean McDonough, Mark Davidson, Geoff Vaughn, Steven Pugliese, Eric Dressler, John Van Buskirk, David Fulton, Karl Lawrence, Ron Rebentish

Back Row: Tom Lowrey, Anthony Guadelope, Jimmy Harris, Alan Grudzinski, Thomas McDonough, Mike Fedigan, Brendan Lynch, Art Friedlander, Kevin Hurdman, David Camus, John Santagata, Sean Jones, Jack Anderson

Not pictured: Joshua Coakley, Mike Bernstein, Andy Elman, Hugh Hardyman, Ron Martin, John Sibley

FRONT OF HOUSE STAFF

Front Row: Eric Paris, Adrian Zambrano, Jessica Carollo, Jesse Gold, Lisa Lamothe, Denise Williams, Trevor Worden (kneeling in front), Brooke Smith, Kristin Netzband, Cristina Marie, Erroll Whittington

Middle Row: Michael Rheinbold, Megan Miller, Alysha Wright, Ashley Baker, Chadd Wilson, Josh Rothberg, Meghann Early

Back Row: Matthew Konigsberg, Tony Lepore, Bill Miller, Glenda Deabreu, Eric Grapatin, Edward Griggs, Jennifer Coolbaugh, Chris Casarino, Jessica Bettini, Jessica Leal, Adam Sarsfield, Orlando Ortiz, Andy Still

Not Pictured: David Toombs, Eric Byrd, Erin Soler, Jesse Gold, John Cormier, Keldya Gordon, Kent Hu, Paul Fiteni, Peter Adamson, Raymond Millan, Rita Wozniak

Spider-Man Turn Off the Dark

STAFF FOR *SPIDER-MAN TURN OFF THE DARK*

GENERAL MANAGEMENT
ALAN WASSER ASSOCIATES

Alan Wasser   Allan Williams
Aaron Lustbader   Mark Shacket

PRODUCTION MANAGEMENT
JUNIPER STREET PRODUCTIONS

Hillary Blanken   Kevin Broomell
Guy Kwan   Ana Rose Greene   Alexandra Paull
Joseph DeLuise

MB PRODUCTIONS
Mike Bauder

TECHNICAL DIRECTOR
Fred Gallo

CASTING
TELSEY + COMPANY
Bernard Telsey CSA, Will Cantler CSA,
David Vaccari CSA
Bethany Knox CSA, Craig Burns CSA,
Tiffany Little Canfield CSA, Rachel Hoffman CSA,
Justin Huff CSA, Patrick Goodwin CSA,
Abbie Brady-Dalton, David Morris, Cesar A. Rocha

COMPANY MANAGER
Marc Borsak

GENERAL PRESS REPRESENTATIVE
O&M CO.
Rick Miramontez
Andy Snyder   Jaron Caldwell
Elizabeth Wagner   Sam Corbett

Production Stage Manager ....C. Randall White
Co-Production Stage Manager ....Kathleen E. Purvis
Second Assistant
    Stage Managers ....Sandra M. Franck,
                 Jenny Slattery, Michael Wilhoite
Sub Stage Managers ....Theresa A. Bailey, Andrew Neal
Associate Company Manager ....Thom Mitchell
Assistant Company Manager ....Lisa Guzman
Assistant Director ....Dodd Loomis
Consulting Executive Producer ....Steve Howard
Production Aerial Supervisor ....Angela Phillips
UK Casting....................................Gillian Hawser

Set Design Creative Team:
Associate Scenic Designer ....Rob Bissinger
Pop-up and Dimensional Design ....Arturs Virtmanis
Illustration and Graphics ....Baiba Baiba
Cityscape Graphics ....Sergei Goloshapov

Assistant Set Design Team:
First Assistant Set Design ....Anita La Scala
Graphic Art ....Sia Balabanova, Rafael Kayanan
Pop-ups ....Nathan Heverin
Model Makers ....Eric Beauzay, Catherine Chung,
              Rachel Short Janocko, Damon Pelletier,
                        Daniel Zimmerman
Draftsmen ....Robert John Andrusko, Toni Barton,
             Larry W. Brown, Mark Fitzgibbons,
             Jonathan Spencer, Josh Zangen

Assistant Set Design ....Tijana Bjelajac,
            Szu-Feng Chen, Heather Dunbar,
        Mimi Lien, Qin (Lucy) Lu, Robert Pyzocha,
            Chsato Uno, Frank McCullough
Previsualization ....Lily Twining

Associate Costume Designer ....Mary Nemecek Peterson
Assistant Costume Designers ....Angela M. Kahler,
                            Katie Irish
Costume Shoppers ....Jennifer Adams, Dana Burkart,
                Cathy Parrott, Jen Raskopf
Assistant Hair Designer ....Cory McCutcheon
Associate Makeup Designer ....Angela Johnson
Associate Lighting Designer ....Vivien Leone
Assistant Lighting Designers.................Caroline Chao,
                           Carolyn Wong
Assistant to the Lighting Designer ......Porsche McGovern
Automated Lighting Programmer ....Richard Tyndall
Assistant Video Designer ....Sarah Jakubasz
Video Programmer ....Phil Gilbert
Associate Sound Designer ....Brian Hsieh
Puppet and Mask Production Supervisor ....Louis Troisi
Assistant Puppet and Mask Coordinator ....Curran Banach
Prosthetics Designed by ....Louis Zakarian
Automated Flying Programmer ....Jason Shupe
Production Carpenter ....Jack Anderson
Assistant Carpenters ....Andrew Elman, Dave Fulton,
               Hugh Hardyman, Kris Keene,
             Matthew J. Lynch, Mike Norris,
                         Geoffrey Vaughn
Production Electricians ....Randall Zaibek,
                          James Fedigan
Head Electrician ....Ron Martin
Production Video Electricians ....Jason Lindahl,
                          Chris Herman
Production Sound Engineer ....Simon Matthews
Assistant Sound Engineer ....Dan Hochstine
Production Properties Supervisor ....Joseph P. Harris, Jr.
Associate Properties Supervisor ....Timothy M. Abel
Production Wardrobe Supervisor ....Michael D. Hannah
Assistant Wardrobe Supervisors ....Christel Murdock,
                          Sonya Wysocki
Dressers ....Robert Belopede, Diana Calderazzo,
           Jackie Freeman, Rachel Garrett, Lyle Jones,
           Rosemary Keough, Carrie Kamerer,
       Shannon McDowell, Leslie Moulton, Daniel Mura,
           Kyle O'Connor, Michael Piscitelli,
         Jack Scott, Kyle Stewart, Ron Tagert,
           Arlene Watson, Cheryl Widner
Seamstress................................Alejandra Rubinos
Laundry ....William Hamilton
Hair Supervisor ....John James
Hairstylists ....Cory McCutcheon, Therese Ducey,
                          Brian Hennings
Production Makeup Supervisor ....Angela Johnson
Assistant Makeup Supervisor ....Tiffany Hicks
Production Photographer/Videographer ....Jacob Cohl
Video Crew ....Ben Nabors, Matt Kazman,
             Nora Tennessen, Greg Emetaz
Key Artwork ....Prologue Films/
                          Kyle Cooper
Lead Guitar Technician ....Dallas Schoo
Additional Guitar Technician ....Mike Vegas
Workshop Audio Engineers ......Carl Glanville, Angie Teo
Vocal Coach ....Don Lawrence
Dialect Coach ....Deborah Hecht

Acting Coach ....Sheila Grey
Technical Production Assistants ....Sue Barsoum,
       Steve Chazaro, Kate DellaFera, Ania Parks,
       Melissa Spengler, Kim Straatemeier
Production Assistants ....Amanda Johnson,
         Samantha Preiss, Danya Taymor,
                         Raynelle Wright
Costume Interns ....Yingshi June Lin,
                       Tomke Von Gawinski
Physical Therapist ....Heidi Green
Official Athletic Trainer ....Prime Blueprint/
                         Dr. Edyth Heus
Consulting Producer ....Jeffery Auerbach
Producing Consultant ....Carl Pasbjerg
Executive Assistant to Michael Cohl ....Jamie Forshaw
Assistant to Jeremiah J. Harris ....Stella Morelli
Assistant to Glenn Orsher ....Tricia Olson
Marketing Director ....Len Gill
Marketing ....Keith Hurd
Marketing Associate ....Mary Caitlin Barrett
Advertising ....Serino Coyne/
            Nancy Coyne, Sandy Block,
          Angelo Desimini, Matt Upshaw
Website Design &
    Internet Marketing ....Situation Interactive/
            Damian Bazadona, John Lanasa,
            Jeremy Kraus, Victoria Gettler,
                        Chris Powers
National Public Relations ....Ken Sunshine/
           Sunshine, Sachs & Associates
Sponsorship Consultant ....Cary Chevat
Ticket Services Manager ....Mike Rafael
Press Associates ....Molly Barnett,
          Philip Carrubba, Jon Dimond,
          Richard Hillman, Yufen Kung
Press Interns ....Chelsea Nachman, Patrick O'Neil,
                 Alexandra H. Rubin
Legal Counsel ....Ron Feiner, Esq.,
           Beigelman, Feiner & Feldman
     Joseph T. Moldovan, Esq., Jack Levy, Esq.,
          Joshua D. Saviano, Esq.,
               Morrison Cohen LLP
Accounting ....Rosenberg, Neuwirth & Kuchner/
          Chris Cacace, Marina Flom,
                Kirill Baytalskiy
General Management Associates ....Mark Barna,
                          Jake Hirzel
General Management Office.............Hilary Ackerman,
          Nina Lutwick, Dawn Kusinski,
               Jennifer O'Connor
Insurance ....DeWitt Stern Group/Pete Shoemaker
Banking ....Signature Bank/Barbara von Borstel,
         Margaret Monigan, Mary Ann Fanelli,
                         Janett Urena
Payroll ....Castellana Services, Inc.
Transportation and Housing ......Road Rebel Touring and
                        Travel Services,
       Alternative Business Accommodations,
               The Mansfield Hotel

Group Sales
Broadway.com/1-800-Broadway

CREDITS AND ACKNOWLEDGMENTS
Scenery and scenic effects built and electrified by PRG
Scenic Technologies, New Windsor, NY. Scenery painted by

Spider-Man Turn Off the Dark

Scenic Art Studios, Cornwall, NY. Show control and scenic motion control featuring Stage Command Systems® by PRG Scenic Technologies, New Windsor, NY. Aerial effects equipment provided by Fisher Technical Services Inc. Video projection equipment, lighting equipment and sound equipment provided by PRG, Secaucus, NJ. Special effects executed by Excitement Technologies, Addison, TX. Softgoods built by I. Weiss and Sons Inc., Fairview, NJ. Props executed by the Spoon Group, Rahway, NJ; the Rollingstock Company, Sarasota, FL; the Paragon Innovation Group Inc., Toronto, ON; Illusion Projects, Las Vegas, NV; Beyond Imagination, Newburgh, NY; Cigar Box Studios Inc., Newburgh, NY; Czinkota Studios, Gardiner, NY; and Hamilton Scenic Specialty Inc., Dundas, ON. Media content created by Prologue Films. Puppets executed by Nathan Heverin, New Paltz, NY; Michael Curry Design Inc., Portland, OR; the Paragon Innovation Group Inc., Toronto, ON; Igloo Projects/Philip Cooper, Brooklyn, NY. Puppet assistance by Ilya Vett. Hauling by Clark Transfer Inc.; Michael O'Brien & Sons, Bronx, NY; and Prop Transport, New York, NY. Excerpt from "Manhattan" written by Richard Rodgers, Lorenz Hart, used by permission of Piedmont Music Company, publisher. Excerpt from "Vertigo," lyrics by Bono with The Edge, music by U2, used by permission of Universal Music Publishing. "The Boy Falls From the Sky" lyrics by Bono and The Edge, music by U2, used by permission.

Costumes constructed by Parsons-Meares Ltd.

Additional costumes by Bill Hargate Costumes, Tom Talmon Studios, Artur & Tailors Ltd., Danielle Gisiger, Valentina Kozhecksy and Arel Studio. Millinery by Monica Vianni, Arnold Levine, Lynne Mackey Studio. Costume crafts by Paragon Innovation Group Inc., Toronto, ON; James Chai, Philip Cooper, New York, NY, Signs and Shapes International. Custom shirts by L. Allmeier. Custom shoes by Jitterbug Boy, LaDuca Shoes, Montana Leather, Capri Shoes and World Tone. Digital printing and screen printing by Gene Mignola. Costume painting by Parmalee Welles-Tolkan, Mary Macy, Margaret Peot, Virginia Clow, Claudia Dzundza. Additional printing by Jeff Fender. Additional dyeing by Eric Winterling. Development painting by Hochi Asiatico.

IN MEMORY OF
Tony Adams

SPECIAL THANKS
Anne Runolfsson, Thomas Schumacher, William Court Cohen, Trevor Bowen, Keryn Kaplan, Shan Lui, Liz Devlin, Catriona Garde, Susan Hunter, Missy Iredell, Michelle Lieu, Jennifer McManus, Principle Management Dublin and New York, David Toraya, Allen Grubman, Gil Karson, Larry Shire, Paul Wachter, Seth Gelblum, Michael West, Stan Lee, Elliot Goldenthal, Jake Bell, Don Lasker, Darryl Scherba, William Dailey, Michael O'Brien and Sons, Derek Mouton of MCD, Vox Amplification, Fender Guitars, Rickenbacker Guitars, to NS Design for the loan of the electric violin and cello, Roland, Tekserve, James Jones Hammered Dulcimers, David S. Weiss, M.D., Bruce Glikas

---

Syfy
Official Media Partner

The Chrysler Building and its image are trademarks of Tishman Speyer Properties, LP and its affiliates and is used herein with permission.

Makeup provided by M·A·C Cosmetics

Rehearsed at the New 42nd Street Studios

Souvenir merchandise designed and created by
S2BN Entertainment
Norman Perry   Brahma Jade   Pete Milano
www.SpiderManOnBroadwaystore.com

Energy efficient washer/dryer courtesy of
LG Electronics

**To learn more about the production please visit
www.SpiderManOnBroadway.com**

HISTORY OF THE FOXWOODS THEATRE

The Foxwoods Theatre combines architectural preservation with state-of-the-art construction and technology. The spirit and character of New York's grandest historic theatres has been maintained and united with the technical amenities of a modern facility.

In 1997 the Ford Center for the Performing Arts was erected on the site of the legendary Lyric Theatre (1903; 1,261 seats) and Apollo Theatre (1920; 1,194 seats). The auditorium's interior design is based on historic elements from the Apollo Theatre. The Apollo's original ceiling dome, proscenium arch, and side boxes were removed, restored and re-installed (upon expansion for the larger scale of the new theatre) in the new auditorium. The side wall panels were created for acoustical considerations and designed to complement the historic features. New murals were commissioned to form a frieze over the new side boxes. Informally titled "Wings of Creativity," they were inspired by ancient Greek myths of Apollo, patron god of musicians and poets.

The lobby's design is based on historical elements of the Lyric Theatre. An elliptical dome from the Lyric was reproduced as the centerpiece of a new two-story atrium. The grand limestone staircase was designed to provide the flow and spirit of a grand theatre or opera house. The staircase railings feature lyre designs that were recreated from the original 43rd Street façade balcony rails. In the floor is a magnificent mosaic featuring comedy and tragedy masks inspired by sculptures on the historic 43rd St. façade. The 650-sq.-ft. mosaic includes 172,800 hand-cut pieces of marble from all over the world. At the top of the stairs is a medallion with the head of Zeus, taken from the Lyric's auditorium, and on the dress circle level, cold-painted windows (a stained glass technique) featuring a cupid design have been restored. The lighting in the lobby features the bare carbon filament light bulb, utilized in the early 20th century, to create a warm candlelight glow.

At 1,932 seats, the new theatre is one of Broadway's largest. The Ford Center opened with the acclaimed musical *Ragtime*, followed by the Broadway revival of *Jesus Christ Superstar* and the award-winning revival of *42nd Street*. In 2005, the Ford Center was renamed the Hilton Theatre. Its premiere production was the musical *Chitty Chitty Bang Bang*, followed by the dance-inspired musical *Hot Feet*, the holiday spectacular *Dr. Seuss' How the Grinch Stole Christmas: The Musical*, *The Pirate Queen* and the new Mel Brooks' musical *Young Frankenstein*. In 2010, the Hilton Theatre was renamed the Foxwoods Theatre. We are pleased to welcome *Spider-Man Turn Off The Dark* to the Foxwoods stage.

FOXWOODS THEATRE

General Manager	Erich Jungwirth
Assistant General Manager	Sue Barsoum
House Manager	Eric Paris
Facility Manager	Jeff Nuzzo
Assistant Facility Manager	David Dietsch
Box Office Treasurer	Spencer Taustine
Assistant Box Office Treasurer	Michelle Smith
Head Carpenter	James C. Harris
Head Electrician	Art J. Friedlander
Head of Properties	Joseph P. Harris Jr.
Head of Sound	John R. Gibson
Staff Accountant	Carmen Martinez
Staff Accountant	Jill Johnson
Shipping/Receiving	Dinara Kratsch
Administrative Assistant	Brian Mahoney

FOXWOODS THEATRE
A Live Nation Venue

LIVE NATION ENTERTAINMENT

President and Chief Executive Officer	Michael Rapino
President, North America Music, North	Mark Campana
President, North America Music, South	Bob Roux
Chairman, Northeast Region	Jim Koplik
President, New York Music	Kevin Morrow
Senior Vice President, Northeast Operations	John Huff
Vice President Marketing, New York	Jim Steen
Vice President Ticketing Operations	Wayne Goldberg
President of Live Nation Network	Russell Wallach
Chief Financial Officer	Kathy Willard
President, North America Venues & Markets	Ben Weeden
Senior Vice-President, North America Finance	Kathy Porter
Vice President, Finance	Dan Casale
Director of Accounting, Northeast	Jennifer Douglas

About Live Nation Entertainment
Live Nation Entertainment (NYSE-LYV) is the largest live entertainment company in the world, connecting 200 million fans to 100,000 events in more than 40 countries, which has made Ticketmaster.com the number-three eCommerce website in the world. For additional information, visit www.livenation.com/investors.

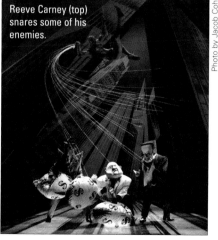

Reeve Carney (top) snares some of his enemies.

Photo by Jacob Cohl

That Championship Season

BOX OFFICE
(L-R): Karen Coscia, Michael Kolbrenner

CREW AND STAGE MANAGEMENT
Front Row (L-R): Scott Sanders, Jenn Molloy, Buster, Mickey Abbate, Cambra Overend, Dave Rogers

Back Row (L-R): Jane Grey, Mike Van Praagh, Herb Messing, Brian McGarity, Terry O'Connor

STAFF FOR *THAT CHAMPIONSHIP SEASON*

GENERAL MANAGEMENT
ROBERT COLE PRODUCTIONS, LLC
Lisa M. Poyer

GENERAL PRESS REPRESENTATIVE
BONEAU/BRYAN-BROWN
Chris Boneau   Matt Polk   Amy Kass

PRODUCTION MANAGEMENT
AURORA PRODUCTIONS INC.
Gene O'Donovan, Ben Heller,
Stephanie Sherline, Jarid Sumner, Liza Luxenberg,
Jason Margolis, Ryan Stanisz, Melissa Mazdra

CASTING
CINDY TOLAN
Adam S. Caldwell

ORIGINAL MUSIC
Michael Barrett

VOICE OF ANNOUNCER
David Garrison

Production Stage Manager ....Jane Grey
Stage Manager ....Cambra Overend
Assistant Scenic
    Designers ....Mikiko Suzuki MacAdams,
                                                    Wilson Chin
Associate Costume Designer ....Wade Laboissonniere
Assistant Lighting Designer ....Keri L. Thibodeau
Associate Sound Designer ....Drew Levy
Assistant Sound Designer ....Will Pickens
Assistant to the Director ....Otoja Abit
Assistant to the Stage Managers ....Bryn Magnus
Assistant to the General Manager ....Lucius Robinson

Advance Carpenter ....Brian Munroe
Production Electrician ....Brian GF McGarity
Light Board Programmer ....Jessica Morton

Sound Operator ....Scott Sanders
Advance Props ....Christopher Pantuso
Wardrobe Supervisor ....Dave Olin Rogers
Dressers ....Mickey Abbate, Jenn Molloy
Assistants to the Producers ....Michael Shapiro,
                                                    Tara Carrozza

Advertising ....SpotCo/
                            Drew Hodges, Jim Edwards,
                    Tom Greenwald, Stephen Sosnowski,
                                                Meghan Ownbey
Interactive Marketing ....Situation Interactive/
                            Damian Bazadona, John Lanasa,
                            Brian Hawe, Victoria Gettler
Legal Counsel ....Fitelson, Lasky, Aslan,
                                                Couture & Garmise/
                                                    Richard Garmise
Accountant ....Fried & Kowgios CPA's LLP/
                                                    Robert Fried, CPA
Comptroller ....Anne Stewart FitzRoy, CPA
Banking ....City National Bank/
                            Anne McSweeney, Sylvia Gibbons,
                                                    Wendy Goin
Insurance ....DeWitt Stern Group/
                            Peter Shoemaker, Robert Stockley
Payroll Service ....Castellana Payroll Services, Inc./
                            Lance Castellana, James Castellana,
                                                    Norman Sewell
Travel ....Altour/
                            Kristine Ljungdahl, Edward Roque
Production Photographer ....Joan Marcus
Rehearsal Studio ....Atlantic Theater Company
Opening Night
    Coordination ....The Lawrence Company Events, Inc./
                                                    Michael P. Lawrence
Theatre Displays ....King Display, Inc.
Group Sales ....Telecharge.com Group Sales/
                            212-239-6262, 1-800-432-7780,
                                                www.telecharge.com/groups

CREDITS
Scenery fabricated and painted by global scenic services,

inc., Bridgeport, CT. Lighting equipment from PRG Lighting. Sound equipment from PRG Audio. Trophy cup courtesy of Brooks Brothers. Various antiques supplied by Centerstage Antiques, Mt. Holly, NJ.

SPECIAL THANKS
Senator Bill Bradley

To learn more about the production, please visit
www.ThatChampionshipSeason.com

 THE SHUBERT ORGANIZATION, INC.
Board of Directors

Philip J. Smith	**Robert E. Wankel**
Chairman	President
Wyche Fowler, Jr.	**Lee J. Seidler**
Michael I. Sovern	**Stuart Subotnick**

Elliot Greene	**David Andrews**
Chief Financial	Senior Vice President –
Officer	Shubert Ticketing
Juan Calvo	**John Darby**
Vice President –	Vice President –
Finance	Facilities
Peter Entin	**Charles Flateman**
Vice President –	Vice President –
Theatre Operations	Marketing
Anthony LaMattina	**Brian Mahoney**
Vice President –	Vice President –
Audit & Production Finance	Ticket Sales

D.S. Moynihan
Vice President – Creative Projects

House Manager ....William Mitchell

That Championship Season
SCRAPBOOK

Correspondents: Jane Grey and Cambra Overend, Stage Managers

Memorable Fan Letter: One fan wrote a letter to "The Stage Managers of *That Championship Season*" and said that *The Country Girl* (which played at this theatre three years ago) was the best play she'd ever seen and she'd love an autographed Playbill.

Opening Night Gifts: Tiffany crystal decanters engraved with the show logo and opening night date from the producers…which went perfectly with the Tiffany crystal glasses engraved with the show logo and opening night date from the stage managers. (And no, they didn't plan that!) Also, bottles of Jameson's with custom-made *That Championship Season* labels from our producer.

Most Exciting Celebrity Visitors: It's hard to top our cast members themselves.

Actors Who Performed the Most Roles in This Show: Two of the understudies learned three roles apiece.

Actor Who Has Done the Most Shows in Their Career: PSM Jane Grey, has more Broadway credits than all the rest combined. Most shows total would be Brian Cox, due to age.

Special Backstage Rituals: At fight call, they each choose one of four colored marbles (from Gregory Mosher's personal childhood collection) out of the trophy in order to determine the order of that evening's curtain call. At "Fifteen Minutes," the stage managers announce a quote for the evening, taken from the show, and Kiefer then Tweets it to all his Twitter followers. At "Places," Jason slaps all the women (there's only three of us) on our asses before every show (and we like it). He also looks at the video monitor of the first few rows of the house, points to a random woman and says "She came, I knew she'd come." During the course of the show, Chris and Jason both gargle with mouthfuls of Jameson's (they swear they never swallow).

Favorite Moment During Each Performance (On Stage or Off): The three aforementioned women enjoy Jason falling down the stairs and being slapped in the face.

Favorite Off-Site Hangouts: Joe Allen's, Angus, Bar Centrale, Sardi's, West Bank… basically any bar we haven't been banned from, and any bar open after 4 a.m.

Mascot: Broadway Buster.

Favorite Snack Food: Liquor.

Favorite Therapy: Liquor.

Memorable Ad-Libs: Chris: "This is the number-one contribution to the environment." (The actual line is "This is the number one threat to the environment.")
Brian: "You boys are like a fine wine." (The actual line is "You boys are like a fine watch.")

Sweethearts Within the Company: Jason and His Ego, Chris and His Ego, Kiefer and his guitar, Brian and his dresser, Jim and his mayoral laugh.

1. Curtain call on opening night (L-R): Jason Patric, Jim Gaffigan, Brian Cox, Chris Noth and Kiefer Sutherland.
2. Tara Wilson and Chris Noth attend the cast party at Gotham Hall.
3. (L-R): Gaffigan, Patric, Noth and Sutherland on the stage of the Jacobs Theatre.
4. (L-R): Gaffigan, Noth, director Gregory Mosher, Cox, Patric and Sutherland at Gotham Hall.

Who Wore the Least: Jason likes to walk around with his shirt off (but it's not a part of the show)…and we like it.

Memorable Directorial Note: "Just talk to each other. You know, like normal people do."

Nicknames: Romeo, Teefer, The Dago, Crankypants, and The Mayor.

Catchphrase Only the Company Would Recognize: "Jewsthesame."

Cellphone Issues: Almost none. We have no announcement and the ushers have to tell the patrons themselves—the ushers at the Jacobs ROCK!

Time Stands Still

First Preview: September 23, 2010. Opened: October 7, 2010.
Closed January 30, 2011 after 16 Previews and 126 Performances.

Wounded and disfigured by a roadside bomb in Iraq, a female photojournalist tries to settle into life back home in New York with her boyfriend, a correspondent who has grown sick of covering war. Though they try to emulate the domesticity of their friends, they find their lives have grown in very different directions.

CAST

(in order of appearance)

James Dodd	BRIAN D'ARCY JAMES
Sarah Goodwin	LAURA LINNEY
Richard Ehrlich	ERIC BOGOSIAN
Mandy Bloom	CHRISTINA RICCI

A loft in Williamsburg, Brooklyn. Recently.

UNDERSTUDIES

For Sarah/Mandy:
HEIDI ARMBRUSTER

For Richard/James:
TONY CARLIN

Editor's Note: *Time Stands Still* was originally presented on Broadway in a limited run from January 5, 2010 to March 27, 2010 under the auspices of the not-for-profit Manhattan Theatre Club. While not technically a revival, the play returned to Broadway September 23, 2010 in an open-ended commercial production with the cast, design and direction largely the same.

☺ CORT THEATRE

138 West 48th Street
A Shubert Organization Theatre

Philip J. Smith, *Chairman*   Robert E. Wankel, *President*

MTC Productions, Inc.   Nelle Nugent   Bud Martin
ARTISTIC DIRECTOR   EXECUTIVE PRODUCER
Lynne Meadow   Barry Grove

Wendy Federman   Ted Snowdon   Max Cooper   Susanne Adamski

Mari Nakachi   Elisabeth Morten/Sharon A. Carr

IN ASSOCIATION WITH
Jack M. Dalgleish   Joseph Sirola

PRESENT

Laura Linney   Brian d'Arcy James   Eric Bogosian   Christina Ricci

IN

TIME STANDS STILL

BY

Donald Margulies

SCENIC DESIGN	COSTUME DESIGN	LIGHTING DESIGN	SOUND DESIGN
John Lee Beatty	**Rita Ryack**	**Peter Kaczorowski**	**Darron L West**
ORIGINAL MUSIC	MAKE-UP DESIGN	STUNT COORDINATOR	PRODUCTION STAGE MANAGER
Peter Golub	**Mindy Hall**	**Thomas Schall**	**Robert Bennett**
ASSOCIATE PRODUCER	MARKETING	CASTING	MTC ASSOCIATE ARTISTIC DIRECTOR
Kenneth Teaton	**aka** **Debra Waxman-Pilla**	**Nancy Piccione**	**Mandy Greenfield**
TECHNICAL SUPERVISOR	PRESS REPRESENTATIVE	GENERAL MANAGER	
Larry Morley	**Boneau/Bryan-Brown**	**Peter Bogyo**	

DIRECTED BY

Daniel Sullivan

Originally commissioned and produced by the Geffen Playhouse, Gil Cates, Producing Director, Randall Arney, Artistic Director.

Originally produced in New York City by the Manhattan Theatre Club,
Lynne Meadow, Artistic Director, Barry Grove, Executive Producer, on January 5, 2010.

The Producers wish to express their appreciation to Theatre Development Fund for its support of this production.

10/7/10

(L-R): Laura Linney, Brian d'Arcy James, Eric Bogosian, Christina Ricci

Photo by Joan Marcus

Time Stands Still

Laura Linney
Sarah Goodwin

Brian d'Arcy James
James Dodd

Eric Bogosian
Richard Ehrlich

Christina Ricci
Mandy Bloom

Heidi Armbruster
u/s Sarah/Mandy

Tony Carlin
u/s James/Richard

Donald Margulies
Playwright

Daniel Sullivan
Director

John Lee Beatty
Scenic Design

Rita Ryack
Costume Design

Peter Kaczorowski
Lighting Design

Darron L. West
Sound Design

Peter Golub
Original Music

Peter Bogyo
General Manager

Lynne Meadow
*Artistic Director,
Manhattan Theatre
Club, Inc.*

Barry Grove
*Executive Producer,
Manhattan Theatre
Club, Inc.*

Wendy Federman
Producer

**FRONT OF HOUSE
STAFF**

Ted Snowdon
Producer

Max Cooper
Producer

Jack M. Dalgleish
Producer

CREW
Seated (L-R): Robert Bennett (PSM), Lauren Klein (Production Assistant), Derek Moreno (Dresser), Scott DeVerna (House Electrician)

Standing (L-R): Ed Diaz (House Carpenter), Paul Trapani (Production Properties), Chris Morey (Company Manager), Natasha Steinhagen (Hair & Makeup), Michael Growler (Wardrobe Supervisor), Jens McVoy (Sound Engineer), Lonnie Gaddy (House Properties)

Joseph Sirola
Producer

Elisabeth Morten
Producer

Sharon A. Carr
Associate Producer

Photos by Brian Mapp

Time Stands Still

Scrapbook

Correspondents: Robert Bennett, PSM, and Denise Yaney, SM

Opening Night Gifts: In addition to flowers and champagne, we got cd mixes of the company's favorite songs and "time" theme oldies.

Most Exciting Celebrity Visitors: Ralph Fiennes and Samuel L. Jackson.

Who Has Done the Most Shows in Their Career: Dan Sullivan

Special Backstage Rituals: Assistant Stage Manager Denise Yaney has a "thumbs up" ritual before every show with Laura Linney and Brian d'Arcy James. The Cort crew has a gesture-specific good show wish as well.

Favorite Moment During Each Performance: "%#$& you...%#$& you."

Favorite In-Theatre Gathering Place: Sunday brunch in the basement is a Cort Theatre tradition that includes front of house staff, crew and cast.

Favorite Snack Food: Vienna Fingers

Mascot: Stage Manager Bob Bennett's little toy horse, Didi.

Favorite Therapy: Eating. Jigsaw puzzles.

Internet Buzz: Most of it looked good to us, frequently great to us. How insightful of the public!

Latest Audience Arrival: Half the house the night we changed Thursday curtain to 7 p.m. We had a great 7:50 p.m. crowd.

Sweethearts Within the Company: Didi and Karen.

Fastest Costume Change: Well, most involved. Laura Linney exits SR and takes off shoes and a sweater, hands off a cane and picks up a hair band, then runs under the stage through the basement (with ASM and props following) to come up SL to change clothes and get sprayed down with water while doing her hair in a ponytail.

Catchphrase Only the Company Would Recognize: "Kissy-Kissy." (Ask the next time you do a show with any one of us.)

Understudy Anecdote: Understudy Heidi Armbruster was followed leaving the theatre after a performance by a fan who asked if she was Laura Linney. She said no, to which the fan replied: "Are you sure?"

STAFF FOR *TIME STANDS STILL*

GENERAL MANAGER
Peter Bogyo

COMPANY MANAGER
Chris Morey

GENERAL PRESS REPRESENTATIVE
BONEAU/BRYAN-BROWN

Chris Boneau	Aaron Meier
Christine Olver	Emily Meagher

TECHNICAL SUPERVISOR
Larry Morley

PRODUCTION STAGE MANAGER .....Robert Bennett
Stage Manager ....Denise Yaney
Assistant Director ....Mia Rovegno
Assistant Set Designer ....Kacie Hultgren
Assistant Costume Designer ....Richard Schurkamp
Assistant Lighting Designer ....Jake DeGroot
Associate Sound Designer ....Charles Coes
Production Electrician ....Shannon January
Production Carpenter ....Edward Diaz
Production Props ....Paul Trapani
Production Sound Engineer ....Jens McVoy
House Electrician ....Scott DeVerna
House Properties ....Lonnie Gaddy
Wardrobe Supervisor ....Growler
Dresser ....Derek Moreno
Hair and Make-up Supervisor ....Natasha Steinhagen
Production Assistant ....Lauren Klein
Assistant to the Technical Supervisor ...Amanda Raymond
General Management Assistant ....John Nehlich
Advertising ....Spotco/Drew Hodges, Jim Edwards,
Tom Greenwald, Beth Watson, Tim Falotico
Marketing Services......................aka/Elizabeth Furze,
Adam Jay, Sara Rosenzweig
Website Design/
New Media Marketing ....Art Meets Commerce/
Jim Glaub, Chip Meyrelles,
Laurie Connor, Kevin Keating,
Ryan Greer, Mark Seeley
Audience Development ....Walker International
Communications Group
Accountant ....Fried & Kowgios CPA's LLP/
Robert Fried, CPA

Controller ....Galbraith & Company, Inc./
Tabitha Falcone
Banking.................................First Republic Bank
Insurance ....DeWitt Stern/Peter Shoemaker
Legal Counsel ....David H. Friedlander, Esq.
Production Photography ....Joan Marcus
Opening Night Coordination ....Serino Coyne LLC/
Suzanne Tobak
Payroll Service ....CSI, Castellana Services Inc.
Car Service ....IBA Limousines/Danny Ibanez and
Broadway Trans/Ralph Taliercio
Rehearsal Space ....Manhattan Theatre Club
Theatre Displays ....BAM Signs, Inc./Adam Miller

THE FOXBORO COMPANY, INC.
Nelle Nugent ....President and CEO
Kenneth Teaton ....SVP Production and Creative Affairs
Patrick Mediate .... Executive Assistant

MANHATTAN THEATRE CLUB STAFF
Artistic Director ....Lynne Meadow
Executive Producer ....Barry Grove
General Manager ....Florie Seery
Associate Artistic Director ....Mandy Greenfield
Director of Artistic Operations ....Jerry Patch
Director of Artistic Administration ....Amy Gilkes Loe
Assistant to the Artistic Director ....Nicki Hunter
Assistant to the Executive Producer ....Emily Hammond
Director of Casting ....Nancy Piccione
Director of Development ....Lynne Randall
Director of Marketing ....Debra Waxman-Pilla
Director of Finance ....Jeffrey Bledsoe
Associate General Manager ....Lindsey Brooks Sag
Company Manager Friedman Theatre ....Seth Shepsle
Theatre Manager Friedman Theatre ....Jim Joseph
Director of Subscriber Services ....Robert Allenberg
Director of Telesales and Telefunding ....George Tetlow
Director of Education ....David Shookhoff
Production Manager ....Kurt Gardner

CREDITS
Scenery fabrication by Hudson Scenic Studio. Lighting equipment supplied by Lights Up & Cue Sound, LLC, West Hempstead, NY. Sound equipment from Masque Sound Inc. Dell laptop computer courtesy of Dell Computers. Macbook Pro computers courtesy of Tekserve.

MUSIC/VIDEO CREDITS
"Bodysnatchers" 100% Interest (Thomas Edward Yorke, Jonathan Richard, Guy Greenwood, Colin Charles Greenwood, Edward John O'Brien and Philip James Selway); ©2008 Warner/Chappell Music Ltd (PRS). All rights administered by Warner-Tamerlane Publishing Corp. All rights reserved. Used by permission. *Friday the 13th Part III* ©Paramount Pictures. All rights reserved. *Invasion of the Body Snatchers* ©Paramount Pictures. All rights reserved. Licensed through Paramount Pictures.

SPECIAL THANKS
Kathryn Appleton, Vanessa Lancellotti

THE SHUBERT ORGANIZATION, INC.
Board of Directors

Philip J. Smith	**Robert E. Wankel**
Chairman	President
Wyche Fowler, Jr.	**John W. Kluge**
Lee J. Seidler	**Michael I. Sovern**

Stuart Subotnick

Elliot Greene	**David Andrews**
Chief Financial Officer	Senior Vice President – Shubert Ticketing
Juan Calvo	**John Darby**
Vice President – Finance	Vice President – Facilities
Peter Entin	**Charles Flateman**
Vice President – Theatre Operations	Vice President – Marketing
Anthony LaMattina	**Brian Mahoney**
Vice President – Audit & Production Finance	Vice President – Ticket Sales

D.S. Moynihan
Vice President – Creative Projects

CORT THEATRE
House Manager ....Joseph Traina

War Horse

First Preview: March 15, 2011. Opened: April 14, 2011.
Still running as of May 31, 2011.

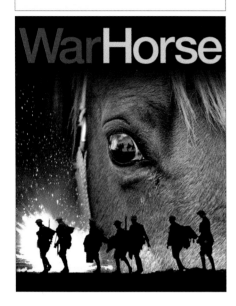

A boy braves the battlefields of World War I in order to retrieve his pet horse who has been sold to the cavalry in Lincoln Center Theater's transfer of the hit National Theatre production, with its arresting physical design.

CAST

THE HORSES

Joey as a foal ....STEPHEN JAMES ANTHONY,
    DAVID PEGRAM, LEENYA RIDEOUT
Joey ....JOBY EARLE, ARIEL HELLER,
    ALEX HOEFFLER, JESLYN KELLY,
    JONATHAN DAVID MARTIN,
    PRENTICE ONAYEMI, JUDE SANDY,
    ZACH VILLA or ENRICO D. WEY
Topthorn .. JOBY EARLE, JOEL REUBEN GANZ,
    ARIEL HELLER, ALEX HOEFFLER,
    TOM LEE,
JONATHAN CHRISTOPHER MacMILLAN,
    JUDE SANDY, ZACH VILLA,
    or ENRICO D. WEY
Coco ...... JOBY EARLE, JOEL REUBEN GANZ,
    ALEX HOEFFLER,
    JESLYN KELLY, TOM LEE,
    JONATHAN DAVID MARTIN,
    ZACH VILLA, or ENRICO D. WEY
Heine ....SANJIT DE SILVA, BHAVESH PATEL

THE PEOPLE *(in order of speaking)*
Song Woman ....KATE PFAFFL
Song Man ....LIAM ROBINSON
Lieutenant James Nicholls .STEPHEN PLUNKETT

Continued on next page

LINCOLN CENTER THEATER AT THE VIVIAN BEAUMONT

under the direction of
André Bishop and **Bernard Gersten**

NATIONAL THEATRE OF GREAT BRITAIN
under the direction of
Nicholas Hytner and **Nick Starr**
in association with
Bob Boyett   War Horse LP
presents

National Theatre of Great Britain production

WarHorse

based on the novel by **Michael Morpurgo**
adapted by **Nick Stafford**
in association with **Handspring Puppet Company**

with (in alphabetical order)

Stephen James Anthony   Zach Appelman   Alyssa Bresnahan   Richard Crawford
Sanjit De Silva   Matt Doyle   Austin Durant   Joby Earle   Joel Reuben Ganz   Ariel Heller
Peter Hermann   Alex Hoeffler   Brian Lee Huynh   Jeslyn Kelly   Ian Lassiter   Tom Lee
Jonathan Christopher MacMillan   Jonathan David Martin   Boris McGiver   Seth Numrich
Prentice Onayemi   Bhavesh Patel   David Pegram   Kate Pfaffl   Stephen Plunkett
Leenya Rideout   Liam Robinson   Jude Sandy   Hannah Sloat   T. Ryder Smith   Zach Villa
Elliot Villar   Cat Walleck   Enrico D. Wey   Madeleine Rose Yen

sets, costumes & drawings **Rae Smith**	puppet design, fabrication and direction **Adrian Kohler** with **Basil Jones** for Handspring Puppet Company	lighting **Paule Constable**
director of movement & horse sequences **Toby Sedgwick**		animation & projection design **59 Productions**
music **Adrian Sutton**	songmaker **John Tams**	sound **Christopher Shutt**	music director **Greg Pliska**

music   songmaker   sound   music director
Adrian Sutton   **John Tams**   **Christopher Shutt**   **Greg Pliska**
associate puppetry director   stage manager   casting
Mervyn Millar   **Rick Steiger**   **Daniel Swee**
NT technical producer   NT producer   NT associate producer   NT marketing   Boyett Theatricals producer
Katrina Gilroy   **Chris Harper**   **Robin Hawkes**   **Alex Bayley**   **Tim Levy**
general manager   production manager   director of development   director of marketing   general press agent
Adam Siegel   **Jeff Hamlin**   **Hattie K. Jutagir**   **Linda Mason Ross**   **Philip Rinaldi**

directed by
Marianne Elliott and **Tom Morris**

Sponsor

Leadership Support from The Jerome L. Greene Foundation.
Major Support from Ellen and Howard Katz in honor of Marianne Elliott,
Florence and Robert Kaufman, The Blanche and Irving Laurie Foundation,
and The National Endowment for the Arts.
Generous Support from Laura Pels International Foundation for Theater and
The Henry Nias Foundation courtesy of Dr. Stanley Edelman.

American Airlines
250 Cities. 40 Countries.
Official Airline

National Theatre is supported by Arts Council England

Supported by
ARTS COUNCIL ENGLAND

4/14/11

The cast with one of the show's signature horse puppets

Photo by Paul Kolnik

War Horse

THE FIRST WORLD WAR — also known as The Great War and The War to End All Wars — took place mainly in Europe between August 1914 and November 1918. The assassination of Archduke Franz Ferdinand of Austria on June 28, 1914, triggered a chain of events that systematically severed the economic alliances and blood ties that held the royal houses of Europe in a mutually beneficial peace. An estimated 10 million soldiers lost their lives during the resulting war, which began with German troops sweeping into Luxembourg and Belgium on August 4.

The United Kingdom, France, Russia, and later Italy and the United States headed the Allied Powers which defeated the Central Powers, led by the Austro-Hungarian, German and Ottoman Empires. World War I caused the disintegration of the Austro-Hungarian, German, Ottoman and Russian Empires, and the cost of the war also began the breakup of the British Empire and left France devastated for more than 25 years. Unresolved questions of who was to blame and who suffered the most in the Great War continued to trouble the old and new nations of Europe, sowing the seeds for the start of World War II more than 20 years later.

Although American involvement in the war was relatively short, the U.S. suffered more than 300,000 casualties. Nonetheless, the U.S. involvement was a decisive factor in the Allied victory of 1918.

The war's western front, which stretched 440 miles from the Swiss border to the North Sea and where the action of *War Horse* takes place, was a line of trenches, dug-outs and barbed-wire fences, with an area known as "no man's land" between them.

The engagement of war was revolutionized during World War I when the surprise, speed, precision and ruthlessness of the horse cavalry was upended by the introduction of barbed wire and automatic machine guns. And towards the end of the war a new weapon emerged. It was mobile, deflected machine gun bullets and crushed barb wire. The horse had been replaced by the tank.

A total of eight million horses died during World War I. One million English horses were taken to France to be used by the British Army. Only 62,000 of them were brought back to England.

Arthur Narracott	T. RYDER SMITH
Billy Narracott	MATT DOYLE
Albert Narracott	SETH NUMRICH
Ted Narracott	BORIS McGIVER
Chapman Carter	AUSTIN DURANT
Allan	ELLIOT VILLAR
Thomas Bone	BHAVESH PATEL
John Greig	JOBY EARLE, JOEL REUBEN GANZ, ALEX HOEFFLER, or JONATHAN DAVID MARTIN
Rose Narracott	ALYSSA BRESNAHAN
Priest	PETER HERMANN
Captain Charles Stewart	BRIAN LEE HUYNH
Sergeant Thunder	RICHARD CRAWFORD
Private David Taylor	DAVID PEGRAM
Paulette	CAT WALLECK
Soldat Schnabel	ZACH APPELMAN
Hauptmann Friedrich Müller	PETER HERMANN
Soldat Klausen	ELLIOT VILLAR
Doctor Schweyk	SANJIT DE SILVA
Oberst Strauss	BHAVESH PATEL
Sergeant Fine	ZACH APPELMAN
Unteroffizier Klebb	STEPHEN PLUNKETT
Emilie	MADELEINE ROSE YEN
Taff	SANJIT DE SILVA
Manfred	AUSTIN DURANT
Matron Callaghan	LEENYA RIDEOUT
Annie Gilbert	HANNAH SLOAT
Veterinary Officer Martin	IAN LASSITER
Goose	JOBY EARLE, JONATHAN CHRISTOPHER MacMILLAN or JUDE SANDY

Villagers of Devon and Soldiers are played by members of the company.

Assistant Stage Managers	LISA IACUCCI, AMY MARSICO

Seth Numrich

Photo by Paul Kolnik

UNDERSTUDIES

For Joey as a foal: BRIAN LEE HUYNH, HANNAH SLOAT, CAT WALLECK
For Song Woman, Song Man: LEENYA RIDEOUT
For Lt. Nicholls, Cpt. Stewart: ZACH APPELMAN, SANJIT DE SILVA
For Arthur: RICHARD CRAWFORD, AUSTIN DURANT
For Billy: STEPHEN JAMES ANTHONY, DAVID PEGRAM
For Albert: STEPHEN JAMES ANTHONY, MATT DOYLE
For Ted: AUSTIN DURANT, BHAVESH PATEL
For Chapman Carter: PETER HERMANN, ELLIOT VILLAR
For Allan: PETER HERMANN, IAN LASSITER
For Thomas Bone: IAN LASSITER, DAVID PEGRAM
For Rose: LEENYA RIDEOUT, CAT WALLECK
For Priest: SANJIT DE SILVA, ELLIOT VILLAR
For Sgt. Thunder: AUSTIN DURANT, BORIS McGIVER
For Pvt. Taylor: STEPHEN JAMES ANTHONY, ZACH APPELMAN

For Paulette: LEENYA RIDEOUT, HANNAH SLOAT
For Soldat Schnabel: BHAVESH PATEL, LIAM ROBINSON
For Hauptmann Müller: T. RYDER SMITH, ELLIOT VILLAR
For Soldat Klausen: IAN LASSITER, STEPHEN PLUNKETT
For Dr. Schweyk, Taff: IAN LASSITER, BHAVESH PATEL
For Oberst Strauss: IAN LASSITER, BORIS McGIVER
For Sgt. Fine: BRIAN LEE HUYNH, BHAVESH PATEL
For Unteroffizier Klebb: RICHARD CRAWFORD, SANJIT DE SILVA
For Emilie: HANNAH SLOAT
For Manfred: BORIS McGIVER, T. RYDER SMITH
For Matron Callaghan: ALYSSA BRESNAHAN, CAT WALLECK
For Annie: KATE PFAFFL, CAT WALLECK
For Vet. Ofc. Martin: STEPHEN PLUNKETT, ELLIOT VILLAR
For Heine: IAN LASSITER

War Horse

Stephen James
Anthony
Joey as a foal

Zach Appelman
*Soldat Schnabel,
Sergeant Fine*

Alyssa Bresnahan
Rose Narracott

Richard Crawford
Sergeant Thunder

Sanjit De Silva
*Heine, Doctor
Schweyk, Taff*

Matt Doyle
Billy Narracott

Austin Durant
*Chapman Carter,
Manfred*

Joby Earle
*Joey, Topthorn,
Coco, John Greig,
Goose*

Joel Reuben Ganz
*Topthorn, Coco,
John Greig*

Ariel Heller
Joey, Topthorn

Peter Hermann
*Priest, Hauptmann
Friedrich Müller*

Alex Hoeffler
*Joey, Topthorn,
Coco, John Greig*

Brian Lee Huynh
*Captain Charles
Stewart*

Jeslyn Kelly
Joey, Coco

Ian Lassiter
*Veterinary Officer
Martin*

Tom Lee
Topthorn, Coco

Jonathan
Christopher
MacMillan
Topthorn, Goose

Jonathan David
Martin
*Joey, Coco,
John Greig*

Boris McGiver
Ted Narracott

Seth Numrich
Albert

Prentice Onayemi
Joey

Bhavesh Patel
*Heine, Thomas Bone,
Oberst Strauss*

David Pegram
*Joey as a foal,
Private David Taylor*

Kate Pfaffl
Song Woman

Stephen Plunkett
*Lieutenant James
Nicholls,
Unteroffizier Klebb*

Leenya Rideout
*Joey as a foal,
Matron Callaghan*

Liam Robinson
Song Man

Jude Sandy
*Joey, Topthorn,
Goose*

Hannah Sloat
Annie Gilbert

T. Ryder Smith
Arthur Narracott

Zach Villa
Joey, Topthorn, Coco

Elliot Villar
Allan, Soldat Klausen

Cat Walleck
Paulette

Enrico D. Wey
Joey, Topthorn, Coco

Madeleine Rose Yen
Emilie

War Horse

Michael Morpurgo
Author

Nick Stafford
Adaptor

Adrian Kohler,
Handspring Puppet
Company
*Puppet Direction,
Design and
Fabrication*

Basil Jones,
Handspring Puppet
Company
*Puppet Direction,
Design and
Fabrication*

Marianne Elliott
Director

Tom Morris
Director

Rae Smith
*Set, Costumes,
Drawings*

Paule Constable
Lighting

Adrian Sutton
Music

John Tams
Songmaker

Christopher Shutt
Sound

Greg Pliska
Music Director

Mervyn Millar
*Associate Puppetry
Director*

Drew Barr
Associate Director

Paul Huntley
*Hair and Wig
Designer*

Thomas Schall
Fight Director

Gillian Lane-Plescia
Dialect Coach

Bob Boyett

Nicholas Hytner,
Director,
National Theatre of
Great Britain

André Bishop and Bernard Gersten,
Artistic Director and Executive Producer,
Lincoln Center Theater

CREW

Front Row (L-R): Juan Bustamante (Deck Automation), Greg Cushna (Flyman), Rudy Wood (Props), Joe Pizzuto (Pyro Technician), Frank Linn (Automation Tech), Kyle Barrineau (Props), Dan Rich (Follow Spot Operator), Adam Smolenski (Deck Sound), John Ross (Props)

Back Row (L-R): Bill Nagle (Production Carpenter), Andrew Belits (Carpenter), Kevin McNeill (Carpenter), Fred Bredenbeck (Carpenter), Bruce Rubin (Electrician/Board Operator), Pat Merryman (Production Electrician), Larry White (Deck Sound), Will Coholan (Props), Jeff Ward (Follow Spot Operator), Bill Burke (Projection Technician), Charles Rausenberger (Props), Marc Salzberg (Production Soundman), Karl Rausenberger (Production Propman)

Not pictured: John Weingart (Production Flyman), Mark Dignam (Props), John Howie (Carpenter), Ray Skillin (Deck Carpenter)

War Horse

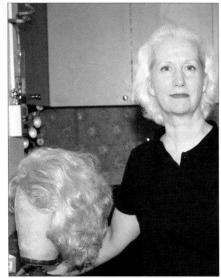

MAKE-UP DESIGNER AND HAIR SUPERVISOR
Cynthia Demand

Photos by Brian Mapp

STAGE MANAGEMENT
(L-R): Rick Steiger (Stage Manager), Amy Marsico (Assistant Stage Manager), Lisa Iacucci (Assistant Stage Manager), Deanna Weiner (Production Assistant), Christopher R. Munnell (Production Assistant)

FRONT OF HOUSE STAFF
Front Row (L-R): Amy Yedowitz, Ann Danilovics, Barbara Hart, Rheba Flegelman (House Manager), Jeff Goldstein, Jared Pachefsky

Middle Row (L-R): Eleanore Rooks, Billie Stewart, Lisa Lopez, Donna Zurich

Back Row (L-R): Security Officer Douglas Charles, Nick Andors, Rezul Hossain, Beatrice Gilliard, Ann Gilles, Heidi Giovine, Nancy Diaz, Margie Blair

WARDROBE
Front Row (L-R): Peggy Danz (Dresser), Kristi Wood (Dresser)

Back Row (L-R): Patti Luther (Dresser), Erick Medinilla (Dresser), Shannon Koger (Dresser), Terry LaVada (Dresser), Adam Adelman (Dresser)

Not pictured: Lynn Bowling (Wardrobe Supervisor), Richard Gross (Dresser), Donna Holland (Dresser), James Nadeaux (Dresser), Sarah Rochford (Dresser), Rosie Wells (Dresser)

War Horse

LINCOLN CENTER THEATER

ANDRÉ BISHOP   BERNARD GERSTEN
ARTISTIC DIRECTOR   EXECUTIVE PRODUCER

ADMINISTRATIVE STAFF
GENERAL MANAGER ....ADAM SIEGEL
  Associate General Manager ....Jessica Niebanck
  General Management Assistant ....Meghan Lantzy
  Facilities Manager ....Alex Mustelier
  Associate Facilities Manager ....Michael Assalone
GENERAL PRESS AGENT ....PHILIP RINALDI
  Press Associates ....Barbara Carroll,
                          Amanda Dekker
PRODUCTION MANAGER ....JEFF HAMLIN
  Associate Production Manager ....Paul Smithyman
DIRECTOR OF
  DEVELOPMENT ....HATTIE K. JUTAGIR
  Associate Director of Development .....Rachel Norton
  Manager of Special Events and
    LCT Young Angels ....Karin Schall
  Grants Writer ....Neal Brilliant
  Manager, Patron Program ....Sheilaja Rao
  Assistant to the Director of
    Development....................Raelyn R. Lagerstrom
  Development Associate/
    Special Events & LCT
    Young Angels ....Jennifer H. Rosenbluth-Stoll
  Development Assistant/
    Individual Giving ....Sydney Rais-Sherman
DIRECTOR OF FINANCE..........DAVID S. BROWN
  Controller ....Susan Knox
  Systems Manager ....Stacy Valentine
  Finance Assistant ....Kristen Parker
DIRECTOR OF
  MARKETING ....LINDA MASON ROSS
  Marketing Associate ....Ashley M. Dunn
  Marketing Assistant ....John Casavant
DIRECTOR OF EDUCATION ....KATI KOERNER
  Associate Director of Education ....Alexandra Lopez
  LEAD Project Manager ....Andrea Dishy
Assistant to the Executive Producer ......Barbara Hourigan
Office Manager ....Brian Hashimoto
Office Assistant ....Stephen McFarland
Messenger ....Esau Burgess
Reception ....Brenden Rogers, Michelle Metcalf

ARTISTIC STAFF
ASSOCIATE DIRECTORS .....GRACIELA DANIELE,
                     NICHOLAS HYTNER,
                     JACK O'BRIEN,
                     SUSAN STROMAN,
                     DANIEL SULLIVAN
RESIDENT DIRECTOR ....BARTLETT SHER
DRAMATURG and DIRECTOR,
  LCT DIRECTORS LAB ....ANNE CATTANEO
CASTING DIRECTOR ....DANIEL SWEE, CSA
MUSICAL THEATER
  ASSOCIATE PRODUCER ....IRA WEITZMAN
ARTISTIC DIRECTOR/LCT3 ....PAIGE EVANS
  Artistic Administrator ....Julia Judge
  Casting Associate ....Camille Hickman
  Lab Assistant ....Kate Marvin

HOUSE STAFF
HOUSE MANAGER.............RHEBA FLEGELMAN
Production Carpenter ....William Nagle

Production Electrician ....Patrick Merryman
Production Soundman ....Marc Salzberg
Production Propertyman ....Karl Rausenberger
Production Flyman ....John Weingart
House Technician ....Linda Heard
Chief Usher ................................M.L. Pollock
Box Office Treasurer ....Fred Bonis
Assistant Treasurer ....Robert A. Belkin

SPECIAL SERVICES
Advertising ....Serino-Coyne/Jim Russek
      Roger Micone, Becca Goland-Van Ryn
Principal Poster Artist ....James McMullan
Counsel ....Peter L. Felcher, Esq.;
            Charles H. Googe, Esq.;
    and Carol Kaplan, Esq. of
  Paul, Weiss, Rifkind, Wharton & Garrison
Counsel ....Lazarus & Harris LLP
Immigration Counsel ....Theodore Ruthizer, Esq.;
          Mark D. Koestler, Esq.
  of Kramer, Levin, Naftalis & Frankel LLP
Labor Counsel .... Michael F. McGahan, Esq.
       of Epstein, Becker & Green, P.C.
Auditor ....Frederick Martens, C.P.A.
              Lutz & Carr, L.L.P.
Insurance ....Jennifer Brown of
             DeWitt Stern Group
Photographer ....Paul Kolnik
Video Services ....Fresh Produce Productions/
                   Frank Basile
Travel ....Tygon Tours
Consulting Architect ....Hugh Hardy,
      H3 Hardy Collaboration Architecture
Construction Manager ....Yorke Construction
Payroll Service ....Castellana Services, Inc.
Merchandising ....Marquee Merchandise, LLC/
                 Matt Murphy
Lobby Refreshments ....Sweet Concessions

STAFF FOR *WAR HORSE*
COMPANY MANAGER ....MATTHEW MARKOFF
Associate Company
  Manager ....Jessica Perlmeter Cochrane
Associate Puppetry Director ....Mervyn Millar
Associate Director ....Drew Barr
Puppetry Associate ....Matt Acheson
Movement Associate ....Adrienne Kapstein
US Associate Set Designer ....Frank McCullough
UK Associate Costume Designer ....Johanna Coe
US Associate Costume Designer ....Sarah Laux
UK Associate Lighting Designer ....Nick Simmons
US Associate Lighting Designer................Karen Spahn
UK Associate Sound Designer ....John Owens
US Assistant Sound Designer ....Bridget O'Connor
UK Puppetry Technician ....Ed Dimbleby
Automated Light Programmer ....Victor Seastone
Projection Programmer ....Benjamin Pearcy
Props ....Faye Armon
Fight Captain ....Ian Lassiter
Make-Up Designer ....Cynthia Demand
Wardrobe Supervisor ....Lynn Bowling
Dressers ....Adam Adelman, Peggy Danz,
        Richard Gross, Donna Holland,
   Shannon Koger, Patti Luther, Erick Medinilla,
    James Nadeaux, Sarah Rochford,
       Rosie Wells, Kristi Wood

Hair Supervisor ....Cynthia Demand
Physical Therapy ....PhysioArts/Jennifer Green
Orthopedist ....David S. Weiss, MD
Production Assistants ....Christopher R. Munnell,
                   Deanna Weiner
Child Guardian ....John Mara

Fight Director ....Thomas Schall

Dialect Coach ....Gillian Lane-Plescia

Vocal Coach ....Kate Wilson

Hair and Wig Design ....Paul Huntley

Official Accordion Sponsorship by Saltarelle

Incidental Music
Recorded at Sear Sound, NY
Recording Engineer: Gary Maurer
Copyist: Steve Cohen
Jim Lake ....Trumpet, Cornet
Angela Gosse ....Trumpet, Cornet
Judy Yin-Chi Lee ....Horn, Alto Horn
Hitomi Yakata ....Trombone, Euphonium
Richard Heckman ....Clarinet, Flute

NATIONAL THEATRE
Nicholas Hytner ....Director
Nick Starr ....Executive Director
Lisa Burger ....Finance Director
John Campbell ....Director of Production,
             Technical and Engineering
Chris Harper ....Producer
Katrina Gilroy ....Technical Producer
Robin Hawkes ....Associate Producer
Racheli Sternberg ....Producing Assistant
Alex Bayley ....Marketing

Supported by the National Theatre's
War Horse Production Office.

Additional thanks to the National Theatre's Marketing,
Digital, Graphics and Finance departments.

CREDITS
Scenery by Hudson Scenic Studio. Tank by Scott Fleary.
Costumes by National Theatre Costume department.
Officer uniform tailoring by Mark Costello. Tailoring by
Roxy Cressy. Additional tailoring by Kirstie Robinson.
Footwear supervision by National Theatre Footware
department. English and German uniforms supplied by
Khaki Devil. U.S. alterations by James Nadeaux. Additional
U.S. alterations by John Kristiansen, NY. Additional
costume supplies by Costume Store, Vintage Shirt
Company and Silvermans. Sound and video equipment by
Sound Associates. Lighting equipment from PRG Lighting.
Props by National Theatre Props department. Technical
drawings by Tim Crowdy. Violin provided by David Gage
String Instruments.

Visit WarHorseOnBroadway.com

For groups of 20 or more:
Caryl Goldsmith Group Sales
(212) 889-4300

War Horse

Scrapbook

Correspondents: Hannah Sloat, "Annie Gilbert" and Matt Doyle "Billy Narracott"

Memorable Opening Night Letter, Fax or Note: Merv Millar, our Associate Puppet Director, went all around the city taking pictures that were specific to a character each of us played and made our opening night card with that image.

Special Backstage Ritual: Just before half-hour, we meet in the hallway off stage right and sing "Roll Us Home" from the show. We sing it in all different styles, depending on what we need that day to get us going.

Favorite In-Theatre Gathering Places: Poker in dressing room #8, chocolate raisins in #4, swear jar in #1.

Favorite Off-Site Hangout: Route 66 (56th and Ninth).

Favorite Snack Food: This cast is now crazy for sugar, whether we like it or not.

Mascot: Bakugon, the rubber ball we use for ball-lee. Ball-lee is a game brought to us by the Brits—it's like Four Squares but with nine squares.

Favorite Therapies: PT, massage, acupuncture, ball-lee.

Memorable Ad-Lib: "29 gui... 39 guineas!!"

Memorable Press Encounter: After Joey's "Regis & Kelly" appearance, someone wrote an e-mail complaining of the mistreatment of the horse, thinking it was real!

Fastest Costume Change: It's hard to say because we almost all have fast changes. The biggest group quick change is going into the first military scene; there are at least ten of us on the deck with dressers.

Busiest Day at the Box Office: The day after opening—also the day they announced an open-ended run!

Heaviest/Hottest Costume: The puppeteers are dealing with the most weight though it's not exactly a costume. Many of us underdress our military outfits under our villager costumes and the wool gets very hot.

Catchphrases Only the Company Would Recognize: "Shelling, oat monkey." "Sizzling barn." "Pliska!" "Schweyk!" "Where are the gaps?"

Memorable Directorial Notes: "You're all brilliant, but...." "Why don't you make us an offer?"

Company In-Jokes: I love it when they applaud the bunting. And "You can buy him back."

Understudy Anecdote: If you're out, five people are in.

Nicknames: "Setharooney," "Schwychy."

Sweethearts Within the Company: We are all in love with Alyssa's beautiful daughter, Shannon (7 months old), who visits on two-show days.

Coolest Thing About Being in This Show: Getting to be with these wonderful people in this beautiful show!!

Also: We often bring food and eat together in the North Lobby of the Beaumont between shows on two-show days.

1. (L-R): Cast members Jude Sandy, Zach Villa and Alex Hoeffler at Avery Fisher Hall for the opening night party.
2. (L-R): Tom Lee, Jonathan Christopher MacMillan and Joel Ganz.
3. Author of original book, Michael Morpurgo.

2010-2011 AWARDS

TONY AWARDS
Best Play
(Author: Nick Stafford)
Best Direction of a Play
(Marianne Elliott and Tom Morris)
Best Scenic Design of a Play
(Rae Smith)
Best Lighting Design of a Play
(Paule Constable)
Best Sound Design of a Play
(Christopher Shutt)
Special Tony Award
(Handspring Puppet Company)

NEW YORK DRAMA CRITICS CIRCLE AWARD
Special Citation: Direction, Design and Puppetry

DRAMA LEAGUE AWARD
Distinguished Production of a Play

THEATRE WORLD AWARD
Loudon Award for Excellence
(Seth Numrich)

DRAMA DESK AWARDS
Outstanding Play
Special Award to the Creative Team
for Thrilling Stagecraft
(Paule Constable, Marianne Elliott, 59 Productions, Adrian Kohler with Basil Jones for Handspring Puppet Company, Tom Morris, Rae Smith, Christopher Shutt, Toby Sedgwick, Adrian Sutton and John Tams)

OUTER CRITICS CIRCLE AWARDS
Outstanding New Broadway Play
Lucille Lortel Award
for Outstanding Director of a Play
(Marianne Elliott and Tom Morris)
Outstanding Lighting Design
(Paule Constable)
Special Award for Puppet Design,
Fabrication and Direction
(Adrian Kohler with Basil Jones
for Handspring Puppet Company)

West Side Story

First Preview: February 23, 2009. Opened: March 19, 2009.
Closed January 2, 2011 after 27 Previews and 748 Performances.

PLAYBILL

WEST SIDE STORY

Shakespeare's tragic romance Romeo and Juliet *is relocated to the streets of 1950s Manhattan, with the warring Montagues and Capulets replaced by teen street gangs, the Anglo Jets and the Puerto Rican Sharks. The bittersweet love story of Tony and Maria is played out against the backdrop of the gangs' deadly rivalry.*

CAST
The Jets

Action	WES HART
Anybodys	SARA DOBBS
A-rab	KYLE COFFMAN
Baby John	RYAN STEELE
Big Deal	MIKEY WINSLOW
Diesel	COLT PRATTES
Graziella	PAMELA OTTERSON
Hotsie	MARINA LAZZARETTO
Kiddo	NATHAN BRENN
	(Tues., Wed., Fri., Sat. eves.)
	MICHAEL KLEEMAN
	(Wed., Sat. & Sun. mats. & Thurs. eve.)
Mugsy	SKYE MATTOX
Riff	JOHN ARTHUR GREENE
Snowboy	MIKE CANNON
Tony	MATTHEW HYDZIK
	JEREMY JORDAN
	(Wed. eve. & Sun. mat.)
Velma	LINDSAY DUNN
Zaza	KAITLIN MESH
4H	SAM ROGERS

The Sharks

Alicia	KRISTINE COVILLO
Anita	NATALIE CORTEZ
Bebecita	MILEYKA MATEO

Continued on next page

⊰N⊱ PALACE THEATRE
UNDER THE DIRECTION OF
STEWART F. LANE, JAMES M. NEDERLANDER AND JAMES L. NEDERLANDER

Kevin McCollum   James L. Nederlander   Jeffrey Seller
Terry Allen Kramer   Sander Jacobs
Roy Furman/Jill Furman Willis   Freddy DeMann   Robyn Goodman/Walt Grossman   Hal Luftig
Roy Miller   The Weinstein Company   Broadway Across America
PRESENT

West Side Story
Based on a conception of JEROME ROBBINS

BOOK BY
Arthur Laurents
MUSIC BY
Leonard Bernstein
LYRICS BY
Stephen Sondheim

ENTIRE ORIGINAL PRODUCTION DIRECTED AND CHOREOGRAPHED BY
Jerome Robbins

STARRING
Matthew Hydzik   Sarah Amengual
Natalie Cortez   John Arthur Greene   George Akram
At certain performances
Jeremy Jordan
plays the role of "Tony."

WITH
Steve Bassett   Nathan Brenn   Mike Cannon   Kyle Coffman   Sara Dobbs   Wes Hart   Michael Kleeman   Ron Piretti
Colt Prattes   Manuel Santos   Lee Sellars   Ryan Steele   Greg Vinkler   Mikey Winslow   Mark Zimmerman

Deanna Aguinaga   Shawn Burgess   Angelica Burgos   Isaac Calpito   Haley Carlucci   Jace Coronado   Kristine Covillo
Desirée Davar   Stephen Diaz   Lindsay Dunn   Michael D. Jablonski   Marina Lazzaretto   Renée Marino
Mileyka Mateo   Skye Mattox   Kaitlin Mesh   Shina Ann Morris   Angelina Mullins   Kat Nejat
Patrick Ortiz   Pamela Otterson   Waldemar Quinones-Villanueva   Alex Ringler   Sam Rogers
Brendon Stimson   Tanairi Sade Vazquez   Michael Williams

SCENIC DESIGN James Youmans	COSTUME DESIGN David C. Woolard	LIGHTING DESIGN Howell Binkley	SOUND DESIGN Dan Moses Schreier
WIGS & HAIR DESIGN Mark Adam Rampmeyer	MAKE-UP DESIGN Angelina Avallone	CASTING Howard/Schecter/Hardt	TRANSLATIONS Lin-Manuel Miranda
ASSOCIATE DIRECTOR David Saint	ASSOCIATE CHOREOGRAPHER Lori Werner	ASSOCIATE PRODUCER LAMS Productions	PRODUCTION STAGE MANAGER Joshua Halperin
ORIGINAL BROADWAY PRODUCTION CO-CHOREOGRAPHED BY Peter Gennaro	ORCHESTRATIONS Leonard Bernstein with Sid Ramin and Irwin Kostal	ARRANGEMENTS Stephen Sondheim Patrick Vaccariello and Garth Edwin Sunderland	GENERAL MANAGEMENT Charlotte Wilcox Company
MUSIC COORDINATOR Michael Keller	TECHNICAL SUPERVISOR Brian Lynch	MARKETING Scott A. Moore	PRESS REPRESENTATIVE The Hartman Group

MUSIC SUPERVISOR / MUSIC DIRECTOR
Patrick Vaccariello
CHOREOGRAPHY REPRODUCED BY
Joey McKneely
DIRECTED BY
Arthur Laurents

New Broadway cast recording available on Masterworks Broadway

10/1/10

"Dance at the Gym"

Photo by Joan Marcus

West Side Story

MUSICAL NUMBERS

ACT ONE

Scene 1: The Neighborhood
    "Prologue" .... The Sharks and the Jets
    "Jet Song" .... Riff and the Jets
Scene 2: Outside Doc's Drugstore
    "Something's Coming" .... Tony
Scene 3: Bridal Shop
Scene 4: The Gym
    "Dance at the Gym" .... Company
    "Maria" .... Tony
Scene 5: Alleyways
    "Tonight" .... Tony and Maria
    "America" .... Anita, Rosalia and Shark Girls
Scene 6: The Drugstore
    "Cool" .... Riff, Jet Boys and Jet Girls
Scene 7: Bridal Shop
    "One Hand, One Heart" .... Tony and Maria
Scene 8: The Neighborhood
    "Tonight" (Quintet) .... Company
Scene 9: Under the Highway
    "The Rumble"

ACT TWO

Scene 1: Maria's Bedroom
    "Me Siento Hermosa" ("I Feel Pretty") .... Maria, Rosalia, Consuela and Fernanda
    "Somewhere" .... Kiddo, Tony, Maria and Company
Scene 2: The Neighborhood
    "Gee, Officer Krupke" .... Action and the Jets
Scene 3: Maria's Bedroom
    "A Boy Like That"/"I Have a Love" .... Anita and Maria
Scene 4: The Drugstore
Scene 5: The Cellar
Scene 6: The Neighborhood

Cast Continued

Bernardo	GEORGE AKRAM
Bolo	STEPHEN DIAZ
Chino	MANUEL SANTOS
Consuela	SHINA ANN MORRIS
Federico	WALDEMAR QUINONES-VILLANUEVA
Fernanda	KAT NEJAT
Inca	ISAAC CALPITO
Indio	PATRICK ORTIZ
Lupe	TANAIRI SADE VAZQUEZ
Maria	SARAH AMENGUAL
Pepe	MICHAEL WILLIAMS
Rosalia	RENÉE MARINO
Tio	JACE CORONADO

The Adults

Doc	GREG VINKLER
Glad Hand	LEE SELLARS
Krupke	RON PIRETTI
Lt. Schrank	STEVE BASSETT

SWINGS

DEANNA AGUINAGA, SHAWN BURGESS, ANGELICA BURGOS, HALEY CARLUCCI, DESIRÉE DAVAR, MICHAEL D. JABLONSKI, ANGELINA MULLINS, ALEX RINGLER, BRENDON STIMSON

UNDERSTUDIES

For Action: COLT PRATTES, BRENDON STIMSON
For Anita: DEANNA AGUINAGA, DESIRÉE DAVAR, KAT NEJAT
For Anybodys: KAITLIN MESH, PAMELA OTTERSON
For A-rab, Baby John: SAM ROGERS, BRENDON STIMSON
For Bernardo: WALDEMAR QUINONES-VILLANUEVA, MANUEL SANTOS

For Big Deal: MICHAEL D. JABLONSKI, SAM ROGERS
For Chino: PATRICK ORTIZ
For Consuela: DEANNA AGUINAGA, DESIRÉE DAVAR, RENÉE MARINO, TANAIRI SADE VAZQUEZ
For Diesel: MICHAEL D. JABLON ALEX RINGLER
For Doc, Krupke, Lt. Schrank: LEE SELLARS
For Fernanda: DEANNA AGUINAGA, HALEY CARLUCCI, DESIRÉE DAVAR, RENÉE MARINO
For Glad Hand: RON PIRETTI
For Graziella: SKYE MATTOX, ANGELINA MULLINS
For Maria: HALEY CARLUCCI, KAT NEJAT
For Riff: MIKE CANNON, WES HART, MICHAEL D. JABLONSKI, COLT PRATTES
For Rosalia: DEANNA AGUINAGA, HALEY CARLUCCI, DESIRÉE DAVAR, RENÉE MARINO, KAT NEJAT
For Snowboy: ALEX RINGLER, BRENDON STIMSON
For Tony: MIKE CANNON
Standby for Doc, Glad Hand, Krupke, Lt. Schrank: MARK ZIMMERMAN

Dance Captain	MARINA LAZZARETTO
Assistant Dance Captain	MICHAEL WILLIAMS
Fight Captain	WES HART

SETTING

Upper West Side of New York City

ORCHESTRA

Conductor: PATRICK VACCARIELLO
Associate Conductor: MAGGIE TORRE
Concertmaster: MARTIN AGEE
Violins: PAUL WOODIEL, FRITZ KRAKOWSKI, DANA IANCULOVICI, KIKU ENOMOTO
Cellos: PETER PROSSER, VIVIAN ISRAEL
Bass: BILL SLOAT
Reed 1: LAWRENCE FELDMAN
Reed 2: LINO GOMEZ
Reed 3: DAN WILLIS
Reed 4: ADAM KOLKER
Reed 5: GILBERT DeJEAN
Lead Trumpet: TREVOR NEUMANN
Trumpets: MATT PETERSON, JEFF WILFORE
Trombone: TIM ALBRIGHT
Bass Trombone: ROB FOURNIER
French Horns: CHRIS KOMER, THERESA MacDONNELL
Piano: MAGGIE TORRE
Keyboard: JIM LAEV
Drums: ERIC POLAND
Percussion: DAN McMILLAN, PABLO RIEPPI
Music Coordinator: MICHAEL KELLER
Keyboard Programmer: RANDY COHEN

West Side Story

Matthew Hydzik
Tony

Sarah Amengual
Maria

Natalie Cortez
Anita

John Arthur Greene
Riff

George Akram
Bernardo

Jeremy Jordan
*Tony at certain
performances*

Steve Bassett
Lt. Schrank

Mike Cannon
Snowboy

Kyle Coffman
A-rab

Sara Dobbs
Anybodys

Wes Hart
Action; Fight Captain

Ron Piretti
Krupke

Colt Prattes
Diesel

Manuel Santos
Chino

Lee Sellars
Glad Hand

Ryan Steele
Baby John

Greg Vinkler
Doc

Mikey Winslow
Big Deal

Mark Zimmerman
Adult Standby

Deanna Aguinaga
Swing

Nathan Brenn
*Kiddo at certain
performances*

Shawn Burgess
Swing

Angelica Burgos
Swing

Isaac Calpito
Inca

Haley Carlucci
Maria Standby

Jace Coronado
Tio

Kristine Covillo
Alicia

Desirée Davar
Swing

Stephen Diaz
Bolo

Lindsay Dunn
Velma

Michael D. Jablonski
Swing

Michael Kleeman
*Kiddo at certain
performances*

Marina Lazzaretto
*Hotsie;
Dance Captain*

Renée Marino
Rosalia

Mileyka Mateo
Bebecita

West Side Story

Skye Mattox
Mugsy

Kaitlin Mesh
Zaza

Shina Ann Morris
Consuela

Angelina Mullins
Swing

Kat Nejat
Fernanda

Patrick Ortiz
Indio

Pamela Otterson
Graziella

Waldemar
Quinones-Villanueva
Federico

Alex Ringler
Swing

Sam Rogers
4H

Brendon Stimson
Swing

Tanairi Sade Vazquez
Lupe

Michael Williams
Pepe

Arthur Laurents
Book, Director

Leonard Bernstein
Music

Stephen Sondheim
Lyrics

Jerome Robbins
Choreography

Joey McKneely and Lori Werner
*Reproduction Choreographer;
Associate Choreographer*

Patrick Vaccariello
*Music Supervisor/
Music Director*

James Youmans
Scenic Design

David C. Woolard
Costume Design

Howell Binkley
Lighting Design

Dan Moses Schreier
Sound Design

Stuart Howard
Casting
Casting

David Saint
Associate Director

Lin-Manuel Miranda
Translations

The Charlotte Wilcox
Company
General Manager

Michael Keller
Music Coordinator

Brian Lynch
*Technical
Supervision*

Kevin McCollum
Producer

James L.
Nederlander
Producer

Jeffrey Seller
Producer

Terry Allen Kramer
Producer

Sander Jacobs
Producer

West Side Story

Freddy DeMann
Producer

Roy Furman
Producer

Jill Furman Willis
Producer

Robyn Goodman
Producer

Walt Grossman
Producer

Hal Luftig
Producer

Roy Miller
Producer

Bob Weinstein,
The Weinstein
Company
Producer

Harvey Weinstein,
The Weinstein
Company
Producer

John Gore,
CEO,
Broadway Across
America
Producer

Thomas B. McGrath,
Chairman,
Broadway Across
America
Producer

Bradley Reynolds,
Lams Productions
Associate Producer

David Siesko,
Lams Productions
Associate Producer

ALUMNI
2010-2011

Kyle Brenn
*Kiddo at certain
performances*

Joshua Buscher
Diesel, Fight Captain

Beth Crandall
Zaza

Sean Ewing
Pepe

Tim Hausmann
Swing

Peter Maloney
Doc

Yanira Marin
Alicia

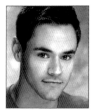
Matthew Marks
Swing

Michael Mastro
Glad Hand

Karen Olivo
Anita

Michael Rosen
Chino

Jennifer Sanchez
Rosalia

Josefina Scaglione
Maria

Phillip Spaeth
Federico

Alex Michael Stoll
Swing

TRANSFER
STUDENTS
2010-2011

Jessica Bishop
Velma, Swing

Karla Puno Garcia
Lupe, Swing

Michael Mastro
Glad Hand

Matt Shingledecker
*Tony at certain
performances*

West Side Story

WARDROBE
Front Row (L-R): Herb Ouellette, Allison Rogers, Sarah Hench, David Grevengoed

Back Row (L-R): Christopher Thorton, Roy Seiler, Hilda Suli-Garcia, Scott Westervelt, Stephanie Fox, Keith Shaw, Aryn Lawrence, Hector Lugo

ORCHESTRA
Front Row: Patrick Vaccariello

Middle Row: Martin Agee

Back Row (L-R): Lawrence Feldman, Igor Scedrov, Karen Banos, Jennifer Baxmeyer, Vivian Israel, Gilbert DeJean, Jeremy Miloszewicz

CREW
Front Row (L-R): Tim Kovalenko, Dan Gaudreau, Rob Toscano, Corey Schmidt, Chuck Fields

Back Row (L-R): Jesse Hancox, Paul Baker, McBrien Dunbar, Chris Kluth, Steve Clem, Keith Buchanan, John Cullen

FRONT OF HOUSE STAFF
Front Row (L-R): Paula Vanderlinden, Maria Agurto, Verne Shayne, Gina Sanabria, Gloria Syracuse

Back Row (L-R): Catherine Larocco, Diana Hosang, Scott Muso, Mike D'Arcy, Jennifer Kina

Photos by Brian Mapp

West Side Story

STAFF FOR *WEST SIDE STORY*

GENERAL MANAGEMENT
THE CHARLOTTE WILCOX COMPANY
Charlotte W. Wilcox
Seth Marquette
Matthew W. Krawiec Dina S. Friedler Margaret Wilcox

GENERAL PRESS REPRESENTATIVE
THE HARTMAN GROUP
Michael Hartman
Wayne Wolfe   Alyssa Hart

COMPANY MANAGER
James Lawson

ASSOCIATE COMPANY MANAGER
Erica Ezold

DIRECTOR OF MARKETING
Scott A. Moore

CASTING
STUART HOWARD ASSOCIATES, LTD.
Stuart Howard   Amy Schecter   Paul Hardt

Production Stage Manager ....Joshua Halperin
Stage Manager ....Lisa Dawn Cave
Assistant Stage Manager ....Jason Brouillard
Assistant to the Director ....Isaac Klein
Assistant to Mssrs. McCollum & Seller ....Kaitlin Fine
Assistant to Mr. Nederlander ....Ken Happel
Fight Director ....Ron Piretti
Associate Scenic Designer ....Jerome Martin
Assistant Costume Designers ....Robert Martin,
    Daryl A. Stone, Maria Zamansky
Assistants to the Costume Designer ....Sara James,
    Yuri Cataldo, Angela Harner
Associate Lighting Designer ....Ryan O'Gara
Assistant Lighting Designer ....Carrie Wood
Associate Sound Designer ....David Bullard
Moving Light Programmer ....David Arch
Head Carpenter/TheatreTech Associate ....Chris Kluth
Production Flyman ....Corey Schmidt
Automation Carpenters ....McBrien Dunbar,
    Robert M. Hentze
Head Electrician ....Keith Buchanan
Moving Light Technician ....Chuck Fields
Spotlight Operator ....Patrick Harrington
Production Properties Supervisor ....George Wagner
Head Properties ....Chuck Dague
Sound Engineer ....Lucas Indelicato
Wardrobe Supervisor ....Scott Westervelt
Assistant Wardrobe Supervisor ....Jessica Dermody
Dressers ....Scotty Cain, Stephanie Fox,
    Kasey Graham, David Grevengoed,
    Sarah Hench, Aryn Lawrence, Hector Lugo,
    Herb Ouellette, Allison Rogers,
    Roy Seiler, Keith Shaw, Hilda Suli-Garcia
Hair Supervisor .. ..Paula Schaffer
Assistant Hair Supervisors ....Armando Licon,
    Pat Marcus
Assistant Keyboard Programmers ....Bryan Cook,
    Jim Mironchik
Production Assistants ....Rachel E. Miller,
    Zac Chandler

Language Consultant ....Desiree Rodriguez
Legal Counsel ....Levin, Plotkin & Menin, LLP
Accountants ....Fried & Kowgios LLP/
    Robert Fried
Controller ....Galbraith & Co./
    Sarah Galbraith
Advertising ....SpotCo/
    Drew Hodges, Jim Edwards,
    Tom Greenwald, Y. Darius Suyama,
    Kristen Rathbun
Website ....SpotCo/
    Sarah Fitzpatrick, Matt Wilstein,
    Marc Mettler
Children's Tutoring ....On Location Education
Children's Guardian ....Libby Stevens
Press Office Associates ....Leslie Baden,
    Michelle Bergmann, Nicole Capatasto,
    Tom D'Ambrosio, Juliana Hannett,
    Bethany Larsen, Matt Ross, Frances White
Marketing Associate ....Joshua Lee Poole
Production Photography ....Joan Marcus
Banking ....JP Morgan Chase/
    Stephanie Daulton
Payroll Service ....Castellana Services, Inc.
Physical Therapy ....PhysioArts/
    Jennifer Green
Massage Therapist ....Russell Beasley
Orthopedist ....Phillip Bauman, MD
Group Sales ....Nederlander Group Sales
Merchandise ....Creative Goods/
    Mike D'Arcy, Pete Milano
Insurance Consultant ......Stockbridge Risk Management
Information Management
    Services ....Marion Finkler Taylor
Travel Services ....Tzell Travel/
    Andi Henig,
    Road Rebel
Tour Booking Agency ....The Booking Group/
    Meredith Blair

CREDITS
Scenery built by Hudson Scenic Studio, Inc.; Show Motion, Inc.; Blackthorn Scenic Studio, Inc.; Scenic Art Studios, Inc.; Blackwalnut; Center Line Studios, Inc. Costumes by Tricorne Inc., Barbara Matera Ltd., Eric Winterling Inc., Timberlake Studios Inc., Giliberto Designs Inc.,

Beckenstein Men's Fabrics Inc. Custom knitwear by Maria Ficalora Knitwear Ltd. Footwear by JC Theatrical & Custom Footwear Inc., Capezio. Millinery by Arnold S. Levine Inc. Undergarments by Bra*Tenders. Costume ageing and distressing by Hochi Asiatico Studio. Accessories by David Samuel Menkes Custom Leatherwear New York. Lighting equipment from PRG Lighting. Sound equipment from PRG Sound. Mannequins and sewing machine provided by Fox Sewing Machines, New York, NY. Cigarette lighters courtesy of Zippo Lighters. Certain props constructed by John Creech Design and Production, Brooklyn, NY. Doc's window and interior shelves set dressing provided by Ann Pinkus, Monmouth Antiques, Red Bank, NJ.

Makeup provided by M•A•C

SPECIAL THANKS
Tom Hatcher, Federico del Piño Gonzales,
Fernando Masorllones

NEDERLANDER

Chairman ....**James M. Nederlander**
President ....**James L. Nederlander**

Executive Vice President
Nick Scandalios

Vice President	Senior Vice President
Corporate Development	Labor Relations
Charlene S. Nederlander	**Herschel Waxman**

| Vice President | Chief Financial Officer |
| **Jim Boese** | **Freida Sawyer Belviso** |

STAFF FOR THE PALACE THEATRE
Theatre Manager ....Dixon Rosario
Treasurer ....Cissy Caspare
Assistant Treasurer ....Anne T. Wilson
Carpenter ....Thomas K. Phillips
Flyman ....Robert W. Kelly
Electrician ....Eddie Webber
Propertymaster ....Steve Camus
Engineer ....Rob O'Connor
Chief Usher ....Gloria Hill

MANAGEMENT
(L-R): Jason Brouillard, Lisa Dawn Cave (in photo), Joshua Halperin, Tom Capps

West Side Story

BOX OFFICE
(L-R): Louie Waldron, Anne Wilson, John Yerkovich

HAIR
(L-R): Pat Marcus, Armando Licon, Paula Schaffer

SCRAPBOOK

Correspondent: Kat Nejat, "Fernanda"

Most Exciting Celebrity Visitor: For me it would be 100 percent CHITA! What an honor!

Actor Who Performed the Most Roles in This Show: I think I am up there…In addition to my regular track, Fernanda, I covered Maria, Anita and Rosalia, and also internally swung every female track EXCEPT Graziella and Anybodys at some point in the show…yes, even the Jet girls!

Actor Who Has Done the Most Performances of This Show: I don't know the number, but I can say that the original cast members who began the show and then also closed it were: George Akram, Steve Bassett, Isaac Calpito, Mike Cannon, Haley Carlucci, Kyle Coffman, Lindsay Dunn, Matthew Hydzik, Marina Lazzaretto, Michael Mastro, Mileyka Mateo, Kaitlin Mesh, Pam Otterson, Sam Rogers, Manuel Santos, Lee Sellars, Ryan Steele, Greg Vinkler, Mark Zimmerman and myself (Kat Nejat) so it must be one of us!

Special Backstage Rituals: Isaac Calpito's chaturanga yoga warmup onstage before every show set to an energizing mix of Madonna staples…George Akram and Jet boys hacky sack….

Favorite Moment During Each Performance: The balcony scene. It's perfect. 'nuff said.

Favorite In-Theatre Gathering Place: We were so lucky to have a greenroom to hang out in backstage, otherwise I honestly think some of the Jets would never have crossed paths with some of the Sharks (and vice versa!). Coming in at a close second would have to be the wardrobe room because they always had delicious snacks cooking (literally!).

Favorite Off-Site Hangouts: Glass House Tavern for the risotto balls, Bond 45 for the pizza and Natsumi for the sushi.

Favorite Snack Food: Twizzlers.

Favorite Therapy: The amazing Russ Beasley (massage therapist) and the team from PhysioArts (physical therapy) kept this company from falling apart. Robbins choreography is no joke! Also, Jennifer Sanchez, our first Rosalia, had a pretty strong Ricola addiction.

Memorable Ad-Libs: Josefina Scaglione (Maria): "I feel pretty, oh so pretty, I feel pretty and……..beautiful YESSSS!!!!!" Doc to Tony in the cellar scene (I believe this was a Doc understudy): "Anita is dead…I mean, MARIA is dead!"

Fastest Costume Change: Maria's change from her "I Feel Pretty" dress to the entrance at the top of the "Somewhere" Ballet. It is all underdressed, but a stuck zipper could be disastrous!

Catchphrase Only the Company Would Recognize: "Tiburones!"

Understudy Anecdote: I had the honor and pleasure of covering both Maria and Anita! The fact that I got to perform both roles multiple times on Broadway blows my mind, but I am brought back to reality remembering the horror of my first time on for either role, being in the middle of a show! Talk about nerves!!! The first time I went on for Maria I was pulled offstage during "America," had the number "Cool" to change costumes/take off wig/prepare and went on for "One Hand, One Heart" to the end of the show, and my first time on for Anita was at intermission, so I went on to perform "A Boy Like That" and the Taunt scene (some of the most emotionally demanding parts of the show)

with very little preparation! Que crazy!

Nicknames: Well I had 2 wigs and I named them after my character, Fernanda's, nicknames: Fern and Nanda! There were also a few female swings, myself included, who would occasionally have to do a Shark/Jet split-track which we lovingly deemed: "Shart" or "Jark."

Coolest Thing About Being in This Show: I think we all knew we were a part of history doing this show. We had the immense responsibility to live up to those who came before us and yet the artistic freedom to make it our own.

Also: I think that none of us in that original company will ever forget sitting in the greenroom in our sweats on Tony night (having already performed the "Dance at the Gym" on the famed Radio City Music Hall stage), watching the Tony awards live on TV together and hearing our own Karen Olivo's name called as the winner of the Tony Award for "Best Performance by a Featured Actress in a Musical"! I'm convinced that our cheers and tears could be heard all the way from the Palace Theatre, where we were, to Radio City Music Hall where Karen was giving her amazing acceptance speech. Similarly, those of us who performed the night of January 2, 2011 will never forget looking out into that packed Palace house on closing night, taking that final bow and knowing that we had been a part of history. I remember thinking, "Now, there will be no more singing that glorious score or dancing that legendary choreography or telling that timeless story…but we DID sing it and dance it and tell it…and it was magical."

Wicked

First Preview: October 8, 2003. Opened: October 30, 2003.
Still running as of May 31, 2011.

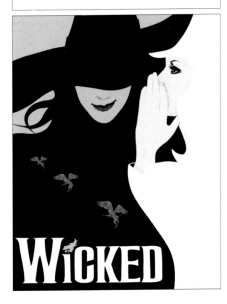

This imaginative "prequel" to The Wizard of Oz *traces the friendship of two young women of Oz, Elphaba and Glinda, and how events beyond their control transform them into the familiar Wicked Witch of the West and Good Witch of the North. Dorothy, the Scarecrow and other beloved Oz characters don't arrive until nearly the end, but reveal fascinating backstories of their own. The show also offers a surprise from the early life of the Wizard himself, and explores what it really means to be "wicked."*

THE CAST

(in order of appearance)

Glinda .... KATIE ROSE CLARKE

Witch's Father .... MICHAEL DeVRIES

Witch's Mother .... KRISTEN LEIGH GORSKI

Midwife .... KATHY SANTEN

Elphaba .... MANDY GONZALEZ

Nessarose .... JENNY FELLNER

Boq .... ALEX BRIGHTMAN

Madame Morrible .... KATHY FITZGERALD

Doctor Dillamond TIMOTHY BRITTEN PARKER

Fiyero .... ANDY KARL

Ozian Official .... MICHAEL DeVRIES

The Wonderful Wizard of Oz ...... P.J. BENJAMIN

Chistery .... TODD ANDERSON

Monkeys, Students, Denizens of the Emerald City,
   Palace Guards and
   Other Citizens of Oz .... NOVA BERGERON,
          AL BLACKSTONE, SARAH BOLT,

Continued on next page

➤N➤ GERSHWIN THEATRE

UNDER THE DIRECTION OF
JAMES M. NEDERLANDER AND JAMES L. NEDERLANDER

Marc Platt
Universal Pictures
The Araca Group *and* Jon B. Platt
David Stone
present

WICKED

Music and Lyrics
Stephen Schwartz

Book
Winnie Holzman

Based on the novel by Gregory Maguire

starring
Mandy Gonzalez   Katie Rose Clarke

also starring
Andy Karl

Alex Brightman   Jenny Fellner   Timothy Britten Parker

Alicia L. Albright Todd Anderson Nova Bergeron Al Blackstone Sarah Bolt
Jerad Bortz Catherine Charlebois Michael DeVries Maia Evwaraye-Griffin Anthony Galde
Kristen Leigh Gorski Kenway Hon Wai K. Kua Kelly Lafarga Kyle McDaniel Jonathan McGill
Joseph Medeiros Lindsay K. Northen Rhea Patterson Nathan Peck Eddie Pendergraft
Alexander Quiroga Kathy Santen Heather Spore Stephanie Torns Brian Wanee
Jonathan Warren Robin Wilner Briana Yacavone

and

Kathy Fitzgerald   P.J. Benjamin

Settings	Costumes	Lighting	Sound
Eugene Lee	**Susan Hilferty**	**Kenneth Posner**	**Tony Meola**
Projections	Wigs & Hair	Production Supervisor	Technical Supervisor
Elaine J. McCarthy	**Tom Watson**	**Thom Widmann**	**Jake Bell**
Music Arrangements	Associate Music Supervisor	Dance Arrangements	Music Coordinator
Alex Lacamoire &	**Dominick Amendum**	**James Lynn Abbott**	**Michael Keller**
Stephen Oremus			
Associate Set Designer	Special Effects	Associate Choreographer	Associate Director
Edward Pierce	**Chic Silber**	**Corinne McFadden Herrera**	**Lisa Leguillou**
Casting	Production Stage Manager	General Management	Press	Executive Producers
Telsey + Company	**Marybeth Abel**	**321 Theatrical Management**	**The Hartman Group**	**Marcia Goldberg & Nina Essman**

Orchestrations
William David Brohn

Music Supervisor
Stephen Oremus

Musical Staging by
Wayne Cilento

Directed by
Joe Mantello

Grammy Award-winning Original Cast Recording on DECCA BROADWAY

10/1/10

(L-R): Katie Rose Clarke
and Mandy Gonzalez

Photo by Joan Marcus

Wicked

MUSICAL NUMBERS

ACT I

"No One Mourns the Wicked" .... Glinda and Citizens of Oz
"Dear Old Shiz" .... Students
"The Wizard and I" .... Morrible, Elphaba
"What Is This Feeling?" .... Galinda, Elphaba and Students
"Something Bad" .... Dr. Dillamond and Elphaba
"Dancing Through Life" .... Fiyero, Galinda, Boq, Nessarose, Elphaba and Students
"Popular" .... Galinda
"I'm Not That Girl" .... Elphaba
"One Short Day" .... Elphaba, Glinda and Denizens of the Emerald City
"A Sentimental Man" .... The Wizard
"Defying Gravity" .... Elphaba, Glinda, Guards and Citizens of Oz

ACT II

"No One Mourns the Wicked" (reprise) .... Citizens of Oz
"Thank Goodness" .... Glinda, Morrible and Citizens of Oz
"The Wicked Witch of the East" .... Elphaba, Nessarose and Boq
"Wonderful" .... The Wizard and Elphaba
"I'm Not That Girl" (reprise) .... Glinda
"As Long As You're Mine" .... Elphaba and Fiyero
"No Good Deed" .... Elphaba
"March of the Witch Hunters" .... Boq and Citizens of Oz
"For Good" .... Glinda and Elphaba
"Finale" .... All

ORCHESTRA

Conductor: DOMINICK AMENDUM
Associate Conductor: DAVID EVANS
Assistant Conductor: BEN COHN

Concertmaster: CHRISTIAN HEBEL
Violin: VICTOR SCHULTZ
Viola: KEVIN ROY
Cello: DANNY MILLER
Harp: LAURA SHERMAN
Lead Trumpet: JON OWENS
Trumpet: TOM HOYT
Trombones: DALE KIRKLAND,
    DOUGLAS PURVIANCE
Flute: HELEN CAMPO
Oboe: TUCK LEE
Clarinet/Soprano Sax: JOHN MOSES
Bassoon/Baritone Sax/Clarinets: CHAD SMITH
French Horns: THEO PRIMIS,
    CHAD YARBOROUGH
Drums: MATT VANDERENDE
Bass: KONRAD ADDERLEY
Piano/Synthesizer: BEN COHN
Keyboards: PAUL LOESEL, DAVID EVANS
Guitars: RIC MOLINA, GREG SKAFF
Percussion: ANDY JONES

Music Coordinator: MICHAEL KELLER

Andy Karl as Fiyero

Photo by Joan Marcus

Cast Continued

JERAD BORTZ, MICHAEL DeVRIES,
MAIA EVWARAYE-GRIFFIN,
KRISTEN LEIGH GORSKI,
KENWAY HON WAI K. KUA,
KYLE McDANIEL, JONATHAN McGILL,
JOSEPH MEDEIROS, LINDSAY K. NORTHEN,
RHEA PATTERSON, NATHAN PECK,
EDDIE PENDERGRAFT,
ALEXANDER QUIROGA, KATHY SANTEN,
HEATHER SPORE, STEPHANIE TORNS,
BRIAN WANEE, ROBIN WILNER

UNDERSTUDIES and STANDBYS

Standby for Elphaba:
JENNIFER DiNOIA
Standby for Glinda:
LAURA WOYASZ

Understudy for Elphaba:
STEPHANIE TORNS
Understudies for Glinda:
LINDSAY K. NORTHEN, HEATHER SPORE
For Fiyero:
JERAD BORTZ, KYLE McDANIEL
For the Wizard and Dr. Dillamond:
MICHAEL DeVRIES, ANTHONY GALDE
For Madame Morrible:
SARAH BOLT, KATHY SANTEN
For Boq:
JOSEPH MEDEIROS, EDDIE PENDERGRAFT
For Nessarose and Midwife:
ROBIN WILNER, BRIANA YACAVONE
For Chistery:
BRIAN WANEE, JONATHAN WARREN
For Witch's Father and Ozian Official:
ANTHONY GALDE, ALEXANDER QUIROGA
For Witch's Mother:
KELLY LAFARGA, ROBIN WILNER
For Witch's Mother/Midwife:
ALICIA L. ALBRIGHT
For Midwife:
CATHERINE CHARLEBOIS

Swings:
TODD ANDERSON, CATHERINE
CHARLEBOIS, ANTHONY GALDE,
KELLY LAFARGA, BRIANA YACAVONE

Dance Captains/Swings:
JONATHAN WARREN, ALICIA L. ALBRIGHT

Wicked

Mandy Gonzalez
Elphaba

Katie Rose Clarke
Glinda

Kathy Fitzgerald
Madame Morrible

P.J. Benjamin
The Wizard

Andy Karl
Fiyero

Alex Brightman
Boq

Jenny Fellner
Nessarose

Timothy Britten Parker
Doctor Dillamond

Jennifer DiNoia
Standby for Elphaba

Laura Woyasz
Standby for Glinda

Alicia L. Albright
Assistant Dance Captain; Swing

Todd Anderson
Swing

Nova Bergeron
Ensemble

Al Blackstone
Ensemble

Sarah Bolt
Ensemble

Jerad Bortz
Ensemble

Catherine Charlebois
Swing

Michael DeVries
Witch's Father/ Ozian Official

Maia Evwaraye-Griffin
Ensemble

Anthony Galde
Swing

Kristen Leigh Gorski
Witch's Mother; Ensemble

Kenway Hon Wai K. Kua
Ensemble

Kelly Lafarga
Swing

Kyle McDaniel
Ensemble

Jonathan McGill
Ensemble

Joseph Medeiros
Ensemble

Lindsay K. Northen
Ensemble

Rhea Patterson
Ensemble

Nathan Peck
Ensemble

Eddie Pendergraft
Ensemble

Alexander Quiroga
Ensemble

Kathy Santen
Midwife

Heather Spore
Ensemble

Stephanie Torns
Ensemble

Brian Wanee
Ensemble

Wicked

Jonathan Warren
Dance Captain;
Swing

Robin Wilner
Ensemble

Briana Yacavone
Swing

Stephen Schwartz
Music and Lyrics

Winnie Holzman
Book

Joe Mantello
Director

Wayne Cilento
Musical Staging

Eugene Lee
Scenic Designer

Susan Hilferty
Costume Designer

Kenneth Posner
Lighting Designer

Tony Meola
Sound Designer

Elaine J. McCarthy
Projection Designer

Tom Watson
Wig and Hair
Designer

Joe Dulude II
Makeup Designer

Thom Widmann
Production
Supervisor

Jake Bell
Technical Supervisor

Stephen Oremus
Music Supervisor;
Music Arrangements

William David Brohn
Orchestrations

Alex Lacamoire
Music Arrangements

James Lynn Abbott
Dance
Arrangements

Michael Keller
Music Coordinator

Edward Pierce
Associate Scenic
Designer

Chic Silber
Special Effects

Corinne McFadden
Herrera
Associate
Choreographer

Bernard Telsey,
Telsey + Company
Casting

Gregory Maguire
Author of Original
Novel

Marcia Goldberg, Nancy Nagel Gibbs and
Nina Essman,
321 Theatrical Management
General Management

Marc Platt
Producer

Michael Rego, Hank Unger and
Matthew Rego,
The Araca Group
Producer

Jon B. Platt
Producer

David Stone
Producer

ALUMNI
2010-2011

Adam Fleming
Ensemble

Wicked

Brenda Hamilton
Swing

Manuel Herrera
Ensemble

Lori Holmes
*Ensemble,
Witch's Mother*

David Hull
Ensemble

Lindsay Janisse
*Dance Captain/
Swing*

Ryan Patrick Kelly
Swing

Eric Jon Mahlum
*Ensemble,
Ozian Official,
Witch's Father*

Brian Munn
Swing

Robert Pendilla
Swing

Rondi Reed
Madame Morrible

Amanda Rose
Swing

Josh Rouah
Ensemble

Mark Shunkey
Chistery, Ensemble

Bryan West
Ensemble

Blake Whyte
Ensemble

Samantha Zack
Swing

TRANSFER
STUDENTS
2010-2011

Aaron J. Albano
Ensemble

Etai BenShlomo
Boq

Richard H. Blake
Fiyero

Kristina Fernandez
Swing

Adam Fleming
Ensemble

Tom Flynn
Doctor Dillamond

Tiffany Haas
Ensemble, Swing

David Hull
Ensemble

Lindsay Janisse
Swing

Kevin Jordan
Swing

Ryan Patrick Kelly
Swing

Kyle Dean Massey
Fiyero

Tom McGowan
*The Wonderful
Wizard of Oz*

Brian Munn
Swing

Robert Pendilla
Swing

Amanda Rose
Swing

Josh Rouah
Ensemble

Libby Servais
Swing

Wicked

Mark Shunkey
Chistery, Ensemble

Betsy Werbel
Ensemble

Teal Wicks
Elphaba

FRONT OF HOUSE STAFF
Front Row (L-R): Kirth Crawford, Alex Kehr, Martha Boniface, Rick Kaye, Mariana Casanova, Carmen Rodriguez

Middle Row (L-R): Jacob Korder, Heather Farrell, Penny Bonacci, Eric Brown, Freddie Rivera, Joyce Pena, Ivan Rodriguez, Miguel Buelto

Back Row (L-R): Leonila Guity, Gregory Woolard, Siobhan Dunne, James Madden, Eileen Roig, Philippa Koopman, David Pena

HAIR/MAKEUP DEPTARTMENT
Front Row (L-R): Cheri Tiberio, Jenny Pendergraft

Back Row (L-R): Ryan McWilliams, Craig Jessup

Not Pictured: Nora Martin

MANAGEMENT DEPARTMENT
Front Row (L-R): Adam Jackson, Susan Sampliner, Christy Ney

Back Row (L-R): Shawn Pennington, Jennifer Marik

Not Pictured: Marybeth Abel

WARDROBE DEPARTMENT
Front Row (L-R): Barbara Rosenthal, Dennis Birchall

Middle Row (L-R): Kathe Mull, Alyce Gilbert, Nancy Lawson

Back Row (L-R): Dianne Hylton, Karen Lloyd, Bobbye Sue Albrecht, James Strunk, Shahnaz Khan, Kevin Hucke, James Byrne, Michael Michalski, Laurel Parrish

Not pictured: Teri Pruitt, Jason Viarengo, Randy Witherspoon

Photos by Krissie Fullerton

Wicked

STAFF FOR *WICKED*

GENERAL MANAGEMENT
321 THEATRICAL MANAGEMENT
Nina Essman   Nancy Nagel Gibbs
Marcia Goldberg

GENERAL PRESS REPRESENTATIVE
THE HARTMAN GROUP
Michael Hartman
Tom D'Ambrosio   Michelle Bergmann

CASTING
TELSEY + COMPANY
Bernie Telsey CSA, Will Cantler CSA, David Vaccari CSA,
Bethany Knox CSA, Craig Burns CSA,
Tiffany Little Canfield CSA, Rachel Hoffman CSA,
Carrie Rosson CSA, Justin Huff CSA, Bess Fifer CSA,
Patrick Goodwin CSA, Abbie Brady-Dalton

TECHNICAL SUPERVISION
JAKE BELL PRODUCTION SERVICES LTD.

COMPANY MANAGER .... SUSAN SAMPLINER

PRODUCTION
STAGE MANAGER .... MARYBETH ABEL

Stage Manager .... Jennifer Marik
Assistant Stage Managers .... J. Jason Daunter, Christy Ney
Associate Company Manager .... Eric Cornell
Assistant Director .... Paul Dobie
Dance Supervisor .... Patrick McCollum
Assistant to Mr. Schwartz .... Michael Cole
Assistant Scenic Designer .... Nick Francone
Dressing/Properties .... Kristie Thompson
Scenic Assistant .... Christopher Domanski
Oz Map Design .... Francis Keeping
Draftsman .... Ted LeFevre
Set Model Construction .... Miranda Hardy
Associate Costume Designers .... Michael Sharpe,
Ken Mooney
Assistant Costume Designers .... Maiko Matsushima,
Amy Clark
Costume Coordinator .... Amanda Whidden
Wig Coordinator .... J. Jared Janas
Associate Lighting Designer .... Karen Spahn
Associate Lighting Designer/
Automated Lights .... Warren Flynn
Assistant Lighting Designer .... Ben Stanton
Lighting Assistant .... Jonathan Spencer
Associate Sound Designer .... Kai Harada
Sound Assistant .... Shannon Slaton
Projection Programmer .... Mark Gilmore
Assistant Projection Designer .... Anne McMills
Projection Animators .... Gareth Smith, Ari Sachter Zeltzer
Special Effects Associate .... Aaron Waitz
Associate Hair Designer .... Charles LaPointe
Fight Director .... Tom Schall
Flying Effects .... ZFX Flying Illusions
Production Carpenter .... Rick Howard
Head Carpenter .... C. Mark Overton
Deck Automation Carpenter .... William Breidenbach
Production Electrician .... Robert Fehribach
Head Electrician .... Brendan Quigley
Deck Electrician/Moving Light Operator .... Craig Aves
Follow Spot Operator .... Valerie Menz
Production Properties .... George Wagner

Property Master .... Joe Schwarz
Assistant Property Master .... Augie Mericola
Production Sound Engineer .... Douglas Graves
Sound Engineer .... Jordan Pankin
Assistant Sound Engineer .... Jack Babin
Production Wardrobe Supervisor .... Alyce Gilbert
Assistant Wardrobe Supervisor .... Kevin Hucke
Dressers .... Bobbye Sue Albrecht, Dennis Birchall,
James Byrne, Dianne Hylton, Nancy Lawson,
Michael Michalski, Kathe Mull, Laurel Parrish,
Teresa Pruitt, Barbara Rosenthal,
Jason Viarengo, Randy Witherspoon
Hair Supervisor .... Nora Martin
Assistant Hair Supervisor .... Ryan P. McWilliams
Hairdressers .... Jenny Pendergraft, Cheri Tiberio
Makeup Design .... Joe Dulude II
Makeup Supervisor .... Craig Jessup
Music Preparation Supervisor .... Peter R. Miller,
Miller Music Service
Synthesizer Programming .... Andrew Barrett for
Lionella Productions, Ltd.
Rehearsal Drummer .... Gary Seligson
Music Intern .... Joshua Salzman
Production Assistants ..... Timothy R. Semon, David Zack
Advertising .... Serino Coyne/Greg Corradetti,
Joaquin Esteva
Marketing .... Betsy Bernstein
Online Marketing .... Situation Interactive
Website .... Istros Media Corporation
Merchandise .... The Araca Group
Theatre Display .... King Displays
Group Sales .... Lisa Goldberg (646-289-6885)
Banking ...... JP Morgan Chase Bank/Salvatore A. Romano
Payroll .... Castellana Services, Inc.
Director of Finance .... John DiMeglio
Production Administrator .... Robert Brinkerhoff
Accountant .... Robert Fried, C.P.A.
Insurance .... AON/Albert G. Ruben Insurance
Legal Counsel .... Loeb & Loeb/Seth Gelblum
Legal Counsel for Universal Pictures .... Keith Blau
Physical Therapy .... Encore Physical Therapy, P.C.
Orthopaedist .... David S. Weiss, MD
Onstage Merchandising .... George Fenmore, Inc.

MARC PLATT PRODUCTIONS
Adam Siegel, Greg Lessans, Joey Levy
Jared LeBoff, Tia Maggini, Dana Krupinski,
Nik Mavinkurve, Conor Welch, Claire Wihnyk

STONE PRODUCTIONS
David Stone   Patrick Catullo   Aaron Glick

321 THEATRICAL MANAGEMENT
Roeya Banuazizi, Amy Merlino Coey,
Mattea Cogliano-Benedict,
Tara Geesaman, Margie McGlone,
Petrina Moritz, Alex Owen, Kat Ramsburg,
Lisa Koch Rao, Greg Schaffert, Ken Silverman

UNIVERSAL PICTURES
President & COO, Universal Studios, Inc. ...... Ron Meyer
Chairman .... Adam Fogelson
Co-Chairman .... Donna Langley
President of Marketing .... Eddie Egan
Co-President, Production
& EVP, Universal Pictures .... Jimmy Horowitz

Wicked is a proud member of the
Broadway Green Alliance

To find out more about the world of *Wicked*
and to take our Broadway survey, visit
www.wickedthemusical.com.

CREDITS
Scenery built by F&D Scene Changes, Calgary, Canada. Show control and scenic motion control featuring Stage Command Systems© and scenery fabrication by Scenic Technologies, a division of Production Resource Group, New Windsor, NY. Lighting and certain special effects equipment from Fourth Phase and sound equipment from ProMix, both divisions of Production Resource Group LLC. Other special effects equipment by Sunshine Scenic Studios and Aztec Stage Lighting. Video projection system provided by Scharff Weisberg Inc. Projections by Vermilion Border Productions. Costumes by Barbara Matera Ltd., Parsons-Meares Ltd., Scafati, TRICORNE New York City and Eric Winterling. Millinery by Rodney Gordon and Lynne Mackey. Shoes by T.O. Dey, Frederick Longtin, Pluma, LaDuca Shoes NYC, and J.C. Theatrical. Flatheads and monkey wings built by Michael Curry Design Inc. Natural herb cough drops courtesy of Ricola USA, Inc. Masks and prosthetics by W.M. Creations, Inc., Matthew W. Mungle and Lloyd Matthews; lifecasts by Todd Kleitsch. Fur by Fur & Furgery. Undergarments and hosiery by Bra*Tenders, Inc. Antique jewelry by Ilene Chazanof. Specialty jewelry and tiaras by Larry Vrba. Custom Oz accessories by LouLou Button. Custom screening by Gene Mignola. Certain props by John Creech Designs and Den Design Studio. Environmentally friendly detergent provided by Arm & Hammer. Additional hand props courtesy of George Fenmore. Confetti supplied by Artistry in Motion. Puppets by Bob Flanagan. Musical instruments from Manny's and Carroll Musical Instrument Rentals. Drums and other percussion equipment from Bosphorus, Black Swamp, PTECH, D'Amico and Vater. Emer'gen'C provided by Alacer Corp. Rehearsed at the Lawrence A. Wien Center, 890 Broadway, and the Ford Center for the Performing Arts.

NEDERLANDER

Chairman	**James M. Nederlander**
President	**James L. Nederlander**

Executive Vice President
Nick Scandalios

Vice President	Vice President
Corporate Development	Labor Relations
Charlene S. Nederlander	**Herschel Waxman**

Vice President	Chief Financial Officer
Jim Boese	**Freida Sawyer Belviso**

STAFF FOR THE GERSHWIN THEATRE
Manager	**Richard D. Kaye**
Assoc. Manager	David Jannone
Treasurer	John Campise
Assistant Treasurer	Anthony Rossano
Carpenter	John Riggins
Electrician	Henry L. Brisen
Property Master	Mark Illo
Flyman	Dennis Fox
Fly Automation Carpenter	Michael J. Szymanski
Head Usher	Martha McGuire Boniface

Wicked
Scrapbook

1. Katie Rose Clarke makes her entrance as Glinda.
2. P.J. Benjamin as The Wizard of Oz.
3. Tom Flynn as Dr. Dillamond
4. The ensemble as Students of Shiz.

Photos by Joan Marcus

Correspondent: Lindsay Northen, "Ensemble"

Memorable Fan Letters: We receive adorable fan letters from children and school groups and enjoy reading them aloud in a voice that we think is suitable for the 7- or 13-year-old that sent it. If it is on the principal hallway callboard it is honored between "Witch Hunters" and the end of the show.

Anniversary Party: We celebrated our seventh anniversary at Tom and Toon across the street this year!

"Gypsy of the Year": Company members sang a song from *Emmet Otter's Jug-Band Christmas*: "Where the River Meets the Sea." We were first runner-up in fundraising this year! The sale of backstage tours and walk-ons has really helped us to raise a lot of money for BC/EFA. This year we raised $181,609.

Actor Who Has Done the Most Performances of *Wicked*: Kenway Kua performed his 2400th and last show on May 22, 2011.

Special Backstage Ritual: The women's ensemble (including standbys) has constructed the "Women's Ensemble Wall of Greatness." Every Wednesday we draw a name out of a hat, and place a "post-it of positivity" next to their name on the chart. It is an excellent self-esteem boost on a two-show day.

Favorite In-Theatre Gathering Place: The Greenroom has been, and always will be, popular. Many a salad, sandwich or homestyle Randy Witherspoon meal has been eaten there. Not to mention a whole lot of cake. *Wicked* loves cake.

Favorite Off-Site Hangouts: Sosa Borella is still going strong as a *Wicked* post-show hangout, but a new favorite is now Medi, the new wine bar on Ninth Avenue (aren't we classy!).

Favorite Snack Foods: The women's ensemble has been known to put away quite a bit of cheese. There was a big kale phase, and the men's ensemble eats a surprising amount of McDonalds for a thin group. The principal hallway candy jar is still going strong thanks to the principals and their dressers. And of course, everyone loves Mark Overton's Munchkin Seeds, now being sold at several neighborhood delis.

Mascot: We don't really have a mascot, but if we did, I think it would be Mimi Merrick, age 2.

Favorite Therapies: We keep Ricola in business. Grether's Pastilles are popular with Elphabas, the Glindas love a glycerin spray, and Pilates is keeping the injury count as low as possible.

Cell Phone Issues: Due to terrible phone service in the Gershwin Theatre, we have minimal cell phone interruption.

Sweethearts Within the Company: We had a lot of weddings in 2010/2011: Heather Spore, Brenda Hamilton, Lindsay K. Northen, Kristen Leigh Gorski and Briana Yacavone all got married! And Lindsay Janisse and Dominick Amendum got married to each other!

Women on the Verge of a Nervous Breakdown

First Preview: October 8, 2010. Opened: November 4, 2010.
Closed January 2, 2011 after 30 Previews and 69 Performances.

PLAYBILL®

This musical depicts a hectic day in the very busy romantic lives of a group of Madrid residents, including a man, his wife, his mistress, his other mistress, his son, his son's girlfriend and a cabdriver who always seems to show up at the right moment.

CAST
(in order of appearance)

Pepa	SHERIE RENE SCOTT
Ivan	BRIAN STOKES MITCHELL
Taxi Driver	DANNY BURSTEIN
Cristina	JENNIFER SANCHEZ
Hector	MURPHY GUYER
Man in Film	CHARLIE SUTTON
Woman in Film	NINA LAFARGA
Doctor	SEAN McCOURT
Candela	LAURA BENANTI
Malik	LUIS SALGADO
Carlos	JUSTIN GUARINI
Marisa	NIKKA GRAFF LANZARONE
Ivan's Concierge	ALMA CUERVO
Lucia	PATTI LuPONE
Paulina	de'ADRE AZIZA
Pepa's Concierge	MARY BETH PEIL
Ana	NINA LAFARGA
Ambite	JULIO AGUSTIN
TV Husband	MURPHY GUYER
Magistrate	MURPHY GUYER
Magistrate 2	ALMA CUERVO
Chief Inspector	MURPHY GUYER
Detective	SEAN McCOURT
Telephone Repairman	CHARLIE SUTTON

Continued on next page

⑧ **BELASCO THEATRE**
111 West 44th Street
A Shubert Organization Theatre
Philip J. Smith, *Chairman*   Robert E. Wankel, *President*

LINCOLN CENTER THEATER
under the direction of
André Bishop and **Bernard Gersten**
in association with
Bob Boyett
presents

WOMEN on the verge of a NERVOUS BREAKDOWN

A New Musical Based on the Film by **Pedro Almodóvar**

Book	Music & Lyrics
Jeffrey Lane	**David Yazbek**

with (in alphabetical order)

de'Adre Aziza   Laura Benanti   Danny Burstein
Justin Guarini   Nikka Graff Lanzarone   Patti LuPone
Brian Stokes Mitchell   Mary Beth Peil   Sherie Rene Scott
and
Julio Agustin   John Carroll   Alma Cuervo   Murphy Guyer
Rachel Bay Jones   Nina Lafarga   Yanira Marin   Sean McCourt
Vivian Nixon   Luis Salgado   Jennifer Sanchez   John Schiappa
Samantha Shafer   Phillip Spaeth   Matthew Steffens   Charlie Sutton

Sets	Costumes	Lighting	Sound
Michael Yeargan	**Catherine Zuber**	**Brian MacDevitt**	**Scott Lehrer**

Projections	Aerial Design	Special Effects	Wigs and Hair	Make-Up
Sven Ortel	**The Sky Box**	**Gregory Meeh**	**Charles LaPointe**	**Dick Page**

Orchestrations	Additional Orchestrations	Music Direction
Simon Hale	**Jim Abbott & David Yazbek**	**Jim Abbott**

Casting	Production Stage Manager	General Press Agent	Musical Theater Associate Producer
Telsey + Company	**Rolt Smith**	**Philip Rinaldi**	**Ira Weitzman**

General Manager	Production Manager	Director of Development	Director of Marketing
Adam Siegel	**Jeff Hamlin**	**Hattie K. Jutagir**	**Linda Mason Ross**

Choreography
Christopher Gattelli

Directed by
Bartlett Sher

Leadership support provided by The Stacey and Eric Mindich Fund for Musicals at LCT.
Major support provided by Debra and Leon Black.
Generous support provided by The New York Community Trust - Mary P. Oenslager Foundation Fund.
Special thanks to the Harold and Mimi Steinberg Charitable Trust for supporting new American work at LCT.
American Airlines is the Official Airline of Lincoln Center Theater.

11/4/10

(L-R): Patti LuPone and Sherie Rene Scott

Photo by Paul Kolnik

Women on the Verge of a Nervous Breakdown

MUSICAL NUMBERS

ACT ONE

"Madrid"	Taxi Driver
"Lie to Me"	Pepa, Ivan
"Lovesick"	Pepa, Ensemble
"Time Stood Still"	Lucia
"My Crazy Heart"	Taxi Driver, Carlos, Marisa, Ensemble
"Model Behavior"	Candela
"Island"	Pepa
"The Microphone"	Ivan, Carlos
"On the Verge"	Lucia, Pepa, Candela, Marisa, the Women

ACT TWO

"Mother's Day"	Pepa
"Yesterday, Tomorrow and Today"	Ivan
"Tangled"	Taxi Driver, Carlos, Candela, Ivan, Pepa, Paulina, Ana, Ambite
"Invisible"	Lucia
"Island" (reprise)	Pepa, Candela, Carlos
"Marisa/The Chase"	Marisa, Ensemble
"Talk to Me"	Pepa's Concierge, Pepa

(L-R): Nikka Graff Lanzarone, Laura Benanti and Justin Guarini

Photo by Paul Kolnik

ORCHESTRA

Conductor: JIM ABBOTT
Associate Conductor: MARCO PAGUIA
Drums: DEAN SHARENOW
Bass: BRIAN HAMM
Guitar: ERIK DELLA PENNA
Keyboard 1: MARCO PAGUIA
Keyboard 2: JAMES ABBOTT
Percussion: JAVIER DIAZ
Trumpet: CJ CAMERIERI
Trombone: TIM ALBRIGHT
French Horn: RJ KELLEY

Reed 1: TODD GROVES
Reed 2: DAN WILLIS
Reed 3: ALDEN BANTA
Violin 1/Concertmaster: LORI MILLER
Violin 2: ENTCHO TODOROV
Viola: JONATHAN DINKLAGE
Cello: ANIK OULIANINE
Synthesizer Programmer: RANDY COHEN
Music Coordinator: DEAN SHARENOW
Music Copying:
EMILY GRISHMAN MUSIC PREPARATION —
EMILY GRISHMAN/KATHARINE EDMONDS

Cast Continued

Ensemble .... JULIO AGUSTIN, ALMA CUERVO,
MURPHY GUYER, NINA LAFARGA,
YANIRA MARIN, SEAN McCOURT,
VIVIAN NIXON, LUIS SALGADO,
JENNIFER SANCHEZ, PHILLIP SPAETH,
MATTHEW STEFFENS, CHARLIE SUTTON

1st Assistant
    Stage Manager .... ANDREA O. SARAFFIAN
2nd Assistant
    Stage Manager .... JENNIFER RAE MOORE
Dance Captain .... JOHN CARROLL
Assistant Dance Captain ....SAMANTHA SHAFER
Swings .JOHN CARROLL, RACHEL BAY JONES,
    JOHN SCHIAPPA, SAMANTHA SHAFER

UNDERSTUDIES

For Pepa:
de'ADRE AZIZA, SAMANTHA SHAFER
For Ana, Cristina:
YANIRA MARIN, SAMANTHA SHAFER
For Pepa's Concierge:
ALMA CUERVO, RACHEL BAY JONES
For Marisa:
NINA LAFARGA, YANIRA MARIN
For Paulina:
NINA LAFARGA, VIVIAN NIXON
For Candela:
VIVIAN NIXON, JENNIFER SANCHEZ
For Lucia:
ALMA CUERVO, RACHEL BAY JONES
For Ivan, Chief Inspector, Hector, Magistrate:
SEAN McCOURT, JOHN SCHIAPPA
For Ambite:
LUIS SALGADO, MATTHEW STEFFENS
For Carlos:
PHILLIP SPAETH, CHARLIE SUTTON
For Detective:
LUIS SALGADO, CHARLIE SUTTON
For Malik:
JULIO AGUSTIN, JOHN CARROLL
For Telephone Repairman:
JOHN CARROLL, PHILLIP SPAETH
For Taxi Driver:
SEAN McCOURT, JOHN SCHIAPPA
For Magistrate 2 and Ivan's Concierge:
RACHEL BAY JONES, JENNIFER SANCHEZ
For Doctor, Man in Film:
JOHN CARROLL, JOHN SCHIAPPA
For Woman in Film:
RACHEL BAY JONES, SAMANTHA SHAFER.

PLACE and TIME

Madrid, 1987

Women on the Verge of a Nervous Breakdown

de'Adre Aziza
Paulina

Laura Benanti
Candela

Danny Burstein
Taxi Driver

Justin Guarini
Carlos

Nikka Graff
Lanzarone
Marisa

Patti LuPone
Lucia

Brian Stokes
Mitchell
Ivan

Mary Beth Peil
*Pepa's Concierge,
TV and Radio
Announcer*

Sherie Rene Scott
Pepa

Julio Agustin
Ambite, Ensemble

John Carroll
*Swing,
Dance Captain*

Alma Cuervo
*Ivan's Concierge,
Magistrate 2,
Ensemble*

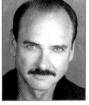
Murphy Guyer
*Hector, TV Husband,
Magistrate, Chief
Inspector, Ensemble*

Rachel Bay Jones
Swing

Nina Lafarga
*Ana, Woman in Film,
Ensemble*

Yanira Marin
Ensemble

Sean McCourt
*Doctor, Detective,
Ensemble*

Vivian Nixon
Ensemble

Luis Salgado
Malik, Ensemble

Jennifer Sanchez
Cristina, Ensemble

John Schiappa
Swing

Samantha Shafer
*Swing, Assistant
Dance Captain*

Phillip Spaeth
Ensemble

Matthew Steffens
Ensemble

Charlie Sutton
*Man in Film,
Telephone
Repairman,
Ensemble*

Jeffrey Lane
Book

David Yazbek
*Music and Lyrics,
Additional
Orchestrations*

Pedro Almodóvar
*Director of original
film*

Bartlett Sher
Director

Christopher Gattelli
Choreographer

Michael Yeargan
Sets

Catherine Zuber
Costumes

Brian MacDevitt
Lighting

Scott Lehrer
Sound

Sven Ortel
Projections

Women on the Verge of a Nervous Breakdown

Gregory Meeh
Special Effects

Evan Collier,
Sky Box
*Technical Aerial
Design*

Charles LaPointe
Wigs and Hair

Dick Page
Make-Up

Simon Hale
Orchestrations

Jim Abbott
*Musical Director,
Additional
Orchestrations*

Bernard Telsey,
Telsey + Company
Casting

André Bishop and Bernard Gersten,
Lincoln Center Theater
Producer

WARDROBE
Front Row (L-R): Claire Verlaet, Leah Redmond, Tom Bertsch, Steve Chazaro

Back Row (L-R): Tree Sarvay, Savana Leveille, Mel Hansen, Laura Ellington, (Christmas Tree), Kathleen Gallagher, Geoffrey Polischuk, Jason Blair

Not Pictured: Pat White, Patrick Bevilacqua

Bob Boyett

STAGE MANAGEMENT
(L-R): Andrea O. Saraffian, Rolt Smith, Jennifer Rae Moore

WIGS
(L-R): Vanessa Anderson, Rick Caroto, Isaac Grnya

Not Pictured: Amy Neswald

Women on the Verge of a Nervous Breakdown

Photos by Brian Mapp

FRONT OF HOUSE STAFF
Front Row (L-R): Powell, Michele Moyna, Eugenia Raines, Marisa Gioffre

Back Row (L-R): Dexter Luke, Pamela Loetterle, Stephanie Wallis (Theater Manager), Joseph Pittman, Kathleen Dunn

CREW
(L-R): Matthew Maloney (House Electrician), Bill Roland (Electrics), Richard Anderson (Props), Brian Mallet (Electrics), George Dummitt (House Carpenter), Colin Roche (Props), Joe Garvey (Electrics), John Alban Jr. (Props), Jeremy Wahlers (Electrics), Mark Hannan (Electrics), Sean Strohmeyer (Electrics), Laura Koch (House Props), Dave Karlson (Production Electrician), J.P. Nord (Carpenter), Rebecca Heroff (Props)

Not Pictured: Andrew Dean (Pyro Technician), Joe Luogo (Carpenter), Joe Moritz (Carpenter), Anthony Moritz (Carpenter), Al Toth (Carpenter), Kevin McNeill (Production Carpenter), John Kenny (Carpenter)

LINCOLN CENTER THEATER
ANDRÉ BISHOP   BERNARD GERSTEN
ARTISTIC DIRECTOR   EXECUTIVE PRODUCER

ADMINISTRATIVE STAFF
GENERAL MANAGER ....ADAM SIEGEL
Associate General Manager ....Jessica Niebanck

General Management Assistant ....Meghan Lantzy
Facilities Manager ....Alex Mustelier
Associate Facilities Manager ....Michael Assalone
GENERAL PRESS AGENT ....PHILIP RINALDI
Press Associates........Barbara Carroll, Amanda Dekker
PRODUCTION MANAGER ....JEFF HAMLIN
Associate Production Manager ....Paul Smithyman

DIRECTOR OF
DEVELOPMENT ....HATTIE K. JUTAGIR
Associate Director of Development ....Rachel Norton
Manager of Special Events and
   LCT Young Angels ....Karin Schall
Grants Writer ....Neal Brilliant
Manager, Patron Program ....Sheilaja Rao

Women on the Verge of a Nervous Breakdown

Assistant to the
Director of Development ....Raelyn R. Lagerstrom
Development Associate/
Special Events &
LCT Young Angels ....Jennifer Rosenbluth-Stoll
Development Assistant/
Individual Giving ....Sydney Rais-Sherman
DIRECTOR OF FINANCE ....DAVID S. BROWN
Controller ....Susan Knox
Systems Manager ....Stacy Valentine
Finance Assistant ....Kristen Parker
DIRECTOR OF MARKETING .LINDA MASON ROSS
Marketing Associate ....Ashley M. Dunn
Marketing Assistant ....John Casavant
DIRECTOR OF EDUCATION ....KATI KOERNER
Associate Director of Education ....Alexandra Lopez
Assistant to the Executive Producer ......Barbara Hourigan
Office Manager ....Brian Hashimoto
Office Assistant .... Stephen McFarland
Messenger ....Esau Burgess
Reception ....Brenden Rogers, Michelle Metcalf

ARTISTIC STAFF

ASSOCIATE DIRECTORS ......GRACIELA DANIELE,
NICHOLAS HYTNER,
JACK O'BRIEN,
SUSAN STROMAN,
DANIEL SULLIVAN
RESIDENT DIRECTOR .... BARTLETT SHER
DRAMATURG and DIRECTOR,
LCT DIRECTORS LAB ....ANNE CATTANEO
CASTING DIRECTOR ....DANIEL SWEE, CSA
MUSICAL THEATER
ASSOCIATE PRODUCER ....IRA WEITZMAN
ARTISTIC DIRECTOR/LCT3 ....PAIGE EVANS
Artistic Administrator ....Julia Judge
Casting Associate ....Camille Hickman
Lab Assistant ....Kate Marvin

---

SPECIAL SERVICES

Advertising ....Serino-Coyne/
Jim Russek, Roger Micone,
Becca Goland-Van Ryn
Principal Poster Artist ....James McMullan
Poster Artwork for *Women on the Verge*
of a Nervous Breakdown ....Juan Gatti
Counsel ....Peter L. Felcher, Esq.;
Charles H. Googe, Esq.;
and Carol Kaplan, Esq. of
Paul, Weiss, Rifkind, Wharton & Garrison
Immigration Counsel ....Theodore Ruthizer, Esq.;
Mark D. Koestler, Esq.
of Kramer, Levin, Naftalis & Frankel LLP
Labor Counsel ....Michael F. McGahan, Esq.
of Epstein, Becker & Green, P.C.
Auditor...........................Frederick Martens, C.P.A.
Lutz & Carr, L.L.P.
Insurance. ....Jennifer Brown of
DeWitt Stern Group
Production Photographer ....Paul Kolnik
Studio Photographer ....Ethan Hill
Video Services ....Fresh Produce Productions/
Frank Basile
Travel ....Tygon Tours
Consulting Architect............................Hugh Hardy,
H3 Hardy Collaboration Architecture

Construction Manager ....Yorke Construction
Payroll Service......................Castellana Services, Inc.
Merchandising .... Marquee Merchandise, LLC/
Matt Murphy

STAFF FOR *WOMEN ON THE VERGE OF A NERVOUS BREAKDOWN*

COMPANY MANAGER ....MATTHEW MARKOFF
Associate Company Manager .... Josh Lowenthal
Associate Director .... Sarna Lapine
Associate Choreographer ....Lou Castro
Assistant Choreographers ....Rebecca Tomas,
Mark Stuart Eckstein
Associate Set Designer ....Mikiko Suzuki MacAdams
Assistant Costume Designer ....David Newell
Associate Lighting Designer .... Jennifer Schriever
Assistant Lighting Designer ....Benjamin C. Travis
Associate Sound Design ....Drew Levy
Associate Projection Designer ....S. Katy Tucker
Projections Programmer ....Michael Kohler
Assistant to Projection Designer ....Lucy Mackinnon
Associate Special Effects ....Jeremy Chernick
Incidental Music, Vocal Arrangements
and Dance Music Arrangements ....Jim Abbott
Music Copyist ....Emily Grishman Music Preparation/
Emily Grishman, Katharine Edmonds
Associate Synthesizer Programmer ....Bryan Crook
Properties Coordinator ....Kathy Fabian
Properties Associates ....Carrie Mossman,
Timothy Ferro
Properties Artisans ....Mary Wilson, Catherine Small,
Eric Berninghausen, Rebecca Perrenod
Show Carpenter ....Kevin McNeill
Production Carpenter ....John Weingart
Production Electrician ....David Karlson
Production Propertyman ....Mark Dignam
Production Soundman ....Scott Sanders
Automated Light Programmer ....Victor Seastone
Wardrobe Supervisor....................Patrick Bevilacqua
Assistant Wardrobe Supervisor ....Tom Bertsch
Dressers ....Alice Bee, Steve Chazaro,
Laura Ellington, Kathleen Gallagher,
Mel Hansen, Geoffrey Polischuk,
Leah Redmond, Tree Sarvay, Mark Trezza,
Claire Verlaet, Patricia White
Hair Supervisor ....Amy Neswald
Assistant Hair Supervisor ....Rick Caroto
Hair Assistant ....Vanessa Anderson
Ms. LuPone's Wig ....Paul Huntley
Ms. LuPone's Make-Up Design ....Angelina Avallone
Production Assistant ....Lisa Chernoff
Music Production Assistant ....Will Reynolds
Assistant to Jeffrey Lane ....Alex Lane
Costume Shoppers .... Ryan Park, Nicole Moody
Rehearsal Pianist ....Adam Ben-David

Dialect Coach ....Deborah Hecht

Technical Supervision by
Bill Nagle and Patrick Merryman

Telsey + Company

Bernie Telsey CSA, Will Cantler CSA, David Vaccari CSA,
Bethany Knox CSA, Craig Burns CSA,
Tiffany Little Canfield CSA, Rachel Hoffman CSA,
Carrie Rosson CSA, Justin Huff CSA,

Patrick Goodwin CSA,
Abbie Brady-Dalton, David Morris, Cesar A. Rocha

CREDITS

Scenery fabrication by PRG-Scenic Technologies. Show control and scenic motion control featuring stage command systems® by PRG-Scenic Technologies, a division of Production Resource Group, LLC, New Windsor, NY. Costumes by Angels the Costumiers, Euroco Costumes Inc., Parsons-Meares Ltd., John Cowles and John Kristiansen. Millinery by Arnold S. Levine Inc. and Rodney Gordon Inc. Men's tailoring by Brian Hemesath. Custom footwear by Capri Shoes, LaDuca Shoes and WorldTone Dance. Custom knitwear by Maria Ficalora. Fabric painting by Jeffrey Fender. Vintage eyewear by Fabulous Fanny's. Hosiery and undergarments provided by Bra*Tenders. Make-up courtesy of Shiseido. Sound equipment by Sound Associates, Inc. Drums provided by Pearl. Latin percussion provided by LP. Keyboards provided by Yamaha. Bass amplification provided by Eden Electronics. Lighting equipment from PRG Lighting. Video projection system provided by Scharff Weisberg, Inc. Special effects equipment by Jauchem & Meeh Inc. Specialty props by Propstar, Tom Carroll Scenery and Aardvark Interiors. Flame treatment by Turning Star Inc. Rehearsed at the New 42nd Street Studios and Roundabout Rehearsal Studios. Natural herb cough drops courtesy of Ricola USA, Inc.

Visit www.lct.org

THE SHUBERT ORGANIZATION, INC.
Board of Directors

Philip J. Smith	**Robert E. Wankel**
Chairman	President
Wyche Fowler, Jr.	**John W. Kluge**
Lee J. Seidler	**Michael I. Sovern**

Stuart Subotnick

Elliot Greene	**David Andrews**
Chief Financial Officer	Senior Vice President – Shubert Ticketing
Juan Calvo	**John Darby**
Vice President – Finance	Vice President – Facilities
Peter Entin	**Charles Flateman**
Vice President – Theatre Operations	Vice President – Marketing
Anthony LaMattina	**Brian Mahoney**
Vice President – Audit & Production Finance	Vice President – Ticket Sales

D.S. Moynihan
Vice President – Creative Projects

House Manager ....Stephanie Wallis
Carpenter ....George Dummitt
Electrician.................................Matthew Maloney
Property Person ....Laura Koch

Women on the Verge of a Nervous Breakdown
SCRAPBOOK

Correspondent: Justin Guarini, "Carlos"

Memorable Opening Night Notes: Opening night was so unbelievably memorable that it's hard to pick just one moment … but if I had to choose one I'd have to say getting such warm, complimentary notes from some of Broadway's most beloved performers (Patti, Stokes, Laura…to name a few) was mind-boggling. Throughout this entire process they have made me feel so welcome, and encouraged me to be better than I thought I could ever be.

Opening Night Gifts: Flowers, plants, books, statues of chickens and ducks, food, some personal treasures.

Most Exciting Celebrity Visitors: I'm actually most excited for my cousins LaTanya and Sam Jackson to see the show. They're coming this week. They're famous, sure, but more importantly they're family. I really respect their opinion and I'm really excited to see what they think of the show.

Special Backstage Rituals: Every night at the "places" call we all circle up onstage and take the time to connect and state our intentions for the night/show. It's such a beautiful experience to be a part of, and really helps to encourage us to be unified in the task of creating a beautiful world onstage for ourselves and, in turn, the audience.

Favorite Snack Food: Good: trail mix with yogurt. Bad: Snickers (damn whoever invented those…I'm a fiend).

Favorite Therapy: Peppermint tea, Yoga, Grether's Pastilles.

Most Memorable Ad-Lib: My favorite was when the darling Laura Benanti and I were doing a number together and she completely mumbled something nonsensical (as opposed to the lyric). I remember looking at her like she had two heads, just before we both started cracking up, and dying in the process of trying not to show the audience we were hopelessly lost. I ended up singing a bit of her line because she was laughing too hard to do it. Needless to say we made it through the number and then promptly fell over once we got off stage.

Fastest Costume Change: I am always completely amazed at the 20-30 second change Patti makes in the first act. She goes from having a full dress, with gloves, bracelets, sunglasses, heels, a purse, and a huge hat…to pearl necklaces, lingerie, different bracelets, rings, earrings, and a beautiful house coat. It takes four dressers to get her whipped in and out of costume. The funny thing is that she's never been late…not once! I hope I didn't jinx it :-/

Who Wore the Least: Originally all the "Women on the Verge" came out in lingerie for the opening number. I can't tell you how much respect I have for all of them for doing that…especially in our society and our business. They all looked beautiful, but each of them was so vulnerable, it was really touching.

Favorite Off-Site Hangout: I love to go right next door to "Un Deux Trois." A great atmosphere and a fun place to hang out and dine.

Catchphrase Only the Company Would Recognize: "Gazpacho!!"

Coolest Thing About Being in This Show: Getting to work with some of the most amazing people in the business right now. Legends, and legends in the making.

1. Toasting opening night (L-R): Mary Beth Peil, Nikka Graff Lanzarone, de'Adre Aziza, Brian Stokes Mitchell, Justin Guarini, Patti LuPone, Pedro Almodóvar, Sherie Rene Scott, Laura Benanti, Danny Burstein and Bartlett Sher.
2. (L-R): Laura Benanti and Pedro Almodóvar at the premiere party.
3. Brian Stokes Mitchell and wife Allyson Tucker.
4. (L-R): Songwriter David Yazbek and librettist Jeffrey Lane.
5. Anna Netrebko and director Bartlett Sher arrive at the Belasco Theatre on opening night.

Wonderland

First Preview: March 21, 2011. Opened: April 17, 2011.
Closed May 15, 2011 after 30 Previews and 33 Performances.

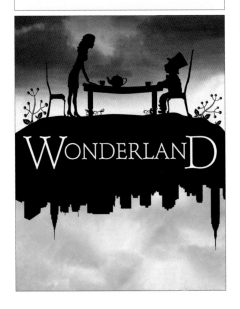

PLAYBILL®

A grown-up Alice goes through the looking-glass in this radical musical reimagining of the Lewis Carroll classic about a dreamlike journey to a magical place.

CAST
(in order of appearance)

Edwina	KAREN MASON
Chloe	CARLY ROSE SONENCLAR
Alice	JANET DACAL
The White Rabbit	EDWARD STAUDENMAYER
Caterpillar	E. CLAYTON CORNELIOUS
El Gato	JOSE LLANA
Jack the White Knight	DARREN RITCHIE
Morris the March Hare	DANNY STILES
The Mad Hatter	KATE SHINDLE
The Queen of Hearts	KAREN MASON
The Victorian Gentleman	DARREN RITCHIE

ENSEMBLE
APRIL BERRY, JOEY CALVERI, SAE LA CHIN,
MALLAURI ESQUIBEL, DEREK FERGUSON,
WILKIE FERGUSON III, LAURA HALL,
NATALIE HILL, LAUREN LIM JACKSON,
MORGAN JAMES, RYAN LINK,
KATE LOPREST, HEATHER PARCELLS,
STEFAN RAULSTON,
JULIUS ANTHONY RUBIO,
TANAIRI SADE VAZQUEZ

Continued on next page

⊱N⊰ MARQUIS THEATRE

UNDER THE DIRECTION OF JAMES M. NEDERLANDER AND JAMES L. NEDERLANDER

DAVID A. STRAZ CENTER FOR THE PERFORMING ARTS   FRANZBLAU MEDIA INC.   NEDERLANDER PRESENTATIONS, INC.
JUDY LISI PRESIDENT AND CEO

THE KNIGHTS OF TAMPA BAY   MICHAEL SPEYER & BERNIE ABRAMS   JAY HARRIS   LARRY & KAY PAYTON
DAVID SCHER HINKS SHIMBERG

JUNE & TOM SIMPSON   INDEPENDENT PRESENTERS NETWORK   SONNY EVERETT PRODUCTIONS LLC

WONDERLAND

Book	Lyrics	Music
GREGORY BOYD & JACK MURPHY	JACK MURPHY	FRANK WILDHORN

Starring
JANET DACAL   DARREN RITCHIE

E. CLAYTON CORNELIOUS   JOSE LLANA   KAREN MASON

KATE SHINDLE   CARLY ROSE SONENCLAR   EDWARD STAUDENMAYER   DANNY STILES

APRIL BERRY   GRADY McLEOD BOWMAN   JOEY CALVERI   SAE LA CHIN   MALLAURI ESQUIBEL
DEREK FERGUSON   WILKIE FERGUSON III   LAURA HALL   NATALIE HILL   LAUREN LIM JACKSON
MORGAN JAMES   RYAN LINK   KATE LOPREST   RENÉE MARINO   HEATHER PARCELLS
STEFAN RAULSTON   JULIUS ANTHONY RUBIO   TANAIRI SADE VAZQUEZ

Set Design	Costume Design	Lighting Design
NEIL PATEL	SUSAN HILFERTY	PAUL GALLO

Video & Projection Design	Sound Design	Hair & Wig Design
SVEN ORTEL	PETER HYLENSKI	TOM WATSON

Musical Supervision & Orchestrations	Vocal Music Arrangements
KIM SCHARNBERG	RON MELROSE & JASON HOWLAND

Casting	Fight Director	Associate Director	Associate Choreographer
CLEMMONS/DEWING CASTING	RICK SORDELET	KENNETH FERRONE	MICHELLE ELKIN

Music Coordinator	Technical Supervisor	Production Stage Manager
DAVID LAI	CHRIS SMITH/SMITTY	DAVID O'BRIEN

Press Representative	Marketing	Advertising	General Management
BONEAU/BRYAN-BROWN	aka MARKETING	SPOTCO	THE CHARLOTTE WILCOX COMPANY

Associate Producers
JUDY JOSEPH   STAGEVENTURES 2010 LIMITED PARTNERSHIP

Executive Producer
WILLIAM FRANZBLAU

Supervising Music Director/Incidental & Dance Music Arrangements
JASON HOWLAND

Choreographer
MARGUERITE DERRICKS

Director
GREGORY BOYD

Original Broadway Cast Recording available on Masterworks Broadway.
The producers wish to express their appreciation to Theatre Development Fund for its support of this production.

4/17/11

Photo by Paul Kolnik

(L-R): Jose Llana,
Darren Ritchie, Janet Dacal,
Edward Staudenmayer,
E. Clayton Cornelious

Wonderland

SCENES

ACT I

1. Chloe's Bedroom/Apartment 8A
2. The Elevator
3. Wonderland
4. The Caterpillar's Den
5. The City Limits
6. A Garden
7. The Mad Tea Party
8. Chloe's Bedroom/The Tulgey Wood
9. Near the Border of
   Looking Glass Land

ACT II

1. The War Room of the Mad Hatter
2. The Grotto
3. The Underground Conservatory of
   Looking Glass Land
4. The Parlour in the Palace of
   the Queen
5. The Hall of Mirrors
6. The Hatter's Prison
7. Chloe's Bedroom

MUSICAL NUMBERS

ACT I

"Overture"
"Worst Day of My Life" ....Chloe, Alice
"Down the Rabbit Hole"..Alice, Unearthly Voice
"Welcome to Wonderland" ....Alice, Company
"Drink Me"..Unearthly Voices
"Advice From a Caterpillar"..Caterpillar, Alice, Legs
"Go With the Flow"...El Gato, Alice, Cats, Kittens
"One Knight"...Jack the White Knight, Fellow Knights
"The Tea Party" ....Company
"The Mad Hatter" ....The Mad Hatter, Company
"Hail the Queen" ....The Queen of Hearts, Company
"Home" ....Alice
"A Nice Little Walk" ....The Mad Hatter, Chloe, Morris
"Through the Looking Glass" ....Alice, Jack the White Knight, Caterpillar, El Gato, The White Rabbit

ACT II

"I Will Prevail" ....The Mad Hatter, Looking Glass Guard
"I Am My Own Invention"...The Victorian Gentleman, Alice
"Off With Their Heads" ....The Queen of Hearts, Ladies-in-Waiting
"Once More I Can See" ....Alice
"Together" ....Jack the White Knight, Caterpillar, El Gato, The White Rabbit, Alice, Chloe
"Home" (Reprise) ....Chloe, Alice, The White Rabbit, El Gato, Caterpillar
"Finding Wonderland" ....Alice, Company

Kate Shindle (center)
and the ensemble

Photo by Michal Daniel

SWINGS

GRADY McLEOD BOWMAN,
RENÉE MARINO

UNDERSTUDIES

For Alice: MORGAN JAMES
For Caterpillar: WILKIE FERGUSON III
For Chloe: APRIL BERRY,
    MALLAURI ESQUIBEL
For Edwina/The Queen of Hearts:
    NATALIE HILL, HEATHER PARCELLS
For El Gato: JOEY CALVERI
For Jack the White Knight/
    The Victorian Gentleman: JOEY CALVERI,
    RYAN LINK
For The White Rabbit: RYAN LINK,
    DANNY STILES
For The Mad Hatter: HEATHER PARCELLS

Dance Captain: MALLAURI ESQUIBEL
Assistant Dance Captain: LAUREN LIM
    JACKSON

Fight Captain: STEFAN RAULSTON

ORCHESTRA

Music Director/Conductor: JASON HOWLAND
Associate Conductor: JEFF LAMS

Concertmaster: KATHERINE LIVOLSI-LANDAU

Violins: LISA MATRICARDI, JENNIFER CHOI,
    ROGER MAHADEEN
Viola: DAVID BLINN
Cello: MAIRI DORMAN-PHANEUF
Trumpet: CJ CAMERIERI
Trombones/Tuba: JENNIFER WHARTON
French Horn/Alto Horn: RJ KELLEY
Woodwinds: KURT BACHER, DANIEL WILLIS
Guitars: MARC COPELY
Acoustic/Electric Bass: CHRIS LIGHTCAP
Keyboards: JEFF LAMS, NICHOLAS CHENG,
    KIRSTEN AGRESTA COPELY
Percussion: BILL LANHAM
Drums: ADAM WOLFE
Music Coordinator: DAVID LAI

Wonderland

Janet Dacal
Alice

Darren Ritchie
*Jack the White
Knight, The Victorian
Gentleman*

E. Clayton Cornelious
Caterpillar

Jose Llana
El Gato

Karen Mason
*Edwina, The Queen
of Hearts*

Kate Shindle
The Mad Hatter

Carly Rose
Sonenclar
Chloe

Edward
Staudenmayer
The White Rabbit

Danny Stiles
*Morris the March
Hare*

April Berry
Ensemble

Grady McLeod
Bowman
Swing

Joey Calveri
Ensemble

Sae La Chin
Ensemble

Mallauri Esquibel
Ensemble

Derek Ferguson
Ensemble

Wilkie Ferguson III
Ensemble

Laura Hall
Ensemble

Natalie Hill
Ensemble

Lauren Lim Jackson
*Ensemble/Assistant
Dance Captain*

Morgan James
Ensemble

Ryan Link
Ensemble

Kate Loprest
Ensemble

Renée Marino
Swing

Heather Parcells
Ensemble

Stefan Raulston
Ensemble

Julius Anthony Rubio
Ensemble

Tanairi Sade Vazquez
Ensemble

Frank Wildhorn
Music

Jack Murphy
Book, Lyrics

Gregory Boyd
Director/Book

Marguerite Derricks
Choreographer

Neil Patel
Set Design

Susan Hilferty
Costume Design

Paul Gallo
Lighting Designer

Sven Ortel
*Video & Projection
Design*

Wonderland

Peter Hylenski
Sound Design

Tom Watson
Hair and Wig Design

Kim Scharnberg
Orchestrations

Ron Melrose
Vocal Arrangements

Jason Howland
Supervising Music Director/Incidental & Dance Music Arrangements/Vocal Music Arrangements

Kenneth Ferrone
Associate Director

Dave Clemmons
Casting
Casting

Rick Sordelet
Fight Director

David Lai
Music Coordinator

Chris Smith/
Theatersmith, Inc.
Technical Supervisor

The Charlotte Wilcox Company
General Manager

James M.
Nederlander,
Nederlander
Presentations, Inc.
Producer

James L.
Nederlander,
Nederlander
Presentations, Inc.
Producer

Michael Speyer
Producer

Bernie Abrams
Producer

Jay Harris
Producer

DOORMAN
Rey Concepcion

COMPANY MANAGER
Alexandra Agosta

HAIR
(L-R): Thomas Augustine, Enrique Vega, Joshua Gericke

STAGE MANAGEMENT
(L-R): Colleen Danaher, David O'Brien, Stephen Gruse

Wonderland

WARDROBE
Front Row (L-R): Graciela Zapata,
Melanie Schmidt, Evelina Nervil, Hector Lugo,
Douglas Earl

Back Row (L-R): Kelly A. Saxon, Scott Westervelt,
Jake Fry, Roy Seiler, Jay Woods, Allison Rogers,
Hilda Garcia Suli, Lilian Colon

STAGE CREW
Front Row (L-R): Joe Sardo, Kenny Sheehan,
Ann D. Cavanaugh, Jason Clark, Jimmy Mayo,
Timothy McIntyre, Rick Poulin, Jesse Stevens

Back Row (L-R): William T. Wright, Jr.,
Fred Mecionis, Neil Rosenberg, David Elmer,
William Ruger, Trevor Ricci

FRONT OF HOUSE STAFF
Front Row (L-R): Jason Mullen, John Clark, Jr.,
Omar Aguilar, Michael Mejias, George Fitze

Second Row (L-R): Odalis Concepcion,
Nancy Diaz, Jean Doty, Donna Flaherty

Third Row (L-R): Lulu Caso,
David R. Calhoun (House Manager)

Back Row (L-R): David Cox, Stanley Seidman,
Cecil Vilar, Paul Morer (Associate House
Manager), Phyllis Weinsaft

Wonderland

GENERAL MANAGEMENT
CHARLOTTE WILCOX COMPANY
Charlotte W. Wilcox
Matthew W. Krawiec
Dina S. Friedler   Seth Marquette
Regina Mancha   Steve Supeck   Margaret Wilcox
Ryan Smillie   Stephen Donovan

COMPANY MANAGER
Alexandra Agosta
ASSISTANT COMPANY MANAGER
Sherra Johnston

GENERAL PRESS REPRESENTATIVE
BONEAU/BRYAN-BROWN
Adrian Bryan-Brown   Susanne Tighe   Kelly Guiod

CASTING
Dave Clemmons CSA   Joy Dewing CSA
Alan Lane

Production Stage Manager ....David O'Brien
Stage Manager ....Stephen R. Gruse
Assistant Stage Manager ....Colleen Danaher
Associate Scenic Designer ....Caleb Levengood
Assistant Set Designers ....Michael Carnahan,
                                            Stephen Dobay
Associate Costume Designer ....Tricia Barsamian
Assistant Costume Designers ....Becky Lasky,
                                            Marina Reti
Associate Lighting Designer ....Craig Stelzenmuller
Assistant Lighting Designer ....Joel Shier
Associate Video Projection Designer ....S. Katy Tucker
Assistant Video Projection Designer ......Lucy MacKinnon
Associate Sound Designers ....Tony Smolenski,
                                            Keith Caggiano
Assistant to Frank Wildhorn/
    Wildhorn Productions ....Nicholas Cheng
Assistant Fight Director ....Christian Kelly-Sordelet
Video/Projections Programmer ....Peter Vincent Acken
Additional Programming by ....Cory FitzGerald
Special Effects ....Chic Silber
Magic Consultant ....Matthew Holtzclaw
Synthesizer Programmer ....Randy Cohen
Assistant Synthesizer Programmers ....Bryan Crook,
                                            Tim Crook
Production Electrician ....Michael Ward
Production Property Master ....Neil Rosenberg
Production Sound Engineer ....Phillip Lojo/
                                            Paul Delcioppo
Head Carpenter ....Jason Clark
Flyman ....David Elmer
Head Electrician ....Evan Vorono
Tampa Moving Light Programmer ....David Arch
NY Moving Light Programmer ....Thomas Hague
Spotlight ....June Abernathy
Assistant Property Master ....Trevor Ricci
Sound Operator ....William Ruger
Assistant Sound Operator... ....Jesse Stevens
Wardrobe Supervisor ....Scott Westervelt
Associate Wardrobe Supervisor ....Kelly Saxon
Dressers ....Douglas Earl, Lillian Colon-Jaramillo,
                    Jake Fry, Hilda Garcia-Suli,
                    Hector Lugo, Evelina Norvil,

Karen Mason (center) and company

Photo by Paul Kolnik

Allison Rogers, Roy Seiler, Jay Woods
Hair Supervisor ....Thomas Augustine
Assistant Hair Supervisor ....Joshua D. First
Hair Dresser ....Joshua Gericke
Make Up Consultant ....Ashley Ryan
Production Assistant ....Aaron Elgart
Legal Counsel ....Franklin Weinrib Rudell
                                    & Vassallo PC/
                                Elliot Brown, Dan Wasser
Accountant ....Fried & Kowgios LLC/Robert Fried
Comptroller ....Galbraith & Co./Sarah Galbraith
Advertising ....Spotco/
                            Drew Hodges, Jim Edwards,
                        Tom Greenwald, Tom McCann,
                                    Josh Fraenkel
Website/Interactive Marketing ....Spotco/
                        Sara Fitzpatrick, Matt Wilstein,
                        Stephen Santore, Christina Sees,
                                    Marc Mettler
Marketing & Sales Direction ....aka/
                        Scott Moore, Liz Furze, Adam Jay,
                        Janette Roush, Erik Alden,
                                    Jacob Matsumiya
Payroll Service ....Castellana Services, Inc.
Banking ....City National Bank/Michele Gibbons
Insurance ....DeWitt Stern/Anthony Pittari
Music Preparation ....Anixter Rice Music Service
Child Tutor ....On Location Education/
                            Leona Casella, Irene Karasik
Child Guardian ....Vanessa Brown
Production Photographer ....Michal Daniel
Group Sales ....Telecharge.com Group Sales
Merchandise ....Creative Goods Design and Supply/
                            Pete Milano, Mike D'Arcy
Information Management
    Services ....Marion Finkler Taylor
Physical Therapist ....Sean P Gallagher/
                        Performing Arts Physical Therapy
Supervising Orthopedist ....Phillip Bauman, MD
Travel Services ....Tzell Travel/Andi Henig
Opening Night Coordination ....Serino Coyne, LLC/
                            Suzanne Tobak, Gail Perlman
Theatre Displays ....King Displays, Inc.

CREDITS
Scenery by Scenic Technologies, Asolo Scenic Shop, Tom
Carroll Scenery and Jupiter Scenic Shop. Specialty soft
goods provided by JC Hansen Co. Costumes by Eric
Winterling, Inc.; Tricorne, Inc.; Giliberto Designs, Inc.;
Adrienne Wells. Shoes by LaDuca Shoes, Worldtone Dance,

Capezio, Handmade Shoes, T.O. Dey. Millinery by Lynne
Mackey Studio, Rodney Gordon, Inc. Custom knitwear by
Maria Ficalora. Custom fabric printing by Gene Mignola,
Inc.; Olympus Flag & Banner. Custom fabric painting by
Hochi Asiatico, Jeff Fender. Custom crafts by Brent
Barkhaus, Costume Armour, Inc. Custom textile artwork by
Christopher Young. Custom crowns by Larry Vrba.
Undergarments and hosiery provided by Bra*Tenders.
Lighting equipment from Production Resource Group.
Video projection system engineered and installed by Scharff
Weisberg. Sound equipment provided by Masque Sound.
Selected songs first workshopped at Broadway Theater
Project; Deb McWaters, Founder Artistic Director

**Originally produced at the David A. Straz, Jr. Center
for the Performing Arts, Tampa, FL.**

**Subsequently produced at the
Alley Theatre, Houston, Texas**

Rehearsed at New 42nd Street Studios and
Pearl Studios

Make-up provided by M•A•C.

NEDERLANDER

Chairman ....James M. Nederlander
President ....James L. Nederlander

Executive Vice President
Nick Scandalios

Vice President   Senior Vice President
Corporate Development   Labor Relations
Charlene S. Nederlander   **Herschel Waxman**

Vice President   Chief Financial Officer
Jim Boese   **Freida Sawyer Belviso**

STAFF FOR THE MARQUIS THEATRE
Manager ....David Calhoun
Associate Manager ....Austin Nathaniel
Treasurer ....Rick Waxman
Assistant Treasurer ....John Rooney
Carpenter ....Joseph P. Valentino
Electrician ....James Mayo
Property Man ....Scott Mecionis

Wonderland

SCRAPBOOK

Correspondent: Heather Parcells, "Ensemble"
"Finding Wonderland is finding who you are."
This cast, crew, and creative team have been the most supportive, patient, exciting, giving, loving, thrilling, talented, creative, accepting, generous, and beautiful group of people I have ever worked with. In a time of intense turmoil in my life, they gave me a place to feel safe and took me on a journey that, like the song says, helped me find who I was. I will be forever grateful.

Opening Night Gifts: Sae La Chin had "Onesies" made for every girl in the ensemble. We all wore them to sing offstage. (See photo, lower right.) Marguerite Derricks, Michelle Elkin, Danny Stiles, Mallauri Esquibel, Kenneth Ferrone, and Wilkie Ferguson gave the cast an original "Squigs" ink drawing of the *Wonderland* cast.

Most Exciting Celebrity Visitors: Wayne Brady. He is so much taller than expected. His energy was infectious. Tyra Banks. We saw her in the audience wearing a hat and sunglasses.

Actor Who Performed the Most Roles in This Show: Renée Marino (female swing) performed five out of the six "dancer tracks." Four of them in one week. Each for the first time.

Who Has Worked on the Most Shows: Vanessa Brown, our child wrangler. She has done 19 Broadway shows including: the original *Ragtime* (ummm...Hello Lea Michele); *Chitty Chitty Bang Bang*; the revivals of *South Pacific* and *The Sound Of Music*. She has wrangled approximately 130 kids to date. The oldest is now 28.

Special Backstage Rituals: 1) Prayer circle led by Janet Dacal at "Places": "For breath, for life, for love, for light."
2) Clayton Cornelious's fist-bumps with each of his "Legs" before his number "Advice From a Caterpillar."
3) During "I Will Prevail": MAD HATTER: sings "Farewell Alice" while OFFSTAGE LEFT CAST MEMBERS sing counter melody: "Farewell Alice, Oh Yeah!"
4) After "Welcome to Wonderland" Derek Ferguson would pat everyone he passed and say "Kill It!"
5) Mallauri and Wigs Josh's Middle School Slow Dance during "Finding Wonderland."
6) Carly & Darren: "Slappin the bass."

Favorite Off-Site Hangout: Glass House Tavern.

Favorite Snack Foods:
-Natalie Hill: Diet Coke.
-Licorice.
-Laura Hall's AMAZING cookies.
-Anything Maggie Shindle, Kate's mom, would bake.
-Hard pretzels in the wig room.
-Lots of birthday cake.

Favorite Therapy: Grether's Pastilles.

Memorable Stage Door Fan Encounters: Five-year-old Keona Skye who saw the show 12 times!
On our closing performance, fans, who were

1. Composer Frank Wildhorn (seated C, cap) with members of the cast and creative team at the recording session.
2. Leading lady Janet Dacal gets a marriage proposal from leading man Darren Ritchie.
3. Prayer circle backstage before a performance.
4. Ladies of the ensemble in their "onesies."

the self-proclaimed "WONDERTARDS," sat in protest of the closing of the show with signs that read: 1) "I blew my voice singing 'I Will Prevail' for NOTHING"
2) "'It's a Beautiful Day in Wonderland'...Too bad we can't see it."
3) "We're all MAD here."
They also made paper flowers for every single member of the cast and handed them to each as they went in the stage door.

Fastest Costume Change: Karen Mason. End of show from Queen to Edwina to Queen

again...all in the span of about 4 minutes. She also wore the heaviest costume...about twenty pounds.

Sweethearts Within the Company: Darren Ritchie and Janet Dacal: Darren proposed to Janet onstage in front of the entire audience after the curtain call...she said yes!
Morgan James and Jason Howland (she papered his dressing room with signed headshots of all the girls).

Company In-Jokes: Kate Shindle: "Something Something Something SMOKE BOMB!"

Wonderland
SCRAPBOOK

Photos courtesy Heather Parcells

1. E. Clayton Cornelious (C) and members of the ensemble attend the Family Festival Street Fair during the 10th annual Tribeca Film Festival April 30, 2011.
2. Darren Ritchie helps Grady Bowman celebrate getting the Gypsy Robe.
3. Janet Dacal recording original cast album.
4. Edward Staudenmayer backstage with the Ladies in Waiting.

"Where's Wilkie?"
"Jack dies???"
"We're Here"—Mallauri Esquibel.
"Woot Woo"—Tanairi Vazquez.
"Sorry, Carly." (Whenever we swore...which was a lot)
"Ninja."
The Vocal Booth lizard.
Huzzle Von Krill (aka the Pink Flamingo Bass).
"That's what *she* said." (We know it's old...but it is still funny).

The famous "Bows" by Marguerite Derricks.
Earthquake Shimmy (Danny/Wilkie).
Wilkie riffing on his "Talking TomCat" app.
Wilkie riffing in general...all the time...it never ended.
"Oh My God!!! A Talking Muffin!"
Fembots
Jose Llana every night saying "Condom" when the Queen would say "Kingdom."
Fembots stomping as loud as they could on the Plexi-glass during the fight.

Swing Table Conversation: Laura Hall: "Jose looks hot in that suit."
Ryan Link: "Like a Filipino Johnny Depp."
Nicknames: 1) Jose Llana—Joser
2) Tanairi Vazquez—Tana
3) The Caterpillar legs: Nee Nee, wee wee, tee tee, etc.
4) Ladies in Waiting:
a. Laides in Hades
b. VBA's (Vocal Booth Assholes)
c. KD Lang
d. Wondertarts
5) The Knights: T-Cup, Rook, Lewis, Ace
Also: 1) New Year's Eve WIG PARTY in Tampa.
2) One day during previews, the cast was handed 70 pages of rewrites.
3) During tech rehearsals, Darren was lying in his "Dead Jack position" and Rupert Holmes said over the God-mic in a very sincere voice, "Darren, I want you to slowly say to Janet...I was tired of my lady...we'd been together too long...." (Insert explosive laughter).
4) Our Musical Director Jason Howland was the master prankster. His escapades:
a) Filled our trumpet player, CJ's trumpet with water.
b) Taped and tied the percussion instruments together to make them unplayable.
c) Enclosed the violinist in a sound-proof cage.
d) Taped people's music together.
e) Changed the accidentals in someone's score so they played in the wrong key.
f) He wore funny hats, Derek Ferguson's opening number suit from Tampa, a tear-away T-shirt with "BAM" for the end of Darren's "One Knight" number.
g) Conducted with an axe, pom poms, and a rose among many other items.
Mishaps Onstage: 1) In Tampa, we had an "All-Access-Pass" to the Tea Party, and Ed (White Rabbit) forgot to bring it onstage, so our Music Director, Jason, handed him his Stage Door Access pass from the pit.
2) Karen forgot to say "Off With Her Head." to Alice...her signature phrase.
3) In Tampa, the "Fembots" did choreographed ninja moves and then were supposed to spin off into the wings. One night, I spun and got dizzy, hit the set and went sprawling like a slip-and-slide into the wings. Lauren Lim Jackson tripped on me and fell right on top of me and we slid together.
4) There used to be a scene in which it snowed at the end after Jack died with ALL the characters onstage. One night every single piece of snow we had dumped on the stage. It was all over the leads and the floor and we just couldn't stop giggling because it was there through the final scene in the bedroom and the bows.
Coolest Thing About Being in This Show: The amazing people...including our Crew, Producers, Creatives, and Stage Managers. We were truly a family

The following shows closed shortly after the start of the 2010-2011 season with no changes to their casts from the previous year's Playbill Broadway Yearbook. *For complete details and photographs from these shows, please consult the 2009-2010 edition.*

First Preview:
February 15, 2010
Opened: March 4, 2010
Schoenfeld Theatre
Closed June 6, 2010 after
20 Previews and
108 Performances.

First Preview:
April 9, 2010
Opened: April 28, 2010
Friedman Theatre
Closed June 13, 2010 after
22 Previews and
54 Performances.

First Preview:
April 19. 2010
Opened: April 29, 2010
American Airlines Theatre
Closed July 11, 2010 after
11 Previews and
85 Performances.

First Preview:
April 14, 2010
Opened: April 26, 2010
Cort Theatre
Closed July 11, 2010 after
13 Previews and
88 Performances.

First Preview:
February 28, 2009
Opened: March 22, 2009
Jacobs Theatre
Closed June 6, 2010 after
24 Previews and
452 Performances.

First Preview:
March 6, 2009
Opened: March 31, 2009
Hirschfeld Theatre
Closed June 27, 2010 after
29 Previews and
519 Performances.

First Preview:
March 12, 2010
Opened: April 4, 2010
Music Box Theatre
Closed August 15, 2010 after
25 Previews and
153 Performances.

First Preview:
February 16, 2010
Opened: March 11, 2010
Hayes Theatre
Closed July 4, 2010 after
26 Previews and
132 Performances.

First Preview:
March 11, 2010
Opened: April 1, 2010
Golden Theatre
Closed June 27, 2010 after
22 Previews and
101 Performances.

First Preview:
March 19, 2010
Opened: April 22, 2010
Studio 54
Closed June 27, 2010 after
37 Previews and
76 Performances.

Events

Broadway Bares XX: "Strip-opoly"

June 20, 2010 at Roseland Ballroom

Photo by Gary J. Cooper

Photo by Rex Bonomelli

Photo by Gary J. Cooper

Photo by Matthew Murray

Photo by Gary J. Cooper

Broadway Bares XX: Strip-opoly, the annual Burlesque-style celebration of Broadway's buffest bodies, broke the million-dollar mark for the first time, June 10, 2010, raising $1,015,985 for Broadway Cares/ Equity Fights AIDS over two performances at the Roseland Ballroom.

Josh Rhodes, assistant choreographer for *The Drowsy Chaperone*, directed the fundraiser.

This year's show featured performances by guest stars from many current and recent shows, including Nick Adams, Kevin Burrows, Charles Busch, Kevin Chamberlin, Kristin Chenoweth, Jennifer Cody, Alan Cumming, Diana DeGarmo, Lea DeLaria, Felicia Finley, Katie Finneran, Barrett Foa, Debbie Gravitte, Julie Halston, Jackie Hoffman, Denis Jones, Jane Krakowski, Sebastian LaCause, Reichen Lehmkuhl, Norm Lewis, Lucy Liu, Julia Murney, Christopher Sieber, Rachelle Rak, Andrew Rannells, Bruce Vilanch, Lillias White and Vanessa Williams.

1. Charlie Williams (*Memphis*) as a bellhop hops to Anita Ward's "Ring My Bell."
2. Kristin Chenoweth (*Promises, Promises*) and Vanessa Williams (*Sondheim on Sondheim*) conclude the opening number by entering on a red velvet swing.
3. *God of Carnage* star Lucy Liu as the "Community Chest," and Reichen Lehmkuhl as "Community Change Purse" in the finale.
4. Rachelle Rak performs "Connecticut Avenue."
5. Euan Morton (top hat) bumps Chenoweth and Williams in "The Best Game in Town," by David Nehls.

Broadway Winners: The Award-Winning Music of Broadway

July 12, 2010 at Town Hall Theatre

Scott Siegel's fourth annual Summer Broadway Festival kicked off with "Broadway Winners: The Award-Winning Music of Broadway," a concert consisting of "thrilling Tony, Grammy, and Academy Award-winning music created on the Great White Way."

Directed by Alexander Gemignani and hosted by Scott Siegel, the cast included Michele Lee, Farah Alvin, Christine Andreas, Kate Baldwin, Christina Bianco, Bill Daugherty, John Easterlin, Marc Kudisch, William Michals, and Terri White. Gemignani also performed.

(L-R): Michele Lee, Christina Bianco, Christine Andreas, Kate Baldwin, Terri White and Farah Alvin.

The American Theatre Wing Spring Gala

June 7, 2010 at Cipriani 42nd Street

The American Theatre Wing's annual spring gala celebrated the centennial of Tony Award-winning composer Frank Loesser.

Titled "Heart and Soul: The Legacy of Frank Loesser," the evening boasted performances by Harry Connick, Jr., Megan Mullally, Kelli O'Hara and others. Loesser wrote scores for *Guys and Dolls*, *How To Succeed in Business Without Really Trying*, *The Most Happy Fella* and *Where's Charley?*, and founded Music Theatre International and Frank Music Corp.

(L-R): Alton F. White, Tshidi Manye, Chauntee Schuler, Gareth Saxe, and Ben Jeffrey at the American Theatre Wing's 2010 Annual Spring Gala at Cipriani 42nd Street.

Broadway Barks 12

July 10, 2010 in Shubert Alley

Broadway Barks 12, the annual dog and cat adopt-a-thon created and hosted by pals Bernadette Peters and Mary Tyler Moore to find homes for pets from city animal shelters, included celebrity presentations of the pets.

Among participants: Fred Applegate, Brooks Ashmanskas, Corbin Bleu, Veanne Cox, Erin Davie, John Dossett, Sean Hayes, Jackie Hoffman, Chad Kimball, Leigh Ann Larkin, Karen Olivo, Loretta Ables Sayre, Kevin Chamberlin, Katie Finneran, Ruthie Henshall, Hunter Ryan Herdlicka, Beth Leavel, Judy McLane, Jan Maxwell, Tony Shalhoub and Richard Thomas.

(L-R): Co-hosts Bernadette Peters and Mary Tyler Moore, with friend.

Actors Fund *They're Playing Our Song*

August 30, 2010 at John Jay College's Gerald W. Lynch Theatre

Photo by Krissie Fullerton

Tony Award winner Sutton Foster and actor-musician-Playbill.com columnist Seth Rudetsky joined forces for a concert version of Marvin Hamlisch, Carole Bayer Sager and Neil Simon's musical *They're Playing Our Song* to benefit the Actors Fund.

Rudetsky played wisecracking veteran songwriter Vernon Gersch; Foster played the kooky and offbeat lyricist Sonia Walsk.

The performance was directed and choreographed by Denis Jones. Steve Freeman was the concert's musical director.

Seth Rudetsky and Sutton Foster played songwriters and lovers in the staged reading.

Broadway in Bryant Park

Summer Thursdays 2010 in Bryant Park

Photo by Krissie Fullerton

Cast members from *Mary Poppins*, *Mamma Mia!*, *American Idiot*, *La Cage aux Folles*, *Million Dollar Quartet*, *The Fantasticks*, *Fela!*, *Avenue Q*, *Lion King*, *The Addams Family* and other Broadway and Off-Broadway shows rocked Bryant Park at lunchtime Thursdays throughout the summer of 2010.

The free outdoor concert series gives the public samples from current shows.

Members of the *Mary Poppins* cast perform "Supercalifragilisticexpialidocious" on the outdoor stage.

Broadway Softball League Championship

August 19, 2010 at Heckscher Fields in Central Park

The team from the Actors' Federal Credit Union beat the Actors' Equity team in a 7-6 squeaker to win the championship of the 2010 Broadway Softball League Koehler Division.

The win came after sixteen weeks of Thursday afternoon softball games in Central Park, played by teams consisting of employees from Broadway shows and organizations at Heckscher Fields. AFCU beat the team from the Nederlander Organization in the semifinals.

The championship game was a full nine-inning game, in contrast to the seven-inning regular-season games.

The Actors' Federal Credit Union team gathers before the championship game.

Photo by Krissie Fullerton

The 19th Annual Broadway on Broadway

September 12, 2010 in Times Square

Kelsey Grammer (*La Cage aux Folles*) hosted the 19th Annual "Broadway on Broadway" concert in Times Square, which drew an estimated 40,000 to hear performers from 20 Broadway shows.

The free lunchtime concert featured current and upcoming shows performing numbers backed by a 30-piece orchestra.

Among those in attendance were cast members of *The Addams Family, American Idiot, Billy Elliot The Musical, Chicago, Elf, Fela!, In the Heights, La Cage Aux Folles, The Lion King, Mamma Mia!, Memphis, Million Dollar Quartet, Priscilla Queen of the Desert, The Phantom of the Opera, Promises, Promises, Rain, Rock of Ages, The Scottsboro Boys* and *West Side Story.*

The concert was presented by The Broadway League and the Times Square Alliance.

1. Sahr Ngaujah of *Fela!* plays the sax.
2. (Center): Dayton Tavares and Alex Ko with members of the *Billy Elliot* ensemble perform "Expressing Yourself."
3. (Center): Charlotte d'Amboise and John O'Hurley with members of the ensemble of *Chicago* sing "We Both Reached for the Gun."
4. Beth Leavel hugs Matthew Gumley in a number from *Elf.*
5. (L-R): Brooks Ashmanskas and Peter Benson perform "Where Can You Take a Girl?" from *Promises, Promises.*
6. Joey Curatolo as Paul McCartney from *Rain.*
7. Karen Olivo and Lin-Manuel Miranda of *In the Heights* perform "Empire State Of Mind" by Jay-Z and Alicia Keys.

Broadway Flea Market and Grand Auction

September 26, 2010 in Shubert Alley

T he 24th Annual Broadway Flea Market and Grand Auction raised a total of $476,917 for Broadway Cares/Equity Fights AIDS.

Seventy-two tables selling a variety of theatre memorabilia raised a total of $239,342. The booths that raised the most money this year were the ones hosted by *Wicked* ($19,834) and "Broadway Beat" ($12,171).

The Silent Auction raised $55,925 by selling 114 items. The top item sold was a musical phrase from the *A Little Night Music* song "Soon" handwritten and signed by Stephen Sondheim. It went for $3,500. A *Wicked* "For Good" musical phrase, handwritten and signed by Stephen Schwartz went for $2,900.

The day ended with a Grand Auction that raised $126,650 from 44 lots, including walk-on roles, backstage visits, and opening night tickets. The top draw was a walk-on in *Wicked*, sold for $16,500.

Among the Broadway and daytime TV stars who raised $9,765 at the Autograph Table and Celebrity Photo Booths: Kate Baldwin, Bryan Batt, Heidi Blickenstaff, Mario Cantone, Kathleen Chalfant, Kristin Chenoweth, Jason Danieley, Malcolm Gets, Mandy Gonzalez, Julie Halston, Ann Harada, Sean Hayes, Gregory Jbara, Andy Karl, Levi Kreis, Andrea McArdle, Marin Mazzie, Julia Murney, Donna Murphy, Bebe Neuwirth, Phyllis Newman, Kelli O'Hara, Denis O'Hare, Orfeh, Carole Shelley, Jordin Sparks, Elizabeth Stanley, John Tartaglia and Julie White.

1. Among this year's treasures, a PLAYBILL apparently autographed by original cast member Barbra Streisand.
2. Montego Glover and Chad Kimball of *Memphis* at the autograph booth.
3. Patrick Wilson of *The Full Monty*.
4. Alice Ripley of *Next to Normal*.
5. Jim Caruso (*Liza's at the Palace...*) has a panicked moment as he interviews Susan Blackwell (*[title of show]*).
6. Cherry Jones (*Mrs. Warren's Profession*) and Bobby Steggert (*Ragtime*).

Broadway Bears XIV

March 6, 2011 at BB King Blues Club & Grill

Broadway Bears XIV, the annual auction of one-of-a-kind, theatrically costumed and celebrity-autographed teddy bears, raised $103,905 for Broadway Cares/Equity Fights AIDS.

Broadway lovers and teddy bear collectors came together for the event, hosted by Bryan Batt with Lorna Kelly reprising her role as auctioneer. More than 40 specially made Broadway Bears, each dressed in original, handmade costumes representing legendary theatrical characters, were auctioned to the highest bidder. Top bids went to:

My Fair Lady—Eliza Doolittle in her pink silk organza dress and hat from Ascot, was designed by Richard St. Clair. Autographed by Julie Andrews, the bear sold for $14,000.

Into the Woods—The Witch, designed by Ariel Pellman and signed by Bernadette Peters and Stephen Sondheim, brought in $6,500.

Rock of Ages—Designed by Karl Ruckdeschel and autographed by Tony Award-nominee Constantine Maroulis, the bear fetched $6,000.

Hairspray—Signed by Broadway's original Link Larkin, Matthew Morrison, now starring on the television hit "Glee," sold for $5,500. The bear was designed by Susan Bolt.

Spider-Man: Turn Off the Dark—Designed by Katie Falk, the Spidey bear earned $5,250.

Spamalot—Designed by Amy Micallef and autographed by original Broadway cast member Hank Azaria, brought in $5,000.

1. Designer Barak Stribling with the bear representing Elizabeth Taylor in *Private Lives.*
2. Host Bryan Batt with the *Spider-Man: Turn Off the Dark* bear.
3. Batt introduces the Jennyanydots bear from *Cats.*
4. Christopher Sieber with the bear representing Sir Lancelot from his show, *Spamalot.*

Broadway Melody Makers

October 15, 2010 at Town Hall Theatre

Town Hall's sixth annual Broadway Cabaret Festival—created, written and hosted by Scott Siegel—kicked off with "Broadway Melody Makers," a concert of Broadway tunes written by Jerome Kern, George Gershwin, Richard Rodgers, Cole Porter, Harold Arlen, Irving Berlin, Jule Styne and Cy Coleman.

The event showcased the talents of Tony winners Judy Kaye, Alice Ripley and Michael Cerveris along with Mary Testa, Tom Wopat and Nellie McKay. Scott Coulter directed with musical direction by Ross Patterson.

Left: Alice Ripley.
Right: Nellie McKay.

Halloween Kids' Night on Broadway

October 31, 2010 at Madame Tussauds and throughout the Broadway Theatre District

Costumed children thronged Times Square for Halloween Kids' Night on Broadway, for which kids ages 6-18 got to attend a Broadway show for free (when accompanied by a paying adult) but also gave access to a pre-theatre costume party at Madame Tussauds and trick-or-treating at Broadway stage doors following the matinees.

The Madame Tussauds party included a tour of the famed wax attraction (including wax figures of Nathan Lane, Rafiki, Matthew Broderick, Frankenstein, Dracula, et al.), plus participation in a "Broadway dance studio" with cast members from Broadway shows; face painting; Broadway costume activities; "Autograph Alley"; a station for distribution of UNICEF donation boxes; games; information about Camp Broadway, Broadway Kids Care, Broadway Green Alliance and more.

1. Laura Michelle Kelly (*Mary Poppins*) embraces Ben Milstein dressed as Michael Jackson.
2. PLAYBILL publisher Philip S. Birsh chucks the wax likeness of Nathan Lane under the chin at the event's kickoff at Madame Tussauds accompanied by trick-or-treaters and (R) Charlotte St. Martin of The Broadway League.
3. Two little girls dressed as Wednesday Addams and one (R) as Morticia from *The Addams Family*.
4. (L-R): Ryan Bastianelli dressed as Bert from *Mary Poppins* meets Gavin Lee, originator of the role on stage.
5. (L-R): Julia, Cheryl, Jessica and Wayne Slaughter trick-or-treat at the Gershwin Theatre.

22nd Annual "Gypsy of the Year"

December 6-7, 2010 at the New Amsterdam Theatre

Photos by Krissie Fullerton

1. To celebrate the 60th anniversary of the Gypsy Robe, several of the robes were displayed in a dance choreographed by Shea Sullivan.
2. Bernadette Peters (C) helped Kristin Chenoweth and Sean Hayes (R) celebrate the award for *Promises Promises* raising the most money of any Broadway show.
3. Carol Channing and dancers recreated the title song from *Hello, Dolly!* for the star's 90th birthday.
4. The Cagelles of *La Cage aux Folles* auditioned for their own version of *Annie*.
5. Lin-Manuel Miranda (C) hosted a reunion of actors who appeared in his *In the Heights* during its three-year run.
6. Best Presentation award went to "The Puppet Master" from the cast of *Rock of Ages*.

A pair of acrobatic dancers performing a sinuous *pas de deux* titled "The Puppet Master" earned *Rock of Ages* the title of 2010 Gypsy of the Year/Best Stage Presentation.

The national tour of *Jersey Boys* proved to be the champion earner, bring in $285,398 for Broadway Cares/Equity Fights AIDS. The annual fundraiser took in a total of $3,776,720, the third-highest gross in the 22-year history of the event.

First runner-up for Best Stage Presentation went to *The Addams Family* for a gag-laced monologue by young Adam Riegler (Pugsley) parodying the "It Gets Better" campaign to stop schoolyard bullying, assuring incoming Broadway shows that they can survive bullying by hostile critics and bloggers and become a hit like *Addams Family*.

Other fundraising awards:

Runner-up National Tour fundraisers: *Wicked* (Emerald City Tour) with $247,571, *Wicked* (Munchkinland Tour) with $236,352, and *Shrek* with $137,888.

Top Broadway musical fundraisers: *Promises, Promises* with $195,011, *Wicked* with $181,609, *Billy Elliot* with $149,268, and *The Addams Family* with $145,915.

Top Broadway play fundraiser was *Driving Miss Daisy* with $94,044, followed by runner-up *A Life in the Theatre*, which collected $72,452.

Judges included Marin Mazzie and Jason Danieley (*Next to Normal*), Alison Fraser (*The Divine Sister*), Boyd Gaines (*Driving Miss Daisy*), Bebe Neuwirth (*The Addams Family*), Patricia White (President, Local 764 Theatrical Wardrobe Union) and Nick Wyman (President of Actors' Equity).

Among the shows that performed dances or skits: *The Addams Family; Billy Elliot; Bloody Bloody Andrew Jackson; Chicago; Fela!; In The Heights; La Cage aux Folles; The Lion King; Mamma Mia; Mary Poppins, Promises, Promises; Rock of Ages; Wicked* and *Women on the Verge of a Nervous Breakdown.*

Broadway Backwards

February 7, 2011 at the Longacre Theatre

The annual "Broadway Backwards" concert, featuring male singers performing songs traditionally sung by women and women singing tunes written for men, raised a record-breaking $281,243 to benefit Broadway Cares/Equity Fights AIDS and The Lesbian, Gay, Bisexual & Transgender Community Center.

The one-night-only event boasted the talents of Tony winners Denis O'Hare, Debra Monk, Len Cariou, Hinton Battle, Karen Olivo and Lillias White, along with F. Murray Abraham, Brooks Ashmanskas, Colman Domingo, Mandy Gonzalez, Clay Aiken, Tituss Burgess, Robin De Jesús, Jose Llana, Bobby Steggert, Tony Yazbeck, Mo Rocca, Jan Maxwell and many others.

1. Bebe Neuwirth (*The Addams Family*) returned to her *Chicago* roots, this time taking on the role of scheming lawyer Billy Flynn on the song "All I Care About is Love," surrounded by fan-whirling chorus girls.
2. As rebuke of the military's "Don't Ask, Don't Tell" policy toward gay troops, Alan Cumming performed a military-themed "Don't Tell Mama" from *Cabaret*, the show in which he won a Tony Award.
3. Male members of the chorus perform "Cell Block Tango" from *Chicago*.

Nothing Like a Dame: A Party for Comden and Green

November 1, 2010 at the Laura Pels Theater

"Nothing Like a Dame: A Party for Comden and Green," featuring Hal Prince, Victoria Clark, Charles Busch and Howard McGillin, celebrated the lifelong collaboration of lyricists and librettists Betty Comden and Adolph Green as a benefit for the Phyllis Newman Women's Health Initiative of The Actors Fund.

A host of actors who appeared in the original and revival casts of Comden and Green's work participated in the event, including Nancy Anderson, Polly Bergen, Charles Busch, Victoria Clark, Debbie Gravitte, Hunter Ryan Herdlicka, Marc Kudisch, Jessica Molaskey, Jennifer Barnhart, Donna McKechnie and Julia Murney.

(L-R): Mary Testa, Liz Larsen and Mario Cantone.

Miscast 2011

March 14, 2011 at the Hammerstein Ballroom

Photos by Krissie Fullerton

Ana Gasteyer, Laura Osnes, Christian Borle, Nicole Parker, Justin Guarini, Alison Jaye Horowitz, Kelsey Fowler and Lisa Howard performed songs from roles in which they would never be cast at "Miscast 2011," the 25th anniversary gala for MCC Theatre, hosted by Andy Cohen.

This year's honorees included MCC alumni Jo Bonney, Patrick Breen, Charles Busch, Norbert Leo Butz, Kathleen Chalfant, Veanne Cox, Rosemarie DeWitt, David Greenspan, Michael Greif, Peter Hedges, T.R. Knight, Swoosie Kurtz, Neil LaBute, Melissa Leo, Judith Light, Joe Mantello, Elizabeth Marvel, Brían F. O'Byrne, Sarah Paulson, Amanda Peet, Piper Perabo, Adina Porter, Connie Ray, Thomas Sadoski, Liev Schreiber, Leigh Silverman, Lucy Thurber, Marisa Tomei, Frederick Weller and Michael Weller.

1. Ana Gasteyer
2. Joshua Henry
3. Laura Osnes
4. Christian Borle
5. Kelsey Fowler and Alison Jaye Horowitz

24 Hour Plays on Broadway

November 14-15 at the American Airlines Theatre

Cheyenne Jackson, Anthony Mackie, Julia Stiles, Sam Rockwell, Gloria Estefan, America Ferrera, Kathy Najimy and Elijah Wood were part of the starry cast of the 2010 edition of "24 Hour Plays on Broadway."

Montblanc sponsors the event, in which actors, playwrights, directors and technicians gather to write, rehearse and perform an evening of short plays in a single 24-hour marathon.

The event benefits the Urban Arts Partnership, a not-for-profit organization that brings arts education programs to New York City public school students.

(L-R): Participants Tracie Thoms, Julia Stiles, Gaby Hoffman and Rachel Dratch

Photo by Joseph Marzullo/WENN

The 25th Annual Easter Bonnet Competition

April 25-26, 2011 at the Minskoff Theatre

The 25th annual Broadway Cares/Equity Fights AIDS Easter Bonnet Competition raised a near-record $3,706,085 in six weeks of nightly curtain-call appeals. The sum was revealed at the the second of two performance of skits, songs and dances that make up the unique fundraiser-show.

The total bested last year's $3.27 million but fell just short of the $3,734,000 record set in 2007. This year's total was raised by 52 participating Broadway, Off-Broadway and touring shows.

Daniel Radcliffe (*How To Succeed in Business Without Really Trying*), Harvey Fierstein (*La Cage aux Folles*) and Sutton Foster (*Anything Goes*) presented the performance/bonnet awards. Radcliffe's show was the top money-maker among Broadway productions, bringing in $271,916.

Various companies of the musical *Wicked* took three major fundraising awards. The show was the first runner-up among Broadway shows, bringing in $165,979. The "Emerald City" touring company was also a big moneymaker among national tours, taking in $242,212. But the "Munchkinland" touring company of *Wicked* flew highest of all, winning the grand fundraising prize for the second year in a row, collecting $360,021 in the fight against AIDS.

The company of Broadway's *La Cage aux Folles* took the top prize for bonnet presentation, with "25 Years of Easter Bonnet," hosted by current co-star Christopher Sieber.

1. (L-R): Sutton Foster, an unidentified *La Cage aux Folles* dancer and Daniel Radcliffe present an award.
2. The winner for bonnet design: from *Bengal Tiger in the Baghdad Zoo*, a replica of the show's cage set containing an incarcerated toy tiger.
3. Don Richard and Jennifer Cody reprise their tart-tongued *Urinetown* characters.
4. A bonnet from the opening number, parodying the TV show "Glee."
5. All the bonnets are displayed in the finale.
6. Runner-up for best performance: *Addams Family* cast members Adam Riegler (Pugsley) and Zachary James (Lurch) do a soft shoe in costume to a Frank Sinatra song.

The Antoinette Perry (Tony) Awards

June 12, 2011 at the Beacon Theatre

The Book of Mormon, War Horse, Anything Goes and *The Normal Heart* won the major production categories at the 2011 Tony Awards.

The 65th annual awards, representing excellence in Broadway theatre for the 2010-2011 season, were presented at the Beacon Theatre in a ceremony hosted by Neil Patrick Harris and broadcast on CBS-TV. The nominees and recipients of the 65th Annual Antoinette Perry "Tony" Awards follow. Winners are listed in **boldface**, with an asterisk (*).

Best Musical
The Book of Mormon
Catch Me If You Can
The Scottsboro Boys
Sister Act

Best Play
Good People by David Lindsay-Abaire
Jerusalem by Jez Butterworth
The Motherf**ker with the Hat by Stephen Adly Guirgis
***War Horse* by Nick Stafford**

Best Revival of a Musical
Anything Goes
How to Succeed in Business Without Really Trying

1. Winners (L-R): co-author Matt Stone, co-author and co-director Trey Parker, producer Scott Rudin, co-director and choreographer Casey Nicholaw, producer Anne Garefino, co-author Robert Lopez, and orchestrators Stephen Oremus and Larry Hochman of *The Book of Mormon*.
2. (L-R): Norbert Leo Butz of *Catch Me If You Can*, Sutton Foster of *Anything Goes* and Mark Rylance of *Jerusalem*.
3. Nikki M. James of *The Book of Mormon*.
4. John Benjamin Hickey of *The Normal Heart*.

The Tony Awards

Best Revival of a Play
Arcadia
The Importance of Being Earnest
The Merchant of Venice
*The Normal Heart

Best Performance by an Actor in a Leading Role in a Musical
*Norbert Leo Butz, *Catch Me If You Can*
Josh Gad, *The Book of Mormon*
Joshua Henry, *The Scottsboro Boys*
Andrew Rannells, *The Book of Mormon*
Tony Sheldon, *Priscilla Queen of the Desert*

Best Performance by an Actress in a Leading Role in a Musical
*Sutton Foster, *Anything Goes*
Beth Leavel, *Baby It's You!*
Patina Miller, *Sister Act*
Donna Murphy, *The People in the Picture*

Best Best Performance by an Actor in a Leading Role in a Play
Brian Bedford, *The Importance of Being Earnest*
Bobby Cannavale, *The Motherf**ker with the Hat*
Joe Mantello, *The Normal Heart*
Al Pacino, *The Merchant of Venice*
*Mark Rylance, *Jerusalem*

Best Performance by an Actress in a Leading Role in a Play
Nina Arianda, *Born Yesterday*
*Frances McDormand, Good People
Lily Rabe, *The Merchant of Venice*
Vanessa Redgrave, *Driving Miss Daisy*
Hannah Yelland, *Brief Encounter*

Best Performance by an Actor in a Featured Role in a Musical
Colman Domingo, *The Scottsboro Boys*
Adam Godley, *Anything Goes*
*John Larroquette, *How to Succeed in Business Without Really Trying*
Forrest McClendon, *The Scottsboro Boys*
Rory O'Malley, *The Book of Mormon*

Best Performance by an Actress in a Featured Role in a Musical
Laura Benanti, *Women on the Verge of a Nervous Breakdown*
Tammy Blanchard, *How to Succeed in Business Without Really Trying*
Victoria Clark, *Sister Act*
*Nikki M. James, *The Book of Mormon*
Patti LuPone, *Women on the Verge of a Nervous Breakdown*

Best Performance by an Actor in a Featured Role in a Play
Mackenzie Crook, *Jerusalem*
Billy Crudup, *Arcadia*
*John Benjamin Hickey, *The Normal Heart*
Arian Moayed, *Bengal Tiger at the Baghdad Zoo*
Yul Vázquez, *The Motherf**ker with the Hat*

1. Tony winner Ellen Barkin of *The Normal Heart*.
2. Nominee Al Pacino of *The Merchant of Venice*.
3. Nominee Patti LuPone (C) of *Women on the Verge of a Nervous Breakdown* flanked by her son and husband on the red carpet.
4. Nominee Victoria Clark of *Sister Act*.

Best Performance by an Actress in a Featured Role in a Play
*Ellen Barkin, *The Normal Heart*
Edie Falco, *The House of Blue Leaves*
Judith Light, *Lombardi*
Joanna Lumley, *La Bête*
Elizabeth Rodriguez, *The Motherf**ker with the Hat*

Best Direction of a Musical
Rob Ashford, *How to Succeed in Business Without Really Trying*
Kathleen Marshall, *Anything Goes*
*Casey Nicholaw and Trey Parker, *The Book of Mormon*
Susan Stroman, *The Scottsboro Boys*

Best Direction of a Play
*Marianne Elliott and Tom Morris, *War Horse*
Joel Grey & George C. Wolfe, *The Normal Heart*
Anna D. Shapiro, *The Motherf**ker with the Hat*
Daniel Sullivan, *The Merchant of Venice*

Best Choreography
Rob Ashford, *How to Succeed in Business Without Really Trying*
*Kathleen Marshall, *Anything Goes*
Casey Nicholaw, *The Book of Mormon*
Susan Stroman, *The Scottsboro Boys*

Best Scenic Design of a Musical
Beowulf Boritt, *The Scottsboro Boys*
Derek McLane, *Anything Goes*
*Scott Pask, *The Book of Mormon*
Donyale Werle, *Bloody Bloody Andrew Jackson*

Best Scenic Design of a Play
Todd Rosenthal, *The Motherf**ker with the Hat*
*Rae Smith, *War Horse*
Ultz, *Jerusalem*
Mark Wendland, *The Merchant of Venice*

Best Costume Design of a Musical
*Tim Chappel & Lizzy Gardiner, *Priscilla Queen of the Desert*
Martin Pakledinaz, *Anything Goes*
Ann Roth, *The Book of Mormon*
Catherine Zuber, *How to Succeed in Business Without Really Trying*

The Tony Awards

Best Lighting Design of a Musical
Ken Billington, *The Scottsboro Boys*
Howell Binkley, *How to Succeed in Business Without Really Trying*
Peter Kaczorowski, *Anything Goes*
*__Brian MacDevitt, The Book of Mormon__

Best Lighting Design of a Play
*__Paule Constable, War Horse__
David Lander, *Bengal Tiger at the Baghdad Zoo*
Kenneth Posner, *The Merchant of Venice*
Mimi Jordan Sherin, *Jerusalem*

Best Sound Design of a Musical
Peter Hylenski, *The Scottsboro Boys*
Steve Canyon Kennedy, *Catch Me If You Can*
Brian Ronan, *Anything Goes*
*__Brian Ronan, The Book of Mormon__

Best Sound Design of a Play
Acme Sound Partners & Cricket S. Myers, *Bengal Tiger at the Baghdad Zoo*
Simon Baker, *Brief Encounter*
Ian Dickinson for Autograph, *Jerusalem*
*__Christopher Shutt, War Horse__

Best Book of a Musical
Bloody Bloody Andrew Jackson, Alex Timbers
*__The Book of Mormon, Trey Parker, Robert Lopez and Matt Stone__
The Scottsboro Boys, David Thompson
Sister Act, Cheri Steinkellner, Bill Steinkellner and Douglas Carter Beane

Best Original Score (Music and/or Lyrics) Written for the Theatre
*__The Book of Mormon, Music & Lyrics: Trey Parker, Robert Lopez and Matt Stone__
The Scottsboro Boys, Music & Lyrics: John Kander and Fred Ebb
Sister Act, Music: Alan Menken. Lyrics: Glenn Slater
Women on the Verge of a Nervous Breakdown, Music & Lyrics: David Yazbek

Best Orchestrations
Doug Besterman, *How to Succeed in Business Without Really Trying*
Larry Hochman, *The Scottsboro Boys*
*__Larry Hochman and Stephen Oremus, The Book of Mormon__
Marc Shaiman and Larry Blank, *Catch Me If You Can*

Special Tony Awards for Lifetime Achievement in the Theatre
Athol Fugard
Philip J. Smith

Tony Honors for Excellence in the Theatre
William Berloni
The Drama Book Shop
Sharon Jensen and Alliance for Inclusion in the Arts

Isabelle Stevenson Award
Eve Ensler

Regional Theatre Tony Award
Lookingglass Theatre Company, Chicago, Illinois

Special Tony Award
Handspring Puppet Company

Here's a tally of the 2011 Tony Award winners:

The Book of Mormon 9
War Horse 5
The Normal Heart 3
Anything Goes 3
Catch Me If You Can 1
Good People 1
How to Succeed in Business Without Really Trying 1
The Importance of Being Earnest 1
Jerusalem 1
Priscilla Queen of the Desert 1

1. On the Red Carpet: playwright (L-R): Larry Kramer, director George C. Wolfe and star Joe Mantello of *The Normal Heart*.
2. Tony host Neil Patrick Harris.
3. Nominee Vanessa Redgrave (*Driving Miss Daisy*).
4. Nominee Arian Moayed (R) with Krissy Shields.

Photos by Joseph Marzullo/WENN

Other Theatre Awards

Covering the 2010-2011 Broadway Season

PULITZER PRIZE FOR DRAMA
Clybourne Park by Bruce Norris

NY DRAMA CRITICS' CIRCLE AWARDS
Best Play: *Good People*
Best Musical: *The Book of Mormon*
Best Foreign Play: *Jerusalem*
Special Citations: Revival of *The Normal Heart*; Mark Rylance for *La Bête* and *Jerusalem;* and the direction, design and puppetry of *War Horse.*

DRAMA DESK AWARDS
Outstanding Play: *War Horse*
Outstanding Musical: *The Book of Mormon*
Outstanding Revival of a Play: *The Normal Heart*
Outstanding Revival of a Musical: *Anything Goes*
Outstanding Actor in a Play: Bobby Cannavale, *The Motherf**cker With the Hat*
Outstanding Actress in a Play: Frances McDormand, *Good People*
Outstanding Actor in a Musical: Norbert Leo Butz, *Catch Me If You Can*
Outstanding Actress in a Musical: Sutton Foster, *Anything Goes*
Outstanding Featured Actor in a Play: Brian Bedford, *The Importance of Being Earnest*
Outstanding Featured Actress in a Play: Edie Falco, *The House of Blue Leaves*
Outstanding Featured Actor in a Musical: John Larroquette, *How to Succeed in Business Without Really Trying*
Outstanding Featured Actress in a Musical: Laura Benanti, *Women on the Verge of a Nervous Breakdown*
Outstanding Director of a Play: Joel Grey and George C. Wolfe, *The Normal Heart*
Outstanding Director of a Musical: Casey Nicholaw and Trey Parker, *The Book of Mormon*
Outstanding Choreography: Kathleen Marshall, *Anything Goes*
Outstanding Music: Trey Parker, Robert Lopez and Matt Stone, *The Book of Mormon*
Outstanding Lyrics: Trey Parker, Robert Lopez and Matt Stone, *The Book of Mormon*
Outstanding Book of a Musical: Adam Mathias, *See Rock City & Other Destinations* (OB)
Outstanding Orchestrations: Larry Hochman and Stephen Oremus, *The Book of Mormon*
Outstanding Revue: *Rain: A Tribute to the Beatles on Broadway*
Outstanding Music in a Play: Wayne Barker, *Peter and the Starcatchers* (OB)
Outstanding Set Design: Derek McLane, *Anything Goes*
Outstanding Costume Design: Tim Chappel and Lizzy Gardiner, *Priscilla Queen of the Desert: The Musical*
Outstanding Lighting Design: David Lander, *Bengal Tiger at the Baghdad Zoo*
Outstanding Sound Design in a Musical: Brian Ronan, *Anything Goes*
Outstanding Sound Design in a Play: Acme Sound Partners and Cricket S. Myers, *Bengal Tiger at the Baghdad Zoo*
Outstanding Solo Performance: John Leguizamo, *Ghetto Klown*
Unique Theatrical Experience: *Sleep No More* (OB)
Outstanding Ensemble Performances: The casts of *In Transit* (OB) and *The Normal Heart*
Special Award to the creative team of *War Horse* for thrilling stagecraft: Paule Constable, Marianne Elliott, 59 Productions, Adrian Kohler with Basil Jones for Handspring Puppet Company, Tom Morris, Rae Smith, Christopher Shutt, Toby Sedgwick, Adrian Sutton and John Tams.
Special Award to The New Group and Artistic Director Scott Elliott
Special Award to The Pearl Theatre Company
Special Award to A.R. Gurney
Special Award to Reed Birney

OUTER CRITICS CIRCLE AWARDS
Outstanding New Broadway Play: *War Horse*
Outstanding New Broadway Musical: *The Book of Mormon*
Outstanding New Off-Broadway Play: *Other Desert Cities* (OB)
Outstanding New Off-Broadway Musical: *The Kid* (OB)
Outstanding New Score (Bway or Off): *The Book of Mormon*
Outstanding Revival of a Play: *The Normal Heart*
Outstanding Revival of a Musical: *Anything Goes*
Outstanding Director of a Play (Lucille Lortel Award): Marianne Elliott & Tom Morris, *War Horse*
Outstanding Director of a Musical: Casey Nicholaw & Trey Parker, *The Book of Mormon*
Outstanding Choreographer: Kathleen Marshall, *Anything Goes*
Outstanding Set Design: Neil Murray, *Brief Encounter*
Outstanding Costume Design: Tim Chappel & Lizzy Gardiner, *Priscilla Queen of the Desert*
Outstanding Lighting Design: Paule Constable, *War Horse*
Outstanding Actor in a Play: Mark Rylance, *Jerusalem*
Outstanding Actress in a Play: (tie) Nina Arianda, *Born Yesterday* and Frances McDormand, *Good People*
Outstanding Actor in a Musical: Josh Gad, *The Book of Mormon*
Outstanding Actress in a Musical: Sutton Foster, *Anything Goes*
Outstanding Featured Actor in a Play: Brian Bedford, *The Importance of Being Earnest*
Outstanding Featured Actress in a Play: Elizabeth Rodriguez, *The Motherf**ker With the Hat*

Presenter Daniel Radcliffe (C) flanked by Joel Grey (L) and George C. Wolfe, co-winners of the 2011 Drama Desk Award as Outstanding Director of a Play for *The Normal Heart.*

Catch Me If You Can cast members Angie Schworer (L) and Rachel de Benedet (R) help Norbert Leo Butz celebrate winning the Astaire Award for Best Male Dancer on Broadway.

Other Theatre Awards

Covering the 2010-2011 Broadway Season

Outstanding Featured Actor in a Musical:
Adam Godley, *Anything Goes*
Outstanding Featured Actress in a Musical:
Laura Benanti, *Women on the Verge of a Nervous Breakdown*
Outstanding Solo Performance: John Leguizamo, *Ghetto Klown*
John Gassner Award (New American Play):
Matthew Lopez, *The Whipping Man* (OB)
Special Achievement Awards: Ellen Barkin for her Outstanding Broadway Debut in *The Normal Heart*
Adrian Kohler with Basil Jones for Handspring Puppet Company for puppet design, fabrication and direction for *War Horse*

THE DRAMA LEAGUE AWARDS
Distinguished Production of a Play: *War Horse*
Distinguished Production of a Musical: *The Book of Mormon*
Distinguished Revival of a Play: *The Normal Heart*
Distinguished Revival of a Musical: *Anything Goes*
Distinguished Performance Award: Mark Rylance, *Jerusalem* and *La Bête*

THEATRE WORLD AWARDS
For Outstanding Broadway or Off-Broadway debuts:
Ellen Barkin, *The Normal Heart*
Desmin Borges, *The Elaborate Entrance of Chad Deity* (OB)
Halley Feiffer, *The House of Blue Leaves*
Grace Gummer, *Arcadia*
Rose Hemingway, *How to Succeed in Business Without Really Trying*
John Larroquette, *How to Succeed in Business Without Really Trying*
Heather Lind, *The Merchant of Venice*
Patina Miller, *Sister Act*
Arian Moayed, *Bengal Tiger at the Baghdad Zoo*
Jim Parsons, *The Normal Heart*
Zachary Quinto, *Angels in America: A Gay Fantasia on National Themes* (OB)
Tony Sheldon, *Priscilla Queen of the Desert*
Loudon Award for Excellence: Seth Numrich of *War Horse*
Lunt-Fontanne Award for Ensemble Excellence: The cast of *The Motherf**ker With the Hat*: Bobby Cannavale, Chris Rock, Annabella Sciorra, Elizabeth Rodriguez and Yul Vázquez

CLARENCE DERWENT AWARDS
From Actors' Equity for "most promising female and male performers on the New York metropolitan scene."
Tracee Chimo, *Bachelorette* (OB)
Santino Fontana, *The Importance of Being Earnest*

Susan Stroman beams after being named Best Choreographer on Broadway at the Fred and Adele Astaire Awards for her work on *The Scottsboro Boys*.

RICHARD SEFF AWARDS
From Actors' Equity, to "female and male character actors 50 years of age or older."
Deirdre O'Connell, *In the Wake* (OB)
Reed Birney, *A Small Fire* and *Tigers Be Still* (OB)

OTHER ACTORS' EQUITY AWARDS
Joe A. Callaway Award for best performances in a classic play in the New York metropolitan area: Lily Rabe of *The Merchant of Venice* and Matthew Rauch of *The Duchess of Malfi* (OB)
St. Clair Bayfield Award for the best supporting performance by an actor in a Shakespearean play in the New York metropolitan area: Charles Kimbrough, *The Merchant of Venice*

ACCA Award for Outstanding Broadway Chorus: the cast of *Fela!*
Extraordinary Excellence in Diversity on Broadway Award: *The Merchant of Venice*

THE IRENE SHARAFF AWARDS
From the Theatre Development Fund, for outstanding costume design
Robert L.B. Tobin Award for Sustained Excellence in Theatrical Design: Robin Wagner
Artisan Award: Michael-Jon Costumes
Lifetime Achievement Award for Costume Design: Lewis Brown
Young Master Award: Olivera Gajic

FRED AND ADELE ASTAIRE AWARDS
Best Choreographer on Broadway: Susan Stroman, *The Scottsboro Boys*
Best Female Dancer on Broadway: Sutton Foster, *Anything Goes*
Best Male Dancer on Broadway: Norbert Leo Butz, *Catch Me If You Can*
Douglas Watt Lifetime Achievement Award: Jacques d'Amboise

HENRY HEWES DESIGN AWARDS
Announced in August 2010 for work in the 2009-2010 Season
Scenic Design: Donyale Werle for *Bloody Bloody Andrew Jackson*
Costume Design: Martin Pakledinaz for *Lend Me a Tenor*
Lighting Design: Kevin Adams for *American Idiot*
Notable Effects: Jeff Cowie, David M. Barber, David C. Woolard, Rui Rita, Jan Hartley and John Gromada for *The Orphans' Home Cycle* (OB)

GRAMMY AWARD
Best Musical Show Album: *American Idiot*

(L-R): Dan Lauria, Judith Light (*Lombardi*), Kathleen Turner (*High*) and Jim Belushi (*Born Yesterday*) at the Drama League Awards.

Faculty

The Shubert Organization

Philip J. Smith
Chairman and co-CEO

Robert E. Wankel
President and co-CEO

Photos by Ben Strothmann

Coalition of Broadway Unions and Guilds (COBUG)

Photo by Brian Mapp

Seated (L-R): Daniel Dashman (Local 798), Mickey Fox (Local 1), Kimberly Rimbold (Actors' Equity), Gene McElwain (Local 751), Anthony DePaulo (IATSE), Tino Gagliardi (Local 802), Patricia White (Local 764), Frank Connolly (Local 817), Bart Daudelin (Local 764)
Standing (L-R):), Mauro Melleno (SDC), Laura Penn (SDC), David Faux (Dramatists Guild), Nick Calledin (ATPAM), Lawrence Paone (Local 751), Carl Mulert (USA Local 829), Mary Donovan (Local 802), Mary McColl (Actors' Equity), Rick Berg (Actors' Equity), Nick Wyman (Actors' Equity), Evan Shoemake (SDC).

Faculty

The Nederlander Organization

James M. Nederlander
Chairman

James L. Nederlander
President

Photo courtesy Nederlander Organization

Nick Scandalios
*Executive
Vice President*

All photos by Anita & Steve Shevett except where otherwise noted.

Freida Sawyer
Belviso
*Chief Financial
Officer*

Jim Boese
Vice President

Susan Lee
*Chief Marketing
Officer*

Jack Meyer
*Vice President
Programming*

Charlene S.
Nederlander
*Vice President
Corporate
Development*

Kathleen Raitt
*Vice President
Corporate Relations*

Herschel Waxman
*Senior Vice
President
Labor Relations*

Tony Award Productions

Alan Wasser
General Manager

Photos by Brian Mapp

Allan Williams
General Manager

Faculty

JUJAMCYN THEATERS

Faculty

The Broadway League

Paul Libin
Chair

Charlotte St. Martin
Executive Director

Seated in Front Row (L-R): Elisa Shevitz, Leslie Dock, Lindsay Florestal, Laura Fayans, Roxanne Rodriguez, Christina Boursiquot, Rachel Reiner
Second Row (L-R): Charlotte St. Martin, Chelsi Conklin, Laura Grady, Kayla Kreidell, Jennifier Stewart, Ed Sandler, Joy Axelrad, Erica Ryan
Back Row (L-R): Neal Freeman, Colin Gibson, Jean Kroeper, Josh Cacchione, Elizabeth Rublein, Chris Brucato, Tom Ferrugia, Chris Brockmeyer, Keith Halpern, Robert Davis

Manhattan Theatre Club

Front Row (L-R): Barry Grove, Lynne Meadow, Mandy Greenfield
Second Row (L-R): Caitlin Baird, Andy Kao, Lindsey Brooks Sag, Darren Robertson, Jeffrey Bledsoe, Nancy Piccione, Amber Wilkerson, Kevin Sullivan, Rosanna Consalvo Sarto, Mark Bowers, Ryan Fogarty
Third Row (L-R): Emily Hammond, Gillian Campbell, Lynne Randall, Emily Fleisher, Diana Buirski, Katie Fergerson, Andrea Gorzell, Josh Martinez-Nelson, Annie MacRae, Jerry Patch, Laurel Bear
Back Row (L-R): Allison Taylor, Alex Barron, Kelly Gillespie, Kristina Hoge, Nora DeVeau-Rosen, Amy Harris, Thatcher Stevens, Becca Kahane, Nicki Hunter, Julia Baldwin, Debra Waxman-Pilla, David Shookhoff, Chad Jones, Amy Loe, Sunil Ayyagari

Faculty

The Roundabout Theatre Company

Front Row (L-R): Julia Levy, Todd Haimes, Harold Wolpert

Second Row (L-R):Jennifer DiBella, Rachel Ayers, Steve Deutsch, Antonio Palumbo, Lynne Gugenheim Gregory, David Steffen, Sydney Beers, Greg Backstrom, Valerie Simmons, Jill Rafson, Amy Ashton

Third Row (L-R): Maggie Cantrick, Joy Magyawe, Stephanie Ward, Susan Fallon, Bobby Dowling, Gavin Brown, Christopher Nave, Sohyun Kim, Yonit Kafka, Carly DiFulvio, Amy Rosenfield, Marisa Perry, Solangel Bido

Fourth Row (L-R): Bobby Wolf, Doug Gaeta, Catherine Fitzpatrick, Wendy Hutton, Liz S. Alsina, Elisa Papa, Sarah Malone, Shannon Marcotte, Aliza Greenberg, Martin Giannini, Steve Schaeffer, Scott Kelly, John LaBarbera

Fifth Row (L-R): Danielle Piendak, Karl Baudendistel, Laura Stuart, Joseph Foster, Cary Kim, Krystin MacRitchie, Kara Harrington, Jessica Pruett-Barnett, Ted Sod, Brett Barbour, Zachary Baer, Tyler Ennis, Bradley Sanchez

Sixth Row (standing L-R): Nicole Tingir, Nicholas Caccavo, Hannah Goldstein, Sherra Johnston, Glenn Merwede, Ewa Cabaj, Reena Bahadur, Grace Eubank, Elise Lebreton, Christina Offley, Holly Sansom, Tiffany Nixon, Erin Monahan, Jaclyn Verbitski, Dee Beider

Back Row (standing L-R): Alex Cadmus, David Flores, Brian Maiuri, Mark Cajigao, Tom O'Connor, Revanth Anne, Joe Clark, Ellen Holt, Jim Roma, Colin Wilson, Nathaniel Tredwell

Faculty

IATSE Local One, Stagehands

Replacement Room Chairperson Daniel Thorn, Administrative Secretary Edmond F. Supple, Sr. and Financial Secretary Anthony Manno

Seated (L-R): Chairman, Board of Trustees John M. Diaz, Sr., Recording-Corresponding Secretary Robert C. Score, President James J. Claffey, Jr., Vice-President William J. Walters, Treasurer Robert McDonough

Standing (L-R): Television Business Manager Robert C. Nimmo, Television Business Manager Edward J. McMahon, III, Theatre Business Manager Michael Wekselblatt, Theatre Business Manager Kevin McGarty, Trustee William Ngai and Trustee Daniel D. Dashman

Stage Directors and Choreographers Society

Front Row (L-R): Kathleen Marshall (SDC Vice President), Julie Arenal, Sue Lawless, Karen Azenberg (SDC President), Leigh Silverman, Moisés Kaufman

Middle Row (L-R): Barbara Wolkoff, Renée Lasher, Elizabeth Miller, Gretchen M. Michelfeld, Seret Scott, Marcia Milgrom Dodge, Michele Holmes

Back Row (L-R): Lena Abrams, Mary B. Robinson (SDC Secretary), Randy Anderson, Laura Penn (SDC Executive Director), Mauro Melleno, Larry Carpenter (SDC Executive Vice President), Walter Bobbie, Kim Rogers, Evan Shoemake, Cole Jordan

Faculty

Actors' Equity Association

Nick Wyman
President

Mary McColl
Executive Director

NATIONAL COUNCIL
Back Row (L-R): Western Regional VP Doug Carfrae, Central Regional VP Dev Kennedy, President Nick Wyman, Eastern Regional VP Kate Shindle, Third VP Ira Mont
Front Row (L-R): First VP Paige Price, Secretary-Treasurer Sandra Karas. Second VP Rebecca Kim Jordan

AEA STAFF SIXTEENTH FLOOR
Front Row (L-R): Joan Glazer, Jennifer Michaud, Marie Gottschall, Chris Williams

Middle Row (L-R): Tom Miller, Jack Goldstein, Anne Fortuno, Stuart Levy, Joe Chiplock

Back Row (L-R): Robert Fowler, Joseph DeMichele, Karen Master, Frank Horak, Megann McManus, David Lotz

STAFF
Front Row (L-R): Karlene Laemmie, Ross Knorr, David Shaerf, John Fasulo
Middle Row (L-R): Allison Plotkin, Kristine Arwe, Calandra Hackney, Angel Wuellner
Back Row (L-R): Keith Howard, Jonathan Black, David Thorn

Front Row (L-R): Kathy Mercado, Jeffrey Bateman, Tripp Chamberlain, Thomas Kaub, Alessandra Williams-Bellotti
Second Row (L-R): Jessica Palermo, Laura Schuman, Chris Bennett, Matthew Summersgill, Melissa Colgan, Louise Foisy
Third Row: (L-R): Cathy Jayne, Zalina Hoosein, Kimberly Rimbold, Jillian Moss, Adeola Adegbola, Michelle Lehrman, Courtney Scott, Mary Kate Gilrein, Joanna Spencer, Sara Gretschel
Back Row (L-R): Pearl Brady, Lawrence Lorczak, Barry Rosenberg, Gary Dimon, Beverly Sloan, Walt Kiskaddon, Michelle Kelts, Jason Clark, Val LaVarco

Faculty

Dramatists Guild

DRAMATISTS GUILD COUNCIL-STEERING COMMITTEE
Standing (L-R): David Ives, David Lindsay-Abaire, Craig Carnelia

Seated (L-R): Peter Parnell (Vice President), Stephen Schwartz (President), Marsha Norman, John Weidman

Not Pictured: Theresa Rebeck (Treasurer), Julia Jordan, Doug Wright, (Secretrary), David Auburn

STAFF
Seated (L-R): Amy VonVett (Executive Assistant), Gary Garrison (Executive Director of Creative Affairs), Ralph Sevush (Executive Director of Business Affairs), Holly Kinney (Director of Finance and Administration)
Standing (L-R): Patrick Shearer (Office Manager), Tari Stratton (Director of Education, Events & Outreach), Roland Tec (Director of Membership), and Rebecca Stump (Membership Associate)

Not Pictured: Robert Ross Parker (Director of Publications), David Faux (Director of Business Affairs), Fred Nelson (Executive Director of the Dramatists Guild Fund)

Association of Theatrical Press Agents and Managers

Seated (L-R): Rina Saltzman, Barbara Carroll, David Calhoun (President), Robert Nolan, Nick Kaledin (Secretary-Treasurer), Penny Daulton (Vice President), Anita Dloniak
Standing (L-R): Jeremy Shaffer, A. Scott Falk, Jonathan Shulman, David Gersten, Adam Miller, Merle Debuskey, Maury Collins, Bill Matson, Jeffrey Pluth and Nance Movsesian

Faculty

Theatrical Teamsters, Local 817

EXECUTIVE BOARD
Front Row (L-R): Francis J. Connolly, Jr.
(Business Agent & Union Trustee),
Jim Leavey (Recording Secretary),
Ed Iacobelli (Vice President).
Back Row (L-R): Mike Hyde (Union Trustee),
Thomas R. O'Donnell (President),
Thomas J. O'Donnell (Secretary-Treasurer),
Kevin Keefe (Union Trustee)

STAFF
Front Row (L-R): Christine Harkerss (Human Resources),
Tina Gusmano (Union Secretary).
Back Row (L-R): Terry Casaletta (Casting Director
Organizer), Marge Marklin (Fund Secretary)

Not Present: Kathy Kreinbihl (Fund Administrator),
Margie Vaeth (Union Secretary)

IATSE Local 306 Motion Picture Projectionists, Video Technicians and Allied Crafts (Ushers)

Back Row (L-R): Roy DuBose, Rafael Cortes, Hugo Capra, Joe Rivierzo, Mike Satrin
Front Row (L-R): Margie Blair, Lorraine Lowery and Rose Ann Cipriano

Faculty

Treasurers & Ticket Sellers Union, IATSE Local 751

Photos by Brian Mapp

THE EXECUTIVE COUNCIL
Seated (L-R): Karen Winer, Diane Heatherington, Fred Santore, Jr., Gene McElwain, Noreen Morgan, Patricia DeMato, A. Greer Bond

Standing (L-R): Harry Jaffie, Dave Heveran, Peter Attanasio, Jr., Frank M. Loiacono, Lawrence Paone, Michael McCarthy, John Nesbitt, Stanley Shaffer

OFFICE STAFF
(L-R): Kathy McBrearty, James Sita, Patricia Garrison, Gene McElwain, Lawrence Paone

Theatrical Wardrobe Union, IATSE Local 764

Seated (L-R): Mary Ferry, Patricia Sullivan, Terry LaVada, Jenna Krempel, Mary Chesterman, Adam Adelman, Dennis Birchall, Mike Gemignani, Patricia White
Standing (L-R): Julie Fernandez, Shelly Friedman, Frank Gallagher, Mark Klein, Shannon Koger, Barbara Hladsky, Scott Harrington, Vangeli Kaseluris, Jane Rottenbach, Warren Wernick, Emily Merriweather

Faculty

Broadway Cares/Equity Fights AIDS

Front Row (L-R): Michael Palm, Chris Davis, Josh Blye, Denise Hurlin, Colyn Fiendel
Second Row (L-R): Aaron Waytkus, Ngoc Bui, Yvonne Ghareeb, Keith Bullock
Third Row (L-R): Tom Viola, Danny Whitman, Carol Ingram, Madeline Reed, Donald Huppert, Meagan Grund, Andy Halliday, Dan Perry, Ed Garrison
Back Row (L-R): Lane Beauchamp, Nathan Hurlin, Rose James, Larry Cook, Michael Simmons-DeFord, Roy Palijaro, Michael Graziano, Chris Economakos, Peter Borzotta, Trisha Doss, Brian O'Donnell, Scott Stevens, Chris Kenney, Kimberly Russell, Dex Ostling, Skip Lawing

American Theatre Wing

BOARD OF DIRECTORS AND STAFF
Seated (L-R): Enid Nemy, Douglas B. Leeds, Sondra Gilman, Theodore S. Chapin (Chairman), Dasha Epstein, Pia Lindström, Anita Jaffe, Ronald S. Konecky
Standing (L-R): Howard Sherman (Executive Director), James Weinman (Staff), Robb Perry (Staff), Gail Yancosek (Staff), Barbara Toy (Staff), Raisa Ushomirskiy (Staff), David Brown (Treasurer), Michael P. Price (Vice President), David Henry Hwang, Peter Schneider, Lucie Arnaz, Alan Siegel (Secretary), Bruce Redditt, William Craver, Jeffrey Eric Jenkins, Joanna Sheehan (Staff), Randy Ellen Lutterman (Staff), Myra Wong (Staff)
Not Pictured: Kate Burton, Mallory Factor, James Higgins, Jo Sullivan Loesser, Jane Fearer Safer, Marva Smalls, Howard Stringer, Sally Susman

Faculty

Theatre Development Fund and TKTS

Photo by Brian Mapp

TDF STAFF

Front Row Kneeling (L-R): Craig Stekeur, Joey Haws, Vickie Alvarez, Mark Runion, Mark Blankenship, Patrick Berger, Erica McLaughlin, Christopher Reichheld, Jonathan Calindas

Second Row Sitting (L-R): Joanne Haas, Marianna Houston, Lisa Carling, Eric Sobel, Victoria Bailey, Michael Naumann, Julian Christenberry, Joy Cooper, Stephen Cabral

Third Row Standing (L-R): JoAnn Gall, Paula Torres, Julie Williams, Ann Matheison, Jane Pfeffer, Richard Price, Catherine Lizima, Sarah Aziz, Howard Marren, Jen Hurlbert, Thomas Westerman

Back Row Standing (L-R): Donald Beale, Joseph Cali, Christophe Mentor, Rob Neely, Michelle St. Hill, Tina Kirsimae, Doug Smith, Tymand Staggs, Ginger Meagher, Fran Polino, Thomas Adkins, Costas Michalopoulos, Sal Polizzi, Sheela Kangal

TKTS TREASURERS

Standing (L-R):
Robert Wilamowski,
Joseph McLaughlin,
William Castellano,
Shari Teitelbaum,
Brian Roeder,
James Divone

Seated (L-R):
William Roeder,
Rajesh Sharma (leaning in),
Stephen Banovich,
Michael Campanella

Photo by David LeShay

Faculty

The Actors Fund

TRUSTEES
Seated (L-R): Honey Waldman, Roberta Reardon, Anita Jaffe, Vice Chair Bebe Neuwirth.
Standing (L-R): Tom Viola, Stewart F. Lane, Edward D. Turen, Assistant Treasurer Steve Kalafer, Lee H. Perlman, Merle Debuskey, Nick Wyman, Thomas Schumacher, Dale C. Olson, Vice Chair Philip S. Birsh, John Breglio, Joyce Gordon, Paul Libin, Secretary Marc Grodman, M.D., Charlotte St. Martin.
Not pictured: Chairman of the Board Brian Stokes Mitchell, Assistant Secretary Abby Schroeder, Treasurer John A. Duncan, Jr., Vice Chair Philip J. Smith, Alec Baldwin, Annette Bening, Jed W. Bernstein, Jeffrey Bolton, James J. Claffey, Jr., Nancy Coyne, Rick Elice, Janice Reals Ellig, Ken Howard, Kate Edelman Johnson, Michael Kerker, Matthew Loeb, Kristen Madsen, Kevin McCollum, James L. Nederlander, Martha Nelson, Phyllis Newman, A.J. Pocock, Harold Prince, David Steiner, Jomarie Ward, Joseph H. Wender, B.D. Wong and George Zuber

NEW YORK STAFF
Front Row (L-R): Wally Munro, Jay Haddad, Louie Anchondo, John Torres
Second Row (L-R): Patch Schwadron, Amy Picar, Dalin Rivera, Joy Pascua-Kim, Ariella Azaraf, Erica Chung, Alice Vienneau, Karissa Krenz
Third Row (L-R): Barbara Toy, Billie Levinson, Tamar Shapiro, Gloria Jones, Rich Renner, Zehava Krinsky, Holly Wheeler, Celia Gannon, Renata Marinaro, Marjorie Roop, Elizabeth Avedon, Margaret Stevens
Back Row (L-R): Courtney Toumey, Judy Fish, Amy Wilder, Cassandra Kohilakis, Carol Wilson, Stephen Joseph, Robert Rosenthal, Chris Nilsson, Sam Smith, Rick Montero, Tim Pinckney, Kent Curtis, David Engelman

LOS ANGELES STAFF
Front Row (L-R): Ted Abenheim, Bonnie Wong, Keith McNutt, Anne Keating, Joey Shanley
Back Row (L-R): Laura Campbell, Meg Thomas, Angelique Prahalis, Heather Vanian, Tracey Downs, Caitlin Moon, Gregory Polcyn, Joanne Webb, Linda Zimmerman, Frank Salamone, John Mattson, Erin Mata, Jan-Kees Van Der Gaag, Tina Hookom, Robin LaBorwit

Faculty

Boneau/Bryan-Brown

Front Row (L-R): Jessica Johnson, Jackie Green, Linnae Hodzic, Adrian Bryan-Brown, Chris Boneau, Susanne Tighe, Amy Kass
Second Row (L-R): Joe Perrotta, Jim Byk, Kelly Guiod, Emily Meagher, Christine Olver, Michael Strassheim, Brandi Cornwell
Back Row (L-R): Heath Schwartz, Matt Polk, Aaron Meier, Kevin Jones

O&M Co.

(L-R): Jaron Caldwell, Sam Corbett,
Rick Miramontez (President),
Philip Carrubba, Molly Barnett,
Richard Hillman, Elizabeth Wagner,
Andy Snyder, Chelsea Nachman,
Jon Dimond

Not pictured: Michael Jorgensen,
Yufen Kung, Alexandra H. Rubin

Faculty

The Hartman Group

Michael Hartman

Nicole Capatasto

Tom D'Ambrosio

Juliana Hannett

Alyssa Hart

Bethany Larsen

Emily McGill

Leslie Papa

Matt Ross

Frances White

Wayne Wolfe

Faculty

Richard Kornberg & Associates

Richard Kornberg

Don Summa

Billy Zavelson

Danielle McGarry

Jeffrey Richards Associates

Standing (L-R): Michael Crea, Will Trice, Jeremy Scott Blaustein, Franco (office mascot), Elon Rutberg, Andy Drachenberg

Seated (L-R): Irene Gandy, Jeffrey Richards, Alana Karpoff and Skye (office mascot)

The Publicity Office

Standing (L-R): Jeremy Shaffer and Michael Borowski

Seated: Marc Thibodeau (with Berger)

Faculty

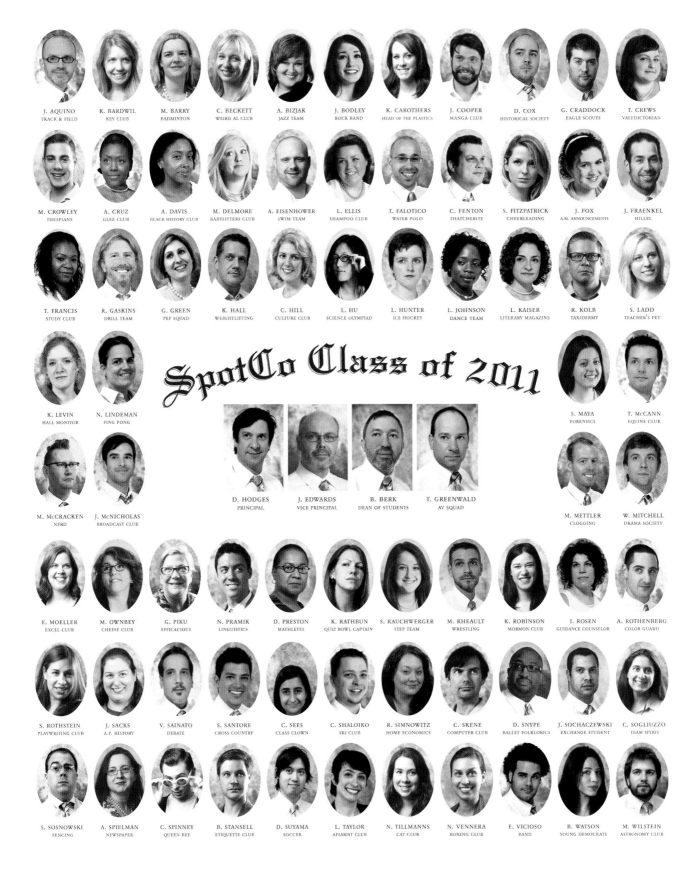

J. AQUINO
TRACK & FIELD

K. BARDWIL
KEY CLUB

M. BARRY
BADMINTON

C. BECKETT
WEIRD AL CLUB

A. BIZJAK
JAZZ TEAM

J. BODLEY
ROCK BAND

K. CAROTHERS
HEAD OF THE PLASTICS

J. COOPER
MANGA CLUB

D. COX
HISTORICAL SOCIETY

G. CRADDOCK
EAGLE SCOUTS

T. CREWS
VALEDICTORIAN

M. CROWLEY
THESPIANS

A. CRUZ
GLEE CLUB

A. DAVIS
BLACK HISTORY CLUB

M. DELMORE
BABYSITTERS CLUB

A. EISENHOWER
SWIM TEAM

L. ELLIS
SHAMPOO CLUB

T. FALOTICO
WATER POLO

C. FENTON
THATCHERITE

S. FITZPATRICK
CHEERLEADING

J. FOX
A.M. ANNOUNCEMENTS

J. FRAENKEL
HILLEL

T. FRANCIS
STUDY CLUB

R. GASKINS
DRILL TEAM

G. GREEN
PEP SQUAD

K. HALL
WEIGHTLIFTING

C. HILL
CULTURE CLUB

L. HU
SCIENCE OLYMPIAD

L. HUNTER
ICE HOCKEY

L. JOHNSON
DANCE TEAM

L. KAISER
LITERARY MAGAZINE

R. KOLB
TAXIDERMY

S. LADD
TEACHER'S PET

K. LEVIN
HALL MONITOR

N. LINDEMAN
PING PONG

S. MAYA
FORENSICS

T. McCANN
EQUINE CLUB

SpotCo Class of 2011

D. HODGES
PRINCIPAL

J. EDWARDS
VICE PRINCIPAL

B. BERK
DEAN OF STUDENTS

T. GREENWALD
AV SQUAD

M. McCRACKEN
NERD

J. McNICHOLAS
BROADCAST CLUB

M. METTLER
CLOGGING

W. MITCHELL
DRAMA SOCIETY

E. MOELLER
EXCEL CLUB

M. OWNBEY
CHEESE CLUB

G. PIKU
EFFICACIOUS

N. PRAMIK
LINGUISTICS

D. PRESTON
MATHLETES

K. RATHBUN
QUIZ BOWL CAPTAIN

S. RAUCHWERGER
STEP TEAM

M. RHEAULT
WRESTLING

K. ROBINSON
MORMON CLUB

I. ROSEN
GUIDANCE COUNSELOR

A. ROTHENBERG
COLOR GUARD

S. ROTHSTEIN
PLAYWRITING CLUB

J. SACKS
A.P. HISTORY

V. SAINATO
DEBATE

S. SANTORE
CROSS COUNTRY

C. SEES
CLASS CLOWN

C. SHALOIKO
SKI CLUB

R. SIMNOWITZ
HOME ECONOMICS

C. SKENE
COMPUTER CLUB

D. SNYPE
BALLET FOLKLORICS

J. SOCHACZEWSKI
EXCHANGE STUDENT

C. SOGLIUZZO
TEAM SPIRIT

S. SOSNOWSKI
FENCING

A. SPIELMAN
NEWSPAPER

C. SPINNEY
QUEEN BEE

B. STANSELL
ETIQUETTE CLUB

D. SUYAMA
SOCCER

L. TAYLOR
APIARIST CLUB

N. TILLMANNS
CAT CLUB

N. VENNERA
BOXING CLUB

E. VICIOSO
BAND

B. WATSON
YOUNG DEMOCRATS

M. WILSTEIN
ASTRONOMY CLUB

Faculty

JOE ALESI · JEFF ALPHIN · ANDY APOSTOLIDES · HAILEY APTER · LESLIE BARRETT · DAVID BARRINEAU · SUMEET BHARATI

SANDY BLOCK · DANIELLE BOYLE · MATT BRITT · DENISE BROWN · TOM CALLAHAN · JOANNE CELAURO · CRYSTAL CHASE

BRAD COFFMAN · LAURIE CONNOR · GREG CORRADETTI · BRUCE COUNCIL · NANCY COYNE · WHITNEY CREIGHTON · RYAN CUNNINGHAM · PETER DALY · ANGELO DESIMINI

ANN DINH · DOUG ENSIGN · JON ERWIN · JOAQUIN ESTEVA · MAUREEN FAY · JOE FIGLIOLA · MOIRA FINNEY · CHERI FONTANEZ · JIM GLAUB

IFAT GOLAN · BECCA GOLAND-VAN RYN · RYAN GREER · PETER GUNTHER · SUSAN HANTMAN · KIM HEWSKI · LAUREN HOULBERG · SCOTT JOHNSON · ROBERT JONES

JACQUI KAISER · MARCI KAUFMAN · KEVIN KEATING · MARY KEKLLAS · ZACK KINNEY · ZHANNA KIRTSMAN · JOHN LAGOMARSINO · JON LAPRADE · JIM LAZOS

JEAN LEONARD · NEHANDA LOISEAU · DANTE LOPEZ · SARAH MARCUS · KAT MAROTTA · CHRIS MARTIN · JOETTE MARTIN · KEVIN McALEER · KEVIN McLEOD

CHIP MEYRELLES · BRANDON MIKOLASKI · ROGER MICONE · SARAH MILLER · DAVID MOLINA · SHAWNA MONSON · MARIA MYLONA · DIANE NIEDZIALEK · SOFIA NISNEVICH

NICK NOLTE · ANDREI OLEINIK · TEE PANTON · BRAD PATTINIAN · LAUREN PRESSMAN · MIKE RAFAEL · CATHERINE REID · JELENA RICHARD · JIM RUSSEK

BETH SCHEFFLAN · MARK SEELEY · JUSTIN STANFORD · JEN STEARNS · CAROLINE THOMPSON · SUZANNE TOBAK · ALHAGIE TOURAY · MATT UPSHAW · DMITRIY USTINOV

IAN WEISS · GINGER WITT · BRIAN WRIGHT · SCOTT YAMBOR · DANA ZELL

SERINO/COYNE 2010-2011
It's **SHOW** TIME.

Faculty

aka*
2011

ADAM KENWRIGHT
ELIZABETH FURZE
SCOTT MOORE
CLINT BOND JR.
ADAM JAY
ADAM NEUMANN
ANDREW DAMER
BASHAN AQUART
CRISTINA MARIE
ELLIE BERKOWITZ
ELIZABETH FINDLAY
ERICA RUFF
ERIK ALDEN
ERIN BECK
GARY MONTALVO
HANNAH SCOTT
JACOB MATSUMIYA
JANETTE ROUSH
JEFF LILLEY
JENNA BISSONNETTE
JOEY BOYLES
JOSHUA POOLE
JULIAN ROCA
KELLY RUSSIN
MAREK RACZKIEWICZ
MEGHAN BARTLEY
MELISSA MARANO
MICHAEL ALTBAUM
RICHARD ARNOLD
SARA ROSENZWEIG
SHANE BROWN
SUZANNE HERETH
TERRY GOLDMAN
TREVOR SPONSELLER
ZOEY JAY

Faculty

Playbill

Philip S. Birsh
Publisher

Arthur T. Birsh
Chairman

Clifford S. Tinder
*Senior Vice President/
Publisher, Classic Arts
Division*

Joan Alleman
*Corporate Vice
President*

MANHATTAN OFFICE
Front Row, Seated (L-R): Blake Ross, Clifford S. Tinder, Clara Barragan, Yadira Mitchell, Anderson Peguero
Second Row, Standing (L-R): Jose Ortiz, Diana Leidel, Jill Boriss, Julie Cohen, Stephanie Bradbury, Tiffany Feo, Theresa Holder, Brynn Cox, Sarah Jane Arnegger, Megan Dekic, Wanda Young
Back Row: Oldyna Dynowska, Ben Finane, Matt Blank, Robert Viagas, Krissie Fullerton, Mark Ezovski, Maude Popkin, Alex Near, Farin Schlussel, Adam Hetrick, Ari Ackerman, James Cairl, David Gewirtzman, Andrew Ku

Not pictured: Louis Botto, Glenn Asciutto, Travis Ferguson, Arturo Gonzalez, Esvard D'Haiti, Kelechi Ezie, Joseph Marzullo, Silvija Ozols, Stella Fawn Ragsdale, Jolie Schaffzin, Glenn Shaevitz, Kesler Thibert, Joel Wyman

Blake Ross
*Editor-in-Chief
Playbill*

PLAYBILL.COM
(Seated L-R):
Kenneth Jones
and Andrew Gans

(Standing L-R):
Adam Hetrick,
Ernio Hernandez
and David Gewirtzman

Not pictured:
Matt Blank
and Andrew Ku

Louis Botto
Columnist

Harry Haun
Columnist

Jennifer Lanter
Columnist

Seth Rudetsky
Columnist

Mark Shenton
*London
Correspondent*

Robert Simonson
*Senior
Correspondent*

Steven Suskin
Columnist

Not Pictured: Tom Nondorf

Faculty

Playbill

CLASSIC ARTS DIVISION and PROGRAM EDITORS

Seated (L-R): Pam Karr, Claire Mangan, Scott Hale, Rori Grable

Standing (L-R): Patrick Cusanelli, Judy Samelson, Amy Asch, Sean Kenny, Ben Hyacinthe, Brian Libfeld, David Porrello

Not pictured: Kristy Bredin, Maria Chinda, Bill Reese, Andrew Rubin

Photos by Brian Mapp

ACCOUNTING
(Clockwise from front left): Lewis Cole, Theresa Bernstein, James Eastman, JoAnn D'Amato, John LoCascio
Not pictured: Beatriz Chitnis

Carolina Diaz
Florida Production Manager

Regional Advertising Salespersons

Kenneth R. Back
Sales Manager
Cincinnati

Elaine Bodker
Sales
St. Louis

Dory Binyon
Sales Manager
Chicago

Bob Caulfield
Sales
San Francisco

Margo Cooper
Sales Manager
St. Louis

Betsy Gugick
Sales Manager
Dallas

Ron Friedman
Sales Manager
Columbus

Tom Green
Sales
Florida/Texas, etc.

Ed Gurien
Sales
Florida/Dallas

Michel Manzo
Sales Manager
Philadelphia

Marilyn A. Miller
Sales Manager
Minneapolis

Judy Pletcher
Sales Manager
Washington, DC

John Rosenow
Sales Manager
Phoenix/Tucson

Kenneth Singer
Sales Manager
Houston

Not Pictured: Nancy Hardin, Karen Kanter, Jeff Ross, Sara Smith and Donald Roberts.

Faculty

Playbill / Woodside Offices

PRODUCTION CHIEFS
(L-R): Louis Cusanelli, Robert Cusanelli and Patrick Cusanelli

PRODUCTION
Standing (L-R): Patrick Cusanelli, Benjamin Hyacinthe, Sean Kenny
Seated: David Porrello

DAY CREW

Back Row (L-R): Robert Cusanelli, Ray Sierra,
Larry Przetakiewicz, Steve Ramlall, Mary Roaid,
Nancy Galarraga, Scott Cipriano, Janet Moti,
John Matthews

Front Row (L-R):
Lennox Worrell,
David Rodriguez,
Chris Toribio, Joseph Lucania

NIGHT CREW

(L-R): Ricardo Garcia,
Anna Rincon,
Frank Dunn, Jim Ayala,
Robert Cusanelli,
Louis Cusanelli II,
Kenneth Gomez,
Lidia Yagual, Elias Garcia

PLAYBILLSTORE.COM

(L-R): Rebeca Miller, Jill Napierala,
Yajaira Marrero, Bruce Stapleton (Manager)

In Memoriam

May 2010 to May 2011

Theoni V. Aldredge
Michael Allinson
Jonathan Anderson
Herman O. Arbeit
Claudia Asbury
Ray Atherton
Edmund C. Balin
Leslie Barrett
John Barry
Frank Bayer
Joseph Bird
Jerry Bock
Gerald Bordman
Tom Bosley
Roger Braun
Maurice Brenner
Oscar Brockett
Joseph Brooks
Lewis Brown
Jean Bruno
Richard Buck
Willis Burks II
David Cahn
Charles Canada
Carmen Capalbo
Thomas P. Carr
Jill Clayburgh
Buff Cobb
John Cossette
Georgia Creighton
Elzbieta Czyzewska
Sylvia Davis
Crandall Diehl
John Dolf
David Doty
Blake Edwards
Hillard Elkins
Gloria Evans
John Ferraro
Mary Fogarty
James Gammon
Stephen Gardner
Jay Garner
Henry Garrard
Betty Garrett
Pam Gems
Carl Gordon

Broadway Dims Its Lights

Broadway theatres dimmed their marquee lights this season upon the passing of the following theatre personalities, listed here along with the date the honor was accorded: *Theatre World* editor John Willis, June 30, 2010. Actress Patricia Neal, August 17, 2010. Librettist/playwright Joseph Stein, October 28, 2010. Composer Jerry Bock, November 4, 2010. Actress Jill Clayburgh, November 9, 2010. Playwright Romulus Linney, January 19, 2011. Producer Ellen Stewart, January 19, 2011. Costume designer Theoni V. Aldredge, January 25, 2011. Stage manager Beverley Randolph, March 16, 2011. Actress Elizabeth Taylor, March 25, 2011. Playwright Lanford Wilson, March 30, 2011. Playwright, librettist and director Arthur Laurents, May 6, 2011.

Mark Gordon
Michael Gough
Farley Granger
Suzanne Grossman
Mary Cleere Haran
Jill Haworth
Israel Hicks
Peter Hobbs
Christine Johnson
Judd Jones
Donald H. Josephson
George Keathley
Larry Keith
Bob Kelly
John Kluge
Jay Landesman
Michael Langham
Harris Laskawy
Arthur Laurents
Douglas B. Leeds
Marcia Lewis
Don Liberto
Romulus Linney
Sidney Lumet
James MacArthur
Kenneth Mars
Hugh Martin
Kevin McCarthy
Rue McClanahan

Charles McClennahan
James McLure
Marian Mercer
Sidney Michaels
Susan Miller
Frances Lee Morgan
Patricia Neal
James Neu
Leslie Nielsen
Darrell Notara
Vince O'Brien
Evelyn Page
Neva Patterson
Arthur Penn
Wally Peterson
Neil Phillips
Nelson Phillips
Pete Postlethwaite
Addison Powell
James T. Pritchett
Thomas C. Proehl
Eddie Pruett
Beverley Randolph
Shelly Rann
Peggy Rea
Dan Resin
Don Ross
Paul Ryan Rudd
Robert Rue

Jane Russell
Craig Sandquist
James Schlader
Sachi Shimizu
Cesare Siepi
Tom Signorelli
Patricia Smith
Alexander "Sandy" Speer
Walter Stane
Joseph Stein
Ron L. Steinbeck
Helen Stenborg
Pat Stevens
Margot Stevenson
Ellen Stewart
Haila Stoddard
James Stovall
Ronald B. Stratton
Sharlie Stuart
Beatrice Dickman Swarm
Allen Swift
Jack Sydow
Shannon Tavarez
Elizabeth Taylor
Noel Taylor
Lindsay Thomas
Robert E. Thompson
Sada Thompson
Michael Tolan
Ian Trigger
Helen Wagner
William Walker
Russell Warner
George David Weiss
Margaret Whiting
Max Wilk
Stanley Williams
John Willis
Dolores Wilson
Doric Wilson
K.C. Wilson
Lanford Wilson
Norman Wisdom
Randall L. Wreghitt
Bob Wright
Jerry Wyatt
Susannah York

Index

A

Aarons, Michael 11, 30, 255
Ababio, Yao 118, 119, 120
Abagnale, Frank Jr. 74-78
Aballi, Alicia 7
Abate, Shelagh 220
Abbandandolo, Brenda 61
Abbate, Mickey 350
Abbott, Christopher 136, 137, 140
Abbott, Eric 15
Abbott, James 8, 370, 373, 378, 379, 381, 383
Abdul-Rahiim, Islah 196
Abel, Marybeth 370, 375, 376
Abel, Timothy 279, 300, 345, 346
Abeles, David 242
Abella, Sheffield 311
Abenheim, Ted 424
Abernathy, June 390
Abit, Otoja 350
Abraham, F. Murray 180, 403
Abrams, Bernard 141, 144, 294, 297, 385, 388
Abramson, Deborah 272
Abramson, Jane 197, 225
Abrazado, Carmen I. 196
Abruzzese, Joe 208
Acciani, Emma 71
Acciani, Emma 252
Accurso, Aaron 329
Accurso, Aron 46, 326, 329, 330
Acevedo, Elisa 105, 106
Aceves, Theresa 138
Acheson, Matt 360
Acken, Peter Vincent 390
Ackerman, Ari 431
Ackerman, Eddie 224
Ackerman, Hilary 33, 147, 279, 346
Ackerman, Hillary 147
Ackert, David A. 258
Acuna, Rita 196
Acuna, Santos 196
Adamian, Daniel 15, 116, 168, 204
Adams, Ashley Kate 185
Adams, Cameron 141-143, 294, 296
Adams, Candi iv, 54, 235, 238
Adams, Jennifer 346
Adams, Katie 204
Adams, Kevin 10, 12, 254, 255, 410

Adams, Nick 184, 287, 289, 293, 395
Adams, Randy 230
Adams, Tony 340, 347
Adamski, Susanne 352
Adamson, Evan 27
Adamson, Peter 345
Adamy, Paul 213
Addams, Charles 1
Adderley, Konrad 371
Addiss, Pat 294, 297
Adegbola, Adeola 418
Adelman, Adam 121, 122, 359, 360, 421
Ademick, Casey 299
Adey, Jenny 185
Adkins, Thomas 423
Adler, Dara 278
Adonna, Emily 277
Agee, Martin 363, 367
Agosta, Alexandra 388, 390
Agosta, Micka 292
Agraz, Raul 57, 155, 159
Aguasvivas, Zipporah 151, 152, 252
Aguchi, Abraham 33
Aguilar, Hector 7
Aguilar, Omar 79
Aguinaga, Deanna 362-364
Aguirre-Sacasa, Roberto 344
Aguirre, Jason 138
Agurto, Maria 292, 367
Agustin, Julio 378-380
Ahrens, Robert 175
Aibel, Douglas 319, 322
Aiken, Clay 403
Ainge, Patrick 292
Aitken, Bobby 212, 215
Akins, Meredith 215
Akram, George 362-364, 369
Al-Kaisi, Fajer 39
Alabado, Krystina 13
Alaio, Rose 228
Alban, John Jr. 382
Albanese, Ron 46
Albano-English, Jessica 27, 317
Albano, Aaron J. 218, 219, 221, 374
Albarracin, Marian 185, 323
Albery, Shana 145, 147, 298, 300
Albrecht, Bobbye Sue 375, 376
Albrecht, Doug 208
Albright, Alicia L. 370-372
Albright, Tim 363, 379
Alcorn, Narda 196
Alden, Erik 135, 390, 430

Alden, Michael A. 133
Alden, Michael A. 134
Aldredge, Theoni V. 434
Alessi, Joseph 66, 67, 68, 72, 73, 106, 429
Alex, Timothy J. 102, 103, 104
Alexander, Graham 308, 309
Alexander, Terence Orleans 224
Alexander, TV 8
Alfred, Roy 94
Alger, Jay 196
Alhadeff, Aaron 227
Alhadeff, Alison 227
Alhadeff, Andi 227
Alhadeff, Emily 227
Alhadeff, Kenny 227, 230
Alhadeff, Marleen 230
Ali, Saheem 122
Alianiello, Diane 89
Alick, Jesse 54, 238
Allain, Stephen 110, 204
Allan, Sara Minskoff 190
Allegro, Joseph 93
Alleman, Joan 431
Allemon, Matt 15
Allen Kramer, Terry 297
Allen, Annette Tapert 33
Allen, Debbie 160
Allen, Heather 80
Allen, Jennifer 227-229, 325-327
Allen, Joey 317
Allen, Jonathan 217
Allen, Mike 151, 152, 251, 252
Allen, Perry "Butch" 95
Allen, Tasha 85
Allenberg, Robert 129, 285, 354
Allers, Roger 190, 192, 193
Allinson, Michael 434
Allison, Drayton 59, 60
Allison, Thom 287-289
Allott, Nicholas 225, 279
Allred, John 142, 146
Almodóvar, Pedro vi, 378, 380, 384
Almy, Tiffany 125
Alper, Steven M. 341
Alphin, Jeff 139, 429
Alsina, Liz S. 21, 70, 152, 251, 271, 416
Alston, Stephanie 129, 285
Altbaum, Michael 430
Alter, Frank 224
Alterman, Charlie 254-256
Altinay, Tia 218, 219,

221, 226
Altman, Matt 121
Altmeyer, Tim 133, 134
Alvarado, Lyanna 128
Alvarez, Bethania 147
Alvarez, Lauren 8, 60, 139, 299
Alvarez, Sandy 157
Alvarez, Vickie 423
Alvarez, Lauren 252
Alverson, Jessica 20
Alves, Clyde 16-18, 23
Alves, Tessa 313, 314
Alvin, Farah 396
Alvord, Megan J. 233, 264
Aman, Brian 167
Amato, Bianca 24, 25
Amato, Joe 173
Amber, Ashley 294-296, 301
Ambjørnsen, Ingvar 108
Ambrose, Kathryn 330
Ambrosi, Mark D' 238
Amendola, Dana 197, 225
Amendum, Dominick 370, 371, 377
Amengual, Sarah 362-364
Amerling, Victor 196, 224
Amma, Aretha 116
Ammerman, Andrew R. 258
Anchondo, Louie 424
Anctil, Matt 181, 183, 186
Anderman, Maureen 97-99
Anders, Kathy 46, 225
Andersen, Kjeld 196
Anderson-Lopez, Kristen 61
Anderson, Cailin 323
Anderson, Cherine 33, 100
Anderson, Happy 235, 236, 239
Anderson, Jack 345, 346
Anderson, Jay 91
Anderson, Jonathan 434
Anderson, Kaitlyn 27, 261, 316
Anderson, Kate 311
Anderson, Nancy 403
Anderson, Randy 417
Anderson, Richard 146, 382
Anderson, Scott 204, 270, 272
Anderson, Stig 212
Anderson, Todd 370-372
Anderson, Tommy 232

Anderson, Vanessa 381, 383
Andersson, Benny 212, 214, 216
Andors, Nick 119, 359
Andos, Randy 2, 7, 57
Andrade, Lance 151
Andrea, Jennie 195
Andreas, Christine 181, 183, 396
Andreas, Sara 74-76
Andres, Emily 46
Andrew, David 215
Andrew, Ronald 132
Andrews, David 27, 34, 47, 54, 66, 100, 110, 125, 135, 172, 176, 179, 185, 189, 217, 233, 238, 248, 258, 261, 279, 300, 306, 323, 330, 350, 354, 383
Andrews, George Lee 274, 276, 280, 281
Andrews, Joan 258
Andrews, Peter 258
Andrews, Steve 172
Andrews, Stuart 225, 279
Andrusko, Robert John 346
Angela, Moya 195
Angelino, Louise 243
Angelou, Maya 62
Angulo, Hector 89, 317
Angulo, Jonathan 89, 317
Angulo, Katherine 316
Aniello, Chris 116, 316
Anikulapo-Kuti, Fela 111-113
Anixter, Russell 147, 330, 341
Anka, Paul 94
Anker, Helen 294, 296, 301
Ann Hould-Ward 269
Annand, Simon 170
Annarumma, Michelina 147
Anne, Revanth 22, 71, 152, 252, 271, 416
Anschutz, Sue 217
Anthony, Bryan 96
Anthony, Julius 385, 387
Anthony, Marc 160
Anthony, Mike 6
Anthony, Stephen James 355-357
Antrim, Chelsea 125
Apostolides, Andy 429
Appelman, Zach 355-357
Appleby, Elspeth 258
Applegate, Fred 184, 325, 327, 331, 396
Appleton, Kathryn 354

Apter, Hailey 429
Aquino, Jim 179, 185, 233, 292, 428
Aquino, Mirjan 147
Arana, Carlos 181, 319
Aravena, Michelle 165
Arbeit, Herman O. 434
Arboleda, Steve 248
Arbuckle, Sean 149, 150
Arcaro, Florence 139
Arcelus, Sebastian 102-104, 107, 165
Arch, David 33, 46, 159, 233, 244, 323, 368, 390
Arch, David John 61
Archer, Beatrix 225
Arditti, Paul 40, 43
Arellano, Lauren 79
Arenal, Julie 417
Arian, Adam 233
Arianda, Nina viii, 63, 64, 66, 407, 409
Arias, Barbara 299
Arlen, Harold 94, 400
Armbruster, Heidi 352-354
Armes, Anastasia 122
Armon, Faye 238, 360
Armstrong, Adrienne 15
Armstrong, Billie Joe 10, 12, 13
Armstrong, David 74, 78, 227, 231
Armstrong, Karen 97, 99, 100, 259, 261
Armstrong, Matt 71
Armstrong, Scott 15
Arnao, Robert 196
Arnaz, Lucie 422
Arnegger, Sarah Jane 431
Arney, Randall 352
Arnold, Jacqueline B. 287, 289, 293
Arnold, Michael 40-42
Arnold, Philip R. 47
Arnold, Richard 135, 172, 430
Aron, Tracy 267, 270
Aronson, Henry 313, 314, 317
Aronstam, Elliott 39, 66, 100, 179, 189, 264, 306
Arsenault, Fred 63, 64, 66
Arsenault, Ghislain 311
Arst, Gregg 45, 46
Arvia, Ann 218-220
Arwe, Kristine 418
Asbury, Claudia 434
Asbury, Cleve 141-143, 148
Asbury, Donna Marie 81-83, 87
Ascenzo, Paul 192

Index

Index

Index

Index

Index

Index

Index

Index

Index

Heveran, Dave 421
Heveran, David 89, 317
Heverin, Nathan 346, 347
Hevner, Caite 89, 233
Hewitt-Roth, Sarah 103
Hewitt, Gary 311
Hewitt, Tom 81, 83
Hewski, Kim 429
Heyman, Edward 94
Heywood, Amelia 100
Hibbard, David 44, 48, 49
Hibbert, Edward 249, 250, 253
Hickey, Joe 8
Hickey, John Benjamin viii, 259, 260, 261, 406, 407
Hickman, Camille 122, 360, 383
Hickman, John 162, 163, 164
Hickman, Kimberly 323
Hicks, Celise 196
Hicks, Erin 121, 122
Hicks, Israel 434
Hicks, Rodney 319-321
Hicks, Tiffany 344, 346
Higgins, Hazel 166, 168
Higgins, James 422
Higgins, Tim 280
Hildebrand, Ray 34
Hildreth, Greg 50, 51, 54, 55
Hilferty, Susan 370, 373, 385, 387
Hilhorst, Alex 264
Hill, Barbara 167
Hill, Christina 428
Hill, Ethan 383
Hill, Faith 211
Hill, Glenn 132
Hill, Gloria 368
Hill, J. Michelle 197
Hill, Jenny 102, 103, 104
Hill, Michael 179, 185, 204
Hill, Natalie 385, 386, 387, 391
Hill, Peggy 303, 304
Hill, Rosena M. 90, 91, 92
Hiller, Jeff 50, 51, 55
Hilliard, Bob 34
Hillman, JJ 54
Hillman, Richard 100, 261, 346, 425
Hillock, Jeffrey 27, 179, 204
Hills, Glenn 185
Hills, Lauren 330
Hilsabeck, Rick 44
Hinchee, Jeffrey 8, 252
Hindelang, Jason 65,

66
Hindman, James 218, 219, 220
Hines, Afra 157, 161
Hingston, Seán Martin 294, 296, 302
Hinrichs, Doug 155, 158, 159
Hinshelwood, Sophia 21, 71, 152, 252, 271
Hirschberg, Carly 225
Hirschhorn, Larry 5, 97, 98
Hirson, David vi, 177, 178
Hirzel, Jake 33, 147, 244, 279, 300, 346
Hitchcock, Ken 228
Hladsky, Barbara 224, 225, 421
Hoare, Charmian 171, 172
Hoban, Jerry 311
Hobbs, Brian Allan 314
Hobbs, Jerry 152, 252
Hobbs, John 172
Hobbs, Peter 434
Hobson, Louis 254, 255, 267-269
Hobson, Verna 60, 61, 115
Hoch, Chris 181-183
Hochman, Larry 1, 4, 56, 58, 62, 319, 321, 406, 408, 409
Hochstine, Dan 345, 346
Hodge, Douglas 184, 186
Hodge, Gaynel 168
Hodges, Drew 22, 33, 39, 46, 71, 80, 94, 100, 110, 129, 132, 152, 159, 179, 185, 233, 244, 252, 264, 272, 285, 292, 311, 323, 330, 350, 354, 368, 390, 428
Hodges, Patricia 63, 64
Hodges, Seena 22, 135, 272, 323
Hodgsen, Peter 60
Hodgson, Martin 282
Hodgson, Michael 282-284, 286
Hodgson, Peter 79
Hodun, James 233
Hodzic, Emir 61, 115
Hodzic, Linnae 135, 217, 425
Hodzic, Rasim 61, 139, 147
Hodzic, Saime 60, 61, 115
Hodzic, Zaim 147
Hoeffler, Alex 355, 356, 357, 361
Hoekstra, Joel 314
Hoerburger, Peter 106, 125, 252
Hoetmer, Deirdre 185

Hoff, Barry 145, 147, 298, 300
Hoffenberg, Julianne 125
Hoffman, Al 94
Hoffman, Anna 79, 80
Hoffman, Anthony 105, 106, 145, 147
Hoffman, Constance 197
Hoffman, Dan 69, 71, 270, 272
Hoffman, Gaby 404
Hoffman, Jackie 1, 3, 9, 395, 396
Hoffman, Lindsay 22, 71, 152, 252, 272
Hoffman, Philip Seymour 180
Hoffman, Rachel 7, 33, 80, 106, 159, 189, 233, 243, 257, 292, 306, 316, 330, 346, 376, 383
Hoffmann, Anna 115, 116
Hofman, Satomi 278
Hofstetter, Bill 89
Hogan, Heather 158, 159, 161
Hoge, Kristina 129, 415
Hoggett, Steven 10, 12, 39
Hoguet, Jennifer 27, 261
Hohn, Jennifer 138, 139, 159
Holbrook, Curtis 5
Holbrook, Morgan 147, 250, 252, 253
Holcenberg, David 215, 217
Holder, Donald 24, 25, 90, 92, 190, 194, 246, 247, 294, 297, 340, 343
Holder, Neville 317
Holder, Oslyn 33
Holder, Theresa 431
Holland, Brian 34
Holland, Donna 121, 122, 359, 360
Holland, Edward, Jr. 34
Hollenbeck, Franklin 33, 105, 106
Holliman, David 196
Hollingworth, Micah 61, 106, 139, 147, 168
Holmes, Chris 85
Holmes, David 217
Holmes, Lori 374
Holmes, Michele 417
Holmes, Mikaela 15
Holst, Richard 251, 252
Holt, B.J. 81, 86, 181, 185, 287
Holt, Ellen 22, 71, 152, 252, 272, 416

Holt, Stacey Todd 102, 103, 104
Holton, Alex 41
Holtzclaw, Matthew 390
Holvath, James 196
Holze, Jennifer 228
Holzer, Leah 106
Holzman, Winnie 370, 373
Hombu, Machiko 204
Hong, Matt 163
Hong, Sooyeon 272
Hood, Andrea 54
Hookom, Tina 424
Hoosein, Zalina 418
Hopkins, Trish 179
Hopper, Luico 288
Horak, Frank 418
Horkey, Maggie 94, 232
Horn, Alan 33, 106
Horn, Alisa 254, 256
Horne, Lena 245
Horner, Laura 225, 291
Hornsby, Ronald 316
Horowitz, Alison Jaye 404
Horowitz, Jimmy 47, 376
Horrigan, Ben 46
Horrigan, Joby 45, 46
Horsley, Allison 168
Horton, Tiffany 47
Horton, William 34
Horvath, J. Samuel 22, 271
Hosang, Diana 367
Hose, Marian Jean 292
Hossain, Rezul 359
Hostetter, Curt 235, 236, 237
Hotel, Dream 300
Houdyshell, Jayne 150
Houghton, Brandon 139, 203
Houghton, Jennilee 15
Houghton, Priscilla Dewey 258
Houlberg, Lauren 429
Hould-Ward, Ann 118, 121, 267
Houlehen, Colleen 27, 167, 210, 261, 316
Hounsel, Ginny 33
Hourigan, Barbara 122, 360, 383
Houseman, Barbara 147
Houston, Doug 2, 8, 320
Houston, Marianna 423
Houston, Mark 196
Howard, Angela 61
Howard, Bart 94
Howard, Joseph 325
Howard, Keith 418
Howard, Ken 424
Howard, Lisa 404

Howard, Peter 81
Howard, Rick 376
Howard, Sherman 36, 37
Howard, Stephen 344, 346
Howard, Stuart 90, 93, 365, 368
Howard, Tiffany Janene 232
Howell, Bruce 61
Howell, Malik 150
Howey, Nicholas 90
Howie, John 121, 358
Howland, Jason 385, 386, 388, 391, 392
Howle, Richard 46
Hoyos, Daniel 122
Hoyt, Lon 75
Hoyt, Tom 371
Hsieh, Brian 346
Hsu, Chen-Win 89, 317
Hsu, Emily 102, 103, 104
Hu, Kent 345
Hu, Lauren 428
Hu, Mina 210
Hubbard, Cristin J. 274, 276
Hubbard, Jeff 14, 15, 147
Hubner, William 185
Hucke, Kevin 375, 376
Huckins, George 330
Hudes, Quiara Alegría 154, 156, 161
Hudson, Don 167
Hudson, Richard 190, 194
Huff, John 347
Huff, Justin 7, 33, 80, 106, 159, 189, 233, 243, 257, 292, 306, 316, 330, 346, 376, 383
Huffman, Brent-Alan 325, 326, 329
Huggins, Richard 279
Hughes, Caroline 185
Hughes, Doug vi, ix, 21, 63, 64, 70, 108, 109, 151, 249, 250, 251, 271
Hughes, Geraldine 170, 171
Hughes, Michael 223
Hughes, Pam 291
Hughes, Van 10, 12
Hughston, Rebekah 204
Hulce, Tom 12
Hull, Charlie 287
Hull, David 141, 142, 143, 374
Hull, Jonathan 279
Hultgren, Kacie 66, 100, 129, 354
Hummel, Mark 325, 328
Humphrey, James 179
Humphris, Caroline

199, 201
Hunt, Caitlin 93, 159
Hunt, Liana 212, 213, 216
Hunt, Mary 21, 151, 271
Hunt, Robb 240, 258
Hunter-Hall, Marc 147
Hunter, Adam John 313, 314, 316
Hunter, Ericka 313, 314
Hunter, Jerry 80
Hunter, Lauren 428
Hunter, Nicki 129, 285, 354, 415
Hunter, Susan 347
Huntley, Paul 16, 19, 71, 74, 77, 121, 122, 149, 150, 199, 201, 267, 269, 358, 360, 383
Huntley, Peter 172
Hunton, Emma 254, 255
Huppert, Donald 422
Hurd, Keith 300, 340, 346
Hurdman, Kevin 345
Hurlbert, Jen 423
Hurlin, Denise 422
Hurlin, Nathan 422
Hurt, Mary Beth 136, 137, 140
Hurwitz, Deborah N. 163, 167, 168
Hurwitz, Isaac Robert 258
Huschle, Christina 225, 238
Huschle, Trini 54
Hushion, Casey 102, 105, 157, 159
Husinko, Greg 15
Huston, Anne 242
Hutchinson, Brian 46
Hutton, Wendy 22, 71, 152, 252, 271, 416
Huynh, Brian Lee 355, 356, 357
Hwang, David Henry 422
Hyacinthe, Benjamin 432, 433
Hyde, Douglas 185
Hyde, Mike 420
Hyde, Terrie Lootens 96
Hyde, Wayne 15
Hydzik, Matthew 362, 364, 369
Hyland, Edward James 24, 25, 28
Hylenski, Peter 102, 104, 313, 315, 319, 321, 385, 388, 408
Hylenski, Suzanne 218-221
Hyler, West 167
Hylton, Dianne 375, 376

The Playbill Broadway Yearbook 2010-2011

449

Index

Index

Index

Index

Index

Index

Index

Index

Index

Index

Index

Index

Index

Index